Agent of Change

Studies in Print Culture and the History of the Book

Agent of Change

Print Culture Studies
after Elizabeth L. Eisenstein

Edited by
Sabrina Alcorn Baron, Eric N. Lindquist,
and Eleanor F. Shevlin

University of Massachusetts Press
Amherst and Boston

in association with
The Center for the Book, Library of Congress
Washington, D.C.

LC 2007004225
ISBN 978-1-55849-593-7 (paper); 592-0 (library cloth ed.)

Designed by Dennis Anderson
Set in Adobe Garamond Pro by Dix Digital Prepress
Printed and bound by The Maple-Vail Book Manufacturing Group

Library of Congress Cataloging-in-Publication Data

Agent of change : print culture studies after Elizabeth L. Eisenstein /
edited by Sabrina Alcorn Baron, Eric N. Lindquist, and Eleanor F. Shevlin.
    p.   cm.
  Includes bibliographical references and index.
  ISBN-13: 978-1-55849-592-0 (alk. paper)
  ISBN-10: 1-55849-592-4 (alk. paper)
  ISBN-13: 978-1-55849-593-7 (pbk. : alk. paper)
  ISBN-10: 1-55849-593-2 (pbk. : alk. paper)
1. Printing—History.   2. Printing—Social aspects—History.   3. Books—History.
4. Books—Social aspects—History.   5. Book industries and trade—History.
6. Eisenstein, Elizabeth L. Printing press as an agent of change.
I. Baron, Sabrina A. (Sabrina Alcorn)
II. Lindquist, Eric N.   III. Shevlin, Eleanor F.
  Z124.A54 2007
  686.209—dc22

                          2007004225

British Library Cataloguing in Publication data are available.

Encouraging the study of books and print culture is a principal aim of
The Center for the Book in the Library of Congress, which was established in 1977
to stimulate public interest in books, reading, and libraries. Its activities include
symposia, publications, and joint projects within the Library of Congress and
with like-minded organizations outside the Library. Its program is sponsored
entirely by contributions from individuals, corporations, and foundations; this
publication is supported by the Daniel J. and Ruth Boorstin Fund. For information
about The Center for the Book's activities, including its publications, state affiliates
program, and its partnership networks throughout the United States and in other
countries, consult its website: http://www.loc.gov/cfbook.

Contents

Acknowledgments

THE EDITORS thank Paul M. Wright, editor, and Bruce Wilcox, director, of the University of Massachusetts Press, as well as John Y. Cole, director of the Center for the Book in the Library of Congress, and Ralph Eubanks, director of publishing at the Library of Congress, for their generous support of this project. We also wish to thank all of the contributors for being a part of this collection; the Press's editorial staff, especially Carol Betsch, for all their varied help; our copy editor, Debby Smith; Genevieve Dell and Samuel P. L. Veissière for their assistance with translations; the two anonymous readers for the Press for their useful comments and advice; Allan A. Tulchin and Carol Armbruster for their help with various queries; Bill Donohue, Tom Magee, and Colin Price; the Department of English and the College of Arts and Sciences, West Chester University of Pennsylvania; the University of Maryland Libraries, especially the Interlibrary Loan Office of the Libraries; the Department of History, American University; and the John W. Kluge Center at the Library of Congress. Finally, we are indebted to Elizabeth Eisenstein and her work.

Agent of Change

Introduction

Eʟɪᴢᴀʙᴇᴛʜ ʟ. ᴇɪsᴇɴsᴛᴇɪɴ's *The Printing Press as an Agent of Change: Communications and Cultural Transformations in Early-Modern Europe* (*PPAC*) [1] was controversial when it was published in 1979, and it continues to be so. But it has exercised an undeniably enormous influence on scholarly inquiry, leaving an imprint on a host of disciplines—not only obviously connected fields such as the history of technology but also disciplines such as anthropology, geography, literary studies, women's studies, and many more whose ties to the printing press are less readily apparent. Perhaps more than any other book, it is responsible for the rise of one of the most significant new fields in recent years, print culture studies.[2] Indeed, it is all but certain that any new book dealing with print culture will, in an early footnote, acknowledge *PPAC* as the *locus classicus* of the importance of print and the concept of print culture. Yet at the outset it was by no means clear that Eisenstein's work would so powerfully sway postmodern academic inquiry. Her two-volume tour de force was from the moment it appeared a book that simultaneously inspired and provoked. Roughly a quarter century after the publication of *PPAC,* we present this volume of essays as a measure of the influence the work continues to exercise.

By Eisenstein's own account, curiosity about the effects of the advent of printing, alongside growing skepticism toward traditional explanations of early modern intellectual and political revolutions, originally inspired her to

---

1. 2 vols. (Cambridge and New York: Cambridge Univ. Press, 1979). All quotations from *PPAC* throughout this book are from this edition.

2. No slight is intended here to other pioneering works, especially Lucien Febvre and Henri-Jean Martin, *L'apparition du livre* (Paris: Éditions A. Michel, 1958), which did not appear in English until almost twenty years later as *The Coming of the Book: The Impact of Printing, 1450–1800,* ed. Geoffrey Nowell-Smith and David Wootton, trans. David Gerard (London: N.L.B., 1976; reissued, London: Verso, 1990). Indeed, the translation of Febvre and Martin appeared in such close conjunction with *PPAC* that the two were sometimes reviewed together. Yet works like *The Coming of the Book* emphasize the "book" and thus have been seen as fostering the field of "book history." Eisenstein's work, in contrast, considers all forms of print, not just the printed book, and thus has been seen as fostering "print culture" studies.

look further into the history of early modern printing. When an initial search failed to uncover "a single book, or even a sizable article which attempted to survey the consequences of the fifteenth-century communications shift" (*PPAC,* xi), she embarked on what would turn out to be a decade of research aimed at rectifying that neglect. In the book this research produced, she argues that the advent of western European printing was not just another Renaissance invention but the crucial invention to come out of that period of ferment. Many historians seemed vaguely aware that printing with move-able metal type and the handpress was important (though many did not), but even those who were aware of printing's import had not really examined how the Renaissance invention of printing had figured in European (and world) history. Thus, Eisenstein's project became a quest to demonstrate the pro-found consequences of the Western European innovation of printing—or, rather, given the magnitude of the task—to begin explaining some of the revolutionary changes wrought by print.

Eisenstein attempted to prepare the way by publishing several lengthy journal articles in the late 1960s and early 1970s exploring many of her ideas, among them a fifty-six-page article for the *Journal of Modern History* in March 1968 entitled "Some Conjectures about the Impact of Printing on Western Society and Thought: A Preliminary Report," which she has said was *PPAC* in embryo.[3] Her "big book" (as she calls it) was published a little over ten years later, in 1979 by Cambridge University Press as two volumes, 794 pages plus preliminaries, in cloth. Now out of print, this first edition sold 2,984 copies.[4] Shortly after its publication the book won two important scholarly prizes: in 1979 the Phi Beta Kappa Ralph Waldo Emerson Prize for a book that con-tributes "significantly to interpretations of the intellectual and cultural con-tribution of humanity," and the following year, the Berkshire Conference of Women Historians' book award. The first paperback edition appeared as one volume in 1980 and was reprinted in 1982, 1985, 1993, 1994, and 1997; total sales figures for this edition and its reprints have reached 7,879—an impres-sive figure for a scholarly book, especially one so ambitious in size and scope. An abridged edition intended for classroom use and a more general audience, entitled *The Printing Revolution in Early Modern Europe,* which first appeared in 1983, then in 1993 as a Cambridge Canto edition (reprinted in 2000), has sold more than 25,000 copies. Cambridge published a second English edition in 2005. Moreover, the abridged edition has been translated into Japanese

---

3. *Journal of Modern History* 40.1 (1968): 1–56. For a complete list of Eisenstein's publications, including the other preliminary articles, see Appendix A.

4. All sales figures are courtesy of Cambridge University Press.

(1987) and most of the major western European languages—French (1991, reprinted in 2003), Spanish (1994), Italian (1995), and German (1997). In 2004 the abridged edition was published in Polish. At a time when most scholarly monographs sell only a few hundred copies, Eisenstein's work has enjoyed uncommon success.

Upon its appearance in 1979 *PPAC* was reviewed in more than eighty publications, an unusually large number for such a book; evocatively, it still attracts reviewers.[5] Interest in the book was not confined to academic circles at publication, nor has it been since. A more general interest was reflected in reviews in newspapers (the *New York Times,* the *Sunday Telegraph,* even the *Birmingham [Alabama] Gazette*) and general-interest periodicals such as *Encounter,* the *New Republic,* and the *New Statesman.* Still, most of the reviews were published in scholarly journals, including an unusual range of specialized journals—*Media, Culture, and Society, ISIS, Papers of the Bibliographical Society of America, Medical History, Terrae Incognitae, Journal of Ecclesiastical History,* to name a few—suggesting the wide array of subjects on which *PPAC* touched. Nor were reviews of the book confined to English-language periodicals; French, German, Dutch, Italian, and Russian journals and newspapers offered commentaries as well. Bibliographers reviewed the book along with historians of science, medicine, and religion; literary and media critics; librarians and book dealers and collectors; publishers, journalists, and cartographers; specialists in information science, technology, and management; and social commentators and pundits.

Some reviewers praised the broad scope as invaluable for new and innovative considerations of the history of technology and the intellectual life of early modern Europe. One noted that the work created a new interpretive framework for medieval and early modern European history in general. Eisenstein was credited with "single handedly" bringing "bibliography out of its ghetto" into "the larger world of intellectual and social history."[6] Such appreciation notwithstanding, the initial response to *PPAC* was decidedly mixed—and in some instances could be characterized as overtly hostile. While the immediate review attention accorded the book when first published signals early acknowledgment of its importance, the academy simultaneously had difficulty comprehending and assimilating Eisenstein's work. What two scholars noted in 1981 about the book's early critical treatment encapsulates

---

5. For a list of reviews, see Appendix B.
6. Peter F. McNally, "' . . . The Eye of the Beholder': Opinions Concerning Elizabeth Eisenstein and *The Printing Press as an Agent of Change,*" in *The Advent of Printing: Historians of Science Respond to Elizabeth Eisenstein's The Printing Press as an Agent of Change,* ed. Peter F. McNally (Montreal: Graduate School of Library and Information Studies, McGill Univ., 1987), 2–3.

its paradoxical reception: "Interestingly, those reviewers who were excited by Eisenstein's work seemed to doubt its contribution to history; critics who disliked it more than they liked it firmly stressed its importance."[7] Certainly there seemed to be an inherent recognition among scholars and reviewers that a book of such size and scope must be significant, but just as certainly there was also inherent tension in the way most of the late 1970s–early 1980s intellectual community responded to the book.

A frequent early criticism was that *PPAC* is too long—one reviewer wrote that it would be "twice as good a book at half the length."[8] (Probably not even the book's most sincere admirers wished *PPAC* longer than it is.) Others complained that it was heavy going, though for every reviewer who complained that the book was "a grueling read" or "impossible to comprehend," others said it was "consistently readable," "highly readable," "delightful reading," "a pleasure to read," or "fresh and engaging."[9] Some scholars, like Anthony Grafton in an article-length review written early in his career, reproached Eisenstein for her reliance on secondary sources.[10] Her "admitted distance from primary sources prompts strong reservations about the value of much of her enterprise," another commented.[11] Although some more recent critics have accused Eisenstein of "technological determinism," few did at the time of publication, and one even absolved her of it explicitly, writing that "she retains technology as the center of social change while she rejects technological determinism."[12] But others thought she put technology too much at the center. Grafton regarded "exaggerated claims of explanatory power" attributed to print as one of the book's major "flaws."[13] Michael Hunter remarked on "a certain reductionist streak running through the book—a tendency to overestimate printing as against other forces of change in the period."[14] A full

---

7. Donald G. Davis and Betsy Vantine, "The Significance of the Printing Press in the West," *Fides et Historia* 13 (1981): 86.

8. Owen Gingerich, review of *PPAC*, *The Papers of the Bibliographical Society of America* 75.2 (1981): 230.

9. Roy Porter, "Printing and Change," review of *PPAC*, *Books & Issues* 1 (1979): 11; Paul Needham, review of *PPAC*, *Fine Print* 6.1 (1980): 24; Peter Laslett, review of *PPAC*, *Renaissance Quarterly* 34.1 (1981): 83; Ashley Montagu, "The Power of the Press," review of *PPAC*, *The Sciences* 20.7 (1980): 21; Ernest G. Schwiebert, review of *PPAC*, *Church History* 49.1 (1980): 84; D. P. Walker, "The Power of the Press," review of *PPAC*, *New York Review of Books* 26.16 (October 25, 1979): 44; Robert S. Westman, "On Communication and Cultural Change," review of *PPAC*, *Isis* 71.3 (1980): 477.

10. Anthony T. Grafton, "The Importance of Being Printed," review of *PPAC*, *Journal of Interdisciplinary History* 11.2 (1980): 269–71.

11. Eric J. Freeman, review of *PPAC*, *Medical History* 25.4 (1981): 425.

12. Roy Atwood, review of *PPAC*, *Media, Culture, and Society* 2.2 (1980): 193.

13. Grafton, "Importance of Being Printed," 285.

14. Michael Hunter, "The Impact of Print," review of *PPAC* and Capp, *Astrology and the Popular Press*, *Book Collector* 28.3 (1979): 341.

twenty years after the appearance of the book, in 1999, Diederick Raven continued to reject definitively Eisenstein's theory of print on the grounds that it treats printing as "a monolithic phenomenon that can be fully understood simply in terms of some de-contextualized technical characteristic."[15]

Several reviewers at the time of publication faulted the book for its "polemical" or even "highly polemical" or "polemical and often pugnacious" tone.[16] Eisenstein's tone was labeled "strident" by others, and her style was characterized as unfocused "eclecticism" run amok. Her ideas were characterized as "quasi-scientific," "impenetrable," and "simple-minded."[17] Only the "great historians," such as Alexis De Tocqueville, Jacob Burckhardt, and Leopold von Ranke, one critic wrote, had the ability to "escape from historiographical forms," strongly insinuating that Eisenstein was reaching beyond her abilities and failing.[18] Yet Eisenstein's "combativeness" won praise from one reviewer.[19] Another called the book "undogmatic," while one more lauded the author's "admirable and unusual sensitivity to possible counterarguments."[20] But there was also a reviewer who faulted the scope of her work as both too narrow and too sweeping![21]

While some criticisms seem fair enough, others now seem decidedly off the mark and reflect a failure to understand what Eisenstein was attempting to do and what she had to overcome in the process. Today it is impossible not to suspect strong gender as well as other biases behind the kinds of comments aimed at her major work. Thirty-five, or even twenty-five, years ago, Eisenstein was a member of a pioneering generation of female scholars in a male-dominated academy, not to mention field (history). These women often faced hostility at worst and condescension at best in their professional lives. If her tone was strident, undoubtedly it needed to be to make her voice heard. When her book appeared, several reviewers insisted (pointedly?) on calling her "Miss" or "Mrs." rather than "Professor" or "Dr." Eisenstein. If she was pugnacious and combative in writing, in reality Elizabeth Eisenstein was a

---

15. Diederick Raven, "Elizabeth Eisenstein and the Impact of Printing," *European Review of History / Revue européene d'histoire* 6 (1999): 234.

16. William J. Bouwsma, review of *PPAC, American Historical Review* 84.5 (1979): 1357; Grafton, "Importance of Being Printed," 275; Hunter, "Impact of Print," 345; Gingerich, review of *PPAC*, 229; Donald R. Kelley, review of *PPAC, Clio: A Journal of Literature, History, and the Philosophy of History* 10.2 (1981): 213.

17. McNally, " 'Eye of the Beholder,' " 2–3.

18. Philip M. Teigen, "A Prolegomenon to the Interpretation of *The Printing Press as an Agent of Change,*" in McNally, *Advent of Printing*, 12–3.

19. J. R. Jacob, "The Medium and the Message in Early Modern Europe," review of *PPAC* and other books, *Annals of Scholarship: Metastudies of the Humanities and Social Sciences* 1.2 (1980): 117.

20. Conor Fahy, review of *PPAC, Italian Studies* 36 (1981): 95; Charles B. Schmitt, review of *PPAC, Journal of Modern History* 52.1 (1980): 111.

21. Raven, "Eisenstein and the Impact of Printing," 234.

wife and mother who was attempting to build a career through half-time positions, the sort to which many female academics were then consigned. She ultimately accepted a situation that brought her much-deserved success and recognition but that nevertheless came at a price, dividing her time between a professorship at a midwestern university and an East Coast spouse. Challenges such as these mark her as a pioneer in more ways than one when she produced *PPAC* a quarter century ago.

Sales figures, awards, and extensive review should not be taken as the only signs of the scholarly significance of *PPAC*. What is more important to note is that this work is widely read and used by scholars as well as students, a status that can be quantified to some degree. A search of the *Arts and Humanities Citation Index,* for example, turned up as of September 2006 no fewer than 564 references to the book. Note that this number does not include monographs. Many of the articles address nontraditional, nonwestern fields and thus attest to the spread of *PPAC*'s influence in areas of inquiry far removed from its central concern with the elite culture of early modern Europe. Examples include Catherine Bell, " 'A Precious Raft to Save the World': The Interaction of Scriptural Traditions and Printing in a Chinese Morality Book," *Late Imperial China* 17 (1996): 158–200; and M. Q. Zaman, "Commentaries, Print, and Patronage: 'Hadith' and the Madrasas in Modern South Asia," *Bulletin of the School of Oriental and African Studies, University of London* 62 (1999): 60–81. Likewise, the *Social Sciences Citation Index* by the same date listed some 333 articles in social sciences journals that cite the book. (The two databases overlap somewhat, but again the SSCI counts only articles, not books.) It is more difficult to quantify citations in monographs definitively, but a Google Book search, which allows a search within the texts of books that Google has digitized, provides some indication. A search in September 2006 produced 249 different titles—monographs about political history, literary history, media studies, the history of science, psychology, and many other subjects. They include such unlikely titles as *Accounting as Social and Institutional Practice*—but perhaps it is not so unlikely after all, given *PPAC*'s reach. A more general Google search of the Internet as a whole (today's benchmark of cultural currency) for the key words "Elizabeth L. Eisenstein" and "The Printing Press as an Agent of Change" returned, respectively, more than 5,200 and more than 8,450 relevant hits (numbers that have in fact increased exponentially while this volume of essays has been in preparation) in diverse languages dispersed over disciplines ranging from the history of printing to the history of religion to law, education, political anthropology, sociology, journalism, romance languages, and economics. Such searches statistically position the book as one of the most widely cited scholarly sources.

Just as some contemporary reviews took Eisenstein to task, some of these monographs and articles cite *PPAC* to take issue with it. But this capacity for sparking debate constitutes its continued relevance. In a 2002 review essay, entitled "Challenging Eisenstein: Recent Studies in Print Culture," Nicholas Hudson frames the five works under assessment as part of "a new stream of studies . . . critically re-evaluating Eisenstein's classic work across a number of fronts," with two taking "issue quite openly with some of the dominant assumptions," two doing so "more subtly," and the last "raising serious questions about the methodologies and founding principles of print-culture research."[22] Although Hudson's title places the reviewed works in opposition to Eisenstein's arguments, it is clear that these scholars have each taken up some of the many challenges for future work that Eisenstein herself set forth. Moreover, the fact that scholars are considering print in the ways that they do today can be traced back to the groundwork she laid nearly a quarter century ago.

This sort of consideration holds true, for example, for Adrian Johns, a historian of science who has come of age in the post-Eisenstein world, and who has offered the most sustained criticism of *PPAC* in a work that matches it in length, *The Nature of the Book: Print and Knowledge in the Making*, published by the University of Chicago Press in 1998. Eisenstein and Johns aired some of their differences in a 2002 *American Historical Review* forum.[23] That the charges Johns mounts emerge most often as differences in approach has invigorated discussions surrounding Eisenstein's central theses rather than invalidated her arguments or rendered her approach obsolete. Moreover, these differences—his micro-investigations versus Eisenstein's large-scale overview of what was then the uncharted territory of print culture studies or his concentration on England (a backwater of the printing industry and book trade well into the eighteenth century) versus Eisenstein's cosmopolitan pan-European focus, to name perhaps the most obvious—often complement rather than discount Eisenstein's work. These and other disagreements help explain not only why her work has sustained an unusually high level of scholarly (and increasingly nonacademic) interest but also why it has generated so many different avenues of exploration. The fact that Eisenstein herself, now in her mid eighties, continues to be a vibrant intellectual and scholarly presence must also be taken into account when considering the manner in which her arguments have both persisted and been resisted.

---

22. *Eighteenth-Century Life* 26.2 (2002): 83–95.

23. Eisenstein and Johns, "How Revolutionary Was the Print Revolution?" *American Historical Review* 107.1 (2002): 84–128.

Twenty-five years on, Elizabeth L. Eisenstein's work continues to inspire and elicit response. The strengths outlined when the study first appeared have endured as its major assets. But perhaps most noteworthy about Eisenstein's study is that much of what was once considered its weaknesses are in today's academy generally viewed as positive attributes. This revised vision is particularly true of the original criticism of eclecticism—the fact that she adhered to no consistent historiographical paradigm or theory in her work but instead adapted and borrowed at will from methods best suited to the material and its analysis. The inability of scholars at the end of the 1970s to characterize her book as either fish or fowl is today acclaimed as the twin virtues of diversity and interdisciplinarity. These traits have in fact contributed to the continued relevance of her work. Eisenstein's study of the print revolution in its various forms is widely cited across the scholarly spectrum, and it appears regularly as required reading on an equally impressive array of course syllabi in numerous disciplines.

For the traditionalist as well as the postmodernist, *PPAC* provides a point of reference for investigating past and present communications revolutions. Witness Andrew Hadfield's recent essay in which he draws parallels between Eisenstein's argument about the import of print and the claims made by the postmodernist Jean-François Lyotard about computerization.[24] Hadfield's piece exhibits a careful, nuanced understanding of her arguments: "What Eisenstein's analysis highlights is that the rising hegemony of printing did not precipitate a transformation based on a change in the means of intellectual production, as technological determinists like Walter Ong and Marshall McLuhan would claim. Rather, the inauguration of cheaply reproducible printed texts altered the relations of intellectual production forever, serving to magnify some significant questions and problems as others faded into the background."[25] Plainly rejecting a view of Eisenstein as a technological determinist, Hadfield also comments on the resemblance between Lyotard's claims of the contradictory "double play" of processes enacted by computerization and claims made by Eisenstein about the conflicting roles of early print.[26] That Eisenstein grapples so thoroughly with the complex, at times

---

24. "National and International Knowledge: The Limits of the Histories of Nations," in *The Renaissance Computer: Knowledge Technology in the First Age of Print,* ed. Neil Rhodes and Jonathan Sawday (London and New York: Routledge, 2000), 106–19.

25. Ibid., 108–9.

26. For Lyotard, computerization has enacted processes that solidify specific identities even as they simultaneously attempt to dismantle them; likewise, Eisenstein noted that print functioned both as a democratically unifying force that cut across national and linguistic boundaries and as a divisive agent that assisted in the development of individual nation-states (ibid., 109).

contradictory, effects of print as a reactive agent explains to a large extent the sustained attraction of her work as a road map for new ways of understanding past communication shifts as well as the technological revolution currently under way.

Eisenstein, in fact, is often embraced as oracular for students and scholars of the Internet revolution. In October 2000, at the turn of a millennium and amid much anxiety about the future of the book, the RAND Corporation and Nanyang Technological University cosponsored a by-invitation conference titled "New Paradigms and Parallels: The Printing Press and the Internet," with Eisenstein's *PPAC* figuring prominently. By assessing parallels between the history and impact of printing in Asia and Europe, the conference organizers sought a more informed basis for developing policies for the Internet and for identifying significant trends as Internet use matures. Eisenstein's "seminal work" served as the cornerstone for studying the general history and impact of printing.[27] Similarly, in June 2002 Eisenstein gave the keynote address, "Old Media in the New Millennium," at the Third Annual Convention of the Media Ecology Association. Others outside the scholarly community have also been drawn to her work's usefulness in contemplating the potential benefits and pitfalls of the Internet. For example, in an online review of the 1983 abridged version, *The Printing Revolution in Early Modern Europe,* the writer for IPS Funds, then a subsidiary of CITCO-Quaker Fund Services, calls her work a " 'Must Read' for anyone wondering how the World Wide Web will affect our civilization." What makes her work such compulsory reading, the review asserts, is its vision: "Many investment professionals, as well as those in the information industry and in government, are trying to understand the longer-term ramifications on our culture of the Internet and the WWW. . . . [Eisenstein's book] was written in 1983, way before the explosion of the WWW onto our civilization, so Eisenstein did not consciously pursue parallels with our current information revolution. However, this makes the incredible number of parallels even more remarkable, since they were not consciously drawn."[28] As these instances suggest, our present proximity to a media revolution and the wake of the dot.com crash allow us to understand better the apparently uncontrolled agency of media and how their technological platforms operate as intellectual, cultural, political, and economic catalysts than could scholars encountering Eisenstein's work in the

27. The Web site for the conference (held October 5–6, 2000) is http://www.rand.org/multi/parallels/SM/index.html.
28. IPS Funds Virtual Bookstore Web site, http://www.ipsfunds.com/bookstore.html#eisenstein. (As of October 2006, IPS Funds appears to be operating independently in Knoxville, TN.)

pre-Internet-explosion world of 1979. What has perhaps contributed most to *PPAC*'s continuing vitality and frequent application—especially to trends and phenomena not explicitly rooted in the western European Renaissance and Enlightenment—is undoubtedly its interdisciplinarity.

THE ESSAYS here speak to the ways in which Eisenstein's work has been an agent of change, within and across scholarly disciplines, for over two and a half decades. Many commentators on *PPAC* have paused to consider the choice of "agent" as a keyword in the book's title. While some have stressed the use of "an" to mark the printing press's status as one among many agents, others have pondered the choice of "agent" over "agency." Within this latter group, some critics have noted that agent bestows anthropomorphic powers on an inanimate object, the press, and have cited the title as evidence for placing Eisenstein in the technological determinist company of Marshall McLuhan, whom Eisenstein acknowledges as an inspiration but from whom she has nevertheless distanced herself. Eisenstein, in the preface to *PPAC*, reflects on her title, and her comments specifically address the issue of human agency. Her concerns, however, center not on the potential interpretations of "agent" but on whether to substitute "early printer" for "printing press." Practicality, she explains, won out in the end when she decided that referring to "the tool rather than its user" would simplify library cataloguing (xv). At the same time, she takes pains to underscore that "the term printing press in the context of this book serves simply as a convenient labeling device; as a shorthand way of referring to a larger cluster of specific changes—entailing the use of movable metal type, oil-based ink, etc." (xv).

Practicalities aside, Eisenstein's use of the term "agent" unavoidably invokes other connotations that in turn suggest analogies worth considering in the light of the ideas her original study sets forth and the revolutions of imagination it has sparked across and within academic disciplines. Specifically, much like a chemical agent whose resulting reactive properties are predicated on the presence of other agents and specific conditions, the Renaissance printing press as an "agent" was a catalyst for major movements and concomitant changes in the structure of knowledge and cognitive operations. Within this connotative frame, the material (paper, moveable metal type, ink, and the like) and the human (printers, financiers, readers, typefounders, et al.) combined at a particular moment with other, specific sociohistorical, economic, and cultural conditions to produce the revolutionary effects Eisenstein details.

In a similar vein, this volume's title, *Agent of Change: Print Culture Studies after Elizabeth L. Eisenstein,* speaks to the power of Eisenstein's *PPAC* as a reactive agent. The twenty essays that follow affirm not only the reactive properties of Eisenstein's study as an agent of scholarly invigoration and change but also the depth and breadth of the effects of these properties. Moreover, this volume profiles on several levels the ways in which her work has shaped the contexts and parameters for viewing printing as a material, social, and psychological practice. In the microcosm, the process of commissioning these essays, from scholars in the field of ancien régime French history, was a fascinating glimpse into the misinterpretations, controversies, and rivalries precipitated by Eisenstein's work. But taken as a whole, in the macrocosm, the collection of essays assembled here demonstrates without doubt the widespread, sustained influence exercised by Eisenstein's original study on conceptions of the intellectual and cultural consequences of print. Whether scholars are in agreement or disagreement with her ideas, there is one certainty throughout—no one would approach print in the ways we do today were it not for her.

While all the essays in this collection illustrate the role that Eisenstein's pioneering study has played in the formation and development of print culture studies, those in Part I, "Agents, Agency, and Print in Early Modern Europe," attend particularly to new directions in scholarly inquiry within the historical era and culture most explicitly addressed by her work. As the introduction to this part details, these opening essays bear witness to the immediate debates and transformations inspired by her treatment of print. The essays in Part II, "Exchange, Agency, and Adaptation in the Cosmopolitan World of Print," ponder the usefulness of her work for understanding cultures of print beyond the geographic and temporal boundaries of her original study. In Part III, "Agency, Technology, and the New Global Media Revolution," the essays apply methods and lessons from *PPAC* to interpreting the intellectual and cultural effects of the current technologically revolutionary moment. Concluding the volume is a conversation with Elizabeth Eisenstein, offering her own recent reflections on the history of her foundational work, the directions it has taken, and the debates it has inspired.

PPAC continues to exert a hold over the imaginations of its proponents and critics alike. Its reactive properties notwithstanding, it has unquestionably endured in a way unusual for a scholarly work. Contrary to the predictions of early critics, Elizabeth Eisenstein is poised to take her place among the most noted of historians. Long a member of the American Academy of Arts and Sciences and a Fellow of the Royal Historical Society, Eisenstein, in January 2003, received the American Historical Association's Award for Scholarly Distinction for "labor[ing] excellently for more than forty years . . . to achieve an international eminence."[29] The University of Michigan (from which she retired as Alice Freeman Palmer Professor of History) in Decem-

---

29. "2002 Book Awards and Prizes," American Historical Association Web site, http://www.historians.org/annual/2003/2002prizes.htm.

ber 2004 awarded her a doctorate of humane letters for her achievements as "one of America's most distinguished historians."[30] Most recently, Eisenstein was honored with a new edition of her primary work (albeit the abridged edition) to mark the twenty-fifth anniversary of the original publication of her ideas on the printing revolution in early modern Europe.[31] This kind of anniversary edition is among the most rare of honors, accorded to very few books at all, much less to a work whose presentation of such challenging and controversial ideas has daunted more than a few readers.[32] Writing on imagination and historiography, the distinguished historian Bernard Bailyn describes a truly visionary work of history as one that generates "a whole area of historical investigation by redirecting it from established channels into new directions, unexplored directions, so that what was once dark, vague, or altogether unperceived, is suddenly flooded with light, and the possibilities of a new way of understanding are suddenly revealed."[33]

Eisenstein's work surely has been a catalyst not only for historical imagination but also for the creation of an entire discipline—print culture studies. Whether viewed as visionary or limited, since the early days of its publication, *PPAC* has dominated and directed conversations about print and its effects. Given our present concerns about the fate of the book and reading in this age of electronic technological revolution, it is clear that the role of print in the historic development of scientific, intellectual, and cultural movements remains central. Illustrating the centrality of print in understanding the past and present, as well as the future, these essays explore the current state of print culture studies and point to its future in particular. At the same time, they reveal the broad influence of Eisenstein's work in enabling both its champions and its foes to envision print and its study in previously unimagined ways.

---

30. "The University Record Online," November 14, 2004, University of Michigan Web site, http://www.umich.edu/~urecord/0405/Nov22_04/06.shtml.

31. Elizabeth L. Eisenstein, *The Printing Revolution in Early Modern Europe,* 2nd ed., with new afterword (Cambridge and New York: Cambridge Univ. Press, 2005).

32. Another contributor to this volume has also been honored with a twenty-fifth anniversary edition of his work: Robert Gross, *The Minutemen and Their World,* 25th anniversary ed. (New York: Hill and Wang, 2001).

33. Bailyn, "History and the Creative Imagination," quoted in *New York Review of Books* 50 (February 13, 2003): 38.

Part I

Agents, Agency, and Print in Early Modern Europe

[Printing] warrants special attention because it had special effects. In this book I am trying to describe these effects and to suggest how they may be related to other concurrent developments. The notion that these other developments could ever be *reduced to nothing but* a communications shift strikes me as absurd. . . . When I take issue with conventional multivariable explanations (as I do on several occasions) it is not to substitute a single variable for many but to explain why many variables, long present, began to interact in new ways.

—Elizabeth L. Eisenstein, *The Printing Press as an Agent of Change*

In the preface to *The Printing Press as an Agent of Change: Communications and Cultural Transformations in Early-Modern Europe* (*PPAC*), Elizabeth Eisenstein characterizes her book as a "large-scale synthetic work" whose "inevitably inadequate, necessarily tentative treatment" of print and its effects is nonetheless far better to attempt than risk the continued neglect of this important topic (xvi–xvii). She again draws attention in her conclusion to the work's provisional character, noting that her "conjectures" are "based on uneven knowledge of pertinent data, much of it drawn from unreliable general accounts, and all of it relevant to very few regions. Too many gaps have been filled in by logical inference" (705–6). An explicit hope she held for the book was that its arguments would effect an extended reconsideration of print as a worthy object of study among historians—a recognition that the ostensibly completed narrative of print's significance, a byproduct of nineteenth-century historiography's grand designs, was instead a crucial, still-unfolding story woefully incomplete in its telling (705). She positioned her book as a reactive agent with its postulations and gaps intended to create a broad outline for subsequent historians to probe, flesh out, fine-tune, validate, or disprove.

Twenty-five years on, the book's reactive capabilities derive, in part, from the status Eisenstein accords to human agency and her focus on what she identifies as particular features, or actions, of print—fixity, standardization, and dissemination—as well as their consequences. In detailing these characteristics, Eisenstein refrains from formal definitions and instead turns to the effects these traits render. Fixity, for example, is intended to describe the broad preservative effects of print, which she considers its "most important" quality (113). As such, the dictionary notion of fixity to "make . . . firm, stable, or stationary . . . permanent . . . definite and settled; . . . to give definite, visible, or fixed form to (something that is intangible, fleeting, or elusive) . . . [to] capture" assumes a surprisingly fluid and dynamic character in her discussions.[1] A cessation of the ebb and flow of ancient languages lost and found, the development and codification of vernaculars and their nationalization, the emergence of new conceptions of authorship and intellectual property rights—all, in Eisenstein's view, are results attributable to the preservative effect that printing fixed on texts through multiplicity rather than durability of copies (114). Through its preservative effect, print in essence "captured" texts, along with the information, or knowledge, contained in them. Indeed, Robert Friedel, a prominent historian of technology, concerned with material culture and the nature of invention, has recently been working to decipher what made technological innovations like the printing press in the West so powerfully transformative and has settled on the notion of capture as the explanation.[2] Moreover, it was primarily the preservative power of print (not just the proliferation of printed copies) that moved information—or knowledge—out of isolated, exclusive conclaves and into a more public

---

1. All standard, formal, and "dictionary" definitions are taken from *Webster's Third New International Dictionary, Unabridged,* consulted online. We have turned to the definitions of the verb forms of these terms not only because the emphasis here and in *PPAC* is on action but also because the dictionary definitions of these qualities refer implicitly to these nouns' verbs. For example, the definition for "standardization" is "the act, process, or result of standardizing."

2. Friedel presented some of this information from a forthcoming book at the Maryland Colloquium for the History of Technology in the fall of 2004. We are grateful to him for sharing his work with us in advance of publication.

sphere where anyone possessed of reading literacy could behold, or read, or be inspired (116).

Likewise, the formal definition of standardization—to "make uniform"—conveys rigid limitation. But, again, this is a concept that is far less static and far more reactive in Eisenstein's discussion than is frequently recognized: "The need to qualify the thesis of standardization is perhaps less urgent than the need to pursue its ramifications" (81). She locates the ramifications of standardization not in the production of numerous identical error-free copies (she recognized that printed copies are neither perfect nor identical) but rather in the stimulus provided by printed paratexts, particularly the "visual aids" so easily assimilated by print (in the form of illustrative images, tables, calendars, and the rest, as well as in more prosaic navigational tools such as page numbers, title pages, and alphabetically arranged indexes) (81). She considers the "repeated encounters with identical images" of such "spatio-temporal" graphic representations most powerful in the rise of print (84). Paratext, a concept explored by the French structuralist Gérard Genette,[3] is at the heart of the Eisensteinian analysis of the strategies of print and figures prominently in all of the accounts in this first section of *Agent of Change*. Elements of paratext constitute sites for transfers of information between producer and consumer, between printer-publisher and reader, that create interpretation. Thus, standardization for Eisenstein was defined by the sea change in style of presentation and the aesthetic of observation triggered by multiple uniform copies and the design elements they imposed on texts. For her, this effect amounted to an unmitigated transformation of interpretive frameworks, nothing short of a revolution in modes of perception and consequently in abilities to identify both the typical and the unique.

Dissemination, or diffusion, is usually defined as to "make widespread; foster general knowledge of; to spread abroad . . . promulgate." Rather than regard dissemination as simple multiplication and distribution of affordable copies, Eisenstein instead perceived it as the more interdependent effect of "cross-fertilization," or "cross-cultural interchange"(72),

---

3. There is no entry for "paratext" in either *Webster's Third New International Dictionary, Unabridged* or *Oxford English Dictionary*, both consulted online.

wrought not solely through diffusion but in conjunction with its opposite, collection. In other words, knowledge, or information, was " 'spread, dispersed and scattered' " by print in radically new ways (72), among vastly different ethnic, socioeconomic, and religious groups, into disparate regions, across geographic and linguistic borders. At the same time dissemination as exemplified by print was simultaneously responsible for the coming together of and collaboration among cosmopolitan intellectual communities, the establishment of large libraries, and the emergence of a plethora of new opportunities for study. Diffusion brought texts together in new ways and in new locations for comparison, correction, expansion of knowledge, and what Eisenstein calls "cultural diffusion," resulting in "entirely new systems of thought" (74–5, 79). Paradoxically, greater recognition of and appreciation for diversity were achieved through collection. For Eisenstein, as for Jean-Dominique Mellot (Chapter 2), diffusion is a much more complex process, full of juxtaposed mirror opposites and a wide range of capacities for permeability.

This emphasis on effects over definition helps explain why these features of Eisenstein's argument in *PPAC* have stimulated so much debate and controversy. Meanings gleaned from reactive properties as opposed to precise definitions create open-ended terminology that invites both further exploration and refutation. More specifically, this approach encourages tactics such as those adopted by Harold Love in Chapter 7. Acknowledging recent challenges to Eisenstein's treatment of "fixity," Love nevertheless is quick to assert that "Eisenstein's position [on fixity and textual transmission] remains persuasive as a statement about capacities," or inherent potential or possibility or power. At the same time, however, he — unlike Eisenstein — delivers a straightforward, dictionary-like definition of fixity based on qualities and parameters as he perceives and employs them in the study of late-seventeenth-century English poetry and manuscript culture. This definition enables him to focus on specific particularities rather than the less-defined, latent power of capacities.

Similarly, that Eisenstein situated human agency within the processes tied to the technological innovation of the printing press rather than foregrounding the human role has also contributed to *PPAC*'s role as a vital agent in scholarly debate. Such positioning has, for example, led to charges of an erasure of the human agent in the processes of print. And indeed in Eisenstein's overall considerations of the production and transmission of scientific knowledge, religious thought, and culture in early modern Europe, networks rather than individuals take center stage. These networks consist of individual human actors performing collectively in the context of technological, commercial, and intellectual trends and transformations. Moreover, she is interested primarily in the nexus among these various arenas of performance.[4] Interestingly just as she posits that these networks and their intersections be examined in ways that transcend specialized divisions of knowledge, throughout the book she appeals to contemporary scholars to move beyond individual, traditional disciplinary specializations. In Eisenstein's view, scholars should instead engage in collaborative networks reminiscent of those she examines, networks created through diffusion that she sees as having transformed the world not only during the Renaissance but also through successive ages. Mellot shares her vision in his essay here, studying diffusion of multiple cheap copies of standard print genres through networks of counterfeiters in ancien régime France. He finds such diffusion to be purely economic in origin but nevertheless vital to accelerating intellectual, political, and religious ferment, or change, leading to reformation, enlightenment, and ultimately political revolution. Diffusion leads the way to multiple levels and extensions of interpretation, which is an uncontrollable force, capable of far-reaching, radical, fundamental transformation.

All of the essays in this part bear out Eisenstein's hypothesis about the primacy of networks in the process of fixing, standardizing, and disseminating information through print in the early modern period, but they also show that the role of human agents, like Paula McDowell's subject Elinor James (Chapter 6) or David Scott Kastan's Humphrey Moseley (Chapter 5) or Margaret Aston's Little Gidding slicers (Chapter 4), cannot be discounted. Agents such as these leave little doubt that we need to know much more about the contributions of contemporary individuals to the early modern information revolution. Elinor James, for example, was printer-publisher and author at a time when that hybrid form of individual

---

4. In *PPAC* see, for example, 143, 150, 332, 359, 443, 447–8, 502, 642–3, 690.

agent was beginning to re-emerge after centuries of guild domination and specialization of function in the printing trade. She composed her political ideas unmediated directly into type, using her printing press to immediately bring information into the sphere of public communication. Where precisely did agency reside? In the printer-publisher, as many scholars have interpreted Eisenstein to be saying and as McDowell, Mellot, Kastan, and others assert here? In the reader, as posited by the structuralist Roland Barthes and the cultural historian Roger Chartier? Or in the technology of printing itself, as Marshall McLuhan and other technological determinists have argued? Is authorial agency visible only in the creation of the ideas that make up texts and not at all in the interpretation of texts? After all, Eisenstein's research, along with that of many other scholars before and since (like Aston, McDowell, and others in this volume), shows that much thought was given to the cues and signs that even Barthes recognized were purposely placed in the text to influence interpretation and establish meaning by someone or some thing other than the reader or the printing press. Both Eisenstein and Ann Blair (Chapter 1) find authorial agency, for example, in the appearance of the printed errata slip, with Eisenstein noting that even in the age of print, only living authors have the opportunity to correct their works (*PPAC,* 80). Blair, however, also points out the significant agency on the part of readers who corrected printed texts not just when they appeared but also during subsequent readings.

The importance of identifying and understanding the functions served by the materiality and form of printed books and texts, whether paratexts such as errata slips, illustrations, and recurring formats, or the physical configuration of the codex, is also reflected in this collection of essays. Writing about the architectural title page, William Sherman (Chapter 3) seamlessly joins the Eisenstein/Genette notion of paratext and also points up the heightened awareness of architecture among early modern readers of print (*PPAC,* 82–83). Sherman concentrates on the graphic representation in printed books of realistic thresholds — steps, porches, porticoes, doors — designed to pull readers metaphorically into printed texts just as their material architectural counterparts conduct visitors into buildings. The deliberate construction and decoration of the printed book as a metaphor of a building, or edifice, facilitates the interpretive transition that

Genette theorized: a more favorable reception and more accurate reading of the text is achieved through the application of paratextual forms familiar from aspects of life outside the construct of print. According to Eisenstein, "layout and presentation . . . reorganize the thinking of readers" (88). While Sherman at first glance might well be seen as highlighting the influence of the paratext and what Genette calls the architext as determined by the printer-publishers and perhaps even author, on further consideration he too recognizes the nexus of multiple agencies that influence interpretations of print and finds agency to some extent also in readers. In a similar vein, Kastan considers the construction of imaginative writing as a distinctive category within an emergent English nationalist literature through economically motivated manufacturing of homogeneous volumes in cumulative matched sets. Deliberate employment of common paratextual elements such as template title pages, frontispiece portraits of the authors, standard dimensions, and the like, was designed by the publisher Moseley not only to ensure marketability of his editions of poetry and drama but also to influence the interpretation or reception of the contents of Moseley's identically designed volumes. Again, this exploration of the activities of an individual printer-publisher shows the multiple, transforming effects of standardization in terms of style and aesthetic through mass production of identical, printed texts. Paratext, or packaging if you will, thus creates both genre and interpretation.

Eisenstein's identification of the impact of exact repeatability of graphic elements looms large in any subsequent consideration of the influence of observation on interpretation, although she points out that the relationship between print and image is one not without potential "disruptions" built in (258). Aston's consideration here of the "new kind of printing" developed in the Christian-utopian community of Little Gidding presents an instance where unrelated "picture and words" could easily have been "at odds" with one another (259). Adolescent girls sliced up printed texts and their illustrations, along with completely unrelated prints, to form component parts, which were then combined and pasted into different configurations to make new "hybrid forms" of books. What Aston found proves to be an illuminating augmentation of Eisenstein's ideas: the "multiple, carefully contrived transpositions" of image and text were not disruptive in the Little Gidding harmony but instead expanded "the reach of the text" as they influenced interpretation by readers. Reproducible (and repositionable) images, custom drawn or not, connected readers and text in ways that were simultaneously unique to and generic in the world of print. Thus once again through layout and format, the printer-publishers shaped interpretation.

These essays also demonstrate the reactivity of studying the historical impact of printing technology and the material object of the printed text in conjunction with literary criticism and reception theory. English literary critics, for example, familiar with the works of twentieth-century-French annales school historians, structuralists, narratologists, and poststructuralists primarily through English translations, appropriated French theories to invigorate their own intellectual milieu. The opportunity to merge the study of social history, sociological theory, and cultural bibliography with the study of literary texts and genres seems key as an explanation for why literary scholars in particular have gravitated so strongly to print culture studies. Lest readers of this volume find an imbalance in favor of Anglophone studies, particularly in this first part, it should also be noted that the English language during the twentieth century asserted a new global hegemony, establishing itself as the postmodern lingua franca and creating an intellectual empire based on English. Not surprisingly then, works in the fields of literary criticism, history, and bibliography, written in or translated into the English language, have the advantage in exercising global impact, as Parts II and III of this volume further illustrate. Even in colonial and postcolonial studies that focus on indigenous populations and deal with non-English material, most of the resulting articles and monographs are published in English. A negative corollary to this assertion, however, also exists: because of the dominance of English today, important work being published by Italian, Spanish, German, and Dutch scholars of early modern European print culture not yet translated into English is regrettably not accorded the attention it deserves. Still, despite the seemingly Anglophone and literary bent of this part, its essays nonetheless provide numerous examples of the interdisciplinary and international confluence that Eisenstein hoped her work would stimulate in the study of early modern western European print culture.

Chapter 1

Errata Lists and the Reader as Corrector

Ann Blair

THE ERRATA LIST counts as one of the trappings of the book that first appeared with printing.[1] It ranks alongside other innovations linked to printing, such as the title page, signatures, and foliation or pagination, in contrast to features (such as the table of contents, the alphabetical index, and the use of headings and textual divisions) that have antecedents in medieval manuscripts. While errors of course occurred in manuscript production and could be multiplied from one exemplar to many copies (for example in *pecia* copying), the errors in printed books were immediately multiplied in many hundreds of copies. Corrections ideally would be made in as many copies again. Stop-press corrections could be made during printing and account for the textual variations that can be found within a single edition. In addition, methods were sought to make corrections after the printing was completed. The earliest solutions included entering manuscript or hand-stamped corrections in copy after copy. A more costly and radical solution, and the only one that rendered the error invisible to the reader, was to reprint a new page (called a "cancel") to be substituted for the faulty one. Although we do not often know why one method of correction was chosen over another, the cancel was likely the optimal response to the intervention of a censor during the printing process, since it erased the offending passage without a trace.[2] But starting in

I am grateful for helpful feedback to Bradin Cormack, Seth Lerer, and the readers for the press, and to the participants of the Folger Institute Conference, "Transactions of the Book," November 2001.

1. Elizabeth Eisenstein, *The Printing Revolution in Early Modern Europe* (Cambridge: Cambridge Univ. Press, 1983), 80–88.

2. David McKitterick, *Print, Manuscript, and the Search for Order 1450–1830* (Cambridge: Cambridge Univ. Press, 2003), 126–7. See also R. W. Chapman, *Cancels* (London: Constable; New York: Richard R. Smith, 1930). Cancels were rare in the sixteenth and seventeenth centuries but more common in the eighteenth. The earliest example Chapman discusses is from 1648 (46–7). In one example he cites from 1800, a cancel was used to enlarge the list of errata (57). For an example of a cancel introduced in a print run probably in response to the demand of a censor, see the two states of Charles Perrault, *Les hommes illustres qui ont paru en France pendant ce siècle* (Paris: Antoine Dezal-

the early sixteenth century, the most common remedy was to include in the book a printed list of errata; these comprised errors noticed once the printing was completed, along with corrections that readers were asked to integrate by hand into their copies of the text after purchase.

Errata lists invite different kinds of study. So far they have been used mostly in editing texts to help determine the ideal state of an edition.[3] To study them from a broader perspective, it would be useful to have statistics about which types of books most often contained them and to reflect on the main reasons why. Clearly some printers and authors were particularly attentive to the quality of production, notably of humanist texts, but one can also find errata lists in vernacular works without great scholarly pretensions. Unfortunately, library catalogues are generally not consistent enough in indicating the presence of errata lists to enable one to study the question without a painstaking examination of vast numbers of individual rare books. One might also be able to use errata lists as a clue to printing methods, to discern common patterns of error. Just as today typing generates inversions of letters and scanning introduces confusions of similar-looking symbols, early modern printing generated peculiar types of error, including letters rotated from their correct position or confused (notably long s and f). Nonetheless, the list of common errors that one sixteenth-century printer included in lieu of a list of specific errata still rings familiar today, with its mix of typographical errors and errors of usage and spelling: confusion of similar letters, double for single consonant or vice versa, wrong punctuation or word division, missing or superfluous letters.[4]

A study of errata was amusingly singled out as the epitome of pointless erudition mocked in Jean Paul's 1795 novel featuring the fifth-form master Quintus Fixlein. "Fixlein had labored—I shall omit his less interesting performances—at a *Collection of Errors of the Press* in German writings: he compared *Errata* with each other; showed which occurred most frequently;

---

lier, 1696), one of which includes descriptions of the Jansenists Blaise Pascal and Antoine Arnauld, the other of which replaces these with descriptions of Thomassin and du Cange, who were orthodox Catholics.

3. For one such study, see Curt Bühler, "Errata Lists in the First Aldine Edition of Caro's *Rime* and of the *Due Orationi* of St Gregorius Nazianzenus," *Studies in Bibliography* 15 (1962): 219–22.

4. Sebastian Fausto, in an edition of Petrarch that he printed (1532), as quoted in Brian Richardson, *Print Culture in Renaissance Italy: The Editor and the Vernacular Text 1470–1600* (Cambridge: Cambridge Univ. Press, 1994), 25. Similarly, the list of errors in Jo. Peckham, *Perspectiva communis* (Venice: Io. Baptista Sessa, 1504) starts with a description of common errors ("inversione litterarum, ut n pro u, u pro n, m pro n, p pro d") and a list of words frequently misprinted, before listing specific corrections to be made by page and line number. This example is discussed in Ruth Mortimer, *Italian Sixteenth-Century Books* (Cambridge, MA: Harvard Univ. Press, Belknap Press, 1974), no. 367.

observed that important results were to be drawn from this, and advised the reader to draw them." [5] This fictional project, with its claims for importance left unsubstantiated, has understandably not elicited any imitators. But in recent decades historians of the book have increasingly attended to aspects of the book long considered insignificant. Focus on the material features of books has shed new light on the roles of authors, editors, printers, and correctors in producing books, as well as on the reception and actual use made of books in different contexts. Errata lists and practices of correction have begun to be included in these studies, though they have not yet been studied systematically.[6]

What I offer here are only some preliminary observations on errata lists and readers' corrections drawn from my reading primarily in sixteenth-century books, with an emphasis on humanist reference works. Errata lists and the prefaces that often accompany them show authors and printers in a last attempt to control the reception of the work, deflecting blame and instructing readers in the corrections to make in the printed text. Annotations in surviving copies show how readers engaged with the text and its errors, with or without attending to the errata lists, to produce the final version of the text in the copy that they owned. The concern for correcting a text was the principal source of the variations that can be observed among the extant copies of most early modern printed books; variations in print were generated by corrections made during the printing process and those in manuscript by readers after the fact.

---

5. Jean Paul Friedrich Richter, "Second Letter-Box," in *Life of Quintus Fixlein,* trans. Thomas Carlyle, intro. Wulf Koepke (Columbia, SC: Camden House, 1991), 146–47 (emphasis original). Of the eight classes of the gymnasium, Quintus taught the fifth class from the bottom and was outranked by the subrector, conrector, and rector; as explained in Carlyle's note 121. I owe this lead to Christian Helmreich, "Du discours érudit à l'écriture romanesque : Recherches sur les cahiers d'extraits de Jean Paul," in *Lire, copier, écrire : Les bibliothèques manuscrites et leurs usages au XVIIIe siècle,* ed. Elisabeth Décultot (Paris: CNRS Editions, 2003), 179–98.

6. See McKitterick, *Print, Manuscript, and the Search for Order,* chap. 4; Seth Lerer, *Error and the Academic Self* (New York: Columbia Univ. Press, 2002), and "Errata: Print, Politics, and Poetry in Early Modern England," in *Reading, Society, and Politics in Early Modern England,* ed. Kevin Sharpe and Steven N. Zwicker (Cambridge: Cambridge Univ. Press, 2003), 41–71; Paolo Trovato, *Con ogni diligenza corretto: La stampa e le revisioni editoriali dei testi letterari italiani (1470–1570)* (Bologna: Il Mulino, 1991). Others have called for a history of correction, including Bernard Cerquiglini, "Variantes d'auteur et variance de copiste," in *La naissance du texte,* ed. Louis Hay (Mayenne: José Cortí, 1989), 109; and Hans Widmann, "Die Lektüre unendlicher Korrekturen," *Archiv für Geschichte des Buchwesens* 5 (1964): 777–826.

The Origins of the Printed List of Errata

Humanist culture was steeped in practices of correction. Even before the invention of printing, humanist scholars labored toward their goal of restoring ancient texts corrupted in transmission to their original purity; they deployed increasingly sophisticated philological methods on the many manuscripts that they recovered and often increasingly sharp invective against colleagues engaged in parallel and competing efforts. In this competitive milieu humanists were worried, too, about the costs to their scholarly reputation of committing errors of their own. As recent work has brought to light, authors in the world of manuscript publication called on "correctors" to edit and improve, then vouch for the quality of their texts before putting them in circulation.[7] This context helps to explain why among the earliest reactions to printing one finds, along with praise and admiration, alarm at the prospect of the errors in poorly edited texts becoming diffused so effectively.[8] A few humanists called for a system of censorship, never implemented, to guarantee that only high-quality editions be printed.[9] Not only did printing introduce new intermediaries and, thus, potential sources of error between the author's manuscript and the printed book (including editor, compositor, and corrector, to name a few), but the errors generated in print would be spread far and wide, whereas "scribes . . . corrupt the text . . . in different ways," as one late-fifteenth-century editor articulated.[10]

The climate of heightened religious controversy and concern for orthodoxy on both sides of the Protestant schism also exacerbated anxieties about errors during the sixteenth century.[11] For many different reasons, ranging from the

---

7. See especially Anthony Grafton, "Correctores corruptores? Notes on the Social History of Editing," in *Editing Texts / Texte Edieren,* ed. Glenn W. Most (Göttingen: Vandenhoeck and Ruprecht, 1998), 54–76, discussing Giannantonio Campano, who served first as a corrector of manuscript works (58–9).

8. Elizabeth Eisenstein is at work on a study of early reactions to Gutenberg's invention.

9. John Monfasani, "The First Call for Press Censorship: Niccolò Perotti, Giovanni Andrea Bussi, Antonio Moreto and the Editing of Pliny's *Natural History,*" *Renaissance Quarterly* 41 (1988): 1–43; Martin Davies, "Making Sense of Pliny in the Quattrocento," *Renaissance Studies* 9 (1995): 240–57.

10. "Nec iidem erunt impressorum futuri errores, qui fuerunt exscriptorum: ii uno exemplari eoque prospecto atque emendato, quot volent codices una opera unoque tenore conficient: illi dum singulus quisque arbitrio abutitur suo, nunquam inter se ita conveniunt, ut ubi paulo sit protractior oratio aut implicatior, non diverse corrumpant." Giannantonio Campano in the preface to his edition of Livy, *Ab urbe condita* (Rome: Ulrich Han, 1470), dedicatory epistle, as quoted in Grafton, "Correctores corruptores?" 59 n. 17.

11. See the insightful analyses of Thomas More's self-correction and use of errata in Seth Lerer, "Errata: Print, Politics, and Poetry in Early Modern England," and *Error and the Academic Self,* chap. 1.

pursuit of an ideal of truth to practical concerns about blame and retribution, sixteenth-century authors and printers were certainly mindful of the virtues of minimizing errors and typically hired correctors (as free-lancers or regular employees) to proofread the compositors' work before each sheet was printed. A description of the Plantin shop in 1534 reports that proof sheets were supposed to be read in the print shop three times, with one person reading aloud from the original manuscript while the corrector checked the printed proof sheet.[12] A French author commented in 1586 that texts were usually proofread twice, first by the corrector, then by the author, but that deficiencies in the process often left numerous errors uncorrected.[13] Careful studies of the procedures of correcting and printing in early modern England suggest that the general sequence (proofs then revises) was similar, but subject to many variations, "not just from century to century in different houses, but from day to day in the same house."[14] Correction was also performed under great time pressure and amid the noise and bustle of the print shop. The variety of states of correction of a text printed within a single edition indicates that corrections were made not only before the sheets were printed in bulk but continually during the printing process. The uncorrected sheets were then used alongside corrected ones, to minimize expenses.[15] A few comments from the late seventeenth century indicate that errors introduced by printing were generally considered normal and inevitable.[16]

---

12. Johan Gerritsen, "Printing at Froben's: An Eye-witness Account," *Studies in Bibliography* 44 (1991): 144–62, esp.149–50, 157.

13. See Etienne Pasquier's account of 1586, as quoted in Jeanne Veyrin-Forrer, "Fabriquer un livre au XVIe siècle," in *Histoire de l'édition française*, vol.1, *Le livre conquérant: Du Moyen Age au milieu du XVIIe siècle* (Paris: Promodis, 1982), 279–301, esp. 292.

14. D. F. McKenzie, "Printers of the Mind: Some Notes on Bibliographical Theories and Printing-House Practices," in *Making Meaning: "Printers of the Mind" and Other Essays,* ed. Peter F. McDonald and Michael Suarez, SJ (Amherst: Univ. of Massachusetts Press, 2002), 13–85, at 53. See also Percy Simpson, *Proof-reading in the Sixteenth, Seventeenth and Eighteenth Centuries* (London: Oxford Univ. Press, H. Milford, 1935).

15. Although a few complained about the practice, the indiscriminate mingling of corrected and uncorrected sheets was "an ordinary part of everyday production." McKitterick, *Print, Manuscript, and the Search for Order,* 123. For a careful identification of stop-press corrections, see Curt Bühler, "Stop-Press and Manuscript Corrections in the Aldine Edition of Benedetti's *Diaria de Bello Carolino,"* in *Early Books and Manuscripts: Forty Years of Research* (New York: Grolier Club and Pierpont Morgan Library, 1973), 138–44, and "A Typographical Error in the Editio Princeps of Euclid," *Gutenberg-Jahrbuch* [41] (1966): 102–4.

16. "Le père Vavasseur n'aiant trouvé qu'une faute dans un de ses ouvrages, consulté s'il faloit mettre Errata ou Erratum. Le Père Sirmond lui dit: donnez-le moi, j'en trouverai encore une et on mettra Errata." *Menagiana ou les bons mots et remarques critiques, historiques, morales et d'érudition de Monsieur Ménage recueillis par ses amis,* 4 vols. (Paris: Veuve Delaulne, 1729), 2:343. Baillet singles out Robert Estienne as the only printer who may have had the honor of printing a book without any errors; Antoine Baillet, *Jugemens des sçavans sur les principaux ouvrages des auteurs,* 4 vols. in 9 (Paris: chez Antoine Dezallier, 1685), 2: pt.1, 18.

Authors could be involved in correcting their works, but because of the great cost and limited supply of type it was not possible to immobilize the type set to print a sheet for long (at most a day or two in the largest printing houses), so that the author had to be present at the print shop every day to correct proof sheet by sheet while the book was being printed—a process that could stretch over months.[17] When great distances separated author and printer—for example, when a book by an author in the American colonies was printed in London—either the sheets went uncorrected, as a printer acknowledged in one instance, or, in one case, a list of errata was printed in the colonies once the author had seen the printed book, producing a hybrid publication.[18] A printing manual of 1664 notes that printers were more inclined to take care in correcting a work when they were funding the publication themselves and less so when another's (the author's or a bookseller's) investment was involved, because a "well-corrected book will fetch a higher price and will sell better and the printer is diligent therefore if his investment is at stake."[19] It is also possible that errata were more often included in books in which blank pages were left at the end of the final quire because the errata filled space that would otherwise have been wasted and thus did not incur any additional costs in paper.[20]

17. Léon Voet, "Plantin et ses auteurs. Quelques considérations sur les relations entre imprimeurs et auteurs sur le plan typographique-littéraire au XVIe siècle," in *Trasmissione dei testi a stampa nel periodo moderno,* ed. Giovanni Crapulli (Rome: Edizioni dell'Ateneo, 1985), 61–76, at 75. Voet reports that only one of the Plantin authors came in every day to correct the sheets of his book. But other authors reported spending months in the place of publication of their works to be able to correct their work in press: Erasmus spent eight months in Venice during the printing of his *Adages* by Aldus; Zuichemus spent two months in Basel while his commentaries were being printed (Gerritsen, "Printing at Froben's," 149). It is likely that Montaigne was involved in proof correction of his *Essays;* see George Hoffman, "Writing without Leisure: Proofreading as Work in the Renaissance," *Journal of Medieval and Renaissance Studies* 25 (1995): 17–31.

18. For a printer's reference to this kind of geographical impediment to authorial correction, see Margaret J. M. Ezell, *Social Authorship and the Advent of Print* (Baltimore, MD: Johns Hopkins Univ. Press, 1999), 92. On the errata sheets printed in Boston for Cotton Mather's *Magnalia Christi Americana* (London, 1702), see Hugh Amory, "Reinventing the Colonial Book," in *A History of the Book in America,* vol. 1, *The Colonial Book in the Atlantic World,* ed. Hugh Amory and David Hall (Cambridge: Cambridge Univ. Press, 2000), 26–54, at 32.

19. "Si liber Typographi impensis imprimitur, magna cura corrigitur: si Authoris aut Bibliopolae, parva, aut nulla: et cur? si sit bene correctus, majori pretio et a pluribus emitur; et ideo Typographus, si rem suam agat, est diligens: si alienam, negligens." Juan Caramuel Y Lobkowitz, *Syntagma de arte typographicae* in *Theologia praeterintentionalis . . . est theologiae fundamentalis tomus IV* (Lyon, 1664), 185–200, art. X, reproduced in V. Romani, *Il "syntagma de arte typographica" di Juan Caramuel ed altri teste secenteschi sulla tipografia e l'edizione* (Manziana: Vecchiarelli Editore, 1988), 46–7. See, from the same period, the complaint of Meric Casaubon that printers neglect to provide "erratas": Casaubon, *Generall Learning,* ed. Richard Serjeantson (Cambridge: Renaissance Texts from Manuscript, 1999), 139.

20. For an example, see note 42.

Even as printers often worked in haste, to maximize the utility of their presses, and rushed the process of correction, or undermined it by using uncorrected sheets, they also realized that errors would come at a cost in reader dissatisfaction. From early on a number of expedients were used to correct errors after impression. Corrections were made by hand in the copies of a 1467 edition of Augustine's *City of God.*[21] Lines omitted were hand-stamped in the margin in one instance; in others, lines were printed on a slip of paper that was either pasted over the erroneous passage in the print shop or inserted loose in the book for the reader to paste in as appropriate.[22] Manuscript insertions, even mimicking the typeface used, are attested for whole pages or for quires missing due to omissions in the supply of sheets.[23] By the early sixteenth century the solution of choice became standardized as a printed list of errata, usually positioned at the end of the text, but occasionally at the end of the front matter and hence near the beginning of a volume.[24]

---

21. C. Frova and M. Miglio, "Dal Ms. Subiacense XLII all'*editio princeps* del 'De civitate dei' di Sant'Agostino," in *Scrittura, biblioteche e stampa a Roma nel Quattrocento: Aspetti e problemi,* ed. C. Bianca et al. (Vatican City: Scuola vaticana di paleografia, diplomatica, e archivistica, 1980), 245–73, as quoted in Anthony Grafton, *Bring Out Your Dead: The Past as Revelation* (Cambridge, MA: Harvard Univ. Press, 2001), 148–9. In Juan de Ortega, *Suma de arithmetica* (Rome: a Stephano Guilleri de Lorena, 1515), the errata lists consists of two parts—the first lists manuscript corrections made in the author's "own hand"; the second errors left uncorrected, as described in Mortimer, *Italian Sixteenth-Century Books,* no. 331. In the copy of this *Suma* at the Houghton Library, at Harvard University, Cambridge, MA, the author's "own corrections" were sometimes made in time for the printing (e.g., fol. 48), sometimes in manuscript after printing (e.g., fols. 50, 59, presumably by the author), and sometimes by pasting on a correctly printed slip (see fol. 31).

22. Lucy Eugenia Osborne, "Notes on Errata from Books in the Chapin Library," *Transactions of the Bibliographical Society,* 2d ser., 13 (1932): 259–60, at 259–60, 263. For the hand-stamping of omitted lines, she cites Marchesinus, *Mammotrectus super Bibliam* (Venice: Nicolaus Jenson, 1479). In Valturius, *Dell'arte militare* (Verona: Boninus, 1483) omissions were printed in the bottom margin of the pages where the error had occurred. For an example of a slip inserted, Osborne cites Albertus Magnus, *De officio missae* (Ulm: Zainer, 1473). Aldus is credited with producing the first printed errata slip, containing a line that had been omitted from an edition of Aristotle; according to Sigfrid Henry Steinberg, *Five Hundred Years of Printing,* rev. ed. John Trevitt (London: British Library and Oak Knoll Press, 1996), 59 (no precise reference is given).

23. McKitterick, *Print, Manuscript, and the Search for Order,* 107–8.

24. Early examples of errata lists include Urbano Valeriani, *Institutiones graecae grammaticae* (Venice: Aldus, 1498), and the edition of Horace by Antonio di Bartolomeo da Miscomini (Florence, 1482), as cited by Paul Saenger, "The Impact of the Early Printed Book on the History of Reading," *Bulletin du bibliophile,* 1996, 237–300, at 240 n. 3. The Augsburg printer Erhard Ratdolt is credited with producing the first list of errata in A. Hyatt Mayor, *Prints and People* (opposite plates no. 74 and 75), as cited in Eisenstein, *PPAC,* 587; but Mayor's claim is hard to substantiate, as Lerer notes in *Error and the Academic Self,* 281 n. 19. For an example of a list of errata positioned at the end of the index, which is positioned at the front of the volume, see Caelius Rhodiginus, *Lectionum antiquarum libri XXX* (Basel: Froben, 1542), sig. [pi4]r.

In the many instances in which the author had not been involved in the correction of proofs (whether the author had not been given the opportunity by the printer or had not taken advantage of it), the errata list could be the result of the author's first contact with the printed version of his manuscript. Errata lists were sometimes prefaced with an outburst of authorial complaints against the printer. But printers might also draw up the errata lists themselves, to forestall the criticism of author or reader. Occasionally we know that the work was delegated to a third party: Isaac Newton, for example, drew up the list of errata for his teacher Isaac Barrow's edition of Archimedes.[25] The complexity of this errata page, divided into three sections, for corrections to the equations, the citations, and the figures, attests to the particular difficulty of identifying the errata to a technical work (see fig. 1.1).[26] Galileo had a conflictual relationship with Tommasso Stigliani, to whom he had entrusted the responsibility of seeing his *Il saggiatore* (1623) through the press. As a result, the work survives in three states: the first with the original list of sixteen errata drawn up by Stigliani; the second with a much longer list of errata that Galileo had printed to paste over the original errata list, notably in copies to give to his friends, in order to remove unauthorized insertions and changes made in the printed text; and the third state with a new printing of the final gathering to include Galileo's long list of errata.[27] More typical are the instances in which the authorship of the errata list is unknown, as in Copernicus's *De revolutionibus* (1543) — a curious case in that the printed list of errata, present only in a minority of copies, stops midway through the book at folio 146 and contains two gaps; but a list of errata for the rest of the work, perhaps drawn up by an expert reader, likely circulated in manuscript.[28]

The method and precision of the references given in the errata list varied, though in general the exercise encouraged the use of specific forms of

---

25. Richard Westfall, *Never At Rest: A Biography of Isaac Newton* (Cambridge: Cambridge Univ. Press, 1980), 258.

26. See Isaac Barrow, ed., *Archimedis opera* (London: Guil. Godbid, 1675), 286.

27. As described in *Ownership of Books: An Investigation into Provenance,* an exhibition in the Thomas Fisher Rare Book Library, University of Toronto, July 18–October 28, 1994 (Toronto: Univ. of Toronto Library, 1994), 40. For an illustration of a page from Galileo's extended list of errata, with a further manuscript addition, see Bradin Cormack and Carla Mazzio, *Book Use, Book Theory: 1500–1700* (Chicago: Univ. of Chicago Library, 2005), 62.

28. On the printed errata sheet, see Noel Swerdlow, "On Establishing the Text of '*De revolutionibus,*'" *Journal for the History of Astronomy* 12 (1981): 35–46, with a reproduction on 41. On the errata for the rest of the text, see Owen Gingerich, "An Early Tradition of an Extended Errata List for Copernicus' *De revolutionibus,*" *Journal for the History of Astronomy* 12 (1981): 47–52; a revised list appears in Owen Gingerich, *An Annotated Census of Copernicus' De Revolutionibus (Nuremberg, 1543 and Basel, 1566)* (Leiden: Brill, 2002), 362–6.

ERRATA *sic corrigantur:*

Pag	Lin	In Argumento.		Pag	Lin	
2	8	A pro B.		54	13	A E pro B E.
2	13	X pro H & G.		58	25	M C pro Z C.
3	2	Z vel Y pro X.		59	ul.	majus pro minus.
8	pe.	C F H pro F G M.		62	16	G I pro C I.
9	19	B M pro D M.		64	22	L E pro L I.
10	34	F N O L pro P X O L.		64	26	O pro I.
11	3	A G pro H G.		64	29	D C pro G D.
16	10	F E ⌐ D E pro G F ⌐ D E.		66	6	B X K pro B X R, & B F pro BE.
16	17	DEq. EB x BA :: Tq . Mq pro DEq. EB x AE t: Mq . Tq.		66	16	A F pro A G.
19	11	C F pro C E.		68	17	D B q pro D K q.
20	ul.	C D pro F B.		68	33	H F x F E pro H F x F D.
21	4	Q. AE——EB pro Q. EB——AE.		68	34	
22	28	B A pro D A.		69	22	G I pro G L.
23	4,5 6,7	A G pro A E.		69	28	T O pro I O.
30	1	L X pro L K.		70	4	sectionum pro contingentium.
31	1	In margine, D E pro D C.		70	8	A E pro A F.
31	14	$\frac{4DEq.}{BX}$ pro $\frac{4FEq.}{BX}$		72	10	LSH pro LSF, & ALN pro ALM.
31	26	B H pro E H.		74	22	Deest + inter AEq & CXxXA.
35	5	F G pro O G.		75	pe.	Deest + inter EXq & CExED.
35	6	F H pro O H.		77	18	E C pro F C.
37	11	C B pro A B.		78	21	Citatur 4 & 22.6 pro 19.5.
37	pe.	Y Z pro V Z.		79	10	A B pro A D.
38		Fig. 49. pro 94.		79	26	K O B pro K O P.
41	13	B H pro B E.		86	5	F A pro D F.
43	pe.	B A C pro B A D.		91	ul.	O P pro O D.
45	25	X V pro X Y.		96	pe.	F G pro F M.
52	22	A, B pro A, E.		99		Ult. duæ lineæ ita corrigantur, FN.FL.::NK.KL. & (ob sect. AMD) NK.KL :: NM . ML quar FN.FL::NM.ML Q.e.a.
				102	8	A D, B G pro A C, B C.

In Citationibus.

*Prop.*9. *nota* f, *pro* 17.6 *lege* 16.6. *pr.*16.*n.*a,13 hujus *l.*12 hujus. *pr.*20.*n.*c,3.6 Libri I. *l.*1.6.*pr.*33.*n.*c,4.*l.*4.2. *pr.*38.*n.*c,21 hujus *l.*37 hujus. *pr.*44. *n.* a, 31 hu,jus *l.*37 hujus. *pr.*45.*n.*f, 7.1 *l.*7.5. *pr.*45.*n.* g, 4.1 *l.*4.6. *pr.* 51. *n.*m, 7.1 *l.* 7.5.

Prop. 2. *nota* g, *pro* 6.5 & 3 ax. 1 *lege* 6 & 5.2. *pr.*4. *n.*g, 53. hujus *l.*53.1 Libri II. hujus. *pr.* 48. *n.* g, *deest hæc citatio* (17 ax. 1.)

Prop. 4. *nota* 2, *pro cor.*44 hujus *lege cor.* 15.2 hujus. *pr.*8.*n.*k, 8.1 *l.*4.3 Libri III. hu,jus. *pr.* 16.*n.*d, & *pr.* 16,17,18,19.*n.* b, *in singulis pro* 16.5 *l.* 4.6. *pr.*20. *n.* c, 16.3 *l.*4.6. *pr.* 21. *n.* b, 46.5 *l.* 4.6. *pr.* 22. *n.* k, 2.6 *l.*6.2. *pr.* 23. *n.*b, 16.5 *l.*4.6. *pr.*23.*n.*d, *l.* facilè deducitur ex 15.3 hujus. *pr.*33. *n.*d, 2.6 *l.*6.2. pr.34.*n.*e, 15.6 *l.*16.6. *pr* 37.*n.*b, 49 & 51. hujus *l.* 2 & 11.3 hujus. *pr.*44.*n.*b, & *pr.*45.*n.*c, *pro* 15.6 *l.*16.6. *pr.*56.*n.*p, ex 2 vel 4.8 *l.* 2 vel 4.3.

*Prop.*14 *nota* 2,*pro cor.*14 hujus *lege* 5 hujus *pr.*15.*n.*b,36.1 hujus *l.*39.3 hujus. Libri IV. *pr.* 21. *n.*a, 6 hujus *l.* 8 hujus. *pr.* 21. *n.*b, 15 hujus *l.* 17 hujus.

In Schematis.

Fig.14. *deest linea* F G. fig.30. *deest* D *ubi* EH *occurrit sectioni.* fig.136. *pro* H *lege* B. fig.148. *deest* D *ubi lineam* AC *bisecat* KB. fig.176. *deest* E. fig. 194. *deest ubi* Y *ubi* LX *diametro occurrit.* fig.276. *deest* E *ubi* DK *sectioni occurrit.*

Fig. 1.1. The errata list in this edition of the works of Archimedes, drawn up by Isaac Newton, is particularly complex, with sections for changes to make in the argument, the citations, and the diagrams. Isaac Barrow, ed., *Archimedis Opera* (London, 1675). Call # *EC65.B2793.675aa. Courtesy of the Houghton Library, Harvard University, Cambridge, Massachusetts.

reference.[29] Some early errata referred to signatures.[30] Others used layout-independent references to book and chapter, although this feature was less useful in a list of errata than it was in an alphabetical index, for example, because a list of errata (unlike an index) is specific to a particular edition and therefore unusable for another one.[31] The errata list figures after the table of contents and the index among the forms of internal reference which are thought to have driven the development of foliation.[32] In an early example of precision, the author Domenico Nani Mirabelli boasts of the care with which he corrected his *Polyanthea* (1503), offering two pages of "castigata" arranged in two columns, each entry of which contained the term to be replaced in addition to the correct term to substitute for it, and a complete reference to folio number, column number (1–2 on the recto, 3–4 on the verso) and line number.[33] In a case where no line numbers were printed in the text, Erasmus was perhaps the first to refer to line numbers by counting from the top or from the bottom of the page, depending on which direction was shorter.[34]

Errata signaled in a list could also include corrections to headings, font choice, or paratext. Thus Conrad Gesner notes in his *Partitiones theologicae* "fol. 54c l. 29 the words 'de bonis spiritibus, de malis spiritibus,' pertain to the previous heading and should be written in small characters."[35] Another author issued an apology for errors in the table of contents.[36] Errors in illus-

---

29. Typically when an error is located only in vague terms, such as by book number, the compiler of the errata is aware of this shortcoming. For example, "est et in octavo libro :: pro =, sed locum non memini" (there is in book eight :: for =, but I don't remember where). *Euclidis elementorum libri xv breve demonstrati,* ed. Isaac Barrow (Cambridge: ex Academiae typographeo, impensis G. Nealand, 1655), list of errata.

30. Paul Saenger, "The Impact of the Early Printed Page on the Reading of the Bible," in *The Bible as Book: The First Printed Editions,* ed. Kimberly Van Kampen and Paul Saenger (New Castle, DE: Oak Knoll Press; London: British Library, 1999), 267.

31. The errata in Rhodiginus, *Antiquarum lectionum libri XXX* (1516), [863–5], refer to book and chapter and sometimes include a general position within the chapter, for example, "in fine."

32. Margaret M. Smith, "Printed Foliation: Forerunner to Printed Page-Numbers?" *Gutenberg-Jahrbuch* 63 (1988): 54–70, at 64. On the role of another kind of list of errors, the index of forbidden books, in developing methods of precise reference, see Paul Saenger, "Benito Arias Montano and the Evolving Notion of Locus in Sixteenth-Century Printed Books," *Word and Image* 17 (2001): 119–37.

33. See Domenico Nani Mirabelli, *Polyanthea opus suavissimis floribus exornatum compositum* (Savona: Franciscus de Silva, 1503), where the colophon boasts that the work was corrected by the author.

34. Erasmus, *Adagiorum opus* (Basel: Froben, 1528), [963]; when counting from the bottom, he specifies "versu a fine." For some discussion, see Saenger, "Impact of the Early Printed Page," 277.

35. Gesner, *Partitiones theologicae, pandectarum universalium liber ultimus* (Zurich: Froschauer, 1549), fol. 157v: "54.c.29 verba, de bonis spiritibus, de malis spiritibus, ad praecedentem inscriptionem pertinent, minutis characteribus scribenda."

36. See Jacob Soll, "The Hand-Annotated Copy of the *Histoire du gouvernement de Venise;* or, How Amelot de la Houssaie Wrote His History," *Bulletin du bibliophile* 2 (1995): 289.

trations could be remedied by inserting at the end of the book the correct illustration with instructions to cut it out and paste it over the illustration to be corrected in the text.[37] Errata lists could also contain errors or could be printed altogether in error.[38] In one book, one errata list was followed by another, to supplement it.[39]

The Forms and Uses of Errata Lists

I would identify two major models in errata lists: the exhaustive list and the general apology, with or without a short list of errors. A central model for the exhaustive list is provided by the errata lists in the works of Erasmus, who worked closely with his publisher Froben of Basel to provide editions of the highest quality. The Froben 1517 edition of the *Adages* includes two addenda (a type of improvement akin to errata) — a supplement to an existing commentary and a new set of adage and commentary. The Froben 1523 edition includes a list of errata, in a densely packed 1½ pages placed at the end of the volume, listing the correct word by page and line numbers at a rate of about 3 to 4 errata per line. At 95 lines this list contains 350–400 errata for 800 pages of print. Most of the errors are minor and are easily recognized — this list of errata clearly aims to be exhaustive. The densely packed and quasi-exhaustive list of errata as practiced by Erasmus constituted one norm for the genre, which was followed in other learned works.[40] The same strategy could be adopted in textbooks for beginners, in which an exhaustive listing of errors in figures, diagrams, punctuation, and spacing was designed to remove any

37. See, for example, Oronce Finé, *La théorique des cieux et sept planètes* (Paris: Cavellat, 1557), copy at Bibliothèque Sainte-Geneviève, Paris. See also Olaus Magnus, *De gentibus septentrionalibus* (Rome: J. M. de Viottis, 1555), where the errata list corrects transposed illustrations. I am grateful to Annie Charon-Parent for these references.

38. For a case of inaccuracies in the errata list, see Stephen B. Dobranski, *Milton, Authorship, and the Book Trade* (Cambridge: Cambridge Univ. Press, 1999), 49; and Gingerich, *Annotated Census,* 265. For editions of a book that included an errata sheet, though the errors listed had been corrected, see the pirated editions of John Hayward, *The Life and Raigne of King Henrie IIII* (1599), as listed in A. W. Pollard and G. R. Redgrave, comps., *A Short-Title Catalogue of Books Printed in England, Scotland, and Ireland and of English Books Printed Abroad, 1475–1640,* rev. W. A. Jackson, F. S. Ferguson, and Katharine F. Pantzer, 3 vols. (London: Bibliographical Society, 1976–1991) (hereafter *STC*) 12995–7a, as discussed in W. A. Jackson, "Counterfeit Printing in Jacobean Times," *The Library,* 4th ser. 15 (1934): 373. I am grateful to David Kastan for this reference.

39. See Thomas Bartholinus, *De libri legendis dissertationes vii* (Copenhagen: Daniel Paul, 1676), errata positioned after the dedication.

40. See, among other examples, the shorter but also densely packed lists in Caelius Rhodiginus, *Lectionum antiquarum libri XXX* (Basel: Froben, 1542), sig. [pi 4]r; or Girolamo Cardano, *De Subtilitate* (Basel: Ludovicus Lucius, 1554). Steinberg reports that Erasmus produced a twenty-six-page list titled *Errata et appendenda* designed to improve all of his works published to date in 1529, but I have been unable to identify this work more precisely; see Steinberg, *Five Hundred Years of Printing,* 59.

source of confusion for the inexperienced reader.[41] The longest errata list I have found so far, in a 115-page treatise *De ratione dicendi,* runs to 10 pages with a total of some 500 errors—those that the author complains the printer had promised to correct in the manuscript but did not, along with "very many new" errors introduced in printing: "Wherefore I exhort and beseech you, friendly reader, to take care to transcribe and note in the margin as soon as possible in their place these corrections as they are noted here in order."[42]

A quicker alternative to the exhaustive list of errata was to offer a general injunction to correct minor errors, in some instances coupled with a short list of major errors. Thus Etienne Dolet's *Commentaria linguae latinae* closes its first volume of some fifteen hundred folio pages with a list of just seven errata, as a short preface to the errata explains: "We could not altogether avoid errors and defects in a work as varied and thick as this one, though we devoted as much diligence and care as we could. The more serious errata that have occurred in reading here and there I put forward for you, but I also ask that if you find some not noticed by us, sweet and benevolent reader, in the name of letters to correct them sweetly and benevolently, as suits a man of letters and a friend of the learned."[43] Dolet pleads for indulgence from the reader and also makes a distinction between serious errors and the smaller "typo" variety that anyone could easily correct. The seven errors listed in Dolet's errata are indeed mostly major word substitutions, such as "Germanorum" for "Gallorum," "Varrones" for "Barones." The latter error makes good sense as an aural misunderstanding and may offer a clue to Dolet's use of dictation in composing the text.[44]

A number of other hefty volumes resort to this distinction between minor and major errors to reduce or even eliminate the need to provide errata. Thus the first edition of Domenico Nani Mirabelli's *Polyanthea* of 1503 notes:

---

41. See Samuel Jeake, *Arithmetick surveighed* (1696), as discussed in McKitterick, *Print, Manuscript, and the Search for Order,* 132.

42. "Quare te, amice lector, hortor et obsecro, ut has castigationes ut suo quaeque ordine notatae sunt, ita transcribendas et in margine exarandas quam primum suis locis cures." Garcia Matamoros, *De ratione dicendi* (Compluti, 1561), sig. P1v; the list of errors runs to sig. P6r. The unusual length of this errata list relative to the text may be a way of putting to use a quire that was otherwise mostly wasted since the text ended on the first page of the quire at sig. P1r.

43. "Erratis, et mendis in opere tam vario, tamque spisso carere omnino non potuimus, tametsi omni diligentia, et cura, quanta maxima potuit, adhibita. Quare quae graviora passim legendo occurrerunt, tibi hic solum subijcio a teque impetratum etiam, atque etiam volo, vel te potius literarum nomine rogo, ut, si qua forte reperias a nobis parum animadversa, tu ipse placate, et benevole, ut virum literatum et literatis amicum in primis decet, placate, inquam et benevole castiges: neque te in gratuito labore supra modum asperum aut ridicule morosum praebeas." Dolet, *Commentariorum linguae latinae tomus primus* (Lyon: Gryphius, 1536), vol. 1, col. 1707–8.

44. For an example of aural errors (made evident by their correction by the author) that provide convincing evidence for composition by dictation, see George Hoffmann, *Montaigne's Career* (Oxford: Clarendon Press, 1998), 47–8.

"Some errors were caused by the inattention of the pressmen [incuria impressorum]: those of some moment I have corrected; others of little moment, such as "aethicorum" for "ethicorum," or that are due to some letters being inverted or transposed, I have left to the prudence of the reader to correct." [45] This general disclaimer is not followed by a list of specific errata. Similarly, the 1565 edition of Theodor Zwinger's *Theatrum vitae humanae,* which opens with an apology by the printer (Oporinus and Froben brothers) explaining the lack of an index (which is promised in the title page), closes with an apology by the same "typographus" in which he explains the lack of a list of errata: "We can bear witness that . . . such a difficult work was undertaken in the most calamitous of times, while others were running wild and thinking about death more than the salvation of the republic [of letters] and was completed through the benevolence of God. In the meantime we should have according to custom noted here the errors that occurred against our will in such a large work: if the hope did not console us that these errors are not so large that they could not be corrected by anyone who was not without learning." [46] In the following edition of Zwinger's *Theatrum,* a half-page list of errata is supplied along with the usual apology for any remaining errors that the reader is enjoined to correct from his own learning.[47] Aware of shortcomings, these printers acknowledged that the text had not been perfected but called on their readers to finish the task.

Errata lists and the blurbs that accompany them were meant to acknowledge or shunt aside the blame for errors. Brian Richardson emphasizes the tensions between editors, authors, and printers in the world of early Italian printing and describes, for example, how the printers Giovanni Battista and Melchior Sessa sought to forestall the criticism of the author they had pub-

---

45. "Postremo quaedam errata impressorum incuria: quae alicuius momenti visa sunt castigavi: Alia levia: qualia sunt Rhoetor pro Rhet. Aethicorum pro Ethicorum: cum aliquibus forsan litteris inversis: aut transpositis: lectoris prudentiae corrigenda reliqui." Domenico Nani Mirabelli, *Polyanthea opus suavissimis floribus exornatum* (Savona: Francisco de Silva, 1503), fol. cccxxxix.

46. "Illud interim vere et ingenue testari possumus, non tam de lucro nos (quod iniquus aliquis calumniari posset) quam de Reipub. literariae commodis sollicitos, Opus tam difficile, tempore omnium calamitosissimo, feriantibus caeteris et de morte potius quam de salute Reipub. cogitantibus, suscepisse: atque illud Dei opt. max. benignitate, ad optatum finem perduxisse. Errata interim, quae in tam operoso Opere invitis etiam contigerunt, pro recepto more hic annotare decuisset: nisi ea nos spes solaretur, quod tanta non sint, quin a quovis non indocto corrigi et emendari queant." Zwinger, *Theatrum vitae humanae* (Basel: Ioan. Oporinum, Ambrosium et Aurelium Frobenios fratres, 1565), sig. [FFF5]r.

47. "Lectori: laboris magnitudo pro nobis deprecatur, si humanus es: si gratus, deprecatione nulla est opus. Et cetera quidem errata, quae vel casu vel negligentia in tam operoso contigerunt opere, tu pro tua eruditione corriges. Quorundam nos te hic admonere voluimus. Nam et nos homines sumus et humani nihil alienum a nobis putamus." Zwinger, *Theatrum vitae humanae* (Basel: Froben, 1571), 3:455.

lished (Girolamo Ruscelli) by producing a long list of errata "even though most of the errors are self-evident, so as not to give Ruscelli reason to make one of his usual attacks at the end of books against 'us poor printers.'"[48] In many instances, as in Zwinger or Mirabelli or Rhodiginus, the errors to be corrected are blamed on the lack of care of the pressmen ("incuria impressorum") in a move that presumably was designed to exculpate the author but that also, in the light of the jockeying for responsibility within the print shop, exculpated the "typographus" sometimes identified as the author of the apology.[49] A common strategy, regardless of the authorship of the lists, was to deflect criticism by flattering the erudition of the reader; thus Gesner explains in the front matter to one of his books that "the more learned and better the reader, the more he will forgive my errors."[50]

Errata lists could also be used to mobilize readers (at least alert ones) to carry out broad "search and replace" tasks that the author may have been unwilling to undertake directly. In some instances these were errors of fact interspersed throughout a large volume and thus time-consuming to correct individually. Gesner for example notes two errors in the opening pages of his large index to theological works, *Partitiones theologicae:* "fol. 7d, line 49 for Joan. Damianus read Joan. Damascenus and similarly wherever else this error may also occur; fol. 8b, line 12: Ulrich Zwingli in the Catechism, read in the Introduction to evangelical doctrine, and elsewhere where a similar error occurs, correct it similarly."[51] In more intentional cases of error-cum-correction, editors used errata lists to attempt to introduce new spellings or to eliminate dialectal forms by introducing systematic substitutions in the errata; cases of this kind are recorded especially in sixteenth-century Italy, where correct usage was the object of controversy and potential disagreement between author and printer.[52] Most spectacularly, the *-ana* attributed to the seventeenth-century

---

48. Richardson, *Print Culture in Renaissance Italy,* 12, discussing Girolamo Ruscelli, *Del modo di comporre in versi* (1559).

49. "Index eorum quae per incuriam sunt insigniter ab impressoribus admissa, peccatum et in alijs, opinor, sed ita, ut operam sibi vel mediocriter possit eruditus in eo praestare." Rhodiginus, *Antiquarum lectionum libri XXX* (1516), [863]; see also quotations from Zwinger and Nani Mirabelli in notes 45 and 46.

50. "Equidem ut quisque doctior et melior vir est, eo procliviorem ad veniam erratorum dandam mihi polliceor." Gesner, *Bibliotheca universalis* (Zurich: Froschauer, 1545), epistola nuncupatoria, fol. 5v.

51. "7.d.49 Ioan. Damianus lege: Damascenus et sicubi etiam alibi similiter forte erratum est. 8.b.12 Huld. Zwingli in Catechismo, lege in Isagoge ad evangelicam doctrinam; et alibi ubi similis error occurret, similiter emenda." Gesner, *Partitiones theologicae,* fol. 157v.

52. See, for example, Richardson, *Print Culture in Renaissance Italy,* 166, discussing Borghini's edition of *Istoria delle cose avenute in Toscana dall'anno 1300 al 1348* (Giunta, 1578). For other examples, see Trovato, *Con ogni diligenza,* 86–93, as cited in Lerer, *Error and the Academic Self,* 20–1.

French scholar Gilles Ménage describes subversive uses of the errata list, which took advantage of its being a widely ignored but potentially powerful feature:

> In those countries where the Inquisition exists, and particularly in Rome, the use of the word "Fatum" or "Fata" in any printed work is forbidden. An author who wished to make use of the latter, adopted this scheme. He printed the word, throughout his book, "Facta"; and then, in the Errata, he placed a notice, "For 'Facta' read 'Fata.'" A similar expedient was resorted to by Scarron. He had composed some verses, to which he had prefixed a dedication, in these words: "A Guilemette, chienne de ma soeur." Sometime after, having quarreled with his sister, just as he was preparing for the press a collection of his poems, he maliciously printed among the errata of the book: "For 'chienne de ma soeur,' read 'ma chienne de soeur.'"[53]

Broad substitutions made in the errata list called on the best readers (with the intention of not reaching all of them) to execute systematic "search and replace" operations that could change a name, a citation, a spelling, or even a word and its semantic thrust. The readers' activity was acknowledged in these instances as producing the final version of the text, which the author tried to direct, although he could never of course control it.

Like many other aspects of early modern printing, the use of errata lists was not consistent. Only a small percentage of books included them, and I have found no obvious pattern to the presence of errata so far. One can surmise that for books such as the Bible and a dictionary like Calepino, the very suggestion that there might be a mistake in the printed text would be too threatening to entertain. In contrast, one can surmise that with some books the concern for textual accuracy did not seem pressing, but then one of the genres where I have found several errata lists is in Italian dialogues on earthquakes, where the need for accuracy would not seem greater than elsewhere.[54] No doubt the presence and style of errata lists depended on the relationship between the printers and authors involved and whether, like Froben and Erasmus, they worked well together or, like some of the printers and authors Brian Richardson studied, they were rivals. Also, a printer or author might feel a competitive need to include a list of errata. I have identified two strategies for errata lists, which, whether they were exhaustive or selective,

---

53. George Moore, ed., *Table Talk or Selections from the Ana* (Edinburgh: Constable and Co., 1827), 23, *Menagiana*, no. 2. For the French original, see *Menagiana* (1729), 3:65–6; for two other similar examples, see *Menagiana*, 2:122. In so doing he no longer addressed the poem to "my sister's [female] dog" but to "my bitch of a sister."

54. See, for example, Lucio Maggio, *Del Terremoto* (Bologna: Benacci, 1571); Iacomo Antonio Buoni, *Del terremoto dialogo* (Modena: Paolo Gadaldini et Fratelli, 1571); and [Filippo de Secinara], *Trattato universale di tutti li terremoti occorsi, e noti nel mondo* (1571).

called on the reader to play an active role in correcting the text and perfecting it to match the author's intention.

Manuscript Corrections by Readers

How well did readers carry out the desires of printers and authors as expressed in errata lists? Certainly I would estimate that the most common kind of annotation left by early modern readers is the correction. It is also the most readily overlooked by modern commentators, because it seems intellectually uninteresting or simply because it is often virtually invisible. Some corrections are so discreet within the text that they easily pass unnoticed: a comma added, a letter capitalized, added, or crossed out, a number changed. More visible are the corrected words or expressions the reader copied out in the margin; these corrections might involve a small change — a space or a single letter added or omitted — or a large one, a word substituted for another, for example.

Readers certainly corrected very many obvious "typographical errors," as the authors of errata blurbs hoped they would. But readers' corrections could also stray from these most obvious corrections to larger interventions in the text. Thus, a nineteenth-century compilation of errors corrected (by hand) in early modern editions of English drama includes many drastic substitutions: "use" for "abuse," "action" for "account," and "anciently" for "accidentally."[55] Similarly aggressive corrections can be found in Latin works; for example, Isaac Casaubon changed "reposuit" to "respondit" in his copy of Jean Bodin's *Universae naturae theatrum.*[56] Close study of each case would be necessary to evaluate when larger corrections of this kind were plausible readings for a text corrupted by composition in haste or from difficult handwriting or dictation and when they constituted instead overzealous or speculative emendation.[57]

---

55. [J. O. Halliwell-Phillips], *A Dictionary of Misprints, Found in Printed Books of the 16th and 17th Centuries, Compiled for the Use of Verbal Critics and Especially for Those Who Are Engaged in Editing the Works of Shakespeare and Our Other Early Dramatists* (Brighton: for private circulation only, 1887).

56. For an exhaustive transcription of annotations in one work of 1597, including many corrections, see Ann Blair, "Restaging Jean Bodin: The *Universae naturae theatrum* (1596) in Its Cultural Context" (Ph.D. diss., Princeton Univ., 1990), 554–609. This transcription would not have been possible without the hospitality and help of Jean Céard.

57. For a reference to the problems posed to the printer by a difficult manuscript, see Adrien Turnèbe's complaint about the errors in his *Adversaria,* which he acknowledges were due partly to the messy state of his manuscript. "Huic tamen libro magna intervenit calamitas. Nam cum exemplar eius subitum et tumultuarium multis esset locis deletum, inculcatum, transpositum, male scriptum, operae librarij in transcribendo saepenumero manum meam adsequi non potuerunt et fere toto eo tempore, quo excusus est liber aut exscriptus, lenta quadam morbi tabe me miserum in modum excruciantis, ac ne nunc quidem dimittentis laboravi: quo factum est, ut qui aliquas mendas alio-

All the questions one can pose about how humanists corrected the ancient texts they edited surface again when one studies the early modern texts they wrote and read and corrected.

Manuscript corrections offer precious evidence about reading practices, with the usual limitation that they tell us nothing about those readers who left no traces of their reading. Readers who made corrections likely read with pen or pencil in hand, though we would often like to know more about the settings and circumstances of such readings.[58] Corrections indicate that a passage was read carefully (particularly when the corrections are not copied out from a printed errata list), even if the passage inspired no other kind of annotation. Some corrections requiring particular effort can be used as an indication of the special importance of an issue to a reader.

Why did readers make manuscript corrections in printed texts? One can imagine that humanist readers, steeped in a culture that staked reputation on practices of emendation and *castigatio,* corrected errors out of habit and out of self-respect (lest others think that they had not noticed the error). Similarly, concern to manifest religious orthodoxy motivated readers to correct errors of doctrine or formulation encountered in reading.[59] Early modern readers, like early modern authors, had multiple motivations to make corrections to improve a text, whether as an abstract good or for future reference for themselves or for others or to protect themselves from blame. By making corrections, readers completed the process of producing a text; despite the guidance of errata lists, readers had the last say, beyond the real control of either printer or author.

How did readers make their corrections? Much of the time readers exercised their own judgment more or less speculatively (and possibly in some instances in concert with others).[60] But readers also followed printed guidelines for correction — those issued by the various indexes of forbidden books

rum auctorum delere voluerim, ultro segetem errorum in scriptis meis obseverim." Adrien Turnèbe, *Adversariorum tomi III* (Basel: Thomas Guarinus, 1581), sig. S2v [approx. 416].

58. Quill and ink were not the only writing implements in use in early modern Europe. For examples of early modern annotations in pencil, see the manuscripts of John Evelyn, British Library (BL), MS Add. 15950, fol. 78v, and Evelyn's copy of Alsted's *Encyclopedia* (1630), vol. 1 (BL Eve.c.6); or, among the holdings in Oxford College libraries: Theodor Zwinger, *Theatrum Humanae Vitae* (1571) at Magdalen College; Domenico Nani Mirabelli, *Polyanthea* (1617) at Jesus College; Johann Jacob Frisius, *Bibliotheca instituta et collecta* (1583) at Balliol College.

59. For example, the copy of Jean Bodin, *Théâtre de la nature universelle* (Lyon: Pillehotte, 1597) owned by the Minims of Besançon is corrected in many places, though not apparently according to official guidelines but to note where Bodin strayed from Roman Catholic orthodoxy. Copy at the Bibliothèque Municipale Besançon, 178, 734, 755, 792 (among others).

60. For some discussion of contexts in which early modern students and scholars worked together, see Ann Blair, "Note-taking as an Art of Transmission," *Critical Inquiry* 31 (2004): 85–107.

and the lists of errata provided by printers. As we know, the impact of post-publication censorship decrees on readers was varied: many Roman Catholic owners of books on the to-be-corrected list left their copies untouched; others copied out the descriptions of the passages to be deleted on a flyleaf but left the text itself intact; others crossed out the offending passages, either lightly in such a way as to leave the text legible or so heavily as to blacken it out; and some even tore out the pages involved. As far as the Catholic Church was concerned, the individual owner of a book condemned in parts was the crucial agent of correction. Although those who had purchased such dubious books in the first place might be less inclined than others to carry out this task of "correction," they could be held accountable for failing to do so.[61]

One can expect less resistance on the part of readers to correcting a text in accordance with a printed list of errata. Errata were most often readily present in the volume itself rather than in a separate book, and they promised to perfect the text according to the author's intentions, rather than the decisions of a censor. There are indeed examples of readers attending carefully to errata lists (see fig.1.2) and introducing the corrections into the text.[62] To facilitate the process of taking errata into account, Samuel Hartlib was proud of what he called a "new contrivance": that "Erratas of printed Book's are Alphabetically to bee inserted into Indices by which meanes they will bee readily found out."[63] These readers were all concerned to perfect the text according to the printer's tacit or explicit injunctions to enter the corrections listed in the printed errata into the text. In my experience, however, corrections of this mechanical kind are surprisingly uncommon.[64] Instead, readers usually made corrections according to their own judgment on matters of substance as well as grammar and usage.

---

61. For recent work on Catholic censorship, see *Church, Censorship, and Culture in Early Modern Italy,* ed. Gigliola Fragnito, trans. Adrian Belton (Cambridge: Cambridge Univ. Press, 2001). For examples of copies of a work in various states of correction according to the Index, see Ann Blair, *The Theater of Nature: Jean Bodin and Renaissance Science* (Princeton, NJ: Princeton Univ. Press, 1997), 184–5.

62. See, for example, Niccolò Perotti, *Cornucopiae* (Venice: Aldus Manutius, 1513) BL C.28.m.3, with very abundant annotations attributed to Aldus; of these only the corrections from the errata list are integrated into the next edition printed by Aldus in 1522. Gesner included the corrections in the printed errata in his annotations of Remberg Dodoens, *Histoire des plantes* (Antwerp: Jean Loë, 1557), e.g., 202, at the Zentralbibliothek, Zurich. I am grateful to Urs Leu for his help during my stay there. For annotations in a copy of the *Encyclopédie* that entered corrections from the errata lists, see Françoise Jouffroy-Gauja and Jean Haechler, "Une lecture de l'*Encyclopédie:* Trente-cinq ans d'annotations par un souscripteur anonyme," *Revue française d'histoire du livre* 96–7 (1997): 329–76.

63. Samuel Hartlib, "Ephemerides," 1656, pt. 2, fol. 29/5/75A, in the electronic version of *The Hartlib Papers, Complete Text and Image Database of the Papers of Samuel Hartlib (c. 1600–1662) Held in Sheffield University Library, Sheffield, England,* 2nd ed. (Sheffield: HROnline Humanities Research Institute, 2002).

64. For McKitterick's similar assessment, see *Print, Manuscript, and the Search for Order,* 142.

» *Hic quia præpropera nobis est morte peremptus:*
  » *Et tamen in lucem plura subinde data:*
  » *Frisius hinc quartus, superaddens plaustra virorum*
    » *Prodit: ut infundat vina quadrima nouis.*
Omnibus his debes magnas apponere grates:
  Hunc quoties fœtum, lector amice, legis.
Blotius in primis te gratum iure requirit:
  Tradita cui regis bibliotheca sacri.
Affluit is quarto, fidus ceu Theseus alter:
  Dum dedit authorum millia fanda typis.

ERRATA.

*Pagina 5. Colum. 2. ad nomen Adami Cratonis lin. 2. pro vt lege & . P. 52. c. 2. lin. 4. à fine dele, Ibidem habentur Amitij quæst. explicat M. S. P. 67. in nomine Antonij Senensis pro famam lege formam. P. end C. 2. lin. 1. ante Ioan. Baptista inser ex-cudeb. P. 84. C. 1. in nomine Arturus Scallaus, (adde) scripsit orationem. ibid. pro Frisij lege Freigij. pro impressus lege im-pressam. Pag. 90. C. 2. lin. 3. dele, * Augustini de Anch. de potest ecclesiast. in fol. P. 99. C. 1. quod post nomē Balthasarū de Lipsia dicitur de Fr. Barthol. & c. transfer ad pag. 105. C. 1. lin. 6. à fine. P. 103. C. 1. lin. 21. lege & ferè. P. 125. C. 1. in medio lege Bruno-nis Quinos. P. 175. C. 2. lin. 11. pro oratio lege ratio. P. 177. C. 1. ad nomen Cosme Rosselij pro lenatem lege tenacem. P. 185. c. 2. lin. 21. pro 1475. leg. 1575. P. 240. C. 1. praua distinctio de autore fecit typographum: ergo lege lin. 7. Per Fran. Iunium Sancto-num, & c. P. 242. C. 2. lin. 28. error in veteri exemplari ex ambiguitate prænominis per Fr. in titulo ascripti, remansit, ergo dele vsq; ad. De Rhetorica, & c. qui dialogi an sint quoq; Francisco vendicandi, an Friderico suo loco relinquendi, à Venetis cognos- NB. cendum. P. 250. C. 1. lin. 16. à fine pro Germanice leg. Germanicu. P. 280. C. 2. lin. 6. post tomos dele punctum. P. 286. c. 2. lin. 5. post, (in II) insere, librat. ibid. lin. 30. pro conserua legend conuersa. ibid. lin. 30. pro illius lege L'Huillier. ibid. lin. 34. post (sacris) adde, sese. P. 291. c. 1. lin. 11. pro commentarij lege Camerarij. P. 292. c. 2. lin. 5. à fine pro stellographicus leg. stellogra-phias. P. 298. c. 2. lin. 5. à fine pro consiliorum & , lege Vespertin. lection. primar. Consiliorum lib. P. 328. c. 2. lin. 32. pro para-disi leg. paralysi. P. 327. c. 2. lin. 23. à fine pro orseum lege Oestrum. P. 339. c. 2. lin. 22. à fine, dele, eodem tempore. P. 372. c. 2. lin. 6. à sine pro Christiani lege Iustiniani. P. 378. c. 1. lin. 23. à fine, pro quilibet lege qui liber. P. 406. c. 2. lin. 34. dele totam. Est enim tantum nomen typographi. P. 418. c. 2. lin. 5. à fine dele, Eiusdem. P. 427. c. 1. lin. 36. pro docendi lege discendi. P. 428. c. 1. lin. 9. post Dialecticam, fac (inde lege) Octaichon varia tractans theologica. P. 435. c. 2. lin. 20. à fine, pro concinnauit lege con-tinuauit. P. 440. c. 1. lin. 17. pro excusus lege excusam. ibid. lin. 27. pro Germanicum lege Germanico. P. 441. c. 1. lin. 10. à fine, dele * Eiusdem Erphordiani hymnor. lib. 8. Substitue in lineam 11. * Ioannes Gallus Erphordianus conscripsit librum hymna-rum quem in 8. P. 443. c. 1. lin. 4. pro Tropi lege Tropos. P. 448. c. 1. lin. 16. post Granij adde, studio. P. 465. c. 2. lin. 7. à fine pro 1547. leg. 1574. ibid lin. 5. à fine pro diuini lege diuina. P. 474. c. 1. lin. 14. dele (postea) ibid. l. 15. post (quem) insere, po-stea. P. 511. l. 19. à fine lege ad decimamquartam vsq; centuriam. P. 517. & 518. sunt transposita & implicita nomina autorum: ea sic emenda. Lineam penultimam pag. 517. c. 2. transfer in lineam 11. à fine pag. 118. c. 1. Lineam vltimam pag. 517. c. 2. & que eam sequuntur, totum scil. nomen Iose. Ludouici Asisio transpone in lineam 10. à fine pag. 518. P. 518. c. 1. lin. 7. dele Iosephi Quercetani. ibid. lin. 10 totum nomen Iosephi Quercetani transfer in columnam secundam. Eiusdem pag. lin. quintam. Et post Lertorium adde eiusdem de curandis vulneribus cæteraq; verba quæ habentur in col. priore lin. 7. Ibid. pa. scil. 518. c. 1. lin. 14. dele, Iosephi Raconditæ & que sequuntur verba scil. epitome, & c. transfer in columnam secundam lineam vudecimam post votem translata. P. 566. c. 1. lin. 29. pro Iulij lege Lelij. P. 606. c. 1. lin. 4. à fine (adde) eiusdem liber receptarum sententiarū in fol. Rostochij anno 1582. p. 607. c. 1. lin. 6. dele totam cum duab. sequentibus. p. 515. c. 1. lin. 5. à fine pro Inuentis lege Iuuen-tutis. p. 620. c. 2. lin. 27. post Ni. Bazelij (insere) prognosticam. P. 625. c. 1. lin. 25. à fine, pro, & . lege earundemq; P. 626. c. 1. lin. 16. à fine post Eiusdem (insere) de. P. 686. c. 1. lin. 5. pro offendant lege non offendant. Ibid. lin. 16. dele (.) post Alchymia. P. 721. c. 2. lin. 12. pro antiquis lege antiquissima. P. 741. c. 2. lin. 15. à fine pro 1590. lege 1390. P. 765. c. 2. lin. 24. lege restitutum & repurgatus. P. 780. c. 2. l. 33. post & , insere, in. ibid lin. 49. lege defenduntur. P. 797. pro Lorm lege Morm. P. 823. c. 2. lin. 11. lege de fide codici. & c. P. 826. c. 2. in Vuo. lege Iuo Episc. P. 818. In Vitali de Cambani. post illa verba, cum hoc titulo amplie-ri: lege quæ post duas insertas lineas sequuntur, Vitalis de Campanis, & c.*

Fig. 1.2 One reader paid close attention to the errata list in this copy of Conrad Gesner's *Bibliotheca instituta et collecta* (Zurich, 1583), probably underlining corrections as he entered them into the text. Call # Z1012.G3.1583. Courtesy, The Lilly Library, Indiana University, Bloomington, Indiana.

Occasionally in this way readers were able to contribute new corrections to later editions of a work. One of the most elaborate instances of reader response I have found involves the indexes to the 1508 edition of Erasmus's *Adages* in a copy at the Houghton Library. In addition to various annotations in the text (providing translations and further references), this anonymous reader made corrections to the two printed indexes. The reader improved the first index (an alphabetical listing of the sayings according to their first word) by correcting page references, adding sayings that were left out, and positioning a proverb under a keyword rather than its initial term.[65] The second index sorted the adages under 257 miscellaneously arranged commonplace headings. This reader, clearly frustrated by the difficulties of finding a particular commonplace heading within the jumbled list of headings, drew up his own alphabetical listing of the headings keyed to the disordered printed list by numbers. The following edition of the *Adages* (Froben, 1515) contained a solution to the very problem experienced by this reader, though with a less elegant way of keying the original jumbled list of commonplace headings to an alphabetical one. The printer was probably not responding directly to this particular reader but more generally to the problem that this reader and other readers experienced and presumably reported on.

Similarly with Diderot's *Encyclopédie,* it is likely that some readers wrote to the editor with their corrections, in a cumulative process of correction that would explain why the errata lists published in many volumes of the *Encyclopédie* include corrections spanning all the previous volumes. Whether directly or indirectly, readers' corrections could contribute to the evolution of a book through subsequent editions. Even when, as in most cases, readers' corrections did not affect later editions, the changes made by readers nonetheless constituted the final stage of production of a printed text, as early modern printers and authors articulated in the errata blurbs. Those who read with pen in hand to correct their copy of a printed book, according to the instructions provided in errata lists or their own best judgment, shaped the transmission of that text, at least through their individual copy. Books annotated by famous scholars were sought out for purchase in learned circles precisely for their annotations and corrections.[66]

---

65. "Arctum annulum, pag 6" is otherwise left out; "nihil cum amaricino 47" is entered under "amaricino," although it also appears under "nil" in the printed index. See Erasmus, *Adagiorum chiliades tres* (Venice: Aldus Manutus, 1508), copy at Houghton Library [*fNC5.Er153A2.1508].

66. Nicholas Heinsius, for example, purchased some two hundred books owned by Julius Justus Scaliger; see *The Auction Catalogue of the Library of J. J. Scaliger,* facsimile ed. H. J. de Jonge (Utrecht: HES, 1977), 4–5, citing F. F. Blok, *Nicolaas Heinsius in dienst van Christina van Zweden* (Delft, 1949), 125.

For the historian readers' corrections are valuable as the first sign of a careful reading. One less-noted consequence of printing was to generate large numbers of books that were left unread. The production of manuscripts was closely related to demand, with manuscripts made on commission or, if produced in a commercial scriptorium, at least with careful anticipation of demand, because of the considerable cost of producing each copy. Printing, on the contrary, produced books in numbers that often far exceeded demand, since a printer could hope to recover the cost of production only by printing and selling hundreds of copies. Much more often than manuscripts, printed books were left unsold and, given their lower price-tag too, were probably more often purchased only to be left unused. One scholar has insightfully concluded that "the majority of the books ever printed have rarely been read."[67] Corrections, the most common form of annotation, thus constitute precious evidence of a careful reading, although they cannot be assumed to be present in all copies that were carefully read.

The prefaces introducing errata lists in early printed books indicate that the producers of the book fully expected the process of correction, already visible at times in the variations among copies in a print run, to continue at the hands of owners and readers. In making corrections in the books that they owned, with or without the guidance of printed errata lists, readers acted beyond the control of authors and printers and played an active role in shaping the final version of the text for themselves and others to whom their annotated copies may have circulated. Occasionally corrections made by readers also had an impact on later editions. The signs of correction left in many early modern books, from variations in the printed text to errata lists and manuscript changes, highlight the collective nature of book production, which involved authors and printers, but also less visible players such as correctors and readers.

---

67. Hugh Amory, "The Trout and the Milk: An Ethnobibliographical Talk," *Harvard Library Bulletin* 7 (1996): 50–65, at 51.

Chapter 2

Counterfeit Printing as an Agent of Diffusion and Change

The French Book-Privilege System and Its Contradictions (1498–1790)

Jean-Dominique Mellot

In *The Printing Press as an Agent of Change: Communications and Cultural Transformations in Early-Modern Europe* (*PPAC*),[1] Elizabeth Eisenstein demonstrates not only that the introduction of printing was the signal for an intensification of written production but also that printing led to progressive and deep cultural change. A print culture began to emerge that required more and more inexpensive and widely available printed books. Nevertheless, because of contemporary structural constraints, this new dynamic of expansion could not operate at full capacity. Soon it came up against the fundamental problem posed by the ambiguous status of the printed book, which, as Lucien Febvre and Henri-Jean Martin note in *L'apparition du livre*,[2] was both commodity (*marchandise*) and force for change (*ferment*). Although it was generally celebrated in principle, the boundless printing boom could not win universal acceptance, whether from the authorities or from the new printers themselves.

From an economic point of view, since the mere printing of a book did not guarantee its sale and a printed edition represented a considerable investment, early printers and bookseller-publishers soon had to find protections against competitors who reproduced their publications, although such competing reproductions had been perfectly acceptable and even encouraged in the

---

This essay was translated from French by Samuel P. L. Veissière.

1. First published in French as the abridged edition, *La révolution de l'imprimé à l'aube de l'Europe moderne,* trans. Maud Sissung and Marc Duchamp (Paris: Éditions La Découverte, 1991).

2. Paris: Éditions A. Michel, 1958; repr., 1971; new ed., 1999; translated by David Gerard as *The Coming of the Book: The Impact of Printing, 1450–1800,* ed. Geoffrey Nowell-Smith and David Wootton (London: N.L.B., 1976; reissued, London: Verso, 1990).

manuscript age. In the search for ways to limit the damage caused by these competing copies, they were soon given a name that would long designate both a phenomenon and a criminal offense belonging to the world of the printed book: counterfeiting (*contrefaçon*). Directly dependent on a dialectic that created an opposition between "legitimate" publishing and "counterfeit," a diverse publishing scene took shape, which would ultimately determine the very nature of the book itself under the ancien régime.

Counterfeiting: Definitions and Early Issues

French lexicographical authorities confirm that the term "counterfeiting" resided in the vocabulary of printing and publishing until at least the early eighteenth century. In the first true dictionary of the French language, Antoine Furetière's *Dictionnaire universel* (1690), the verb "to counterfeit" (*contrefaire*) is defined as a "printing term": "it is to print a book, an image, a drawing, in order to deprive the author of the right of privilege he has obtained to have it printed (by whomever he may elect)." The *Dictionnaire de Trévoux,* in its 1704, 1721, 1732, 1740, and 1752 editions, replicates this definition word for word. In Diderot and D'Alembert's *Encyclopédie* (vol. 4, 1754, col. 133b), *contrefaçon* is defined as a "*bookselling term* that signifies the publication or part of the publication of a counterfeit book, that is, printed by somebody who does not own the right to the detriment of those who own it."

In the meantime, only the *Dictionnaire de l'Académie* (1718 edition) seems to have begun to broaden the concept of *contrefaçon:* "a commercial term referring to the fraud committed in counterfeiting either the printing of a book or the manufacture of a fabric to the prejudice of those who own the right and the privilege." This broadening in time led to the situation of today, when the word *contrefaçon* in French refers more to brand-name products that are fraudulently imitated in developing countries for worldwide distribution at low prices than it does to publications reproduced to the detriment of their authors and publishers. This does not mean, however, that counterfeit publishing has disappeared at the international level—far from it. The chief merit of earlier definitions is to direct our attention to the pre-industrial manufacturing context in which counterfeiting developed under the ancien régime. Without the technology that makes possible the sequential production and reproduction of multiple copies, one cannot speak about counterfeiting but rather only about specific reproductions, more or less innocently intended—copies, imitations, pastiches, fakes, and forgeries.

In other words, the fact that printing was primarily associated with the phenomenon of counterfeiting in the minds of old lexicographers is not necessarily because it made possible the reproduction of works of the mind—an idea that is nonetheless present in the current French reference dictionary, *Le Robert* (*Le nouveau Petit Robert,* 2004), in which literary and artistic contexts are chiefly evoked in the definition of *contrefaçon* as "the act of counterfeiting a literary, artistic, industrial work to the detriment of its author, its inventor." In fact, if printing was so intimately connected with the phenomenon of counterfeiting, it was mostly because it was one of the first modern commercial activities relying on partially mechanized production[3]—a commercial activity, moreover, that, with the imprint (for example, "A Paris, chez Iehan Petit, libraire iuré de l'Université, rue Sainct Iacques"), presented the first explicit form of what is nowadays called "industrial traceability." Yet, as the future would show, this form of traceability would not be less susceptible to mass-produced misappropriation that usurped the identity and reputation of established printers and booksellers.

If, then, the definition of "counterfeiting" appeared a legal one above all (as usurpation of a right), the underlying issues were mainly economic. The commercial logic that governed the circulation of written work underwent radical modifications during the transition from handwritten to printed books. While a scribe or a copyist generally labored on one work at a time, to fill an order for an individual client, printed editions are sold to an a priori anonymous clientele.

The difficulty lay not with production, which is easily increasable, but with diffusion. And to aggravate this difficulty, if an edition financed by a bookseller-publisher was soon reproduced more cheaply by a rival operating near the original place of publication, sales of the original were likely to suffer. Nevertheless, in the early years of printing, there were no laws to prevent the occurrence of such a nasty trick, just as there had been none in the manuscript age. In those days, no corporate body existed to impose a professional code of practice on the printing professions. If booksellers and printers sought the favor of the political power, it was therefore not to protect intellectual property and the rights of authors. These intellectual property rights did not exist and would not exist for a long time yet: until the end of the eighteenth century, authors were content most of the time to sell their manuscripts to a bookseller for a lump sum.[4] More prosaically, booksellers and printers sought

---

3. Carrying the argument further, some scholars—see, for example, François Moureau, *Les presses grises. La contrefaçon du livre (XVIe–XIXe siècles)* (Paris: Aux Amateurs de livres, 1988)—further argued that Gutenberg's invention itself was the archetype of counterfeiting. Incunabular printing did indeed undertake to reproduce handwritten books cheaply and in numerous copies.

4. For a useful evolutionary account of the status, living conditions, and remuneration of authors under the ancien régime, see Alain Viala's classic *Naissance de l'écrivain: sociologie de la littérature à l'âge classique* (Paris: Éditions de Minuit, 1985).

favor to avoid the business debacles of having their publications reprinted at a lower cost before they profited from the editions they had financed.

Book Privilege and Counterfeiting: Dialectic and Parallel Development

Origins of the System: Temporary Publishing Protection Covering a Minority of Publications

In several European states, the late fifteenth century saw the birth of book privileges, the origins and early decades of which have been reconstructed in Elizabeth Armstrong's interesting study.[5] After two short-lived experiments in Germany (in the dioceses of Würzburg in 1479 and Ratisbon in 1480), the idea of protecting some editions with privileges spread to Italy (the duchy of Milan, 1481; republic of Venice, 1486; kingdom of Naples, 1489; the Papal States sometime later). The idea met with undisputed success, notably in Venice. By the end of 1498, France had taken up the idea, though at first applying it mainly to the duchy of Milan, which it occupied as a result of the Italian Wars. The development of the practice in France itself dates from 1504. Meanwhile, the first occurrences of what was to become a near-universal phenomenon were recorded in the rest of Europe: Spain (1498), Portugal (1501), the Holy Roman Empire (1501), Poland (1505), Scotland (1507), Sweden (the diocese of Uppsala, 1510), the Netherlands (duchy of Brabant, 1512), England (1518), followed by Switzerland (Basel), Denmark, and elsewhere.

For a fee, the ruling authorities of these countries—but sometimes also the bishops or certain sovereign courts—agreed to protect, within their jurisdictions, the exclusive rights to an edition produced by a particular bookseller for the length of time judged necessary for its sale (the term was generally rather brief; in France it was six years and often less). This exclusive protection gave a bookseller who had been wronged by an act of counterfeiting the right to sue the counterfeiter in the appropriate courts and to obtain redress (in the form of confiscation of the counterfeit edition to the benefit of the holder of the privilege, a fine imposed on the offender, and payment of court costs by the latter). Hence the success of this procedure in states that, like the kingdom of France, had the advantage of extensive territory, subject to an acknowledged central authority, and populated by many competing printers and booksellers, in the capital as well as in a number of important provincial centers.

---

5. Armstrong, *Before Copyright: The French Book-Privilege System, 1498–1526* (Cambridge: Cambridge Univ. Press, 1990). Despite its title, Armstrong's study does not limit itself to France and gives an overview—at least of the first years—of the European book-privilege situation.

By protecting certain editions and systematizing what would later be called "copyright" (*droit de copie*) or, according to the *Encyclopédie* (vol. 5, 1755), "right of property in a work" (*droit de propriété sur un ouvrage*), the book privilege identified a kind of offense. It gave birth at the same time to the notion of counterfeiting in the strictly legal sense: the fraudulent reproduction of a protected edition for illicit competition. Privileges were sought, at least in the beginning, only for those promising works that were likely to be profitable, but naturally these privileged editions were most likely to be reprinted. The famous Venetian printer Aldus Manutius was one of the first to complain publicly, in 1502, of the counterfeiting of his bestselling editions of the classics, despite protection by a double privilege from the Venetian Senate and the Pope. A little later, Martin Luther and Erasmus saw their works become in some sort bestsellers through more or less uncontrolled counterfeiting.

By an axiom characteristic of ancien-régime bookselling, privilege, which condemned counterfeiting legally, at the same time made it economically necessary if a popular work was to achieve its highest possible sales. Exclusive rights granted to a particular bookseller for a particular title did not necessarily give him the means of production and distribution needed to meet the demand for a popular work. Only the advent of counterfeiting enabled the fullest commercial success, locally and beyond. By an all-too-apparent paradox, book privileges called for and justified counterfeiting.

That said, the privilege system, relying on voluntary resort to public authority, was nowhere near applied to the whole range of printed production. The statistics established in Armstrong's *Before Copyright* for the period 1498–1526 show that the first 295 known French privileges, corresponding to 463 effective editions, represent only about 5.25 percent of editions appearing in Paris alone.[6] Although these figures give only a general picture, they suggest that the proportion of protected works encroached only marginally on the mass of freely reprinted editions (*réimpressions libres*) belonging to what would later be called the "public domain."

A Change of Logic and Its Limits: The Norm of Royal Privilege for All New Works

Because early book privileges were not concerned with the control of text and content, the "book as commodity" emerged as a production that was surprisingly free or, at any rate, subject to very little constraint. However, this

---

6. Armstrong refers to Brigitte Moreau, *Inventaire chronologique des éditions parisiennes du XVIe siècle d'après les manuscrits de Philippe Renouard*, published by the City of Paris, from 1972 (years 1501–35 covered so far).

relatively free system began to evolve in a more restrictive manner in the mid sixteenth century, when regulation of the "book as commodity" in France began to be coupled with a desire to control content, or the "book as force for change." This evolution owed much to the development of demands for censorship. After March 18, 1521, facing the threat of an invasion of "heresy," French royal legislation prescribed prepublication examination, by the faculty of theology of the Sorbonne, of every printed book that dealt with religion. After several reiterations of this requirement, the king, judging the university procedure too ineffective for such critical times, decided to follow the example of Philip II of Spain and extended the privilege system to every new work, religious or not (letters patent of January 24, 1562). Despite resistance from the parlements and the Sorbonne, the new law was imposed once and for all by the decree of Moulins, in February 1566.[7] Thus, royal privilege, hitherto an optional protection for new publications, became obligatory as the result of a desire for centralized control over all new publication for political rather than economic reasons. The notion of privilege and that of permission, the notion of commercial protection and that of approval of content, hence became conflated. "Book as commodity" and "book as force for change," taken hostage by one another, as it were, found themselves subjected to the same system of centralized surveillance, and the new situation had great consequences for the subsequent organization of publishing.

At the end of the sixteenth century and during a great part of the seventeenth, however, the new norm of exclusive royal privilege met with resistance that greatly limited its impact. Although the parlement of Paris finally accepted the principle of this new publishing regime (except for the two periods of crisis of the Ligue and the Fronde), the provincial parlements, notably those of Rouen, Toulouse, and Bordeaux, refused for a very long time—until 1678–83—to relinquish the "provincial privileges" they had themselves established in the early sixteenth century to protect printers and booksellers in their jurisdictions.[8] Why such resistance? Contrary to what one may think a priori, it was not a matter of revolt by provincial notables, jealous of their prerogatives and challenging the authority of the central power. In fact, the most prominent provincial parlements were demonstrating their intention

---

7. For the process that led to the decree of Moulins, see, esp., Geneviève Guilleminot-Chrétien, "Le contrôle de l'édition en France dans les années 1560: la genèse de l'édit de Moulins," in *Le livre dans l'Europe de la Renaissance. Actes du XXVIIIe colloque international d'études humanistes de Tours . . .* (Paris, Promodis-éditions du Cercle de la Librairie, 1988), 378–85.

8. See, esp., for Rouen, Édouard-Hippolyte Gosselin, "Simples notes sur les imprimeurs & libraires rouennais (XVe, XVIe et XVIIe siècles)," in *Glanes historiques normandes à travers les XVe, XVIe, XVIIe et XVIIIe siècles* (Rouen: E. Cagniard, 1869), 53–175.

to continue exercising one of the regulatory powers officially vested in them: maintaining and watching over the equity and welfare of the economic life of their jurisdictions. In the name of that principle, explicitly claimed more than once, they strove to preserve affordable prices and a public domain of free competition, as well as to protect the integrity of the book guilds of which they had charge in their jurisdictions. Provincial parlements, that of Normandy (Rouen) in particular, hence refused to ratify royal privileges, which, in their view, were too onerous, long lasting, and damaging to an entire trade under the pretense of favoring certain authors or well-established Paris booksellers with individual monopolies. During a court hearing on May 14, 1659, the judges of the parlement of Normandy went on to denounce the monopolistic tendencies of the central authority in very direct terms: "If we were to follow these privileges, so easily obtained in Paris, Rouen's printers and all others would have nothing left to print." To counter these trends within their jurisdictions, provincial parlements strove to restrain the portion of book privileges that seemed to them exorbitant and that wrongfully reduced the area of the public domain. Themselves issuing *petit sceau,* or privy seal, privileges effective in their provinces, they played the role of "guilty conscience" confronting the arbitrary tendencies of royal policies. In other words, until the beginning of Louis XIV's personal rule, not only were the exclusive rights of the Great Seal not respected but they were openly contested in court by a legal institution emanating from royal authority.

Privilege or Monopoly? The Privilege System Compromised by Arbitrary Extensions

If royal authority did not yet have the means to enforce this overly ambitious legislation, especially outside the capital, probably the worst thing, from the point of view of principles, was that it did not respect its own rules. In fact, from the end of the sixteenth century, there was on the part of the central power a dual tendency that turned out to be of significant consequence. Despairing of imposing on everyone and everywhere the logic of the exclusivity of its privileges, the monarchy preferred in effect to turn privilege into a reward for nearby, docile, and trusted booksellers and authors. Thus, royal privileges, created as the symbol of an all-powerful monarchy and the sign of a new publishing rationality across the kingdom, became in these conditions the instrument of a feeble power, reduced to using favoritism, or even clientism, and to preferring the "infiltration" of publishing into its realm of effective control. Privileges also became, in this manner, the favorite weapon of a redoubtable centralization in publishing matters because it was established, as if by default, on the arbitrariness of proximity: Paris publishers were favored because it was hoped that, being close by the seat of central power, they could be more easily watched and controlled; it was even envisaged, in due time, to reserve for them the bulk of French printing.[9] In this way, the formation around 1585 of companies of Paris booksellers who held a collective and renewable monopoly on certain categories of works (such as the liturgy reformed by the Council of Trent[10] and patrologies) represented a first step in that direction.

Nevertheless, facing the opposition of a major part of the Paris booksellers' guild and the repugnance of the parlement of Paris to register the renewal of such monopolies, the royal authorities preferred to increase their hold on publishing by more discreet means. The Royal Chancellery of France (*la Grande Chancellerie*) thus imposed a practice whose mechanism was well dissected by Henri-Jean Martin, in *Livre, pouvoirs et société à Paris au XVIIe siècle:* the continuation of privilege. Not content to grant privileges only for new editions, at the end of the sixteenth century royal authorities began to extend the protection of works whose initial privilege had expired, even if those titles had undergone no "appreciable addition" according to the formula of the time. Despite the resistance of the Paris and provincial parlements, and despite the very text of the statutes of the Paris book trade guild (1618, article 33),[11] the practice of continuation evolved and imposed itself more and more markedly over the course of the seventeenth century. The chancellor Pierre Séguier, who held office from 1635 to 1672, did not hesitate to make it the instrument of his policy. At his instigation the Chancellery of France began to issue royal privileges that for the time were of very long duration (as long as fifteen to twenty years) to great Paris printer-booksellers who were among the

---

9. In 1645, the French chancellor Pierre Séguier was very seriously planning to limit print production to Paris and to assign it to a sort of royal super-printing-press housed in several disused colleges of the Montagne Sainte-Geneviève in the Latin Quarter. He abandoned that idea only in the face of the hue and cry of all the members of the profession and its representatives. In 1717, the guild of booksellers and printers of Paris envisaged another solution: it demanded of the kingdom's book trade administration that printed production be forbidden, at least temporarily, in the provincial cities that, following Rouen's example, were specializing in the counterfeiting of Parisian privileged editions. This time, the royal administration refused to grant such a measure.

10. This market above all was considerable. Around 1630 the Compagnie des usages, which held a privilege for printing liturgical books of Roman use, reformed by the Council of Trent, employed in Paris twelve to fifteen printing presses and forty to fifty journeyman printers, according to Antoine Vitré, one of the king's printers in Paris. See Henri-Jean Martin, *Livre, pouvoirs et société à Paris au XVIIe siècle (1598–1701),* 2 vols. (Geneva: Droz, 1969; new ed., 1999), vol. 1, esp. 52, 106. This work was published in English as *Print, Power, and People in 17th-Century France,* trans. David Gerard (Metuchen, NJ: Scarecrow Press, 1993).

11. Which prohibited the obtainment of a continuation of privilege for a work whose initial privilege had reached its expiration date, except in the case of an "increase by at least a quarter."

closest to power, such as Sébastien Cramoisy, Pierre Rocollet, Antoine Vitré, and Pierre Blaise. Yet these privileges also frequently covered old titles or titles already published abroad, and others with very strong sales in this time of the Counter-Reformation (such as works by Louis de Grenade and *Fleurs des vies des saints*). Facing protests from the book trade, Séguier indeed made concessions to further his main objectives—in March 1647, he announced his intention to require authors and booksellers to obtain privileges for "old books" as well, a measure withdrawn immediately—but he maintained and increased the practice of granting monopolies without limit to trusted members of the Paris booksellers' guild.

In the mid seventeenth century, when this policy succeeded in becoming a permanent feature, counterfeiting was not yet considered an alarming problem. It is true that counterfeiting gave rise to relatively frequent proceedings against individual counterfeiters—usually initiated by wronged Paris booksellers[12]—but it was not necessarily considered a general phenomenon. When the leading lights of the Paris guild denounced provincial competition, they complained about the undue freedom to reprint in the provinces, at minimal cost, titles that had already fallen into the public domain. The point was not yet to stigmatize an illicit practice but to bemoan the development, in all legality, of formidable competition. In the words of Antoine Vitré in 1662: "Rouen, Troyes, Lyon, Orléans and other cities of the kingdom . . . could, for four francs, supply printing that Paris could not do for ten. . . . The printers and booksellers of other cities possessed the same character as those of Paris and could perform as well . . . , rents, labor, food and paper were reduced by more than half in price [for the provincials]. If this freedom was not taken away by privileges, the ruin of Paris printing could not be avoided."[13] In Rouen, a provincial capital (and also at this time, the kingdom's second city in population and probably in printing output as well) that was soon to become the bastion of French counterfeiting, counterfeits represented only about 5 percent of local production between 1600 and 1670 while reprints of works that had fallen into the public domain represented nearly 44 percent.[14]

---

12. Martin, *Livre, pouvoirs et société;* also Roméo Arbour, *Un éditeur d'œuvres littéraires au XVIIe siècle: Toussaint Du Bray* (Geneva: Droz, 1992); and Georges Lepreux's still useful *Gallia typographica ou Répertoire biographique et chronologique de tous les imprimeurs de France . . .* , 6 vols. (Paris: H. Champion, 1909–14), especially the last volume, dedicated to the king's printers in Paris.

13. *Memoire d'un ancien imprimeur et libraire pour conserver l'employ aux maistres et compagnons imprimeurs de la ville de Paris* (Paris, 1662), most probably by the Parisian bookseller and king's printer Antoine Vitré. Bibliothèque nationale de France (hereafter Bib. nat.), Fol. Fm. 12467.

14. See Jean-Dominique Mellot, *L'édition rouennaise et ses marchés (vers 1600–vers 1730): dynamisme provincial et centralisme parisien* (Paris: École des chartes, 1998), esp. 166.

"Continuation of Privileges" and the "Great Booksellers' War"

In attacking the important business activity that this public domain represented for the provincial printers and booksellers, who acted as *relais multiplicateurs* (that is, main multipliers of copies), the state would, almost automatically, elevate the phenomenon of counterfeiting to previously unknown levels. In fact, it was soon no longer a question of being satisfied with "nibbling" progressively on the public domain. On December 10, 1649, letters patent from the king sought to legitimize permanently the "privilege to reprint old books" (articles 26–29).[15] This measure gave way to a chorus of protests from the majority of members of the book trade, the university, and above all from the parlement of Paris, which refused to record the offending articles. A little later, on the occasion of a ruling of September 20, 1657, the sovereign court, referring to the statutes of the Paris book trade guild (1618), even reaffirmed the requirement to increase "by at least a quarter" the content of every new edition claiming a new privilege. By then, the "Great Booksellers' War"[16] had begun. This "war" in the 1650s and 1660s was undertaken, with the support of contradictory legal precedents, by the competitors of the Paris beneficiaries of the "continuation of privileges," who were protected by the monarchy. The competitors, often provincials, were by contrast actively supported by the parlements.[17] But this series of "privilege prosecutions" and jurisdictional conflicts (parlements against the king's Council of State) did not involve only private interests — in fact, booksellers from Rouen and Lyon were not fooled: they joined forces themselves in a number of privilege prosecutions before the Council of State. What was principally at stake in these repeated prosecutions was the future of the entire French publishing system, the viability of an entire business, and beyond that, the peculiar dynamic of print culture — hence, the litigious tenacity of the parties proceeded against and the stubborn determination of the royal power to impose the legalization of the continuation of privileges. On February 27, 1665, a Council decree sought to make a final ruling on this point, but its formulation was ambiguous, and, especially in the provinces, it continued to be challenged by the ruling of the Paris parlement of September 20, 1657, which was founded on the Paris guild statutes of 1618.

In Rouen, for example, to every notification of continuation of privilege

---

15. See Henri Falk, *Les privilèges de librairie sous l'Ancien Régime. Étude historique du conflit des droits sur l'œuvre littéraire* (Paris: A. Rousseau, 1906; repr., Geneva: Slatkine, 1970), esp. 84.

16. In the words of Martin, *Livre, pouvoirs et société*.

17. See, particularly, Lepreux, *Gallia typographica . . . Province de Normandie*, 2 vols. (1912).

that arrived from Paris, the local guild of printers and booksellers responded with a "protest of nullity," invoking precedents of the parlements, particularly the famous ruling of September 20, 1657. The Rouennais did not limit themselves to formal protests. Supported by the parlement of Normandy, they sued beneficiaries of privilege continuations on the grounds that they were a "surprise" (obtained against the spirit of the laws), and, to denote the small consideration they had for such privileges, they immediately launched a collective "anti-edition" by reprinting the wrongfully privileged edition.[18] To counter this provocation, which they associated with counterfeiting, the privileged booksellers of the capital undertook prosecutions of their own. This little judicial game could have lasted a long time if corporate finances and resources had been unlimited, but they were far from it at that time. By allowing these proceedings to be drawn out, the royal authorities played for exhaustion by both parties with a view to imposing their preference without completely disowning the parlements. From the late 1660s, with the sometimes inextricable stalemate of privilege trials, the Great Booksellers' War seemed irremediably lost for the opponents of continuations. Moreover, in the meantime, Louis XIV had set about bringing the parlements to heel, in Paris as well as in the provinces.

French Publishing between "Legal Allowance" and Real Fraud

Although the legal battle seemed lost, the economic struggle for the survival of publishing activities outside the capital would long continue to rage. The victory of the Chancellery of France and the Paris bookselling oligarchy did not result in the disappearance of editions competing against those protected by privilege continuations. In most cases, this rival production merely underwent a massive shift underground into counterfeiting and clandestineness.

At the height of Louis XIV's reign, the monarchy and the Chancellery found themselves relatively free in the institutional domain to impose the continuation of privileges as a more imperative norm than the privileges themselves. As of 1675, as Martin has emphasized, the practice of continuation was systematized arbitrarily, even if it meant destabilizing the official publishing system. Great Paris printer-booksellers who were overtly favored, like Pierre Le Petit, Jean-Baptiste II Coignard, André Pralard, François Muguet, Étienne Michallet, and others, obtained renewals of their privileges for a

---

18. No fewer than forty-eight of these "editions of protest" were counted in the archives of the guild of printers and booksellers of Rouen between 1656 and 1669, particularly for literary and religious successes, including numerous school reference books that sold well. Departmental Archives of Seine-Maritime, Rouen, 5E 483–90.

series of works among the most in demand, for renewable terms of twenty, twenty-five, or even fifty years.[19] From the last quarter of the seventeenth century, and during most of the eighteenth, the system turned the continuations into a sort of "publishing allowance" reserved not to the authors or their assignees but to a patriciate of Paris booksellers close to power, who would end up forgetting the origin of this allowance and think themselves "owners" of the titles for which they had been granted renewable privileges decades before.[20] It was those "sons of booksellers, assured of their fortune through this odious monopoly, proprietors . . . of the exclusive privilege of most of the books that are printed, [who] enjoy[ed] their position without care and without work, as one enjoys a plot of land that produces a large income" and of whom Mr. de Malesherbes, director of the book trade administration from 1750 to 1763, painted a less than flattering portrait in his *Mémoires sur la librairie* (1758–9). Although Denis Diderot, in his *Lettre sur le commerce de la librairie* (1763), leapt to the battlements to justify this logic of monopolistic property—mostly because he was hired by the oligarchy of great Paris booksellers to defend the principle of their allowance against any form of legal competition from the provincials—his efforts only marginally elevated the position of authors.[21]

In the meantime, as the prolongations of privileges for the most profitable titles multiplied (to the benefit of the Parisians), the Direction de la Librairie—a new administrative department emerging out of the Chancellery of France and placed under the leadership of the Abbé Jean-Paul Bignon, nephew of the chancellor, Louis Phélypeaux de Pontchartrain—had under-

---

19. Martin, *Livre, pouvoirs et société*, esp. 2:693–5. "Most of the texts published from the 1660s [would remain] . . . the property of the publishers who [had] . . . published them for the first time." Among the works with a flow that was "frozen": various dictionaries; the works of Louis de Grenade, Robert Arnauld d'Andilly, Louis Abelly, and Saint Augustine; and the catechism of the Council of Trent.

20. On this particular point, see Raymond Birn's interesting study, "The Profits of Ideas: *Privilèges en Librairie* in Eighteenth-Century France," *Eighteenth-Century Studies* 4 (1970–1): 131–68, esp. 144–6, on the demand presented in 1726 by the Parisian guild to the keeper of the seals, Joseph-Jean-Baptiste Fleuriau d'Armenonville (Bibl. nat., ms. fr. 22072, no. 62): "It is certain . . . that it is not the privileges granted by the King to the booksellers that give them ownership over the works they print, but exclusively the acquisition of the manuscript, the ownership of which is transmitted by the author by means of the price he receives for it. . . . [The bookseller] must remain the permanent owner of this work's text, him & his descendants, as a plot of land or a house which he would have acquired, because the acquisition of an inheritance does not differ in nature from that of a manuscript. . . . The King, having no rights over the works of authors can pass them on to no one without the consent of those that are the legitimate proprietors." This text particularly infuriated the keeper of the seals and disqualified this first attempt from the Parisian guild.

21. Even by contenting themselves with selling their manuscripts once and for all, the authors were guaranteed to make considerably more money with the capital city's great booksellers.

taken in 1701 to eradicate de facto all that was left of the public domain open to competition. A council ruling of September 7, 1701, followed by letters patent of October 2 of the same year, henceforth made it compulsory to obtain a privilege or a permission (prepublication censorship examination) for the publication of any book, even an old one, that exceeded two printed sheets.[22] For the least of opuscules, for the most insignificant of reprints—including at first the "literature of hawkers," pamphlets or simple chapbooks (*livrets de colportage*)[23]—one thereafter had to go to Paris to undertake a lengthy procedure before the Chancellery of France.

Needless to say, had these new regulations been fully honored, they would have been more than dissuasive, prohibitive even, for the activities of most provincial printer-booksellers. Yet because they could choose only between financial ruin and illegality, it is not surprising that most provincial printer-booksellers preferred the second option, seeing no advantage from a system of privileges that was supposedly universal but that in fact was unrealistic and unjust. By making privileges obligatory for all publications and by simultaneously seeking to preserve the private preserve (*chasse gardée*) of the tycoons of Parisian bookselling, the authorities actually encouraged outsiders to flout the privilege system. Beginning in the last years of the reign of Louis XIV, despite threats of interdiction, severe prosecution, and internment in the Bastille for the most defiant printers and booksellers, the book-privilege system was completely undermined. In Rouen, whose case is best known, more than 40 percent of print production located from the 1690s was illicit (fictitious imprints make the task of identification particularly difficult and involve a systematic resort to analytical bibliography), and the phenomenon only increased after the 1701 extension of the privilege system and permission to reprint. In this situation, the proportion of counterfeits, estimated to be at least 15 percent of local print production in the very beginning of the eighteenth century, experienced a growth for which there are not yet reliable figures but that apparently reached great heights.

At that point, counterfeiting was no longer simply a series of individual infringements of the system. A veritable "counterfeiting culture" had been born. As a "disgraceful double" of the privilege system, it was a necessary evil

---

22. In 1707, Chancellor Pontchartrain thought to subject even booklets of fewer than two sheets (for which until then only the permission of a subaltern jurisdiction was required) to an identical procedure (Bibl. nat., ms. fr. 21126, fols. 880–1).

23. See Jean-Dominique Mellot, "La Bibliothèque bleue de Rouen: l'émergence d'une production indésirable et très demandée (fin XVIIe–début XVIIIe siècle)," in *La Bibliothèque bleue et les littératures de colportage. Actes du colloque organisé par la Bibliothèque municipale . . . de Troyes . . . 12–13 novembre 1999 . . .* (Paris: École des chartes; Troyes: Maison du Boulanger, 2000), 23–39.

and ultimately essential to sufficient distribution of the titles most in demand. Why? Because book privileges that were in force in the French kingdom did not present, as historiography has tended to insist until now, only a censorial and ideological obstacle to publication. If this were true, it would always have been possible to circumvent this roadblock. René Descartes, among others, had shown the way to circumventing censorship in the first half of the seventeenth century, and most authors who were the least bit innovative did not forgo this route. Indeed, all one had to do was publish unorthodox writings in a neighboring country that was freer, at least where publishing was concerned, to escape the brake of French government control on texts and wait until public opinion did its job and the new work was sufficiently digested to be reprinted in the Most Christian Kingdom, with or without "tacit permission"[24]—a process that became ordinary in the eighteenth century. The obstacle presented by the privilege system as consolidated in the reign of Louis XIV was above all economic but also social. By reducing to nothing the proportion of free reprints, it prevented the resumption in the province of reprinting successes and works that had become usual, and it de facto deprived the national public residing in the kingdom of these titles or at least delayed the public's access to them. Counterfeiting, which was illegal, was no less legitimate, a distinction that needed to be understood in high places.

Justifications and Institutionalization of an Alternative Production

From the reign of Louis XIV forward, counterfeiting, justified in practice, also began to be justified in discourse, in much the same way that free copies had been defended in the seventeenth century by the voice of the parlements. For a good part of the eighteenth century, the provincial printers' and booksellers' guilds, standing together, demanded from the book trade administration the legalization of their counterfeits in the name of public utility or, at least, the right to reprint editions whose privileges had been wrongfully turned into permanent monopolies to benefit Paris booksellers. The arguments invoked were simple, with both an economic and a civic aspect. First, because of the monopoly system resulting from the continuation of privileges, "books from Paris" were "extremely high-priced," as the booksellers of Toulouse wrote in 1767. Furthermore, they said, "only rich people can buy them. . . . A poor arti-

---

24. The tacit permission, conceived by Abbé Bignon, director of book trade administration (*la Librairie*), authorized initially the reprinting in the kingdom of works published abroad, and for which the backing of a royal privilege would not have been embarrassing. It was applied, in the mid eighteenth century and under the influence of Malesherbes, to an increasing quantity of writings that were not very compatible with the granting of a formal approval and a Great Seal privilege.

san supporting a family sends his children to charity schools, he needs . . . a *Nouveau Testament* translated into French, the *Figures de la Bible, Imitation de Jésus Christ* and the *Catéchisme historique* by Fleury, these . . . volumes cost 12 livres [in the] Paris edition, he buys them for 12 sols per volume[25] [in the] provincial edition. Can this artisan ever be in a position to give for these . . . volumes the value of two quintals [200 kg] of wheat that he needs to feed his family?"[26] The monopoly system maintained artificially high prices that paralyzed the book market and encouraged fraud. In the eighteenth century, which was keen on political economy, the remedy was simple, as a memorandum from Rouen's printers and booksellers composed at the time put it. The name of this remedy was competition.

> It is only fair that a bookseller . . . who buys [an author's] manuscript enjoy for a certain period the advantage of not having any competitors; but when this time has expired, what are the reasons for not allowing competition? . . . It is really for the good of the state that after the expiration of its privilege, a work should be common to all the kingdom's booksellers and printers. Competing editions would employ a greater number of workers, would stimulate manufactures. . . . The whole goal [of provincial booksellers] is to overcome the discouraging position in which the Paris booksellers and printers have placed them with the unlimited possession of exclusive privileges. As true citizens, they ask for the means to live while working for the good of the state.[27]

Moreover, Parisian booksellers were incapable of making the most of the exclusive privileges that royal benevolence had granted them. It was a well-known fault, emphasized by another memorandum from Toulouse, undated but from a little later: "Often [Parisians] . . . obtain renewal of privileges for books which they know they shall never reprint, with the [sole] object of preventing thereby their reprinting by provincial booksellers . . . , without paying attention to the fact that if the latter were to reprint these works, they would supply them with the reprints in exchange, and . . . by this means, the consumption of printed books in Paris could only become much more considerable, and would equal, for the Paris booksellers, the reprinting of numerous good books for which the printing houses of Paris would never suffice."[28]

---

25. That is, a price per volume of five times less (one pound was worth twenty sols).

26. Bibl. nat., ms. fr. 22127, fols. 233–5: *Memoire sur l'etat actuel de la librairie et imprimerie de Toulouse,* September 1767. For a general presentation of provincials' memoirs and grievances, see Birn, "Profits of Ideas," esp. 158.

27. Memo addressed to the king and Council of State, n.d. [c. 1767] (Bibl. nat., ms. fr. 21832, fols. 41–6).

28. Bibl. nat., ms. fr. 22127, fols. 319–24.

These highly official pleas did not in any way aim to call into question the principles of book privilege: it was simply a question of reforming the abuses, primarily recognizing the seizure of the public domain to the prejudice of provincial printers and booksellers. But what these texts did not address, and which was a product of the time, is that during the wait for the end of such abuses, counterfeiting often enabled the authors of these reports and their colleagues to do better than merely survive.

Fortuné-Barthélemy de Felice, a printer established in Yverdon, Switzerland, allowed himself, in the article on counterfeiting in his revision of the *Encyclopédie* (1772), to justify and even to extol the practice. In his view, it was indisputable that counterfeiting, whatever one might think of it, represented an incomparable agent of diffusion: "The experience of manufactures [*fabriques*] of all kinds in all European states . . . decided the question long ago in favor of counterfeiting, and this decision is well in keeping with justice, . . . for one will never opt to counterfeit a product . . . that does not sell well. . . . Counterfeits are excellent . . . because . . . , when prices are reduced, many people who perhaps might not even have heard of the original edition can now buy it. . . . How do [booksellers] dare say [that a book] . . . is a good that belongs to them [and] that the trade of those who counterfeit it is piracy? . . . Any exclusive privilege could tend only toward the ruin of the state" (11:264–5). In the eighteenth century, even if they did not go as far as approving overt defiance of the royal privilege system, many local and provincial authorities tolerated (a few did support) the activity of counterfeit printers in their jurisdictions. This tolerance was particularly true of judges of provincial parlements—who showed signs of restiveness after the death of the Sun King—and certain police lieutenants in cities and bailiwicks. By their accommodating attitude, and at times their encouragement (Pierre de Boisguilbert, lieutenant of police in Rouen and founding father of political economy,[29] showed the way from the 1690s with his incitements to "economic disobedience"), these officials contributed to a form of institutionalization of counterfeiting practices, or at the very least to making them commonplace.

The case of Rouen was, no doubt, the most conspicuous, since during most of the eighteenth century, the first president of the parlement was the official overseer of bookselling in the province of Normandy. And, in the name of the economic interests of his jurisdiction, he did not hesitate to proclaim his role as the defender of Rouennais counterfeiting. Thus, in August 1764, Armand-Thomas Hue de Miromesnil, first president at the parlement of

---

29. See *Pierre de Boisguilbert et la naissance de l'économie politique*, preface by Alfred Sauvy, 2 vols. (Paris: Institut national d'études démographiques, 1966).

Rouen, appealed to the director of the book trade of the kingdom, Antoine de Sartine, lieutenant general of the Paris police: "The ease with which Parisian printers increase the number of their privileges and the exorbitant prices they place on their books, restraining this branch of commerce in the provinces to very narrow limits, have, so to speak, forced those that do it to counterfeit new books . . . and [to] print other books whose privileges dated back 15 or 20 years and sometimes more. . . . [This practice] on some occasions excited the outcries of Parisian booksellers. . . . I admit that most provincial booksellers only stock counterfeit books . . . but is it fair to seize them and to punish them?" [30] Miromesnil added further that he "always allowed these kinds of printing" under the condition that he was informed of them. Coming from a high official who had the confidence of the Chancellery, such excuses for the illicit activities of the counterfeit printers and booksellers of Normandy were a veritable acknowledgment of their legitimacy, as well as, in passing, a denunciation of a privilege system perverted by favoritism and economic irrationality.

Toward a Reevaluation

One must be careful in attempting to evaluate Francophone print production during the century of the Enlightenment. Until relatively recently, French research remained, on this point, conditioned by the Parisian character of the principal standard sources and little inclined to question the imprints, themselves Parisian, of a great part of French eighteenth-century publications. [31] French publishing could in this way be identified with privileged Parisian production, duly screened and registered by the centralizing monarchy. [32]

Not until the late 1970s and the early 1980s did several contributions from Henri-Jean Martin, [33] such as *Histoire de l'édition française*, [34] call for a read-

---

30. Letter, August 8, 1764, published by Georges de Beaurepaire, *Le contrôle de la librairie à Rouen à la fin du XVIIIe siècle* (Rouen: A. Lainé, 1929), 12–22.

31. The investigation *Livre et société dans la France du XVIIIe siècle,* ed. François Furet, 2 vols. (Paris: La Haye, Mouton et Cie, 1965–70), notably the contribution of Furet, "La 'librairie' du royaume de France au 18e siècle," 3–32, and Alphonse Dupront's afterword, 185–238, as well as Robert Estivals, *La statistique bibliographique de la France sous la monarchie au XVIIIe siècle* (Paris: La Haye, Mouton et Cie, 1965), illustrate particularly this point of view.

32. Furet, in "La 'librairie'" (12–3), admits that not seeing "the Parisian and central character of the sources of book trade administration . . . , for the 18th century at least, as a major disadvantage." Dupront in his afterword (205), adds, "The investigation is almost exclusively Parisian; *even if the provinces produced little, we do not know how much. Despite hawking literature . . . it did not go beyond a society of notables*" (emphasis added).

33. See, esp., "La librairie française en 1777–1778," *Dix-huitième siècle* 11 (1979): 87–112.

34. Henri-Jean Martin and Roger Chartier, eds., *Histoire de l'édition française,* 4 vols. (Paris: Promodis, 1982–6; repr., Paris: Fayard, 1989–91), esp. "Conjonctures: le licite et l'illicite," 2:92–3.

justment in the light of the expansion and more critical use of sources. After
the works of René Moulinas on the printing presses of the papal enclave of
Avignon,[35] those of Robert Darnton on the Société typographique de Neuchâ-
tel (STN)[36] confirmed the value of exploring the activities of "peripheral
printing presses" established to exploit French and Francophone markets all
along the eastern borders (in the Low Countries, Liège, Bouillon, Deux-Ponts,
Kehl, Neuchâtel, Lausanne, Geneva, Yverdon, Avignon, Nice, and elsewhere).
In *Grub Street Abroad,* Elizabeth Eisenstein also advanced the idea that the
busiest bookselling centers "were to be found outside the borders of well-
consolidated dynastic States" and that "the eighteenth-century francophone
press was unexceptional in this regard," insisting rightly on the important
extraterritorial contribution to the French periodical press.[37] Under the influence of Darnton, a hypothesis advanced in *Histoire de l'édition française* even
claimed that perhaps "in the second half of the eighteenth century . . . one
French book out of two or even more was published outside the kingdom." [38]

These findings do not mean, however, that the "hypnotic effect" of Parisian
sources[39] should give way to an excessive fascination with external sources.
The idea that the STN and its similar copies profited abundantly from the
French book market is undeniable but this is not the whole story. The intensive activity of other centers of production and diffusion located within the
borders of the kingdom must also be borne in mind, especially in the light of
what is beginning to become known of "counterfeiting culture." [40] Between
the privileged editions, which were monopolized by Parisian booksellers and
prohibited, and the daring editions launched on the periphery of French territory, there was still a great deal of room, in the final century of the ancien
régime, for a supply at least equally important—a supply responding to the

35. Moulinas, *L'imprimerie, la librairie et la presse à Avignon au XVIIIe siècle* (Grenoble: Presses universitaires de Grenoble, 1974), and "La contrefaçon avignonnaise," in Martin and Chartier, *Histoire de l'édition française,* 2:294–301.

36. See, esp., Darnton, "Le monde des libraires clandestins sous l'Ancien Régime," in *Bohème littéraire et Révolution* (Paris: Gallimard-Seuil, 1983), 111–53, "Le livre prohibé aux frontières: Neuchâ-tel," in Martin and Chartier, *Histoire de l'édition française,* 2:343–59, and *Édition et sédition. L'univers de la littérature clandestine au XVIIIe siècle* (Paris: Gallimard, 1991).

37. Eisenstein, *Grub Street Abroad: Aspects of the French Cosmopolitan Press from the Age of Louis XIV to the French Revolution* (New York: Clarendon Press, 1992), esp., "Perspectives on Extraterritorial Publishing," 1–35, "The Cosmopolitan Enlightenment," 101–30, and "Grub Street Abroad," 131–63. Eisenstein rightly reminds us: "There is general agreement that almost all the main works of the French Enlightenment—from Montesquieu's *Lettres persanes* (Amsterdam, 1721) to d'Holbach's *Système de la nature,* 1770)—were first published outside France" (105).

38. "L'édition en français hors de France," 2:302–3.

39. The expression is Dupront's, in his afterword to Furet, *Livre et société,* 208.

40. On this point, see Jean-Dominique Mellot, "Entre 'librairie française' et marché du livre au XVIIIe siècle: repères pour un paysage éditorial," in *Le livre et l'historien. Études offertes en l'honneur du professeur Henri-Jean Martin* (Geneva: Droz, 1997), 493–517.

basic needs of the French market that could be satisfied neither by the thirty-six authorized printer-booksellers in the capital nor by their competitors scattered beyond the borders for various reasons, such as overly strict control (of the Parisians), excessively high prices, or distance from the realities of local demand. It so happened that provincial counterfeiting mostly took on the task, and for this reason, it was far from neutral. The printing presses of big provincial centers, such as Rouen, Lyon, Toulouse, Caen, and others, despite *numerus clausus* (restricted number) imposed successively in 1704, 1739, and 1759, maintained a capacity for production that was far superior to what the laws still allowed them to print.[41] Putting this capacity at the service of reprinting at a lesser cost the titles that were underexploited because of either Paris monopolies or prior publication abroad was a matter of public utility for which, as discussed earlier, the provincials lacked neither commonsense arguments nor institutional support.

Certainly the sources for establishing the extent of this provincial contribution are more fragmentary than the rich archives of the STN on which Darnton's studies are based. But many indications enable us to suspect that an enormous quantity of counterfeits were produced in the provinces during the eighteenth century, based on the evidence that is continually found in French public libraries (who preserved them despite their origins), as long as one is not confused by false imprints or the lack of imprints altogether. Moreover, numerous letters in the STN correspondence itself attest that the Neuchâtel editions were seriously challenged by provincial counterfeiters capable of producing books more cheaply, faster, and on the spot, and who were better able to gauge the expectations of the French public.[42] In Rouen, the small archives of the Machuel family of booksellers — particularly the correspondence of the widow of Jean-Baptiste III Machuel, surviving for the years 1768–73[43] — draw a geography of the production of counterfeits where the principal points of support of the Rouennais sales network are Lyon, Toulouse, Rheims, or Avignon, not forgetting Liège and Amsterdam.

---

41. Twelve printers were still allowed in Rouen and Lyon after the restrictive legislation of May 1759. From 430 in 1701, the number of French printers fell to 285 as a result of the Council of State's ruling of July 21, 1701, and to 250 by virtue of that of March 31, 1739.

42. See, esp., Darnton, *Édition et sédition*, 93–6, 98, 100, on the printer-booksellers Jacques Manoury the elder from Caen, Gabriel Regnault from Lyon, and Pierre Machuel and Jacques-Jean-Louis-Guillaume Besongne from Rouen.

43. Bibliothèque municipale de Rouen, ms. g. 190 bis: 534 letters partially exploited in Jean-Dominique Mellot, "Rouen et les libraires forains à la fin du XVIIIe siècle: la veuve Machuel et ses correspondants (1768–1773)," *Bibliothèque de l'École des chartes* 147 (1989): 503–38, and "Libraires en campagne: les forains normands du livre à la fin du XVIIIe siècle," in *Le livre voyageur. Constitution et dissémination des collections livresques dans l'Europe moderne (1450–1830). Actes du colloque*

To sell their counterfeit (and sometimes banned) editions, the Rouennais resorted to the use of dozens of itinerant booksellers (*libraires forains*)[44] who came from several villages in the region of Coutances, in Lower Normandy. These substantial peddlers, often traveling in small groups and equipped with carts, ordered and sold thousands of volumes in a vast northwestern quarter of the kingdom, occasionally haunting Paris but mostly frequenting the market towns and fairs, the country houses and vicarages of the Paris Basin, Normandy, and the North. The commercial success of these specialized traveling salesmen was such — Noël Gille, for example, ordered from the widow Machuel alone two hundred to six hundred volumes (nearly half of which were bound) a month, not counting new releases, at the same time he was contacting other important suppliers on Rouen's main square — that they confirmed the promise of this relatively close market on which the Paris booksellers, because of the excessively high prices of their privileged editions, had hardly any hold.

What kind of books, then, were mostly circulated by these itinerant booksellers whose role was approved by Malesherbes himself?[45] They themselves gave an apparently obvious answer when they spoke of "all of our counterfeits (*contrefaçons*)" (letter from Nicolas Alboi[s]'s wife to Jean-Baptiste Machuel's widow, October 28, 1771). And if we are to judge by the numerous surviving orders, a large part of these counterfeits consisted of "everyday" religious or practical books, sold bound — *Journée du chrétien, Imitation de Jésus-Christ*, lives of the saints, sermons, pastoral works, François Barrême's *Comptes faits, Cuisinière bourgeoise, Dictionnaire de santé*, as well as countless other specialized dictionaries — historical, geographical, religious, botanical, agronomical, and so forth. At the same time, softcover books, representing roughly half of all orders, offered rather recent literary successes: Voltaire's *Précis du siècle de Louis XV,* Marmontel's *Contes moraux* and the novel *Bélisaire*, Rousseau's *Julie ou la Nouvelle Héloïse*, and others, as well as apologies for Christianity and refutations of Voltaire by the Abbés Nonnotte and Bergier. Let us not forget the "philosophical" side of the Enlightenment:

---

international . . . Lyon . . . 23 et 24 mai 1997, ed. Dominique Bougé-Grandon (Paris: Klincksieck, 2000), 153–76.

44. The itinerant booksellers and their practices were brought to light by Anne Sauvy's pioneering article on one of them, the Normand Noël Gille, native of Montsurvent near Coutances: "Noël Gille dit la Pistole, 'marchand foirain libraire roulant par la France,'" *Bulletin des bibliothèques de France* 12 (1967): 177–90.

45. "Preventing this type of commerce," Malesherbes wrote, "would deprive of a great commodity the Seigneurs who live on their lands, the country priests and many other individuals who are secluded in their burg and the villages where there is no bookseller." Cited in Anne Sauvy, "Le livre aux champs," in Martin and Chartier, *Histoire de l'édition française,* 2:431.

Parnasse libertin; Honni soit qui mal y pense ou Histoire des filles célèbres du XVIIIe siècle; Le Sopha; Tableau de l'amour conjugal; or even *Thérèse philosophe.* This mixed catalogue, probably destined for an equally heterogeneous and disparate audience, clearly reveals the extent of the request for cheap productions that have nothing to do, however, with street literature (*Littérature de colportage*).

The satisfaction of this market, so promising and useful to the diffusion and popularization of the Enlightenment in what would now be called rural France (*la France profonde*), relied only secondarily on suppliers from the peripheries, such as the STN, and usually did not involve Paris suppliers, who were too expensive and unresponsive—a point constantly emphasized in the correspondence of itinerant booksellers. The provincial counterfeiting centers in large part supplied this market, proclaiming their socially useful character for doing so, as the aforementioned memoranda, themselves dating from the 1760s, attest. Rouen played a pioneering role in this domain, but it was far from being the only city to prosper at it. In Lyon, according to the testimony of a contemporary, of the twelve print shops in business at the end of the eighteenth century, "three quarters dealt only with counterfeits."[46] Similarly, Toulouse, in the words of Malesherbes in his *Mémoires sur la librairie,* had become a formidable counterfeiting center. Caen, Rheims, and a growing number of secondary printing centers (Montargis, Châlons, Orléans, Marseille) on which there still is insufficient light shed, strove with the passing century to take their share of the spoils. Diderot, taking up his pen on behalf of the Paris guild, denounced in his *Lettre sur le commerce de la librairie* the attitude of those who said, "If they are going to be robbed anyway, our owners [of Paris privileges] might as well be robbed by a neighboring Frenchman than by a Dutchman." But the royal administration itself was not far from approving such a principle. "It is still better if French booksellers and workers make the profit," Malesherbes wrote in 1757.[47]

The Reforms of 1777: Legalization as a Necessary Prelude to the Disappearance of Counterfeits

Still remaining to be considered in this logical progression is the transforming of "patriotic fraud" into a practice legally permitted under royal legislation.

---

46. Émeric David, *Mon voyage de 1787,* Bibliothèque de l'Arsenal, Paris, ms. 5947, fols. 15–6.

47. *Lettre à l'intendant de la généralité de Lyon,* cited in Jean-Paul Belin, *Le commerce des livres prohibés à Paris de 1750 à 1789* (Paris: Belin frères, 1913), 30.

This step would not be taken until 1777, at the initiative (and it was no coincidence) of the old first president of the parlement of Normandy, the marquis of Miromesnil, who had, in the meantime, become Louis XVI's keeper of the seals (*garde des sceaux*). Under his authority six Council decrees were passed on August 30, 1777, profoundly reforming the French publishing system. The Chancellery and the book trade administration chose to satisfy the insistent demands of the provincials. The preamble to the decrees announced that it was a matter of providing "the provincial printers with the legitimate means to employ their presses" and to "reduce [the price of books] to a value proportional to the means of those who want to procure them." A decision was then taken to abolish continuation of privileges, to the great displeasure of the Paris guild: all the old privileges reverted to the public domain, which made their lawful reprinting possible in the provinces, under the streamlined system of "simple permission" ("simple" because of the absence of monopoly).[48] Authors, for their part, saw the recognition of their right to take advantage, during their lives, of the privileges connected to their works. At the same time, inspectors of bookselling in the provinces were charged with legalizing, by a procedure known as stamping or marking (*estampillage*), the millions of counterfeit volumes that printer-booksellers had in stock—which of course incited a general outcry in Paris and a joyous outburst in the provinces.[49] With masses of counterfeit editions, for the most part provincial, bearing the stamp of "Rouen," "Lyon," "Toulouse," "Nancy," "Marseille," as a mark of manufacture, the extent of the fraud appeared for the first time in broad daylight. Because the registers of stamping are neither complete nor reliable,[50] we are reduced to crediting a contemporary estimate (1777) that, apparently without exaggeration, placed the number of counterfeit copies that were legitimized in this way at six million.

What were the titles that were estimated by this stamping procedure? A

48. On the issue of simple permission and its application, see Julien Brancolini and Marie-Thérèse Bouyssy, "La vie provinciale du livre à la fin de l'Ancien Régime," in Furet, *Livre et société*, 2:3–37; and, more recently, Robert L. Dawson, *The French Booktrade and the "Permission Simple" of 1777: Copyright and the Public Domain, with an Edition of the Permit Registers* (Oxford: Voltaire Foundation, 1992). A total of 1,500 simple permissions were registered, representing approximately 2,158,400 copies, 96 percent of which were produced by provincial printers (principally in Rouen at 25 percent and Toulouse, Lyon, and the cities of Lorraine).

49. On stamping, see Anne Boës and Robert L. Dawson, "The Legitimation of *Contrefaçons* and the Police Stamp of 1777," *Studies on Voltaire and the Eighteenth Century* 230 (1985): 461–84; and Jeanne Veyrin-Forrer, "Livres arrêtés, livres estampillés, traces parisiennes de la *contrefaction*," in Moureau, *Les presses grises*, 101–12.

50. Only eight of those guild registers out of twenty remain, and those that survive give lists that include neither all the cities nor all the involved printers and booksellers.

survey undertaken in the collections of the Bibliothèque nationale de France[51] allows us to form an idea. Of eighteen counterfeits bearing the stamp of 1777 (thirteen from Rouen, three from Lyon, one each from Marseille and Nancy) that have been identified, the majority (fourteen) consist of reprints of established literary successes—Abbé Prévost's *Histoire du chevalier des Grieux et de Manon Lescaut;* Mme de Grafigny's *Lettres d'une Péruvienne;* Alain-René Lesage's *Histoire de Gil Blas de Santillane;* Voltaire's *Candide ou l'Optimisme;* Crébillon fils's *Les egaremens du cœur et de l'esprit,* as well as recent plays. Three others are religious steady sellers: Abbé Fleury's *Histoire ecclésiastique;* the so-called Catechism of Montpellier; and Abbé Baudrand's *L'âme sur le calvaire.* All were reprinted in the provinces[52] under false Paris or foreign imprints, or without any imprints at all on the title page.

Even though the preceding sample is limited, it is sufficiently representative to allow the conclusion that the measures of liberalization adopted in 1777 were certainly not a luxury for French publishing. They enabled the provincials to relay, legally from then on, the successes of established men or women of letters, whose influence would have been delayed or limited if the privileges of Paris booksellers had continued. As Raymond Birn has noted, "In one instance at least, the Ancien Régime saw how imperative it was to adapt an institution to social needs."[53] Politically, it was actually, as Henri Falk observed, the "first decentralization measure of the Ancien Régime."[54] These assessments are admittedly tempered by the fact that the Paris lobby succeeded in partially renegotiating the adopted reforms to its advantage.[55] Counterfeiting, moreover, did not completely disappear in the following years. But with the reach of the privilege system reduced, its pernicious effects on print production were automatically stopped. The millions of counterfeit copies that were legitimized from 1777 or authorized to appear by simple permission bear witness to this. Legality and equity scored points and at the same time drove back fraud and the logic of monopoly. In the last years

---

51. Jean-Dominique Mellot and Élisabeth Queval, "Pour un repérage des contrefaçons portant l'estampille de 1777 au département des Livres imprimés," in *Mélanges autour de l'histoire des livres imprimés et périodiques,* ed. B. Blasselle and L. Portes (Paris: Bibliothèque nationale de France, 1998), 178–94.

52. Only one of these editions is attributable to the printing presses of Avignon, eight belong to those of Rouen, one to those of Caen; all the other counterfeits taken into account are, according to a study of the materials used, from the French provinces, without the possibility of further specificity.

53. Birn, "Profits of Ideas," 168.

54. Falk, *Les privilèges de librairie* (Paris: A. Rousseau, 1906), 142.

55. See Sabine Juratic, "Le monde du livre à Paris entre absolutisme et Lumières. Recherches sur l'économie de l'imprimé et sur ses acteurs," 2 vols., Ph.D. diss., École pratique des hautes études, Paris, 2003.

of the ancien régime, the new privilege formula experienced an undeniable success: the demand for privileges reached levels unprecedented since their inauguration—almost a thousand a year in the 1780s—before disappearing permanently with the coming of the French Revolution in 1789–90.[56]

On the eve of the Revolution, a movement to "institutionalize counterfeiting" and reform privilege, directly inspired by provincial experience, ended up reaching the higher echelons of the government, largely thwarting the projects of the Paris lobby. It incidentally transformed itself into a liberalizing movement, a reasoned reconstitution of the public domain of freely reprinted editions. Access to works in the greatest demand thus increased in a spectacular way. In this sense, the movement initiated by the growth of counterfeiting paradoxically only prepared for the astounding explosion of press freedom proclaimed on August 26, 1789 in the *Declaration of the Rights of Man and the Citizen*.

From the beginning of the Revolution, privileges, permissions (tacit or simple), were abolished, and with them disappeared not only what was left of counterfeiting but also the peripheral printing presses and, for a while, the embryonic rights that had at last been recognized for authors. Before the first clear attacks on this proclaimed freedom of the press in 1792, printers, authors, journalists, private individuals, and institutions produced and reproduced whatever they chose, as fast and as inexpensively as possible, even if it meant rough handling of what was beginning to be called intellectual property. The silence imposed by absolutism was succeeded by the noise and shock of opinions elicited by a system of national representation. A logic of frantic competition and urgency to disseminate political information exploded, from one day to the next, sweeping away not only burdensome prepublication licensing and publishing monopolies but also protections (of authors, of the print trades, of texts, of quality) and balance (notably the distribution of book guilds throughout France) patiently established through three centuries of what Roger Chartier characterized a few years ago as the "Ancien Régime typographique."[57] Multiple bankruptcies, the disqualification of the book trades, the employment crisis, the hypercentralization of the country, the return in force of an arbitrary power and its bloody persecutions under the Terror, after several years of revolution, did not take long to cause people to recall with nostalgia the paradoxes of the "golden age of the book," an

---

56. On July 27, 1790, precisely, the last book privilege was granted, according to Falk, *Les privilèges de librairie,* but the practice had been considerably curtailed since July 1789.

57. See the article Chartier dedicated to this formula and what it recovers in the *Dictionnaire encyclopédique du livre,* ed. P. Fouché, D. Péchoin, P. Schuwer, J.-D. Mellot, A. Nave, and M. Poulain, vols. 1– (Paris: Éditions du Cercle de la Librairie, 2002–), 1:93–4.

era when privileges immoderately favoring the Paris booksellers simultaneously stimulated the activity of provincial counterfeiters and foreign competitors in the name of public interest and social benefit. The ambition to stamp out counterfeiting had caused an accelerated diffusion, which, in turn, created an imperative to liberalize the practices governing the press. However, during the Revolution that followed, under the dictatorship of political information drawn from topical satires and the newspaper, one could no longer claim, outside of Paris, to publish or read anything essential to the opinion and the life of the "Great Nation."

Chapter 3

On the Threshold

Architecture, Paratext, and Early Print Culture

WILLIAM H. SHERMAN

I feare I haue too much presumed on your idle leisure . . . to stand talking all this while in an other mans doore.
—Thomas Nashe, Preface to Sir Philip Sidney, *Astrophil and Stella* (1591)

No more dawdling on the threshold of the threshold.
—Gérard Genette, *Paratexts: Thresholds of Interpretation* (1987)

THIS ESSAY is the product of an imaginary dialogue, of the sort favored by Renaissance writers and facilitated by printing itself, between two authors who never refer to each other but who have much to say to each other about a topic of enduring interest. The authors are the historian Elizabeth Eisenstein and the narrative theorist Gérard Genette, and the topic is what title pages, prefaces, and other liminal devices can reveal about what we imagine we are doing when we pick up and make our way into a printed book. With two classic studies, both published in 1979 and extended in subsequent works, these two scholars have done as much as anyone in their generation to define the terms with which we approach the printed text and its technological and cultural legacies.

In *The Printing Press as an Agent of Change: Communications and Cultural Transformations in Early-Modern Europe* (*PPAC*), Eisenstein considers the impact of printing not just on the appearance and distribution of books but on scholarly inquiry and communication, professional and economic relations, and religious and political reformation. Thanks to the breadth of its scope and the boldness of its claims, the book has provoked two and a half decades of fruitful discussion about the relationship between "scribal culture" and "print culture" and about the role played by the printing press in the major movements associated with the emergence of modernity.

In *The Architext: An Introduction*,[1] Genette began his equally ambitious project of mapping the system of relations linking all texts to other texts (both within and between individual works), producing a series of books devoted to different aspects of what he labels "transtextuality." In the study that has arguably made the greatest impact on the widest range of readers, *Paratexts: Thresholds of Interpretation*,[2] Genette coined the term "paratext" to describe the verbal and visual accessories that accompany texts and present them to the public (including covers, title pages, prefaces, and tables of contents), calling for new attention to their role in mediating between authors, printers, and readers. Not the least of Genette's achievements is to have given a collective name to a cluster of textual components that had needed one for half a millennium: "paratext" does not yet appear in the standard lexicons of the English language, but it has so successfully entered the scholarly vocabulary that it is now applied — without quotation marks or pause for thought — to texts of every period and genre. Genette himself, however, is careful to acknowledge his limited chronological and generic scope; and few of the scholars who take his terms into other contexts have stopped to consider the influence of his almost exclusive focus on nineteenth- and twentieth-century French fiction on his discussion of what printed paratext is and does — or, more pointedly, what it was and did in the formative years of printing.[3] After all, it was during these years (as Eisenstein and others have pointed out) that the paratextual apparatus underwent many of its most profound and lasting transformations.[4]

For Genette, the paratext is a "group of practices and discourses," mobilized by "the author and his allies," that "enables a text to become a book

---

1. Translated by Jane E. Lewin (Berkeley and Los Angeles: Univ. of California Press, 1992); originally published as *Introduction à l'architexte* (Paris, 1979).

2. Translated by Jane E. Lewin (Cambridge: Cambridge Univ. Press, 1997); originally published as *Seuils* (Paris, 1987). All page references in the text and notes are to the English-language edition. For a lucid summary of Genette's "poetics of transtextuality," see Richard Macksey's Foreword to *Paratexts*, esp. xiv–xix.

3. A rare exception is J. W. Binns's discussion of the paratext found in early Anglo-Latin texts printed at Oxford and Cambridge, where he suggests that "such texts modify and enrich [Genette's] argument considerably." "Printing and Paratext in Sixteenth-Century England: The Oxford and Cambridge Presses," *Cahiers Élisabéthains* 50 (October 1996): 5.

4. See, for a start, *PPAC*, 52 (and the sources cited there). A. F. Johnson's sketchy essay, "Title-Pages: Their Forms and Development [1928]," in *Selected Essays on Books and Printing*, ed. Percy H. Muir (Amsterdam: Van Gendt, 1970), 288–97, has now been fleshed out by Margaret M. Smith's *The Title-Page: Its Early Development, 1460–1510* (New Castle, DE: Oak Knoll Press, 2000) — the subject of Nicolas Barker's useful review essay, "The Title-Page," *The Book Collector* 52 (Winter 2003): 447–58. And there has been important new work, in recent years, on the title itself; see, esp., Eleanor F. Shevlin, "'To reconcile *Book* and *Title*, and make 'em kin to one another': The Evolution of the Title's Contractual Functions," *Book History* 2 (1999): 42–77.

and to be offered as such to its readers and, more generally, to the public" (1–2).[5] The paratext is not only distinct from the text proper but "always subordinate to [it]" (12). It may be found in the interstices of a text (chapter titles or notes) or outside the book altogether (diaries, correspondence, interviews, or reviews); but most of the components Genette identified and examined constitute what is sometimes called the "the front-matter" (titles, epigraphs, dedications, or prefaces). The paratext marks out a preliminary space where readers are brought to the edge of the text, invited to enter it, and given important information about it—its title and genre, its author and the circumstances of its composition, its relationships to other texts and the appropriate methods for digesting or applying it. As Genette explains in his first chapter, "More than a boundary or a sealed border, the paratext is, rather, a *threshold,* or—a word Borges used apropos of a preface—a 'vestibule' that offers the world at large the possibility of either stepping inside or turning back. It is . . . a zone between text and off-text, a zone not only of transition but also of *transaction*" (1–2). At the end of his exhaustive survey, looking back over the liminal territory he has charted, Genette resorts to another set of metaphors to underline the paratext's primary function: "The paratext provides a kind of canal lock between the ideal and relatively immutable identity of the text and the empirical (sociohistorical) reality of the text's public (if I may be forgiven these rough images), the lock permitting the two to remain 'level'. Or, if you prefer, the paratext provides an airlock that helps the reader pass without too much respiratory difficulty from one world to the other" (407–8). Such images are signs of Genette's critical power and creativity, and in passages like these Genette's account is at its most quotable and portable. These metaphors, then, should certainly be "forgiven," but they should not be simply taken as a given: while the threshold and the vestibule were vital metaphors for early modern writers and readers (who reinvented them for the new culture of print), the canal lock and airlock bring with them a whole series of anachronistic assumptions.

Were Genette more interested in moving back in time to trace the emergence and evolution of the paratext, he would quickly reach a point where "authorial responsibility" is too embryonic and diffuse to be considered a

---

5. Genette's definition of paratext as authorial becomes gradually more explicit and absolute. On p. 2 he notes that paratext is "always the conveyor of a commentary that is authorial or more or less legitimated by the author"; on p. 3 he describes it as the province of "authorial intention and responsibility"; and on p. 9 he asserts that "by definition, something is not a paratext unless the author or one of his associates accepts responsibility for it." By the end of the text the "authorial point of view" has become nothing less than "the implicit creed and spontaneous ideology of the paratext" (408).

universal (or at least defining) feature. He would stumble over instances in which it is by no means clear where the paratext ends and the text begins, or where the paratext crosses the threshold and interrupts or even undermines the text it is supposedly serving,[6] instances where the text is subordinate to the paratext rather than the other way around, simply spelling or spinning out the primary message conveyed by a title, frontispiece, or preface.[7] And he would find it increasingly difficult to sustain his sense that "the identity of the text" is inherently more stable than the public to which it is presented.[8]

If Genette went all the way back to the first century or so of printing, he would discover that the period's own textual producers and consumers had a surprisingly sophisticated understanding of both the pragmatic and the symbolic functions of paratext. And he would, in turn, supply Eisenstein with unexpected support for her argument that printing marked a revolutionary change in the world of the book. As texts themselves crossed the threshold into the culture of print, the appearance and the function of paratext evolved in response to new socioeconomic pressures and possibilities, gradually fixing the presentational apparatus into a form that has remained remarkably consistent throughout the history of printing. But from the start the new medium encouraged (or perhaps forced) its creators and users to approach the book with a creative self-consciousness that all but disappears as printing becomes established. Early paratext, in particular, is marked by a sense of spatial and

---

6. Laurence Sterne's *Tristram Shandy*, with its notorious marble page that literally turns the text inside out, is the best-known example. But the traditional device of the dreaming author — in which the text itself shuttles between the fictional world and the real world — is one of the most common narrative frames in medieval and early modern literature and it is equally difficult to fit into Genette's scheme. Another pervasive practice that would cause problems for Genette is the undermining marginalia often printed in English Renaissance books. See William W. E. Slights, *Managing Readers: Printed Marginalia in English Renaissance Books* (Ann Arbor: Univ. of Michigan Press, 2001), chaps. 1, 3, 7.

7. The title of John Bunyan's heavy-handed allegory, *The Holy War, Made by Shaddai Upon Diabolus, for the Regaining of the Metropolis of the World. Or; the Losing and Taking Again of the Town of Mansoul* (London, 1682), makes clear its point. The primary purpose of the text is to spell out the schematic message of the pictorial frontispiece, showing the anthropomorphic town of Man's Soul (with its "Eare-gate," "Eye-gate," and "Heart Castle") besieged on one side by a monstrous "Diabolus" and protected on the other by "Shaddai's Army."

8. Genette adds a note to his claim about the "relatively immutable identity of the text," acknowledging that "immutable" should be understood "very relatively, of course, and very diversely: one has only to think of those medieval works of which no two texts are absolutely alike" (408 n. 10). But the mutability I have in mind here is not just the variability of individual copies of texts — a phenomenon that extends, at any rate, well into the age of printing and is exemplified by the often-repeated observation that no two copies of Shakespeare's 1623 First Folio are identical. I am thinking, further, of the kinds of forces and circumstances that led (for instance) to the extraordinary differences between the First Quarto and Second Quarto of *Hamlet,* or the A-Text and B-Text of Marlowe's *Doctor Faustus,* where the paratext does little to stabilize texts that are so radically divergent they now demand to be edited separately.

metaphorical play that writers tend no longer to deploy, and readers no longer to require or desire, in what Genette describes as the "making present" of the printed book.[9]

In a recent study of French Renaissance *conteurs* and the prologues they penned to introduce their books, Deborah N. Losse recovers an elaborate repertoire of what she calls (following Genette) "liminary strategies." In some of the period's most common tropes, the book was described as an orphan or fledgling in search of a patron's protective wings, a shop offering new wares to eager consumers, and a table furnished with tasty morsels.[10] These metaphors crossed the Channel to England, where they remained current throughout the sixteenth and seventeenth centuries and where, as Kevin Dunn has explained, they were generally put to the service of justifying the author's move from private meditation or coterie circulation to public discourse — as well as the more practical and pressing matter of securing patronage.[11] By the end of the sixteenth century texts offered without epistles to the reader and other "paratextual vestibules" were considered "inherently defective or incomplete."[12]

---

9. There are many exceptions to be found in contemporary literature — particularly at the experimental edges of fiction. Perhaps the most extreme example is the Polish science-fiction writer Stanislaw Lem's *Imaginary Magnitude* (San Diego, CA: Harcourt Brace Jovanovich, 1984), which consists of five fictional introductions to twenty-first-century books. Lem begins, appropriately enough, with an introduction on the art of writing introductions — in which prefatory texts are described as "a richly carved doorframe chased in gold and surmounted by counts and griffins on a majestic lintel" (9). Peter Handke's *Across* (New York: Farrar, Straus, and Giroux, 1986) — as its name implies — also plays to great effect on the poetics of the threshold, while the Scottish novelist Alasdair Gray has established himself as a paratextual connoisseur with *The Book of Prefaces* (London: Bloomsbury, 2000). For the paratextual play in Gray's fiction, see Glyn White, "The Critic in the Text: Footnotes and Marginalia in the Epilogue to Alasdair Gray's *Lanark: A Life in Four Books* [1981]," in *Ma(r)king the Text: The Presentation of Meaning on the Literary Page*, ed. Joe Bray, Miriam Handley, and Anne C. Henry (Aldershot, Hants.: Ashgate, 2000), 55–70. In the context of this essay it is worth pointing out that Gray explicitly revives the Renaissance paratextual strategies explored here: *Lanark*'s opening frontispiece wittily mimics the engraved title page from Sir Walter Raleigh's *The History of the World* (London, 1614).

10. Losse, *Sampling the Book: Renaissance Prologues and the French Conteurs* (Lewisburg, PA: Bucknell Univ. Press, 1994), chap. 3. Another pervasive trope was the book-as-mirror, with the ornamental border on the title page invoking the frame of a looking glass. See Shevlin, "'To reconcile *Book* and *Title*,'" 50–2; and Rayna Kalas, "The Technology of Reflection: Renaissance Mirrors of Steel and Glass," *Journal of Medieval and Early Modern Studies* 32 (2002): 519–42.

11. Dunn, *Pretexts of Authority: The Rhetoric of Authorship in the Renaissance Preface* (Stanford: Stanford Univ. Press, 1994), chap. 1.

12. Randall Anderson, "The Rhetoric of Paratext in Early Printed Books," in *The Cambridge History of the Book in Britain*, vol. 4, *1557–1695*, ed. John Barnard and D. F. McKenzie, with the assistance of Maureen Bell (Cambridge: Cambridge Univ. Press, 2002), 637, where Anderson quotes Michael Drayton's complaint, in the preface to *The second part . . . of Poly-Olbion* (London, 1622), that printers issuing texts without "Epistles to the Readers . . . haue cousoned the Buyers with vnperfected Bookes."

None of these accounts prepares us as well as Genette's own "rough images" for the extent to which early modern textual thresholds were understood in spatial—and often specifically architectural—terms. Sometimes paratexts were used to describe the world of the text as a particular type of outdoor or indoor space—one fitted, on one hand, to the content offered by the author, compiler, or printer, and, on the other, to the kinds of activities imagined for the reader. One of the most common metaphors (particularly for anthologies of poems, aphorisms, and other texts harvested from the world of books) was the cultivated garden, as in the epistle "To the Reader" from John Bodenham's *Belvedere* (London, 1600): "It shall be sufficient for me then to tell thee, that here thou art brought into the Muses Garden, (a place that may beseeme the presence of the greatest Prince in the world.) . . . The walkes, alleys, and passages in this Garden are almost infinite; every where a turning, on all sides such windings in and out: yet all extending both to pleasure and profit, as very rare or seldome shalte thou see the like. Marke then, what varietie of flowres grow all along as thou goest, and trample on none rudely, for all are right precious."[13] Perhaps the most common architectural container for Renaissance texts was the theater—especially for collections of moralistic poetry such as Samuel Rowlands's *A Theater of Delightfull Recreation* (London, 1605), with its emblematic theater depicted on the title page. Another common textual edifice, particularly for didactic or polemical titles, was the schoolhouse. Stephen Gosson called his diatribe against contemporary vices *The School of Abuse* (London, 1579), and in his dedicatory epistle to Philip Sidney he encouraged his reluctant reader literally to be taken to school: "The Schoole which I build, is narrowe, and at first blushe appeareth but a doggehole. . . . I perswade my selfe, that seeing the abuses which I reveale, trying them thorowly to my hurt, and bearing the stench of them yet in my owne nose, I may best make the frame, found the schoole, and reade the first lecture of all my selfe, too warne every man to avoyde the perill. . . . If your Worshippe vouchsafe to enter the School doore, and walke an hower or twaine within for your pleasure, you shall see what I teach." Gosson invites his reader to "enter the School doore" (i.e., open the book) and "walke an hower or twaine within" (i.e., read for an hour or two). As these metaphors suggest, it was not just the text proper but also the threshold itself that was an architectural space—a gateway, arch, portico, or porch through which the reader entered the text.[14]

---

13. Clara Gebert, ed., *An Anthology of Elizabethan Dedications & Prefaces* (Philadelphia: Univ. of Pennsylvania Press, 1933), 135.

14. Ibid., 46–7.

Few Renaissance writers had a more powerful sense of paratextual play than the Elizabethan author Thomas Nashe: one of history's great dawdlers on the threshold, Nashe filled his prefatory texts with elaborate metaphors, intertextual references, and in-jokes.[15] One of his most brilliant (if most ephemeral) productions was the prefatory letter he provided for the first printing of Sidney's great sonnet sequence *Astrophil and Stella*.[16] Sidney himself showed no interest in publishing these poems during his life (which ended prematurely in 1586), and for some time the text that would do more than any other to launch the Elizabethan sonnet-publishing craze was available in only a small number of closely held manuscript copies. In 1591 the enterprising bookseller Thomas Newman issued John Charlewood's unauthorized (and badly garbled) printing of Sidney's text, prefaced by letters from himself and Nashe and followed by a set of what the title refers to as "sundry other rare Sonnets of diuers Noble men and Gentlemen." The "Sonnets" include an early version of Samuel Daniel's *Delia* sequence, published in revised and expanded form the following year, with an architectural title page inviting the reader into a classical temple (fig. 3.1) — though it is one copied from the Elizabethan translation of the late-fifteenth-century Italian romance the *Hypnerotomachia Poliphili*.[17] Newman's messy text was almost instantly recalled, at the insistence of Sidney's family, with the support of the highest authorities, and replaced with a completely new version, correcting many of the errors from the first version and cutting both of the prefatory letters and all of the poems by other authors.[18]

This brief but charged publication history captures an important moment in the gradual legitimation of printed literature, and in the transformation of Sidney into the public model for the Protestant soldier-poet. In Henry

---

15. His "Preface to *Menaphon,*" a long letter addressed "To the Gentlemen Students of both Vniuersities" and printed before Robert Greene's pastoral romance *Menaphon* (London, 1589), is one of the most quotable pieces of literary criticism from the Elizabethan period — all the more remarkable because it was his first publication. For useful overviews of Nashe's literary career, see Charles Nicholl, *A Cup of News: The Life of Thomas Nashe* (London: Routledge & Kegan Paul, 1984); and Lorna Hutson, *Thomas Nashe in Context* (Oxford: Clarendon Press, 1989). For an important attempt to grapple with his authorial rhetoric, see Jonathan V. Crewe, *Unredeemed Rhetoric: Thomas Nashe and the Scandal of Authorship* (Baltimore: Johns Hopkins Univ. Press, 1982).

16. *Syr P. S. His Astrophel and Stella* (London, 1591). The most detailed account of *Astrophil and Stella*'s textual history is H. R. Woudhuysen, *Sir Philip Sidney and the Circulation of Manuscripts, 1558–1640* (Oxford: Clarendon Press, 1996), 365–84.

17. Samuel Daniel, *Delia* (London, 1592). The woodcut of the temple was prepared for book 2 of *Hypnerotomachia: The strife of loue in a dreame* (London, 1592), a translation of [Francesco Colonna], *Hypnerotomachia Poliphili* (Venice, 1499).

18. See Woudhuysen's reconstruction of the affair (*Sir Philip Sidney,* 367–9). Nicholl adds some important details (*A Cup of News,* 83).

Woudhuysen's words, "What was private and inward, for the eyes of just a few, now became available to all. It was not just Sidney's image which was to be changed by this: the words he wrote in his fine italic hand were to be selected, edited, and altered in ways which can ultimately no longer be recovered. In the next hundred or so years the culture of print finally triumphed over the manuscript culture: the transference of Sidney's works . . . from the one medium to the other was to play a significant part in this process."[19] Nashe's contribution to the process was extremely modest—in effect if not in tone. His letter did not reach many sixteenth-century readers beyond Sidney's displeased sister, the countess of Pembroke, and few of its modern readers have been impressed by it. Mona Wilson, in her 1931 edition of *Astrophil & Stella,* describes Nashe's preface as "an egregious puff . . . relieved only by the pretty conceit that this 'tragicommody of love is performed by starlight'" (in which Nashe plays on the star-related names of Sidney's lovers and sets up an elaborate sequence of theatrical tropes). More recently, G. R. Hibbard complained that "much of the preface is quite frankly padding, and it is not surprising that when Newman . . . brought out a second and much improved edition . . . Nashe's contribution was omitted from it."[20] But if we approach the letter in terms inherited from early modern liminary strategies, rather than modern marketing strategies, Nashe's short text has much to teach us about paratextual performativity in early print culture.

Entitled "Somewhat to read for them that list," Nashe's letter begins with a bold act of scene-setting: "*Tempus adest plausus aurea pompa venit,* so endes the Sceane of Idiots, and enter *Astrophel* in pompe" (A3r). Sidney's original readers would have recognized that Nashe was appropriating a line from Ovid's *Amores* (translated by Christopher Marlowe as "The shout is nigh; the golden pompe comes heere") to depict Sidney and his alter ego, Astrophel, as the true revivers of the Ovidian arts of love.[21] He immediately invites his gentlemen readers, put off already by an outpouring of inferior amatory verse, to enter this new "Theater of pleasure": "Gentlemen that haue seene a thousand lines of folly . . . let not your surfeited sight, new come from such puppet play, thinke scorne to turn aside into this Theater of pleasure, for here you

---

19. Woudhuysen, *Sir Philip Sidney,* 384.

20. Mona Wilson, ed., *Astrophil & Stella,* by Sir Philip Sidney (London: Nonesuch Press, 1931), xxxi; G. R. Hibbard, *Thomas Nashe: A Critical Introduction* (London: Routledge & Kegan Paul, 1962), 50.

21. Nashe is quoting Ovid, *Amores,* 3.2.44. Marlowe's translation can be found in *All Ovids Elegies,* vol. 3, *Bookes* (Middlebourgh [i.e., London], 1603). I cite vol. 1 of Roma Gill's edition of *The Complete Works of Christopher Marlowe* (Oxford: Clarendon Press, 1987), 64. I am grateful to Sean Keilen for his assistance with this passage.

shal find a paper stage streud with pearle, an artificial heau'n to ouershadow the faire frame, & christal wals to encounter your curious eyes, whiles the tragicommody of loue is performed by starlight" (A3r). Nashe then proceeds to elaborate on the genre and plot of Sidney's "play": "The chiefe Actor here is *Melpomene* [the Muse of tragedy], whose dusky robes dipt in the ynke of teares, as yet seeme to drop when I view them neere. The argument [is] cruell chastity, the Prologue hope, the Epilogue dispaire" (A3r). All too aware of his own obscurity and Sidney's fame, Nashe here imagines himself "taxt with a margent note of presumption" — that is, a reader's angry annotation accusing him of arrogance — "for offering to put vp any motion of applause in the behalfe of so excellent a Poet" (A3r). And yet, he hopes to be "excused, [as] I open the gate to his glory" (A3r).

After an extravagant series of analogies — describing his pen as a picklock used to open the poetic treasures "imprisoned in Ladyes casks" (A3r), Astrophel as "Englands Sunne" coming to dissolve the "cloude of sorrow" from English letters (A3v), the readers as merchants who have come "to fill vp their boate" (A4v), and the countess of Pembroke as the "eloquent secretary to the Muses," "a second *Minerua,*" and the inheritor of both the "lirick Harpe" of Sappho and the "Laurel Garlande" of Sidney himself (A4r) — Nashe finally breaks off and returns to the gateway through which he points his readers into Sidney's text: "Gentlemen, I feare I haue too much presumed on your idle leisure, and beene too bold, to stand talking all this while in an other mans doore: but now I will leaue you to suruey the pleasures of *Paphos,* and offer your smiles on the Aulters of *Venus*" (A4v). These tropes — in which a book is a building and the paratext its doorway — became a commonplace in the prefaces of Renaissance writers. Perhaps the clearest example can be found in another playful epistle from another virtuoso pamphleteer of the English Renaissance, John Taylor ("The Water Poet"). In *Taylors revenge,* the author included a prefatory letter "to Any that can Read": "To shew thee the meaning of this little Building, Imagine this *Epistle* to be the doore, and if thou please to come in and see what stuffe the whole Frame is made off." [22]

Nashe's self-consciousness about taking too long to lead his readers across the threshold was itself a common conceit in early paratext. As John Bunyan concludes his four-page verse epistle "To the Reader" in the allegorical poem *The Holy War* (1682), he writes:

> But I have too long held thee in the Porch,
> And kept thee from the Sun-shine with a Torch.
> Well, now go forward, step within the dore. (A4r)

---

22. John Taylor, *Taylors revenge* (London, 1615), A3r, cited in Anderson, "Rhetoric of Paratext," 638.

These lines recall the volumes of George Herbert (*The Temple*) and Christopher Harvey (*The Synagogue*), whose poems took their readers on architectural tours, and suggest that Bunyan's paratextual "porch" is a specifically ecclesiastical space. In English churches, from at least the early sixteenth century, the term "porch" is used for the "transept or side chapel" (*OED,* "porch," 2). For Catholics and Protestants alike, this space provided the starting point for most of the ceremonies marking important events in the life cycle (from baptism through marriage to burial). For early modern readers, then, the porch would be a familiar threshold—they would be used to moving through it as a transitional zone between inside and outside and between the quotidian and the sacred—and it would provide a particularly effective vestibule for readers being prepared for new textual content or form.

In both Herbert and Harvey, the porch is not just a devotional space but a preliminary space. In Herbert, "The Church-porch" is the first poem the reader encounters inside the book/building; and in Harvey, we begin with "A stepping-stone to the threshold of Mr. *Herberts* Church-porch" (which almost certainly wins the prize for the most liminal images in a single title) before pulling back to view "The Church-yard," "The Church-stile," "The Church-gate," "The Church-wals," and "The Church" itself and finally entering "The Church-porch" proper.[23] But Bunyan, in his preface to *The Holy War,* is clearly speaking about a space outside the building—more precisely, a transitional space just outside the door—and this was, in fact, the more common meaning and function of the "porch" in English architecture (both sacred and secular) from the Middle Ages on. As the *OED* reminds us, the word derived from the Latin *porticus,* and its primary sense was "an exterior structure forming a covered approach to the entrance of a building; sometimes applied to an interior space serving as a vestibule" (*OED,* "porch," 1a). In the middle of the seventeenth century there was a veritable vogue for textual porches that use those terms to represent entryways in the most general sense: the great educator Comenius, for example, called one of his introductions to the Latin language *Vestibulum Novissimum Linguae Latinae [or] Joh. Amos Comenius his Last Porch of the Latin Tongue* (London, 1647). But the image was always open to extended architectural metaphors, perhaps the most drawn-out of which was Ezekias Woodward's 1640 treatise on the instruction of children, directed to both parents and the preachers who instruct them. Woodward's full title advertises a vestibule: *Vestibulum or, A Manuduction Towards a Faire Edifice*

---

23. George Herbert, *The Temple* (London, 1633); [Christopher Harvey], *The Synagogue* (London, 1640). Cf. Randall McLeod's brilliant readings of Herbert's architectural paratext: "Enter *Reader,*" in *The Editorial Gaze: Mediating Texts in Literature and the Arts,* ed. Paul Eggert and Margaret Sankey (New York: Garland, 1998), 3–50, and "FIAT fLUX," in *Crisis in Editing: Texts of the English Renaissance,* ed. Randall McLeod (New York: AMS Press, 1993), 61–172.

by Their Hands, who are designed to open the way thereunto. The title page also acknowledges the text's oddest feature—the placement of the dedicatory epistle, "To the Common Reader," before those to the dedicatee and "the Ministers"—and explains that "The Epistle to the Reader is as a *Light* in the *Porch,* therefore *set*-out first to bee seene." [24]

RICHARD RIDELL'S entry on "portico" in the Grove *Dictionary of Art* explains that the term is "used in Western architecture for a covered area before the entrance . . . and usually forming the central element in the façade." He suggests that the "portico" tended to be "of grander proportions than the simple porch." [25] But Doreen Yarwood's survey of British architecture reveals that even in the late Middle Ages porches could be "profusely ornamented with sculpture, paneling, tracery, and pinnacles," and her examples of Elizabethan and Jacobean entrance porches are as grand as the most elaborate portico—though less ornate, perhaps, than the most fanciful architectural title page. [26] Ridell's description of the function of the portico and Yarwood's of the porch are especially useful for helping modern students to recover the early modern connections between the entrances to buildings and the entrances to books. [27]

> [The portico] constitutes an intermediary or transitional space—covered, but open at the sides—between the exterior and the fully enclosed interior of a building, and between public and private spaces. (265)

---

24. All that survives of Woodward's text is its unusually elaborate paratext—a five-page letter, "To the Common Reader"; a five-page dedicatory epistle; a seventy-nine-page letter, "Epistle to the Ministers"; and a forty-seven-page preface. The "Epistle to the Reader" picks up and extends the title page's architectural metaphors: "A very grave Dr. was pleased to liken my work to an *Edifice,* well grounded and raised. . . . I crave a faire way for entrance, and *dedicate* that also, being (in my sense) the chief part of the *structure,* and gives us admittance thereinto: for if the *building* be never so *faire,* yet, if we cannot enter, the beautie is nothing to us, or but a mere outside only" (2v).

25. Ridell, "Portico," *The Dictionary of Art,* ed. Jane Turner (New York: Grove's Dictionaries, 1996), 25:264–5; hereafter cited in text.

26. Yarwood, *The Architecture of Britain* (New York: Charles Scribner's Sons, 1976), 58, 100; hereafter cited in text. I am grateful to Georgianna Ziegler for bringing Yarwood's book to my attention.

27. So, too, is the recent work of Christy Anderson—particularly "Learning to Read Architecture in the English Renaissance," in *Albion's Classicism: The Visual Arts in Britain, 1550–1660,* ed. Lucy Gent (New Haven: Yale Univ. Press, 1995), 239–86, but also "Monstrous Babels: Language and Architectural Style in the English Renaissance," in *Architecture and Language: Constructing Identity in European Architecture, c. 1000–c. 1650,* ed. Georgia Clarke and Paul Crossley (Cambridge: Cambridge Univ. Press, 2000), 148–61. Especially interesting for my purposes here are Anderson's examples of classical columns on ornamental title pages in the English Renaissance—some of which were actually made up of books stacked end-to-end.

> The *entrance porch* or frontispiece was an Elizabethan development from the early Tudor gatehouse. As the main entrance to the building it was the focal centre for the employment of new Renaissance forms and ornament. Here the designers interpreted the classical orders and used them, not as structural elements, but in ornamental manner. (98)

When Yarwood refers to the porch as a frontispiece, she is not speaking figuratively: in architectural terminology, the word refers to "the principal face or front of a building." This sense of "frontispiece" entered the English language in the 1590s and just over a decade later was first used in a textual context to describe "the first page of a book, . . . the title-page including illustrations and table of contents . . . [or] an introduction or preface." Not until the end of the seventeenth century did the term take on its current sense of "an illustration facing the title-page of a book or division of a book."[28]

The connections I have been tracing between books and buildings—and, more generally, between cognitive activity and physical space—have a very long history, stretching back through the Middle Ages into classical antiquity. The book-as-building may well sit alongside the book-as-body as the longest-serving and widest-ranging metaphorical repertoire.[29] In medieval Europe, as Mary Carruthers has shown, cogitation, meditation, and communication depended on the interplay between words and architecture: books and monasteries presented their users with what she calls "an architecture for thinking."[30] And as the culture—and vocabulary—of printing takes shape in the sixteenth century and beyond, anthropomorphic terms such as "spine" and "foot" are joined by architectural terms such as "sill" and "gutter" (both dating from the mid nineteenth century, one referring to the space at the bottom of the page and the other to the trough where the two pages of an opening come together). But almost immediately, and for a couple of centuries, printed texts regularly turn the opening page(s) of the book into an architectural entryway.

Architectural frames for pages are not new in the age of printing: some of the most artful examples can be found in illuminated manuscripts. But

---

28. *Oxford English Dictionary,* s.v., ""frontispiece."

29. The classic survey is Ernst Robert Curtius, "The Book as Symbol," in *European Literature and the Latin Middle Ages,* trans. Willard R. Trask (Princeton, NJ: Princeton Univ. Press, 1953), 302–47.

30. Carruthers, *The Craft of Thought: Meditation, Rhetoric, and the Making of Images, 400–1200* (Cambridge: Cambridge Univ. Press, 1998), 7. See also Carruthers, *The Book of Memory: A Study of Memory in Medieval Culture* (Cambridge: Cambridge Univ. Press, 1990); and Lina Bolzoni, *The Gallery of Memory: Literary and Iconographic Models in the Age of the Printing Press,* trans. Jeremy Parzen (Toronto: Univ. of Toronto Press, 2001).

the "architectural title-page" as an identifiable and increasingly common type seems to date from the transitional years of book production when individual copies of printed texts could be hand illuminated. "The most important composition," in Lilian Armstrong's account,

> developed to decorate the opening of Venetian incunables was the so-called 'architectural frontispiece'. The illusionistic devices and classicizing components of this composition were present in North Italian manuscript illumination of the 1460s, but the compositional type was popularized by the Veneto-Paduan illuminators in the early years of printing. . . . The Veneto-Paduan architectural frontispiece revels in the Albertian illusion of three-dimensional space, so prized by Renaissance artists, while at the same time acknowledging the inherent flatness of the printed page. The imagery invokes the world of Classical Antiquity through which one enters the glorious history of Rome, or memorials raised to the learning of the past.[31]

These practices are carried over into the English printed book from an early date, forming one of the most common frames for title-page woodcuts and (from the 1540s on) engravings.[32] While these printed architectural frames look crude compared with the brilliant and fanciful spaces produced in individual manuscripts and incunables by Armstrong's illuminators, they serve the same functions—for a much broader readership. During the Renaissance, many of the most influential books were entered through increasingly elaborate visual thresholds, adding to the ornamental repertoire of vegetation and strapwork cartouches "fanciful, even fantastic, essays on architectural themes"—including the triumphal arch, the theatrical stage, the funereal monument, and the Classical and Christian temple.[33]

Victor Hugo's *Notre Dame de Paris* (1831) is now remembered primarily for its bell-ringing hunchback, Quasimodo; but its central concern is the relationship between texts and buildings, and book 5 offers its readers a long digression on the fate of the cathedral in the age of the printing press. Chap-

31. Armstrong, "The Hand-Illumination of Printed Books in Italy 1465–1515," in *The Painted Page: Italian Renaissance Book Illumination, 1450–1550*, ed. Jonathan J. G. Alexander (Munich: Prestel, 1994), 42. Cf. Armstrong's *Renaissance Miniature Painters and Classical Imagery: The Master of the Putti and His Venetian Workshop* (London: Harvey Miller, 1981), esp. "The Architectural Title-Page," 19–26.

32. The quickest way to survey the architectural frames found on many of the period's title pages is to leaf through two classic reference books: R. B. McKerrow and F. S. Ferguson, *Title-page Borders Used in England and Scotland, 1485–1640* (London: Oxford Univ. Press for The Bibliographical Society, 1932); and Alfred Forbes Johnson, *A Catalogue of Engraved and Etched English Title-Pages* (London: Oxford Univ. Press for The Bibliographical Society, 1934).

33. Margery Corbett and R. W. Lightbown, *The Comely Frontispiece: The Emblematic Title-page in England, 1550–1660* (London: Routledge & Kegan Paul, 1979), 5–9.

ter 2 is an extended historical meditation on the phrase used for its title, "Ceci tuera cela" ("This will destroy that") — glossed by the narrator first as "the book will destroy the church" and then as "printing will destroy architecture." Hugo's formulation has been quoted in most major studies of the two "communications revolutions" — brought on by the advent of, first, the printed book and, now, the electronic text. Eisenstein quotes it in *PPAC* (66) in the chapter titled "Defining the Initial Shift" — or rather quotes its being quoted by Frances Yates in her classic study *The Art of Memory*. In Yates's version of the passage, "a scholar, deep in meditation in his study high up in the cathedral, gazes at the first printed book which has come to disturb his collection of manuscripts. Then, opening the window, he gazes at the vast cathedral, silhouetted against the starry sky, crouching like an enormous sphinx in the middle of the town. 'Ceci tuera cela', he says. The printed book will destroy the building." [34] If the printed book brought an end to the age of the cathedral, one of the ways in which it did so was by *becoming* the building. Printed paratexts took a wide range of textual edifices across the threshold and into even the humblest home.

---

34. Yates, *The Art of Memory* (London: Routledge & Kegan Paul, 1966; repr., London: ARK Paperbacks, 1984), 124.

Chapter 4

Moving Pictures

Foxe's Martyrs and Little Gidding

Margaret Aston

In the history of printing, John Foxe's *Acts and Monuments* or "Book of Martyrs" has come to seem more important than ever during the quarter century since the appearance of Elizabeth Eisenstein's *The Printing Press as an Agent of Change: Communications and Cultural Transformations in Early-Modern Europe* (*PPAC*). As understanding of the relationships between script and print, texts and readers, word and image has increasingly engaged our attention, Foxe's great work is telling us more and more. Eisenstein was pointing the way toward future fields of study when she wrote about the ability of "ordinary men and women to participate vicariously" in the great epic of Foxe's Protestant martyrology, and the "new interplay between pictures and words." What follows amounts to a footnote exemplification of her remark that "relationships between text and illustration, verbal description and image were subject to complex transpositions and disruptions." [1] The focus here is on an illustration in a great book of conjoined texts and images, which was designed to make its impact through deliberate artful transposition.

The great book in question is one of the large biblical concordances produced by the Ferrar family at Little Gidding. By the mid 1630s the small family community established by Nicholas Ferrar in the Huntingdonshire countryside had gained fame not only as a religious retreat but also for its book production. If in some quarters the following of a religious regime, even of so informal and domestic a kind, seemed to reek of old monasticism, others, including Charles I, who visited Little Gidding in 1642, some nine years after his first contact with the community, was evidently sympathetic to the

I am very grateful for the generous help I have received from Trevor Cooper, Tom Freeman, and Joyce Ransome.

1. *PPAC*, 258, 260, 423. See also p. 415 on Foxe's title page and Protestants with books on their laps, and p. 423 n. 399 on "the outpouring of tracts contributing to a new Protestant martyrology which culminated in Foxe's successive editions."

spirituality of this place of Christian work and prayer, as well as admiring of its books. The daily services of the family group (which included three generations) were—like the books they made—closely scriptural, and their routine was structured to provide time and space for the work of the Concordance Room and, from 1631 on, for dialogue and debate in their Little Academy. The participants in these discussions, which aimed to amuse as well as improve the community as a whole, were given names that reflected their character or standing, such as the Chief, Mother and Guardian, the Cheerfull, Affectionate and Patient, thereby inculcating a degree of formality, as well as moral intent. The large volumes of gospel harmonies so laboriously created at Little Gidding were a new form of handmade book, which combined printed letter-face and engraving to produce texts with extraordinary trompe l'oeil effect. This unique hybrid perhaps still awaits its due in the history of bookmaking. That it had any connection with Foxe's celebrated work has not hitherto been suspected.

Foxe was no stranger in that community. Indeed, the hostile pamphlet *The Arminian Nunnery*, which attacked the community so venomously in 1641, paid what amounted to a backhanded compliment to the influence of Foxe's work by alleging that "for another shew that they [the 'fond and fantasticall *Family of Farrars*'] would not bee accounted Popish, they have gotten the *Booke of Martyrs* in the *Chappell;* but few or none are suffered to read therein, but onely it is there (I say) kept for a shew."[2] This was in fact about as far from the truth as it was possible to be.

Quite apart from English Protestant credentials at large, the Ferrar community had a strong and specific bonding to the *Acts and Monuments*. The founder's upbringing and innate convictions were grounded in reading "the Lives of all the Holy men of old time, and Saynts of God, the good Fathers of the Church, and of those good Men, in our later times, even in the Church of England, the Saynts and Holy Martyrs." Nicholas Ferrar's mother ensured that her children were brought up in her own fullness of "love to God's word" through daily scripture reading and psalm singing, and according to her son John's account, this devotion included, "when she satt at work [i.e. needlework] with her Children and Mayds about her, . . . hearing them read Chapters, and her often reading in the Booke of Martyrs." Nicholas grew up, as his elder brother attested, with these central books most dear to his heart:

---

2. *The Arminian Nunnery* (1641), 9; cited in Alan L. Maycock, *Chronicles of Little Gidding* (London: SPCK, 1954), 55. For John Ferrar on the distortions of the pamphlet, see Lynette R. Muir and John A. White, eds., *Materials for the Life of Nicholas Ferrar, Proceedings of the Leeds Philosophical and Literary Society, Literary and Historical Section* 24, pt. 4 (1996): 110–1 [394–5].

¶ The cruell burnyng of Maifter Farrar,
Martyr.

The Mar=
tyrdome of
D. Robert
Farrar. B.
and Martyr,
at Carmar-
then. Anno
1555.March
32.

fide of the market croffe, the xxx.day of March, beyng Sa-
terday next before Paffion fonday, moft conftantly fuftey-
ned the tozments and paffion of the fire.

Fig. 4.1. The martyrdom of Bishop Ferrar of Saint David's. John Foxe, *Actes and Monuments* (1583), 1555. Courtesy of the British Academy John Foxe Project.

first the Bible, and, after that "the next Book—the Book of Martyrs, he took great delight in—and the story of Bishop Ferrar he had perfect, as for his names sake"[3] (fig. 4.1). According to one later report, the memory training of the Ferrar children included daily reading and reciting by rote "some portion

3. From John Ferrar's "Life of Nicholas Ferrar," in *The Ferrar Papers,* ed. B. Blackstone (Cambridge: Cambridge Univ. Press, 1938), 10, 66, 82; Muir and White, *Materials,* 41, 42–3, 100. John Ferrar (1590–1657), about two years older than Nicholas (born February 22, 1593), whom he outlived by twenty years, probably wrote this not long before 1655.

of the Scriptures, and parts of the book of martyrs"[4]—and it would have been natural (despite the lack of family relationship) for their learning to have included some part of Foxe's account in book XI of Dr. Robert Ferrar, bishop of St. David's, who died at the stake in Carmarthen on March 30, 1555.[5]

Reading from the Book of Martyrs formed part of the weekly observance in the ordered life at Little Gidding. It was the custom (which might have struck a visitor like Edward Lenton—had he been invited to dinner, as he had hoped, in vain[6]—as a reflection of monastic life) to have a chapter of the Bible read aloud at meal times. And at supper on Sunday in the great parlor (which was preceded by organ playing, singing, and grace), there were readings that included stories from Foxe. "Grace was sayd, and all satt downe, and a while after one read a Chapter, and then another, that had first supped, went to the Desk, and read a Story out of the Booke of Martyrs."[7] The community seems indeed, like their founder, to have embraced Foxe's martyrology as second only to scripture.

What edition, or editions, of the *Acts and Monuments* were read at Little Gidding? If finding an answer to that question seems unlikely, we can at least be sure of one thing. The community came into possession of a large engraved version of the *Table of the First Ten Persecutions of the Primative Church* that remodeled the woodcut illustrating Foxe's treatment of that subject in book I of the *Acts and Monuments*. From the second edition of 1570 on, this woodcut was by far the largest illustration in Foxe's work (a fold-out that was printed from three substantial woodblocks, each bigger than one folio page), and it was at risk for that very reason. It was all too inviting an object for domestic decoration and has often disappeared from surviving copies of the book. In the seventh edition of the work, printed in 1632, the printers themselves seem to have lost one of the blocks and simply included two-thirds of the whole panorama. But by then it was possible for readers to buy independent reproductions of the print. Indeed the popularity of this gruesome representation

---

4. Blackstone, *Ferrar Papers*, 9 n. 4; P. Peckard, *Memoirs of the Life of Mr. Nicholas Ferrar* (Cambridge, 1790), 9.

5. Bishop Ferrar's story appears in John Foxe, *Actes and Monuments* (London, 1583), 1544–56, with an illustration on p. 1555 that was also present in the first edition (1563) on p. 1100.

6. Transcriptions of Edward Lenton's letter (from different sources) are in Maycock, *Chronicles*, 40–8; and Muir and White, *Materials*, 128–36, including (respectively, at 46–7 and 133): "Being now neere 12 a Clock we ended our discourse and I called for my Horses, hoping thereuppon that he would have invited me to stay dinner. . . . But insted of making me stay, he also helpt me in calling for my horses accompanying me even to my stirrup." For the considered policy of Nicolas Ferrar and his mother not to offer such hospitality, see Blackstone, *Ferrar Papers*, 51–2; and Muir and White, *Materials*, 88.

7. Blackstone, *Ferrar Papers*, 40; Muir and White, *Materials*, 74.

of multiple tortures is indicated by the fact that in the early seventeenth century, woodcut prints, as well as the engraved version of this large *Table,* may
have been produced for separate sale.[8]

While the woodcut "tables" of the *Ten Persecutions* included by the printers
of the sixth and seventh editions of Foxe in 1610 and 1632 were printed from
the 1570 blocks (showing some signs of wear), the engraved version, which
has been dated to about 1625, was quite different (fig. 4.2). Though still large,
it was smaller than the original *Acts and Monuments* woodcut from which it
was copied, and it rearranged the scenes that it reproduced, as well as reversing some of them (such as Saint Lawrence on his gridiron and Christians in
burning oil in the bottom corners).[9] But it remains plain that the engraved
Table was intended to accompany Foxe's book, to which page references
(from the 1610 edition) were given, scene by scene, in the copied headings.
The title and explanatory text beneath are also reproduced, including the
final injunction about the kingdom of the Turks "wasting and destroying the
Churches of Asia, and afterward of Europe: read the acts and Monuments."
Additional texts, however, reveal that this print is free-standing. At the bottom, a new heading calls it a "most fit and requisit table, both for ornament,
and alsoe to stirre up Christians, to stand to the faith, and likewise to be had
in Remembrance, with a Continuall Thankfulnesse to god for our peace,"
while an inset note beside Saint Lawrence's gridiron in the bottom right cor-

---

8. On the persecutions print of 1570, see M. Aston and Elizabeth Ingram, "The Iconography
of the *Acts and Monuments,*" in *John Foxe and the English Reformation,* ed. David Loades (Aldershot,
Hants.: Ashgate, 1997), 101–14, 140–2. For the woodcut tables that survive on their own, produced
by the printers of the sixth and seventh editions (respectively, H. Lownes, 1610, and A. I[slip],
F. K[ingston], and R. Y[oung], 1632), see *STC* (see Chap. 1, n. 38) 11227.3 and 11228.3; and Tessa
Watt, *Cheap Print and Popular Piety 1550–1640* (Cambridge: Cambridge Univ. Press, 1991), 158–9.
The complete copy of 1632 in the British Museum, Department of Prints and Drawings ("British
Large Atlas XVIc": 186-12-776) cannot be proved to have been produced for sale separated from the
book, but this is the last known printing of the whole, for which the three blocks were given new,
heavier framing lines. For the truncated version in the edition of that year, in which the loss of the
third block seems clear from the wide white margin where it should be, see John Foxe, *Acts and
Monuments* (London, 1632), between 44 and 45 (B[ritish]L[ibrary] 4824 k 5; *STC* 11228). Before this
point was reached, however, the text at the bottom of the whole (which is truncated like the images)
had been reset in different typeface from the 1610 edition. The loss was apparently definitive since,
interestingly, in the next (eighth) edition of the *Acts and Monuments* in 1641, the large print that
appears in book I between pp. 44 and 45 is no longer the 1570 woodcut but instead an engraved copy
of the seventeenth-century engraving, *A Most Exact and Accurat Table,* which follows the revised
arrangement of imagery it had adopted, now all reversed through the copying process. A complete
example of this large foldout (about 52 x 59 cm) bearing the name of the engraver, John Droeshout,
appears in the Cambridge University Library copy of this edition (shelfmark P.1.10).

9. The 1570 woodcut, reprinted entire for the last time in 1632, measures 416/7 x 865/7 mm. The
engraving of c. 1625 is 395 x 488/92 mm (the size of the whole contained within its own framing line
is 15 x 19 inches).

ner (a scene transposed there from the bottom left in the original) advises the reader: "Are to be sould by William Riddiard at the Unicorne in Cornehill neare the Exchange." [10]

At some point between about 1625 and 1635, this print reached Little Gidding and joined the collection of pictorial sources in the Concordance Room. Did Nicholas Ferrar buy it himself in London to add to the pool of prints he had already been collecting during his years abroad? [11] It was surely valued as potential material for the Ferrars' "new kind of printing" rather than as an admonitory ornamental picture: it was to be cleverly cut and pasted for a full-page spread in the 1635 New Testament concordance. This large impressive volume is described on the title page as *The Actions & Doctrine & Other Passages touching Our Lord & Saviour Iesus Christ as they are Related by the Foure Evangelists. Reduced into one Complete Body of Historie . . . by way of Comparison And . . . Composition And . . . Collection.* And the illustrations that played so important a part are presented here as "Sundry Pictures expressing either the Facts themselves Or their Types & Figures Or other Matters appertaining thereunto." [12]

The "Life of Nicholas Ferrar," which John Ferrar wrote near the end of his own life in the 1650s, tells of the importance that the Gospel harmony or concordance (as its makers called it) held for the community:

> The concordance was a year in making at first, when they only said psalms and epistles and gospels. There was a fair large room near the great chamber wherein he spent one hour of the day in the contriving of it and gave directions to his nieces that then attended him how and in what manner with their scissors they should cut out [of] each evangelist such and such verses and thus and thus lay them together to make and perfect such and such a head or chapter. Which when they had first roughly done, then with their knives and scissors they neatly fitted each verse so cut out to be pasted down on sheets of

---

10. British Museum, Department of Prints and Drawings (previously filed in Foreign History A.D. 31, now Historical Prints ROY 55BC–1350, *Persecution of Christians in the Roman Empire:* C1–4AD, 1868–8–8–13419). It is dated c. ?1625 in the *STC* 11227.5.

11. According to Peckard, while Nicholas Ferrar was abroad, he bought "a very great number of Prints engraved by the best masters of that time; all relative to historical passages of the old and new Testament. Indeed he let nothing of this sort that was valuable escape him" (*Memoirs,* 88). Cited in Blackstone, *Ferrar Papers,* 60 n. 3; see xvii, and Muir and White, *Materials,* 9, for Peckard's access to now-lost manuscript sources.

12. C 23 e 4 title page. Exactly the same words on the role of the pictures were used in the title of the lesser concordance in the British Library of about the same date (C 23 e 2). On this volume and the Little Gidding concordances in general, see the invaluable discussion by George Henderson, "Bible Illustration in the Age of Laud," *Transactions of the Cambridge Bibliographical Society* 8 (1982): 173–204, at 185–95.

Fig. 4.2. *Table of the First Ten Persecutions.* Engraving (c. 1625). © Copyright the Trustees of the British Museum.

paper. And so artificially they performed this new-found-out way, as it were a new kind of printing, for all that saw the books when they were done took them to be printed the ordinary way, so finely were the verses joined together and with great presses for that purpose pressed down upon the white sheets of paper.[13]

So successful was this method of cutting and pasting, their "new devised way of printing," that its originator was anxious when he knew his end was near that the family should continue this work, both "the thing and the pictures" that went with it.[14] Anyone who has inspected the pages of the great concordances, with their expert layout of text and picture — "the sublimation of scissors and paste," in George Henderson's words[15] — can readily endorse the enthusiasm of contemporary admirers of this new type of illustrated book.

The first Gospel concordance initiated by Nicholas Ferrar was designed as a form of productive employment that would directly benefit the community's daily services. The book was arranged in 150 chapters or headings that were "said over" at the allotted hours and days of each month as the family gathered for prayer, so that the whole was repeated twelve times a year.[16] The content of this New Testament concordance became as familiar as daily bread to the community of Little Gidding, and word soon spread of the extraordinary new bookmaking that was going on in the Concordance Room. The 1635 version, now in the British Library, in which images from the *First Ten Persecutions* print featured, was made to order for Charles I. At some point, probably in 1633, the king (who may have been in the neighborhood of Little Gidding on his progress northward), sent one of the gentlemen of his household over to the community with a request — that seemingly would brook no refusal — to borrow the celebrated harmony he had heard about. The result was that the volume, so much to royal taste, was impounded for months, during which the monarch had no scruples about annotating it in his own hand.[17] The

---

13. Muir and White, *Materials,* 76; see also Blackstone, *Ferrar Papers,* 42–3.

14. Muir and White, *Materials,* 113–4.

15. Henderson, "Bible Illustration," 187.

16. Muir and White, *Materials,* 76; C. Leslie Craig, "The Earliest Little Gidding Concordance," *Harvard Library Bulletin* 1 (1947): 312–3; Maycock, *Chronicles,* 19. John Ferrar's account makes clear that the person who spoke the "head" each time did so "without book." See Joyce Ransome, "Monotessaron: The Harmonies of Little Gidding," *Seventeenth Century* 20 (2005): 23–30, for this and the following paragraph. I am most grateful to the author for allowing me to read this piece before publication.

17. There are problems about the dating and details of this event, on which see Muir and White, *Materials,* 19–20 [303–4], 77 [361]; Craig, "Earliest Concordance," 313, but the date 1633 is now generally accepted.

community regained possession only after promising to make the king his own copy, which was duly done, and finely bound in gilded Morocco.[18]

Remarkably, there still survive not only the grand concordance, dated 1635, made to satisfy Charles I's regal importunity, but two simpler "house" copies antedating it, made in about 1628–30 and 1631. One, which turned up only in 1933, is now at Harvard, and the other reached the Bodleian Library in Oxford earlier in the twentieth century. The former can actually be identified (by its annotations) as the copy loaned to the king, and the latter, which also has notes in the royal hand, may have been produced as a temporary replacement for the loaned book, and possibly played some role in the preparation of the 1635 presentation volume. Neither of these versions has any direct bearing on the illustrated page of 1635 with which we are concerned. The Bodleian concordance is not illustrated, and the pictorial content of the Harvard version consists of prints after Martin de Vos by Hieronymus Wierix and others, and engravings by Adriaen Collaert, Hans Collaert II, Jean Baptiste Barbé, Jacques de Bie, and Cornelis Galle.[19]

Columns 417–8 in the 1635 concordance formed part of chapter 122, which combined passages from the first three Gospels that foretold wars, famines, plagues, and the persecution and tribulation of the disciples. It bore the heading "The Predictions."[20] Expertly spliced and cut as they were, the ten small scenes that occupy half this page (fig. 4.3) would not necessarily have prompted a reader to think of Foxe. The illustrations on this spread were in fact a selection of twelve of the thirty-four forms of martyrdom depicted in the original print, ten of which were set in three rows filling the top half of the page. Beneath the scriptural text at the bottom, two more images come from the same source (but without their attached labels) of "Christians hands and feete cut off" and "Their braines beaten out with Maules" (fig. 4.4). The seventeenth-century *Persecutions* print, like the 1570 woodcut it followed, adopts a vaguely perspectival formula in that the scenes and figures in the foreground are on a larger scale than those at the top of the page. The later engraving is more erratic in this respect, for although the figures on the top line are roughly half the size of those in the lowest register, scenes of miniature people mingle with larger ones at the sides and in the middle. The cutters

18. Not in crimson velvet—as royal books often were—as John Ferrar later said it was (Muir and White, *Materials,* 77). On this copy and its presentation, see Ransome, "Monotessaron," 31 n. 69, 36 n. 91.

19. Craig, "Earliest Concordance," 315–28; Nancy G. Cabot, "The Illustrations of the First Little Gidding Concordance," *Harvard Library Bulletin* 3 (1949): 139–43.

20. The verses in this chapter are drawn from Matthew 24:6–14, Mark 13:7–13, and Luke 21:9–19.

Marturus and Son whot fry'ed at om from Chains

Furnace

Christians burn'd in a Furnace

Some burnt with their intrals torne out

Roasting Christians and pouring Vinegar and Salt upon their Members

Christ hans tossed upon bulls hornes

Christians cruelly thrust t under the Naties with sharp pricker

Lawrence laid upon the Gridiron

The tearing of Womens Breasts

Christians right eyes bored out

Christians cast to Swine to be devoured

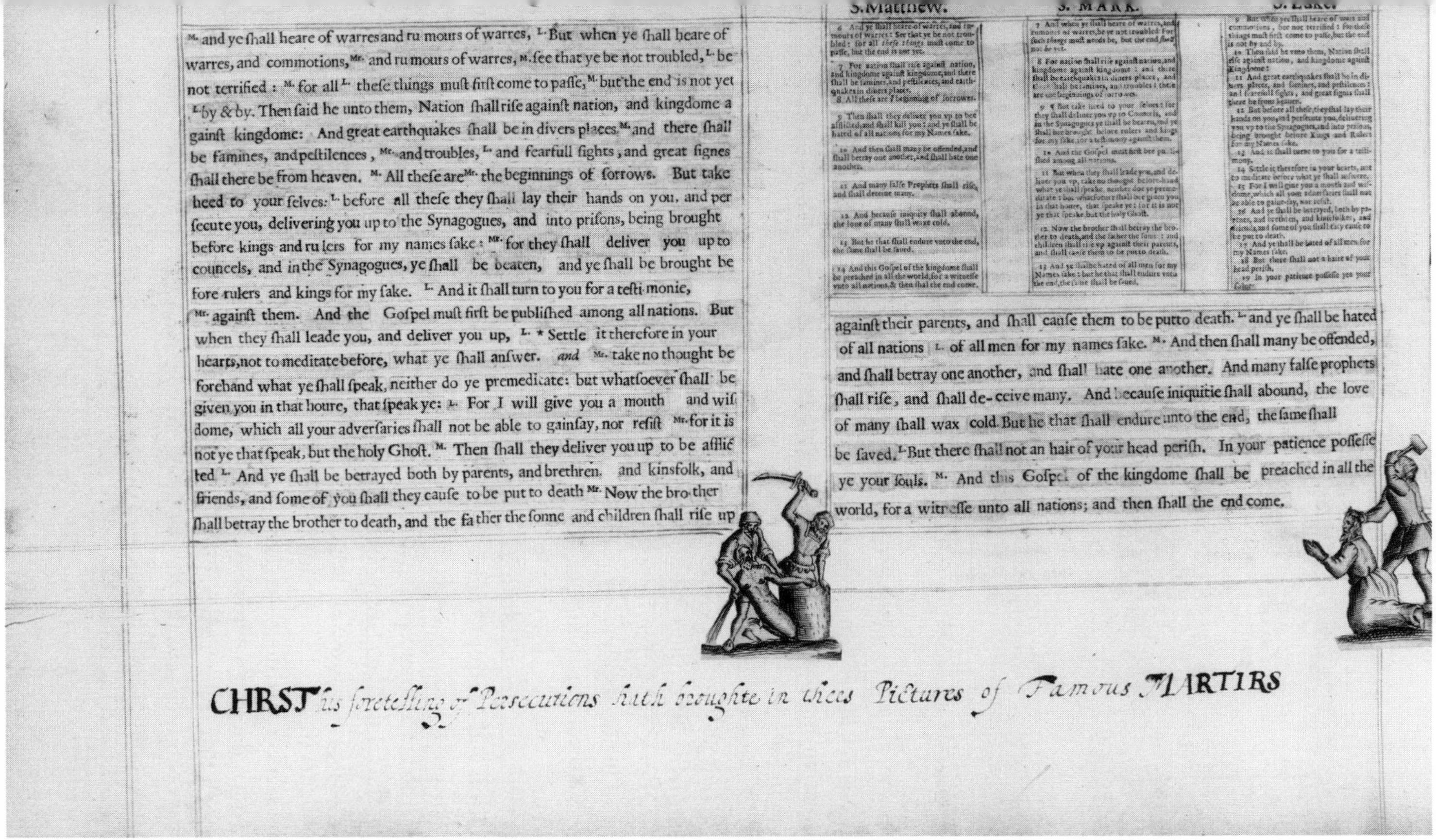

...and ye shall heare of warres and rumours of warres, ᴸ But when ye shall heare of warres, and commotions, ᴹᵏ and rumours of warres, ᴸ see that ye be not troubled, ᴸ be not terrified : ᴹᵏ for all ᴸ these things must first come to passe, ᴹᵏ but the end is not yet ᴸ by & by. Then said he unto them, Nation shall rise against nation, and kingdome against kingdome: And great earthquakes shall be in divers places, ᴹᵏ and there shall be famines, and pestilences, ᴹᵏ and troubles, ᴸ and fearfull sights, and great signes shall there be from heaven. ᴹᵏ All these are ᴹᵏ the beginnings of sorrows. But take heed to your selves. ᴸ before all these they shall lay their hands on you, and per-secute you, delivering you up to the Synagogues, and into prisons, being brought before kings and rulers for my names sake: ᴹᵏ for they shall deliver you up to councels, and in the Synagogues ye shall be beaten, and ye shall be brought be-fore rulers and kings for my sake. ᴸ And it shall turn to you for a testimonie. ᴹᵏ against them. And the Gospel must first be published among all nations. But when they shall leade you, and deliver you up, ᴸ ⁂ Settle it therefore in your hearts, not to meditate before, what ye shall answer. ᴬⁿᵈ ᴹᵏ take no thought be-forehand what ye shall speak, neither do ye premeditate: but whatsoever shall be given you in that houre, that speak ye: ᴸ For I will give you a mouth and wisdome, which all your adversaries shall not be able to gainsay, nor resist ᴹᵏ for it is not ye that speak, but the holy Ghost. ᴹᵏ Then shall they deliver you up to be afflic-ted ᴸ And ye shall be betrayed both by parents, and brethren and kinsfolk, and friends, and some of you shall they cause to be put to death ᴹᵏ Now the bro-ther shall betray the brother to death, and the father the sonne and children shall rise up

against their parents, and shall cause them to be put to death. ᴹᵏ and ye shall be hated of all nations ᴸ of all men for my names sake. ᴹᵏ And then shall many be offended, and shall betray one another, and shall hate one another. And many false prophets shall rise, and shall de-ceive many. And because iniquitie shall abound, the love of many shall wax cold. But he that shall endure unto the end, the same shall be saved. ᴸ But there shall not an hair of your head perish. In your patience possesse ye your souls. ᴹᵏ And this Gospel of the kingdome shall be preached in all the world, for a witnesse unto all nations; and then shall the end come.

CHRIST his foretelling of Persecutions hath taught in these Pictures of Famous MARTIRS

Fig. 4.3. Page of the 1635 Gospel Concordance made for Charles I. British Library C 23 e 4. By permission of the British Library.

Fig. 4.4. Scenes of early Christian torments. Detail from *Table of the First Ten Persecutions.*

in the Concordance Room mixed their scales judiciously, taking four of the smallest images from the top line and right side of the *Table*. They placed these with a certain symmetry; "Christians cast to Swine to be devoured" on the left is matched by "Christians tossed upon buls hornes" to the right, while the mutilation and braining are set as untitled *bas de page* ornaments below.

Thought certainly went into the choice and arrangement of the twelve scenes cut out of the seventeenth-century engraving for the concordance page of "famous martirs." Not only were the scenes set in a new order, but the identifying texts (now without their accompanying page references to the 1610 "Book of Martyrs") were also neatly realigned above each scene. If there is a hint of apology, or justification, in the title at the bottom of the page—"Christ his foretelling of Persecutions hath broughte in thees Pictures of Famous Martirs"—these scenes themselves clearly imply the early church context that was the stated subject of Foxe's original. Saint Lawrence upon the gridiron and Marturus and Sanctus fried in an iron chair are given fresh prominence at the top. Between these two was set the depiction of Christians being burned in a furnace, unsatisfactory though it was with its peculiar missing side, the result of its having been at the edge of the engraving (unlike the 1570 original, where it was at the center of the right section of the large tripartite woodcut) (fig. 4.5). Comparison with the engraving suggests a deliberate focus on scenes of burning and death by fire. All six scenes in the top two rows of the concordance page involve persecution by fire of one kind or another, and though that still left several images of this kind unused, the emphasis on this form of torment stands out in a more obvious way here than in the *Ten Persecutions* print of the Book of Martyrs.

These observations are supported by the Little Gidding Story Book report of the Academy's Christmastide dialogue of 1632. The celebration of Christ-

Fig. 4.5. Christians burn in a furnace. Detail from *Table of the First Ten Persecutions.*

mas that year had become a matter of some debate in the community, thanks to the earnest austerity if not puritanical persuasions of the Cheerfull (Hester Collett, one of the younger Collett sisters). She played the leading role in the Advent debate, a "Dialogue on the Austere Life," which resulted in an effective Christmas fast.[21] Among the sources contributing to the arguments, Foxe made an appearance through the references both to Pico della Mirandola (called on by the Guardian and the Mother) and to Saint Cyprian. What "Mr Fox hath registred in his Book of Acts & Moniments" concerning Cyprian's being admonished to be sober in eating and drinking lest he be distracted from heavenly meditations, was quoted verbatim from the passage in book 1 on the eighth persecution of the church in 259.[22] This was one of the ten persecutions illustrated in the oversize illustration.

---

21. A. M. Williams, ed., *Conversations at Little Gidding* (Cambridge: Cambridge Univ. Press, 1970), xxxii, lxxiii–iv, 159, 163, 165, 181–2. Williams—who makes astute observations on the characters of the various speakers—differs from E. Cruwys Sharland, who in *The Story Books of Little Gidding* (London, 1899), xliv, proposed Margaret and Elizabeth Collett for the Cheerfull and the Affectionate, by instead identifying the former as Hester Collett (xiv, xxxii).

22. The Mother (Mary Ferrar/Collett), questioned by the Guardian (John Ferrar) about her admiration for Pico, referred to "Mr Fox" to extol this model, using some of the martyrologist's own words. Williams, *Conversations,* 169–71; Foxe, *Acts and Monuments* (1583), 778. The Mother also

When Christmas arrived, such examples were needed. Words now had to compete with rumbling stomachs. As the Mother (Mary Collett) put it, opening the Christmastide meeting of the Little Academy, "the Belly, you know, hath no cares; and therefore I know not how you can apply your stories to quiet its grudgeings for those delicacies which you have robbed it of." [23] Once again the Book of Martyrs proved a useful resource. The "Banquet of Stories" for this occasion gave first place to Saint Lawrence, bearing in his name the laurels of victorious suffering, whose story was chosen for including all the appropriate "ingredients" for this festival of feast and flame. Christmas fire and light singled out this martyr, and the concentration on his pattern was in part to use delights of the mind to compensate for a reduction of gastronomic pleasures. As the Cheerfull put it: "St. Augustine sayth that St. Laurence his Passion was a Candle set up to enlighten the whole world"; and as far as good cheer was concerned, "St. Laurence is rost meat for our soules to feed on." It was Foxe's own term in his account of Saint Lawrence, which paraphrased Prudentius's *Peristephanon,* a source Saint Augustine also used to describe how "this triumphant martyr," pressed down with fire pikes, had challenged his persecutor to turn him over and "Assay whether rosted or raw, thou thinkst the better meat." [24] The Cheerfull proceeded to give a full version of Saint Lawrence's history and martyrdom, culminating in his roasting alive on "a great Instrument of Iron made in fashion of a gridiron," and the saint's direction to Decius to turn him over for thorough roasting on his other side. [25] This was the scene carefully cut out for pasting at the top

---

quoted Foxe on Saint Cyprian (Williams, 182), again with the martyrologist's *ipsissima verba,* this time from his description of the ten first persecutions in the primitive church (*Actes and Monuments* [1610], i, 62) on how Cyprian "sheweth . . . of another revelation of his, wherin he was admonished to be spare in his feeding, and sober in his drinke, lest his mind given to heavenly meditation might be carried away with worldly allurements, or oppressed with too much surfet of meates and drinkes, should be lesse apt or able to prayer and spirituall exercise." The quotations from Foxe necessarily raise questions about the composition and recording of the speeches in the Little Gidding conversations: how much preparation beforehand and editing afterward there may have been. The familiarity with Foxe could certainly have owed much to earlier reading and rote-learning, and Nicholas Ferrar's role seems to have been limited to that of note-taker and editor (Muir and White, *Materials,* 17–8).

23. Sharland, *Story Books,* 246.

24. Ibid., 248–9; Foxe, *Actes and Monuments* (1610), 65. The martyr's words in Prudentius's account, "coctum est, devora, et experimentum cape sit crudum an assum suavius" (*Peristephanon,* bk. 11, ll. 406–8), were rephrased by Saint Augustine (Sermo 303; In Natali martyris Laurentii); "Iam, inquit, coctum est; quod superest, versate me, et manducate." Migne, *Patrologia Latina,* 38; Saint Augustine, *Opera Omnia,* 5, col. 1394. (I thank Tom Freeman for help here and for the reference to Prudentius). For deductions about the Christmas celebrations of 1631 and 1632, see Williams, *Conversations,* xxviii–xxix.

25. Sharland, *Story Books,* 257–8. In Foxe's account (*Actes and Monuments* [1610], 65), Saint Lawrence's words to "the tyrant" as he was pressed down on the gridiron were "This side is now rosted enogh, turne up o tyrant great: / Assay whether rosted or raw, thou thinkst the better meat."

of the page in the king's concordance, when the cutters included only the opening identification of the original captions saying "Lawrence laid upon the Gridiron by Galienus or Decius," and the martyr's words "This side is now rosted enough turne me O Tyrant great, &c" [26] (fig. 4.6). The Book of Martyrs, in mind if not eye, was on call for this Christmas storying that made so much of Saint Lawrence.

Foxe's account of Saint Lawrence ends with the saint's being given honorable burial by Christians, one of whom, Hippolytus, was thereafter "torne in pieces by wild horses." "The Christian drawne in pieces with wilde horses" (mentioned on page 54 of the 1610 edition of the *Actes and Monuments*) was one of the illustrations in the *Ten Persecutions* engraving that was not chosen for pasting into the concordance. But Foxe was an immediate presence in the story of Saint Lawrence, and Cheerfull ended her recounting of it with "Mr Fox his conclusion"—a prayer to learn through this saint to live and die for Christ.[27] The Mother then inaugurated a discussion on the power of Christ to turn the worst pains of fire into delight in Christ. "He that lies broyling on a Gridiron in others eies, lies in his owne Conceit upon a Bed of Pleasure." In the exchanges that followed, some of the examples cited to show that "fire should not paine, though it burnt, nor torments afflict when they were most felt" came straight from Foxe. The Mother herself related the case of James Bainham, paraphrasing the martyrologist's description of how he revoked his abjuration and was brought to the stake in 1532. Bainham's own words, as given by Foxe, are cited to show that he was another Lawrence in his endurance of the fire: "Heare his owne words, and see the selfe same tender mercy of God which St. Laurence acknowledged, made good on him likewise. When the fire had devoured halfe his legs and Armes, he calls out to the lookers on, Oh, yee Papists, Behould you looke for miracles, and here now you may see a miracle: for in this fire I feele no more paine then if I were in Bed of Downe; but it is to mee as sweet as a Bed of roses." [28]

---

26. For these words on the engraving (with references to p. 65 in the 1610 *Actes and Monuments*), see fig. 4.6.

27. "This is the story of St. Laurence, which I will end with Mr Fox his conclusion: The God of might and mercy graunt us grace by the life of St. Laurence to learne in Christ to live, and by his death to learne for Christ to dy. Amen." Sharland, *Story Books,* 258; Foxe, *Actes and Monuments* (1583), 72, and (1632), 93.

28. Sharland, *Story Books,* 258, 260; Foxe, *Actes and Monuments* (1583), 1027–30 (cited 1030)—in part Foxe's *ipsissima verba.* For Foxe's account of Bainham and the probably apocryphal nature of these words (important, like the story of Bishop Ferrar's end, as demonstrating stoical suffering comparable with that of early church martyrs), see Thomas S. Freeman, "The Importance of Dying Earnestly: The Metamorphosis of the Account of James Bainham in 'Foxe's Book of Martyrs,'" in *Studies in Church History* 33 (1997), *The Church Retrospective,* ed. R. N. Swanson, 267–88, esp. 279–81. See also on Bainham, Stephen Greenblatt, *Renaissance Self-Fashioning* (Chicago: Univ. of Chicago Press, 1984), 74–6.

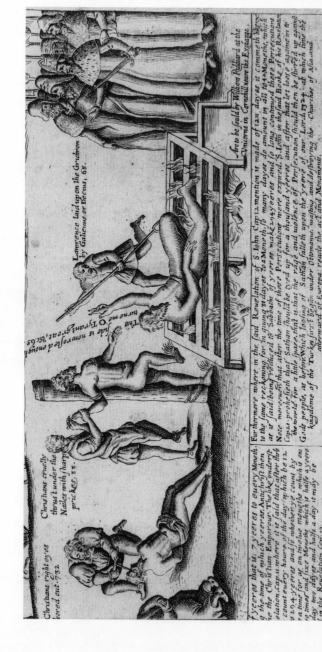

Fig. 4.6. Saint Lawrence on the gridiron. Detail from *Table of the First Ten Persecutions*.

The Affectionate (another of Nicholas Ferrar's Collett nieces) added two more examples from the Book of Martyrs (not naming her source) to the same effect. The first was that of Bishop Ferrar, who (as we have seen) was of special interest to the Little Gidding family. Again the words used are a close paraphrase of Foxe's own, suggestive of the familiarity with the *Acts and Monuments*. "When Richard Jones, a knights sonne, bemoaned the painfullnes of his death to Bishop Farrer a little before his burning, If you see mee once to stirre in the fire, sayd the Bishop, then give no Creditt to my doctrine. And what he sayd he well performed: for he stood without moving to the last, holding up his stumps till one Richard Gravell beat him downe with a Staffe."[29] The Affectionate's other example, from the same year (1555), was that of Thomas Haukes and again was to show that though "fire is intolerable," fears of its "unsufferable" pain were confounded. Once more Foxe's words are repeated with the small changes of one who knows them surely enough to make such variations, telling how Haukes's friends received the signs they earnestly desired to show that even in the pain of burning, man could "keep his mind quiet and patient." They were given the agreed sign, as Haukes lifted his hands above his head and clapped them thrice to the applause of the onlookers. The Moderator (Mrs. Susanna Collett) added the rider that the "little paine" of the fire put to the holy martyrs in Queen Mary's time was well known and attested by the persecutors themselves, witness Bishop Bonner's words: "A vengeance light on them, said Bishop Bouner; I thinke they take a delight in burning, and then what shall we gaine by the match?"[30]

While this scene shows the familiarity with the stories in the Book of Martyrs shared by members of the Little Gidding community, it also suggests some of the thoughts that might have been in the heads of those in the Concordance Room who picked out and arranged the martyrdom scenes to adorn Charles I's concordance. Although by 1633 the discussions and privations of Advent 1632 were over, the dietary rigors of that season continued—anyway for some—and might still have had some physical bearing on workers who snipped and set the pictures of roasting Christians. They had heard and discussed stories of the martyrs and turned over the pages of Foxe's great

---

29. Sharland, *Story Books*, 261; Foxe, *Actes and Monuments* (1583), 1555.

30. Sharland, *Story Books*, 261–2; Foxe, *Actes and Monuments* (1583), 2044. Again, citation from Foxe indicates close familiarity. "They call me bloudy Boner. A vengeaunce on you all. I would faine be rid of you, but you have a delite in burnyng. But if I might have my will, I would sowe your mouthes, and put you in sacks, and drowne you." See Deborah Burks, "Polemical Potency: The Witness of Word and Woodcut," in *John Foxe and His World*, ed. Christopher Highley and John N. King (Aldershot, Hants.: Ashgate, 2002), 266.

book with its woodcuts of Bishop Ferrar and Thomas Haukes and others. It seemed to the Guardian (John Ferrar), who took up the Moderator's observation about Bonner, that the Marian bishop was cast in the same mold as the persecuting Emperor Decius. The mental link between Marian martyrs and martyrs of the early church was securely forged. The Guardian then went on to make some remarks about the differing demeanors of persecutors and persecuted, in a way that suggests close observation of the *Acts and Monuments* woodcuts: "Make comparison of demeanor both in the comming unto and the continuance of the execution it selfe, and you shall see it evident, by the difference of tempers, that you shall perceive the Martyrs full of Confidence, of cheerefulnes, of Charity, leaping, singing, praying: they that condemne them, and they that carry them away to death, goe raging, cursing, quarelling, with bent brows, hanging lips, and staring eies. The ones talke is all of joy, nothing but Heaven, Angells, happines; the others tongues runne all upon Devills, Hell, and damnation."[31]

The work that produced the Little Gidding concordances reflects close knowledge and careful study of the large print collection that went into the making of the Ferrars' books. Much thought was given to both text and illustration on every page, and something can be learned about the bookmaking processes from the numerous loose prints that survive among the Ferrar papers in Magdalene College, Cambridge. These are almost without exception the works of Continental printmakers (from the late sixteenth century on), some in duplicate or triplicate, and a few still in the sewn gatherings in which they may have been purchased. Some which have details carefully snipped out tell where the "knives and scissors" have done their work.[32]

The print used for the page of "Pictures of Famous Martirs" was definitely an odd man out among the sophisticated illustrations on hand in the Concordance Room. Given the pictorial riches the cutters had to choose from, it is no surprise to find that they appear to have had no further use for the discarded portions of the *Persecutions* "table." Its recognizably simplistic English technique and naive figure drawing would have consorted ill with the

31. Sharland, *Story Books,* 262. For the impact that the illustrations and heroical examples (including Bainham and Haukes) had on Bunyan, see Thomas S. Freeman, "A Library in Three Volumes: Foxe's 'Book of Martyrs' in the Writings of John Bunyan," *Bunyan Studies* 5 (1994): 47–59. The woodcut of the ten first persecutions seems to have "made a deep impression on Bunyan and he kept visualising it when he wrote about martyrdom and persecution" (52).

32. For this print collection, see David Ransome, *The Ferrar Papers 1590–1790* in *Magdalene College Cambridge: Introduction/Finding List* (Wakefield: Microfilm Academic Publishers, n.d.), 117–54, reels 13–4. I am grateful to Trevor Cooper for the loan of this list.

refined details they singled out elsewhere.[33] That this engraving went into the composition of a whole spread in the New Testament concordance might be taken as a tribute to the importance of Foxe's work for England's reformed tradition, and the proven capacity of the *Acts and Monuments* to play a role alongside scripture itself.

Yet there could not be complete serenity about such amplitude of picture accompanying scripture. There were spreads in Charles's great concordance where picture dominated and the word was barely present. This very indulgence in the visual, as if it was the glory of the book and what made it so fat and rich, was open to criticism. Perhaps it was difficult to resist the temptation of doing the utmost for the king's aesthetic delight. But it entailed going beyond the reach of the text. That was freely acknowledged. For instance, a double spread is headed "A Summary Recapitulation of all the Former stories of our Lord and Saviour Iesus Christ To which are added Divers other Conjecturals touching his Infancie," with a positive riot of twenty-one illustrations including the infancy theme.[34] There were some to whom such "conjecturals" would have seemed like the worst fictions of medieval gospel harmonies. A positively zoolike page of variously sized snakes (one "a snake casting her skin") and wolves and birds, arranged to illustrate the text "Behold, I send you foorth as sheepe in the middest of Wolves: be yee therefore wise as serpents and harmlesse as Doves" (Matt. 10:16) is thus explained: "thees Pictures express the Cruelty of wolves And the Subtility of Serpents." Images of a man hanging, people in the stocks, and amputated limbs are annotated: "Thees Pictures are to express the Torments in Prison" in the chapter on the imprisonment of St. John.[35] If the page of Martyrs was excused for its nonscriptural content, it was not alone in that, though its resonances extended further beyond the gospel context than the amplifying pictures justified elsewhere. Not that one should read any kind of guilt or apology into these explications but rather a desire to proclaim that such pictorial varying was firmly attached to the Word.

The aim of presenting "one Complete Body of Historie" consisting of complementary word and image took some of the concordance pages beyond the gospel text into subsequent Christian history. The Ferrars were clear about the role of illustrations in extending and extrapolating from the text. As the 1635 title page explains, they had added "Sundry Pictures expressing either the Facts themselves or their Types and Figures or other Matters apper-

---

33. Comparison with the title page of the *Acta Apostolorum* (BL, C 23 e 3), which has comparable small cut-outs of the torments of Christ and the Apostles (including a figure praying in a burning cauldron), points up this contrast.

34. BL, C 23 e 4, cols. 33–6.

35. Ibid., cols. 183–4, 57–8, and for other such justifications, cols. 241–2, 319–20, 351–2, 473–4.

taining thereunto," and in the 1635 book these "other matters" seem to have been allowed particularly generous freedom of expression. Perhaps too, the royal harmony was composed with its own expectations of the king's understanding and use of the complex cross-reference system explained at length in the "Advertizements" opposite the title. Arranging the texts so that the four evangelists could be read both individually and comparatively to arrive at a coherent composite narrative, Nicholas Ferrar made plain his debt to the system invented at Douai about 1570 and exemplified by Cornelius Jansen, whose Gospel harmonies appeared in numerous editions, with a method of identifying the evangelists by letters that was followed at Little Gidding. The layout of the harmony enabled the reader to appraise the variant texts and construct his own version through the system of "Comparison, Composition, and Collection," which described the textual methodology. The page of "Famous Martirs" includes a reminder of these distinctions with its headings "Composition" and "Comparison," just as an earlier page on "The steward" of Luke 16 points out that "the Collection — serves both for Comparison and Composition." It seems that the recipient of this volume (expressly prepared for one set of eyes and hands) was being given special treatment to help him meditate on the gospel texts. The workers in the Concordance Room never lost sight of the royal user whose private thoughts and reflections would come to rest on their collocation of words and images.[36] They surely knew that he (if not they themselves) was untroubled by images in places of prayer and was accepting of their role in scriptural study.[37]

Was this pictorial spread of famous martyrs a one-off, unique to the concordance made for Charles I?[38] Further research may answer that question. In the meantime deductions may be drawn from the great book that was so carefully made, not for group use and reading but for the personal study of

---

36. BL, C 23 e 4, title page and facing "Advertizements," cols. 317–8. This paragraph is owed largely to Joyce Ransome, who has alerted me to the significance of the "Composition" and "Comparison" notices, observing that "this particularly elaborate version of the cross-reference system . . . only occurs in the royal harmony. (The others had just the Collection composed of Context and Supplement, which is also in the king's.) That being the case, the Foxe print, like the Comparison and Composition sections themselves, would likely have been a one-off image as you suggest." For elucidation of this and other aspects of the Gospel concordances, see Ransome, "Monotessaron."

37. See Joyce Ransome, "Little Gidding in 1796," *Records of Huntingdonshire* 3 (2001–2): 13–28, for a 1796 report of wall paintings of the sacrifice of Isaac and the Fall, which were found in the Ferrars' manor house on the walls of a room called the oratory or "Paradise Chamber" — conceivably the Great Chamber.

38. Apart from Robert Peake's Bible illustrations, Antony Griffiths did not find a single English print in the three Little Gidding concordances he examined. Griffiths, *The Print in Stuart Britain 1603–1689* (London: British Museum, 1998), 22.

King Charles I. The Ferrars' lavish gratification of royal enjoyment of the visual joined forces with their expectations of royal readiness to meditate on the humanity and sufferings of Christ and the continuum of suffering in Christian history. The application of Foxe's pictures of early martyrs to the theme of Christian persecution presented vivid material for the king's contemplation. He was not short of time or occasion to reflect on the theme of martyrdom, from the start of his reign, when John Donne told him of the church's delight in the commemoration of martyrs, until his final letter to the Prince of Wales nearly twenty–four years later, suggesting that his own sufferings held "the honour of a kind of martyrdom." [39] If Charles had the Book of Martyrs beside him to read during his captivity, his musings about the many whose endurance was recorded in that great work could have included recollections of "The Predictions" and the "Pictures of Famous Martirs," who had earned their spiritual crowns so long before through physical sufferings infinitely worse than his own. He was well prepared to construct his own rhetoric of martyrdom, and the constructed page of his great concordance could have contributed to the formulation of the final royal self-image.

Looking at this page in the concordance made for Charles I enables us to see something of the novelty of the Ferrars' "new device" of printing that managed subtly to subvert (or convert) the relationship of text and image through multiple, carefully contrived transpositions. Some engravings were harnessed unchanged to the freshly designed page; others gave up details to illuminate a new theme or to be reformulated for a chosen topic. This labor-intensive form of bookmaking simultaneously undermined the apparent stability of print and remodeled it with the help of script. The combined deconstruction (in the word's original, literal sense) of printed texts and sets of engraved images, yielded fresh meanings for both on pages that were essentially hybrid forms. Slicing up texts and images to reassemble them in a new context conferred a new life and meaning which, if not at variance with the original from which they came, had a fresh voice. The page borrowed from the *Ten Persecutions* of the "Book of Martyrs" shows the subtle shifts of emphasis that might be achieved in this way; by selection and rearrangement, removing individual

---

39. E. M. Simpson and G. R. Potter, eds., *The Sermons of John Donne,* 10 vols. (Berkeley and Los Angeles: Univ. of California Press, 1953–62), 6:241; Charles Petrie, ed., *The Letters, Speeches, and Proclamations of King Charles I* (London, 1935), 265–6; Pamela Tudor-Craig, "Charles I and Little Gidding," in *For Veronica Wedgwood These: Studies in Seventeenth-Century History,* ed. Richard Ollard and Pamela Tudor-Craig (London: Collins, 1986), 187. See Charles Carlton, *Charles I: The Personal Monarch,* 2nd ed. (New York: Routledge, 1995), 340–1, for an uncorroborated statement that Charles read the Book of Martyrs during his imprisonment at Carisbrooke; followed by Andrew Lacey, *The Cult of King Charles the Martyr* (Woodbridge: Boydell and Brewer, 2003), 9, 52.

images from their corporate context and impressing them to serve a gospel argument. Foxe was sublimated into the scriptural design.

The story behind this single page in the great volume prepared for Charles I shows, then, something of the ability of the printed page to move between different worlds. The image, printed as woodcut or engraving, with or without accompanying explicatory words, moved readily from study to cottage wall, from individual meditation to shared viewing or corporate discussion, from closable book to tearable poster. The collective imagery of the *Table of the First Ten Persecutions of the Primative Church* had been conceived in 1570 as integral to the great volume of church history. From that origin, it found an independent life, more akin to a broadsheet or domestic ornament, even if still produced as a page-referenced index to the widely read book from which it had become separated. Thence some of the images, by means of the Ferrars' innovative form of bookmaking, were incorporated in the carefully crafted pages of the huge tome that was designed for elevated private royal perusal. It was almost a case of stepping from the sublime to the ridiculous and back again to the sublime. One could hardly ask for a better example of the chameleon capacity of print.

Yet there remains an unanswerable question. Had seventy years' circulation of the well-imaged text of Foxe's famous Book of Martyrs made such an indelible mark on English consciousness that these pictures of famous martyrs could not but recall that work? Would most faithful English men and women, had they been able to look over the king's shoulder as he reached this page (whether or not they had ever seen the *Ten Persecutions* print) at once have thought of England's martyrs dispatched by the fires of Marian persecution? If that is an unreal question, the page of the rich book that was as fine and private as any illuminated manuscript still gives us plenty to think about. And those thoughts owe much to all that has flowed from Eisenstein's provocative work.

Chapter 5

Humphrey Moseley and the Invention of English Literature

DAVID SCOTT KASTAN

The categories of human thought are never fixed in any one definite form; they are
made, unmade and remade incessantly: they change with places and times.
—Emile Durkheim, *The Elementary Forms of Religious Life* (1915)

It is one thing to describe how methods of book production changed after the mid-
fifteenth century and to estimate rates of increased output. It is another thing to decide
how access to a greater abundance or variety of written records affected ways of learning,
thinking, and perceiving among literate élites.
—Elizabeth L. Eisenstein, *The Printing Press as an Agent of Change*

ENGLISH LITERATURE WAS invented early in the winter of 1645.
But before that date is committed to memory, I should, in fairness, admit that
at least two other competing narratives of its invention exist: one, that literature was invented some two hundred years earlier, sometime in the late
fourteenth century, when the word "literature" first entered English from the
French and referred generally to the field of humane learning, available to,
and in some ways defining, an early modern cultural elite. "In the beginning
literature was just books," as David Bromwich has said,[1] or at least in that
beginning. Literature, in Bromwich's sense, referred to what was necessary to
be read rather than to what was written. It was what Raymond Williams calls
"a category of use and condition rather than of production."[2] Thus, in 1521
Henry Bradshaw would muse, "What were mankynde without lytterature"

---

1. Bromwich, "The Invention of Literature," *A Choice of Inheritance* (Cambridge, MA: Harvard
Univ. Press, 1989), 2. See also John Guillory, *Cultural Capital: The Problem of Literary Canon Formation* (Chicago: Univ. of Chicago Press, 1993), esp. 71–9.
2. Williams, *Marxism and Literature* (Oxford: Oxford Univ. Press, 1977), 47.

and find his answer in his account of "the comyn people, simple and neclygent," who "without lytterature and good informacyon / Ben lyke to Brute beestes."[3]

Certainly it is some such conception of literature that recently allowed James Simpson to write of John Bale's *Catalogus* (1557–9) as "the beginning of English literary history both as a whole, and, by the same token, for the period 1350–1550," though Simpson recognizes that even the "handful of 'literary' writers" that do appear in Bale's list merit their place "for their polemical positions on religious questions rather than for their contribution to a 'literary' tradition."[4] Simpson's scare quotes around the word "literary" are telling, and he admits that "it is not until Thomas Warton's brilliant *History of English Poetry* (1774–81) that England produces a history of specifically 'literary' discourse"[5] (though again it is worth noting that here too the word "literary" appears in quotation marks). Still, Warton's *History* indicates a new cultural confidence in the very category of literature, even as Simpson's scare quotes reveal how fragile is our own.

Indeed, it is that confidence that the second influential history of English literature has taken as its defining logic. This history locates the origins of English literature some four hundred years later than the first, around "the turn of the eighteenth century," as the cultural theorist Terry Eagleton has claimed,[6] when a notion of literature understood as a discrete set of imaginative writings formed and was confirmed not only in studies like that of Warton but in a variety of institutional settings (and as a part of a larger cultural trend in which "art" became the accepted category for imaginative works in all forms).[7] Literature was increasingly recognized and identified as a field of more or less autonomous aesthetic experience. "Literature cannot, I think," John Clarke said in 1731, "be made subservient to any *important* Purpose of Life."[8] Or, as Isaac Disraeli insisted in 1796: "the concerns of mere literature are not very material in the system of human life. . . . Literary investigation is allied neither to politics nor religion; it is . . . abstracted from all the factions on earth; and independent of popular discontent, and popular delusions."[9]

---

3. Bradshaw, *The Holy Lyfe and History of Saynt Werburge* (London, 1521) sig. l8v.
4. Simpson, *Reform and Cultural Revolution*, vol. 2 of *The Oxford English Literary History* (Oxford: Oxford Univ. Press, 2002), 23–4.
5. Ibid., 24.
6. Eagleton, *Literary Theory: An Introduction* (Oxford: Blackwell, 1983), 18.
7. See Larry Shiner, *The Invention of Art: A Cultural History* (Chicago: Univ. of Chicago Press, 2001).
8. Clarke, *An Essay Upon Study* (London, 1731), 194.
9. Disraeli, *Miscellanies; or, Literary Recreations* (London, 1796), vii, xxi.

If works of literature were, then, widely thought in themselves to be (and indeed to be distinguished by the fact they were), as Vicesimus Knox said, "harmless in their consequence to society,"[10] their study was nonetheless seen to be valuable as part of a process of moral and imaginative improvement. "The exercise of taste and of sound criticism is in truth one of the most improving employments of the understanding," Hugh Blair said in one of the most influential accounts of the new belletristic conception of imaginative writing. "To apply the principles of good sense to composition and discourse; to examine what is beautiful and why it is so; to employ ourselves in distinguishing accurately between the specious and the solid, between affected and natural ornament, must certainly improve us not a little in the most valuable part of all philosophy, the philosophy of human nature."[11] High minded and abstract, such expressions worked predominantly to mystify the nature of literature, giving rise to assertions like that of Elizabeth Cooper, who admitted: "Of what Value polite Literature is to a Nation is too sublime a Talk for me to meddle with; I therefore chuse to refer my Readers to their own Experience."[12]

I am similarly reluctant to "meddle with" questions of the value of "Polite Literature to a Nation." What I want here to consider is a question that is happily simpler and also logically prior: how was it that readers of literature could be referred "to their own Experience"? Cooper's modest retreat from the sentimental enthusiasms of the age comes in the preface to her anthology of "English Poetry, from the Saxons to the Reign of King Charles II," published in 1737 as *The Muses Library*. Whatever might be thought the nature and the value of literature, it depended on a body of available texts to be read. Cooper's anthologizing is at the forefront of an eighteenth-century vogue for affordable reprints and miscellanies, establishing literature as an increasingly broad, if also increasingly autotelic, imaginative field, available for readers to test and refine their taste and judgment. Trevor Ross has even attempted to date this conception precisely, finding on February 22, 1774, in the action of the House of Lords to overturn the idea of "perpetual copyright," so long asserted by English stationers, the moment when "literature in its modern sense began."[13] The Lords were persuaded that literature needed to be available to general readers, every bit as accessible a public domain as were the green spaces of London. As a contemporary witness to the debates noted: "the

---

10. Knox, *Essays, Moral and Literary*, 2 vols. (London, 1795), 1:217.

11. Blair, *Lectures on Rhetoric and Belles Lettres*, 2 vols. (London, 1783), 1:9–10.

12. Cooper, ed., *The Muses Library* (London, 1737), ix.

13. Ross, "The Emergence of 'Literature': Making and Reading the English Canon in the Eighteenth Century," *ELH* 63 (1996): 409.

Works of *Shakespeare*, of *Addison, Pope, Swift, Gay* and many other excellent Authors of the present Century are, by this reversal, declared to be the property of any Person."[14]

It was easy, in one sense, for the Lords to so decide, for literature had been safely marked off from the field of political activity, as it was similarly being set apart from history, philosophy, and science, and indeed refined out of a serious engagement with ideas of any sort. It had become (or at the very least been almost uniformly described as—admittedly not at all the same thing) an isolated and autonomous cultural arena with no public consequences among its potential effects. If Ross's date for its invention is correct, literature becomes Literature, we might say, when the government agrees it is no more than a personal diversion or sentimental stimulus, a cultural accoutrement available to "refine the taste, rectify the judgment, and mould the heart to virtue," in the words of one eighteenth-century anthologist.[15] Literature pointedly becomes identifiable as the canon of works that, as W. H. Auden would later say, "makes nothing happen," except for the honing of the private sensibilities of its readers.

Both of these versions of the invention of literature—the fourteenth-century articulation of it as aristocratic learning and the eighteenth-century insistence of it as bourgeois accomplishment—are plausible and interesting accounts of its conception, though neither is the one I propose here. The first, however, accounts for the invention of literature only by seeing it as something it no longer is; if it successfully accounts for the presence of the word "literature" in English, it does not account for the specific category the word has come to define. And, if the second history effectively does attempt to account for that category by charting the segregation of literature from other discursive forms, it does so without recognizing how much this aestheticizing is itself a reaction to a prior moment in its disarticulation from other modes of discourse rather than an originary one. The move to aesthetic autonomy is a secondary history, a history less of literature than of literature's irrelevance, which happily could not be sustained even as it was asserted. Imagined, however, as belletristic, and subtly but unmistakably feminized, the English literature invented by the eighteenth century was a civilized remaking of the literature invented a century before.

An intermediary history might be sought in the laureate model, a notion

---

14. "The Cases of the Appelants and Respondents in the Cause of Literary Property" (1774), in *The Literary Property Debate: Six Tracts, 1764–1774*, ed. Stephen Parks (New York: Garland, 1975), sig. A5r.

15. *Sentimental Beauties and Moral Deliniations from the Writngs of the Celebrated Dr. Blair and other much admired Authors* (London 1782), t.p.

of English literature forming around and within a canon of English authors. Chaucer, Gower, Lydgate, and Skelton at the beginning; Spenser, Sidney, Daniel, Jonson, and Milton (and with Shakespeare high-jacked by the 1623 Folio to the project) marking its maturity. This story has been often and well told: Richard Helgerson and Kevin Pask are but two of its chroniclers.[16] English literature, in this account, comes into being as the poetic ambitions of some English poets, mimetically constructed on classical models, are realized in print. Much of this history is compelling, and in important ways fills the gap between the fourteenth century's appropriation of the word "literature" and the eighteenth century's aestheticization of it.

But this history too will not quite do. In part, because, though the laureate logic can arguably be said to produce the English author, it is not so obvious that it constructs a field of English literature; but also, and more immediately, because the narrative of laureate ambition—"the ambition," as Helgerson writes, "not only to write great poems but also to fill the role of the great poet"[17]—simply allows authors more agency in that cultural project than they prove to have. Helgerson revealingly calls his book *Self-Crowned Laureates,* but one might wonder whether self-crowning is capable of effecting the elevation it intends and announces.

The difficulty can be clearly seen in the early history of the Bodleian Library. Notoriously, Sir Thomas Bodley in 1612 had warned his librarian, Thomas James, against collecting playbooks and other "idle bookes, & riffe raffes," which would only take up shelf space from more worthy volumes and even embarrass the Library: "Were it so againe, that some litle profit might be reaped (which God knowes is very litle) out of our playbookes, the benefit therof will nothing neere conteruaile, the harme that the scandal will bring vnto the Librarie, when it shalbe giuen out, that we stuffe it full of baggage bookes."[18] Plays, of course, were perceived as scandalous in many quarters: for example, William Prynne's notorious *Histrio-mastix,* published in 1633, which is only the best known, and perhaps the most hysterical, of the antitheatrical tracts. But Bodley's fear of scandal does not obviously relate to the fear of moral contagion that motivates Prynne and other antitheatricalists. Bodley's resistance is social and intellectual rather than moral: playbooks do not count

16. Helgerson, *Self-Crowned Laureates: Spenser, Jonson, Milton, and the Literary System* (Berkeley and Los Angeles: Univ. of California Press, 1983); Pask, *The Emergence of the English Author: Scripting the Life of the Poet in Early Modern England* (Cambridge: Cambridge Univ. Press, 1996).

17. Helgerson, *Self-Crowned Laureates,* 1.

18. G. W. Wheeler, ed., *The Letters of Sir Thomas Bodley to Thomas James, First Keeper of the Bodleian Library* (Oxford: Clarendon Press, 1926), 219, 222. Subsequent references to this work are cited parenthetically in the body of the text.

as potentially collectible items not because they risk the infection of the stage but because they are ephemera, like "Almanackes . . . & proclamations," the dominant product of the print trade, yet unworthy of preservation.

Although it has often been observed that none of the more than five thousand titles of the first Bodleian catalogue of 1605 were playbooks, it has less often been noticed that of the books in the catalogue only three would now count as English literature (single copies of Gower, Lydgate, and Chaucer are the only vernacular examples that appear). So to the degree that plays were already identifiable as literature, their absence from the library speaks to the general lack of interest in English literary production, and, to the degree they were not yet so identifiable, their absence alerts us to the fact that the scholarly overemphasis on early modern drama in its accounts of the literary achievement in England has distracted us from seeing that English literature had not yet even formed as a category of collection and organization. It was not that plays were thought immoral or that poetry lies, it was that English imaginative writing was not thought important enough to be preserved and studied, unworthy to be, in Bodley's phrase, "vouchsafed a rowme, in so noble a Librarie" (222).

As late as 1611, Bodley wrote his librarian dismissive of "some of your Englishe bookes, very barely worth the buieng" (203). Books of English literature were chief among these, and although Samuel Daniel's *Works* (1601) would eventually find a place in the library, its absence from the 1605 catalogue is telling. Sometime after 1605, the library accepted a copy of Daniel's *Works,* with its original published dedication to Queen Elizabeth replaced by a unique cancel with the poem to Bodley, apparently a one-off printing either to thank Bodley for its inclusion or to urge him to it.[19] The dedicatory poem praises Bodley, "him whose care hath beene / To gather all what euer might impart / Delight or Profite to posteritie," as well as his library, "This storehouse of the choisest furniture / The worlde doth yeeld."[20] But Daniel's *Works* at the time of its publication had to wait to be so gathered. It clearly did not seem either to Bodley or to his librarian part of "the choisest furniture" that the library was committed to preserve. In the event, Daniel's *Works* eventually did find a place in the library, and the dedicatory poem seems apparently a strategy to accomplish its inclusion. Daniel's poem is revealing in many ways, not least because it insists on the institutional conditions that

---

19. See John Pitcher, "Editing Daniel," in *New Ways of Looking at Old Texts,* ed. W. Speed Hill (Binghamton, NY: Renaissance English Text Society, 1993), 68–9.

20. Daniel, *The Works of Samuel Daniel, Newly Augmented* (London, 1601), Bodleian copy, Shelfmark Arch. G d.47 (1).

determine poetic immortality rather than on the literary qualities of the work itself. The library is praised as that "exquisite and rare monument that doth immure / The glorious reliques of the best of men." But relics, Daniel knows, are not self-determining of their dignity; they demand reliquaries, or other communal validations, to be seen as something more than fragments of old bones. Daniel thus acknowledges that poets cannot canonize themselves: they cannot by themselves turn their work into literature through their own agency. The agency of a collector such as Bodley was needed to effect canonization. "Most noble Bodley!" Henry Vaughan would later apostrophize: "we are bound to thee / For no small part of our Eternity," where "our eternity" refers at once to the rich heritage preserved in the library and now thankfully available to contemporaries to read, and to the immortality that contemporary poets will achieve through their inclusion ("On Sir Thomas Bodley's Library: The Author being then in Oxford").

Abraham Cowley, similarly, would write a poem to mark the occasion of the entry of his published *Works* into the Bodleian collection. Cowley's "Ode. Mr Cowley's Book presenting it self to the University Library" has his published book itself wondering whether the library will into its "Sacred throng admit / The meanest British wit" (ll. 25–6) and hoping for a time when it might find itself chained to the Bodleian shelves, "A chain which will more pleasant seem to me / Than all my own Pindarick Liberty" (ll. 4–5). Institutional incorporation is recognized finally as of greater value than poetic inspiration, as Cowley's book eagerly seeks a place, even if a secondary one, among the texts canonized by their inclusion in the library: "Will you to bind me with those mighty names submit, / Like an Apocrypha with holy Writ" (ll. 36–7).

Cowley understood, as did Daniel apparently, that the literary canon was reluctant to include these vernacular Johnnies-come-lately, but also that, through the mediation of what Cowley called "the mysterious Library," their entry might somehow be secured. Though the authorization offered by the Bodleian collection began, however, to allow English writers into the canon of literature, it did not itself define a canon of English literature. The Bodleian slowly and unsystematically responded to the ambitions of English authors, adding their work to a field of literature defined by and for a social and cultural elite. But it certainly did not effect a widespread understanding of what the organizing principles of the field of English literature might be or even provide a sense of what texts might constitute it.

What, however, finally would allow an idea of English literature to form and be generally recognized was largely the work of one publisher and bookseller in the middle of the seventeenth century, Humphrey Moseley. Moseley was a successful London stationer.[21] On March 27, 1620, he was apprenticed to Matthew Lownes. He was made a freeman of the Stationers' Company by translation on May 6, 1627, and soon set up a shop with Nicholas Fussell in Saint Paul's Churchyard at the sign of the Ball. Their first publication was Christopher Lever's *The Historie of the Defenders of the Catholique Faith,* and in the nine years they were in partnership, they published only four additional books, all religious or devotional, of which the best known was John Donne's *Sermons Upon Several Occasions* (1634). They worked mainly as booksellers.

In October 1633 Moseley was admitted to the livery of the Stationers' Company. For another seven or eight months he worked with Fussell, but by July 1634 he appears for the first time in the Stationers' Register entering a book on his own as "Master Mozeley."[22] The book, a translation by James Hayward of Giovanni Biondi's romance, *Donzella Desterada, or, The Banish'd Virgin,* was eventually published in 1635, with the imprint "Printed at London, by T. Cotes, for Humphrey Moseley, and are to be sold at his shoppe, at the three Kings in Pauls Churchyard 1635." This is the only surviving title that Moseley issued from the Three Kings, and soon thereafter he moved to the shop he would occupy for the rest of his life: The Prince's Arms, "over against Pauls greater north door," as his imprint specifies.

We know little about his life, not when he was born or when he was married. We know his father was a cook and that his wife's name was Anne (and that she took over his business for a time after his death). We also know that at least four children were born to the couple, but only one lived to maturity. Moseley's business thrived, and he was elected a warden of the Stationers' Company in 1659, though apparently against his own wishes. He rarely attended meetings of the Company's Court; his characteristic absence on one October 3, for example, was noted "by reason of some distemper of the body." He died on January 31, 1661, and four days later he was buried in London at Saint Gregory's Church.

That is about the extent of the information we have, except for the extraordinary record of Moseley's publishing. He was responsible for perhaps three hundred titles in the twenty-five years he worked alone, few of which were the newsbooks, sermons, or polemical pamphlets that provided the steady

---

21. For details of Moseley's life and professional activities, I am indebted to John Curtis Reed, "Humphrey Moseley, Publisher," *Oxford Bibliographical Society Proceedings and Papers* 2.2 (1928): 57–142; and Peter Lindenbaum, "Humphrey Moseley," in *The British Literary Book Trade, 1475–1700,* ed. James K. Bracken and Joel Silver, *Dictionary of Literary Biography* (Detroit, MI: Gale, 1996), 170:177–83.

22. Edward Arber, ed., *A Transcript of the Registers of the Company of Stationers of London, 1554–1640 A.D.,* 5 vols. (1875–94; repr., Gloucester, MA: Peter Smith, 1967), 4:24.

income for most of his fellow stationers. His publications were mainly literary and historical, most important, what would be later recognized as the central literary achievement of mid-seventeenth-century England. In 1659, Moseley said proudly that he had "annually published the Production of the best Wits of our, and Foreign Nations,"[23] a professional commitment virtually unique among the community of stationers. His interests can be seen in the lengthy catalogues of what was for sale at The Prince's Arms that appeared in many of the books he printed, the first, in a translation of Corneille's *The Cid* (1650), divided into three categories: "Various Histories, with curious discourses in Humane Learning, &c," "Choyce Poems, with excellent Translations," and "Incomparable Comedies and Tragedies, written by severall Ingenious Authors." Eventually these catalogues were issued separately in various formats, many containing quite extensive lists of publications. In 1656, for example, the catalogue filled twenty pages with 246 titles, including a section of "Books . . . I do propose to Print very speedily," and his last catalogue, issued in 1660, has 363 items on thirty-two pages and ends with a section headed, "These books I propose to print, Deo Volente." But "God, alas, was not willing," as Peter Lindenbaum wryly observes, and none of the twenty-three books in the section was ever published with Moseley's imprint.[24]

Unquestionably what is most remarkable about Moseley's career is the degree to which he recognized and developed a market for literary works, an interest perhaps first established while he was apprenticed to Matthew Lownes, who had published the works of both Sidney and Spenser. Between 1645 and 1656, Moseley produced editions of Milton, Waller, Crashaw, Shirley, Suckling, Cowley, Denham, Carew, Davenant, Cartwright, Stanley, Quarles, and Vaughan. In 1647, he published the folio of Beaumont and Fletcher's collected works, and throughout the 1650s he produced, in addition to individual play books, a series of small collections of plays: Brome's *Five New Plays,* Shirley's *Six New Plays,* Massinger's *Three New Plays,* Carlell's *Two New Plays,* and Middleton's *Two New Plays.* In 1653, he entered some forty plays in the Stationers' Register,[25] a mark of his considerable publishing ambitions.

The poetry was almost all printed in octavo, similarly bound, and with

---

23. H[umphrey] M[osley], "The Stationer to the Reader," in *The Last Remains of Sr John Suckling. Being a Full Collection of All His Poems and Letters Which Have Been So Long Expected, and Never till Now Published,* by Sir John Suckling (London, 1659), sig. A3r.

24. Lindenbaum, "Humphrey Moseley," 178.

25. G. E. Briscoe Eyre, ed., *A Transcript of the Registers of the Worshipful Company of Stationers of London, 1640–1708 A.D.,* transcribed by H. R. Plomer, 3 vols. (London: Privately printed, 1913–4; repr. Gloucester, MA: Peter Smith, 1967), 1:428–9.

almost identical layouts and typefaces for the title pages. Most of the volumes contain similarly posed frontispiece portraits of the author (usually engraved by William Marshall), and the Milton, Shirley, and Carew volumes regularly appear sequentially in Moseley's catalogues with virtually the same title, *Poems, with a Mask.*[26] The play collections were similarly uniform, sharing the prominence of the author's name on the title page, an engraved portrait as the frontispiece, and a publisher's address and commendatory verse, all calculated to establish the playwright, in Paulina Kewes's words, "as a central, unifying presence which binds together and confers value upon a corpus of disparate and hitherto dispersed texts."[27] Moseley's individual playbooks were usually printed in quarto, unless he had already issued plays by that author in one of his octavo collections, in which case the single play was published in octavo so that it could be conveniently bound into the collected volume.

Moseley, through his regularization of the appearance of the volumes of poetry and plays, produced a recognizable series of the best writing of his generation. Though the motives for the unprecedented standardization and uniformity were inevitably commercial — to encourage readers to buy more than one volume, perhaps even the entire series — the effect was to make a coherent literary field visible. Indeed I would say the effect was to make contemporary literature visible, as authors, even as they were constructed and confirmed by the paratexts of the individual volumes, were denied their singularity and displayed as an organized body of texts with common characteristics. The commercial success of the project is confirmed by the volumes' inclusion in William London's catalogue "of the most vendible books in England" (1658), but its cultural success is more accurately measured in the degree to which his authors have come to define the literary achievement of the seventeenth century, as well as by the degree to which publication was what enabled that achievement to be recognized as literary (that is, disparate and idiosyncratic exemplars of imaginative writing could now be seen as a unified and coherent cultural project). Not all of Moseley's authors have assumed a place in the pantheon of immortal writers (Thomas Stanley, for example), but they do mark the existence of an incredibly vital literary world at the time; and although its achievement was not (or only belatedly) canonized by high priests of elite culture, it was in that moment impressively constructed and validated by the bourgeois desires that the book trade, in every sense, represents.

---

26. Each book, as Peter Lindenbaum notes, was by "various means made to look like part of a series: Moseley's English Poets." See Lindenbaum, "Milton's Contract," *Cardoza Arts & Entertainment Law Journal* 10 (1992): 451.

27. Kewes, "'Give Me the Sociable Pocket-Books . . .': Humphrey Moseley's Serial Publication of Octavo Play Collections," *Publishing History* 38 (1995): 11.

Moseley's interest in literature was clearly driven by concerns beyond market logic. In his preface to the 1645 edition of Milton's *Poems,* he assures the "Gentle Reader" that his incentive to publish was "not any private respect of gain, . . . for the slightest Pamphlet is now adayes more vendible then the Works of learned men."[28] Rather, what motivated the publication "is the love I have to our own Language," a love that made Moseley "diligent to collect and set forth such peeces both in Prose and Vers, as may renew the wonted honour and esteem of our English tongue" (sig. a3r–v). One might well assume this statement is disingenuous, mere publisher's puff, if it were not for the fact that in 1645 a volume of English and Latin poems by the then almost unknown John Milton was not an obvious best-seller. Still, Moseley trusts his instincts in putting it forth, convinced that he is "bringing into the Light as true a Birth, as the muses have brought forth since our famous Spencer wrote" (sig. a4v).

It is important, however, to see how much of a risk it was. Moseley was betting his money on his own taste and judgment, and though posterity has proven him correct, the marketplace did not, since the volume was not reprinted until 1673. In part, Moseley's willingness to take the risk was based on the success of what was his first literary publication, earlier that year in 1645 — the publication that I take to mark his invention of English literature. Early in the year, Moseley issued the *Poems* of Edmund Waller.[29] Waller today is largely forgotten, but, as Thomas Rymer wrote (in Latin) on his tomb, "Of the poets of his day, he was easily the first."

The publication history of Waller's poems is complex and has recently been brilliantly re-examined by Timothy Raylor, correcting the errors of the *Short Title Catalogue (STC).*[30] In late 1644, Thomas Walkley had begun work on a collection of Waller's poems and parliamentary speeches that he would publish as the *Workes of Waller,*[31] identifying the author on the title page as

---

28. John Milton, *Poems of Mr. John Milton Both English and Latin, Compos'd at Several Times. Printed by His True Copies* (London, 1645), sig. a3r. Subsequent references to this work are cited parenthetically in the body of the text.

29. Edmund Waller, *Poems, &c., Written by Mr. Ed. Waller of Beckonsfield, Esq.* (London, 1645). Subsequent references to this work are cited parenthetically in the body of the text.

30. For *STC,* see Chap. 1 n. 38. Raylor, "Moseley, Walkley, and the 1645 Editions of Waller," *The Library,* 7th ser., 2 (2001): 236–65. I accept his reordering of the Waller editions from the familiar Wing numbering and also thank him for his generosity in permitting me several informative discussions about these issues.

31. D. G. Wing and A. W. Pollard, *Short-Title Catalogue of Books Printed in England, Scotland, Ireland, Wales, and British America and of English Books Printed in Other Countries, 1641–1700,* 3 vols. (New York: Index Society, 1945–51), 495. Subsequent references to this work are cited parenthetically in the body of the text.

"Lately a Member of the Honourable House of Commons, in this present Parliament." Walkley's edition included, in addition to seventy-three poems, three speeches that Waller had given in Parliament between 1641 and 1643, which in the volume are bibliographically continuous with the poems, beginning on signature G7r.[32]

Soon after Walkley's edition appeared, Moseley published his own version of Waller and justified the new publication on the grounds that the poetry had previously been available only "in loose imperfect Manuscripts" and in "an adulterate Copy, surreptiously and illegally imprinted, to the derogation of the Author and the abuse of the Buyer" (sig. A4r). Certainly this last charge refers to the Walkley edition, but we may wonder how surreptitious this edition was, since it names Walkley as its publisher on the title page, and also how "illegal," since it appeared in print before Moseley's edition, and, on at least one state of its title page, prominently displays the imprimatur of a licenser, Nathaniel Brent, dated December 30, 1644.

The copy, however, may indeed be "adulterate," and Moseley offers his own edition (Wing W513, following Raylor) to remedy its faults, so Waller's poems can now, as the publisher claims, "appear in their pure originals and true genuine colours" (sig. A4r). The authenticity of the texts is seemingly guaranteed by the title-page claim that the poems are "Printed by a Copy of his [i.e., Waller's] own hand-writing." But, though the edition is indeed based on a scribal copy and not all dependent on Walkley's text, the underlying manuscript was unlikely to have been in the poet's own hand. It was almost certainly one of several manuscript collections made by friends and patrons (the accuracy of which would have reflected the inevitable debasements of scribal transmission). Waller wrote in an italic hand, and the printed text shows unmistakable evidence of compositorial misreading of secretary script.[33]

Waller was unlikely to be thinking much about publishing his verse at this time, however, having been arrested on May 31, 1644 and exiled to France in late November, following the discovery of what become known as "Waller's Plot," an effort to secure London for the king. What Henry Herringman says in his 1664 edition of the poems seems almost certainly true: that the earliest publications of Waller's poems were undertaken without the poet's knowledge and were discovered with surprise and displeasure when Waller

---

32. Edmund Waller, *The VVorkes of Edmond VValler, Esquire, Lately a Member of the Honourable House of Commons in This Present Parliament* (London, 1645).

33. For example, "*Tagry Arthurs* shield" for "fairy *Arthurs* shield," as it appears in Walkley's edition; see Raylor, "Moseley, Walkley," 250.

"returned from abroad" in the summer of 1652 and "was troubled to find his name in print but somewhat satisfied to see his lines so ill rendered, that he might justly disown them, and say to a mistaking Printer, as one did to a mistaking Reciter, — *Male dum recitas, incipit esse tuum.*"[34] And Herringman claims on his title page that his edition of 1664 presents the poems "Never till now Corrected and Published with the approbation of the Author."

Nonetheless, though Moseley has misunderstood or misstated the provenance of the manuscript he prints, his avowed concern for the authenticity of the text is at least characteristic. His edition of Abraham Cowley's *The Mistress* (1647), for example, says that he is publishing his text from "A Correct Copy of these verses and (as I am told) written by the Authour himselfe" mainly because he has heard "the same is likely to be don from a more imperfect one."[35] In another of his books the publisher says that this edition is "now made publick to prevent false Copies: for really if you have not these, you will be abus'd with others, so imperfect and mangled, that we may justly pronounce them to be none of the Authors own."[36]

It does seem that Moseley indeed cared about the authenticity of the texts he printed and took, as he said in his edition of the Digby *Letters,* the "greatest care to publish nothing but what is genuine";[37] nonetheless, if he did so, he displayed no concern at all for his authors' rights. He published Vaughan's *Olor Iscanus,* despite the poet's expressed desire to have the manuscript destroyed, admitting, *"I have not the Author's Approbation to the Fact, but I have Law on my side."*[38] In his 1647 edition of Cowley's *The Mistress,* Moseley confesses, "It is not my good fortune to bee acquainted with the Authour any farther than his fame . . . and to that I am sure I shall doe a service by this Publication" (sig. A2r). A service to his fame, perhaps, though not a payment to his pocket; but Moseley hopes Cowley will be "so well contented, as to forgive at least this my boldnesse, which proceedes only from my Love of Him, who will gaine reputation, and of my Countrey, which will receive delight from it" (sig. A2r). Ironically, when Moseley published Cowley's collected

---

34. Edmund Waller, *Poems, &c. Written upon Several Occasions, and to Several Persons, by Edmond Waller . . . , Never till Now Corrected and Published with the Approbation of the Author* (London, 1664), sig. A3r. The Latin is from Martial's epigram 38: "when you recite [my verse] badly, it begins to be yours."

35. Abraham Cowley, *The Mistresse, or Seuerall Copies of Love-Verses* (London, 1647), sig. A2r. Subsequent references to this work are cited parenthetically in the body of the text.

36. George Digby, earl of Bristol, *Letters between the Ld George Digby and Sr Kenelm Digby kt Concerning Religion* (London, 1651), sig. A2r–v.

37. Ibid., sig. A2v.

38. Henry Vaughan, *Olor Iscanus: A Collection of Some Select Poems and Translations* (London, 1651), [sig. (a)1r].

poetry in 1656, the poet contributed a preface in which he complains against "the publication of some things of mine without my consent or knowledge" and puts the blame at the feet of either "the indiscretion of . . . *Friends*" or "the unworthy avarice of some *Stationers*." [39] In his edition of Waller's *Poems,* Mosley claims that the text is superior to the degraded form in which it had previously been available because his is derived from a putatively authorial manuscript. His claim is thus merely the first example of an editorial principle that Moseley used to distinguish his publications, even if his misreport of the nature of the underlying manuscript reveals his no less characteristic, though perfectly legal, practice of publishing without the approval or even the awareness of the author.

Moseley includes the seventy-three poems that appear in Walkley's edition of Waller's *Workes,* essentially in the same sequence as they appear there, with the exception of Walkley's fourth poem, which appears first in Moseley's edition; otherwise the order is the same. Moseley also prints seven poems not in the Walkley edition. Most of the surviving copies of Moseley's first edition of the *Poems* include the three parliamentary speeches that had appeared in the Walkley edition, though, as Raylor notes, they are "printed on new sheets with fresh headlines and fresh pagination (sig. O8-P2; pp. 1–20) despite the fact that the last quire of poems employed only a half sheet." [40] The evidence of the printing, coupled with the fact that at least one surviving copy of Moseley's first edition does not include the speeches, makes it almost certain that they were afterthoughts for Moseley's volume and added sometime after the edition was first available in print.

No doubt Waller's celebrity made it likely that a volume of his writings might find an eager audience, especially a Royalist one, and Moseley is happy to capitalize on this; but his edition, unlike Walkley's, carefully constructs Waller as a poet rather than as a political figure. His title identifies the book not as Waller's *Workes* but as Waller's *Poems, &c.,* and indeed the book has become primarily a book of poetry rather than an edition of a public figure's miscellaneous writings. In various ways Moseley marks the book as a literary production; for example, he adds on the title page that "All the Lyrick Poems in this Book were set by Mr. Henry Lawes Gent. of the Kings Chappel and one of his Majesties Private Musick," and he prints Waller's dedication to Lady Sophia Murray, in which Waller seeks to "defend the attempt I have made upon Poetrie" (sig. A2r). Moseley includes his own "advertisement to the Reader," which introduces "This parcell of exquisit Poems" (sig. A4r) and

---

39. Abraham Cowley, *Poems Written by A. Cowley* (London, 1656), sig. A2r.
40. Raylor, "Moseley, Walkley," 249.

insists on its textual authority. Indeed, rather than exploit Waller's political notoriety, Moseley puts forth the superior basis of his text as this volume's chief selling point. "The reputable stationer," as Randall Ingram has recently written, advertises the fact that he has "restored" Waller's poems "so that they accurately represent the author's authentic work,"[41] and he does so to help sell his book.

Certainly Ingram's observation is true for Moseley's first edition, but, because of the emphasis of his advertisement, it is unquestionably strange to discover that Moseley's next edition of Waller's *Poems,* also dated 1645 (but, as Raylor has demonstrated, almost certainly a publication of the early 1650s), is neither a reprint nor a revised edition of the first. It is in fact largely identical to the denigrated Walkley edition, though it includes the very "Advertisement to the Reader" that attacks the Walkley text as corrupt and illegal. The new title page again makes the change from Waller's *Workes* to his *Poems,* and the volume again includes the seven additional poems that Moseley had previously published. The order and the texts of the first seventy-three poems, however, are not those of Moseley's first edition; they are exactly the same as they appear in the denigrated Walkley text. But it is not that Moseley has now for some reason decided to use Walkley's edition as the basis of his own text; the situation is even more surprising: the seventy-three poems, which fill pages one through ninety-two, appear on the very sheets that Walkley had printed.

Somehow the remaining, unbound sheets of Walkley's edition had come into Moseley's possession, possibly following a dispute over title, though no explicit record of such a dispute survives. What is clear is that on December 14, 1644, Moseley registered, "under the hands of Master Rushworth & Master Whitaker warden, *Poems,* by Master Edw. Waller."[42] Walkley's edition was never entered. Although his title page prominently displayed its license, which insured approval of the book's content, that was different from entry, which established a stationer's right to the copy. It seems as though Moseley and Walkley had each obtained a distinct manuscript of Waller's poems, and that the two publishers were virtually simultaneously working on a printed edition to sell. Walkley, however, for whatever reason, never entered his copy (it is worth noting that this was neither illegal nor unusual; indeed fewer than 20 percent of the 978 titles published in 1645 were ever entered). Moseley, however, did enter his copy of Waller's *Poems,* and that entry effectively con-

41. Ingram, "First Words and Second Thoughts: Margaret Cavendish, Humphrey Moseley, and 'the Book,'" *Journal of Medieval and Early Modern Studies* 30 (2000): 107.

42. *Stationer's Register 1640–1708,* 1:140.

stituted his right to the edition and, from the point of view of the Stationers' Company, rendered Walkley's (which must have already been in the press) unauthorized.

That at least ten copies of the Walkley edition have survived and some fourteen of Moseley's suggests, however, that both editions remained available for purchase. (If Walkley's had been in some way suppressed, the ratio of surviving copies presumably would tilt more heavily in favor of Moseley's.) But in 1653 Moseley purchased from Walkley his "right & title to a booke or copie called, *Poems, &c* by Mr Edm. Waller. Licensed by Sr Nath: Brent, & alredy printed." [43] The assignment formally resolved whatever dispute may have existed between the two stationers, and, as Raylor, notes, the phrase "already printed" suggests that what Moseley actually sought and acquired was the surviving stock of pages of Walkley's first edition [44] rather than the right to the text, which technically already belonged to him. Moseley then published the old sheets as his own book (Wing W511), canceling the original title page and printing half sheets with his own earlier edition's prefatory matter, which had denounced Walkley's edition, and the seven additional poems that had also appeared in Moseley's first edition. Seemingly, the financial advantage of issuing a new edition from already printed sheets now outweighed the bibliographical scruple that had been the original Moseley edition's chief selling point. And the new book, with its misdated title page, sold well, for a second edition (Wing W512) was soon issued.

It is perhaps not a story that reflects particularly well on Moseley, though it is hardly the most shocking story in that ever-amusing sit-com called "Stationers Behaving Badly" (and in truth Moseley's purchase of the rights to a book he had himself entered may not have been, as has been suggested, an effort to take advantage of a vulnerable competitor but may instead have been a gratuitous act generously designed to help a colleague whose business was clearly in decline and with whom he had several times worked in better years). In its unmistakable evidence of Moseley's violation of his own oft-proclaimed textual commitments, however, the edition testifies to how ardent was the publisher's interest in keeping Waller in print, as he again turned Waller's *Workes* into *Poems* and consolidated the transformation of Waller from a political figure into a poet, a poet who would become a significant influence on the next literary generation.

In the period leading up to the Civil War, Waller's poems already were widely circulating in manuscript. In 1642, three years before the poetry had appeared in print, John Denham could write in *Cooper's Hill* that Waller was

---

43. Ibid., 1:423.
44. Raylor, "Moseley, Walkley," 258.

"the best of Poets."[45] But, though Waller's literary excellence was recognized by his contemporaries, his influence increased dramatically after the poems were printed. "Unless he had written," John Dryden wrote, "none of us could write."[46] Dryden's hyperbolic praise, however, even as it acknowledges Waller's extraordinary impact on the next generation of poets, ignores the means that enabled Waller to escape his contemporary coterie reputation. Perhaps what Dryden should have said was, "Unless he had been published, none of us could write," for the powerful effect Waller's poetry exerted on the literary taste of the second half of the seventeenth century was achieved only through its circulation in print. Though Moseley could not have anticipated that influence, at least we must say that his editions of Waller made it possible and indeed mark the beginning of the publisher's extraordinary commitment to literary works, the moment, one might say (at least I will say), that English literature was invented.

William Stansby's publication of Ben Jonson's *Works* in 1616 familiarly is taken as a decisive step toward the development of the idea of the English author, as many have convincingly argued, but Moseley's publication of Waller's *Poems* is a no less decisive moment in the development of English literature. If the very title of Jonson's *Works* sought to elevate the demotic drama to elite cultural status, the title of Waller's *Poems* sought to segregate an aesthetic arena from other discursive modes. In the event, it was not quite this clean. As we have seen, Walkley's edition of Waller included three parliamentary speeches and the title page identified Waller as a member of Parliament. Although Moseley's would eventually do the same, nonetheless, his title and, even more insistently, his advertisement mark how purposefully Moseley worked to depoliticize the book—to make it a book of poetry rather than a political pamphlet.

This is not to say that Moseley's conception of literature was disinterested. Contemporaries did praise him for his role in recognizing and preserving the best of English imaginative writing, but the recognition of an aesthetic realm distinguishable from other discursive modes was not, as it would eventually be—or at least be asserted to be—in the eighteenth century, self-consciously emptied of its politics. Indeed it was quite the opposite. What Ann Baynes Coiro engagingly has called Moseley's "position as a guerilla fighter on the front line of high culture"[47] was motivated, as has often been remarked, by Moseley's unconcealed Royalist sympathies. Joseph Leigh's commendatory

---

45. Denham, *Coopers Hill. A Poeme* (London, 1642), sig. A2v.

46. Dryden, preface to William Walsh's *A Dialogue Concerning Women* (1691), in *The Critical Opinions of John Dryden,* ed. John M. Aden (Nashville, TN: Vanderbilt Univ. Press, 1963), 275.

47. Coiro, "Milton and Class Identity: The Publication of *Aeropagitica* and the 1645 *Poems,*" *Journal of Medieval and Renaissance Studies* 22 (1992): 277.

poem in the edition of William Cartwright's works (1651), interestingly not in praise of the author but addressed "To the Stationer (Mr Moseley) on his Printing Mr Cartwright's Poems," begins by marking Leigh's own dispiriting Interregnum experience: "I that have undergone the common Fate / In making shift to lose my own Estate, / Have felt that which did Thousands more befall," and then turns to announce his subject. I "am now just strong enough to make a Rime / Not to write Wit, which I pretend not to, / But to admire those Noble Souls that do: / Whose high Atchievments Thou hast brought to light / Setting forth Wits who best knew how to write." And after tediously listing Moseley's publications ("Then raised brave Suckling . . . Then gavst us melting Carew . . . Then Waller's muse . . . Then fam'd Newcastle's choice variety"), Leigh praises the decision to publish Cartwright, and he goes on to urge Moseley to continue his publishing ventures: "And since thy hand is in, gather up all / Those precious Lines which brave Wits have let fall . . . For times approach wherein Wit will be dear." [48]

For Royalists in the vertiginous world of the Civil War and following, when the king would first be challenged, then defeated, and finally executed, "Wits" became a code word for those of not only talent and taste but also shared Royalist sympathies. Leigh's clunky poetic catalogue of Moseley's literary publications reflects this set of cultural assumptions, and it cannot then be accidental that the one poet Leigh omits from his list of the "high Atchievments" that Moseley has "brought to light" is John Milton. Though in 1645 Moseley might well not have known Milton's republican politics, by 1651 it would have been impossible not to know. Moseley had carefully located Milton's poetry in the 1645 edition in a Royalist context, noting on the title page (as on the Waller title page) that "The SONGS were set in Musick by Mr. HENRY LAWES Gentleman of the KINGS Chappel, and one of HIS MAIESTIES Private Musick.," and reminding potential buyers that the book was for sale at the (well-named) Prince's Arms. But by 1651 Milton had long since escaped his publisher's design, and the poet's presence in the unabashedly Royalist publishing project of 1645 could only be an embarrassment for both men.

The impulse originally to publish Milton, however, was primarily to follow on the success of the Waller volumes. Moseley admits in his epistle "to the Reader" in his edition of Milton's poems that the "incouragement I have already received from the most ingenious men in their clear and courteous entertainment of Mr. Wallers late choice Peeces, hath once more made me adventure into the World, presenting it with these ever-green, and not to

---

48. Cartwright, *Comedies, Tragi-comedies, with Other Poems, by Mr William Cartwright, Late Student of Christ-Church in Oxford, and Proctor of the University* (London, 1651), sig.*1r–v.

be blasted Laurels" (sig. a4r). Apparently Moseley approached Milton for the manuscript: "the Authors more peculiar excellency in these studies, was too well known . . . to keep me from attempting to solicit them from him" (sig. a4r). This was a decision, like Milton's to accept Mosley's solicitation, that perhaps seems almost inexplicable now when we think of the two men's opposed political commitments.[49] But neither in 1645 could have been certain about the politics of the other. In 1645, to Milton, Moseley might well have seemed the only active publisher with any interest in poetry; and certainly to Moseley, Milton would have seemed no more than a little known but obviously ambitious and talented poet,[50] and the edition of his works imagined as a worthy addition to Waller's *Poems,* one that might well confirm and consolidate the cultural and commercial project the Waller edition had begun.

Sometime early in the winter of 1645, Moseley's edition of Waller's *Poems* initiated the process of distinguishing literature from other forms of serious writing and organizing it as a recognizable field of cultural activity, though clearly not one yet divorced from political concerns, as the eighteenth century would later try to insist it should be. Indeed, the eighteenth century's determination that literature be isolated from the public sphere, recognized as a polite achievement rather than a political one and imagined as an arena of no consequence "to any important purpose of life," in the eighteenth-century schoolmaster John Clarke's phrase, is not in fact an originary understanding of the nature of literature but a decidedly anxious reaction to an old one. It is a determined resistance to the royalist aesthetic and polemical thrust of literature at the (or at least, at one) moment of its origin.

A telling mark of Moseley's success can be found in the self-presentation of the book trade itself. In 1656 the publisher Robert Pollard began to work at his shop on Threadneedle Street, which was called the Ben Jonson's Head; in 1661 Francis Kirkman was selling books at the backside of St. Clements in his shop, the John Fletcher's Head; and, of course, in the early eighteenth century, Jacob Tonson's shop was called the Shakespeare's Head. Publishers who had once worked in shops with names like The Saracens' Head, The Pope's Head, and (Moseley's own) The Prince's Arms, now inhabited shops that bore the names of English literary figures that advertised the activities of

---

49. Of Milton's pamphlets, only *Reason of Church-Government* and *Areopagitica* displayed Milton's name on the title page, while several others included his initials. *Tetrachordon* and *Colasterion,* for example, identified the text as "By the former Author, J. M."

50. Moseley's role in the Milton volume has been generally ignored or at least underestimated. Characteristic is David Hale's phrasing, "Two views prevail about Milton's action in 1645, presenting himself for the first time to a general public by name as a poet," in "Milton's Self-Presentation in *Poems . . . 1645," Milton Quarterly* 25.2 (1991): 37, erasing the actual agency of presentation in print.

their publishers (and, not incidentally, these particular names testified to how successfully print had turned drama into a recognizably literary mode). The publishers who had invented English literature were now able to use their creations to sell their books.

A FINAL CAVEAT: I do not believe that English literature has a single history and a single point of origin; it has many histories, at least as many as there are definitions and potential uses of what we can conceive of as "English literature." Nor do I think that one could not find significant anticipations and precursors of Moseley's publishing strategies and commitments. But if Moseley was not the first person to conceive of English literature as a coherent discursive field (and in truth I think he was), he was certainly the first person to make that field visible and, more important, to make it vendible and thus available to a broad community of readers. Whatever we think English literature might be once it entered the age of print, it seems clear that it could not have become that merely through the ambitions of its authors or the interests of its readers. It also required the activity of the book trade, as Humphrey Moseley realized one winter day in 1645.

Chapter 6

"On the Behalf of the Printers"

A Late Stuart Printer-Author and Her Causes

Paula McDowell

"Whoever is for making Printing a Free Trade are Enemies to God, their King, and their Country." So declared the printer-author Elinor James (c. 1645–1719) in her petition *To the Honourable House of Commons. Gentlemen, Since You have been pleased to lay such a heavy Tax upon Paper,* n.d. (c. 1696–8), a broadside that she not only printed but also wrote and distributed herself. James in fact wrote and printed more than ninety broadsides and pamphlets over a period of at least thirty-five years from 1681 to 1716. A self-educated tradeswoman with a press in her own home, she addressed print trade issues such as the economic *dis*advantages of a free press, labor relations in printing houses, and the infringement of what we would now call "copyrights." She advised City of London leaders on issues such as the enforcement of City by-laws, and she routinely printed her opinions on the major national political events of her time. (In 1689, she was arrested, tried, and fined for "dispersing scandalous and reflecting papers" condemning William III for accepting the English crown.)[1] Satirized as "London City-Godmother," this self-appointed spokesperson for her trade nevertheless declared proudly in *Mrs. James's Advice to all Printers,* n.d. (c. 1715), "I have been in the element of Printing above forty years, and I have a great love for it, and am a well-wisher to all that lawfully move therein, and especially to you that are masters."[2]

In her pioneering study of the advent and implications of printing in early modern western Europe, Elizabeth L. Eisenstein explains her decision to focus

---

1. Narcissus Luttrell, *A Brief Historical Relation of State Affairs from September 1678 to April 1714* (Oxford: Oxford Univ. Press, 1857), 1:617. For further information, see Paula McDowell, *The Women of Grub Street: Press, Politics, and Gender in the London Literary Marketplace 1678–1730* (Oxford: Clarendon Press, 1998), and McDowell, ed., *The Early Modern Englishwoman: Essential Works: Elinor James* (Aldershot, Hants.: Ashgate, 2005).

2. Reprinted in John Nichols, *Literary Anecdotes of the Eighteenth Century,* 9 vols. (London, 1812–6), 1: 306–7. This broadside does not appear to have survived in the original.

on the larger social and cultural consequences of printing rather than on the human agents involved:

> I would have liked to underline the human element in my title by taking the early printer as my 'agent of change.' But although I do think of certain master printers as being the unsung heroes of the early-modern era and although they are the true protagonists of this book, impersonal processes involving transmission and communication must also be given due attention. In the end, practical considerations became paramount. I decided that cataloguing would be simplified if I referred to the tool rather than its user.[3]

While Eisenstein chose not to focus on "the human element" in printing, scholars have since agreed that we know far too little about the men and women who manufactured printed texts and about their understandings of printing as a social force. This essay contributes to what Adrian Johns has recently heralded as a "new historical understanding of print"[4] by introducing a new source for publishing historians: Elinor James's broadsides addressing print trade issues between c.1695 and c.1715. James routinely petitioned the Houses of Lords and Commons concerning bills and legislation affecting her trade, and, as we have seen in her *Advice to all Printers,* she also petitioned her peers in the trade. Her petitions shed new light on the British book trade at a key transitional period in its history: one that saw the end of official prepublication censorship in 1695, the first copyright statute enacted in 1710, and the consolidation of important ongoing shifts in the organization and economics of the trade. One of only a few early modern printers who were also prolific authors (others include Benjamin Franklin and Samuel Richardson), James provides us with an insider's view of the printing house and the political and economic factors—and human personalities—that affected it. While the extant originals of her broadsides and pamphlets are widely dispersed in archives throughout Great Britain and North America, the inaugural collection and reprinting of known texts as of 2005[5] has recently made facsimiles available to scholars of political, economic, and publishing history, and further archival discoveries are likely to result from wider recognition of this outspoken female printer-author as a figure worthy of our attention.

---

3. Eisenstein, *PPAC*, xv.

4. Johns, *The Nature of the Book: Print and Knowledge in the Making* (Chicago: Univ. of Chicago Press, 1998), 28.

5. McDowell, *Elinor James.*

"A Mad Woman . . . at the Doors of the House of L[or]ds & Commons"

Elinor Banckes James was married in 1662 at "about seventeen years"[6] to the twenty-six-year-old journeyman printer Thomas James, who set up as a master printer in about 1675. She worked alongside her husband for thirty-five years, then succeeded him as head of the business in 1710. Upon her death in 1719, her property passed to her eldest daughter, Jane James Ilive (1670–1733), who later succeeded her own husband, Thomas Ilive, then passed down the business to their son Jacob. In 1705, the bookseller John Dunton described Elinor James's husband as "a competent printer and well-read man" but added that he was "something the better known for being husband to that *She-State Politician* Mrs. *Elianor* [sic] *James.*"[7] As the great-grandson of Thomas James, the first Bodleian librarian, Thomas James Jr. was perhaps most notable for having possessed an extraordinary inherited library of some three thousand books. Yet there is little evidence that his wife had access to these books during his lifetime, and indeed, his will specifies that she should inherit the printing house only on two conditions: first, that "no part of my Library of Books . . . be taken by my said Wife," and second, that "she dos [sic] not molest my Executors in the Execution of this my Will."[8] Yet Elinor James somehow managed to gain control of her husband's books after his death, and she chose to donate them to Sion College Library.[9] She also donated a striking portrait of herself labeled "Eleonora *Conjux Thomae James,*" which may have been painted on the occasion of her great bequest (fig. 6.1). This portrait shows her holding a magnificent book (most likely the "Sion College Book of Benefactors 1629–1888," which records her bequest in detail) and displaying one of her own works, *Mrs. James's Vindication of the Church of England* (1687).[10]

The concerns that James expresses in her broadsides demonstrate her hands-on familiarity with the printing business. In her *Advice to all Printers,*

---

6. Corporation of London, Guildhall Library, MS 10,091/26, marriage license of Thomas James and Elinor Banck(e)s, October 27, 1662.

7. Dunton, *The Life and Errors of John Dunton Citizen of London,* 2 vols. (London, 1705; repr., New York: Burt Franklin, 1969) 1:252–3.

8. London, National Archives, PROB 11/515, fols. 148v–149v, will of Thomas James, proved May 9, 1710.

9. These books, forming the "Thomas James Library," are now housed at Lambeth Palace Library, London.

10. The Benefactors Book, now catalogued as the "Sion College Book of Benefactors 1629–1888" (London, Lambeth Palace Library, MS L40.2/E.64), lists by title and size each of the thousands of books that James donated. Sample pages are reproduced in McDowell, *Elinor James,* 290–3.

for instance, she complains of apprentices "flinging their houses into pie"—that is, "pieing" their type, or upsetting the wooden "houses," or typecases, in which printers stored their fonts. As the mistress of a printing house, she almost certainly oversaw the printing of her own texts if she did not physically print them. While one of her earliest extant works shows the imprint "Printed by *Tho. James* at the *Printing-press* in *Mincing-Lane.* 1682,"

Fig. 6.1. "Eleonora *Conjux Thomae James,*" n.d. [c. 1711], painting. Artist unknown. Reproduced by permission of the National Portrait Gallery, London.

the majority show her name in imprints or do not have imprints. For her, a formal imprint was redundant, because she typically signed her papers with the phrase, "Your Soul's Well-Wisher, Elinor James," and she often gave them titles such as *Mrs. James's Advice, Mrs. James's Reasons,* or *The Petition of Elinor James.*

James's broadsides are best understood in the context of early modern petitioning. Petitions were formal requests for favors or redress of grievances addressed to monarchs, members of Parliament, and other public bodies and private individuals. In England, petitioning was a right theoretically available to the meanest subject.[11] James intended her petitions as interventions in particular political crises and legislative debates. Timing was more important to her than aesthetics, and she shows little interest in writing for posterity or cultivating a reputation as an author. As a petitioner with a press in her own home, James could produce her petitions more rapidly than most. On at least one occasion, she responded — in print — to parliamentary debates within less than twenty-four hours, as the phrase "Yesterday . . . I did hear" in one of her petitions suggests.[12]

James addressed her petitions chiefly to three different groups: six successive monarchs (Charles II, James II, William and Mary, Anne, and George I), the Houses of Lords and Commons, and the Lord Mayor and Aldermen of the City of London. Petitioners often tried to gain an audience with the addressees of their papers, and James preferred to distribute her petitions herself. She describes delivering the first of her numerous petitions to Charles II in about 1671 or 1672 and she claims to have obtained audiences with James II and William III.[13] Most of her extant petitions, however, are addressed to the Houses of Lords and Commons. For thirty-five years, she petitioned Parliament on average *at least once a year.* The essence of parliamentary petitioning was attendance in person at the doors or lobby of the Houses of Parliament, and James appears to have done considerable "lobbying" of her own, for a manuscript notation on one of her broadsides in what looks like a contemporary hand describes her as "A Mad Woman who used to attend at the Doors of the House of Lds & Commons."[14]

---

11. On petitioning conventions, see David Zaret, *Origins of Democratic Culture: Printing, Petitions, and the Public Sphere in Early-Modern England* (Princeton, NJ: Princeton Univ. Press, 2000).

12. *I Can assure Your Honours, that I have always been for the Peace of King and Kingdom,* n.d. (1698 or 9).

13. For further discussion of these claims, see McDowell, intro., *Elinor James.*

14. This copy of *June the 21th 1715. Mrs. James's Reasons, to the Lords Spiritual and Temporal,* currently housed at the Harry Ransom Humanities Research Center at the University of Texas, Austin (shelfmark Ak.J232+715m), is reproduced in McDowell, *Elinor James,* 223.

"An Art and Mistery that ought . . . not to be made . . . common"

The period of James's career was a decisive one in the history of the British book trade. In 1695, the Printing or Licensing Act of 1662 (14 Charles II, cap. 33) was allowed to lapse for good, ending prepublication censorship and government restrictions on the number of printers and presses throughout England. Printing was no longer confined to London, York, and the two university towns, and controls on the importation of books were relaxed. Today we understand this event as a landmark in the history of freedom of the press, but to James it was at once unexpected and undesired. Parliament had tried to revive licensing in 1695 but failed to agree on specifics before the end of the session. At least eight further bills would be introduced over the next decade, but none would become law.[15] It is important to note, however, that although most stationers wished for licensing to be revived, many (including James) argued against the particular bill put forward in 1695. For while this bill revived prepublication licensing, it made no mention of the ancient privileges of the Stationers' Company (particularly the right to control the registration and ownership of copies) or of any need to restrict the number of printers. For the first time in English history, the printing trade was opened to all.

James argued in support of licensing in numerous petitions, most notably *Mrs. James's Application To the Honourable the Commons Assembled in Parliament, On the behalf of the Printers*, n.d. (c. 1695) (fig. 6.2); *Mrs. James's Reasons that Printing may not be a Free-Trade; because it is not for the Peace of the Kingdom, nor the Good of the People*, n.d. (c. 1695–1702); and *To the Honourable House of Commons. Gentlemen, Since You have been pleased to lay such a heavy Tax upon Paper*, n.d. (c. 1696–8). The sweeping omissions in the 1695 bill help to explain her tone of astonishment here:

> I Can assure Your Honours, I could not have thought that any one could have dared to have given such a Bill against Printing (till I saw the *Printers* Reasons). Sure it must be a 𝕱𝖎𝖗𝖊-𝖇𝖗𝖆𝖓𝖉 of Hell that presumed it? For it wholly aims at the ruin of *Printers, Book-sellers* and *Stationers;* and it is as if they designed to destroy the whole Nation: Indeed the *Messenger* that preferr'd this unreasonable Bill told me, *That he would hang up half the* Printers, and at this rate he may hang them all. (*On the behalf of the Printers*)

---

15.   John Feather, "The Book Trade in Politics: The Making of the Copyright Act of 1710," *Publishing History* 8 (1980): 19–44; and *A History of British Publishing* (London and New York: Routledge, 1988), 73. See also Raymond Astbury, "The Renewal of the Licensing Act in 1693 and Its Lapse in 1695," *The Library*, 5th ser., 33 (1978): 296–322. John Feather, in *Publishing, Piracy, and Politics: An Historical Study of Copyright in Britain* (London: Mansell Publishing, 1994), provides a table titled "Book trade bills 1695–1710" (table 2.1) and notes that there were "fifteen [bills] in all between 1695 and 1714, which, in one form or another, sought to regulate the affairs of the book trade" (51).

Mrs. *JAMES's* Application

To the HONOURABLE the

COMMONS

Aſſembled in PARLIAMENT,

On the behalf of the PRINTERS.

I Can aſſure Your Honours, I could not have thought that any one could have dared to have given ſuch a Bill againſt Printing (till I ſaw the *Printers* Reaſons) Sure it muſt be a **fire-brand** of Hell that preſumed it? For it wholly aims at the ruin of *Printers, Book-ſellers* and *Stationers*; and it is as if they deſigned to deſtroy the whole Nation : Indeed the *Meſſenger* that preferr'd this unreaſonable Bill told me, *That he would hang up half the* Printers, and at this rate he may hang them all. For,

I. What an unreaſonable thing it is to expoſe Printing? That any one may Work at it, that have not ſerved an Apprentiſhip to it. When,

II. There is not half Imploy for them that are already, and a great many are gone off for want of Imployment.

III. And for the moſt part of thoſe Journey-men that do remain, when they come to be Sick they cannot ſupport themſelves, but are forced to have a gathering in their own Trade, which is but ſmall Relief for a Sick Man and his Family; beſides it is a great ſhame, ſince they have ſo many Privileges to keep them from want (if the Company of *Stationers* did not detain them) that they might live like Men and be happy.

IV. The ſpreading of Printing over the whole Kingdom, will Ruin the *Book-ſellers*, for no Man will ſend to *London* for Books, if he can have the Privilege of Printing them, and any Book that ſells moſt, they will Print, not regarding any Mans Right, tho' ſometimes the Copy coſt the *Book-ſeller* a great deal of Money; Beſides the hazard of Printing, which if they ſell not their Impreſſions off, it would be their great loſs; ſo by this means the *Book-ſeller* will loſe his Countrey Trade, and by conſequence have little imploy for the *Printer*.

V. As for bringing Books from Forreign Parts ready Printed, it will deſtroy both *Printers, Book-ſellers* and *Stationers*, beſides the inavoidable inconveniency of Importing Treaſon.

I don't doubt but when Your Honours conſiders the ill Conſequences of this *BILL*, but that you will abhor it, and fling it out : And if Your Honours will Eſtabliſh Printing right, according to *Acts of Parliament* on that behalf provided,

I. That there ſhall be but Twenty-four Maſter *Printers*, beſides the KING's *Printers*.

II. That the greateſt of them ſhould have no more than Three Apprentices at a time, and others leſs.

III. That they ſhould employ none but Free-men, and their Privileges was to have Copy Money and Holy-days : But by the Multiplication of *Printers*, they Under-work the Trade ſo much, that the Maſter cannot afford to give it as formerly. For indeed the Maſter *Printers* by this means becomes Slaves to the *Book-ſellers*, fearing to offend them, leaſt they ſhould have no Work at all; I can aſſure Your Honours, it is not ſelf-intereſt, but the Publick Good, and the Peace of the Kingdom, and the great love I bear to Juſtice and Equity, that moves me to trouble Your Honours in this matter.

And I humbly beſeech Your Honours (ſince the moſt High GOD hath given you Power) to Redreſs the great Grievances of the *Printers*; ſeeing the Company of *Stationers*, have all the Copys that belongs to *Printers* divided among themſelves, which are very conſiderable, and were given for their Incouragement becauſe they were confin'd from ſetting up. And if Your Honours would vouchſafe to Order the Company of *Stationers* to reſtore their Copys (or make better Proviſion for them) which they cannot juſtly deny, then will You be like *Mordecai*, that ſaved his People from Ruin and Deſtruction.

And by doing good and ſettling the *Printing-Trade*, Your Honours will ſecure the Peace of this Kingdom; and there's none will preſume to go into holes and corners to Print Treaſon : But theſe that are here will admire Your Honours, and the Generations to come will be bound to bleſs GOD for You, and Your Memories will be precious.

And the Moſt High God grant that you may not only be precious to Men, but that you may find favour before GOD, and be eternally happy. Which is the deſire of your Humble Servant and Souls-well-Wiſher,

ELIANOR JAMES.

Fig. 6.2. *Mrs. James's Application To the Honourable the Commons*, n.d. (c. 1695). Reproduced, by permission, from the copy in The Crawford (Bibliotheca Lindesiana) Collections at the National Library of Scotland (shelfmark Crawford MB 694).

James saw the 1695 bill as "against Printing" because it lifted restrictions on printing that helped to ease chronic unemployment for printers and journeymen. As she explained: "There is not half Imploy for them that are already, and a great many are gone off for want of Imployment. . . . And for the most part of those Journey-men that do remain, when they come to be Sick they cannot support themselves, but are forced to have a gathering in their own Trade." She advised members of Parliament: "if Your Honours will Establish Printing right, according to *Acts of Parliament* on that behalf provided," there should be "but Twenty-four Master *Printers,* besides the KING's *Printers.* . . . the greatest of them should have no more than Three Apprentices at a time, and others less" (*On the behalf of the Printers*). Multiplying printers would have dire economic and ideological consequences, for recurring unemployment meant that some desperate printers would be tempted to break the law: "great Numbers of Printers must needs be very destructive to the Kingdom; by reason all that set up take Apprentices, and then their Necessity makes them do any thing that offers to Employ them" (*That Printing may not be a Free-Trade*). If a limited number of printers could make an honest living, then none would find it necessary to "go into holes and corners to Print Treason" (*On the behalf of the Printers*). Accordingly, James urged, "I would have Printers to have full Imploy, for that is the only way to make them honest and above Temptations" (*Such a heavy Tax upon Paper*).

Recalling the royal charter of incorporation granted to the Stationers' Company by Queen Mary I in 1557 and confirmed by Queen Elizabeth in 1558, with its frequent references to the "Mistery or Art of Stationery,"[16] James suggested that printing should not be a "Free-Trade" because it was not really a "trade" at all. She urged: "Printing is not a Trade as other Trades are, but it is an Art and Mistery that ought . . . not to be made so common, as that it should be slighted and trampled under Foot" (*Such a heavy Tax upon Paper*). In her view, the crown had granted the stationers corporate legal status with the understanding that they would limit their own numbers for the good of the nation: "for as [printing] is an Art that may do much good, so it may be injurious and destructive; and Queen *Elizabeth*'s Princely Wisdom foresaw the Evil, and therefore restrain'd their Number, knowing that was the only way to secure Her Government, and keep Her Kingdom in Peace" (*Such a heavy Tax upon Paper*).[17] In return for their privileges, the stationers were bound to the crown by ties of fidelity and service—that the govern-

16. The Stationers' Company Charter is reprinted in Edward Arber, ed., *A Transcript of the Registers of the Company of Stationers of London; 1554–1640 A.D.,* 5 vols. (London: privately printed, 1875–94), I:xxviii–xxxii.

17. An ardent Protestant who idolized Queen Elizabeth, James tends to erase Queen Mary I, a Catholic, from the history of the granting of the charter.

ment in 1695, James warned, now threatened to undermine. Prepublication licensing should be revived, for "there's not any thing can corrupt the Minds of the generality of the People more than Vain Books and Pamphlets" (*That Printing may not be a Free-Trade*). The stationers themselves could not be entrusted to censor the press, for they could not be disinterested judges in these matters: "As to Things relating to Church and State, neither Booksellers nor Printers are sufficient Judges; for they depend one upon another; therefore it must be done by a Power above them" (*That Printing may not be a Free-Trade*). Finally, for both economic and ideological reasons, controls on the importation of books must be reintroduced: "As for bringing Books from Forreign Parts ready Printed, it will destroy both *Printers, Book-sellers* and *Stationers,* besides the inavoidable inconveniency of Importing Treason" (*On the behalf of the Printers*). For all of these reasons and more, James expressed her desire that Parliament would revive some version of the Licensing Act but not pass the inadequate bill put forward in 1695: "I don't doubt but when Your Honours considers the ill Consequences of this *BILL,* but that you will abhor it, and fling it out" (*On the behalf of the Printers*).

"Slaves to the *Booksellers*": Copyright and the Consolidation of Capital

Since the incorporation of the Stationers' Company in 1557, the printers' power and status within the company had substantially declined. While one central concern of James's trade petitions is the need to revive licensing, another is the changing relationship between printers and booksellers, and specifically, what she saw as the role played by the major booksellers' accumulation of copyrights in the deterioration of the printers' status. James frequently addressed issues of copyright in a variety of contexts. In arguing against the lifting of restrictions on the number of printers, for instance, she informed Parliament that the spread of printing beyond London would dramatically increase the infringement of these "Right[s]":

> The spreading of Printing over the whole Kingdom, will Ruin the *Book-sellers,* for no Man will send to *London* for Books, if he can have the Privilege of Printing them, and any Book that sells most, they will Print, not regarding any Mans Right, tho' sometimes the Copy cost the *Book-seller* a great deal of Money. (*On the behalf of the Printers*)

The geographical spread of printing would make restitution for stolen property even more difficult to obtain: "Printers having the Liberty to set up in every Corporation, the Bookseller being at a great distance will not be sensible presently, but when he does know what Restitution can be made, they can never recover the damage" (*Such a heavy Tax upon Paper*). "Booksellers and others" needed to have their "Propriety" protected,

> for their Copies is their cheif [*sic*] Support, and they have as much Right to them as any Man that Builds a House and pays the Workman for Building it. And when Printers are set up and have Apprentices, they will not regard any Man's Propriety, but if there be any Saleable Books, they will Print them for their own Support. (*Such a heavy Tax upon Paper*)

As her phrasing here suggests, in her writings about copyright James tended to represent bookseller-publishers as proto-capitalist employers and printers as their vulnerable "Workm[e]n" (rather than as the dignified custodians of an ancient "Art and Mistery" entrusted to them by the queen). The infringement of rights to copies, she stated, hurt printers not because printers owned major copies but because the major copy-holders, the booksellers, would "lose [their] Countrey Trade, and by consequence have little imploy for the *Printer*" (*On the behalf of the Printers*). In James's view, the most pressing problem with copyright in her time was not the occasional infringement of these rights by needy printers but the systematic concentration of copies in the hands of a small number of powerful booksellers. By the early seventeenth century, booksellers had already become the major copy-holders, but in the eighteenth century there was an even greater concentration of capital — thus giving James the impression that "the Company of *Stationers,* have all the Copys that belongs to *Printers* divided among themselves" (*On the behalf of the Printers*). Looking back to what she saw as the halcyon days of the incorporation of the Stationers' Company, she suggested that the sovereign originally granted printing privileges to printers in return for their limiting their own numbers: "the Copys that belongs to *Printers*" were "given for their Incouragement because they were confin'd from setting up" (*On the behalf of the Printers*). Concerned that the booksellers were gaining far too much control, James worked to clarify for members of Parliament the relationship between the printers and the other stationers:

> Booksellers and Stationers should not directly, nor indirectly, set up Printing-Houses; for indeed, the Printer has nothing to live upon but his Printing, when Booksellers and Stationers have their several Imployments to live on: Printing indeed, is part of the Booksellers Business, so far as to Employ the Printer; but Stationers have nothing to do with Printing. (*That Printing may not be a Free-Trade*)

James urged Parliament to "Order the Company of Stationers to restore [the printers'] Copys (or make better Provision for them)." She also noted that lifting restrictions on the number of printers would benefit only booksellers, not printers: "the Master *Printers* by this means becomes Slaves to the *Book-sellers,* fearing to offend them, least they should have no Work at all" (*On the behalf of the Printers*).

Although today it is commonly suggested that the eighteenth-century struggle over copyright was "essentially . . . a battle between two groups of booksellers," [18] James's writings on copyright remind us just how intimately this battle affected diverse sectors of the trade. In her view, these struggles were about the evolution of relationships among a wide number of groups (printers vs. booksellers, London-based vs. provincial booksellers, and so on). At the same time, though, it is significant that despite her awareness of the number of groups affected, James only once mentions the writers of texts, and she never actually uses the word or employs the concept of an "author." As historians of copyright have observed, the first modern copyright law, the Statute of Anne (8 Anne cap. 19), legally empowered authors by recognizing them as possible proprietors of their works, yet the most powerful players in copyright debates, the booksellers, employed the concept of "author's rights" chiefly to protect their own property. James argued that the increased infringement of copyrights due to the multiplication of printers "will make the Bookseller afraid to buy any Copies, and so Ingeninus [*sic*] Men that might do the Nation good, will be disencouraged for Writing, by reason no man [i.e., Bookseller] will care to buy, because he cannot call it his own" (*Such a heavy Tax upon Paper*). As this quotation suggests, a more urgent issue for her than the rights of "Ingeninus Men" was the readiness of booksellers to buy copies and finance their printing. The writers of texts were thus in no better or worse situation than their printers: both were at the mercy of a small number of major property-owners who had the capital to finance the printing of texts—just as "any Man that Builds a House and pays the Workman."

Paper Taxes and Printing-House Practices

By 1705, "the revival of licensing in its old form was a dead issue," [19] and the government was looking for new ways to control the press. Between 1690 and 1713, a need to finance almost continuous foreign wars led to the introduction of new taxes on domestic and imported paper and the first-ever taxes on

---

18. Mark Rose, *Authors and Owners: The Invention of Copyright* (Cambridge, MA: Harvard Univ. Press, 1993), 4.

19. Feather, *History of British Publishing,* 85.

certain classes of printed matter.[20] Well into the eighteenth century, England was still heavily reliant on continental sources for high-quality paper. While the cheaper grades of brown paper could be manufactured domestically, white paper required expensive linen rags, and as James informed Parliament, "the *English* Paper Makers cannot make Paper so Good, nor so Cheap; neither can they make enough; for they have not the Linnen-rags here, as they have in those Countries with whom we deal for Paper, by reason we consume not so much Linnen, as they do."[21] In 1696, Parliament passed a bill taxing both domestic and imported paper for a term of two years, from March 1, 1696/7 to March 1, 1698/9 (Stat. 8 & 9 Wm. III, cap. 7, "An Act for granting to His Majesty several Duties upon Paper Vellum and Parchment"). There was a great deal of pamphleteering both at the passing of this act and later when the government tried to renew it, for paper was an enormous expenditure for printers. James protested against paper taxes in *To the Honourable House of Commons. Gentlemen, Since You have been pleased to lay such a heavy Tax upon Paper*, n.d. (c. 1696–8); *To the Honourable House of Commons. May it please your Honours, Seriously to consider, That Trade is the Life of the Nation*, n.d. (1701 or 1702); and *March 7. 1702, To The Honourable House of Commons*. In c. 1696–8, she expressed her astonishment at the government's actions: "Gentlemen, Since you have been pleased to lay such a heavy Tax upon Paper, as the like was never known" (*Such a heavy Tax upon Paper*). In c. 1702 when the government considered reviving the two-year tax, she observed, should "this Paper Act pass, . . . it will destroy the Booksellers, Stationers, and Printers, that I have a kindness for . . . it will be a continual Grief to me to hear their Complaints, which the dearness and scarceness of Paper will occasion" (*Trade is the Life of the Nation*). She acknowledged Parliament's need to raise revenue to support the war, yet she took every opportunity to remind Parliament that the earlier paper tax had failed miserably to serve this purpose. As an act of 1702 pointed out, the 1696 "Act for granting . . . Duties upon Paper Vellum and Parchment" had proved wholly "insufficient to satisfie all the Monies which were borrowed upon Credit of that Act."[22] James observed "how prejudicial the Taxe [*sic*] upon Paper was, and how little Advantage it brought to the Kingdom" (*Trade is the Life of the Nation*). Reviving this tax would "prove utter ruin to a great many; for it will undo the Stationers,

---

20. See John Bidwell, "French Paper in English Books," in *The Cambridge History of the Book in Britain*, vol. 4, *1557–1695*, ed. John Barnard and D. F. McKenzie, with the assistance of Maureen Bell (Cambridge: Cambridge Univ. Press, 2002), 583–601; D. C. Coleman, *The British Paper Industry 1495–1860: A Study in Industrial Growth* (Oxford: Clarendon Press, 1958); and Rupert C. Jarvis, "The Paper Makers and the Excise in the Eighteenth Century," *The Library*, 5th ser., 14 (1959): 100–16.

21. *March 7. 1702, To The Honourable House of Commons*.

22. 1 Anne, cap. 7: "An Act for making good Deficiencies & for preserving the Publick Credit."

Booksellers, Printers, Book-binders, and Paper-makers, &c. who already have been great Sufferers" (*Trade is the Life of the Nation*). Paper taxes were unpatriotic, giving an additional advantage to Continental paper makers on whom England already relied: "what have we to do with the Dutch, for to destroy ourselves, to promote their Interest?" (*Trade is the Life of the Nation*). Instead of introducing new taxes, the government should "study to promote Trade, that the People may be able to live and pay the Taxes" (*Trade is the Life of the Nation*). Rather ingeniously, James concluded one petition by suggesting that Parliament tax men's wigs instead of paper: "I don't doubt but your Honours Wisdom will find out a more easier way. . . . For what if your Honours laid Six pence upon every Perewigg [*sic*], this will raise a great deal of Money, and it will not undoe any Man" (*Trade is the Life of the Nation*).

In 1711 and 1712, acts were passed imposing duties on certain classes of printed matter (stat. 9 Anne cap. 23 and 10 Anne cap. 19). The so-called Stamp Taxes were yet another effort to raise revenue after nearly twenty years at war, but it may also have been hoped that these new taxes would help to control the press. In January 1712, Queen Anne asked Parliament to consider remedies to the licentiousness of the press, and that spring, the crown prosecuted a succession of libel cases. James seized this opportunity to suggest her own remedy to this problem. In *March 27th 1712. To the Honourable House of Commons. The Grief of Elenor James*, she acknowledged that "the Printers Sins has been very great" yet expressed her hope that the government "would punish the Guilty, and let the Innocent go free." Reiterating a theme of her earlier petitions, the relationship between unemployment and a temptation to break the law, she proposed that the Queen should "allow a small Sallery [*sic*]" to printers "to tie them to Obedience." If printers could support themselves and their families, she suggested, they would not be tempted to publish libelous and seditious works: "then Your Honours will find that Printing will be regulated" (*March 27th 1712*).

While James addressed the majority of her petitions concerning printing and bookselling to Parliament, she also addressed at least one petition on this topic to her peers in the trade. In *Mrs. James's Advice to all Printers*, she assumed that her fellow printers were already familiar with the problem she outlined: the increasing conflict between the traditional, guild-based system of apprenticeship, with its codes of mutual agreement among printers, and the illicit but evidently common practice of printers hiring others' apprentices on a freelance basis:

> You cannot be ignorant of the great charge in bringing up of servants [apprentices] in the art of printing; neither can you be insensible how remiss, provoking, and wasteful some servants are, especially when they are encouraged

therein, by the unjust hope of getting away from their masters, and having over-work from other masters that have not had the charge and trouble of bringing them up.

Hiring other printers' apprentices seriously undermined the system of apprenticeship, for "giving [an apprentice] money makes him a journeyman before his time." Perhaps drawing on her own personal experience, she observed:

> When a boy has served half his time, and has gained some experience in his trade, he presently begins to set up for conditions with his master; then he will not work unless he has so much for himself . . . which if his master denies, . . . away he runs with great complaints, . . . it is no wonder to hear a boy that wants an honest principle to do his own duty, rail against and bely his master *and mistress*. [My emphasis]

She urged printers to "take no man's servant from him, and then a master may (as he ought) have the benefit of the latter part of his time, to make him amends for his trouble and charge." She also urged them to limit the number of their apprentices, and "not to bind any boy except he be above the age of fourteen." She then went on to address her journeymen "brothers": "Now to you, journeymen; you are my brothers, for my husband was a journeyman before he was a master, and therefore I wish you well." Expressing her solidarity with these men while also reminding them of their subordinate position as employees, she advised, "take care that you are not guilty of any ill-thing, as shewing servants ill examples, and giving bad counsels, for if you should, you would be like Judas, in betraying your master." She especially reminded the journeymen of their duties as husbands and fathers: "For what benefit have you in starving your wives and children, and making yourselves sots only fit for hell?" Twenty years earlier, as we have seen, she expressed her sympathy with the journeyman's economic struggles. (Perhaps she remembered the thirteen years that her own husband had spent as a journeyman before being able to set up his own shop.) As always, she blamed these struggles on a shortage of work for printers: "by the Multiplication of *Printers,* they Under-work the Trade so much, that the Master cannot afford to give it as formerly" (*On the behalf of the Printers*).

The Local Labors of Printing and the Challenge of Disciplinary Boundaries

Elinor James was a middle-class tradeswoman whose mental life revolved around issues of business, faith, and politics. Her ninety extant broadsides and pamphlets show her to be, in number of works printed, one of early modern England's most prolific women writers. Her petitions concerning the book trade are a rare (and in some ways unique) source for the study of the mental world and material practices of printing. While we know a good deal about a few deservedly renowned printers, we know far less about the day-to-day activities and struggles of the more typical, but no less determined men — and especially women — responsible for printing the bulk of early modern printed texts. If our attempts to understand the printing press as an agent of change have too often rendered the printers themselves "strangely ethereal,"[23] then greater attention to England's first woman printer-author (fl. 1681–1719) will make an important contribution to our understanding of early printers' local labors.

Yet James's broadsides will reward the attention not only of historians of printing but also of political and economic historians, literary scholars, and others. Indeed, they are especially useful precisely because they challenge our own ideological assumptions (such as the benefits of a free press) and our own disciplinary boundaries and critical frames. James's papers address a staggeringly broad range of concerns, from issues of commerce to national and local politics to religious debates, and they will demand the collective efforts of many different types of scholar to "unpack." (Only a historian of printing, for instance, is likely to decipher immediately her complaint about apprentices "flinging their houses into pie.") These "ephemeral" texts are densely topical, yet also often undated; in addition, James typically assumed that she was writing to an audience that already knew what she was talking about. She seldom bothered to specify which bill before Parliament she was objecting to, which speech she was responding to (and so on). These cheaply printed, hastily produced broadsides also challenge existing critical models of intelligibility and value. What do literary scholars, for instance, do with a prolific author who may never have "written" her works at all but composed them directly at the printing-press with type? What do literary scholars do with an author who always signed her texts, yet was largely uninterested in them after their immediate strategic goals had been achieved (or not)? How are feminist literary scholars to understand a prolific woman writer who intended her works neither for private coterie circulation nor (chiefly) for sale in the literary marketplace but rather for a different sort of audience altogether? It is precisely because James's texts raise provocative questions like these ones that they will reward the attention of diverse scholarly audiences — audiences as diverse as those that this determined petitioner of monarchs, ministers, master printers, and others addressed three hundred years ago.

---

23. Johns, *Nature of the Book*, 18.

Chapter 7

Fixity versus Flexibility in "A Song on Tom of Danby" and Dryden's *Absalom and Achitophel*

Harold Love

Elizabeth eisenstein's endorsement of textual stability or "fixity" as a primary advantage of transmission through the press over manuscript transmission has been challenged in separate studies by Adrian Johns and David McKitterick.[1] Both dissenting writers, arguing from different perspectives but within a broadly McKenzian framework, would see the claim for the fixity of the printed text as a retro-projection of nineteenth-century attitudes that we cannot assume to have been shared by earlier authors and readers. Both also reflect a retreat from the dichotomizing assumptions of studies, including some of my own, reliant on Walter J. Ong's partly anthropological and partly phenomenonological modelings of chirographic and typographic modes of knowing. Yet Eisenstein's position remains persuasive as a statement about capacities: the press, when properly governed, was indeed capable of sustaining a higher level of fixity than all but the most scrupulously supervised kinds of scribal transmission. The difficulty is that the existence of a capacity does not mean that it was always exercised or that it can be assumed to have been operative in any given historical instance of authorship, publishing, or reception. Often it was not. My examples in what follows are mostly from British practice; however, it would not be difficult to find parallel examples from the Continent.

In order not to be misunderstood I must make clear that "fixity" in what follows covers the entire process of textual production of a given work, not only the replication of a single setting of type. At the beginning of the process it includes the crucial transition from author's fair copy to first-edition

---

1. Johns, *The Nature of the Book: Print and Knowledge in the Making* (Chicago: Univ. of Chicago Press, 1998), 10–20; McKitterick, *Print, Manuscript, and the Search for Order, 1450–1830* (Cambridge: Cambridge Univ. Press, 2003).

pages, and at the other end it would embrace such events as the annotation, erasure, or defacement of copies and alterations that might be introduced, either deliberately or involuntarily, in reading them aloud at a time when texts were probably as often listened to as silently perused. Instructive evidence on this last point is given in recent work by Adam Fox.[2] This is *not,* of course, Eisenstein's definition.

Fixity as a property of texts in transmission is dependent on two factors: the degree of cultural respect afforded to presumed authorial readings, and the capacity of any given technological practice to protect the text from progressive deterioration through the inevitable errors of replication. Cultural respect, or rather the lack of it, is the concern of an influential chapter by Arthur Marotti on the scribal transmission of lyric verse in early modern England, in which he illustrates that transcribers would sometimes assume a right to recreate, extend, or contract the text of their exemplar to suit their own tastes and interests.[3] I have encountered numerous examples of the same attitude in my work on scribally circulated satires and lampoons; a particularly striking one is examined in a later discussion. This practice reflected a then quite widespread view of authorship for the scribal medium as continuous throughout the life of the text rather than ending with the placing of a definitive authorial version into circulation. There was certainly a much weaker conception of the scribally circulated text as being somehow an "owned" one in the sense enforced for printed texts by the Stationers' Company. But we must also recognize that some early transcribers were so deeply imbued with cultural respect for the work as to collate their fortuitously encountered copies with other manuscripts or even to construct a critical apparatus from a variety of sources. One striking example is the collection of viol music copied late in the Caroline era by Sir Nicholas L'Estrange, in which he has entered the variants of several other manuscripts, now lost.[4] We are dealing, in other

---

2. Fox, *Oral and Literate Culture in England, 1500–1700* (Oxford: Oxford Univ. Press, 2000), 36–9.

3. Marotti, *Manuscript, Print, and the English Renaissance Lyric* (Ithaca, NY: Cornell Univ. Press, 1995), 135–208. Dame Sarah Cowper was another example of a transcriber whose copying was often a form of recomposition. See Harold Love, "How Personal Is a Personal Miscellany? Sarah Cowper, Martin Clifford and the 'Buckingham' Commonplace Book," in *Order and Connexion: Studies in Bibliography and Book History,* ed. R. C. Alston (Cambridge: D. S. Brewer, 1997), 111–26; and Anne Kugler, *Errant Plagiary: The Life and Writing of Lady Sarah Cowper: 1644–1720* (Stanford, CA: Stanford Univ. Press, 2002).

4. See Andrew Ashbee, "A Further Look at Some of the Le Strange Manuscripts," *Chelys* 5 (1973–4): 24–43, and "The Transmission of Consort Music in Some Seventeenth-Century English Manuscripts," in *John Jenkins and His Time: Studies in English Consort Music,* ed. Andrew Ashbee and Peter Holman (Oxford: Clarendon Press, 1996), 243–70.

words, with a liberty of recomposition that might or might not be taken, depending on the circumstances of copying and the interests of the individual copyist. A humble paid scribe would have no incentive to recompose a text, whereas a poetical squire or a learned lady, such as Sarah Cowper, entering materials in a personal miscellany, would have had no pressing reason not to do so, should the whim take them.[5]

We deceive ourselves, however, when we assume that such a lack of cultural respect for the authorial text was unique to the scribal medium. Print publishers were capable of taking liberties with their exemplars that were equal to or sometimes much greater than those taken by the majority of copyists— something that, through the mediation of agents and editors, they continue to do today. One incentive to revision was the strict censorship exercised in earlier times over the printed work. While the scribally circulated text was in most early instances an uncensored one, and sometimes, as in the verse of Rochester, took breathtaking advantage of this freedom, the printed text, in all but a few peril-fraught examples of surreptitious printing, was subject to the rewritings of censors, such as Sir Nicholas L'Estrange's more famous brother, Sir Roger, or precautionary revisions by bookseller-publishers designed to forestall censorship. A damning list of examples might be extracted from, for instance, the publishing of almanacs, as described by Bernard Capp; but the problem was endemic to all writing for the press.[6] Censorship was not always political or religious: anything regarded as likely to displease members of a book's target audience or reduce sales was likely to be excised or softened by the work's publisher. Reprints were frequently shortened, enlarged, re-titled, or further censored to meet the expectations of new audiences without any reference to the authors, who before 1709 enjoyed neither a copyright nor a recognized moral right in the printed copies of their works. One famous example of a stationer's postpublication revisions is the edition of Shakespeare's sonnets published by Benson in 1640; others are copiously recorded in Adam Smyth's eye-opening study of the printing of verse miscellanies.[7] There might also be ideological reasons for a text, once out of its author's control, being

---

5. On the fidelity to their exemplars of many early-modern scribes, see Steven W. May, "Renaissance Manuscript Anthologies: Editing the Social Editors," *English Manuscript Studies 1100–1700* 11 (2002): 203–16. May's more complex argument about the origin and significance of scribal change cannot be considered here. See also note 12.

6. Capp, *English Almanacs, 1500–1800: Astrology and the Popular Press* (Ithaca, NY: Cornell Univ. Press, 1979), 44–50.

7. See David Baker, "Cavalier Shakespeare: The 1640 *Poems* of John Benson," *Studies in Philology* 95 (1998), 152–73; Adam Smyth, *"Profit and Delight": Printed Miscellanies in England 1640–1682* (Detroit, MI: Wayne State Univ. Press, 2004).

rewritten: Johns gives examples from the field of scientific and technological publication.[8] Eisenstein, in her response to Johns, attempts to deal with this issue by dividing printers into "technically proficient masters" and "ignorant craftsmen," the former being more protective of the stability of the text; but in real life, the "good" printer (think of Aldus, or Eisenstein's own example of Regiomontanus) was the more likely to edit and revise author's copy.[9] In any case, the vast majority of printers and stationer-publishers were neither good nor bad but came somewhere in the middle.

It is curious that we still have no comprehensive study of book-trade editing practices of the early period — or perhaps not so curious when we reflect that no such study exists of the same practices as they affect present-day popular fiction. Let us hear from one eighteenth-century preface:

> I hope you will be ready to own publicly, whenever you shall be called to it, that by your great and frequent Urgency you prevailed on me to publish a very loose and uncorrect Account of my Travels; with the Direction to hire some young Gentlemen of either University to put them in Order, and correct the Style. . . . But I do not remember I gave you Power to consent that any thing should be omitted, and much less that any thing should be inserted: Therefore, as to the latter, I do here renounce every thing of that Kind; particularly a Paragraph about her Majesty the late Queen *Anne,* of most pious and glorious Memory . . . Likewise, in the Account of the Academy of Projectors, and several Passages of my Discourse to my Master *Houyhnhnm,* you have either omitted some material Circumstances, or minced or changed them in such a Manner, that I do hardly know mine own Work. . . . I find likewise that your Printer hath been so careless as to confound the Times, and mistake the Dates of my several Voyages and Returns; neither assigning the true Year, or the true Month, or Day of the month: And I hear my original Manuscript is all destroyed, since the Publication of my Book. Neither have I any Copy left.[10]

This is a fictional account, but the experience it recounts was that of many authors whose work was not sufficiently adjusted to the demands of the times or the marketplace. The rage to revise and modify is flagrantly evident even in the editing of classical Greek and Latin texts, the very field of publishing where we would least have expected to see it. Medieval transcribers had done everything they could to copy their ancient sources faithfully, restricting

---

8. Most blatantly Newton's and Halley's revision of Flamsteed's star charts. See Johns, *Nature of the Book,* 543–621.

9. Elizabeth L. Eisenstein, "An Unacknowledged Revolution Revisited," *American Historical Review* 107.1 (2002): 92.

10. Jonathan Swift, *Gulliver's Travels,* in *Prose Works,* ed. Herbert Davis (Oxford: Blackwell, 1965), 5–7.

their own interventions to the correction of apparent mistakes and anomalies. The arrival of the press brought a vogue for heroic and often capricious
emendation, of which Swift's contemporary Richard Bentley was a celebrated
example. One could argue that the printed edition had become an arena for
competitive self-display, luring editors on to more and more far-fetched dem-
onstrations of ingenuity; but is it not as likely that such editions were merely
opening practices to public inspection that were endemic to the medium?
Bentley's notorious edition of Milton in which he questioned hundreds of
perfectly correct original readings suggests that it well might have been.[11]
Bentley simultaneously betrayed that he had no confidence whatsoever in
the fixity of print. Print and scribal reproduction each offer instances both
of profound cultural respect for the assumed authorial reading and of a profound lack of respect. The distinction between them lies not in the extent of
intervention but in the fact that print publishers felt obliged, in a way that
was not generally felt by scribes, to feign the first of these and to conceal the
second, often by barefaced lies (think of the First Folio's title-page claim to be
"Published according to the True Originall Copies").

On the second factor affecting fixity—the protection of the author's text
from transcriptional alteration—printer and copyist differ little in either
attitude or capacity. Accuracy of transcription varied considerably from scribe
to scribe, exactly as it did from compositor to compositor. The scribe and the
first-edition compositor faced identical problems of deciphering manuscript
copy and were prone to exactly the same kinds of misreading. The compositor
of a second or subsequent edition had the advantage of setting from printed
copy, which was generally more legible than handwritten transcripts, though
this distinction may not have been so strongly felt by those for whom the
early written hand was a natural medium of expression, and for whom a considerable part of reading was done from script rather than print. We should
also remember that most early readers even of printed texts read more slowly
and with greater attention than we do, frequently with the aim of consigning
the substance of the discourse to memory.

What is more important is that compositors took it upon themselves, almost
routinely, to adjust many minor details of language and presentation to the
prevailing book-trade norms. Here, as W. J. Cameron has demonstrated, the
practice of first-edition compositors was often much more interventionist than
that of scribes.[12] Many, possibly most, scribes of vernacular texts would uncon-

---

11. See R. G. Moyles, *The Text of Paradise Lost: A Study in Editorial Procedure* (Toronto: Univ. of
Toronto Press, 1985), 59–71.

12. Analysis of the variants of hundreds of late-seventeenth-century satires transmitted in
manuscript "demonstrated quite clearly that professional scribes introduce fewer variants than are

cernedly impose their own spelling and punctuation preferences on those of the exemplar; changes of this kind, however, would remain within an agreed range of orthographical possibilities common to handwritten texts. The existence of individual variation did not mean the absence of an acknowledged system but simply that the system was more tolerant of inconsistency than that subscribed to by the printing trade. Individual scribal stylings, like individual handwriting, paralleled the liberties one took with one's dress or public behavior, the ideal being to express personal identity within a wider conformity.

Print compositors, in contrast, were trained to adjust scribal accidentals into an increasingly invariant set accepted by metropolitan stationers as proper for printed books: the analogy here would be closer to that of the military uniform. In English, this system was in part dictated by the limitations of the compositor's case, particularly the need to economize on *e*'s, which occur much more frequently in scribal spellings. By 1700 the trade had agreed on a standardized English spelling not much different from that taught today; but even during the seventeenth century, printers' spelling was usually a whole generation "ahead" of that used by scribes, as can be seen in instances where copy can be compared with the published edition or when the characteristic spellings of an author are compared with those of the printed editions of his or her works. Those young learners, like Alexander Pope at the century's end, who taught themselves to write by imitating print forms, were likely to imbibe the printers' spellings at the same time, but most were taught by often elderly dames' school mistresses or writing masters who had their own clear ideas about spelling and, like Holofernes in *Love's Labour's Lost,* must often have deplored the current printed forms. The long survival in written documents of such phonetically indicative forms as "hee," "shee," and "wee" against the printers' favored shorter variants is one example: dozens of others could be cited. It is rare before the early eighteenth century to find manuscripts, even when they are copied from printed books, written throughout in "printers' spellings." The authors and scribes, in other words, exploited the liberty of a variable and unstandardized but coherent and widely accepted system, while the compositor was in the position of having to translate that system into a different one that was a less accurate register of the sounds of the spoken language (in Walter Ong's terminology a grapholect rather than a phonetic record of a dialect).[13] The printers' routine reformulation of the accidentals of manuscript copy was another mark of the movement toward standardization

---

introduced during the normal processes in the printing shop." George de F. Lord, gen. ed., *Poems on Affairs of State: Augustan Satirical Verse 1660–1714,* 7 vols. (New Haven, CT: Yale Univ. Press, 1963–75), 5: 529.

13. Ong, *Orality and Literacy: The Technologizing of the Word* (London: Methuen, 1982), 106–8.

remarked by Eisenstein, but it also represented a further assault on the fixity of the handwritten exemplar.[14]

The compositor setting a second or subsequent edition from printed copy was expected further to modernize the spellings and punctuation of the exemplar, as well as certain minor features of expression, in order to bring them into line with developments in the collegial sense of what was acceptable for print publication and to reassure purchasers that they were acquiring a completely up-to-date product. The Watts/Tonson printing house of the early eighteenth century regularly standardized the semantically determined emphasis capitalization of earlier editions to the system still used in present-day German under which all nouns are capitalized and other parts of speech de-capitalized; later in the century came the stripping away of all capitals apart from those still observed in modern book production. Because changes of this kind were a progressive process in which the updatings of one edition were to be taken over and augmented in the next, new printed editions were almost invariably set from the immediate predecessor, a practice that institutionalized the perpetuation of error. The need to be guided in the choice of an exemplar by the up-to-dateness of its accidentals was not usually felt by the scribe or copyist, who was free to return to much earlier copies of the work in question. The selection of a scribal exemplar, when choice was possible, was less likely to be determined by the quality of its accidentals than by an estimate of its textual probity. A second task imposed on both scribe and compositor was that of repairing real or apparent errors, a process that in both media often led to sophistication. But, since scribes were under no compulsion to emend a text to the high standards of accuracy and consistency demanded by the press, many were prepared to let errors stand for the reader to repair as seemed fit. (Printers frequently do the same, inviting the "courteous reader" to emend any uncorrected errors, but this has never been ideal trade practice.) Moreover, scribal corrections often remained visible on the page while those made by the compositor are determinable only from collation of successive editions and those of the printing house proofreader through the laborious analysis of variant states of the sheets concerned. Even when a scribe has scraped over a reading, the fact that erasure has taken place remains visible to the eye.

What really decides the question of fixity in favor of the printed text is the mathematics of transcription. That works in scribal circulation show more extreme kinds of variability is the result of the obvious fact that to produce two thousand copies of a printed book in the early modern period would require only two or three resettings, each giving rise to a separate edition, with

---

14. See Elizabeth L. Eisenstein, *The Printing Revolution in Early Modern Europe* (Cambridge: Cambridge Univ. Press, 1983), 50–63.

the second and third transcriptions eased by being performed from already printed copy, but that for two thousand copies of a scribally circulated text to be produced would require that number, minus one, acts of transcription, each in effect a separate edition. The results of this practice are everywhere apparent in debased copies standing at the end of a long process of transmission. And yet scribal culture had ways of mitigating these problems through the production in scriptoria of closely supervised batches of transcriptions, all derived from a single exemplar; through skill in emendation (based on a practical understanding of the kinds of mistakes likely to be made in transmission); and through the common practice of basing a text on more than one exemplar. The circulation of manuscript newsletters in the reign of Charles II affords examples of the first practice and John Oldham's marginal emendations in his transcriptions of poems by Rochester the second, while any stemmatical analysis of a large ancient, medieval, or early-modern textual tradition will yield abundant evidence of the third. On a wider historical scale, the descent of the "Paris Basin" text of the Vulgate or of the Mazoretic text of the Torah demonstrates how effective such socially sustained disciplines of correction could be. Anomalies would regularly arise but would just as regularly be identified and corrected. In instances where the text was already firmly embedded in the scribe's memory, there would be little danger of radical alteration; moreover, copies perceived as seriously defective would simply cease to be copied (though they might linger to puzzle modern editors).[15]

Many widely copied secular texts developed similar "vulgate" traditions that, in the absence of culturally legitimated recomposition of the kind discussed earlier, might hold remarkably stable across decades or even centuries of transmission, with good readings regularly driving out bad. Of course the "good" reading might well be the more plausible one rather than the authorial one; but our concern here is with stability not authenticity. Eisenstein's general point must be regarded as broadly true as it affects young, rapidly radiating scribal traditions, such as those of the Renaissance and early-modern lyric and lampoon, and instances of careless or inattentive copying, but need not hold true of more mature traditions, when effective institutional protocols for verifying the accuracy of transcription were adequately sustained. Possessing a collective awareness of the problem, scribal culture had long-standing methods of dealing with it.

To sum up, differences between the two media in fixity and stability are, first, likely to be overstated and, second, a question of probabilities and capacities, which might or might not be realized in particular circumstances of copying. Against present-day assumptions, scribal transmission could

---

15. Ibid., 78–9.

sometimes be more protective of authors' intentions than the press, while the press, behind the fiction of cultural respect for the authorial name, was often highly re-creative in its reformulation of texts in both first and subsequent editions. Awareness of this situation should encourage us to be more careful in distinguishing between different genres and varieties of both print and scribal transmission. Yet it is undeniable that, in particular cases, scribally transmitted texts can be observed mutating during transmission at a rate inconceivable in the press. Two political poems illustrate this mutation. The first, from 1679, circulated entirely through manuscript copies and the second, from 1681, exclusively through print.

THE VARIOUSLY titled satire beginning in some versions "What a devil ails the parliament" and in others "Zounds what ails the parliament" was a Whig lampoon directed at Thomas Osborne, earl of Danby, at the time of his impeachment in the winter of 1678–9. The first four stanzas indicate the method of the whole:

A Song on Thomas Earl of Danby

1

What a Devil ailes the Parliament
Sure they were drunck with Brandy
When they did thinck to circumvent
Thomas Earl of Danby.

2

But they ungratefull will appeare
As any thing that can be
For they recieved Fidlers fare
From Thomas Earle of Danby.

3

Sr John Coppleston did Invite
All those he thought would bandy
In any thing both wrong & right
For Thomas Earl of Danby

4

But Shaftsbury doth lye & lurke,
That litle Jack a Dandy
And all his Engines sett at worke
'Gainst Thomas Earle of Danby [16]

---

16. Princeton Univ. Library, Princeton, NJ, MS Taylor 4, p. 38. A complete text of the poem with a full analytic record of variants will be available in the second volume of the edition of Buckingham's

While a squib in its manner and form, it was far from squiblike in its intention, which was to send Danby to the block. An attribution to George Villiers, second duke of Buckingham, is late and, even if true, could hardly apply to more than part of the poem as it grew in circulation. That it was perfectly in accordance with Buckingham's view of Danby (a former protégé who had turned against him) is hardly of significance when that view was shared by the larger part of the nation. The poem's mutability in transmission is extreme. Possibly beginning as six or seven stanzas, it had expanded to forty stanzas in the version here quoted, while an additional nineteen stanzas are found in other sources. The twenty-one currently known sources probably represent many hundreds originally in circulation. The poem was also sung to at least two tunes—"Black Jack" and "Pretty Peggy Benson." Only an early seven-stanza version ever entered print circulation and that nearly two decades after its first appearance in manuscript.

The early "political stanzas" were soon supplemented with new ones attacking members of Danby's family—before long his wife, his four daughters, their husbands, his daughter-in-law, and his two sons had each acquired one or more stanzas of denigration, much of it grossly sexual. Further stanzas continued to be added in response to the development of the parliamentary campaign against the unfortunate Lord Treasurer. The growth of the poem from version to version can be dated from these allusions. The Whig parliamentary attack on Danby took formal shape when articles accusing him of high treason were presented to Parliament on December 23, 1678. The earliest form of the piece seems to have been written at about this time. Parliament was dissolved on January 25, 1679, necessitating new elections. On March 3 the duke of York departed for exile in Brussels, and shortly afterward a stanza was written containing an allusion to that event:

> his Reedemer James swimmes downe ye Thames
> And past the Goodwin Sand by
> The Crowne or heirs hee never spares
> To Shelter Tom of Danby

On March 6 the new parliament met and a stanza appeared about a squabble over an attempt to elect Sir Edward Seymour to the speakership, which was vetoed by the king. A version transcribed by Peter Le Neve around March 20 already contained sixteen stanzas, including five attacking members of Danby's immediate family.[17] A stanza found in four sources refers to the

---

literary works, *Plays, Poems, and Miscellaneous Writings Associated with George Villiers, Second Duke of Buckingham,* ed. Robert D. Hume and Harold Love (Oxford: Oxford Univ. Press, 2007), 2:20–30.

17. British Library, MS Add. 61903, fols. 33r–34r.

remarriage of Danby's daughter Sophia on March 26. Some thought Danby should be allowed to go into exile, a possibility canvassed in yet another new stanza; however, on April 16, 1679, he was sent to the Tower, where he was to remain for several years. Even then new stanzas continued to be written, including two referring to an attempt made in the early months of 1680, with the connivance of Danby's secretary, to have Buckingham prosecuted for sodomy.

This confused and creative history of addition and revision is reflected in an astonishing amount of difference across the tradition. As well as varying in the number of stanzas they transmit, the sources also disagree over the order of those stanzas and in innumerable verbal details. The variations in order result from chance encounters with new material (in several instances stanzas have been squeezed into the margins of already existing versions) and attempts by scribes to impose logical sequence on disordered materials. The following list of variant orders was prepared with the assistance of Felicity Henderson for the Hume and Love edition of Buckingham.

B[ritish] L[ibrary] MS Add. 61903 — 1, 2, 3, 4, 23, 12, 10, 7, 5, 6, 17, 13, 41, 26, 27, 28, 33, 34, 35, 36, 37, 38, 39, 40.

BL MS Sloane 3516 — 1, 2, 3, 4, 5, 6, 7.

BL MS Sloane 194 — 1, 2, 3, 4, 5, 6.

BL MS Sloane 655 — 12, 10, 11, 8, 7, 14, [*marg.* 15, 17, 13, 41, 26], 27, 28, 20, 21, 19 [*marg.* 42]. [The marginal stanzas on fol. 65r appear to have been meant to be read counterclockwise down the left side (15, 17) and up the right (13–26).]

Edinburgh Univ. Library, MS Dc.1. 3/1 — 1, 2, 3, 4, 5, 6, 7, 12, 10, 11, 8, 14, 15, 17, 13, 41, 26, 27, 28, 20, 21, 19.

Univ. of Leeds Library, Brotherton Collection, MS Lt. q. 52 — 1, 2, 3, 4, 5, 6, 7, 12, 10, 11.

Lincolnshire Archives Office, MS ANC 15/B/4 — 1, 2, 3, 4, 5, 6, 7, 8, 12, 10, 11, 14, 15.

National Library of Scotland, MS Advocate 19.1.12 — 1, 2, 3, 4, 5, 6, 22, 23, 24, 7, 9, 43, 12, 10, 11, 13, 16, 17, 18, 44, 25, 26, 27, 28, 29, 30, 31, 32.

Univ. of Nottingham Library, Portland Collection, MS Pw V 42 — 1, 2, 3, 4, 5, 6, 51, 19, 27, 45, 52, 53, 46, 23, 24, 29, 47, 48, 49, 7, 8, 12, 10, 11, 14, 15, 32, 50.

Oxford, Bodleian Library, MS Don. b. 8 — 1, 2, 3, 4, 5, 6, 12, 10, 11, 14, 15, 27, 28, 54.

Oxford, Bodleian Library, MS Douce 357 — 1, 2, 3, 4, 5, 6, 19, 20, 21, 12, 10, 11, 8, 7, 14, 17, 13, 41, 26, 27, 28.

Oxford, Bodleian Library, MS Eng. poet. c 25—1, 2, 3, 4, 5, 6.

Oxford, Bodleian Library, MS Eng. poet. e 4—1, 2, 3, 4, 5, 6, 7, 12, 10, 11, 55,
56, 53, 26, 27, 28, 17, 13, 52, 23, 24, 57, 41, 58, 59, 8, 19, 15.

Oxford, Bodleian Library, MS Firth c 15—1, 3, 4, 5, 6, 19, 20, 21, 7, 8, 14, 15.

Oxford, All Souls College, Codrington Library, MS 116—1, 2, 3, 4, 5, 6, 23,
24, 7, 12, 10, 11, 8, 51, 14, 17, 13, 27, 41.

Princeton Univ. Library, MS Taylor 2—1, 2, 3, 4, 5, 6, 19, 20, 21, 7, 8.

Princeton Univ. Library, MS Taylor 4—1, 2, 3, 4, 5, 6, 7, 8, 9, 10, 11, 12, 13,
14, 15, 16, 17, 18, 19, 20, 21, 22, 23, 24, 25, 26, 27, 28, 29, 30, 31, 32.

Yale Univ., Beinecke Library, MS Osborn b 327—1, 2, 3, 4, 5, 6, 7, 8, 12, 10,
11, 14, 15.

Yale Univ., Beinecke Library, MS Osborn b 54—1, 2, 3, 4, 5, 6, 7, 23, 24, 9,
43, 12, 10, 11, 8, 14, 13, 16, 18, 44, 25, 26, 27, 28, 29, 30, 31, 32.

Yale Univ., Beinecke Library, MS Osborn b 371—1, 2, 3, 4, 5, 6, 19, 20, 21, 7,
8, 12, 10, 11, 14, 15, 17, 13, 41, 26, 27, 28, 55, 56, 52, 23, 24, 57, 53.

Poems on Affairs of State (London, 1704), vol. 3—1, 2, 4, 5, 6, 7.

Absence of fixity could hardly be more graphically indicated. Through its distributed system of replication, under which any reader might become a scribe, editor, or coauthor, and through its freedom from political and religious regulation, the scribal medium possessed a capacity for textual transformation that was denied the more cumbrous, public processes of the press. Of course, to repeat my earlier point, to observe this capacity spectacularly realized in one situation is not to say that it was realized in all. Against the amazing transformations of the Danby skit it would be easy to set other examples of scribal transmission of satires that display a high degree of fixity in their preservation of the original. Moreover, it is often when these works eventually find their way into print that the most radical alterations take place. The versions of Restoration political lampoons that appeared from the 1690s in the various *State Poems* and *Poems on Affairs of State* collections, like the versions of Rochester's poems in the first "legal" edition of 1685, were all heavily rewritten to meet the expectations of the new medium.[18]

To illustrate the advantages but also the limitations of fixity it is helpful to turn for comparison to a slightly later text, whose political influence was no less considerable but that circulated wholly through the press. Dryden's *Absalom and Achitophel* appeared late in 1681 in a large, carefully printed edition using the impressive folio format that had been exploited for the Popish Plot

18. For these changes see Harold Love, "Refining Rochester: Private Texts and Public Readers," *Harvard Library Bulletin,* n.s., 7 (1996): 40–9.

narratives it criticizes.[19] Circulated throughout the country in copies from seven London editions of 1681–2, two Dublin ones, and Oxford editions of two rival translations into Latin, the poem gave valuable support to the king's campaign to rule by prerogative alone without dependence on Parliament. Although it appeared anonymously, there was no secret about who its author was or what that author's political views were, since they were detailed in a short preface. (Dryden's earliest open assumption of authorship came with the inclusion of the work in *Miscellany Poems* [1684].) Both the substance and the content of its message were tightly controlled throughout the processes of replication and re-imposition.

In this respect the poem exemplifies the capacity of print under appropriate circumstances to support fixity as graphically as "A Song on Tom of Danby" illustrates the capacity of the scribal text to move to the other extreme. This fixity is one of the reasons we regard *Absalom and Achitophel* as literature while "What a devil ails the parliament" remains evanescent popular culture. And yet the fixity, even of *Absalom and Achitophel,* was not uncompromised, and it is helpful at this point to consider certain other aspects of its transmission and reception. We know nothing of the work's history prior to its appearance in print, but in view of its evident political mission of influencing the outcome of the earl of Shaftesbury's trial before a grand jury, it is likely that it was carefully read by the Tory managers and revisions suggested. (One version has it that it was a direct commission from the king, another that it was "writ at the instance of our great Minister, Mr Seymour"—the Sir Edward mentioned earlier, who had now changed his loyalties.)[20] A suggestion of revision in proof is given by oddities in the make-up of the first edition. The first six leaves were originally imposed as three bifoliar gatherings; at a later stage, however, the decision was made to insert the third sheet inside the second, a practice known as quiring, which is common in large folios to reduce the amount of stitching required but rare, and indeed unnecessary, in such slim ones. Anomalously the second leaf of the outer fold of the quire still carries its original signature, "C," and was originally printed with the catchword "Not" on its verso rather than the correct "Oh." An additional unsigned leaf was then inserted between the leaf signed "C" (bibliographically A2) and leaf D1. This insertion occurs at the exact point where in the second edition an additional twelve lines are added. Hugh Macdonald notes that "it may be a mere

---

19. Discussed in Harold Love, "The Look of News: Popish Plot Narratives 1678–1680," in *The Cambridge History of the Book in Britain.* vol. 4, *1557–1695,* ed. John Barnard and D. F. McKenzie with the assistance of Maureen Bell (Cambridge: Cambridge Univ. Press, 2002), 652–6.

20. *The Works of John Dryden,* ed. Edward Niles Hooker, H. T. Swedenberg Jr., and Vinton A. Dearing, 20 vols. (Berkeley and Los Angeles: Univ. of California Press, 1956–2000), 2:209.

coincidence that this inserted leaf should occur at this place, but its presence here and the strange arrangement of the preceding leaves, suggest that the printer was faced with some last-minute problems."[21] The California editors are in no doubt that politically motivated adjustment to the text was still taking place after it had already been set up in type.[22] Once in print the poem became subject to textual slippage of another kind: the variants of fourteen early editions occupy a full ten, densely packed pages of the California edition.[23] In a subsequent stage of textual production, the fixity of the text was further attacked by annotating readers, expressing assent with or dissent from its views, and inscribing real names besides the Biblical ones. In 1682 a key was published to assist them.

We might also note that the textually "fixed" *Absalom and Achitophel* was, in a sense different from those considered by Eisenstein and Johns, a shifty and untrustworthy text. Its shiftiness arises from the way in which it anchors itself in the archetypal printed text, the Bible, while at the same time performing a subversion of its source through the distortions necessarily produced by its application of biblical names and anecdotes to modern political circumstances. Where Dryden's present-day story could not be paralleled through the biblical narrative, that narrative had to be changed. Textual stability masks an ideological instability manifest in a radical reconstruction of sacred story conducted in a spirit that borders on the libertine. In the same spirit, the comparison of Charles II with David was used as an implied justification of the king's de facto polygamy. This was recognized by its early readers, one of whom responded shortly after its first publication with a splenetic piece called *A Whip for the Fool's back, who styles Honorable Marriage a Curs'd Confinement, in his Profane Poem of Absalom and Achitophel.*[24] By contrast the textually labile "What a devil" retained an ideological consistency that at first sight seems at odds with the freedoms that it invited from its readers and transcribers but viewed from another perspective can be seen to flow from them. The force of the template inviting the readers to a game whose aim was to create more and more ingenious insults directed at the unfortunate TED, his wife, and family was irresistible. That the Danby stanza with its invariant final rhyme could be adapted to purposes of praise as well as blame is demonstrated by Kenneth Grahame's use of it for Mr. Toad's song of self-praise in

---

21. Macdonald, *John Dryden, a Bibliography of Early Editions and of Drydeniana* (Oxford: Clarendon Press, 1939), 21.

22. *Works of John Dryden,* 2:411–2.

23. Ibid., 2:415–24.

24. London, 1681. The work is attributed to Christopher Nesse.

The Wind in the Willows, but no contemporary is known to have produced a version along the lines of

> God save our good Lord Treasurer
> The best that ever can be
> We all may live the merrier
> With Thomas Earl of Danby

The fixity here was one of attitude. Even Tory readers were forced to join in the game of denigration. Moreover, in studying the textual heritage of the poem, we unexpectedly become aware of other kinds of fixity. One group of manuscripts emanates from a single source, the "Cameron" scriptorium, which specialized in high-priced anthologies of state and libertine verse. As we would expect, they are virtually invariant. It is also fair to say that, even in the more adventurously altered copies, although expression varies considerably, basic sense—the particular joke or taunt of a stanza—is usually preserved and sometimes sharpened.

Once again we are dealing with capacities that will sometimes be pushed to their extremes, sometimes neutralized by countervailing impulses, sometimes reversed, and sometimes delicately shaded. While accepting Eisenstein's prescription in respect of these two works and others of the same kind, we are not entitled—as she would be the first to agree—to extend those to all script and all print. Rather, we need to consider each historical case of authorship, manufacture, and dissemination on its own merits within its own particular context of events and media practice, remembering that for a capacity to exist does not mean that it will always be exercised. We should also be alert to signs of flexibility in the fixed and fixity in the flexible, whether at the textual or paratextual level.

It might also be helpful to point out that fixity is not always a virtue, nor is its absence always a vice. Fixity in the reproduction of a debased and inaccurate or politically doctored text is hardly commendable, even if it provokes the continuation of textual production through annotation by outraged readers. The processes of print production (seen as extending over the full cycle of authorship, editing, publishing, manufacture, distribution, and consumption) were inherently slow-moving and inflexible.[25] Regarded as a political text rather than as a timeless reflection on human political behavior, *Absalom and Achitophel* spoke to its moment but was quickly left behind once that moment had passed. Insofar as the poem remained a contributing element in

---

25. This cycle is considered in Harold Love, "Early Modern Print Culture: Assessing the Models," *Parergon* 20 (2003): 45–64.

the onward movement of politics, it was through its being supplemented by a series of further works of a similar kind, some favorable and some opposed to its point of view, each of which was parasitic on Dryden's poem in the same way as *Absalom and Achitophel* was itself parasitic on the Old Testament. These included Tate's *The Second Part of Absalom and Achitophel,* Samuel Pordage's *Azaria and Hushai* (1682), Elkanah Settle's *Absalom Senior* (1682), *The Tribe of Levi* (1691), and *The Tribe of Issachar* (1691). There were also similar poems based on ancient narratives, such as *The Conspiracy of Aeneas and Antenor* (1682) and *Agathocles, the Sicilian Usurper* (1683). By the time each of these answers had made its way through the cumbrous processes of print authorship and manufacture, it was likely that they were no longer enunciating genuinely pressing issues; moreover, being unredeemed by Dryden's wit and deep human insight, they soon disappeared forever. (We should note that the authorial fixity of Tate's piece was compromised by Dryden himself, who added two satirical portraits to ginger it up and may well have made other changes.) But their appearance does indicate a benefit of print's characteristic mode of dissemination, in that their authors could always assume that Dryden's poem, with which they were in dialogue, was obtainable for reference. Only on this basis could such a secondary tradition be created. Scribal retorts of the same kind, though they certainly existed, were a hit–or–miss affair, since it could not be assumed that readers had seen or had access to the forerunner. The only certain way of overcoming this was to circulate the reply in a linked-group together with the forerunner, as happened with Rochester's poetic jousts with Scroope and Mulgrave.[26]

By the same token "What a devil ails the parliament" must be conceded a far greater degree of political success, arising from its very flexibility, and the way in which it enrolled its readers into the ongoing process of composition. Day by day and week by week it was modified to press its case in a consistently topical form. Readers might make their own selection of stanzas for copying and add new ones at will; yet even a reduced text might expand again when it was brought into contact with differently descended versions through the communal processes of social transmission. The poem in transmission was a living, fecund organism not a beached political Behemoth — another reminder that absence of fixity is not always a drawback.

---

26. *The Works of John Wilmot, Earl of Rochester,* ed. Harold Love (Oxford: Oxford Univ. Press, 1999), 92–108.

Part II
Exchange, Agency, and Adaptation in the Cosmopolitan World of Print

This impulse to end tales that are still unfolding owes much to the prolongation of nineteenth-century historical schemes, especially those of Hegel and Marx which point logical dialectical conflicts toward logical dialectical ends. The possibility of an indefinite prolongation of fundamentally contradictory trends is not allowed for in these grand designs. Yet we still seem to be experiencing the contradictory effects of a process which fanned the flames of religious zeal and bigotry while fostering a new concern for ecumenical concord and toleration; which fixed linguistic and national divisions more permanently while creating a cosmopolitan Commonwealth of Learning and extending communications networks which encompassed the entire world.
—Elizabeth L. Eisenstein, *The Printing Press as an Agent of Change*

Expanding on the early-seventeenth-century formulation of Sir Francis Bacon, Elizabeth Eisenstein distinguished the printing press as ultimately the most important of the three Renaissance technological innovations he thought had "changed the whole face and state of things throughout the world." [1] More precisely, Eisenstein considered that print-

---

1. Bacon did not distinguish between what he considered the three most important of recently developed technologies—printing, gunpowder, and the compass: "Again, we should notice the force, effect, and consequences of inventions, which are nowhere more conspicuous than in those three which were unknown to the ancients; namely, printing, gunpowder, and the compass. For these three have changed the appearance and state of the whole world; first in literature, then in warfare, and lastly in navigation: and innumerable changes have been thence derived, so that no empire, sect, or star, appears to have exercised a greater power and influence on human affairs than these mechanical discoveries." Bacon, *Novum Organum,* ed. and trans. Basil Montague, in *The Works of Francis Bacon,* 3 vols. (Philadelphia: Parry & MacMillan, 1854), 3:370. See Eisenstein's distinction

ing played a crucial role in creating a cosmopolitan world, which by the dawn of the Enlightenment exhibited characteristics she viewed as more "ecumenical" and "tolerant," if not strictly secular (*PPAC* 443). These qualities are distinctly "modern" and progressive, transcending both parochial ways of thinking and territorial frontiers. But as the opening quotation shows, she recognized as well the contradictions inherent in both print and its effects, visible even while the early-modern communication revolution was taking place: the agency of print could (and can) be simultaneously expansive and restrictive, uplifting and repressive. Just as print promoted a self-conscious, cosmopolitan western European intellectual community whose lingua franca, first Latin and later French, collapsed geographical and linguistic borders, so too it promoted vernacular tongues whose "fixing" helped construct and solidify narrower national parameters, real and imagined. Put in broader terms, just as print broke down one set of ancient, enduring, limiting boundaries, so too it helped create and erect new limits that would continually need to be broken down and overcome in successive ages, across cultures as well as around the globe.

The explicit, nationalist identities fostered by print in the Renaissance and later periods operated at both the individual and collective levels. The emergence of these attributes provided the first glimpse of what the historical-materialist Benedict Anderson (building on the work of Lucien Febvre and Henri-Jean Martin, as well as early presentations of Eisenstein's ideas) called "imagined communities," which characterize human existence, especially in the modern world. Indeed, Anderson's work may be viewed in many ways as an extension of the notions about the impact of print that Bacon postulated and the exploration of print and its effects that Eisenstein initiated. Communities at the level of nations are described as "imagined" by Anderson on the grounds that "members of even the smallest nation will never know most of their fellow-members, meet them, or even hear of them, yet in the minds of each lives the image of their communion." Such bonds are constructed through the act of solitary silent

---

in *PPAC,* 3. Dame Frances Yates agreed with Eisenstein that the press was more important than gunpowder and the compass because of the support it provided to the function of memory. See *Times Literary Supplement,* November 23, 1979, 5.

reading. In other words, the sense of simultaneity and "deep, horizontal comradeship" that nourish modern national identity are the end product of the agency of print.[2] Eisenstein notes this same relationship emerging in early modern England when she writes of a "vicarious participation by a mass-reading public in a national historical drama," describing large numbers of English Protestants simultaneously reading Foxe's Book of Martyrs, and as a result, forming a group identity (*PPAC*, 423). Fast-forwarding to the twentieth-century work of Marshall McLuhan, he defines communication by whatever media as "participation in a common situation."[3]

Print's facilitation of "vicarious participation" "in a common situation" expanded especially as the spatial parameters of imagined communities were extended. If Bacon really meant the larger world instead of just western Europe when he wrote in the *Novum Organum* (1620) about the trio of transforming technologies (and the work's title page, which depicts ships embarking westward beyond the Pillars of Hercules, is a strong indication that he did), he was somewhat premature in assessing the full effects of the printing press. Although printing had certainly wrought many profound changes in Europe by then, most of the world remained unaffected by it. Exceptions were China, Korea, and some other parts of Asia, which, as Kai-wing Chow shows in Chapter 8, had developed economical and efficient printing that did not require use of a press long before the European invention of movable metal type. The implementation of printing within western Europe, moreover, was not a uniform phenomenon. In the early seventeenth century, for example, Scotland, which shared an island and a crown with England, did not have much of an indigenous publishing industry though printing had been introduced there as early as 1507. Scottish writers made extensive use of printing presses in other nations, but as Arthur Williamson writes in Chapter 9, "only with the Cromwellian period of the 1650s do we see the beginnings of the Scottish publishing industry" on any scale. If the printing press had not "changed the whole

---

2. Anderson, *Imagined Communities: Reflections on the Origin and Spread of Nationalism* (1983; London and New York: Verso, 2003), 6, 35, 7.

3. McLuhan, "Notes on the Media as Art Forms" (1954), quoted in Paul Barker, "Medium Rare: With Big Brother Bestriding the Global Village, a Chance to Read What McLuhan Really Wrote," *Times Literary Supplement*, March 17, 2006, 3.

face and state of things" in Scotland and other peripheries of Europe by 1620, then just as certainly, it had not changed the vast regions of the globe barely touched by Europeans at that time.

Premature though Bacon may have been, he was correct in the long run. The printing press did eventually become a global reactive agent, as the essays in this part illustrate through examples spread widely over time and territory. As it happened, the printing revolution in early modern Europe coincided with the beginnings of European exploration and colonization. By Bacon's time, the European printing press was operating in regions whose existence had been unknown to its inventors. In 1539, little more than fifty years after renewed European contact with the Americas, as Antonio Rodríguez-Buckingham reminds us in Chapter 10, a printing press was established in Mexico City. A decade and a half later, another press began operating under Portuguese colonizers on the other side of the globe at Goa in the Indian subcontinent.

Despite these early beginnings, as European printing technology and conventions flowed across time and territory, this dissemination encountered a vast array of social, cultural, intellectual, and linguistic practices that slowed the pace of the global printing revolution. Chow notes that parts of Asia had an established printed literary tradition that was highly developed by the time Europeans began to print. In other regions, aboriginal cultures had only nonliterate traditions and modes of communication. Even in literate cultures a bewildering variety of writing systems was in use, ranging from *kanji* in the Far East to pictographs among the Aztecs and Incas to alphabetic Arabic scripts. Thus, the degree and success of adaptation necessary to spread printing across these widely differing regions, societies, and customs depended on a number of variables in the colonies (such as cultural compatibility and the type and extent of European domination) and in the metropolis (notably the reigning political philosophy of the moment). The absolute nature of Spanish conquests in the Americas encouraged the early and successful introduction of the printing press for a specific state-sponsored purpose: converting the indigenous population to Christianity. On the other side of the world in South Asia, printing was initially introduced under regimes with a similar agenda. But it was rather under the later dominance of Anglo-Saxon imperialists that South

Asia proved most hospitable to the printing press and ultimately achieved a highly evolved print culture. Anderson has written of the impact on British India wrought by the policy of "Macaulyism," a long-range education program, based on English texts, designed to create individuals, indeed entire social classes, who "culturally" identified with their English overlords more than with fellow natives.[4] Vinay Dharwadker, quoted by Vivek Bhandari in Chapter 13, has argued that in the nineteenth century, colonial South Asia produced the first "fully formed" print culture to appear outside Europe and North America, "distinguished by its size, productivity, and multilingual and multinational constitution, as well as by its large array of Asian languages and its inclusion of numerous non-Western investors and producers among its active participants."

Accordingly, as west met east, the double helix of print's agency — the coalescing of opposing strands of imperial and indigenous cultures through the effects of fixity, standardization, and dissemination — emerged in hybrid forms of cosmopolitanism, which, in turn, nurtured the dormant seeds of independence and new forms of nationalism in cultures under the control of colonial powers. Jane McRae demonstrates this phenomenon in her discussion in Chapter 14 of the nationalizing agency of print during the nineteenth century in New Zealand's traditionally oral and harshly subjugated Maori population. Print preserved and diffused both a culture and a language that had previously existed only in spoken words and face-to-face interactions. The qualities of print allowed regular, simultaneous access to Maori myths and traditions by a larger sector of the population over a far-flung territory, contributing to the formation of stronger Maori group identity.

In contrast, much of the Muslim world (although bordering on and even partly in Europe, as well as being one of the three Abrahamic cultures of "the book") long resisted printing because it perceived text imprinted on paper as a graphic image rather than a representation of ideas. Print as an image was therefore potentially idolatrous. As a result, the introduction of printing into Egypt, perhaps the most cosmopolitan Muslim state at the time, did not come until 1798. It arrived in the midst of the Enlighten-

---

4. Anderson, *Imagined Communities*, 90–3.

ment, on the cusp of conquest by Europeans who remained Christian but were moving to embrace toleration and who no longer held religious conversion as a centerpiece of their colonial policy. As Geoffrey Roper notes in Chapter 12, print "did not become a normal method of text transmission among Arab Muslims until the second half of the nineteenth century, despite the much earlier triumph of the print revolution elsewhere."

Likewise, in what might be thought a polar opposite to Muslim areas, the North American colonies after the first century of conquest were dominated by Anglo-Saxons who emigrated from Protestant areas of northern Europe with a well-evolved print tradition, if one less sophisticated than some on the Continent. Moreover, prominent among the earliest settlers of New England were William Bradford and William Brewster, who had practiced the printing trade in England and in the Low Countries. But Anderson and others have noted a striking similarity between the North American colonies and the Muslim world: although a press began operating in Cambridge, Massachusetts, in the late 1630s, its output was predominantly ephemeral and utilitarian into the early decades of the eighteenth century. Further south, in the Virginia colony, printing was prohibited during the same period. It was not until the size of the population and the formation of creole identity had reached a critical mass sometime in the third decade of the eighteenth century that printing exploded in Anglophone North America, becoming the same kind of transformative force it had been in the communications revolution of the Renaissance chronicled by Eisenstein. From this juxtaposition of the Muslim world and British America, it might be argued that although areas colonially dominated by more liberal European cultures embraced the worldwide diffusion of print culture at different paces, these areas eventually developed independent, nationalist identities fostered through the agency of print. Yet in regions where political forms were more absolute and repressive or more directly linked to religious aspirations, diffusion of printing was both slow to develop and less reactive. Indeed, another part of this argument may be that because of traditional fettering of print in the Muslim world, its part in the global communications revolution is yet to be written. As Eisenstein observes, "In a different cultural context," the technology of printing might be used "for different ends" (*PPAC,* 702). She also notes that "efforts to summarize changes wrought by printing in any one statement or neat formula are likely to lead us astray" (*PPAC* 70). If this is true for printing in early modern Europe, which was culturally a relatively homogeneous region (despite very real internal linguistic, ethnic, and religious differences), it is all the more true for printing in the larger, radically diverse world over a longer period as this set of essays explores. Changes wrought by the printing press in sixteenth-century Spanish America were vastly different from the changes wrought by the printing press in nineteenth-century British India. As the contributions in this volume show, it would be folly to attempt to summarize them neatly or succinctly.

Nor can we reduce the agency of print in human society simply to production of printed books. As Eisenstein has stressed, what was "new in fifteenth-century Western Europe [was] not 'l'apparition du *livre*' but 'l'apparition de l'*imprimerie.*'"[5] In other words, it was not primarily the printed book that effected dramatic changes in early modern Europe but rather it was many other forms of printed matter, less visible to scholars in later ages because most were ephemeral and utilitarian, and consequently have not survived. Although printing figures largely in these essays, printed books do not. The essays here are generally concerned with other kinds of print products. Peter Stallybrass in Part III writes about the most famous colonial North American printer Benjamin Franklin, who printed voluminously. But most of his printing was job printing of ephemera: Franklin "was only marginally a printer of books." Among the essays in this part addressing the practices of printing in other areas of the world, Roper notes that "the printed book . . . has never been quite as significant among Arabs and Muslims as it was in Europe. Popular devotional texts, pamphlets, 'pavement literature,' and, above all, newspapers and journalism tended to loom larger in the Middle East." The "above all" applies in many of the discussions in *Agent of Change* and perhaps in any discussion of printing since the eighteenth century.

While the revolutionary force of Renaissance printing technology from the fifteenth to the seventeenth centuries received primary emphasis in the

---

5. Elizabeth L. Eisenstein, "In the Wake of the Printing Press," *Quarterly Journal of the Library of Congress* 35.3 (1978): 187.

formulations of Bacon and Eisenstein, Eisenstein also looked forward to the developments of the Enlightenment. In fact, Benedict Anderson and other scholars, notably the neo-Marxist philosopher and critical theorist Jürgen Habermas,[6] saw the Enlightenment era of the eighteenth century as the period of ferment that produced the modern world, or at least the modern print communication revolution and the political transformations concomitant to it. Anderson recognized the importance of Renaissance antecedents, particularly humanism and the politicized readers (and writers) of vernacular during the Reformation, but what was most important for Anderson was the melding of the printed book, "the first modern-style mass-produced industrial commodity," with the true capitalist markets and economies of the largely colonial eighteenth century, resulting in what Anderson termed "print capitalism." And print capitalism "made it possible for rapidly growing numbers of people to think about themselves, and to relate themselves to others, in profoundly new ways," in other words, to become national communities.[7]

The ultimate commodification of print and its power to be intensely transformative in human society are evident, as Anderson notes, in the emergence of a crucial if ephemeral eighteenth-century genre, the newspaper. Paradoxically it was the fictive and arbitrary nature of the newspaper, especially its "calendrical coincidence,"[8] imposing the rituals of anonymous simultaneity on individuals, which created collective, homogeneous identity among the larger group of numerous and scattered citizens of modern states. This notion clearly reflects Eisenstein's conception of the effects of diffusion and collection, as well as her observations that the periodical newspaper press replaced the pulpit in early modern society as a medium for disseminating news and information, as well as providing psychological reinforcement (*PPAC*, 131, 553–4). She points out the incongruity in the necessity for the well-informed active citizen to retreat to internalized, solitary reading of the newspaper in order to participate in

---

6. See Habermas, *The Structural Transformation of the Public Sphere: An Inquiry into a Category of Bourgeois Society,* trans. Thomas Burger with Frederick Lawrence (Cambridge, MA: MIT Press, 1989), among other works.

7. Anderson, *Imagined Communities,* 39, 34, 25, 36.

8. Ibid., 33.

the larger, public group political processes of modern society. Anderson reinforces this characterization by citing Hegel's view that "newspapers serve modern man as a substitute for morning prayer," and observing that reading, or interacting with, the medium of the newspaper requires resort to "silent privacy, in the lair of the skull."[9] In a later article, Eisenstein quotes the Welsh utopian socialist Robert Owen (1771–1858), who described the newspaper as "'the most powerful engine for good or evil that has been brought into action by human creation.'"[10]

As an example, we can look to the British North American colonies of the eighteenth century where there is no doubt that the newspaper became an important—perhaps the most important—form of publication. News publications played a significant role, from the English civil wars of the mid seventeenth century on, in breaking up the first British empire. This opinion was held by contemporaries as well as modern scholars. Witness Eisenstein's citation of the soon-to-be French revolutionary Jacques Pierre Brissot, who traveled in the North American colonies during the 1780s and published an account of his travels. Brissot asserted "that 'without newspapers and gazettes, the American Revolution would never have occurred.'"[11] Printing in the British colonies had remained confined to a few northern cities until around 1720, and even then, few books were printed on colonial printing presses. Colonial American printers more commonly printed newspapers. Calhoun Winton writes in Chapter 11 about the effects of print in the mid-Atlantic and southern colonies at the time of the American Revolution through a case study of two presses, one operated by a Loyalist and the other by colonial patriots. Despite their different political allegiances, both provided news that was "essentially timely and accurate about the advent of the Revolution and its unfolding." "The major consequence" of their collection and dissemination of information, Winton argues, "was, inevitably, to buttress the patriot cause." In the British North American colonies, the unifying simultaneity of collected information printed in newspapers contributed to attaching inhabitants

---

9. Ibid., 35.
10. Eisenstein, "The End of the Book? Some Perspectives on Media Change," *American Scholar* 64.4 (1995): 549.
11. Ibid., 550.

more to the creole cause of independence than to the metropolitan ambition of centrally administered subordinate colonies. In the next century, on the other side of the world in a different kind of society altogether (though another British colony), newspapers became an equally important part of Maori culture. Just as colonial American newspapers contributed to a sense of national unity, the Maori producers of the newspaper *Te Wananga* hoped that something similar would happen among the various Maori tribes: that it would, as McCrae quotes from the first edition, "bring them together in one mind.'" Similarly, although dealing with a group of subjugated individuals "who came from different backgrounds," Bhandari finds a parallel phenomenon in nineteenth-century Punjab, where newspapers created a community of the like-minded by using "the existing, deeply drawn lines of communication within [the native] society to which the colonial authorities had only minimal access."

One other factor should be noted: print operated as a reactive agent only in favorable economic conditions. Printer-publishers required market demand for their products if their businesses were to succeed. Indeed, if we look back to Gutenberg's printing enterprise in fifteenth-century Mainz, it is notable that he went bankrupt after he abandoned job printing of indulgences to produce instead massive expensive tomes like the Bible. Even the early-sixteenth-century Antwerp printing entrepreneur Christophe Plantin, who operated as many as fifteen presses at a time, nearly suffered the same fate when he undertook the immense task of printing the polyglot Bible. Rodríguez-Buckingham shows in his discussion of printing in colonial Spanish America that economic realities or necessities caused the printing press there to stray from its original purpose as an instrument of conversion. Mexican printers, for example, could not support themselves by printing only catechetical materials; they had to resort to turning out other print products, such as playing cards and job printing as well as nonreligious books. A similar pattern characterizes printing activities in British America, where lack of an adequate market also dictated that print serve more utilitarian purposes into the 1720s and beyond. In Muslim areas, Roper tells us, the same was true. Thus, for print to be a catalyst for cultural or political change in any place, in any age, it also needed to be a marketable commodity. Print must serve or create a demand, whether ideological or economic, real or imagined.

The plastic, adaptive qualities of print, both as a market commodity and as a medium for transmitting information, outside the metropolis (as well as inside it) held the potential to undermine the very culture and context that had created it. Newspapers in the colonial age nurtured the centralized control of various empires and incubated the nationalist impulses of a wide diversity of indigenous cultures, from the oral, antipodean Maori to the scientifically advanced pre-Columbian Inca to the ancient literate Asian societies and the ephemera-reading creole populations of America and India. No matter the culture of the colonized, and likewise no matter the culture of the metropolis, print exercised transformative power. Printing technology is a demonstrably vital agent in the reactions necessary to eradicate empires and their agendas, in other words, what McLuhan called an "instrument of effect." [12]

Metropolitan governments typically did not exercise absolute monopolies over print in their colonies (certainly not in later colonial periods). As a result, they found themselves challenged in various ways by print in the hands of natives as well as creoles. This failure, or inability, of imperial overlords to adequately control the power of the press is not easy to explain. Perhaps European conquerors made naive cultural assumptions about the agency of print in colonial environments; perhaps they failed to recognize the potential for co-option that is inherent in the printed word; or perhaps they simply could not grasp the capacity of print to stimulate the desire for self-determination. But whatever the explanation, in case after case, it was indigenous populations who employed this "instrument of effect" to establish autonomous identities and communities rather than uphold the metropolitan state and its culture.

The effects of printing framed by Eisenstein were (and are) diverse, and as a result, often contradictory. While the multiplication of printed materials may have weakened the "traditional sense of community" in some ways,[13] she recognizes that print also encouraged new forms of associa-

---

12. McLuhan, quoted in Barker, "Medium Rare," 5.

13. "By its very nature, a reading public was not only more dispersed; it was also more atomistic and individualistic than a hearing one" (*PPAC*, 132).

tion, often across national boundaries and sometimes across vast distances: "Even while communal solidarity was diminished, vicarious participation in more distant events was also enhanced; and even while local ties were loosened, links to larger collective units were being forged. Printed materials encouraged silent adherence to causes whose advocates could not be found in any one parish and who addressed an invisible public from afar. New forms of group identity began to compete with an older, more localized nexus of loyalties" (*PPAC*, 132). As the essays in this part also show, the study of an array of both print phenomena and human cultures across temporal and territorial boundaries demonstrates that the agency of print could—and did—create a variety of real and imagined communities, from the Renaissance to the present day. Initially, print created elite, intellectual communities of the Latin-literate possessed of pseudo-nationalistic names—the republic of letters, or the commonwealth of learning—that transcended distance through access to and exchange of information. At first, such communities existed primarily in the minds of Europeans, but, later, as print spread around the globe, so too did more tangible national communities formed through the agency of print. Print possessed the power to transform entire cultures and reconfigure nations.

Chapter 8

Reinventing Gutenberg

Woodblock and Movable-Type Printing in Europe and China

KAI-WING CHOW

"GUTENBERG REVISITED from the East" is the title of the introduction Roger Chartier wrote for a special issue of *Late Imperial China* on
printing. He calls for "a more accurate appreciation of Gutenberg's invention"
because it "was not the only technique capable of assuring the wide-scale
dissemination of printed texts."[1] Moreover, as a historian of books and a
cultural historian interested in the study of print culture, Chartier recognizes
the importance of images and illustrations in European books. His approach
to the history of books transcends the narrow focus on the "printed word"
characteristic of the works of conventional book historians.[2] This sensitivity
enables him to appreciate the long history and far-reaching impact on print
culture of woodblock printing in China and Japan. The same appreciation of
the role of illustrations in European print culture is also evident in Elizabeth
L. Eisenstein's classic study *The Printing Press as an Agent of Change* (*PPAC*),
published a little over twenty-five years ago. Eisenstein's insight warrants special commemoration in the light of recent interest in visual culture in print.
The study of printed images and book illustrations demonstrates the importance of the woodblock in producing images. It presents a timely opportunity
to revisit the narrative of Gutenberg, which has been predominantly logocentric and exclusively typological.

The narrative of the invention of movable-type printing by Gutenberg needs
to be reinvented not because "the name of Gutenberg does not appear on the

---

1. Roger Chartier, "Gutenberg Revisited from the East," *Late Imperial China* 17.1 (1996): 2.

2. Roger Chartier, *The Cultural Uses of Print in Early Modern France,* trans. Lydia G. Cochrane
(Princeton, NJ: Princeton Univ. Press, 1987), and *The Cultural Origins of the French Revolution,* trans.
Lydia G. Cochrane (Durham, NC: Duke Univ. Press, 1991).

imprint of any book"[3] or because he was only one of several European printers who claimed to be the inventor[4] but because the narrative of the history of printing in Europe has been skewed so that many significant aspects of the cultural history of the book — in Europe and in China — have been obscured. To reinvent the Gutenberg narrative is to be "wary of such ethnocentrism" with which Western historians have judged woodblock printing "against the standard of Gutenberg's invention."[5] To rescue the role of woodblock printing in European printing after the mid-1450s, is to call into question the idea that movable-type printing was the only technology capable of bringing about revolutionary change in Europe and the idea that woodblock printing had not brought any significant change to China and East Asia.[6] Conventional accounts of the history of printing in Europe systematically privilege movable-type printing as a major factor in creating conditions of modernity: the spread of the Enlightenment, the dissemination of scientific knowledge, the rise of national languages and literatures, and the growth and spread of nationalism, as well as the expansion of critical publics that were crucial to the development of representative forms of government. I would argue that this standard narrative has systematically disparaged the importance of woodcut before and after the invention of movable-type printing, resulting in a profoundly logocentric approach to the study of the history of printing.

There are, however, exceptions. Eisenstein points out that woodcut engraving used to print illustrations was "an innovation which eventually helped to revolutionize technical literature by introducing 'exactly repeatable pictorial statements' into all kinds of reference works."[7] Even though she refers only to "woodcut engraving," not specifically to woodblock printing, the two are

3. Lucien Febvre and Henri-Jean Martin, *The Coming of the Book: The Impact of Printing, 1450–1800,* ed. Geoffrey Nowell-Smith and David Wootton, trans. David Gerard (London: New Left Books, 1976), 56.

4. In *The Nature of the Book: Print and Knowledge in the Making* (Chicago: Univ. of Chicago Press, 1998), Adrian Johns devotes a chapter, "Faust and the Pirates: The Cultural Construction of the Printing Revolution," to competing accounts of the origins and early history of print. According to Johns, the construction of these accounts of the invention of the movable-type printing press underscores on one level the struggle between printers and royal power over the control of printing rights. Johns notes as well that "in practice the history of the press was being written by printers, booksellers, and hacks, by antiquarians and amateurs" (344–5).

5. Chartier, "Gutenberg Revisited," 2.

6. There is a growing literature on the social and cultural impact of print in China before the nineteenth century when European movable-type technology was introduced. See, for example, Dorothy Ko, *Teachers of the Inner Chamber: Women and Culture in Seventeenth-Century China* (Stanford, CA: Stanford Univ. Press, 1994); Robert E. Hegel, *Reading Illustrated Fiction in Late Imperial China* (Stanford, CA: Stanford Univ. Press, 1998); Kai-wing Chow, *Publishing, Culture, and Power in Early Modern China* (Stanford, CA: Stanford Univ. Press, 2004).

7. Eisenstein, *PPAC,* 53.

indistinguishable in their capacity to multiply texts and images. I return to this point later in the chapter. First, I identify the specific roles woodblock printing had played before Gutenberg's movable type and how it continued to be an integral part of the history of European printing until the twentieth century. Then I address another widely held misconception about the history of Chinese printing, that movable type did not develop into a practical printing technology and was abandoned early on because of the large number of Chinese characters. Contrary to the common view, not only did Chinese printers experiment with different materials in making movable type (*huozi*, meaning "living or moving characters"), but beginning in the sixteenth century, the number of publishers using movable-type printing also grew despite the predominance of woodblock printing in the Ming (1368–1644) and Qing (1644–1911) periods.

Xylography: The Orphan of European Printing

Woodblock printing, or xylography, has been ignored by the narratives of the history of Western printing. In most standard histories of western European printing, the advent of print is fixed at the point when Gutenberg printed a Bible with movable type no later than 1456.[8] While all scholars of the book know that woodblock printing was used in Europe several decades before 1456, few regard what have been called "block books" as the ancestor of the Gutenberg Bible. "If the first block-books appeared before the invention of printing, can we then establish a filiation between xylography and the printed book?" Lucien Febvre and Henri-Jean Martin ask this question in their classic *The Coming of the Book,* only to answer in the negative.[9] It is worthy of note that in contrasting xylography" with "the printed book," they do not regard the former as a true printing method.

Many standard accounts of European printing take pains to disown woodblock as the precursor of movable-type printing. In a general survey of the history of European printing, Colin Clair explains his dismissal of block books: "One should bear in mind that the purpose of the block-book had nothing to do with the dissemination of literature. It was merely an extension of the single leaf block print aimed at providing the illiterate with visual concepts of the Christian religion. These early block-books are therefore either Biblical in subject or moralizing discourses. . . . The one exception to this general

---

8. S. H. Steinberg, *Five Hundred Years of Printing,* new ed., rev. John Trevitt (London: British Library; New Castle, DE: Oak Knoll Press, 1996), 5.

9. Febvre and Martin, *Coming of the Book,* 48.

rule seems to have been the Latin grammar of Donatus." [10] Nothing betrays more unequivocally the common bias against woodblock printing than these remarks. Was not the first book printed by Gutenberg with movable type the Bible? Were not most of the books printed in Europe in the fifteenth and sixteenth centuries devoted to religious and moralizing discourses? How then was the intention of block-book printers different from that of those using movable type?

Xylography, compared with typography, is considered a primitive and inferior method of reproducing text, incapable of producing large editions. Some scholars point out that the woodblock was replaced by metal movable type because of the inferior capacity of xylography in producing large runs to "supply the educational needs of Renaissance Europe." [11] This view distorts the actual practice of movable-type printing in the first three hundred years of European printing because it is a teleological explanation. As Febvre and Martin have shown, down to the eighteenth century the average print run of books in most genres remained small. Only religious books and a few language tools would reach editions of 1,500 or 2,000 copies. If textbooks and chapbooks are excluded, even in the eighteenth century "print runs remained comparatively modest." [12] The majority of European printers would have found the capabilities of xylography more than adequate in meeting the need of small runs for most books.

Another technological explanation that disowns woodblock printing as a forefather of the movable-types printing press is also advanced by Febvre and Martin in *The Coming of the Book*. They insist that "the technique of the wood-cut did not in any sense inspire printing, which was the result of a quite different technique." [13] They argue that since wood engravers were "ignorant of the techniques of casting and making fonts from type metal,"

---

10. Clair, *A History of European Printing* (New York: Academic Press, 1976), 3. Clair's view, however, is simply an echo of a view long established among scholars of printing. Otto W. Fuhrmann, for example, comments: "The purpose of the block books was not the dissemination or preservation of literature, but the pictorial dramatization to semiliterate people of legends and miracle stories, of moralizing tendency, with explanatory captions and brief texts; their technique was the Chinese method, suitable for this kind of work in which the text played only a minor role." Fuhrmann, "The Invention of Printing," in *A History of The Printed Book*, ed. Lawrence C. Wroth (New York: Limited Editions Club, 1938), 35.

11. George Walton Williams, *The Craft of Printing and the Publication of Shakespeare's Works* (Washington, DC: Folger Shakespeare Library, 1985), 20.

12. According to Febvre and Martin, a few runs at the end of the fifteenth century reached 1,500. At the end of the sixteenth century, a few Bible editions were as large as 3,000. A Latin-French dictionary printed in the sixteenth century was pirated in a run of 6,500. Even though Voltaire's *Essai sur les moeurs* was published in an edition of 7,000, publishers in the eighteenth century "hesitated to order really large editions." Febvre and Martin, *Coming of the Book*, 216–20.

13. Ibid., 46.

"the printed book cannot be thought of as a refinement introduced by wood engravers."[14] It is indisputable that the techniques of making fonts by casting metal type were not the same as wood engraving. But this explanation locates the essential conditions of printing not in the effect of multiplying texts but in terms of the specific method of reproducing them. As such, their definition logically excludes woodblock printing as a method of printing. But several pages later, they acknowledge that those printers in Mainz, Haarlem, and Avignon had been experimenting with the movable metal types "between 1430 and 1450 when the success of the xylographs had demonstrated the utility and prospects of such an invention."[15] Here they seem to acknowledge that woodblock printing did inspire European printers' experiment with metal movable types.

At least one scholar familiar with stereotype printing has recognized the logical inspiration woodblock printing offered to early European printers. George Kubler points out that from printing "one-piece wood-cuts to the idea of printing with movable letters is indeed only one step; if one visualizes the printing block cut up in single letters, it becomes evident that one can assemble these letters to one's liking in other ways and thereby form a new text."[16] Indeed according to the common myth recounted by Kubler, that is what Gutenberg did in the beginning: " Out of a piece of hard wood, Gutenberg sawed some thousand tiny blocks. . . . After having thus furnished himself with a number of the letters of the alphabet, he placed whole words tighter, arranged them in lines on a string, until they form a page. . . . It was the Lord's Prayer with which he made his first attempt at printing with movable types."[17]

A recent study of the development of printing in China, Korea, Japan, and Europe has demonstrated that once woodblock printing was in use, printers experimented with movable type, first using wood movable type, then metal types. The same stages of development were seen in China, Korea, and Europe. Printers developed clay, tin, and copper types in China in the eleventh through the thirteenth centuries and in Korea in the thirteenth and fourteenth centuries. To argue that the problems with which European printers struggled before the invention of metal movable types were unique is untenable.[18] The experiment with movable types in China as in Europe

---

14. Ibid., 48–9.

15. Ibid., 54.

16. Kubler, *A New History of Stereotyping* (New York: J. J. Little and Ives, 1941), 16.

17. Ibid., 19.

18. Pan Jixing, *Zhongguo, Han'guo yu Ouzhou zao qi yin shua shu di bi jiao* (A comparative study of early printing technology in China, Korea, and Europe) (Beijing: Ke xue chu ban she, 1997), 61–88, 120–30, 76–86, 183–96.

was prompted by the desire to lower the cost of printing. That movable types were developed in China, Korea, and Europe after block printing came into use is evidence for a universal set of problems printers had to grapple with in their attempt to improve the quality of print and to lower its cost. I have more to say about woodblock printing in fifteenth-century Europe in a later section.

By making the experiments a uniquely European development, Febvre and Martin try to deny a technological connection between woodblock and movable-type printing, forestalling any possible theory linking Gutenberg's invention to Chinese printing. It is not possible to present a discussion to refute their argument here. Instead, it is sufficient to say that the current dominant view as exemplified by Febvre and Martin is but one view in the controversy over whether the Gutenberg printing method owed anything to Chinese printing. Dissenting views have simply lost their battle without the participation of scholars who are familiar with the history of both European and Chinese printing. To deny any connection with woodblock printing is to preclude any linkage with Chinese influence. This is the ideological background that prompted Febvre and Martin and others to explain so painstakingly why the Gutenberg method was not inspired by woodblock printing.[19]

Before we continue, it is necessary to discuss the usages of some terms in the narratives of European printing. In most works on European printing, the term "woodcut" is not synonymous with woodblock. Woodcut is generally taken to mean an illustration or picture carved on a piece of wood. In the European discourse on printing, "woodblock" has assumed a specific meaning. Woodblock printing refers to the printing of an entire page, consisting of illustration or text or both, from a single block of wood. This distinction between woodcut and woodblock, I would argue, is insignificant in terms of the condition of carving symbols permanently on a wood block. The symbols fixed in the block—whether a full page or a part thereof—can be letters or scripts or nonliterary icons. The essential features of woodblock printing are that the printing block is made of wood and that immovable symbols—text or otherwise—are carved into the block. Size, therefore, is not a relevant element in distinguishing woodcut from woodblock. Since the page or block is carved and can be stored away, its advantage is its reusability. In these senses, woodcut and woodblock can be regarded as the same method of multiplying

---

19. Thomas Francis Carter documented the views of scholars who argued for Chinese influence on Gutenberg in *The Invention of Printing in China and Its Spread Westward*, 2nd ed., rev. L. Carrington Goodrich (New York: Ronald Press, 1955). Febvre and Martin refer to this work without an outright refutation of the evidence Carter presents (*Coming of the Book*, 334 n. 27). For the antecedents to Febvre and Martin's argument, see Carter, *Invention of Printing in China*, 207 n. 2.

symbols, whether text or images, and therefore wood engraving and woodcut should not be treated as different printing methods. They are only different methods of carving, not printing. Whether one is printing a full page or part of a page, insofar as text and illustrations are permanently carved into the wood block, the printing method is block printing. For the same reason, whether an entire page or only part of a page is printed from movable type, the method is still the same. As discussed in the next section, these two methods as they were practiced in Europe were not mutually exclusive.

The Bifurcated History of European Printing: Woodblock Printing as an Art

As I have been indicating, the role of woodblock printing as an object of study has been greatly depreciated in the history of European printing. Historians often mention block printing as a crude method promptly replaced by the more sophisticated Gutenberg printing press. Woodblock printing is misrepresented in European histories of printing by two narrative strategies. First, woodblock printing is depicted as most suitable for producing images, and not an effective method for producing letters and texts. Second, even in producing images, it is depicted as inferior to copperplate engraving.

The first strategy has resulted in, or facilitated, the establishment of the study of woodcut and block books as a form of art history. The study of printed images in the fifteenth and sixteenth centuries in Europe has been the specialty of art historians, and the woodcut is long established as a form of art. This fact is reflected in the magisterial study of woodcuts by Arthur Hind, keeper of prints and drawings at the British Museum in the mid twentieth century. The discursive framework in which he undertook his two-volume study of the history of woodcut from the fifteenth through the twentieth centuries is that of his field of study, art history.[20] Thus, the relegating of woodblock printing to art history has created a bifurcated approach to European print culture.

This undesirable division has long influenced how historians study the Reformation, for example. As Christiane Anderson points out, "German Reformation broadsheets and pamphlets have figured among the stepchildren of historical research. Composed of image and text in a variety of combinations, these polemical tracts, when studied at all, have generally been considered in terms of either the image or the text, but rarely both at once." Studies based

---

20. Arthur M. Hind, *An Introduction to a History of Woodcut, with a Detailed Survey of Work in the Fifteenth Century* (London: Constable and Co., 1935).

on separating the image from the text fail to appreciate the "highly symbolic and often humorous meanings of these broadsheets and thus provide a vivid glimpse of the daily concerns and larger social issues of the audience they were calculated to address." Anderson notes that because of the low literacy rate, ranging from 10 percent to 30 percent in the German towns and no more than 5 percent in the German-speaking lands as a whole, "the major burden of publicizing Protestant views fell upon nonliterate means of communication, upon oral and visual culture. Printed propaganda was either read aloud to the illiterate by those who could read or was transmitted visually. Woodcuts manifestly played a crucial role in the spread of Lutheran ideas." [21] Given these facts, the logocentric approach to the history of printing needs to be challenged.

The second strategy that misrepresents woodblock printing is the view that woodblock was incapable of producing refined and precise scientific illustrations. This strategy has produced a skewed account by completely eclipsing woodblock printing in the history of European printing. The privileging of technology in our modern hierarchy of knowledge has marginalized any intellectual endeavor that is not regarded as science or technology. Movable-type printing in European consciousness is regarded as a technology, but woodblock printing has been treated as an art or craft. The relocation of the history of woodblock printing to the field of art history has resulted in its erasure as a printing technology, obscuring the important role of printed images in the early phase of European printing. As Eberhard Konig has noted, "In the study of the fifteenth-century book a peculiar distinction is still maintained: art historians study decoration in the handwritten book but pay less attention to the printed illustrations in printed books or to printed illustrations." [22]

The relegation of illustrations or woodcuts to the domain of art reinforces the idea that woodcuts are incapable of presenting precise scientific information. Until recently this bias was taken for granted in most works on the history of the woodcut and publishing in late Renaissance Europe. In the introduction to *The Art of the Woodcut in the Italian Renaissance Book*, Bennett Gilbert displays these long-held assumptions about the advantages of metal engraving: "Finally, toward the end of the period there arose a demand for a

---

21. Anderson, "Popular Imagery in German Reformation Broadsheets," in *Print and Culture in the Renaissance: Essays on the Advent of Printing in Europe,* ed. Gerald P. Tyson and Sylvia S. Wagonheim (Newark: Univ. of Delaware Press; London and Toronto: Associated Univ. Presses, 1986), 120–1.

22. Konig, "New Perspectives on the History of Mainz Printing: A Fresh Look at Illuminated Imprints," in *Printing the Written Word: The Social History of Books, circa 1450–1520,* ed. Sandra Hindman (Ithaca, NY: Cornell Univ. Press, 1991), 143.

precision and level of details in technical illustration that woodcutting could not produce. . . . As the printed text took on the job of preserving data, and with this teaching the skills of architecture, music, artillery, etc., it required the enhanced precision and detail possible only with engraving in metal." [23]

Yet Gilbert's statement about the inferior ability of wood engraving compared with metal is at odds with the evidence. The choice of metal types and the growing use of metal engraving during the sixteenth, seventeenth, and eighteenth centuries were the result of a convergence of many conditions, including limited papermaking technology and the adoption of the press to increase pressure in the transference of ink. European paper, produced by the laid method, had an uneven surface that could not produce a good impression from a fine wood engraving and thus required the use of the press. Woodblock often broke under the pressure from the press. Chinese paper, in contrast, was, as Theodore DeVinne observes, "soft, thin, and pliable, and a quick absorbent of fluid ink." It did not require the pressure of the printing press but only the application of a brush to transfer the ink successfully. "If American book papers were substituted for Chinese paper, the process of printing by the brush and with fluid ink would be found impracticable. . . . The brush would not give enough pressure to transfer the ink." [24] Although the handmade paper of early modern Europe was far superior to that of later, nineteenth-century machine-made paper, DeVinne's point still holds true for the early period; it was undoubtedly the strength of copperplates under pressure that prompted their use rather than a greater ability to produce precise illustrations. After its spread among European printers in the sixteenth century, metal engraving did not completely eliminate the use of woodcut in producing illustrations or other types of images. Metal engraving had its own disadvantages: metal plates took longer to produce and were more expensive.

As the skill of European woodcutters grew more sophisticated, woodblock was adequate to reproduce most scientific illustrations. Gilbert's view of the inferiority of woodblock in printing precise technical illustrations is at odds with that of Elizabeth Eisenstein. Her study stresses the role of printing in the dissemination of knowledge and ideas; she refers to the "significant role played by printed illustration in anatomy texts" and to "how illustrating text books helped to guide scientific observation." [25] Eisenstein points out that woodcut engravings used to print illustrations were "an innovation which

---

23. Gilbert, *The Art of the Woodcut in the Italian Renaissance Book* (New York: Grolier Club; Los Angeles: UCLA Special Collections, 1995), 7.

24. DeVinn, *The Invention of Printing* (1876; repr., Detroit, MI: Book Tower, 1969), 115.

25. Eisenstein, *PPAC*, 266–7, 485–6.

eventually helped to revolutionize technical literature by introducing 'exactly repeatable pictorial statements' into all kinds of reference works." Stressing the interdependence of text and images in conveying knowledge, she notes: "The fact that identical images, maps and diagrams could be viewed simultaneously by scattered readers constituted a kind of communication revolution in itself." These observations on the importance of illustrations led her to conclude that "even though block-print and letterpress may have originated as separate innovations and were initially used for diverse purposes, . . . the two techniques soon became intertwined."[26] Eisenstein's view of the communicative role of illustration in scientific publications, however, is not fully fleshed out and is being called into question by philosophers and historians of science,[27] though her observation of the important role of woodblock illustration in the production of scientific knowledge remains accurate.

Scientific illustrations have long been treated as a form of art. Until Thomas Kuhn's study of the production of scientific knowledge, philosophers and historians of science had considered abstraction and theory the ultimate concern of scientists. As pointed by out by Ronald N. Giere, under the influence of logical empiricism, science had been thought to be axiomatic systems. The proper modes of representation of genuine scientific knowledge are linguistic and logical. Within this framework of logical empiricism, nonlinguistic modes of representation such as pictures and diagrams play a negligible role, if they are accorded one at all. Visualization and its graphic tools have received little attention from historians and philosophers of science.[28] As David Topper has remarked, "Scientific illustration is customarily viewed as a form of art. Only recently, and in a few disparate sources, has scientific illustration been studied as a branch of science — as a means of conveying information." But the information conveyed by scientific illustration always depends on "styles, motifs, or conventions from the 'fine arts.'"[29]

This bifurcated approach to the study of European books is misguided in the light of new scholarship in many areas. From several perspectives, it is imperative to abandon this bifurcation in order to understand fully the impact of illustrations and all the iconic elements in the early modern book

---

26. Ibid., 53–4. She refers to publishers' extensive practice of recycling of illustrations and images cut on woodblocks (258–9).

27. For a discussion of the complexity of the relationship between illustration and text in scientific books, see Brian S. Baigrie, ed., *Picturing Knowledge: Historical and Philosophical Problems Concerning the Use of Art in Science* (Toronto: Univ. of Toronto Press, 1996).

28. Giere, "Visual Models and Scientific Judgment," in Baigrie, *Picturing Knowledge,* 269–302.

29. Topper, "Towards an Epistemology of Scientific Illustration," in Baigrie, *Picturing Knowledge,* 246–7.

in Europe. Historians of science, literary historians, historians of the book, and cultural historians of various strains have examined the diverse roles that images have played in the production and dissemination of knowledge, the marketing and organization of books, and the shaping and spreading of attitudes and sensibilities.

Those historians of science attentive to the illustrations produced by woodcuts in science books have warned against the assumption that illustrations merely provide useful information supplementing texts. In his study of "naturalistic illustrations," Bert S. Hall has pointed out that borrowing woodblocks from other works to illustrate a different work was common in the sixteenth century.[30] This transposition between text and illustrations in books raises an important issue regarding the critical role of the economics of commercial publishing in the production of knowledge. The complex role of woodblock illustrations in the production and dissemination of scientific knowledge casts doubt on the uncritical acceptance of the primacy of movable-type printing and the discursive denial of the sustained importance of woodblock printing.

Scholars interested in the economic and cultural dimensions of European publishing have found illustrations to be an invaluable source of information about printing practices. Illustrations and iconic elements in the book have become an important source for understanding publishing strategies as well as the significance of patronage for publishers and the various forms of patronage publishers sought to secure.[31] Woodblock illustrations have been analyzed by cultural historians as an important factor in the molding of attitudes and shaping of practices.

Roger Chartier's study of the images depicting death scenes in *Ars moriendi*, for example, has shown the important role of printed images in the study of attitudes toward death in the fifteenth and sixteenth centuries.[32] The study of woodcut illustrations is no longer the exclusive subject of the art historians as scholars in various disciplines have expanded these objects of investiga-

---

30. Hall, "The Didactic and the Elegant: Some Thoughts on Scientific and Technological Illustrations in the Middle Ages and Renaissance," in Baigrie, *Picturing Knowledge,* 19.

31. English and foreign publishers in the sixteenth century used various iconic elements associated with Saint George and England to market their books and to create reputations for themselves. See Yu-Chiao Wang, "The Image of St. George and the Dragon: Promoting Books and Book Producers in Pre-Reformation England," *The Library,* ser. 7, 5.4 (2004): 370–401. For the study of patronage through analysis of publishers' iconic devices, see John A. Buchtel, "Book Dedications and the Death of a Patron: The Memorial Engraving in Chapman's *Homer,*" *Book History* 7 (2004): 1–29.

32. Chartier, "Texts and Images: The Arts of Dying, 1450–1600," in *Cultural Uses of Print,* 32–70.

tion beyond the concerns of art history. In recent years the rapid growth of scholarship on visual elements, especially illustrations in books published in the early modern period, calls for a re-examination of our standard narrative of the history of European printing, an account that privileges words over images, texts over illustrations, and movable-type printing over woodblock printing. The time is ripe for the appreciation of the impact of woodblock printing on the transformation of European culture and practices.

European Printing: A Mixture of Xylography and Typography

As Febvre and Martin have remarked, in *Biblia pauperum,* the Apocalypse, Lives of the Virgin, the Passion, and the *Ars moriendi,* "the text was of equal importance to the illustrations."[33] These "block-book[s] with text," as one nineteenth-century scholar called them, continued to be printed more than a half century after metal movable type became the dominant method of reproducing text.[34] Some scholars point out that the printing of block books did not cease entirely until nearly sixty years after the invention of movable type.[35] Still others observe that woodblock printing as a method of reproducing playing cards and illustrated broadsheets continued well into the eighteenth century.[36] But few consider that even though block-books — books printed exclusively from woodblocks — ceased to be produced in the early sixteenth century, woodblock printing was not completely replaced. It is essential to differentiate between the two practices: the production of block books and the use of woodblocks in printing literary and iconic symbols. The cessation of the former did not mean the discontinuation of the latter.

Even though Febvre and Martin deny any connection between woodblock printing and metal movable-type printing from a technological perspective, when they begin to discuss illustration, they do not fail to mention woodcuts and wood engravings: "Originally we saw that the illustrated book, successor to the block book, had the same aim and the same clientele."[37] For them, the "illustrated book" is a book printed with movable metal types and its illustra-

---

33. Febvre and Martin, *Coming of the Book,* 47.

34. DeVinne, *Invention of Printing,* 251.

35. It is generally recognized that the latest block book was printed at Venice by Andrea Vavassore in 1510. Frederick W. Goudy, *Typologia: Studies in Type Design and Type Making, with Comments on the Invention of Typography, the First Types, Legibility, and Fine Printing* (Berkeley and Los Angeles: Univ. of California Press, 1940), chap. 3; Steinberg, *Five Hundred Years of Printing,* 3–4; DeVinne, *Invention of Printing,* 251.

36. Steinberg, *Five Hundred Years of Printing,* 70.

37. Febvre and Martin, *Coming of the Book,* 96.

tions printed from woodcuts. The continuity Febvre and Martin recognize between the block book and the woodcuts in the "illustrated book" is limited to only the purpose of printing and the targeted reader, and does not extend to the technology of reproduction. But, to repeat, woodcuts are no different from woodblock that produced both text and illustrations of a block book. Such a practice is more accurately characterized as a mixture of woodblock and movable-type printing.

Woodblock printing had simply become an integral part of European printing. Here we are referring to the continued use of woodblock to print images and texts on the same page in a single book. There are two points that need to be underscored. First, text in books printed after the mid-1450s was not printed exclusively with metal types. Texts fixed permanently in wood blocks were not confined to initials, colophons, publishers' trademarks, coats of arms, title pages, borders, and writer's marks. Exceptionally large fonts and calligraphy were also printed from woodblocks. If we expand our objects of study beyond books, the role of woodblock in producing text was even greater. Broadsides, for example, often were printed from woodblocks.[38] Second, woodcuts continued to be used extensively for illustrations or iconic decorations. Nonetheless, a general division of labor was adopted by most commercial publishers: woodcuts for illustrations and movable metal type for text. If viewed from the perspectives of both publisher and reader, the initials, page borders, and illustrations not only enhanced the visual appeal of the book while providing reading aids and additional information on the text but compensated for the loss of the aesthetics associated with calligraphic writing of manuscripts. These visual elements helped to mitigate the monotony of uniform letters of a page printed with movable type.

After Gutenberg's perfection of the movable-type printing press, printers for various reasons continued to depend on woodblock printing for the production of illustration as well as texts.[39] In the sixteenth century the dissemination of scientific and geographical knowledge depended on extensive use of woodcuts. The first edition of Nicholas Copernicus's *De Revolutionibus orbium coelestium,* published by Rheticus, contained 142 woodcut illustrations. Moreover, the small and large initials that open the chapters were printed with xylography.[40] The books published by the Dutch printer

---

38. See, for examples, the German Reformation broadsheets included in Anderson, "Popular Imagery in German Reformation Broadsheets," 120–47.

39. For examples, see *A Library of Woodcut Books of the 16th Century: Illustrations by the Famous Old Masters* (Vienna: Gilhofer & Ranschburg, 1930).

40. Owen Gingerich, "Copernicus's *De Revolutionibus:* An Example of Renaissance Scientific Printing," in Tyson and Wagonheim, *Print and Culture in the Renaissance,* 55–6.

Peter Apian (Petrus Apianus, 1495–1552) provide some of the best examples of the contribution of woodblock to the spread of geographical knowledge. His map of the world in *Cosmosgraphiae* printed in 1524 had place names that could not have been printed with movable type. They are permanent text, engraved on woodcut.

Even though most texts were printed with metal movable type after the mid-1450s, printers often found it convenient and practical to carve letters into woodcut illustrations. In illustrations where letters appeared in a curved space, in a ribbon style, it was particularly difficult to typeset letters.[41] Many illustrations in books printed in Antwerp included both engraved and type-set texts.[42] In many instances it was extremely difficult, if not impossible, to typeset letters inside woodcut images. When text was needed in a nonlinear space in images such as the human body in medical manuals, carving text as a permanent part of the illustration would be more practical than typesetting letters.[43] The anatomical diagram "Double Skeleton Print," printed by Peter de Wale in 1530, is a good example of the need to engrave text as part of the image. The frontispiece of William Tyndale's English translation of the New Testament (1536) contained typeset letters as well as letters carved into a block whose large border was filled with images.[44] Thus, not only images but text continued to be printed from woodblock.

In his study of the Renaissance book, Martin Davies praises the achievement of *Hypnerotomachia Polophili,* printed by the Venetian printer Aldus Manutius. "The high distinction of *Hypnerotomachia* lies in its blending of type, woodcut capitals and woodcut illustrations in a harmonious whole."[45] This characterization of Aldus's *Hypnerotomachia* applies generally to books printed after the invention of metal movable type. European books were printed with both metal movable type and woodblocks. Even though woodblocks were used primarily to produce illustrations and other iconic elements, it was not uncommon to find texts permanently engraved in the woodblock.

---

41. For examples of such letters in fifteenth-century books, see Hind, *History of Woodcut;* Martin Davies, *Aldus Manutius: Printer and Publisher of Renaissance Venice* (Malibu, CA: J. Paul Getty Museum, 1995), 41. For examples in sixteenth-century books, see Jan van der Stock, *Printing Images in Antwerp: The Introduction of Printmaking in a City: Fifteenth Century to 1585* (Rotterdam: Sound and Vision Interactive, 1998), 79, 80; and Steinberg, *Five Hundred Years of Printing,* 50, 66.

42. For examples of such illustrations, see Van der Stock, *Printing Images in Antwerp,* 61–3, 68, 75, 79–80, 82, 84–5; and Steinberg, *Five Hundred Years of Printing,* 50–1.

43. For examples of such illustrations, see Hind, *History of Woodcut,* 595, 673, 680, 684, 704, 727.

44. Steinberg, *Five Hundred Years of Printing,* 49–50.

45. Davies, *Aldus Manutius,* 17.

The End-Grain Wood Engraving Method
in the Nineteenth Century

Metal engraving surely allowed for the production of very detailed and very fine illustrations. But this process was much more expensive and took longer to produce than wood engraving. An even greater disadvantage was the need for special handling. Metal engravings could not be printed side by side with letter types. In contrast, wood engraving was fast and inexpensive. Wood engraving, I would argue, is a refined method of woodblock printing. Both the idea of fixing an image with or without text and the material on which they are produced are the same as in woodblock printing. Wood engraving is therefore an improvement on woodblock printing that cannot be possibly considered a development of the movable-type method. Xylography continued to be a part of European printing in the eighteenth and nineteenth centuries. In fact, with the development of a new method of wood engraving and advances in papermaking, woodblock became widely popular among British printers.

Thomas Bewick (1753–1828) developed a method of woodcutting that produced much finer engraving in the latter half of the eighteenth century. By cutting on the end-grain, rather than on the plank of a woodblock, Bewick was able to produce finely detailed woodcuts that could endure much better than traditionally produced woodcuts when subjected to the pressure of the printing press. The improvement of wood engraving by Thomas Bewick allowed publishers to print letterpress type side by side with images on woodblock so that "image and text could be attractively and relevantly integrated on the page." [46] But there was another factor that contributed significantly to the success of Bewick's new engraving method, the adoption of a new type of paper—wove paper, which provided a smooth surface. Because of the rough print surface of laid paper, printers printing from copperplates in the late 1700s began to use wove paper.

Before the invention of wove paper, printers used laid paper whose surface had minute ripples, which created irregularities. The British printer and type founder John Baskerville had been dissatisfied with the uneven surface of laid paper. His training in japanning and metal-work prior to his becoming a printer must have exposed him to Chinese wallpaper on wove stock, made

---

46. Michael Hancher, "Gazing at *The Imperial Dictionary*," *Book History* 1 (1998): 156. With wood, the height of the block can be aligned with the metal types, whereas metal plates were very thin compared with the metal types. The discrepancy in height required separate handling of the illustration printed from metal plates.

from cloth mesh. Wove paper was first manufactured in Europe by the British papermaker James Whatman in 1756, and the first book printed in Europe on wove paper was subsequently produced in 1757 in England. By 1779 or 1780, wove paper was being made in France as well. By 1805 wove paper had supplanted laid paper for many printing purposes in Europe.[47] With the new technique of end-grain wood engraving and the new wove paper, many printers after Bewick used woodblock engraving as "an increasingly precise and mechanical means for printing facsimile images."[48] Woodcuts continued to be used by various presses down to the twentieth century. Notable among them were the Essex House Press (1898–1901) of C. R. Ashbee, the Eragny Press (1894–1914), the Doves Press (1900–17), the Ashendene Press (1894–1935), and the Golden Cockerel Press (1920–61).[49]

The Imperial Dictionary published by Blackie and Sons, a British publishing house with branches in Glasgow and London, contained some two thousand images produced by wood engravings. This dictionary was the first to bring "visual imagery so heavily to bear on lexical definition." It provided a model that dominated the manufacture of general-interest dictionaries, "forcing the problematic question whether, or how, visual reproduction can indeed elucidate verbal concepts."[50] End-grain wood engraving was the prevalent method in England as well as in France.[51] Wood engraving, according to Gerard Curtis, "dominated reproductive processes for most of the century." The refinement of woodblock printing enabled magazines such as the *Penny Illustrated Magazine, Weekly Chronicles,* and *Illustrated London News* to boost their sales. "These illustrated journals were one of the great cultural achievements of the Victorian period." As Curtis points out, "woodblock and typographic pressing not only technologically wedded the two lines [that is, the lines of written text and those of drawn images], but fostered a revival of the graphic union between image and word."[52] Woodblock printing continued to be a major method for printing illustrations in Europe through the twentieth centuries. It was not replaced completely until computerization of printing rendered movable type, copperplates, and woodblock obsolete.[53]

---

47. Jacob Kainen, "Why Bewick Succeeded: A Note on the History of Wood Engraving," *United States National Museum Bulletin* 218 (1959): 192–4. The first book on wove paper was a Latin edition of Virgil produced by Baskerville, but part of the book was still printed on laid paper.

48. Hancher, "Gazing at *The Imperial Dictionary,*" 156.

49. Steinberg, *Five Hundred Years of Printing,* 175–87.

50. Hancher, "Gazing at *The Imperial Dictionary,*" 158–9.

51. Kainen, "Why Bewick Succeeded," 192.

52. Curtis, *Visual Words: Art and the Material Book in Victorian England* (Aldershot, Hants.: Ashgate, 2002), 16–17.

53. Kainen, "Why Bewick Succeeded," 188. The recent abandonment of woodblock by modern printers can be seen in the large number of woodblock letters and images that are for sale on eBay.

Misconceptions about Chinese Printing Technology

Just as European printing is associated with movable type, Chinese printing is thought to be confined to woodblock printing. One is amazed at the ignorance about the history of printing in China found even among experts on the history of printing. A newly revised edition of S. H. Steinberg's popular history of printing states that for Chinese printers "the block-book had for centuries been the only known medium of printing." [54] In the first chapter of *A History of European Printing*, titled "The Birth and Infancy of Printing," Colin Clair refers in a footnote to the invention of movable-type printing in China in the eleventh century, opining: "but no development was *possible* [emphasis added] at that time owing to the peculiar characteristics of the Chinese language." [55] Clair and others assume that only phonetic languages are suitable for the development of the modern form of movable-type printing.[56]

The discussion of Chinese printing in Febvre and Martin's widely acclaimed book presents an elaborate discussion of this "problem." The section's author, M. R. Guignard, is interested in explaining how woodblock printing was an obstacle to the development of metal-type printing. She narrates the history of the development of printing in China as an example of failure to overcome the technical problems encountered in the development of movable-type printing. The explanation focuses on the enormous cost and the technical difficulties involved. First, she assumes that the huge number of Chinese characters required capital investment beyond the reach of private printers. But the only example she gives is the exceptionally voluminous project of *Gujin tushu jicheng* (Compendium of books past and present), an "encyclopedia"

---

54. Steinberg, *Five Hundred Years of Printing*, 70.

55. Clair, *History of European Printing*, 1.

56. The same argument is put forth in James L. Huffman's explanation for the abandonment of movable-type printing by Japanese publishers in the seventeenth century. It is well known that Toyotomi Hideyoshi had books printed from copper movable types captured from Korea. And Ieyasu reportedly gave 300,000 pieces of wooden movable types to the Ashikaga family and had in his possession 200,000 copper type cast in 1614. Despite this early use of a "new technology, movable type" by the shogunate, Huffman explains that "the complexity of the *kanji* [Chinese characters] used in Japanese writing and the aesthetic sterility of materials produced by interchangeable type fonts disturbed most Tokugawa-era printers, so after a few years they threw out the printing presses, just as they discarded the foreign guns and religions, and shifted back to the traditional slate and woodblock techniques." Huffman, *Creating a Public: People and Press in Meiji Japan* (Honolulu: Univ. of Hawai'i Press, 1997), 20. There is no question that the relatively larger number of the Chinese characters would present problems to the printers. But what is perhaps the more important reason is not addressed. How economical was movable type compared with woodblock? How much more investment did a commercial printer need to set up a movable-type printing shop in comparison with a woodblock printing shop? The factors of cost and scale of economy are not addressed.

commissioned by the Kangxi emperor in 1720.[57] She takes pains to point out that it was printed with ten thousand copper characters, engraved, rather than cast. But the cost problem, she says, was too great to be overcome:

> No individual could have financed such an enterprise, or engaged such a work force, or kept such a vast number of characters in a usable order. Further, the fluid quality of the ink used in China hardly lent itself to printing in metal; and lastly, the book was unattractive on aesthetic and sentimental grounds, since it deprived the reader of the pleasure of fine calligraphy and of the style of such a calligrapher working in *harmony* [emphasis added] with his text. Woodblock engraving and block-printing, by contrast, make possible a faithful reflection of the calligrapher's style. . . . [P]ublication in China was often subsidized by private individuals who *insisted* [emphasis added] on traditional wood-block method.[58]

The author has considered the disadvantages of woodblock printing only from the point of view of movable-type printing. She discusses woodblock printing as "a precedent," or as the "infancy," of movable-type printing, which eventually emerged to be the only "standard" or "modern" method of printing. But it is precisely the cost of making a large number of copper-character types that made woodblock printing a favorable choice for Chinese printers before the nineteenth century. Even during the nineteenth century, the cost of making books from woodblocks was still very low.[59] The low cost of production was responsible for the generally low prices of books in Ming Qing (1368–1911) China. As S. Wells Williams, author of the most popular nineteenth-century work on China, observed: "The cheapness with which books can be manufactured, brings them within the reach of the poorest."[60]

The abundance of wood and cheap labor for carving in Ming Qing China made it much more economical and practical for Chinese printers to continue to use woodblock printing.[61] Even though some printers like the Hua

---

57. Cf. Zhang Xiumin, *Zhongguo yin shua shi* (Shanghai: Shanghai ren min chu ban she, 1989), 717–8.

58. Guignard, "The Chinese Precedent," in Febvre and Martin, *Coming of the Book*, 75.

59. Chow, *Publishing, Culture, and Power in Early Modern China*, 59–62.

60. S. Wells Williams, *The Middle Kingdom: A Survey of the Geography, Government, Education, Social Life, Arts, Religion, & etc., of The Chinese Empire and Its Inhabitants* (New York: Wiley, 1876), 477. Williams's account was highly influential in shaping American understanding of China in the nineteenth century. Similar views on the extensive reach of printed books to the lowest strata in late imperial China were echoed by James Legge in a letter written in 1849 when he was in Hong Kong: "In no country are books so cheap as in China." Helen Edith Legge, *James Legge: Missionary and Scholar* (London: The Religious Tract Society, 1905), 75. Like Williams, Legge was referring to the low price of books for the Chinese, not for foreigners like himself.

61. For a discussion of production costs for Chinese printers in the sixteenth century, see Chow, *Publishing, Culture, and Power in Early Modern China*, chap. 1.

and An families in the mid sixteenth century had printed many books using movable metal type, woodblock remained the most attractive technology for most Chinese printers without substantial resources. Guignard's use of the example of the multivolume encyclopedia also fails to take into consideration that many books printed in the late Ming period, especially popular novels and informative texts, were written in a simple and plain, nonclassical style that required far fewer characters than the encyclopedia, which included many rare and obsolete words. The cultural explanation Guignard advances in her section is also noteworthy. Her explanation for why movable-type printing did not develop in China as it did in western Europe is lodged in the metahistorical narrative that privileges technological progress as an agent of historical change. This technological approach also prompts the author to offer a cultural explanation for why, even though the Chinese had invented movable type, they failed to develop it into a practical method of printing. Instead of explaining the relative advantages and disadvantages of woodblock printing in economic terms, Guignard says that Chinese printers "insisted" on using woodblock printing because it allows a calligrapher to work in a deep intellectual and aesthetic "harmony" with a text. For her, the Chinese print- ers' "cultural" preference for aesthetics over technological progress explains why the movable-type method was not adopted widely in China. Guignard is entirely oblivious to the economic advantages of woodblock printing.

Movable Type in Chinese Printing

As previously noted, movable-type printing was invented in China in the eleventh century. It did not become the dominant method of printing there, but neither was it abandoned or forgotten. Recognizing the high cost of mak- ing metal type, Chinese printers experimented with cheaper materials and developed copper, tin, lead, and clay movable type. Zhou Bida (1126–1204) printed a book with clay type in 1193, and the technique continued into the Qing dynasty (1644–1911).[62] It was also "logical" for Chinese printers to cut up woodblock with characters so that they could be reassembled for print- ing different books. In the early fourteenth century, Wang Zhen succeeded in printing books with movable wooden type.[63] Movable-type technology spread also to frontier societies in the northwest and to Korea in the east.

In the early twentieth century, the French Sinologist Paul Pelliot discovered several hundred wooden types for the Uighur language dating from around

---

62. Zhang Xiumin and Han Qi, *Zhongguo huo zi yin shua shi* (A history of movable-type print- ing in China) (Beijing: Zhongguo shu ji chu ban she, 1998), 10–3, 52–60.

63. Ibid., 14–20.

1300 on the floor of one of the caves in Dunhuang. These types are excellent evidence of Wang Zhen's 1313 description of movable-type printing in use during the Yuan period. Even though Uighur is a phonetic language, these types were carved not into individual phonetic letters but into individual words of varying sizes. As Carter and Goodrich aptly remark, they are "in slavish imitation of the Chinese system, whose characters can be taken to be individual words." This discovery is significant because it demonstrates that printing with movable type, whether in the form of individual characters or whole words, had already spread to Central Asia by 1300.[64] Similarly, movable-type printing was introduced into Korea in the thirteenth century. The Korean court had experimented with both wooden and metal type as early as the thirteenth and fourteenth centuries. Lead and even iron types were made in 1436 and 1684, respectively.[65]

The development of movable type did present technical problems for Chinese printers that differed from those of European printers. Chinese printers, for example, had to organize a large number of distinctive characters. Though this was a major problem, it was overcome by the use of rhythm, topics, and a combination of both methods. Chinese printers, however, because they used the brush method with all except metal types, did not have to deal with the difficulty of transferring ink onto the paper without pressure.

European printers faced two different but related problems. As pointed out above, European printers in the fifteenth century used laid paper made from rags, whose surface was rough and would not take the ink evenly with the brush method used in block printing. Also, with the brush method and water-based ink, only one side of a sheet could be used for printing. Using both sides of the paper, however, would have resulted in a 50 percent reduction in the cost of paper.[66] The adoption of the wine press and later the development of oil-based ink solved these two problems. With more pressure from the press, the impression made by the ink on the paper was sharper, clearer, and more defined.[67] But the use of such a press presented a different problem. When subject to regular pressure from the press, woodblocks with small or fine carving often broke. Indeed, copies of books printed from the same blocks have yielded evidence of repairs made to broken blocks: on the same page, it is possible to find instances where the "spelling is different and the shapes of

---

64. Carter and Goodrich, *Invention of Printing in China,* 213–7.

65. The earliest extant book printed from copper type in Korea dates back to 1377. Pan Jixing, *Zhongguo, Han'guo yu Ouzhou zao qi yin shua shu di bi jiao,* 122–43.

66. Kubler, *History of Stereotyping,* 15.

67. Pan Jixing, *Zhongguo, Han'guo yu Ouzhou zao qi yin shua shu di bi jiao,* 193.

the letters are different."[68] However, the regular damage caused by the press more often required that new letters be cut to replace broken blocks. The easy and frequent breaking of text and images in the block prompted European printers to experiment with metal types and later copperplate, which could far better withstand the pressure exerted by the press than woodblocks.

To almost all historians of European printing, the printing press and metal movable type are inseparable. The word "letterpress" is clear evidence of such thinking. But this is so only because of the specific conditions in medieval Europe. The history of printing in China and Korea demonstrates that metal movable-type printing did not necessarily require the use of a press. Nor did the wooden handpress print significantly faster than printing from woodblock. Woodblock printing in China developed and continued to be preferred by printers because the paper produced in China provided a smooth print surface that did not require pressure to transfer the ink. When wooden type was developed, it was practical because the method of applying ink remained the same.

By the sixteenth century both woodblock and movable-type printing were in use in China.[69] Despite the continued predominance of woodblock printing, the number of books printed with movable type gradually increased.[70] Like printers in Korea and Europe, Chinese printers understood the advantage of movable type. And though the relatively large number of distinctive characters compared with dozens of phonetic letters to a certain extent discouraged publishers with limited resources and small circulation from adopting movable type, many Chinese publishers found it advantageous to develop and adopt movable-type printing. Furthermore, the cost of making copper-metal type did not force Chinese printers to abandon casting metal types.[71]

In the Ming period (1368–1644), publishers in Wuxi, Suzhou, Changzhou,

---

68. DeVinne does not have any satisfactory explanation for these discrepancies. But they happened regularly in Chinese printing using woodblock. Chinese printers could change some of the text of a book using the same set of blocks. The example DeVinne provides, the fifty-two-page *Chiromancy of Doctor Hartlieb*, is a block book. DeVinne, *Invention of Printing*, 238–9.

69. It is a common view in European scholarship that movable type after its invention in China was not further developed and fell out of use until the nineteenth century, when the Europeans brought their movable-type method to China. See, for example, Hind, *History of Woodcut*, 66.

70. K. T. Wu, "Ming Printing and Printers," *Harvard Journal of Asiatic Studies* 7.3 (1943): 212–20.

71. There is no reason for Guignard and others to argue that all the metal types made in China were hand carved. That there were different characters in the same book is not enough to support the idea that Chinese metal types were hand carved. The advances in bronze metallurgy from the time of the Shang dynasty provided Chinese printers with the necessary technology to cast types. See Pan Jixing, *Zhongguo, Han'guo yu Ouzhou zao qi yin shua shu di bi jiao*, 91–3.

Nanjing, Zhejiang, Jianning, and Jianyang in Fujian had published books using copper-tin alloy movable types.[72] Publishers in Changzhou also experimented with lead movable scripts.[73] The high cost of copper prompted publishers to use wooden movable type. Wooden type was used by publishers in Hangzhou, Suzhou, Nanjing, Fuzhou, and even in remote provinces such as Sichuan and Yunnan. There are over a hundred extant books from the Ming era that were published using wooden type.[74]

Despite the growing use of movable type in the Ming period, woodblock remained the dominant method of printing. The flexibility of woodblock offered many advantages: low level of investment, simple skill, and great mobility. The greatest skills necessary in the production of a Chinese book were those required in the carving of blocks. The carvers needed only a set of carving knives. The skill required to print from the blocks was relatively simple, and it was not difficult for a carver to master the skill of printing and sewing the pages together. The carver did not need to be literate. Illiterate workers, including women and children, could and did become carvers. A book could be produced by one person—from copying the text to the block to printing copies and finally stitching up the pages.

European entry into the business of printing was a very risky venture, requiring a relatively high level of capital investment. Many European printers in the sixteenth and seventeenth centuries had to depend on patronage support for their operation.[75] In contrast, it was much less risky for Chinese businessmen to venture into publishing. The abundant supply of cheap paper and labor in the sixteenth and seventeenth centuries and the absence of a licensing system and prepublication censorship allowed easy entry into commercial publishing. Woodblock printing offered novice printers an attractive and less risky option than movable-type printing, which required more resources and greater technical expertise. The simplicity of woodblock printing allowed the spread of not just the products of printing but the technology itself throughout East and Central Asia.

---

72. Zhang Xiumin, *Zhongguo yin shua shi*, 686–91; Zhang Xiumin and Han Qi, *Zhongguo huo zi yin shua shi*, 32–49.

73. Zhang Xiumin, *Zhongguo yin shua shi*, 695.

74. Xiao Dongfa, *Zhongguo bian ji chu ban shi* (A history of editing and publishing in China) (Shenyang: Liaoning jiao yu chu ban she, 1996), 343–4. This number is evidently an underestimate. Methods for identifying movable-type editions need to be improved. Relying on the discovery of "upside down" or "sideways" characters as the basis for identifying such editions systematically rules out editions with no typesetting mistakes.

75. For discussions of book producers and forms of patronage in England, see Wang, "Image of St. George"; and Buchtel, "Book Dedications."

Toward a Global History of Printing

The differences in European and Chinese printing technology have been exaggerated to create a false dichotomy: that European printing after the mid fifteenth century had outgrown woodblock printing and that Chinese printing never developed movable type into a practical technology because of the large number of characters in Chinese languages and the culture's aesthetic preference. This reductionist view has fostered a preference in Western narratives of printing history for text over illustration, word over picture, written line over drawn line, and language over image, and, in turn, has glossed over the much more complex relationship between text and picture, information and aesthetics. The long shadow that Gutenberg's invention has cast over the study of European printing and the history of the book has imbued them with a deep-rooted logocentrism that privileges a linguistic approach. Accounts of the technological advantage of movable-type printing have been produced with little attention to the economic and commercial advantages of publishers using woodblock printing.

Publishers in Europe and China printed books for sale. The cost of production and the vendibility of their books were important factors in their choice of technology. Both Chinese and European printers chose their methods based on similar economic considerations. They sought to maximize profits by keeping production costs low. The use of wood in illustration and types was determined by economic reasons for both Chinese and European printers. After the movable-type method was invented in Europe, woodblock printing was not replaced but integrated into European printing technology. Printers needed woodblocks to produce illustration and other iconic elements to accompany the text, and they needed woodblock initials to mimic calligraphy in manuscripts as well as to break the monotony of uniform typecast letters. Woodblocks in the form of printers' marks and other iconic devices were important means for generating publicity for businesses engaged in selling books and other forms of print. The copperplate engraving by European printers never completely replaced the woodcut. In fact, the nineteenth-century perfection of the end-grain engraving method developed by Bewick in the latter decades of the eighteenth century lent a new life to woodblock printing.

The continued use of woodblock in printing initials, illustrations, and other decorative as well informative images, however, inspired printers to search for a method to produce a permanent printing block or template so that they could print any run in response to market demands. The development of stereotype printing, lithography, and, most recently, computer printing all fulfill the ideal of producing a relatively permanent and yet easily altered printing template, from which any number of copies can be printed as the need arises. The template method combines the advantages of both movable-type and woodblock printing.

In the light of the preceding discussion, the various "cultural" explanations for the differential impact of printing in Europe and China need to be reconsidered and the history of printing rewritten from a truly comparative perspective. In brief, it is time to reinvent the narrative of Gutenberg, rescuing the obscured role of woodblock in European printing in the post-Gutenberg period. Resuscitating the importance of woodblock printing in Europe will encourage investigation into the similarities in the history of printing in Europe and in Asia. In this sense I find it exciting to commemorate the twenty-fifth anniversary of the classic work of Elizabeth Eisenstein, who has long given due credit to woodblock illustrations in European printing.

The history of printing is being rewritten by scholars across a wide spectrum of disciplines, and the growing interest in visual modes of representation and their media underscores the need to investigate the nonlinguistic, nonpropositional, and iconic representation of knowledge in print. The confluence of interests in the study of the visual aspects of cultural production behooves us to revisit the standard account of European printing and its logocentric privileging of movable-type printing for its superior capacity in reproducing text. The importance of woodblock illustrations in the study of religion, science, literature, and politics in early modern Europe calls for a new appreciation of the role woodblock printing played in the making of European books. More important, this new understanding calls into question the bifurcated approach to the history of European printing. By re-inserting woodblock printing into the history of European printing after the invention of movable type in the mid fifteenth century, we gain a better perspective for understanding the similar reproductive capacity of both woodblock and movable-type printing before the nineteenth century. The knowledge that both woodblock and movable-type printing were employed by European and Chinese printers facilitates endeavors in examining the differential impact of printing in Europe and China. If woodblock printing is an essential component of European printing, the beginning of European printing can hardly be fixed in the mid fifteenth century. The temporal origin of printing in Europe needs to be moved back several decades to include block books and playing cards. Only by moving out of the shadow of Gutenberg can a historical account of European printing be attained and a truly global history of printing become possible.

Chapter 9

Scotland

International Politics, International Press

ARTHUR WILLIAMSON

Had *Cain* been *Scot,* God would have chang'd his Doom,
Not forc'd him wander but confin'd him home.
—John Cleveland, "The Rebell Scot" (1643)

I N 1594 ANDREW Melville composed a Latin pastoral celebrating the birth of King James's son and heir, Prince Henry. Melville was no ordinary figure, but Scotland's leading court poet, its leading minister, and, as rector of the University of St. Andrews, its leading educator. The poem, *Principis Scoti-Britannorum Natalia,* was also far from ordinary. The *Natalia* envisioned James and Henry succeeding to the English Crown, creating a united Britain, and, now empowered with "Scoto-Britannic champions," turning the tide in the great struggle against Spain. At the head of the Protestant communities, the new Britain would overthrow the Habsburg global empire and its papal ally. Thereby would arise a new era of justice and righteousness—one that did nothing less than work the historical redemption.[1] The poem would be printed at Edinburgh with the king's express approval.

But something else happened, and in a way it too was extraordinary. Melville's colleague at St. Andrews, the distinguished jurist William Welwood, immediately arranged to have the poem also printed at The Hague and from

I am most grateful to Paulina Kewes, Waldemar Kowalski, Allan Macinnes, Steve Murdoch, Jason Peacey, David Scott, as well as to Suzanne Tatian and her colleagues at the William Andrews Clark Memorial Library, for their help and insight.

1. Paul J. McGinnis and Arthur H. Williamson, *George Buchanan: The Political Poetry* (Edinburgh: printed for the Scottish History Society by Lothian Print, 1995), 276–81. For a discussion of this poem, see the introduction. Also see *The British Union: A Critical Edition and Translation of David Hume of Godscroft's "De Unione Insulae Britannicae,"* ed. and trans. Paul J. McGinnis and Arthur H. Williamson (Aldershot, Hants., and Burlington, VT: Ashgate, 2002), 11–3.

there distributed to the world, including England.[2] Scotland's vision emanated not from the realm itself but from the Netherlands. Scotland's emphatically European horizon was actually immersed within Europe. The same was true of Scottish learning and language, matters closely associated then with the realm's religious and political aspirations. Even Scottish pedagogy spoke to an international audience. Andrew Simson's state-promoted *Latinae Grammatices Rudimenta* appeared in Edinburgh as well as Antwerp in 1580. Just as official and semi-official publications were printed outside Scotland, so too were more controversial works, such as George Buchanan's *De Jure Regni apud Scotos: Dialogus* (Edinburgh, 1579; London in the following year; and again in 1581). John Johnston, another colleague at St. Andrews, would send his poetry directly to the Continent: his "Iambi Sacri" would see publication at Leiden and, apparently, also at Saumur. His *Inscriptiones Historicae Regnum Scotorum* appeared only at Amsterdam. Giants at both ends of the Scottish Renaissance such as Hector Boece and David Hume of Godscroft often went to the Continent to publish their most serious writings. The late medieval scholastic John Mair published an enormous amount of work, but not a single volume within Scotland. With the partial exception of Mair, none of these authors was an exile when he produced his work. Much of the time neither government repression nor censorship had caused them and so many like them to send their works overseas. Rather, we have here a pattern that typifies much Scottish writing throughout most of the early modern period.[3]

Why then did Scots look abroad? Why did this highly literate people develop only a limited national press? Modern scholars have long noted that Scotland was a small country and that its market for books was correspondingly restricted.[4] When Robert Boyd at Saumur received half the press run

---

2. A. I. Cameron, ed., *Calendar of the State Papers relating to Scotland and Mary, Queen of Scots, 1547–1603, Preserved in the Public Record Office, the British Museum, and Elsewhere in England* (Edinburgh: H. M. General Register House, 1936), 11:430–1. The poem did create a diplomatic flap, for it made Britain a Scottish project and effectively sidelined Elizabeth.

3. The experience of Scots genuinely in exile confirms this pattern. In 1584, Scottish Presbyterian exiles in England sought to have their declaration printed secretly in London and, significantly, also at Antwerp (where it would appear under the name *"incerto authore et typographo"*). A secret press in Scotland seems never to have occurred to them. David Calderwood, *The History of the Kirk of Scotland,* ed. Thomas Thomson, 8 vols. (Edinburgh, 1842–9), 8:262.

4. Leicester Bradner, *Musae Anglicanae: A History of Anglo-Latin Poetry, 1500–1925* (New York: Modern Language Association; London: Oxford Univ. Press, 1940), 157; David Stevenson, "A Revolutionary Regime and the Press: The Scottish Covenanters and Their Printers, 1638–1651," *The Library,* 6th ser., 7.4 (1985): 317, reprinted in Stevenson, *Union, Revolution, and Religion in 17th-Century Scotland* (Aldershot, Hants.; Brookfield, VT: Variorum, 1997); M. L. Ford, "Importation of Books into England and Scotland," in *The Cambridge History of the Book in Britain,* vol. 3, *1400–1557,* ed. Lotte Hellinga and J. B. Trapp (Cambridge: Cambridge Univ. Press, 1999), 199, 200–1.

of Johnston's poems, he apparently saw a far greater demand at the Frankfurt book fair than in Scotland.[5] Although Walter Chepman and Andro Myllar had imported the new technology from Rouen in 1507, indigenous Scottish printing remained limited throughout the century. More works saw print in Scotland after the 1560 Protestant triumph, and yet, ironically, modern studies suggest that only with the Cromwellian period of the 1650s do we see the beginnings of the Scottish publishing industry.[6] Earlier, powerful neighbors with developed printing trades met Scottish needs and preempted local printers—a high proportion of whom were not natives anyway. Scots wanted books, Scottish governments wanted them to have books, at least selectively, but Scotland barely supplied them.

Something quite different was going on. The answer to our questions lies elsewhere, and its implications for the history of printing and print culture are significant. It has been recently claimed that only by adopting "a local perspective" and through "local researches" can we understand the creation of the systems of values, conventions, and assumptions that made print a cogent social reality.[7] The essay that follows suggests that preoccupation with the local will prove misleading. Early modern Europeans created and participated in multiple public spaces and were extremely conscious of so doing. Their cosmopolitanism can only be distorted when viewed through our post-romantic preoccupation of "identity," and, still more, simplistic post-modern notions of social construction. Probably no print experience can illustrate this proposition more forcefully than that of Scotland.

With the exception of the Jews, no other European people was more dispersed throughout Christendom and beyond. From Moscow to Madrid,

---

5. Robert Wodrow, *Collections upon the Lives of the Reformers and Most Eminent Ministers of the Church of Scotland,* 2 vols. (Glasgow: Maitland Club, 1834–48), 2:100. Boyd received 360 copies. Two hundred went to the Frankfurt fair via Amsterdam, a hundred went to Rochelle, and only sixty went to Scotland "to be given to the authors relations." Johnston died before the volume could be published but had agreed to take a hundred copies "to encourage the printer"—presumably for sale in Scotland (2:99). The other half of the press run could have gone entirely to Scotland. But since Boyd was Johnston's colleague in France, this seems unlikely.

6. As early as 1509, Chepman complained that merchants were importing books he had been licensed to print. Alastair J. Mann, *The Scottish Book Trade, 1500–1720: Print Commerce and Print Control in Early Modern Scotland* (East Linton, East Lothian, Scotland: Tuckwell, 2000), 129. Regarding Scottish printing after 1560, see Arthur H. Williamson, "Education, Culture, and the Scottish Civic Tradition," in *Shaping the Stuart World, 1603–1714: The Atlantic Connection,* ed. Allan I. Macinnes and Arthur H. Williamson (Boston: Brill, 2006), 33–54.

7. Adrian Johns, "How to Acknowledge a Revolution," in AHR Forum, "How Revolutionary Was the Print Revolution?" *American Historical Review* 107.1 (2002): 124–5. Also note Elizabeth Eisenstein's contribution to the forum, "An Unacknowledged Revolution Revisited" and her rejoinder to Johns. Ibid., 87–105, 126–8.

from Amsterdam to Smyrna, and, increasingly, from Amboina to Virginia, Scots turned up in extraordinary numbers. They were highly visible in France during the wars of religion, and in large numbers they continued to attend French universities and to participate in French intellectual life well into the seventeenth century. They would always be prominent in the Netherlands. They were hugely important to North Sea and Baltic commerce. They were hugely important to that region's religious life. Thousands and possibly tens of thousands settled in Poland, Lithuania, and Germany. They became influential in Sweden and Denmark-Norway economically, militarily, diplomatically. During the Thirty Years' War it is now credibly estimated that as many as fifty thousand Scots enlisted for the Protestant cause in the service of the Bohemians, the Dutch, and especially the Swedes.[8]

The on-going Scottish migrations reach back into the later Middle Ages, and they would continue into modern times. But during the years between 1550 and 1650, the Scots abroad possessed sufficient interconnection and coherence as to have a dramatic impact on British and European politics. In 1639 and 1640, these connections enabled the Scots to defeat Charles I militarily while they outmaneuvered him diplomatically. Long-standing Scottish associations with the Swedish court, the Swedish aristocracy, the Swedish military, the Swedish mercantile elites all helped to turn the Swedish kingdom into a tacit but active ally of the revolution in Scotland.[9] Analogous connections and determined Scottish efforts combined in the Netherlands to create another crucial ally. Even Denmark-Norway, though its ruler Christian IV was Charles's uncle, showed itself ambivalent and appears at moments to have colluded with the Scots. Above all, the Scots competed with the king for the hearts and minds of the English people, and there too their historical connections and common purposes proved decisive. The Scottish revolution succeeded, and in turn it shook the British Isles to their foundations. It opened the vista of world change that Andrew Melville had imagined some fifty years before.

Historically, Scotland produced more soldiers, more merchants, more peddlers, more philosophers, more clergy, more students, more professors, more poets, more intellectuals—*and* more books—than Scottish society could ever hope to absorb. This circumstance made the Scots an all but uniquely international people. No less would they emerge a uniquely crusading people.

---

8. Robert I. Frost, "Scottish Soldiers, Poland-Lithuania, and the Thirty Years' War," in *Scotland and the Thirty Years' War*, ed. Steve Murdoch (Boston: Brill, 2001), 191.

9. Alexia Grosjean, "General Alexander Leslie, the Scottish Covenanters, and the *Riksråd* Debates, 1638–1640," in *Ships, Guns, and Bibles in the North Sea and the Baltic States, c. 1350–c.1700*, ed. Allan I. Macinnes, Thomas Riis, and Frederik Pedersen (East Linton, East Lothian, Scotland: Tuckwell, 2000), 115–38.

Scottish economic and political survival demanded a thorough-going cosmopolitanism. That necessity merged easily—almost naturally—with Scottish hopes for world reform, with Scotland's apocalyptic vision, with its aspirations for universal renewal. The Scottish press would be configured accordingly.

The new demographic evidence is arresting, but in some ways the cultural evidence is still more compelling. In Poland large communities of Scots settled in port cities, such as Gdansk, where some would become wealthy and highly influential. From there they penetrated into virtually all parts of the vast Polish commonwealth. They served in the military at all levels. Some became well connected at court. Although Scots became involved on both sides of the confessional conflict, most were militant Calvinists, and their role was considerable in the Polish economy and, simultaneously, in the Polish Reformation. Moreover, links with Scotland were maintained in part through successive waves of migration, in part through commercial interconnection, and a surprisingly high level of travel back and forth. Money earned in Poland helped fund the Scottish Church, Scottish hospitals, and Scottish universities, perhaps most notably the University of Aberdeen.

By far the most visible and commented-upon Scots in Poland were peddlers who traded in towns and also in the countryside, where they carried goods to the great latifundia of the commerce-despising Polish nobility.[10] So prevalent were such Scottish peddlers that the term Scot—"Szot" or "Szkot"—became a synonym for "trader" or perhaps "tinker."[11] For some two centuries the Scottish peddler would be a stock character in Polish literature, cropping up in the works of such poets as Jan Kochanowski, Wladyslaw Stanislaw Jeżowski, Wacław Potocki, Sebastian Fabian Klonowicz, among others.[12] Scottish observers, such as the jurist John Skene, Scotland's clerk

---

10. To be sure, peddlers in early modern Poland came from just about everywhere: there were Germans, Italians, Hungarians, Armenians, Tartars, and, increasingly prominent, Jews. But, except for the Jews, the Scots were more numerous, more widespread, and more organized than the others. Anna Biegańska, "A Note on the Scots in Poland, 1550–1800," in *Scotland and Europe, 1200–1850*, ed. T. C. Smout (Edinburgh: J. Donald; Atlantic Highlands, NJ: distributed by Humanities Press, 1986), 159. The Scottish presence in Poland was apparently such that Englishmen there were normally identified as Scots. Antoni Krawczyk, "The British in Poland in the Seventeenth Century," *The Seventeenth Century* 17.2 (2002): 254, 256.

11. See "szot" in the glossary to Jan Kochanowski, *Dzieła polskie,* 2 vols. (Warsaw: Państ. Instytut Wydawniczy, 1976), 2: 310; Anna Biegańska, "Scottish Merchants and Traders in Seventeenth- and Eighteenth-Century Warsaw," *Scottish Slavonic Review* 5 (1985): 20–1; Frost, "Scottish Soldiers," 193; Gershon David Hundert, "On the Jewish Community of Poland during the Seventeenth Century: Some Comparative Perspectives," *Revue des études juives* 142.3–4 (1983): 367 and n. 60; Krawczyk, "British in Poland," 256.

12. Biegańska, "Scottish Traders," 29; Krawczyk, "British in Poland," 256. Some of this literature has been discussed and even translated in Waldemar Kowalski, "The Placement of Urbanised Scots in the Polish Crown during the Sixteenth and Seventeenth Centuries," in *Scottish Communities*

register, and the travel writer William Lithgow found themselves amazed by the numbers of their countrymen that they encountered there. The Scot in Poland would become a commonplace in English politics and even occurred in contemporary English literature.[13]

In Poland, Scottish traders, and in theory all Scottish residents, were governed through formal "brotherhoods," with highly articulated constitutions, and these organizations were emphatically Protestant. Inevitably, the brotherhoods established their own churches and consequently became in effect Protestant networks within Poland, often funding the training of ministers, both Scots and Poles, for the Polish Reformed Church.[14] The Scots in Poland

---

Abroad in the Early Modern Period, ed. Alexia Grosjean and Steve Murdoch (Boston: Brill, 2005). Cf. Maria Bogucka, "Scots in Gdansk (Danzig) in the Seventeenth Century," in Macinnes, Riis, and Pedersen, *Ships, Guns, and Bibles,* 41. Typically in Polish writing, an idealized aristocratic agrarian world (one powered by servile peasant labor, it might be added) would be contrasted in passing with the cheapened, narrow, grasping world of the Scot and the Jew.

13. John Skene, *De Verborum Significantione. The Exposition of Termes and Difficill Wordes, Conteined in the Four Buiks of Regiam Maiestatem and Uthers, in Acts of Parliament, Infeftments, and Used in Practique of This Realme . . .* (Edinburgh, 1597), sig. P3v; William Lithgow, *Scotlands VVelcome to Her Native Sonne, and Soveraigne Lord, King Charles . . .* (Edinburgh, 1633), sig. A4v. Lithgow has mother Scotland claim (and exaggerate): "For *Polland* shee's my Nurse, brings up my Youth, / Full Thritty thousands, yearely, of a trueth; / Than loades them with the fatnesse of her Soyle, / Which I, in their due time, doe still recoyle." The passage is often noted, but unnoticed are the surrounding lines that celebrate the large-scale Scottish presence in France, the Low Countries, Germany, Sweden, Denmark, and Ireland. Still, the sheer number of Scots in Poland had captured the public imagination. Both sides of the 1606 debate on Anglo-Scottish union in the House of Commons noted the extensive Scottish presence in Poland. In *The White Devil* (1612), 3.3.6–7, John Webster has Flameneo declare that he would rather "be enter'd into the list of the forty thousand peddlers in Poland" than give up his place at court. The "list" he refers to is doubtless the self-governing brotherhood of Scottish traders in Poland, an organization that ostensibly regulated and represented all Scots in the country. See Arthur Wilson, *The History of Great Britain, Being the Life and Reign of King James the First, Relating to What Passed from His First Access to the Crown, Till His Death* (London, 1653), 34–5; Archibald Francis Steuart and Beatrice C. Baskerville, eds., *Papers Relating to the Scots in Poland, 1573–1793* (Edinburgh: printed at the University Press by T. and A. Constable for the Scottish History Society, 1915), ix.

14. Th. A. Fischer (Ernst Ludwig Fischer), *The Scots in Eastern and Western Prussia* (Edinburgh: O. Schulze & Co, 1903), 24, 158; Th. A. Fischer, *The Scots in Germany: Being a Contribution towards the History of the Scots Abroad* (Edinburgh: O. Schulze & Co., 1902), 40 and n. 1, 54–5; Kowalski, "Placement of Urbanised Scots," 83–4; Wacław Potocki, *Dzieła,* ed. Leszek Kukulski, 3 vols. (Warsaw: Państwowy Instytut Wydawniczy, 1987), 2:351; and Anna Biegańska, "In Search of Tolerance: Scottish Catholics and Presbyterians in Poland," *Scottish Slavonic Review* 17 (1991): 43–4. Given this prominent Scottish presence and visibility, it is surely no accident that the radical Protestant community at Raków sent its confession to King James VI and I. Nor should it surprise us that to the north in the wilds of Lithuania arose a Scottish colony at Kedainiai, apparently inspired by Calvinist utopianism no less than by commerce—a community that survived into the eighteenth century. Linas Eriksonas, "The Lost Colony of Scots: Unravelling Overseas Connections in a Lithuanian Town," in Macinnes, Riis, and Pedersen, *Ships, Guns, and Bibles,* 173–87; Steve Murdoch, "The Scottish Community in Kedainiai in its Scandinavian and Baltic Context," paper presented at the

promoted reformation both at home and abroad, even when it ceased to be clear which realm actually was home.

Early modern Scots had penetrated Polish economic, social, and religious life so thoroughly as to become a cultural fixture. They would do no less in Germany. There too the term Scot—"Schotte"—came to mean trader or peddler. There too, especially in the northeastern provinces of Mecklenberg, Pomerania, Brandenburg, East and West Prussia, Scottish traders became as widespread as in Poland.[15] Again as in Poland, Scots were identified with Protestantism and dramatically so through their large-scale participation in the Thirty Years' War on behalf of the reformed cause. By the time of Gustavus Adolphus's intervention in 1630–32, the Scottish soldier had become a commonplace figure—and also the subject of brutal verbal and visual caricature by the German Counter-Reformation.[16] As in Poland, here too Scots played a prominent role both in the Reformation and in the economy, the former seen as part of the common, universal cause.

From the outset, Scots were active in the English Reformation and in subsequent movements there for further reform. They figured significantly in the 1584 upheaval, the greatest challenge the reformers were to mount against the Elizabethan regime. But in the revolutionary years 1638–43, Scottish political activity within England and elsewhere surged to altogether new levels. The National Covenant (1638) emerged, in the Scottish view, as the model for nations. The subsequent Solemn League and Covenant with England (1643) provided the model for foreign relations, arrangements that promised to initiate a redeemed world much as Melville had hoped. As in Germany and Poland, conservatives in England railed against Scottish activism and radicalism. The royalist bigot John Cleveland fulminated about the Scots' involvement in England with a voice that would have been immediately recognizable in central and eastern Europe:

> Like Jews they spread, and as Infection fly,
> As if the Devil had Ubiquity.
> Hence 'tis they live like Rovers and defie
> This or that place, Rags of Geography.
> They're Citizens o'th World; they're all in all,
> Scotland's a Nation Epidemicall.[17]

"Colloquium Balticum: Baltijos regionas Europos mastu," Kendainiai, June 16, 2001. My thanks to Dr. Murdoch for sharing his forthcoming essay with me.

15. Fischer, *Scots in Prussia,* 5, 15; Fischer, *Scots in Germany,* 50.

16. See Arthur H. Williamson, "Scots, Indians, and Empire: The Scottish Politics of Civilization 1519–1609," *Past & Present* 150 (February 1996): 46–83, esp. 50–2, 55.

17. *The Poems of John Cleveland,* ed. Brian Morris and Eleanor Withington (Oxford: Clarendon Press, 1967), 30–1.

Royalists in these years typically were virulent Scotophobes and often enough, such as the playwright John Tatham, decried the corruption of the British Isles through the doctrines of the Scottish political theorist George Buchanan.[18]

Though the language of conservative opposition to Scottish aspirations turns out to have been remarkably similar both in England and in eastern Europe, there were also important differences. In contrast to their experience in Poland, Germany, and other Baltic lands, Scots participated much more visibly within the print dimension of England's public life. To be sure, Scots disseminated the National Covenant in eastern Europe. The Covenanting government also maintained continuous contact with their off-shore communities, just as it did with the countries they inhabited. As late as 1647, with Scotland's power and prestige now in visible decline, the regime still directed a special exhortation from the clergy specifically "unto the Scots merchants and other their country-people scattered in Poland, Swedland, Denmark and Hungary."[19] But in 1638, the Scottish government went well beyond any of its activities in eastern Europe and entered upon an extraordinary media campaign in England and the Netherlands. Described by a recent commentator as "the most concerted and effective use of media propaganda by a Scottish government or party in the early modern period," the Edinburgh regime overwhelmed royalist apologia in England and frustrated royal efforts to secure thorough-going censorship in the United Provinces.[20] Titles like

---

18. Tatham, *The Distracted State* (1641), in *The Dramatic Works of John Tatham* (Edinburgh: W. Paterson; London: H. Sotheran & Co., 1879), 93–4. See Arthur H. Williamson, " 'A Pil for Pork-Eaters': Ethnic Identity, Apocalyptic Promises, and the Strange Creation of the Judeo-Scots," in *The Expulsion of the Jews: 1492 and After,* ed. Raymond B. Waddington and Arthur H. Williamson (New York: Garland, 1994), 247. Scottish radicalism had long been attacked by conservative English playwrights, perhaps most memorably in Ben Jonson's *Bartholomew Fair* (1614; revived and produced, significantly, in 1661). See Williamson, "Pil for Pork-Eaters," 246.

19. As part of a larger justification of the regime's policies: *A Declaration of the Convention of Estates in Scotland, Concerning Their Armie with Their Reasons for Continuance Thereof Untill March Next; and in What Manner the Officers and Souldiers Shall Be Paid. Dated at Edinburgh October 15, 1647. Together with an Exhortation of the General Assembly of the Kirk of Scotland, unto the Scots Merchants and Other Their Country-People Scattered in Poland, Swedland, Denmark and Hungary* (Edinburgh, 1647). The concern of the *Exhortation,* unsurprisingly, was to maintain religious solidarity, supply ministers, and disseminate the new Westminster accords. Nearly a decade earlier, no less than Alexander Leslie himself apparently delivered a copy of the National Covenant to the Swedish Council. Riksarkiv (Stockholm): Oxenstiernska samlingen, Axel Oxenstierna av Södermöre/E772. Again, my thanks to Steve Murdoch for drawing these documents to my attention. Dr. Murdoch very kindly translated and summarized the Swedish materials.

20. Mann, *Scottish Book Trade,* 84. Also see Alastair J. Mann, "The Press and Military Conflict in Early Modern Scotland," in *Fighting for Identity: Scottish Military Experience c. 1550–1900,* ed. Steve Murdoch and Andrew Mackillop (Boston: Brill, 2002), 282; Joad Raymond, *The Invention of the Newspaper: English Newsbooks, 1641–1649* (Oxford: Clarendon Press; New York: Oxford Univ.

The Intentions of the Army in Scotland, An Information to All Good Christians within the Kingdome of England, or *The Lawfulness of Our Expedition into England* will seem cumbersome today. In context they proved compelling. The role of emigré Scots in disseminating them is beyond doubt. The significance of these activities is difficult to overestimate. For a century and more, historians have commented on the extraordinary "explosion" of publication that began in London during the summer of 1641 with the collapse of royal authority. Joad Raymond, a modern historian of the English newspaper, has argued persuasively that these developments must be seen as a continuation of events begun in Scotland.[21]

The issue was never simply to secure the revolution at home. The networks that had made the revolution a success also ensured that the Scottish government never lost sight of a European horizon, and the subsequent struggles that took place throughout the British Isles, it is increasingly clear, need to be seen as but one theater within the Thirty Years' War. A great many contemporaries saw it that way, and none more so than the Scots. Beginning in 1640, revolutionary Scotland made determined efforts to form a tripartite confederation that joined the Estates General of the United Provinces with the Scottish and English Parliaments. By 1643, the Scottish Covenanters were working to create a British confederation with Sweden as well as with the Dutch republic. It is no accident that the Solemn League and Covenant was immediately published in Latin and French, for the Scots hoped that the Dutch would not only join the new confederation but also "invite all other Christian princes to doe the lyke."[22] Yet in the end, only in England did a

Press, 1996), 120; Peter Donald, *An Uncounselled King: Charles I and the Scottish Troubles, 1637–1641* (New York: Cambridge Univ. Press, 1990), 128–33, 185–93, 200; Dagmar Freist, *Governed by Opinion: Politics, Religion, and the Dynamics of Communication in Stuart London, 1637–1645* (London and New York: Tauris Academic Studies; New York: distributed by St. Martin's Press, 1997), 52, 217–8, 220, 222, 224–6, 229, 258; Conrad Russell, *The Fall of the British Monarchies, 1637–1642* (Oxford: Clarendon Press; New York: Oxford Univ. Press, 1991), 61; David Stevenson, "A Revolutionary Regime and the Press," 325. Mann has in mind the Scottish-Dutch interaction, but, as he recognizes, the two form part of a single undertaking.

   21. Raymond, *Pamphlets and Pamphleteering in Early Modern Britain* (Cambridge: Cambridge Univ. Press, 2003), 187.

   22. John R. Young, "The Scottish Parliament and European Diplomacy 1641–1647: The Palatine, the Dutch Republic, and Sweden," in Murdoch, *Scotland and the Thirty Years' War,* esp. 77, 87, 90–1; *Convenant & alliance saincte pour la reformation & defense de la religion, l'honeur & prosperité du Roy, la paix & seurté de trois Royaumes, D'Angleterre, Ecosse & Irlande, faicte solennellement par les estats & peuple desdits royaumes* (London, 1643). The British Library copy has a handwritten note on it with the date October 20, 1643. B[ritish]L[ibrary], E72 (9). There appear to be two Latin renderings published that year. Harry G. Aldis, *A List of Books Printed in Scotland before 1700, Including Those Printed Furth of the Realm for Scottish Booksellers* ([Edinburgh]: printed for the Edinburgh Bibliographical Society, 1904), 30 (nos. 1082, 1089).

formal arrangement actually come about, and as a result Scottish penetration into the emerging British confederation became truly extraordinary. In England, and also in the Netherlands, there existed an exceptionally large and expanding print-supported public life, far more developed than anything in eastern Europe, and within them a Scottish press burgeoned as never before. The number of copies printed can be amazing: one Covenanting pamphlet appeared in an English edition of ten thousand and a Dutch run of three thousand—numbers, Raymond tells us, that exceeded anything produced in London even after 1641. The Covenanter Robert Baillie may have been smug, but he was also right when in 1646 he looked back on the Scottish pamphleteering campaigns and commented: "Allwayes paper-debates are the least of our care; we never yet lost at that game." [23]

Charles I had brought a printing press with him to Newcastle when he and his forces confronted the Scots in 1640. Oliver Cromwell would bring a press with him into Scotland when the republic made its pre-emptive strike against Charles II in 1650. However, the Scottish general Alexander Leslie did not bring along a press when he led the Covenanting army south in 1644 to support Parliament in the English Civil War. He did not need to. Scots had already set up a military press, logically enough, in London. The first Scottish newspaper, *The Scottish Dove*—primarily (though far from exclusively) concerned with news of the expeditionary forces—appeared in London between late 1643 and late 1646. That is, exactly during the period of the Solemn League and of direct Scottish involvement in English affairs. There lies no small irony in this development. The first newspaper actually printed in Scotland, *Mercurius Scoticus,* arrived with the English republican armies nearly a decade later.[24] The first Scottish paper produced within Scotland, *Mercurius Caledonicus,* appeared only in 1661, after the Restoration. The Scottish newspaper began life as a multi-national publication, born out of the cosmopolitanism inherent within Scottish politics. It arose from a world that completely fit the assumptions of Andrew Melville and the later sixteenth century.

Contrary to the caricature popular in today's accounts of the period,

---

23. Raymond, *Pamphlets,* 183; Baillie cited in ibid., 187.

24. Mann, "Press and Military Conflict," 274. *Mercurius Scoticus* is discussed briefly in C. H. Firth, ed., *Scotland and the Commonwealth: Letters and Papers relating to the Military Government of Scotland from August 1651 to December 1653* (Edinburgh: printed at the University Press by T. and A. Constable for the Scottish History Society, 1895), xiv, 315 n. 1; a number of excerpts are quoted in the appendix. Although it is occasionally used as a source, there appears to be no serious analysis of the origins and purposes of this republican paper—or why the parliamentary commissioners arriving from London shut it down in early 1652.

Scotland's revolutionary leadership realized that it would be no easy matter to secure the aspirations of the Solemn League and Covenant in England.[25] They knew full well that the two churches had grown apart, that "Anglican" innovations, arising from the 1590s, had acquired a powerful following during the decades of the early seventeenth century. Archibald Johnston of Warriston, arguably the lynchpin among the leaders, recognized from the beginning that there were Englishmen who had "doubts & scruples anent the kirk government."[26] Further, the leadership understood that Scottish interference in these matters would prove offensive and counterproductive. Accordingly, Scots would work as much as possible through English agents. In 1642–43, at the outset of their involvement, the Scots also found it useful to present themselves as an honest broker within the southern war and sought to repair the breach between Crown and Parliament — though of course in ways that would lead to reform. So too, they emphasized common ground with the English Parliament and vigorously promoted prominently shared concerns for zeal, for reform, for militant confrontation with the Counter-Reformation, while leaving specific, if all important matters of doctrine, church government, and Anglo-Scottish union for negotiation and subsequent agreement. Far from being arrogant naïfs or proto-imperialists, the Scots saw clearly that the future lay with collaboration rather than coercion, confederation rather than conquest. For a small nation, no other way was available, and by 1643, highly developed vocabularies of sacralized confederation had emerged for just such a purpose.

So too, in these circumstances, "paper-debates" could only be of paramount importance. Scotland's major apologia for its revolution, Samuel Rutherford's *Lex Rex,* appeared in 1644 in a London as well as in an Edinburgh edition. Earlier Scottish classics that spoke to the same point, such as George Buchanan's political writings, also saw print. His highly political

25. Most notoriously by H. R. Trevor-Roper, "Scotland and the Puritan Revolution," in *Historical Essays, 1600–1750, Presented to David Ogg,* ed. H. E. Bell and R. L. Ollard (London: A. & C. Black, [1963]), 78–130. Even vastly more sophisticated and truly important works, such as Brian P. Levack, *The Formation of the British State: England, Scotland, and the Union, 1603–1707* (Oxford: Clarendon Press; New York: Oxford Univ. Press, 1987), esp. 108–11; and Conrad Russell, *The Causes of the English Civil War* (Oxford: Clarendon Press; New York: Oxford Univ. Press, 1990), esp. 16, 31, can speak of a Scottish imperial vision. Much Scottish political thought, especially in its Presbyterian form, emphatically rejected the Roman Empire and especially Constantine as a norm. In this context, Scottish "empire" could only be Athenian, not Roman, a confederal Achaian League rather than a more centralized, hierarchical structure.

26. Cited by Peter Donald, "The Scottish National Covenant and British Politics, 1638–1640," in *The Scottish National Covenant in its British Context,* ed. John Morrill (Edinburgh: Edinburgh Univ. Press; New York: distributed by Columbia Univ. Press, 1990), 99.

drama *The Baptist* would be translated in England for the first time.[27] In 1644, the Scots would also arrange for the publication in London of John Knox's history of the Scottish Reformation (with an important new introduction by David Buchanan). Yet again in that year, from Edinburgh (but with an eye for distribution in London) appeared David Hume of Godcroft's *History of the House of Douglas,* a work that promoted civic responsibility, resistance, and "the good patriot." The last two writings had hitherto appeared only in incomplete editions and normally circulated in manuscript.[28]

As early as October 1643, an altogether new kind of publication appeared for the purpose of promoting the Scottish agenda: *The Scotch Mercury,* a diurnal or newspaper that undertook to communicate "the affairs of Scotland and the Northern Parts." Specifically, it reassured its readers that the Scottish forces were "restlesse till they be upon the march and expedition for England" and looked to the impending, all-important siege of Newcastle. "Our gude nobility, our gude Gentry and Commons are all for you." All that was needed was "a little advance-money." "Were we not poor our selves, we would not ask a penny." Here emerged the major ongoing themes of the Scottish and Scottish-oriented press in England: apologia for the Scottish army, promoting of the Holy League and Covenant, hope of joining "our Publique Faiths together." The *Mercury* concluded with a stirring peroration: "And now be couragious, good Brethren of England, we come with all speed; Your cause is the best that ever was; And, love [for] your gude Parliament, you never had sike another."[29] In a manner so characteristic of Scottish attitudes during 1643, the newspaper's opening remarks tried to adjudicate between the royalist and parliamentary press, and thereby the two causes. No surprise, it found for the latter.

We may never know for certain who produced this first Scottish news-

---

27. By order of the House of Commons, in 1642. *Tyrannicall-Government Aanatomized: or, A Discourse concerning Evil-Councellors* appeared in February 1643. The work was originally titled *Baptistes, sive calumnia trageodia.* Buchanan's *Rerum Scoticarum historia* also appeared that year, apparently published in Amsterdam (see D. G. Wing and A. W. Pollard, *Short-Title Catalogue of Books Printed in England, Scotland, Ireland, Wales, and British America and of English Books Printed in Other Countries, 1641–1700,* 3 vols. [New York: Index Society, 1945–51], B5296). Regarding efforts to reprint Buchanan's *De Jure Regni apud Scotos: Dialogus* in 1639, see Keith L. Sprunger, *Trumpets from the Tower: English Puritan Printing in the Netherlands, 1600–1640* (New York: Brill, 1994), 116 n. 142; Donald, *Uncounselled King,* 188.

28. An incomplete version of Knox's *History* was published in 1587. The year 1644 witnessed two London editions of the history and an Edinburgh reprint. A brief, truncated version of Godscroft's history had appeared in 1633. Published with difficulty and in limited numbers, it too did not supplant the manuscript versions. The 1640s edition has remained the standard version until the 1996 variorum.

29. *Scotch Mercury,* October 5, 1643, 5–6, 8.

paper, with its evident knowledge of the north, its preoccupation with the Scottish forces, its frequent Scotticisms, and its painfully anglicized title. One candidate is the well-known Scottish travel writer William Lithgow (c.1582–1650), who surveyed English fortifications in 1643. (Scots also appear to have undertaken a similar survey of Northumberland, notably Newcastle and Tynemouth, before the 1640 campaign).[30] Lithgow had already published a detailed account of the siege of the Dutch city of Breda (1637). Once Scotland entered the English Civil War, he produced a similar narrative of the Scottish role in the struggle for Newcastle. These writings have a distinctly journalistic character. Lithgow insists that he will only recount what he had actually seen: "this work [derives] from my owne occular experience, whereof I am a daily Testator." His accounts clearly came from the front lines, where he seems to have been one of the earliest "embedded" reporters: "If this familiar stile seeme not to thee so accurate and elegant, as I have done heretofore in other works, impute the fault thereof to . . . my miserable lying on cold straw, in straw huts, and unshifted apparrell, to the clangor of armour, the ratling of pikes, the clamour of tongues, the sounding of trumpets, and the noise of drums: where, when, and whilst I was writing this experimental [i.e., experiential] discourse."[31] A severe moralist and committed Covenanter, Lithgow believed, like so many Scots, that England needed to become fully reformed to be Scotland's "true sister." But he was no less exercised that Scottish military achievement, and especially the achievements of General Leslie, not go unrecorded—and be lost to these "ingrateful times."[32]

Lithgow rather than the Scottish commissioners in London most likely also continued as Scotland's main conduit to *The Scottish Dove,* which appeared the following week as successor to the *Mercury.*[33] Now with an English edi-

---

30. William Lithgow, *The Present Surveigh of Londons and Englands State* (London, 1643). Lithgow had departed Scotland from Prestonpans in April of that year. Roger Howell, *Newcastle upon Tyne and the Puritan Revolution: A Study of the Civil War in North England* (Oxford: Clarendon Press, 1967), 106. My thanks to Allan Macinnes for drawing my attention to William Lithgow.

31. William Lithgow, *A True and Experimentall Discourse, upon the Beginning, Proceeding, and Victorious Event of This Last Siege of Breda* (London, 1637), sig. A4r. He makes the same point in *A True Experimentall and Exact Relation upon That Famous and Renovvned Siege of Nevvcastle . . .* (Edinburgh, 1645), 5.

32. Lithgow, *Surveigh,* sig. C2v, *Siege of Breda,* 49, 51, and *Siege of Newcastle,* 4.

33. Joseph Frank believed there might well have been some connection between the *Scottish Dove* and one or more of the Scottish commissioners in London. But, as Frank recognizes, the *Dove* tended to look past the doings at Westminster. Frank, *The Beginnings of the English Newspaper* (Cambridge, MA: Harvard Univ. Press, 1961), 55, 63, 316 n. 80. It seems unlikely that the *Dove* was merely a paper that just happened to endorse Scottish views. Raymond, *Newspaper,* 34; Lawrence Kaplan, *Politics and Religion during the English Revolution: The Scots and the Long Parliament, 1643–1645* (New York: New York Univ. Press, 1976), 88.

tor, George Smith, the new weekly no longer had a specifically Scottish voice. Nor would Scottish usages occur. But for the next three years, it offered, as its name indicated, a consistently and resolutely Scottish perspective on English politics and the affairs of the two kingdoms.[34] One of its prime aims was to describe, defend, celebrate, and, when necessary, apologize for the Scottish expeditionary force. It passionately promoted the Covenant and subsequently, as the issue emerged, a Presbyterian Church settlement. The new diurnal also offered more effective public relations, surely the main reason for the change. Unlike the *Mercury,* the *Dove* maintained that the real concern of the Scottish army was English slowness in taking the Covenant (comment on "advance money" became buried).

With its striking masthead, the new newspaper looked different from the other London diurnals. It sounded different as well. Modern studies of the early newspaper have observed that Smith had a far more declared agenda and a more pronounced ideological edge than "any other editor of his time." When the Scots wanted censorship of selected London diurnals, indeed their closure, the *Dove* wanted censorship and closure. When the Scots sought a remodeling of the parliamentary army, so too did the *Dove.* Scotland's commissioners in London did not like the celebration of Oliver Cromwell at the expense of the Scottish forces. Neither did the *Dove.* The *Dove* would even adopt typically Scottish attitudes toward witchcraft.[35] The farewell issue in late 1646 listed as its first two reasons for shutting down that there was now "little news" and no need simply to repeat the reports of others—that is, Scottish news (especially Scottish military news), Scottish sources, and, quite possibly, Scottish counsel had just ceased. The whole point of the paper had been to provide "an Intelligencer between England and Scotland." Smith had insisted all along that Scotland was "our Doves chief Errand." Now the Scots had withdrawn and, for Smith, were no more. Raymond is certainly right when he says that "there were no signs of foul play" in the demise

---

34. Our knowledge of Smith extends no further than what he tells us. At the outbreak of the English civil war, he made his way to London to enlist in the parliamentary armies. Being unfit for service, he went into printing and produced a series of tracts (seemingly no longer extant) before taking up with the *Dove.* Frank has speculated that he came from the north. If so, we might further speculate that he came from Newcastle, where there existed a large Scottish population and where Scottish Covenanters and English Puritans seem to have collaborated at least from the late 1630s. Frank, *Newspaper,* 55; Howell, *Newcastle,* 97–107, esp. 106.

35. Frank, *Newspaper,* 93, 109, 110–1. Modern commentators have not responded well to the *Dove's* style and militancy. For Frank, Smith was "verbose" and "unctuously pious" (*Newspaper,* 56). For Raymond, Smith showed a "cloying piety" (*Newspaper,* 34). See also Joad Raymond, ed., *Making the News: An Anthology of the Newsbooks of Revolutionary England, 1641–1660* (New York: St. Martin's, 1993), 110.

of the *Dove:* with the Scottish departure, it had died an altogether natural death.[36]Appropriately enough, the final issue included a jeremiad on behalf of the Covenant. Yet, in significant ways, the jeremiad is directed to Scotland, and we sense a voice grown distant. During its lifetime, the *Dove* did not concentrate on the doings at Westminster but focused on military affairs, Scottish honor, and Scottish spirituality. Perhaps it should not surprise us that at moments Smith sounds remarkably like Johnston of Warriston.[37]

Though the *Mercury* and the *Dove* presented Scottish news, Scottish attitudes, and a Scottish agenda to an English audience, nothing like them existed north of the border. During that fateful year 1642, some English newspapers would actually be reprinted in Edinburgh.[38] Efforts were apparently made to make them look like the London versions. Ostensibly, it would be difficult to imagine anything more provincial. Such a view of Scotland finds itself further reinforced by the reprinting of parliamentary petitions, declarations, remonstrances, ordinances, and even a speech by John Pym. Still more striking is the reprinting of the petition of the "gentlewomen and trades-mens wives" in London and of two petitions from the county of York. And yet in a way all these reprints are not in the least provincial but just the reverse. Scots read English papers and English political literature because they felt connected with the great events taking place in London. Whether the purpose was simply to secure Scotland or, from there, to transform the world—and the former might well require the latter—it did not take much to perceive that decisions in England would determine the course of the British Isles and beyond. In a real sense the south was their world and their future, a world and a future in which they needed to participate.

Scotland in itself, however, offered a very different kind of environment,

---

36. *Scottish Dove,* n.d. (probably December 1646), 2, 4; ibid., October 20, 1643, 22; and Raymond, *Newspaper,* 51.

37. For example, October 11, 1644 (no. 52). To be sure, the *Dove* did indeed comment on corruption in parliamentary committees (perpetrated by those hostile to the Scottish agenda) and on recruiter elections, among other items. But the newspaper never lost sight of its original, larger purposes, and, in line with those purposes, sought to address a broader audience that extended beyond London and politics within the capital. Smith and Lithgow also share a similar tone. See Lithgow, *Surveigh,* sig. A2r–v.

38. Specifically, two issues: *The Diurnal Occurrences, Touching the Dayly Proceedings in Parliament,* December 27–January 3, 1641/42; *A Continuation of the True Diurnall Occurrences in Parliament,* January 10–24, 1642; possibly also *A Continuation of the True Diurnall Occurrences,* February 7–14, 1642. Noted by David Stevenson in "Scotland's First Newspaper, 1648," in Stevenson, *Union, Revolution, and Religion,* 123; described more fully by William James Couper, *The Edinburgh Periodical Press, Being a Bibliographical Account of the Newspapers, Journals, and Magazines Issued in Edinburgh from the Earliest Times to 1800,* 2 vols. (Stirling: E. Mackay, 1908), 1:56–7, 163–6; Frank, *Newspaper,* 278, 279.

a much more face-to-face society, in which scribal and oral communication remained hugely important. Internally, justifications for the revolution, most notably the works of Johnston of Warriston, Alexander Henderson, and Robert Baillie, would be read from the pulpit. Alternatively, they would circulate among "well affected professors in private conference." In the spring of 1639, Henderson's "Instructions for Defensive Arms" circulated in manuscript and was read aloud to congregations. Only with the outbreak of hostilities in England three years later did it see publication, as *Some Speciall Arguments Which Warranted the Scotch Subjects Lawfully to Take up Armes in Defence of Their Religion and Liberty.* Characteristically, it appeared simultaneously in both London and Amsterdam, but not in Scotland.[39] In at least the early stages of the revolution, there appears to have been considerable concern that statements of radical ideology not fall into the wrong hands. Timing was key, control essential. Eventually every press in Scotland would be turning out copies of the National Covenant, but initially they circulated for signature throughout the country in manuscript. No Scottish newspaper ever emerged. The modern historian David Stevenson claims that the royalist Engagers tried to create one as they launched their ill-fated invasion of England in 1648.[40] But the title, tone, and structure of their publication, *Ane Information of the publick Proceedings of the Kingdom of Scotland . . . ,* locate it squarely within the tradition of the earlier Covenanting media campaigns of 1639–40. It may have been intended as the first in a series of such tracts — no follow-up ever appeared — but no one on either side of the border would ever have mistaken it for a diurnal. Something much closer to an early newspaper seems to have been undertaken at Aberdeen in 1657. In July of that year, the city council decreed the creation of "ane weekly diurnall to be sellit for the wse of the inhabitants." The city accounts indicate that some "fyften diornalls" (apparently issues) were actually produced.[41] The Aberdeen diurnal is hard to assess

---

39. Donald, *Uncounselled King,* 128; Hugh Dunthorne, "Resisting Monarchy: The Netherlands as Britain's School of Revolution in the late Sixteenth and Seventeenth Century," in *Royal and Republican Sovereignty in Early Modern Europe: Essays in Memory of Ragnhild Hatton,* ed. Robert Oresko, G. C. Gibbs, and Hamish M. Scott (New York: Cambridge Univ. Press, 1997), 139 n. 59.

40. Stevenson, "Scotland's First Newspaper," 123–6. Cf. *Information from the Estaits of the Kingdome of Scotland, to the Kingdome of England* ([Edinburgh], 1640); *Information from the Scottish Nation, to All the True English, Concerning the Present Expedition* ([Edinburgh], 1640]); *An Information to All Good Christians vvithin the Kingdome of England . . .* (Edinburgh, 1639).

41. John Stuart, ed., *Extracts from the Council Register of the Burgh of Aberdeen, 1625–1747,* 2 vols. (Edinburgh, 1871–2), 2:165–6; John Stuart, ed., *The Miscellany of the Spalding Club,* 5 vols. (Aberdeen: printed for the Club by W. Bennet, 1841–52), 5:181; J. P. Edmond, *The Aberdeen Printers: Edward Raban to James Nicol, 1620–1736,* 4 vols. (Aberdeen, J. & J. P. Edmond & Spark, 1884–6), 2: xxxv, xxvi, 91–2.

because no copies of it are now extant, but, whatever the case, these events occurred in the drastically changed world of the English conquest and the first Britain. Then a large-scale, print-based public culture within Scotland did begin to appear. A. J. Mann argues persuasively that the 1650s are the axial moment in the rise of the domestic Scottish press.[42]

Perhaps nothing more fully illustrates the contrast between Scotland's internal press and its international press than the campaign for the Netherlands. With the growing authoritarianism from the 1590s on in both England and Scotland, as well as in Europe generally, printing in the Low Countries became increasingly a press in exile. The great Presbyterian writers—Samuel Rutherford, Alexander Leighton, David Calderwood, Robert Baillie, among numerous others—would all have their (proscribed) works published there. Over a dozen of Calderwood's religious writings were printed at Leiden and Amsterdam between 1618 and 1624—some of them proving hugely influential. Small wonder the London government issued a proclamation in 1625 against forbidden books produced in the Netherlands. The government continually pressured Dutch authorities to introduce and enforce censorship. It sent in its own agents to discover, expose, and disrupt the clandestine presses. Today it is often forgotten how severely exercised James and his son became at what was happening in the Netherlands. Essential to the radicals' success were the sizeable Scots emigré communities whose ministers, such as Robert Dury at Leiden, Alexander Leighton at Utrecht, John Forbes with the Merchant Adventurers, Alexander Petrie at Rotterdam, and, most important, William Spang at Vere and then Middelburg, maintained close links with the Presbyterian leadership in Scotland. No less important were the long-standing connections with Dutch printers and Dutch Calvinism.[43]

To be sure, the Netherlands would also host a substantial English Puritan press as well, no less large and at least as important. The works of the great scholars and philo-Semites Thomas Brightman and Hugh Broughton would appear there, along with that of many significant lesser lights. Brightman and Broughton enduringly reshaped all the Anglophone cultures. But English Puritanism in the Low Countries, however influential, however important, was slow to become more than a press in exile, one seeking change

---

42. Mann, *Scottish Book Trade,* esp. 33, 103, 128, 157, 232. It is noteworthy that throughout 1657, the Aberdeen city council promoted the publication of a wide range of books—while also trying to prevent the publication and dissemination of Quaker writings.

43. Mann, "Press and Military Conflict," 268; Sprunger, *Trumpets,* 115; Mann, *Scottish Book Trade,* 80, 82, 57–8. See A. H. Williamson, *Scottish National Consciousness in the Age of James VI: The Apocalypse, the Union and the Shaping of Scotland's Public Culture* (Edinburgh: John Donald, 1979), 32–3.

in England, serving the exiled English churches. Naturally enough, English scholars, like all scholars, sought to speak to the world, and Broughton's claim — "Francfurt Mart shall beare me witnesse" — is well known.[44] By the 1630s, however, the Scottish press, or, perhaps better, the Scoto-Dutch press, tried to enter into the high politics of the Netherlands and did so with considerable success. Virtually every tract on behalf of the Covenanters — and outstandingly the Covenant itself — soon appeared in a Dutch translation, at times simultaneously. After a point it no longer becomes clear when a Dutch edition was produced at Edinburgh or in the United Provinces. Initially their visible purpose was to secure Dutch armaments and formal Dutch diplomatic neutrality, but, with success on the battlefield, the Netherlands' participation in the Solemn League and Covenant became the central objective.

The Crown reacted furiously. Scotland confronted a naval blockade. All mail from Scotland into England would be intercepted and examined at the border. Scots in England and Ireland found themselves constrained to swear a ferocious oath of loyalty to the king and renounce the Covenant. Often their homes would be searched by government agents. Potential sympathizers were interrogated. Renewed and determined pressure was placed on the Dutch Republic. Royalist agents moved into action. Often enough they met with some success, and the clandestine presses were forced to suspend operations, go underground, or move to other cities. Between 1638 and 1640, the most prominent agent, John Le Maire, hunted down at least seventeen subversive books in Amsterdam, Leiden, and Rotterdam. At one point, Le Maire congratulated himself for having foiled a French translation of one work but feared that thousands of copies in English had gotten off to Scotland. If there were a Dutch version, its whereabouts remained a question. Royalist censorship, interception, and disruption ultimately did not prove effective, and in the end the London government found it necessary to produce and disseminate a Dutch translation of Charles's 1638 proclamation.[45] Revolutionaries and royalists dueled in Dutch before the people of the republic — surely a pamphlet war unprecedented in British history.

---

44. Only Henry Finch's extraordinary work of apocalyptic philo-Semitism, *The Calling of the Jews* (1621), actually seems to have been translated into Dutch before 1640 (*Een schoon prophecye,* 1623). Sprunger, *Trumpets,* 59, 70. During the 1640s, English revolutionaries increasingly recognized the importance of addressing the Dutch in print, and by mid century a number of English works would see translation. Jason Peacey notes that Walter Strickland, Parliament's ambassador at The Hague, was understandably sensitive to this need. My thanks to Dr. Peacey for drawing Anglo-Dutch printing to my attention. Revolutionary Scotland, however, was much more vulnerable than the south and, as it happens, better connected to northern Europe.

45. Sprunger, *Trumpets,* 122; Donald, *Uncounselled King,* 188.

The Scots were certainly successful to the extent that they secured muni-
tions and still other assistance from the Netherlands. A number of Dutch
ministers attended the 1638 Glasgow Assembly that abjured episcopacy, and as
early as 1639, the University of Leiden expressed support for the Scots' struggle
for liberty. Relations continued to improve in the wake of the Covenanter triumph. The year 1643 marks the high point of Scottish power and influence,
whether in Britain, in the North Sea, in the Baltic, in central Europe, or in
Ireland. Although there would be no Dutch counterpart to the *Scottish Dove,*
something almost as telling did emerge. That year the Zeeland Synod formally
endorsed the Westminster Assembly and, more generally, the Scottish agenda.
The Scottish Parliament was so delighted that it immediately published the
Latin letter with English translation. And well they might be delighted, for
it was almost as if the Covenanters themselves had written the letter. The
Zeelanders called on the Scots to repair "the deplorable division between the
Kings most Excellent Majestie and his Parliament." At the same time, they
told of their "anxiety and sorrow" for "the lamentable condition of the kirk in
Irland and the troubled estate of the kirk in England." If the English church
were subverted (an implicit, though obvious reference to William Laud and
his policies), then the forces of the Counter-Reformation would "overturn
the kirks of Scotland, [and also] . . . bring the kirks of the Netherlands to
the same desolation." "The kirks within our bounds are so united [with the
English Church], that we judge if the kirks of England perish, they cannot
escape ruine." The future of Protestantism depended on Scottish-led reform
in Britain — as, presumably, did the outcome of the Thirty Years' War. "Goe
on constantly and couragiously in helping the afflicted [British] kirks." It was
high time for the reformed churches to "joyne their counsells, courage and
strength." [46]

The Scottish-Dutch connection was close in many ways. The Dutch revolt
against an absentee king spoke to the Scottish context, as did the political
thought of their prominent theorist Johannes Althusius.[47] Though royalist-

46. David Stevenson, *The Scottish Revolution, 1637–44: The Triumph of the Covenanters* (New
York: St. Martin's Press, 1974), 99, 128, 189; Kevin Sharpe, *The Personal Rule of Charles I* (New Haven,
CT: Yale Univ. Press, 1992), 833 n. 68; *A Letter from the Synod of Zeland, to the Commissioners of the
General Assembly of the Kirk of Scotland . . .* (Edinburgh, 1643), 14, 13, 18.

47. Edward J. Cowan, "The Making of the National Covenant," in Morrill, *Scottish National
Covenant,* 74–81, 89 n. 77. Cowan argues that Rutherford's *Lex Rex* draws extensively on Althusius, but more recently, John Coffey has noted that Rutherford's sources are wide-ranging and also
depend heavily on Catholic resistance theory. Coffey, "Samuel Rutherford and the Political Thought
of the Scottish Covenanters," in *The Celtic Dimensions of the British Civil Wars: Proceedings of the
Second Conference of the Research Centre in Scottish History, University of Strathclyde,* ed. J. R. Young
(Edinburgh: J. Donald Publishers, 1997), 75–95.

inspired lampoons of "the Scottish Nation" may or may not have occurred, anti-Scottish sentiment in the Netherlands seems to have possessed neither the scale nor the virulence, anti-Semitism, and anticommercialism that informed Scotophobia in Poland, Germany, and England. From the Netherlands the Scots would launch much of their published voice to the world, in at least four languages, with the intent of "filling all of Europe with their books." And from the Netherlands they would launch John Dury (1596–1680), probably the greatest Protestant irenicist of the seventeenth century. Born in Edinburgh but the son of an exiled Presbyterian minister, he grew up in Holland. Great nephew of Andrew Melville and his sometime student, the author of more than 228 works, Dury spent his long life tirelessly traversing Europe trying to create a Protestant theological union—and thereby the basis for political union. In a real sense, he was an heir to Melville, in significant ways a manifestation of the values in Melville's *Natalia*. It is hard to imagine a more complete product of Dutch and Scottish culture.

Still, for all their commonalty, in the end the connection between the two countries ultimately did not prove close enough. The year 1643 may have been the high point for Scottish aspirations both within Britain and in the United Provinces, but by 1645, Scotland's power and influence experienced a precipitous decline on both sides of the Channel, and in that year the Estates of Holland refused to sign the Solemn League and Covenant in order, they said, to preserve their neutrality.[48]

Scottish successes in seventeenth-century Europe are truly remarkable by any standard. Across the Continent, they shaped the course of events religiously, militarily, diplomatically, culturally. They shifted forever the history of the British Isles. The English republic—undoubtedly the century's most dynamic, radical, and creative state—drew heavily on Scottish thought, Scottish experience, Scottish ideals.[49] In still further ways the great republic paralleled the aspirations of the Scots, and not least with their apocalyptic hopes

---

48. Sprunger, *Trumpets,* 124; Mann, *Scottish Book Trade,* 77. A convenient summary of Dury's extraordinary career appears in Richard L. Greaves and Robert Zaller, eds., *Biographical Dictionary of British Radicals in the Seventeenth Century,* 3 vols. (Brighton, Sussex: Harvester Press, 1983–4).

49. This is not to say that English radicalism and republicanism were a Scottish import or simply replicated Scottish experience. Though the Parliamentarians drew on Scottish theorists such as Buchanan, adopted Scottish tactics such as the Triennial Act, reorganized their armed forces on the Scottish model, more frequently found the Covenant congenial than is commonly admitted, or often shared similar visions of world reform, English radicalism remains nevertheless a deeply indigenous phenomenon. The first republic, 1649–53, Sean Kelsey has shown, grew directly out of English experience and institutions. Kelsey, *Inventing a Republic: The Political Culture of the English Commonwealth, 1649–1653* (Manchester: Manchester Univ. Press, 1997). My thanks to David Scott for drawing my attention to this volume.

for an integration of British and Dutch societies.[50] The Scots had stimulated, politicized, and promoted public life in societies throughout much of Europe, and they had done so as a matter of coordinated policy.

The phenomenon becomes highlighted when printing is considered. The Scots connected with John Canne in Amsterdam and created the famous "Cloppenburgh press." They connected with George Smith in London and created the *Scottish Dove*.[51] Scottish radicalism long had a pan-British dimension. Yet there was an unmistakable downside. Scotland's international publication contrasted dramatically with the domestic. This Janus-faced experience with print may have been built into Scottish society, but it also entailed a grave cost to Scottish public life. Not one of Dury's 228 publications saw print within his native land. The growing royalist authoritarianism in Scotland from the later 1590s forced Melville to give over state poetry, lay aside the "Gathelus," his Scottish national epic, and concentrate on political-religious epigrams, mini-pamphlets easily disseminated and hard to suppress.[52] Many of Hume of Godscroft's major Latin treatises, much of his poetry, and all of his vernacular works could not be published during his lifetime. The second part of his remarkable treatise on Anglo-Scottish union was stopped in the press, even at Bordeaux. Clandestine presses never did well in seventeenth-century Scotland; efforts to set up one at Leith in 1607 proved short-lived.[53] There is no equivalent to England's Martin Marprelate and his successors. During the first decade of the seventeenth century, a furious and also surprisingly rich debate took place about King James's policy of reintroducing bishops into Scotland. Today it seems remote not because the issues no longer excite us but because so little of it has survived. William Cowper, the new bishop of Galloway, published an apology for accepting the office and what was for him

---

50. Described by Steven C. A. Pincus, *Protestantism and Patriotism: Ideologies and the Making of English Foreign Policy, 1650–1668* (New York: Cambridge Univ. Press, 1996), chap. 3. It should be noted that by the mid 1640s, the hostility of radical Englishmen toward the Scots could become arrestingly intense. But radical Scotophobia could never truly replicate the royalist variety. The Scottish revolutionary and civic tradition was too much a part of their intellectual furniture. In 1649 Marchamount Nedham could write violently anti-Scottish verse and yet consistently turned to that archetypal Scot George Buchanan as a republican icon. Nedham was no Cleveland, and modern historians, such as Joad Raymond and Conrad Russell, have missed this extraordinary irony. Raymond, *Newspaper*, 47–8; Russell, *The Crisis of Parliaments: English History, 1509–1660*, corrected ed. (New York: Oxford Univ. Press, 1990), 259.

51. Sprunger, *Trumpets*, 116.

52. See McGinnis and Williamson, *Buchanan: Political Poetry*, 31–6, 284–97. Also see James Doelman, *King James I and the Religious Culture of England* (Cambridge: D. S. Brewer, 2000), chap. 4.

53. David Masson, ed., *Register of the Privy Council of Scotland* (Edinburgh: H.M. General Register House, 1887), 8:84, 499–500.

a drastic volte-face. "Sindrie answered him in writt, becaus the presse was not patent to them as to him." By far the most notable of these was Godscroft, who went on to conduct a widely circulated correspondence with a number of the new bishops and soon emerged the terror of the Jacobean episcopal establishment. Godscroft's letters, effectively pamphlets, are remarkable and raised issues of striking precocity and sophistication. The letters could circulate only in manuscript because Godscroft "wanted the commoditie of the presse," and, tragically, only a handful of more than two dozen now survive.[54] Later on, the hugely prodigious Calderwood noted in one of his circulating manuscripts, "I confes I have only pointit at mony thingis quhilk I would have writt more fullie . . . if the prese war alse fre to us as to our opposits."[55] Not even the print shops of Amsterdam could compensate completely for the want of an indigenous industry. The cultural cost to Scotland can only have been enormous.

Among the manuscript writing that does survive, formal Latin treatises stand out rather than vernacular pamphlets, universal statements rather than the immediate claims of local political exchange. Neo-Latin literary culture and even Latin as the language of learning acquired a more central position than it would in Scotland's larger neighbors. It also remained important far longer. When Scottish scholars did have recourse to the vernacular—one thinks of Robert Pont and John Napier of Merchiston—it often resulted from unexpected needs, not authorial intention.[56] A huge amount of Scottish writing was geared for foreign consumption and only incidentally for domestic audiences. Scotland's deep international involvements underwrote the long survival of Scottish Latinity. Scottish priorities were ordered accordingly.

Scotland's great strength was also its great weakness. Both were built into the very tissues of early modern Scottish society, and change would not occur before the close of the seventeenth century. Just as relatively few books were imported on speculation into Scotland during earlier years of the sixteenth century—not because Scots chose not to read but because they were so deeply

---

54. Calderwood, *History,* 7:180. For a detailed discussion of Godscroft and the early seventeenth century, see McGinnis and Williamson, *British Union,* 24–53; Williamson, *Scottish National Consciousness,* chap. 4.

55. National Library of Scotland: Wodrow MS, quarto 84, no. 23 ("Reply of a Dotatyst"), f. 174.

56. See Arthur H. Williamson, "Number and National Consciousness: The Edinburgh Mathematicians and Scottish Political Culture at the Union of Crowns," in *Scots and Britons: Scottish Political Thought and the Union of 1603,* ed. Roger A. Mason (New York: Cambridge Univ. Press, 1994), 187–212.

immersed into the intellectual world of the Continent[57] — so later Scottish cosmopolitanism ensured that Scotland's press would be a transnational, European phenomenon. In this respect, the Scottish experience anticipates the French intellectual world at the end of the century and the dynamics of the early Enlightenment.[58] To understand them all, we need to look not at "the nature of the book" but at the varied, wide-ranging, and interacting cultures that produced the book. Andrew Melville has provided the key.

---

57. Ford, "Importation of Books," 200–1.

58. See Eisenstein, *PPAC,* 145; Jonathan Irvine Israel, *Radical Enlightenment: Philosophy and the Making of Modernity, 1650–1750* (New York: Oxford Univ. Press, 2001), 22.

Chapter 10

Change and the Printing Press in Sixteenth-Century Spanish America

ANTONIO RODRÍGUEZ-BUCKINGHAM

THE FIRST known printing press in the western hemisphere was established in Mexico City in September 1539 by Juan Pablos (1500?–60).[1] An Italian from Brescia, Pablos represented the Cromberger firm of Seville, one of the largest printing establishments in Spain during the sixteenth century.[2] A printer by the name of Esteban Martín is known to have resided in Mexico

I wish to express my gratitude to the Bernard Mendel Foundation of the Lilly Library at the University of Indiana for granting me the first Mendel Fellowship. The data I collected while at the Lilly Library was of crucial importance for the writing of this essay.

1. The following sources provide the best information on the history of the establishment of the first presses of the Americas and on the lives and production of the first printers. For Mexico and Peru, see José Toribio Medina, *La imprenta in Mexico: 1539–1821*, 8 vols. (Santiago de Chile: Casa del Autor, 1912; repr., Amsterdam: N. Israel, 1965), vol. 1; José Toribio Medina, *La imprenta en Lima, 1584–1824*, 2 vols. (Santiago de Chile: Casa del Autor, 1904; repr., Amsterdam: N. Israel, 1965), vol. 1; and José Torre Revello, *El libro, la imprenta y el periodismo en América durante la dominación Española* (Buenos Aires: Casa Jacobo Peuser, 1940). For Mexico, see Joaquín García Icazbalceta, *Bibliografía Mexicana del siglo XVI, catálogo razonado de libros impresos en Mexico de 1539 a 1600*, new ed. by Agustín Millares Carlo (Mexico City: Fondo de Cultura Económica, 1954); Henry R. Wagner, *Nueva bibliografía Mexicana del siglo XVI, suplemento a las bibliografías de don Joaquín García Icazbalceta, don José Toribio Medina y don Nicolás León*, trans. Joaquín García Pimental and Federico Gómez de Orozco (Mexico City: Éditorial Polis, 1940); and Emilio Valtón, *Impresos Mexicanos del siglo XVI (incunables Americanos) en la Biblioteca Nacional de México, el Museo Nacional y el Archivo General de la Nación* (Mexico City: Impr. Universitaria, 1935). For Peru, see Rubén Vargas Ugarte, *Biblioteca Peruana*, 12 vols. (Lima: Editorial San Marcos, 1935–58), vol. 7. For information on individual printers, see Agustín Millares Carlo and Julián Calvo, *Juan Pablos, primer impresor que a esta tierra vino* (Mexico City: Librería de M. Porrúa, 1953); Alexandre A. M. Stols, *Antonio de Espinosa, el segundo impresor Mexicano* (Mexico City: Universidad Nacional Autónoma de México, 1962); Alexandre A. M. Stols, *Pedro Ocharte, el tercer impresor Mexicano* (Mexico City: Imprenta Nuevo Mundo, 1962); and Antonio Rodríguez-Buckingham, "Colonial Peru and the Printing Press of Antonio Ricardo" (Ph.D. diss., University of Michigan, 1977).

2. For a definitive study on Juan Cromberger, see Clive Griffin, *The Crombergers of Seville: The History of a Printing and Merchant Dynasty* (Oxford: Clarendon Press; New York: Oxford Univ. Press, 1988).

216

City in 1535, and some scholars believe he exercised the trade there. An *Escala espiritual para llegar al cielo* of Saint John Climax and a *Catechismo mexicano* dated 1537 have been attributed to him, but neither a copy of these books nor any other work with Martín's imprint has ever been found.

Juan Cromberger (1500?–40), head of the firm, died in Seville, and from 1548 to 1559, Pablos became the exclusive printer in the colonies. Nine other printers are known to have worked in Mexico before the end of the century. The first was Antonio de Espinosa, a Spaniard from Jaén who moved to Mexico in 1554 to work for Pablos. Realizing there was room in Mexico for more than one printer, he returned to Spain to seek permission from the king to break Pablos's monopoly. Espinosa obtained the desired license from the king on September 7, 1558, and returned to print in Mexico. His production there lasted from 1559 until 1576, the year he is thought to have died. Pedro Ocharte, a Frenchman from Rouen who printed from 1563 until 1592, followed Espinosa. Accused of heresy before the Inquisition, he was forced to stop working between 1572 and 1576. While facing serious difficulties after the trial, he was able to continue printing until his death in 1592. Pedro Balli, either a Frenchman or a Spaniard of French origin who went to Mexico as a book dealer, followed Ocharte, printing between 1574 and 1600. The fourth printer after Pablos was Antonio Ricardo. He was an Italian from Turin who printed in Mexico between 1577 and 1579, the year before he moved to Peru, where he was the first and only printer in South America until his death in 1605. Maria Sansoric, Ocharte's widow, followed Ricardo. She printed two books, one in 1594 and another with Cornelio Adriano Cesar in either 1597 or 1598. Melchor Ocharte, probably a son of Pedro and Maria who printed one book in 1597, followed her. For reasons unclear, his work was interrupted until 1599, after which it continued until 1601. The seventh printer after Pablos was Fleming Enrico Martinez, an engineer by training, who printed from 1599 to 1611. Luis Ocharte Figueroa, another member of the Ocharte family who printed from 1600 to 1601, followed him. Cornelio Adriano Cesar, a Dutchman who worked for Christophe Plantin (1514–89) in Leiden, had a press in Mexico toward the end of the century, but before he could function, the Inquisition tried him for being a Lutheran. He appears in 1594 and 1597, associated with the press of Maria Sansoric. After the trial, and most likely cleared of all charges, he took over the press of Santiago Tlatelolco, a Franciscan school for the children of prominent native families. Most of his work was done during the seventeenth century. Presumably Antonio Alvarez, a Spaniard, also worked in Mexico during the sixteenth century, but no imprints have been found to support reports of his work. This study considers the activities of those sixteenth-century printers whose materials have been found.

Elizabeth Eisenstein, in her seminal study of the press as an agent of change, addresses the topic of dissemination as an issue of print culture. Two of her comments are of particular importance to my research and provide a starting point for this essay. The first is a call for historical studies to clarify the specific effect created by an increased supply of texts when directed at different markets.[3] Without questioning this need, it seems equally important to clarify the effect of such an increase if directed at a single market. The second comment refers to the interplay between text and illustrations made possible by the printing press.[4] The illustrated initial letters used by the printers of Mexico and Peru are an example of this interplay. Their presence in the early books of the Spanish colonies suggests connections with printing houses in and out of Spain hitherto not considered. In this essay, I examine the content of the first printings of Spanish America, taking into account the press's mission to disseminate Christianity among the natives of the viceroyalties of Mexico and Peru. I also study the provenance of some of the illustrated letters shown in the books and underscore the importance of the illustrated letter as a device with dual quality of text and image.

The kings of Spain, first Charles V (1500–58) and later his son and successor, Philip II (1527–98), were reluctant to allow printing presses in their viceroyalties of Nueva España (Mexico) and Nueva Castilla (Peru).[5] They understood the connection between the spreading of Martin Luther's writings and the capabilities of the press for wide and fast dissemination of ideas. For them, it was a matter of utmost importance that the production and circulation of books, particularly to the colonies, be made under close supervision.

Royal control over the printed book in Spain had surprisingly liberal beginnings. Queen Isabella (1451–1504), grandmother of Charles V, issued a royal decree on December 25, 1477, exempting one of the first printers of Spain from paying taxes. The mandate was reiterated in 1480, when both Isabella and Ferdinand (1452–1516) extended these privileges to all foreign books entering Spain. By the early sixteenth century, however, the attitude had changed. Even before Luther, the Church had objected to the printing of certain items, notably Bibles.[6] Isabella and Ferdinand signed a stern decree

---

3. Eisenstein, *PPAC,* 71.

4. Ibid., 55.

5. Reacting to the spread of Protestant ideas, Charles V in 1546 commissioned the faculty at the University of Louvain to prepare a list of "dangerous" books printed in Germany. The list was the basis for the *Index Librorum Prohibitorum,* the official list of works whose reading was forbidden by the Roman Catholic Church. In 1558, Philip II issued a mandate placing considerable restrictions on the permission to print books. The king was reacting to a request from the Council of Castile to allow the reading of only religious books. Torre Revello, *El libro, la imprenta y el periodismo en América,* 23, 25.

6. Eisenstein, *PPAC,* 347.

on July 8, 1502, requiring a license before any book could be printed. Until the introduction in 1551 of the official list of objectionable books known as the *Index Librorum Prohibitorum,* the process for obtaining the license was the major tool for censoring books in Spain and its colonies. The processes varied, but it involved extensive and repeated page-by-page examinations of the prospective manuscript by a body of members of chancelleries and bishoprics backed by the Inquisition. While examining the manuscript, the censors prepared a list of errors and recommended deletions and submitted it with the manuscript to a royal clerk, who handed them to the printer after confirming that the process had been carried out. A version showing the corrections was prepared by the printer and sent back to the clerk with the manuscript and the original documents. The censors and the clerk verified the accuracy of the version. If it was approved, two printed copies were ordered from the printer for revision before approval for the final printing was granted.[7]

Books on various subjects had been taken to the Americas since the early years of the Spanish presence. Often the traffic of books created reactions from the authorities that reveal their apprehension. Books of chivalry and in particular the stories of Amadís of Gaul were considered especially noxious. A royal decree dated April 4, 1531, signed by Empress Isabel of Portugal (1503–39), wife of Charles V, minces no words in expressing the empress's dissatisfaction. She states that many books in the Spanish language dealing with "vain and profane subjects such as Amadís and others of its kind have been circulating to the Indies with bad consequence to the Indians." She ordered that the traffic be stopped immediately and that only "books on religion and other pious subjects" be allowed to enter.[8] Lists of objectionable books registered in the logs of captains of ships entering the colonies draw attention to the difficulties involved in controlling the traffic of books across vast distances.[9] Studies of holdings in monastic libraries and private collections during colonial times reveal scores of books on questionable topics, as well as books from regions of the world that were unacceptable at the time.[10] Clearly the traffic of books was difficult to control.

The difficulties involved in controlling the influx of books fueled royal

---

7. Torre Revello, *El libro, la imprenta y el periodismo en América,* 26.

8. José Toribio Medina, *Biblioteca Hispano-Americana, 1493–1810,* 7 vols. (Santiago de Chile: Casa del Autor, 1898–1907), 6:xxvii.

9. Irving A. Leonard, *Books of the Brave, Being an Account of Books and Men in the Spanish Conquest and Settlement of the Sixteenth-Century New World* (New York: Gordian, 1964).

10. See Miguel Mathes, *Santa Cruz de Tlatelolco: La primer biblioteca académica de las Américas* (Mexico City: Secretaría de Relaciones Exteriores, 1982); and Antonio Rodríguez-Buckingham, "Monastic Libraries and Early Printing in Sixteenth-Century Spanish America," *Libraries and Culture* 24.1 (1989): 33–56. Teodoro Hampe Martínez has done extensive work on the private libraries of Peru during the sixteenth and seventeenth centuries. See his "Una biblioteca cusqueña confiscada por la

apprehensions regarding the establishment of local presses. Nonetheless, it was evident that books were needed in the colonies to support the efforts to catechize the Native Americans. The principle of *patronato real* (royal patronage), a relationship between the Church and the Crown where the king had the upper hand, gave the king the leverage to resist the demands by the clergy to print the books in situ. But the same principle made the king responsible for facilitating every effort directed at saving the souls of his subjects. Native Americans came under royal patronage through a bull obtained by the missionaries and the Spanish crown from Pope Paul III on April 17, 1537, proclaiming that as human beings and not by nature slaves, Native Americans were capable of receiving the Christian faith. The dilemma now was how to support the catechizing effort without exposing the natives to the heresies that circulated in Europe at the time.

A solution that appealed to both Charles V and Philip II was to provide the required books while keeping the control of their content in Europe by using the services of recognized printers in Europe whose work they knew. They commissioned the firms of Cromberger and Christophe Plantin to print religious materials for use in the Americas. Predictably, however, this solution did not satisfy the need for religious books in the native languages, a major consideration.

The problems of ensuring accuracy and issuing licenses to materials destined to be used across the seas presented managerial obstacles of nightmarish proportions. Revisions by individuals with expertise in theology and in languages hitherto unknown were necessary at both ends of the process to ensure that the message in the book had not been distorted. Even under the best conditions, the process could take decades. Nonetheless, Charles continued his reluctance to allow a press in Mexico, and Philip felt the same way about Peru years later. A Christian *doctrina* in Spanish and a Mexican language (probably Náhuatl) was commissioned in 1537 from a printer of Seville, most likely Cromberger. Years later, the first imprint of Peru was issued days before the permit from the king actually arrived in Lima. Even after the presses in both Mexico and Peru were functioning, some printing of books in native tongues continued in Spain. For example, one of the editions of a grammar and vocabulary in Quechua, a language of Peru, was printed in Seville in 1603. In these cases, the likely reason was that the best-qualified expert had been transferred from the colonies and was living in a monastery in Spain.

When permission was finally granted to the press of Mexico, the main

Inquisición: El proceso al doctor Agustín Valenciano de Quiñones, hereje reconciliado (1574–1595)," *Revista Andina* 10 (December 1987): 527–64.

purpose was to issue religious books in native tongues. While other uses were not clearly specified, both the emperor and the Church left no doubt that regardless of language, any book issued in the colonies had to be an artifact intimately associated with the dissemination and defense of Catholic dogma and the policies of the Spanish Crown. Nevertheless, the reality in the world the printers encountered soon made them search for alternatives to the limited market for their books. The list of subjects studied here reveals that from the start not all the books printed were in compliance with the original mission of the press. The third item printed by Pablos was an account of a devastating earthquake that destroyed Guatemala City the night of September 10, 1541: *Relación del espantable terremoto que agora nueuamente ha acontecido en la cibdad de Guatimala* (1541). (Mexican imprints are identified parenthetically in the text by their numbers in Joaquín García Icazbalceta's *Bibliografía Mexicana del siglo XVI,* which readers should consult for complete information. The *Relación* is García Icazbalceta 3.) The first imprint of Peru was a royal mandate calling for the implementation of the Gregorian calendar: *Pragmática sobre los diez días del año* (1584). (Peruvian imprints are identified parenthetically in the text by their numbers in Rubén Vargas Ugarte's *Biblioteca Peruana,* vol. 7. The *Pragmática* is Vargas Ugarte 1.)

Royal apprehensions were justified years later when new printers appeared on the scene, and some encountered serious difficulties with the Inquisition. It is not my purpose here to revisit the horrors and abuses perpetrated by the Inquisition and its predecessors since the early years of the conquest in both viceroyalties.[11] But it is important to mention some of the activities of the Holy Office in matters concerning the printers. Between 1571, when the Inquisition was officially established in Mexico, and 1600, two major printers faced serious charges before the Holy Office: the French-born Pedro Ocharte, whose original name was probably Pierre Charte, son-in-law of Juan Pablos, and the Dutch-born Cornelio Adriano Cesar, probably Cornelis Adriaen de Keyser. Juan Ortiz, an engraver, was also accused. In Peru, Antonio Ricardo was summoned by the Inquisition in 1605 to answer questions regarding an incident in which Ricardo was involved. The Holy Office had arrived in Lima in 1570.

The charges against all of these people do not relate directly to the books they printed but to their being foreign with suspicious leanings and possible

---

11. Extensive studies on these subjects are published in José Toribio Medina, *Historia del Tribunal del Santo Oficio de la Inquisición en Mexico,* 2nd. ed., suppl. Julio Jiménez Rueda (Mexico City: Ediciones Fuente Cultural, 1952); and Ricardo Palma, *Anales de la Inquisición de Lima: Estudio histórico* (Lima: Tipografía de Aurelio Alfaro, 1863).

connections with areas of Europe considered dangerous. That they worked in a new and sensitive technology did not help their cases. All of them were at one time associated with the house of Ocharte. Pedro, the head of the family, was brought before the Inquisition in 1572 to face charges of harboring Lutheran feelings, and after a painful trial, was released in 1573. Juan Ortiz, a Frenchman and an associate of Ocharte, was also accused of being a Lutheran.[12] Before moving to Peru, Ricardo and Ocharte were partners in printing one of the books in native tongues (García Icazbalceta 91). Evidence of their partnership remains in a will Ricardo made in 1586 in Lima leaving twenty-three hundred pesos to pay a debt to Ocharte.[13] Later, between 1594 and 1596, Cornelio Adriano Cesar began to work for Maria Sansoric, Ocharte's widow.[14]

Ricardo was the only one in the group who was not accused of heresy. His predicament had a more mundane origin. Luis Antonio Eguiguren, one of his biographers, reports an unpublished bill of sale dated April 1605, before Francisco Dávila, notary public, which describes the following incident. Martín Díaz de Contreras, secretary of the governing body known as Real Audiencia, was present in the main plaza of Lima while Alonso de la Paz, auctioneer, was auctioning the property of a woman named María Cardona. Among the items auctioned were some engraved portraits that the auctioneer advertised as representations of "twelve emperors, twelve popes, and twelve apostles at four pesos of eight reales each." Ricardo was in the audience accompanied by an unnamed Andalusian, who remarked aloud, "Take away the emperors, my good man. All together, they are not worth half a peso." According to Eguiguren, the rest of the buyers withdrew because of the Andalusian's poorly chosen remark. Ricardo and the Andalusian had to appear before the Inquisition to testify about their role in the incident. Eguiguren states that only Ricardo's prestige saved him from serious difficulties.[15]

Much attention has been given over the years to the subject of printing in the native languages, and it is a subject that merits exclusive and extensive treatment. To facilitate this study of the general production of the presses, however, I include just a brief background of the languages in question. Of

---

12. Archivo General de la Nación, *Libros y libreros del siglo XVI* (Mexico City: Tipografía Guerrero, 1914), 85–90.

13. Márquez Abanto, "Don Antonio Ricardo, introductor de la imprenta en Lima; su testamento y codicilio," *Revista del Archivo Nacional del Perú* 19 (1955): 295.

14. Alexandre A.M. Stols places the time Cesar began to work for Maria Sansoric between 1595 and 1596. See his "The Harlem Printer Cornelio Adriano César Tried before the Mexican Inquisition 1598," in *Studia Bibliographica in Honorem Herman de la Fontaine Verwey,* ed. S. van der Woude (Amsterdam: Menno Hertzberger, [1968]), 356–63.

15. Luis Antonio Eguiguren, *Las calles de Lima* (Lima, 1945), 341.

the many languages spoken in Mexico and Peru at the time of the Spanish Conquest,[16] the earliest missionaries dealt primarily with the major ones. Their task was monumental, for there were no original support materials about these languages in the form of grammars or dictionaries. Many of the early religious books were translated into the native tongues with the help of bilingual natives and the personal notes the missionaries took in the field. The native language found most commonly in sixteenth-century books printed in Mexico was Náhuatl, often referred to as Mexican. It is part of the Uto-Aztecan family and was the language spoken by the Aztecs who entered the Valley of Mexico around A.D. 900. It was the lingua franca of the Aztec Empire and of the people the Spaniards encountered in their conquest of Mexico. Náhuatl, which at the time was written in hieroglyphs, is still spoken in some parts of central Mexico. Other books were printed in the Tarascan language (often referred to as *lengua de Michuacan*), which belongs to the Tarasco-Insolate family, still spoken in the state of Michuacan in western Mexico; in *lengua Zapoteca, still* spoken by the Otomanguean group of the states of Oaxaca and Tehuantepec and in the southern Sierra region of Mexico; and. in the Chuchona language. Part of the popoloca-chocha, Chuchona was spoken in the state of Puebla and is still spoken in that region of Mexico.

The languages that appear in the early books from Peru are the two main languages spoken there at the time, the Quechua (or Quichua) and the Aymara. The first is part of the Quichuan family of South American languages and was the lingua franca of the Inca Empire. It is still spoken in the central Andes of South America, including parts of Bolivia and Ecuador. Aymara is part of the family of languages of the same name, and was spoken in southeastern Peru in the areas of Puno, Titicaca Lake, and Bolivia. Aymara is still spoken in those regions.

The importance the missionaries gave to printing religious books in native languages invites responses about the result of their efforts, the native reception of the printed texts, the extent of the production of the early presses, and the subjects selected for printing in the Americas. Scholars have assumed that religious books in native languages are to be found in significant numbers, and that the production of the early presses was limited to those books. They have also assumed that, because of the reluctance of the Spanish monarchs to relinquish European control over the colonial printing process, the position of Seville as the crossroads to the Americas, and the fact that for nearly twenty years Juan Pablos used gothic type and illustrations from Cromberger, that

---

16. Margaret Bunson and Stephen M. Bunson, *Encyclopedia of Ancient Mesoamerica* (New York: Facts on File, 1996).

the typography used in the early presses was identical to that used in Seville, mostly by Cromberger.[17] These assumptions render a view of the Spanish American books as unidimensional artifacts and discourage further analysis of their intellectual content or physical characteristics. The direction of this research allows only brief comments about the outcome of the catechizing effort of the missionaries and the natives' reception of the book; my observations about the numbers, content, and format of the early imprints are more conclusive.

The remarkable vigor with which the natives of Mexico and Peru held on to their mythologies and world views is noted in the campaigns to change them marshaled during the sixteenth and early seventeenth centuries by the Church and the Crown. The main object of councils of bishops held in Mexico and Peru during that time was to discuss issues related to the catechizing of the native populations. The outcome of the effort did not give the Church reasons to be satisfied. More than the failure to indoctrinate, the main problem seemed to be that the natives incorporated their views into the Christian message.[18] For sixteenth-century minds, deeply committed to the meaning of that message, blending Christianity with other world views was an anathema and thus totally unacceptable. Such labels as "superstition" or "idolatry" appear in many of the books studied here as prelude to the campaigns of *extirpación de la idolatría* that acquired momentum in the seventeenth century.

Written reports called *informes* or *visitas* by authorities from both viceroyalties reveal Spanish concerns with the results of their Christianizing efforts. Good examples are a treatise on the superstitions and idolatry from Mexico by Hernando Ruiz de Alarcón, titled *Tratado de las supersticiones* (1629), and *Manual de ministros* (1659), a manual for priests by Jacinto de la Serna.[19] In Peru, a report titled *Informaciones acerca de la religion y gobierno de los Incas,* by Juan Polo de Ondegardo, a lawyer, informed the authorities about the religion and government of the viceroyalty. It includes a section called "Mitos y surpersticiones de los indios," which deals with subjects such as the mythology of the Incas, their sacred shrines in Peru, the cult of the dead, sorcery, and "idolatry." The section is included in the *Confessionario para los curas de Indios,* printed by Ricardo in 1585 (Vargas Ugarte 3).

Mexicans and Peruvians recognized the book as an icon of power of the

---

17. Daniel B. Updike, *Printing Types, Their History, Forms, and Use: A Study in Survivals,* 2 vols. (Cambridge, MA: Harvard Univ. Press, Belknap Press, 1966), 2:60.

18. Charles Gibson, *The Aztecs Under Spanish Rule: A History of the Indians of the Valley of Mexico, 1519–1810* (Stanford, CA: Stanford Univ. Press, 1964), 100.

19. Jacinto de la Serna, "Manual de ministros de los indios para el conocimiento de sus idolatrias, y extirpación de ellas," *Anales del Museo Nacional de México,* epoca 1, 6 (1892–9): 261–480.

dominant group. Before the arrival of Europeans, there was a tradition of writing in books in Mesoamerica, but only a few of those handwritten books survived the conquest. Paradoxically, some of the same zealots who destroyed them also trained young Mexicans to help them translate the texts into the Roman alphabet. Several early colonial books, such as the Codex Mendoza, were lavishly illustrated under the supervision of Spanish clerics to inform the king of Spain about his new subjects. Included in this book and others, such as the Codex Telleriano-Remensis, are depictions of rituals, divination, calendars, deities, scenes of daily life, and more. They were part of the message to Charles V that assistance for the Christianizing effort was seriously needed.

A later group of manuscripts called Techialoyan is believed by some scholars to date from the sixteenth century, though more date them considerably later. They are no different in shape from European manuscripts with leaves sewn at the spine. The paper was made from a native fir-bark called *amate,* and their illustrations are watercolors depicting individuals, maps, and landmarks. Supposedly, their purpose was to support legal arguments in land ownership and inheritance disputes.[20]

The European book was a totally foreign artifact to the ancient Peruvians. Their means for distant communication included the *quipus,* a complex system of color-coded cords and knots.[21] Yet Felipe Guamán Poma de Ayala began his *Nueva crónica y buen gobierno* the same year (1585) that a *Doctrina Christiana* was printed by Antonio Ricardo (Vargas Ugarte 2).[22] This remarkable linguistic, ethnographic, and artistic document, intended for the king of Spain, is an Andean exposé of the Spanish presence in Peru between 1565 and 1615. In 1,189 pages, 398 of which are illustrated, Guamán Poma records the relations in the viceroyalty between conquerors and conquered through scenes of everyday life. The book opens a window into the native resistance to acculturation by the dominant society through the interplay of the native conception of the world expressed in images and text.[23] It is important here because it reveals that a native Peruvian author, shortly after the conquest, recognized the book as an icon of power and used it to make his point to the

---

20. Donald Robertson, *Mexican Manuscript Painting of the Early Colonial Period: The Metropolitan Schools* (New Haven, CT: Yale Univ. Press, 1959).

21. Marcia Ascher and Robert Ascher, *Code of the Quipu: A Study in Media, Mathematics, and Culture* (Ann Arbor: Univ. of Michigan Press, 1981).

22. Rolena Adorno, expert on this subject, dates the composition of the text between 1585 and 1615. Mercedes López-Baralt, *Icono y conquista: Guamán Poma de Ayala* (Madrid: Hiperión, 1988), 74.

23. Rolena Adorno, *Guamán Poma: Writing and Resistance in Colonial Peru* (Austin: Univ. of Texas Press, 1986), 27.

king of Spain. Mercedes López-Baralt, in her study of the manuscript, notes one of the drawings showing Guamán Poma with his book in hand, kneeling before King Phillip III. López-Baralt points out the perfectly bound European format of the book drawn by Guamán Poma. Unfortunately, the book never reached the king's hands, and the scene never took place.

In the discussion that follows, I examine 220 titles, 180 from Mexico, printed before 1601, and 40 from Peru, printed before 1606. The titles are classified by subject for a study, first, of their intellectual content, then, of their physical characteristics for clues to the diversity of their provenance.

Subject Study: Mexico

Eighty-one of the imprints of Mexico are classified under the subject of religion. Thirty-nine of these are exclusively in a native language or a native language combined with Spanish or Latin, while forty-two are in either Spanish or Latin. Twenty-five of the religious books are *doctrinas,* printed for use in indoctrinating the natives and others in religious matters. Not all are in a native language. While the first book Pablos printed, Juan de Zumárraga's *Breve y muy compendiosa doctrina Christiana* (1539) (García Icazbalceta 1), is in Spanish and Náhuatl, the fourth book, Zumárraga's *Doctrina breue muy prouechosa* (1543) (García Icazbalceta 4), for children, is only in Spanish. The remaining religious books are for activities such as prayer or singing. Two of these are in Latin. One is a fragment of a religious calendar in Spanish (1577?) (García Icazbalceta 83).

Other children's books, not always religious, were printed in native languages. In 1559, for example, *Cartilla para los niños en lengua Tarasca* by Maturino Gilberti (García Icazbalceta 36) was published in Tarascan to teach children how to read. This *Cartilla* was reissued in two other native languages, once in 1575 as part of Gilberti's *Thesoro spiritual de pobres en lengua de Michuacán* (García Icazbalceta 73) and then in 1580 in Chuchona (García Icazbalceta 100).

Sixteen Mexican imprints identified as linguistics are studies of native languages. Twelve are about the vocabulary or grammar of the native tongues. Most significant among them are Maturino Gilberti, *Arte en lengua de Michoacán* (1558) (García Icazbalceta 32), a study of the grammar of the Michuacan language; Alonso de Molina, *Arte de la lengua Mexicana y Castellana* (1571) (García Icazbalceta 65), a comparative study of Náhuatl and Spanish grammars; and Juan de Cordova, *Vocabulario en lengua Zapoteca* (1578) (García Icazbalceta 91), a dictionary of the Zapotec language. Some of these books contain information about attitudes or even policies of the time. For example, in *Arte en lengua de Michoacán,* Gilberti discusses the importance of communicating with the natives in their own language, and Cordova's *Vocabulario* includes statements granting authority to the author to regulate the printing of his own work. Finally, not all books classified under linguistics were studies of native languages. Gilberti's *Grammatica* (1559) (García Icazbalceta 37) is a Latin grammar, written for the students of the Royal and Imperial College for the Indians of Santiago Tlatelolco.

The third subject represented among sixteenth-century Mexican imprints is information and entertainment. Even though legislation forbade the colonies to print materials about themselves, the subject appears in both Mexico and in Peru. According to José Torre Revello, these laws were broken so often that a royal mandate was issued in the next century directed at the viceroys of Mexico and Peru.[24] *Relación del espantable terremoto* (1541) (García Icazbalceta 3) is the narrative of an earthquake that devastated Guatemala City, written by an eyewitness, Juan Rodríguez, who gives the precise date and time of the event (Saturday, September 10, 1541, at 2:00 A.M.) and the names and occupations of the victims. Under the same subject is Francisco Cervantes de Salazar, *Commentaria in Ludovici Vives excercitationes lingua Latinae* (1554) (García Icazbalceta 23). In this work, Vives, who taught Latin to the young Mary Tudor, later queen of England, describes the University of Mexico, the city and its attractions, and the country. *Tvmvlo imperial de la gran ciudad de Mexico* (1560) (García Icazbalceta 40), also by Cervantes de Salazar, documents what was perhaps the most luxurious *túmulo,* or burial altar, in Mexico, that honoring Charles V. Luis de Velasco, viceroy of Mexico, gave permission to Antonio de Espinosa to print the book, which includes many descriptions of Mexico City and New Spain. Espinosa was a punch-cutter and engraver of considerable skill who arrived in Mexico in the early 1550s to work for Pablos. Joaquín García Icazbalceta considers this work to be the first literary production of Mexico.[25] Another book clearly intended to inspire awe and impress the reader about the land is Juan de Cárdenas, *Primera parte de los problemas y secretos maravillosos de las Indias* (1591) (García Icazbalceta 119), a three-part work that describes the climate, minerals, plants, and such "strange properties of the land" as volcanoes and earthquakes, the various maladies that attacked the Spaniards living in the colonies, and habits of the inhabitants, such as tobacco smoking.[26] Two books under this subject were intended for sophisticated audiences. In 1577, Antonio Ricardo printed Ovid's *De tristibus*

---

24. Torre Revelo, *El libro, la imprenta y el periodismo en América,* 45–6.
25. García Icazbalceta, *Bibliografía Mexicana del siglo XVI,* 161.
26. Ibid., 399.

(García Icazbalceta 84), the first book of Latin poetry printed in the western hemisphere. The other book is *Carta del Padre Pedro de Morales* (1579) (García Icazbalceta 97), a narrative describing the festivities that took place in Mexico upon the relocation of the relics of Saint Gregory XIII. The main part of the festivity covered in the book was a literary contest that included a play or *acto sacramental* called *Triunfo de los santos*. The first play printed in the western hemisphere, the *acto* deals with the triumph of the saints and the Church upon the crowning of Emperor Constantin.

Theology, medicine, and military science are found only in Mexican imprints. Most of the imprints classified as theology are abstracts of position papers in Latin referred to as theses. They are broadsides of only one or two leaves each, on a point of philosophy or religion, presented for discussion at the university by a scholar. The distinction is made between the subjects of theology and religion to separate the former from books of instruction and prayer. Five titles are on medicine and two on military science. Alonso Lopez de Hinojosos, *Summa y recopilación de chirugia* appeared first in 1578 (García Icazbalceta 93) and then again in 1595 (García Icazbalceta 131). Agustín Farfán, *Tractado breve de anathomía y chirugía* was printed in 1579 (García Icazbalceta 95), and Farfán's *Tractado brebe de medicina y de todas las enfermedades* in 1592 (García Icazbalceta 122). On the imprints on military science, one, Diego García de Palacio, *Dialogos militares, de la formación, e información de personas, instrumentos, y cosas nescessarias para el buen vso dela guerra* (1583) (García Icazbalceta 103), is on army matters and the other, by the same author, *Instrvción navtica, para el bven vso, y regimiento de las naos, su traza, y y* [sic] *gouierno conforme a la altura de Mexico* (1587) (García Icazbalceta 114), is on navy issues.

Subject Study: Peru

Of the forty imprints recorded from Peru, only six are religious, of which four are in Spanish and the native languages. The first book printed in Peru, *Doctrina Christiana y catecismo para instrucción de los Indios* (1584) (Vargas Ugarte 2), is in the three major languages of the country, Spanish, Quichua, and Aymara. Much like the first book printed in Mexico, this *doctrina* addresses precisely the mission assigned to the press. Two other religious books in the three languages were printed in the following year: *Confessionario para los curas de Indios* (Vargas Ugarte 4) and *Tercero cathecismo y exposición de la doctrina Christiana por sermones* (Vargas Ugarte 3). The *Confessionario* is a book of instructions for the priests to counterbalance the religious rites of the natives and contains a wealth of information for the historian and ethnographer. Inserted within the instructions are descriptions of native religion, costumes, beliefs, and social interaction. Also under this subject is Luis Gerónimo de Oré, *Symbolo Cathólico Indiano* (1598) (Vargas Ugarte 19). Combining religious instruction and a large body of ethnohistoric information, with parts in Quichua and Aymara, *Symbolo* contains what may be the first post-contact poem in a Native American language, printed in roman characters. It also possesses the first copyright granted to an author in South America.

Books on the languages (linguistics) are well represented in the Peruvian press. *Arte y vocabulario en la lengua general del Piru llamada Quichua* (1586) (Vargas Ugarte 5) is the first book in this category. Ricardo printed a second edition in 1604 (Vargas Ugarte 38). The 1586 edition is printed entirely in roman type, while in the 1604 edition, the Spanish section is printed in italics. Though considerably larger than the first, the second edition occupies about the same number of leaves, enabling the printer to save a substantial amount of paper.[27] While there are other example that show Ricardo's skill as a printer, this one underscores his knowledge of the latest trends and shows that his equipment was on a par with that of contemporary Europe.

Information and entertainment is represented by five titles. In a style that resembles a news article, the first three items recount the attack of the buccaneer Richard Hawkins on Chilean towns, his capture, and his imprisonment in Lima. *Traslado de una carta* (1594) (Vargas Ugarte 11) is the printed Spanish translation of a letter Hawkins wrote to his father in London. As in Mexico, some books under this subject were intended to entertain sophisticated audiences. Pedro de Oña's *Primera parte de Arauco domado* (1596) (Vargas Ugarte 16) is an extensive epic poem in octaves, the first written by an American author, and the first about an American subject written and printed in the Americas. Abounding with ethnographic and geographic descriptions, the work deals with the settlement of the region of Chile populated by the Araucaneans. The subject complements the famous epic *La Araucana* by Alonso de Ercilla (1533–94). Diego de Avalos y Figueroa, *Primera parte de la miscelanea austral* (1602) (Vargas Ugarte 20) is largely an assortment of unrelated trivia, such as the pleasures of music, the qualities of a wife, and a few noteworthy descriptions of Peru. It contains many poems, including "Defensa de damas," an apology for women, in octaves, published by itself the following year (Vargas Ugarte 20). *Primera parte* includes in the author's statement (*dedicatoria*) that his purpose is the "agreeable entertainment and pleasure of the reader."

There are three imprints under the subject of law. *Pragmática sobre los diez*

---

27. Guillermo Escobar Risco, ed., *Vocabulario y phrasis en la lengua general de los Indios del Perú, llamada Quichua y en la lengua Española* (Lima: Universidad Nacional Mayor de San Marcos, Instituto de Historia de la Facultad de Letras, 1951); and Medina, *La imprenta en Lima,* 1:30–6.

dias del año (1584) (Vargas Ugarte 1) is the first imprint of South America.[28] It is a royal mandate requiring promulgation of the papal decree by which Gregory XIII had reformed the old Julian calendar. The second legal imprint, Miguel de Agia's *Tratado que contiene tres pareceres graves en derecho* (1604) (Vargas Ugarte 37), is a legal interpretation of a royal decree dealing with labor imposed on the natives.

Many items under administration, all in Spanish, are mandates by the viceroyalty regarding labor and the treatment of the natives. Nearly all are broadsides and were probably produced in large numbers. Unfortunately, only a few have survived (Vargas Ugarte 23–36). Specialized administration is represented by one book on educational administration, *Constituciones y ordenanzas de la universidad* (1603) (Vargas Ugarte 21), and in two on economic administration, *Aranzel real de la alcavala* (1592) (Vargas Ugarte 7), and Juan de Belveder, *Libro general de las reducciones de plata y oro* (1597) (Vargas Ugarte 17).

In contrast to Mexico, Peru produced only two works in Latin classified under linguistics: Julian Martel, *Praecepta grammatices ex variis collecta* (1594) (Vargas Ugarte 13), and Juan Vega, *Instituciones grammaticae Latino carmine* (1595) (Vargas Ugarte 15).

Physical Characteristics of the Imprints: The Initial Letter

Used to open chapters and paragraphs from the early manuscripts to the printed books of the nineteenth century, the initial letter possesses the singular quality of being both illustration and text. The initials in illuminated manuscripts often depicted situations that complemented the content of the book. This duality achieved during the High Middle Ages levels of sophistication and beauty exquisite enough to be considered an artistic genre. After Gutenberg's invention, the tradition of including illustrated letters in books was so strong that the early printers would leave spaces at the beginning of chapters for the rubricator to include by hand the appropriate illustrated initial letter. As the process of printing developed, the initial letter was produced in quantity from images of letters of the alphabet cut on wood blocks.[29]

The blocks were like pieces of a puzzle, each with a separate letter and

---

28. For a comparison of the only two existing copies of *Prágmatica*, see Antonio Rodríguez, "First Printings of South America in the Harvard Library," *Harvard Library Bulletin* 16.1 (1968): 38–48.

29. Arthur Mayger Hind, *An Introduction to a History of Woodcut, with a Detailed Survey of Work Done in the Fifteenth Century,* 2 vols. (London, Constable and Company, 1935; repr., New York: Dover, 1963).

design, whose common theme was selected when the book was at its planning stage. Some sets were used for adornment, others to complement the text with visual messages. Once a book was printed, the pieces of the set were kept in the printing office for later use. But because many sets were borrowed or purchased by other printers, the woodblocks became scattered throughout the printing shops of Europe. Some traveled to Mexico and Peru with the early printers.

Physical Characteristics of the Imprints: Mexico

An examination of the physical format of the imprints in Mexico shows that after 1550, the typography changed from gothic to roman and italic type. New illustrations and illustrated initial letters appear in some of the books, showing motifs identical to those used by printers outside of Spain. Aristotle's *Dialectica resolutio* (1554) (García Icazbalceta 22), printed by Pablos, for example, exhibits a title page so close to one used by the English printer Edward Whitchurch in his 1549 edition of the *Book of Common Prayer* that it includes his signature (EW) (figs. 10.1–10.2).[30] Pablos and the other Mexican printers also used illustrated letters quite similar to some used by Whitchurch.[31] An edition of Apianus's *Cosmographia* printed in Antwerp in 1540 and a *Psalterium chorale,* dated 1563 or 1564 and attributed to Pedro Ocharte, used initials with identical motifs (figs. 10.3–10.4). A copy of the latter book, which is not described in the major bibliographies, is housed at the Lilly Library of the University of Indiana. The same letter with an identical motif also appeared in the English Bible printed in Antwerp in 1537 and known as the Matthew or Matthew's Bible.

Physical Characteristics of the Imprints: Peru

In Peru, the quality of Ricardo's output from the start demonstrates state-of-the-art techniques. His knowledge and skill are shown in the similarity of motifs of the initials used in his *Arauco domado* with those in Ramusio's *Delle navigationi et viaggi,* printed in Venice by the Giunta family.[32] The identical

---

30. The frontispiece was first reported in the *Times* (London), June 10, 1881, in an article about the acquisition of books by the British Museum. It was discussed extensively in Mexico before two articles were published about it: Lucy Eugenia Osborne, "The Whitchurch Compartment in London and Mexico," *The Library,* 4th ser., 8.3 (1927): 303–11; and, more recently, Rodríguez-Buckingham, "Monastic Libraries."

31. See Rodríguez-Buckingham, "Monastic Libraries," 39–40.

32. Ibid., 47.

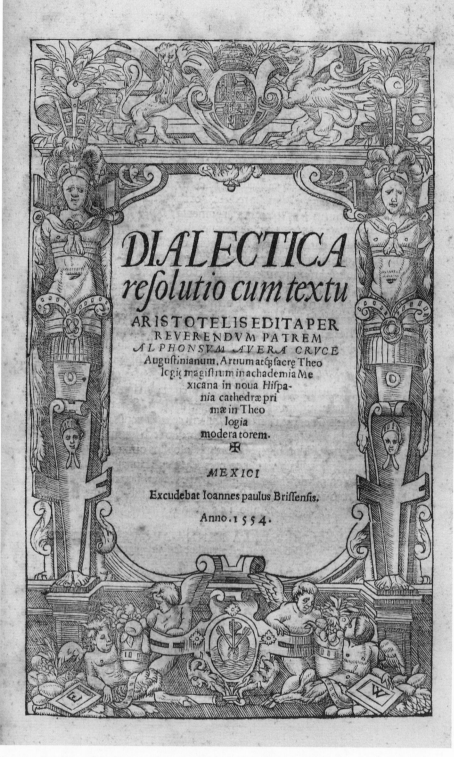

Fig. 10.1. Title page of *Dialectica resolutio,* printed by Juan Pablos (Mexico City, 1554). Courtesy, The Lilly Library, Indiana University, Bloomington, Indiana.

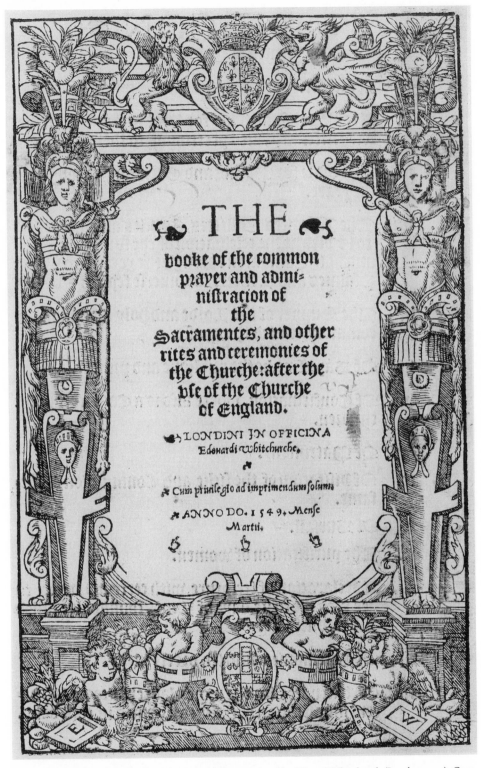

Fig. 10.2. Title page of *The Booke of the Common Prayer*, printed by Edward Whitchurch (London, 1549). Courtesy of Princeton University Library.

Fig. 10.3. Initial letter from Apianus, *Cosmographia* (Antwerp, 1540). Courtesy of the Smithsonian Institution Libraries.

motif of the initial used in Agia's *Tratado* and the one used in a Bible printed in Lyons in 1542 by Jean Crespin is also noteworthy.[33] Crespin is known to have left Lyons in 1548 to operate a press in Geneva to promote Protestantism.[34]

THERE IS no satisfactory answer in this essay to the question of the effectiveness of the first colonial presses as tools in Christianizing the natives in the viceroyalties. The Church's reaction in subsequent years, however, suggests that the new technology did not give the results expected by the missionaries. Furthermore, the difficulties involved in producing books forced printers to find alternative ways to supplement their income, and from the start the press diverged from its original mission. The third imprint from Mexico and the first from Peru, for example, fall outside the original objective of the press. This change of direction becomes more noticeable as the century progresses, and it involves other areas of the culture.

This study recognizes that while bibliographers disagree on the actual count, the evidence shows that the total output of the presses in Mexico and

33. Ibid., 48.
34. Jean François Gilmont, *Jean Crespin: Un éditeur réformé du XVIe siècle* (Geneva: Droz, 1981).

Fig. 10.4. Initial letter from *Psalterium chorale,* printing attributed to Pedro Ocharte (Mexico City, 1563 or 1564). Courtesy, The Lilly Library, Indiana University, Bloomington, Indiana.

Peru in the sixteenth century was very low.[35] Moreover, one may say in general that the printing enterprise was not lucrative, at least not in its beginnings. In his work on the Crombergers, Clive Griffin states that while Juan Pablos continued to print until 1560, "his output is not sufficient to allow us to assume that his presses were always fully occupied."[36] Another clue is provided by Antonio Ricardo, who in his 1586 will mentions the large numbers of unsold imprints he had in stock.[37]

The observations made of 180 titles from Mexico and 40 from Peru show the number of religious books in the native languages is very limited. A reason may be that while higher authorities purchased the books, the audience was limited to the friars who dealt with the natives. It is germane to ask

35. Antonio Rodríguez-Buckingham, "The First Forty Years of the Book Industry in Sixteenth-Century Mexico," in *Iberian Colonies, New World Societies: Essays in Memory of Charles Gibson,* ed. Richard L. Garner and William B. Taylor ([University Park, PA]: privately printed, 1985), 37–61.

36. Griffin, *Crombergers,* 128.

37. Márquez Abanto, "Don Antonio Ricardo," 302.

how the early printers survived in the face of such meager production. It seems likely that only after they arrived in Mexico or Peru did they become aware of the realities of the limited market and the need to diversify. Even though a large number of subjects has been identified, few imprints are on record.

Previous research on Ricardo suggests that printed broadsides, loose engraved images, and particularly playing cards were very likely additional sources of extra income for the early printers.[38] Aside from studies of Pablos's press, however, which was apparently a failure as an economic venture,[39] little has been done on this subject for other printers. A government monopoly, the making of playing cards must have been a lucrative endeavor for Ricardo. His ownership of the press guaranteed a contract to make them on a regular basis. In his will he stated that he had registered fifty-seven decks of playing cards, some of which apparently were hand colored. Another activity of the first printing shop was the printing of holy images. In his will, Ricardo declared that in addition to printing paraphernalia, large numbers of loose engravings were in his shop.

The high number of broadsides printed in both viceroyalties to supply demands from the administrative bodies of the Church or the government suggests that job printing at the local level may have provided the printers with additional income.

The encounter of some of the printers with the Holy Office of the Inquisition does not demonstrate a direct intervention of the tribunal in the publishing of their books, but it does substantiate royal apprehensions regarding influences from areas of Europe that challenged the authority of the Church. Significantly, these influences are noted in the diversity in the design and motifs of the initials used in the books more than in their intellectual content. The origins of this diversity are areas of Europe other than Spain and, in some instances, areas in conflict with Spain. The illustrated letter provides evidence in the study of the book as a physical artifact. Although initials are frequently regarded as meaningless adornments, the influences of their design or motifs expand into areas otherwise impossible to reach. Their provenance is frequently obscured, however, because as a single block they can be easily separated from the set to which they originally belonged.

The interplay between picture, number, or letter, Elizabeth Eisenstein states, is perhaps more significant than the change undergone by each ele-

---

38. Rodríguez-Buckingham, "Colonial Peru," 65–74.

39. García Icazbalceta, *Bibliografía Mexicana del siglo XVI,* 47 (item 16). See also Griffin, *Crombergers,* 91–2.

ment alone.[40] In the words of typographer Harry Carter, it is the task of the typographic historian "to group typefaces, to find resemblances, to depict printer's letters moving from time to time, from place to place, to fit their history to histories of more general or different scope, to make sense."[41]

---

40. Eisenstein, *PPAC,* 55.

41. Harry Graham Carter, *A View of Early Typography up to about 1600* (Oxford: Clarendon Press, 1969), 4.

Chapter 11

The Southern Printer as Agent of Change in the American Revolution

CALHOUN WINTON

When historians discuss the role of the printer in the American Revolution, they usually look at political orientation: how the printer aided or impeded the progress of that movement. The *locus classicus* of this attitude—and strongly influential in its development—is the well-known remark of Thomas Jefferson to Isaiah Thomas about William Rind and Virginia: "Until the beginning of our revolutionary disputes, we had but one press, and that having the whole business of the government, and no competitor for public favor, nothing disagreeable to the governor could be got into it. We procured Rind to come from Maryland to publish a free paper." [1] And so Virginia joined the Revolution.

The inference one could draw, and that many have drawn, is that because the Revolution succeeded, the printers must have supported the process. Their importance is taken to have been as acolytes of—or apostates from—the patriot cause. In this essay I argue, however, that their principal importance lies not in what they conveyed but in how they conveyed it: the means or mechanism by which they were agents in the flow of information. This is, of course, an elaboration of Elizabeth Eisenstein's thought as she considered an earlier revolution in *The Printing Press as an Agent of Change* (*PPAC*): "I would have liked to underline the human element in my title by taking the early

---

1. Jefferson to Thomas, July 1809, as quoted in Isaiah Thomas, *The History of Printing in America,* ed. Marcus A. McCorison from the 2nd ed. (New York: Weathervane Books, 1970), 556n. Since this edition is well-indexed and annotated, further quotations by or references to Thomas may be assumed to be from this source. The pioneering work on the press, and still relevant, is Philip G. Davidson, *Propaganda and the American Revolution, 1763–1783* (Chapel Hill: Univ. of North Carolina Press, 1941). An influential essay collection has been Bernard Bailyn and John B. Hench, eds., *The Press and the American Revolution* (Worcester, MA.: American Antiquarian Society, 1980). An important essay on the southern printers in this collection is Robert M. Weir, "The Role of the Newspaper Press in the Southern Colonies on the Eve of the Revolution: An Interpretation," 99–149.

printer as my 'agent of change.'" The mechanism printers embody might in today's jargon be termed an "information system." In Colonial America, this information system was essentially in place by 1775, having been created from nothing in the southern colonies, in fewer than eight decades.[2]

The ideology of the printer did matter, of course, especially in colonies where there was no, or only one, printer. This significance is in accordance with James N. Green's important dictum (which refers to the middle colonies but is applicable to the southern as well) that the arrival of a second printer insured competition and multiplied the problems of those in authority, whether political or religious, in enforcing conformity.[3] The events in the Virginia press that Jefferson described thus confirm the dictum: Jefferson and his colleagues brought in Rind to multiply the problems of the royal governor. By the time of the Revolution, however, the mainland colonies without a printer or with just one amounted, in those south of Pennsylvania, only to the Floridas, Georgia, and Delaware. Delaware, moreover, was entirely in the orbit of the large Philadelphia marketplace, well supplied in information by its numerous competitors.

These southern printers were not at all united in support of the patriot cause. The largest entrepreneur of them all, Robert Wells of Charleston, was in fact a staunch loyalist who early in the war returned to Britain. His activities, and those of his competitors, are worth examining in some detail. Since treatment in the present form cannot be encyclopedic, they are compared, as in a case study, with the activities of Robert and his sister Mary Katherine Goddard in Maryland. Although Wells was a loyalist to the core, and the Goddards thoughtful, even learned patriots, the effect of their activities, I argue, was the same: providing information that was essentially timely and accurate about the advent of the Revolution and its unfolding. The major consequence of this process was, inevitably, to buttress the patriot cause.

As I have noted elsewhere, Wells came to South Carolina in 1752 from his native Scotland, where he had been apprenticed as a bookbinder and bookseller.[4] Printing and bookselling in South Carolina were then domi-

---

2. Eisenstein, *PPAC*, xv. A recent book that presents a theoretical view of information flow in a broad context is Daniel R. Headrick, *When Information Came of Age: Technologies of Knowledge in the Age of Reason and Revolution, 1700–1850* (New York: Oxford Univ. Press, 2000).

3. Green, "English Books and Printing in the Age of Franklin," in *The Colonial Book in the Atlantic World*, vol. 1 of *A History of the Book in America*, ed. Hugh Amory and David D. Hall (Cambridge: Cambridge Univ. Press, 2000), 248.

4. See Calhoun Winton, "The Southern Book Trade in the Eighteenth Century," in Amory and Hall, *Colonial Book*, 232–8. See also David Moltke-Hansen, "The Empire of Scotsman Robert Wells, Loyalist South Carolina Printer-Publisher" (master's thesis, Univ. of South Carolina, 1984);

nated by the Timothy family, Benjamin Franklin's former partners. The royal governor, James Glen, was, however, also a Scot, and South Carolina had a well-established Scottish community, which was prospering. The extent and power of the local prejudice against them, though no doubt real, has perhaps been exaggerated. Scots were being snubbed all over the English-speaking world. As Linda Colley and others have pointed out, Scots in their homeland and abroad were becoming rapidly assimilated into the British empire and tended to support the governing apparatus of that empire, to the point that John Wilkes and his supporters in London were accusing the Scots of being downright un-English.[5] Association with the South Carolina Scottish community and with the royal government must have seemed as natural to Wells as breathing. His son William Charles recalled years later that his father had him wear "a tartan coat . . . and a blue Scottish bonnet," to emphasize his heritage, and perhaps attract the favorable attention of the Jacobite refugees who were settling in considerable numbers in the Carolina up-country.[6]

Wells started a dry-goods business—a natural venue for casual book-selling—and in the mid 1750s opened his "great Stationary and Book Shop on the Bay," which evolved into the largest bookselling establishment in the southern colonies.[7] He became one of the early members of the Charleston Library Society, founded in 1748,[8] and in 1757 added a bookbindery to his bookselling enterprise. The following year Wells engaged a fellow Scot, David Bruce, as printer and began a printing business and a newspaper (in which he advertised his other activities), the *South-Carolina Weekly Gazette*. By this time he was acquiring patronage appointments: marshal of the vice-admiralty court in 1758 and public auctioneer—vendue master as his title read—in 1759. At the vendues, Wells sold, principally, slaves but also and character-istically books. He was, according to Isaiah Thomas (who served Wells as a journeyman), using slaves as pressmen in his printing office.

Wells had competitors, of course, some no doubt drawn by the very exam-ple of his prosperity. The South Carolina economy was flourishing, riding to

---

and Christopher Gould, "Robert Wells, Colonial Charleston Printer," *South Carolina Historical Magazine* 79 (1978): 23–49.

5. Linda Colley, *Britons: Forging the Nation 1707–1837* (New Haven, CT: Yale Univ. Press, 1992), 117–32. Weir emphasizes the "widespread hatred and fear" of the Scots in the South ("Role of the Newspaper Press," 122–3). This must be tempered by the fact that many southerners were Scots or the descendants of Scots.

6. Wells, *Two Essays . . . with a Memoir of his Life* (London: Archibald Constable & Co., 1818), viii–ix.

7. See Winton, "Southern Book Trade," 236–8.

8. James Raven, *London Booksellers and American Customers: Transatlantic Literary Community and the Charleston Library Society, 1748–1811* (Columbia: Univ. of South Carolina Press, 2001).

a large extent like Wells's enterprises on the back of slave labor. General merchants and specialized booksellers imported and sold books and pamphlets, and by 1765 Wells's weekly newspaper, now entitled the *South-Carolina and American General Gazette* had two other competitors, both also weeklies, in Charleston: Charles Crouch's *South-Carolina Gazette and Country Journal,* and the oldest, Peter Timothy's *South-Carolina Gazette.* The *American General* of Wells's title signals the widening of his ambitions. During the early 1770s he was taking part in publication-by-subscription projects that included both the island and mainland colonies of the British Atlantic world and was importing books from Britain for publication and sale with his own title page, as if they were his imprints.

An observer in January 1775 might have remarked that Wells appeared to be in an enviable position. He was in close touch with the royal authorities and held patronage appointments made by them. He also associated with the colonial elite, and he knew the opinions of both groups. He was cognizant of the latest ship arrivals and departures in South Carolina ports (his paper printed shipping news in every issue). He was prospering from his intra- and intercolony printing and publishing ventures. The observer might feel that here was a man who figured to be well-placed for an eminent career in the emerging Anglo-American empire.

The career, however, never materialized; nor did the empire. Events of the ensuing spring and summer that year, at Concord and Bunker Hill, disposed of both dreams. But the conduct of Wells's newspaper in those months, which must have been traumatic for him, is remarkable. Although it was only a weekly, the coverage of transatlantic and colonial news was detailed and, within the limits of possible knowledge, accurate. Under the bylines of "European Intelligence" and "American Intelligence" Wells printed factual news and opinion more or less informed, always citing the date and source of the information. Sometimes the "Intelligence" would fill two or even three full pages of his four-page paper.

In the February 17, 1775, issue, for example, he quotes a letter received on that date from Bristol, relaying "advices from London," of late December that "a Change in the Ministry was likely to take Place which, it was thought, would effect a Reconciliation between Great Britain and her Colonies." Bristol as a source of news was significant: the town was Edmund Burke's parliamentary constituency, for whom he would shortly speak, memorably, about reconciliation with those colonies. Bristol was also a major trading partner with the colonies. In the same paper, under "American Intelligence," Wells reports on the actions of the general assemblies of New Jersey, Pennsylvania, and Virginia regarding the Continental Congress and quotes a statement "heartily approving of the Proceedings" of that Congress. The hearty approval did not extend to the management of the *South-Carolina and American General Gazette.*

In similar manner, the January 6, 1775, issue carried an item about some Whig supporters of John Wilkes getting drunk at a ball at the London Guildhall and being ejected. But it also reported, as if in compensation, the recent actions of the South Carolina Provincial Congress naming delegates to the Continental Congress in Philadelphia. These actions were attested to as a true copy and signed by the Secretary of the Congress, Peter Timothy, who was Wells's newspaper and bookselling competitor, and strong political opponent. Timothy, a longtime supporter of Wilkes, had indeed participated in the successful movement to have the South Carolina Commons vote a gift of fifteen hundred pounds sterling to Wilkes in 1765 for his legal defense, a gift that had grievously offended royal authorities in Charleston and in the metropolis.[9]

Wells, it is true, was fueling loyalist hopes where he could, as in his reference noted earlier to the possible change of ministry in London. This reference was intended to raise the thought that a new ministry might be more cautious about initiating hostilities. Many colonists, by no means all of them loyalists as such, would have welcomed this step, as would Burke and his associates in opposition in Britain, who hoped to regain public office. Wells continued this strategy in the April 18, 1775, issue by quoting Lord Chatham's plan of the previous February to "avert impending calamities." But when news arrived in Charleston of those calamities, which were unfolding in Massachusetts on that very day, Wells's paper reported them. The May 12, 1775, edition carried a story from the *Essex (Massachusetts) Gazette* of April 25: "Last *Wednesday,* the 19th of April, the troops of his Britannick Majesty commenced hostilities upon the people of this province." A detailed account of the opening engagements follows, reporting from Concord: "Here about a hundred and fifty men going toward a bridge of which the enemy was in possession, the latter fired and killed two of our men, who then returned the fire and obliged the enemy to retreat back to Lexington." The shot by the rude bridge, heard round the world, was thus heard in Charleston about three weeks later.

Wells's competitors and political foes, Charles Crouch and Peter Timothy, had also been bringing news of the gathering storm to South Carolinians. Wells had, in this instance, not managed to scoop the opposition; perhaps he did not wish to do so. Charles Crouch's *South-Carolina Gazette and Country Journal* had broken the story on Tuesday (the paper's normal day of publica-

9. See Hennig Cohen, *The South-Carolina Gazette, 1732–1775* (Columbia: Univ. of South Carolina Press, 1953), 218; and Robert M. Weir, *Colonial South Carolina: A History* (Millwood, NY: KTO Press, 1983), 303–7.

tion), May 9. Crouch carefully reported its source: "By the brigantine Indus-try, Captain Allen," which sailed from Salem, Massachusetts, on April 25, "we have the following alarming Intelligence." It is word for word the same account from the *Essex Gazette,* Concord Bridge and all, that Wells was to use later in the week. Note that both Crouch and Wells, coming from opposite ends of the political spectrum, learn the story, verify its source, accept the story as true, and quote it verbatim from the same source. War had com-menced.

The news, which must have hit Charleston and South Carolina like a hur-ricane from the north, caused practical difficulties for Peter Timothy's own *South-Carolina Gazette.* After the issue of May 29, with a spirited letter from "Caroliniensis" calling on the citizenry for a "resolve of LIBERTY or Death," the paper fell silent until September. The reasons for the silence may be sur-mised: Timothy, by virtue of his position and because of the same sequence of events, had become a vital cog in the new provisional government's opera-tion. The next issue, on September 7, printed an appeal from the Council on Safety, asking for "good spare Muskets," for which the donor would receive "reasonable Satisfaction," and contained the latest resolutions of the Gen-eral Committee, then the de facto government of the province, signed by Timothy as secretary. The secretary had been attending committee meetings instead of meeting newspaper deadlines. Crouch, meanwhile, was trying to slake the public's thirst for news by publishing during the ensuing months what modern journalists would call "extras," while continuing his regular Tuesday issues. The news-filled paper of Tuesday, May 16, was followed on Friday by an abbreviated paper headlined, "Crouch's South-Carolina Gazette *Extraordinary.*"

In the months before the battles of April the three papers had kept Caro-linians well-informed of events both coastal and transatlantic, with particular attention to British politics. Although it is difficult to generalize, one might say that Timothy's *South-Carolina Gazette* attempted a studiedly neutral stance while Wells and Crouch fought it out from opposing sides. On January 23, 1775, for example, Timothy published the names of the delegates to the Provincial Congress held ten days earlier in Charleston, characterizing them as "the most complete Representation, of all the good People throughout the Colony, that ever was," and printed their resolutions, certifying the resolu-tions as true copies by his signature. In the same issue he printed Governor Bull's reply that he does not recognize the Provincial Congress. "I know," the governor writes, "no legal Representatives of the good People of the Province, but the Commons House of Assembly [which] stands prorogued," that is, not in session.

The amount of news arriving by overland post, as distinguished from coastal shipping, is uncertain but was strictly limited. Both means were available in 1775. There was some use of the overland post in Charleston: Wells from time to time printed the names of those having unclaimed mail at the post office. The network, though under royal control and supervision, had largely been engineered and fostered in the southern colonies by the printers. Benjamin Franklin's role in this is well known, but his contemporary William Parks played an equivalent part in developing a network in the beginning years of the process. Parks was an early printer in both Maryland and Virginia and oversaw the extension of the postal system south from Pennsylvania to those colonies. Parks's former apprentice James Davis became the first printer to operate in North Carolina and the colony's first postmaster.

By 1774 the postal link, at least in principle, extended as far south as Savannah.[10] But only in principle. In June of that year Hugh Finlay, newly appointed surveyor of the royal postal system in North America, completed a journey, on foot and horseback, from Quebec to the Georgia port. Finlay was an old hand in the postal service, having in 1763 been named postmaster in Quebec, by Benjamin Franklin. His report of the heroic trek was not made public for almost a hundred years and is still too little consulted by students of history. As he demonstrates, in these southern colonies, because of the long distances involved and the poor roads, coastal and transatlantic shipping were the major means of communication and source of news, though the colonists preferred the land route. "No man in these parts," Finlay wrote in Charleston, "wou'd think of forwarding a letter by water if there was opportunity by land." But the difficulties were formidable, as he discovered. "On the whole," he wrote, "the road from Charles Town to Wilmington [North Carolina] is certainly the most tedious and disagreeable of any on the Continent of North America; it is through a poor, and barren, country without accommodations for travelers."[11]

It was different in the colonies farther north surrounding the Potomac

---

10. A history of the post office in North America that incorporates a transatlantic perspective and recent scholarship is much needed. Earlier accounts, still valuable, are William Smith, *The History of the Post Office in British North America 1639–1870* (Cambridge: Cambridge Univ. Press, 1920); and Fairfax Harrison, "The Colonial Post Office in Virginia," *William and Mary Quarterly*, 2nd ser., 4 (1924): [73]–92. A recent excellent book by Richard R. John, *Spreading the News: The American Postal System from Franklin to Morse* (Cambridge, MA: Harvard Univ. Press, 1995), focuses on the postcolonial American experience, but, significantly, the first chapter is entitled "The Post System as an Agent of Change."

11. *Journal kept by Hugh Finlay, Surveyor of Post Roads on the Continent of North America, during his Survey of the Post Offices between Falmouth and Casco Bay in the Province of Massachusetts, and Savannah in Georgia; begun the 13th Sept. 1773 and ended 26th June 1774* (Brooklyn, NY: Frank H. Norton, 1867), 56, 67.

River and Chesapeake Bay, and the differences are instructive. Parks's overland postal network between the middle and New England colonies and the Potomac area was becoming increasingly efficient as the crisis approached, and the royal network could be supplemented by enterprising printers. Such a one was William Goddard, who moved from Philadelphia to the growing town of Baltimore, to establish in August 1773, a newspaper that he entitled the *Maryland Journal and Baltimore Advertiser*. News had been provided to Marylanders for decades by the *Maryland Gazette,* founded in Annapolis by William Parks and continued there by the Green family. In the August 20 issue of his *Maryland Journal,* Goddard revealed his plan for establishing a direct, exclusive postal link leaving Philadelphia early Monday morning, to arrive in Baltimore Tuesday evening. "Whereby," he continued, "I shall receive the *Massachusetts, Connecticut, New York, Pennsylvania,* and sometimes the *British* and *Irish* Papers and publish the freshest Advices . . . and forward [the paper] to Annapolis and the Lower Counties on Thursday morning, Several Hours before the arrival of the King's Post." He would thus scoop the *Maryland Gazette* in both Baltimore and its hometown.

Goddard, though perhaps a cantankerous individual, was an experienced printer and newsman. He also possessed the resource, an invaluable one as it turned out, of having a sister with him, Mary Katherine, who was a master printer in her own right.[12] That he began his paper, almost as if by instinct, with a reference to the overland postal system reflects his long working acquaintance with that system. He was, one might say, born into it: his father, Giles, a prosperous physician in New London, Connecticut, was also postmaster of the town. William served his apprenticeship with James Parker, printer and postmaster of New Haven, and when he was made free, established a printing office in Providence, Rhode Island. There he began the town's first newspaper in 1762, the *Providence Gazette and Country Journal,* and in 1764 was appointed postmaster.

In the first issue of his paper, Goddard published an unsigned installment of the history of the town. The author, we now know, was a local man, Stephen Hopkins, and their association was to be as important in Goddard's life as was, in a different way, the acceptance at about the same time by Robert Wells of royal places in South Carolina's governing class. For Hopkins wrote

---

12. Biographical information is derived from Goddard's publications and from Ward L. Miner, *William Goddard, Newspaperman* (Durham, NC: Duke Univ. Press, 1962). Information about Mary Katherine Goddard is also from Martha J. King, "Women Printers of the Colonial South: Mary Katherine Goddard as a Case Study," paper presented at annual meeting of the Society for the History of Authorship, Reading and Publishing, Worcester, MA., 1996. I am indebted to Dr. King for permission to use this paper, which she kindly supplied me.

and Goddard published a pamphlet during the Stamp Act debate of 1764, which placed Goddard right in the eye of the Stamp Act storm. *The Rights of Colonies Examined* is, however, anything but inflammatory, in either rhetoric or in manner of typographic presentation. It is a neat quarto, handsomely printed with type purchased for Goddard by his mother and perhaps set by his sister Mary Katherine, who was working around the printing office at the time. Printed, the title page announces, by William Goddard and "PUBLISHED BY AUTHORITY." By whose authority his opponents were quick to inquire. The author, P— (i.e., Patriot?), presents a reasoned, and very temperate, analysis of the history of taxation, reviewing the "revolution principles" of the British constitution, "confessed by all, to be founded by compact, and established by consent of the people." [13] What Whig could disagree? Because the Stamp Act, as proposed, does not have the consent of the people who are being taxed, it is manifestly unfair.

The intention of Hopkins and Goddard may have been reasoned debate, but the effect of their pamphlet was to raise a firestorm of letters and pamphlets on both sides of the Atlantic. The deed was done: within a few months Goddard took, as his biographer notes, "not merely an active but a leading role in the fight of the colonies against the Stamp Act," in the guise of a journalist who signed his writings as "a British-American." [14] He was a marked man, though he perhaps did not know it, as marked as his contemporary Robert Wells in Charleston.

What the two men shared was not beliefs or ideology but a comprehensive knowledge of the printing press, its strength, scope, and limitations. A principal limitation of the colonial press was that it consumed money, capital. Wells, as we have seen, with true entrepreneurial spirit, fed his press funds from a variety of sources in addition to newspaper subscriptions and advertising: job printing, government printing, bookbinding, bookselling, and even book auctions. But Charleston was a larger market than Providence, and Goddard's rival paper, the *Newport Mercury,* had the government business in Rhode Island. Goddard's mother was generous, but her resources were not unlimited. He decided to try his vocation in Philadelphia.

The story of Goddard in Philadelphia, though gripping, is beyond the scope of this essay. Suffice it to say that there, in the teeth of fierce competition from David Hall (Franklin's former partner) and William Bradford, he brought out the *Pennsylvania Chronicle and Universal Advertiser* in 1767 and quickly made it into one of the best newspapers in North America. He

---

13. Providence, RI, John Carter Brown Library, shelfmark A40e, 4.
14. Miner, *William Goddard,* 49.

planned a subscription and distribution system for the paper that included representatives, totaling seventy-seven, in all thirteen mainland colonies, the West Indies, Canada, and London. On December 2, 1767, he published, in a special number, the first of John Dickinson's *Letters from a Pennsylvania Farmer* and followed this by publishing the remaining letters serially, week by week. Why Dickinson chose the *Chronicle* for initial publication of the famous letters is unknown, but the decision probably had to do with Goddard's distribution system: these would be read. In November 1768 Goddard maintained that he had "the most numerous subscribers that any paper has on this continent." No one offered to contradict him.

When Goddard elected to try his hand in Baltimore, then, he brought a large amount of professional experience to the provincial town that was rapidly growing into a small city. For a while he managed to keep both of his newspaper enterprises running, by dint of having Mary Katherine put out the *Chronicle* in Philadelphia while he saw to providing a home for the *Maryland Journal* and getting that paper started. Advertisers came forward. In the first number, a developer with access to twenty thousand acres on the Ohio River proposes to divide and lease the acreage, signing himself simply, "George Washington." In the same paper Goddard promises, "I shall always publish with Pleasure whatever is sent to me in Favour of Liberty and the Rights of Mankind, provided the Language is decent and compatible with good Government, but I am resolved that my Paper shall be FREE and of NO PARTY." Easier said than done. Politics and party were everywhere. In December of the *Journal's* first year, 1773, the controversy over the importation of tea was at the boil. In December Goddard consulted his sources up and down the coast and informed his readers: "It seems to be the general Voice of the People in Philadelphia, that THE TEA SHALL NOT BE LANDED THERE—The same patriotic Spirit prevails in Charlestown, South-Carolina, and in the Colony of Rhode-Island." Goddard followed up on this in the next issue: "Yesterday evening Mr. Butler, one of the post riders lately established by the Printer of this Paper, arrived here, express from New York, with the following interesting intelligence" about the tea controversy.

The detail about the post riders is significant. Goddard was turning over in his mind the idea of proposing a postal system independent of the royal mail. To this end he wound up the *Pennsylvania Chronicle* and brought Mary Katherine in to take over the *Maryland Journal.* This she did, on February 17, 1774, with characteristic aplomb, announcing over her signature that the *Maryland Journal* "at a period of Time not far distant [will] become a Chronicle of Intelligence and literary Entertainment." If this seemed to disparage her older brother's achievement with the paper so far, so be it. He was out of town, off on his quest that was eventually successful, for the new postal system, traveling through the colonies and new states for the next several years. The story of the *Maryland Journal* and the coming of the Revolution thus becomes Mary Katherine's.

It is a remarkable story. This unmarried, thirty-four-year-old woman, who was now alone in the world (their mother had died in Philadelphia in 1770), wrote and edited, composed the type, and supervised the production and distribution of the paper; kept the books; billed the subscribers; and paid the bills, even as war came on. Isaiah Thomas, who knew her well, judged that she was an "expert and correct compositor" and characterized her as "a woman of extraordinary judgment, nerve, and strong good sense." She also had entrepreneurial flair: within a few years she had opened a dry goods store near her Market Street office, bought into a local paper mill, and established a bookselling and bookbinding operation to go with her newspaper. Her business career thus paralleled, on a smaller scale, that of Wells in Charleston.

Like Wells, she provided in her newspaper a wide spectrum of news and opinion. Considerable attention was naturally devoted to the efforts, ultimately successful, of her brother to establish an alternative postal system in the mainland colonies. This system was given official sanction by the Continental Congress in July 1775, and later that year Mary Katherine became the first postmistress of Baltimore, or perhaps anywhere. Earlier, before the events of Lexington and Concord, her paper had frequently expressed hope for reconciliation. In June of 1774 "Amor Patriae," perhaps William himself, called for "a happy and honourable reconciliation between us and the mother country."

The *Maryland Journal* followed closely the activities of the Continental Congress, as had Wells and his competitors in Charleston, reporting, for example, about the resolution voted by the Congress in October 1774 affirming that the colonists "are entitled to life, liberty, and property." The *Journal's* advertiser George Washington, incidentally, was a delegate from Virginia voting for this phrase, but Thomas Jefferson was not present. In January 1775 Mary Katherine Goddard quoted Edmund Burke's speech to the freeholders of Bristol in which he said, "I consider the commercial interests of England and her Colonies as one and the same; they are reciprocal and perfectly coincident."

Coincidentally, on the day when the fatal news from Lexington arrived at the printing office, that is, April 26, Mary Katherine was putting the paper together and had already set on page one a letter of the previous February from the merchants of Birmingham to Burke, thanking him for his efforts at reconciliation. The news from Massachusetts (headlined "We have just received the following important INTELLIGENCE") was conveyed to the readers in a single paragraph on page three signed by J[oseph] Palmer, a member along with John Hancock of the Massachusetts Committee of Safety, and attested as a true copy by Nathan Balding, the Town Clerk of Worcester.

This document, which had been printed the day before in Philadelphia in three newspapers and by William Bradford as a broadside, has been identified by John H. Scheide and Frank Luther Mott as the very first account in print of the event at Lexington.[15] The longer and more circumstantial account published by the *Essex Gazette,* which brought the news to South Carolina, was not yet available in Baltimore. More news was coming in all the time, however. Mary Katherine issued a broadside extra (calling it a "Postscript") the next day, and in another dated May 22 published affidavits and depositions from observers on the scene "Relative to the Commencement of the late HOSTILITIES."

Mary Katherine's scrupulosity illustrates once again the concern already observed among the Charleston printers to get it right, to make as certain as possible that the record was straight. Colonial printers had been referred to as "meer mechanics," and some scholars have generalized from this reference, portraying printers as lower-class artisans, buffeted about by the winds of political faction.[16] By the time of the American Revolution southern printers at any rate certainly did not see themselves in this way. They knew their printing press was an agent of change.

---

15. John H. Scheide, "The Lexington Alarm," in *Proceedings of the American Antiquarian Society* 50 (1940): [49]–79; Frank Luther Mott, "The Newspaper Coverage of Lexington and Concord," *New England Quarterly* 17 (1944): 489–505.

16. Stephen Botein was a proponent of this interpretation. See his "Printers and the American Revolution," in Bailyn and Hench, *Press and the American Revolution,* 127–225, and his earlier article, "'Meer Mechanics' and an Open Press: The Business and Political Strategies of Colonial American Printers," *Perspectives in American History* 9 (1975): 130.

Chapter 12

The Printing Press and Change in the Arab World

GEOFFREY ROPER

IN 1937 the Arab American historian Philip Hitti published his *History of the Arabs,* which quickly established itself as a classic; through its many subsequent editions up to the present, it has introduced generations of students and general readers to the broad outlines of Arab history. Its final chapter, dealing with the past two centuries, and the changes brought about by modernization and westernization, opens with a brief account of the import of a printing press by the French into Egypt in 1798. Subsequent pages give prominence to the establishment of other presses in Cairo, Beirut, and elsewhere. Clearly, for Hitti, printing was an essential ingredient of modernization in the Arab world. Nor was he alone in this view: in the following year (1938), the celebrated Arab nationalist historian George Antonius, in his influential book *The Arab Awakening,* laid great stress on the introduction of printing as a factor in that awakening. "The installation of a printing press equipped to emit books in the Arabic language," he wrote, "opened out new horizons . . . without [it], the making of a nation is in modern times inconceivable." [1]

But neither they nor most subsequent historians of the Arab world down to the last quarter century explained why printing was so important, nor did they devote any significant space or effort to tracing its progress or

This survey covers, in addition to the Arab countries, that is, those where Arabic is the main written language, some aspects of Arabic printing history in the broader sense, involving book production in all languages using the Arabic script, a historic vehicle of Islamic culture. But the many detailed studies of Ottoman Turkish printing history are not considered: for a comprehensive list of publications in this field in the period 1981–95, see M. Bülent Varlık, *Türkiye basın-yayın tarihi bibliyografyası* (Ankara: Kebikeç Yayinlan, 1995). Nor has it been possible to survey the fewer but significant specialized contributions on Persian, Urdu, Malay, and other Muslim languages.

1. Hitti, *History of the Arabs from the Earliest Times to the Present* (1937; 7th ed., London: Macmillan, 1960); Antonius, *The Arab Awakening: The Story of the Arab National Movement* (London: Hamish Hamilton, 1938), 40.

elucidating the effects that it had. Even studies of intellectual history, such as Albert Hourani's masterly and seminal *Arabic Thought in the Liberal Age* (1962), despite dealing intensively with printed texts, paid scant regard to the means and processes by which intellectual production reached its readers and achieved its potent effects. The relatively few studies of Arabic book history tended to concentrate their attention on the manuscript production of earlier eras, with printing added, if at all, merely as a postscript. The key work in this field was Johannes Pedersen's *Den Arabiske Bog* (1946; translated by Geoffrey French as *The Arabic Book,* 1984): only the last of its ten chapters considers the printed book, and this deals only with the outline history of the establishment of presses and the nature of some of the texts printed. Among the Arabs themselves, the situation was little better. Khalīl Ṣābāt's useful survey of the history of Arabic presses[2] took for granted their historical role and did not attempt to analyze the relationship between the printed output and changes in social and intellectual patterns. In 1979, the date that also marks the appearance of Elizabeth L. Eisenstein's *The Printing Press as an Agent of Change: Communications and Cultural Transformations in Early-Modern Europe (PPAC)*, a major history of the Arabic book by Maḥmūd ʿAbbās Ḥammūda allocated a mere 11 of its 280 text pages to the printed book and used them to give no more than a bare chronological summary.[3] As late as 1982, the Tunisian scholar Abdelkader Ben Cheikh, in a report to UNESCO, commented that "discontinuité et rareté des approches caractérisent l'état actuel des recherches sur le livre et la lecture dans les pays arabes."[4]

So Elizabeth Eisenstein's observation that "almost no studies are devoted to the consequences that ensued once printers had begun to ply their new trades"[5] certainly applied in full measure to the historiography of the Arab Middle East. In 1982, fresh from the excitement of reading Eisenstein, I pointed out, at the annual conference of the Middle East Librarians' Committee (MELCom) in Paris, that the systematic study of early Arabic printed books and the impact of printing on the Arab world had yet to achieve any significant recognition as a discipline to be pursued by either historians or bibliographers, and I appealed for new initiatives in

---

2. Ṣābāt, *Tārīkh al-ṭibāʿa fī 'l-Sharq al-ʿArabī* [History of printing in the Arab East], 2nd ed. (Cairo: Dar al-Maʿārif, 1966).

3. Ḥammūda, *Tārīkh al-kitāb al-Islāmī* [History of the Islamic book] (Cairo: Dār al-Thaqāfa, 1979).

4. ["discontinuity and scarcity of approaches characterize the current state of research on the book and reading in Arab countries."] Ben Cheikh, *Production des livres et lecture dans le monde arabe* [Production of books and reading in the Arab world] (Paris: UNESCO, 1982), 49.

5. Eisenstein, *PPAC,* 4.

this field.[6] Three years later, Michael Albin of the Library of Congress corroborated some of what I had said by setting out, in a paper to the American Oriental Society,[7] the parameters of the discipline of Islamic book history, which he claimed did not then exist. By "Islamic" he was referring not to the religion as such but to Muslim culture in all its manifestations, as mediated through the Arabic script and the texts written in it; he gave the term "book history" as a direct translation of *histoire du livre,* the discipline developed by French scholars, particularly Lucien Febvre and Henri-Jean Martin.[8] But he also pointed especially to Elizabeth Eisenstein, whose work he considered would "shape the discipline of book history for decades to come" and therefore "might point the way for students of the Islamic book." There was, however, a note of ambivalence in this recommendation: as well as firmly rejecting "technological determinism" (although he did not, like some others, openly accuse Eisenstein of this), Albin noted that it was "not her certainties which illuminate our studies, but her doubts."[9] This ambivalence is reflected in some subsequent work in the history of Arab and Muslim modernization, and the role of printing in it, as I indicate in what follows.

The Historiography of Arabic Printing since 1979

In the past two decades the state of knowledge in this field has been transformed, quantitatively and qualitatively. The historical incidence and development of Arabic printing and presses, since their introduction to the Arab world in the eighteenth century, have attracted a steady procession of researchers where previously they were few and far between. There is space here to mention only a few highlights and examples. In 1982 the major reference manual *Grundriss der arabischen Philologie* included a section titled "Die Anfänge der arabischen Typographie und die Ablösung der Handschrift durch den Buchdruck," by the noted German scholar of Islamic studies Gerhard Endress. Although somewhat sketchy and inaccurate, it presented to the traditional world of European philological scholarship a useful survey of the print revolution in Arab countries as it affected the physical presentation of texts.[10]

---

6. Geoffrey Roper, "Arabic Incunabula," *L'arabisant* 21 (1982): 21–4.

7. Albin, "Islamic Book History: Parameters of a Discipline," *International Association of Orientalist Librarians Bulletin* 26–27 (1985): 13–16.

8. Febvre and Martin, *L'apparition du livre* (Paris: A. Michel, 1958), edited by Geoffrey Nowell-Smith and David Wootton, translated by David Gerard as *The Coming of the Book: The Impact of Printing 1450–1800* (London: N.L.B., 1976; reissued, London: Verso, 1990).

9. Albin, "Islamic Book History," 13–15.

10. Endress, "Die Anfänge," in *Grundriss der arabischen Philologie,* vol. 1, ed. Wolfdietrich Fischer and Helmut Gätje (Wiesbaden: Reichert, 1982), 291–6, 312–4.

In 1985 the Tunisian scholar Wahid Gdoura took a major step forward with his study of the beginnings of Arabic-script printing in eighteenth-century Syria, Lebanon, and Turkey. Although most of his book was devoted to the background, initiation, and development of the early presses, and an enumeration of their output, the final section did give a brief assessment of the place of printed books in the intellectual milieu of the time, their use as an agent of reform and modernization, and their limited role until the later, more widespread adoption of printing became "le facteur moteur des grandes rénovations intellectuelles . . . du XIXème siècle."[11] Written in French, it later gained a wider Arab readership in an Arabic version.[12] In the same year (1985), the Iraqi writer and educator Bihnām Faḍīl 'Affāṣ produced a substantial synoptic account of the history of printing and presses in his country, providing much useful new data. Although he notes in his introduction that printing was the "foundation stone" of the nineteenth-century Arab Renaissance (*Nahḍa*), in Iraq as elsewhere, he did not attempt any analysis of its specific role in intellectual or social change.[13] The same was true of later studies such as those of Aḥmad Muḥammad al-Qalāl (1994) on publishers and publishing (with particular reference to Libya) and Maḥmūd Muḥammad al-Ṭanāḥī (1996) on the Egyptian printed book in the nineteenth century. This last was also the theme of a major monograph by the distinguished Egyptian librarian and bibliographer 'Ā'ida Ibrāhīm Nuṣayr (1994). Drawing on her previous work on the enumerative bibliography of the period,[14] she set out at some length the intellectual currents discernible in the printed books and their physical characteristics. She also analyzed the nature and role of their publishers: governmental presses, private individuals, learned and literary societies, commercial companies, and the like, as well as the channels of distribution.[15] By doing so, she has made a significant contribution to our knowledge and understanding of early Egyptian printed book production;

---

11. ["the driving factor in the great intellectual renewals . . . of the 19th century."] Gdoura, *Le début de l'imprimerie arabe à Istanbul et en Syrie: Évolution de l'environnement culturel (1706–1787)* [The beginning of Arabic printing in Istanbul and Syria: Evolution of the cultural environment (1706–1787)] (Tunis: Institut Supérieur de Documentation, 1985), 247.

12. Waḥīd Qadūra, *Bidāyat al-ṭibā'a al-'Arabīya fī Istānbūl wa-Bilād al-Shām: Taṭawwur al-muḥīṭ al-thaqāfī* (Zaghouan: Mu'assasat al-Tamīmī lil-Baḥth al-'Ilmī wa-al-Ma'lūmāt, 1992).

13. Bihnām Faḍīl 'Affāṣ, *Tārīkh al-ṭibā'a wa-'l-maṭbū'āt al-'Irāqīya* [History of Iraqi printing and printed publications] (Baghdad: Maṭba'at al-Adīb al-Baghdādīya, 1985).

14. Nuṣayr, *Al-kutub al-'Arabīya allatī nushirat fī Miṣr fī 'l-qarn al-tāsi' 'ashar* [Arabic books published in Egypt in the nineteenth century] (Cairo: Qism al-Nashr bi-'l-Jāmi'a al-Amirīkīya bi-'l-Qāhira, 1990).

15. Nuṣayr, *Ḥarakat nashr al-kutub fī Miṣr fī 'l-qarn al-tāsi' 'ashar* [The book-publishing movement in Egypt in the nineteenth century] (Cairo: al-Hay'a al-Miṣrīya al-'Āmma li-l-Kitāb, 1994).

but she did not attempt any Eisensteinian analysis of how this production may have, in itself, been an agent of change.

The physical characteristics of early Arabic books printed in Egypt were more particularly the focus of a major and groundbreaking study in analytical bibliography by Jīhān Maḥmūd al-Sayyid, published in 2000.[16] Her detailed treatment ranges from title pages to colophons and includes tables of contents, preliminaries, text-blocks, and watermarks. But there is little discussion of the cognitive and social effects of these features and their development. More recently, two significant monographs, by Yaḥyá Maḥmūd ibn Junayd and ʿAbbās ibn Ṣāliḥ Ṭāshkandī, have added greatly to our knowledge of the history of printing in the Arabian peninsula.[17] But, like the others already mentioned, they do not try to trace the emergence of print culture in the area.

Apart from such monographic treatment, the growth of interest in Middle Eastern printing history has also been reflected in several conferences and exhibitions. In 1989 Eleazar Birnbaum and a group of his colleagues organized a major exhibition in the Thomas Fisher Rare Book Library of the University of Toronto, with seventy-nine exhibits carefully chosen to illustrate the transition from the scribal to the printed production of Muslim texts.[18] In 1995 the Jumʿa al-Mājid Centre in Dubai and the Cultural Foundation in Abu Dhabi jointly convened a symposium (*nadwa*) on the history of Arabic printing up to the end of the nineteenth century. Twelve papers by distinguished Arab scholars covered different Arab countries and areas, Europe, the Americas, the Indian subcontinent, Iran, and the Russian empire, as well as the role of orientalists and trends in text editing in the late nineteenth century. But the stated aims of the symposium did not include consideration of the effects of the spread of printing, nor did this consideration feature, to any great extent, in the contributions.[19] It did, however, in another conference held the fol-

---

16. Sayyid, *Al-bibliyūjrāfiyā al-taḥlīliya: dirāsa fī awāʾil al-maṭbūʿāt al-ʿArabīya* [Analytical bibliography: A study in early Arabic printed books] (Alexandria: Dār al-Thaqāfa al-ʿIlmīya, 2000).

17. Ibn Junayd, *Al-ṭibāʿa fī shibh al-jazīra al-ʿArabīya fī ʾl-qarn al-tāsiʿ ʿashar al-Mīlādī (1297–1317 H)* [Printing in the Arabian Peninsula in the nineteenth century] (Riyadh: Maktabat al-Malik Fahd al-Waṭanī, 1998); Ṭāshkandī, *Al-ṭibāʿa fī ʾl-Mamlaka al-ʿArabīya al-Saʿūdīya 1300 H–1419 H* [Printing in Saudi Arabia, 1882–1999] (Riyadh: Maktabat al-Malik Fahd al-Waṭanī, 1999).

18. Birnbaum, Virginia Aksan, Michael McCaffrey, and Noha Sadek, *From Manuscript to Printed Book in the Islamic World: Catalogue of an Exhibition, Thomas Fisher Rare Book Library, University of Toronto* (Toronto: Univ. of Toronto, 1989).

19. *Nadwat Tārīkh al-ṭbāʿa al-ʿArabīya ḥattá intihāʾ al-qarn al-tāsiʿ ʿashar . . . 1416 H . . . 1995 M.: al-waqāʾiʿ wa-ʾl-buḥūth allatī ulqiyat fīhā* [Symposium on the history of printing up to the end of the nineteenth century, 1995: Documents and studies delivered] (Abu Dhabi: Cultural Foundation, 1996).

lowing year (1996) in Copenhagen on the topic "The Introduction of the Printing Press in the Middle East." There a small group of mainly Western scholars presented papers that analyzed in some detail the role of printing in eighteenth- and nineteenth-century Islamic culture, and the use that was made of it by rulers and ruled in a number of different countries of the Middle East.[20] Some of them are considered in the discussion that follows.

The opening years of the twenty-first century have seen further activity in this arena. In 2001 the twenty-first Deutscher Orientalistentag of the Deutsche Morgenländische Gesellschaft, held in Bamberg, included a special panel, "Zur frühen Druckgeschichte in den Ländern des Vorderen Orients." As in Copenhagen, a select group of specialist scholars, in this instance German, considered analytically the impact of the earlier presses and the role of their protagonists.[21] This was accompanied by a notable exhibition of early imprints, organized by Klaus Kreiser, which included a few carefully chosen rarities in Arabic from Italy and Lebanon, described in detail in the catalogue.[22]

Then in 2002 Middle Eastern printing history came to the very birthplace of the printing press, when a major exhibition was installed at the Gutenberg Museum in Mainz, titled "Middle Eastern Languages and the Print Revolution: A Cross-Cultural Encounter." Organized jointly by the director of the museum, Eva Hanebutt-Benz, and two Arabic specialists, Dagmar Glass and Geoffrey Roper, the exhibition aimed to present not just the earliest imprints (although these were present) but also representative specimens of the range and development of printed material, in Arabic and other Middle Eastern languages, as it spanned the revolutionary transition from scribal to print culture.[23] At the same time, a symposium was held in the museum, as part of the First World Congress of Middle Eastern Studies, on the topic "History of Printing and Publishing in the Languages and Countries of the Middle East." This symposium was on a larger scale than the other gatherings so far mentioned, bringing together thirty-two specialists, whose papers covered a wide range of historical and technical aspects, including some post-Eisensteinian

---

20. The papers were published in a special issue of *Culture & History* 16 (1997).

21. Ulrich Marzolph, ed., *Das gedruckte Buch im Vorderen Orient* (Dortmund: Verlag für Orientkunde, 2002).

22. Klaus Kreiser, ed., *The Beginnings of Printing in the Near and Middle East: Jews, Christians and Muslims* (Wiesbaden: Harrassowitz in Kommission, 2001).

23. Eva Hanebutt-Benz, Dagmar Glass, and Geoffrey Roper in collaboration with Theo Smets, eds., *Middle Eastern Languages and the Print Revolution: A Cross-Cultural Encounter / Sprachen des Nahen Ostens und die Druckrevolution: Eine interkulturelle Begegnung*, Gutenberg Museum Mainz, Internationale Gutenberg-Gesellschaft (Westhofen: WVA-Verlag Skulima, 2002).

studies of print culture.[24] In 2005 a second international symposium on the same topic was convened at the Bibliothèque nationale de France in Paris, at which twenty-eight papers were presented. So, Arabic and Middle Eastern printing history can fairly be said to have lost its Cinderella status of twenty-five years or so ago, at least in part because of the change in the general intellectual climate stimulated by Eisenstein in 1979.

The Study of Arab Print Culture

As well as histories of the introduction of printing and of the early presses and their output, such as those mentioned previously, some scholars in this period have also attempted the more demanding task of tracing the emergence of print culture in the Arab world and its effects on patterns of awareness and social interaction. In 1986 the Tunisian information scientist Abdelkader Ben Cheikh approached the subject from the perspective of literacy and education. In his book on the role of reading in social development, he devoted a substantial section to the historical impact of printing, especially in Tunisia, in which he traced the emergence of two kinds of reading in Islamic culture: sacred and ritual recitation (*qarāʾa*) and desacralized, internalized reading (*muṭālaʿa*). Printing spread the latter to a much wider public, opening the way to the extension and modernization of education and, ultimately, of the wider literate society.[25]

This topic was also the theme of Carter Vaughn Findley's 1989 essay on the transition to modern patterns of knowledge and education in the Middle East. He traced the passing of the "magic garden" mentality in Muslim culture, its replacement by a more rationalist discourse, and the subsequent movement toward "mass mobilization." He attributed this change to, among other factors, the nineteenth-century arrival of the "Gutenberg age" in the area and the consequent "media revolution."[26]

The 1990s saw a quickening pace in the pursuit of such lines of enquiry, although major monographic treatment was still lacking. In 1992 Brinkley Messick devoted a chapter to print culture in his book on the role of textual transmission and "textual domination" in Yemen. Some of his insights have

---

24. Philip Sadgrove, ed., *History of Printing and Publishing in the Languages and Countries of the Middle East, Journal of Semitic Studies,* suppl. no. 15 (2005).

25. Ben Cheikh, *Communication et société: Pouvoir lire et développement culturel* (Tunis: Publications du Centre de recherches en bibliothéconomie et sciences de l'information, 1986), 115–59.

26. Findley, "Knowledge and Education in the Modern Middle East: A Comparative View," in *The Modern Economic and Social History of the Middle East in its World Context,* ed. Georges Sabagh (Cambridge: Cambridge Univ. Press, 1989).

a much wider relevance and validity, such as his observation that, unlike traditional oral and scribal educational materials, "printed textbooks [pertained] to a curriculum system of public instruction, and the associated sociopolitical, citizen-based universe of nationalism"; nevertheless, the relatively isolated and untypical nature of Yemeni society perhaps limits the applicability of his findings to the study of the print revolution elsewhere in the Arab Middle East.[27]

The British Muslim intellectual and information scientist Ziauddin Sardar went perhaps to the other extreme in his 1993 article on the role of communication technologies in "the making and unmaking of Islamic culture." Writing in very broad terms about the whole of "Muslim history," he traced three transformations that have revolutionized the creation and transmission of knowledge (*'ilm*): the introduction, respectively, of paper, printing, and electronic media. The second of these, he considered, effectively led to the unmaking of the old knowledge-based Islamic culture because it brought about a split between traditional knowledge, which the conservative-minded Islamic scholars (*'ulamā*) were reluctant to see in print, and the modern secular texts widely disseminated from the presses.[28] While unsupported by any systematic analysis of what texts were in fact produced by the nineteenth-century presses, this thesis perhaps reflected a synthesis of certain revisionist approaches to the emergence of Muslim print culture that can also be found in the work of several other scholars.[29]

The distinguished Arabic literary and philosophical scholar Muhsin Mahdi, in his 1995 essay, also treated printing as just one of the transitions undergone by Muslim literate culture: in his opinion, the earlier emergence of the written book was more important and "printing has simply fixed and diffused" many texts of no greater significance or value than their manuscript forerunners. He did, however, acknowledge that printed books eventually imparted "a degree of solidity and authority that went far beyond the solidity and authority of the manuscript copy or copies of the same book"; he went on to summarize some of "the numerous social and cultural implications of the transition," such as the rise of national sentiment and secular culture, the emergence of professional writers, the changing ratio of new works to old ones, the use of books as instruments of state policy, the buttressing of

27. Messick, *The Calligraphic State: Textual Domination and History in a Muslim Society* (Berkeley and Los Angeles: Univ. of California Press, 1992), 115–31.

28. Sardar, "Paper, Printing and Compact Disks: The Making and Unmaking of Islamic Culture," *Media, Culture and Society* 15 (1993): 51–5.

29. E.g., Abdullah Schleifer and Timothy Mitchell, considered in later discussions.

popular religion through the use of printing by the Sufi (mystical) orders, and the impact on the Arabic language. On nearly all these Eisensteinian topics, however, he raised questions without giving answers.[30]

In a more specialized study published in 1999, Ulrich Marzolph, after observing that "probably the most decisive event for cultural production in the Arab Middle East in the nineteenth century was the introduction of printing," went on to assert the essential continuity in the content of some kinds of book from manuscript to print production, in particular the issuing of compilations of stories. But he then traced how within print culture these compilations underwent significant shifts and changes and became "sanitized step by step in order to give way to a domesticated fantasy," presumably more in keeping with the requirements of the new middle-class market for printed books.[31]

The present century has already seen further notable contributions to the study of Middle Eastern print culture. Two examples must suffice, both from German scholars who are prominent in this field. At the 2001 Bamberg conference mentioned earlier, Dagmar Glass traced the essential role of Arabic printing presses in the nineteenth-century Renaissance (*Nahḍa*) and in the renewal of Arabic written culture.[32] Looking at the question from the point of view of the consumption of printed material, Johann Strauss has traced the development of print culture through a detailed analysis of different readerships among the various linguistic and religious groups of the Ottoman Empire, including Arabs, in the nineteenth and early twentieth centuries.[33]

Eisenstein in Studies of the Arab World

All of the studies mentioned in the previous section seem to have been written at least partly under the indirect influence of Elizabeth Eisenstein, insofar as they deal with questions of the kind originally raised in *PPAC,* and that consequently were "in the air" at the time they were written. None of them, however, cites her book or explicitly acknowledges her influence. Nor has

30. Mahdi, "From the Manuscript Age to the Age of Printed Books," in *The Book in the Islamic World: The Written Word and Communication in the Middle East,* ed. George N. Atiyeh (Albany: State Univ. of New York Press; Washington, DC: Library of Congress, 1995), 1–15.

31. Marzolph, "*Adab* in Transition: Creative Compilation in Nineteenth-Century Print Tradition," *Israel Oriental Studies* 19 (1999): 161–72.

32. Glass, "Die *Nahḍa* und ihre Technik im 19. Jahrhundert: Arabische Druckereien in Ägypten und Syrien," in *Das gedruckte Buch im Vorderen Orient,* ed. Marzolph (Dortmund: Verlag für Orientkunde, 2002).

33. Strauss, "Who Read What in the Ottoman Empire (19th–20th Centuries)?" *Middle Eastern Literatures* 6.1 (2003): 39–76.

there appeared any major monographic study of Arab print culture drawing wholly or partly on her insights, like the notable study of Russian printing history by Gary Marker.[34] There are, however, a few smaller-scale contributions that do mention her, and wholly or partly adopt a framework of inquiry that reflects her approach.

J. S. Szyliowicz in his 1986 article pointed to two of Eisenstein's findings on the role of printing in changing "the way in which people think and perceive reality": first, the reorganization of texts and reference guides to enable their more systematic use and the more rational presentation of data, and second, the reorganization of time and effort among scholars and students, away from copying and memorization toward "more productive intellectual work." He indicated, although without detailed analysis, that these trends were present also in early Ottoman printed-book production in the eighteenth and nineteenth centuries.[35] The German scholar Reinhard Schulze took up another Eisensteinian theme in a ground-breaking 1987 article on nineteenth-century Islamic cultural production. In this essay he pointed out that the concept and feeling of modernity were necessarily predicated on a rejection of the immediate past in favor of reclaiming a semi-mythical "golden age" of "timeless universality." Just as in Renaissance Europe, this shift was made much easier, and less reversible, by the use of the printing press to establish, propagate, and canonize the texts of that earlier age — those of classical antiquity in western Europe, early Islamic ones in the Arab Middle East.[36] Schulze did not mention Eisenstein here but was unmistakably influenced by her; in a later article (based on a paper at the 1996 Copenhagen conference) he made his debt clearer, citing her in support of his assertion that "printing fundamentally changed the attitudes in the Muslim world toward history." [37]

In a more specialized context, I made some use of Eisenstein's insights in my 1988 thesis on Arabic printing in nineteenth-century Malta. In it I tried to place the subject — and Arabic printing history in general — in the context of communication and book history overall: tracing its development from

---

34. Marker, *Publishing, Printing, and the Origins of the Intellectual Life in Russia, 1700–1800* (Princeton, NJ: Princeton Univ. Press, 1985).

35. Szyliowicz, "Functional Perspectives on Technology: The Case of the Printing Press in the Ottoman Empire," *Archivum Ottomanicum* 11 (1986): 257–8. Also in Ekmeleddin İhsanoğlu, ed., *Transfer of Modern Science & Technology to the Muslim World* (Istanbul: Research Centre for Islamic History, Art and Culture, 1992), 251–60.

36. Schulze, "Mass Culture and Islamic Cultural Production in 19th-Century Middle East," in *Mass Culture, Popular Culture, and Social Life in the Middle East,* ed. Georg Stauth and Sami Zubaida (Frankfurt am Main: Campus Verlag; Boulder, CO: Westview Press, 1987), 205–7.

37. Schulze, "The Birth of Tradition and Modernity in 18th- and 19th-Century Islamic Culture: The Case of Printing," *Culture & History* 16 (1997): 41.

Innis through McLuhan, Febvre and Martin, and culminating in Eisenstein, while noting the absence of such analysis by Middle East historians. I tried also to cast my description and analysis of the Malta output in such a way as to facilitate the consideration of those features highlighted by Eisenstein as important in the development of print culture, and I concluded with some, necessarily provisional and tentative, discussion of Eisenstein's "clusters of changes," involving the accelerated dissemination, standardization, and preservation of texts brought about by the early Arabic presses in Malta and elsewhere.[38] In later published articles, I applied these concepts to the work of one particular famous Arab writer of the period, Fāris al-Shidyāq, who worked at the Malta press and later became a leading proponent of the print revolution in the Ottoman Empire: I attempted to show how he not only transformed the delivery of both classical and modern Arabic texts but also embodied in himself, as a former scribe who became a professional author and journalist, the transition from scribal to print culture. He himself, more than a hundred years before Eisenstein, had emphasized elements of dissemination, standardization, and preservation to justify the adoption of what was still in some Arab and Muslim eyes a suspect novelty.[39] In addition, I pointed to his role in, and his opinions on, the use of the printing press in developing national awareness and civic rights, along with those of some of his contemporaries.[40] Interestingly, though, the example of Fāris al-Shidyāq has subsequently been adduced elsewhere to make a tentative counterargument against Eisensteinian notions of print-induced cultural change.[41]

Another doctoral thesis, presented by the Iraqi American librarian and scholar Fawzi Abdulrazak in 1990, also drew inspiration from Eisenstein. This was a study of early Arabic printing in Morocco, and its very title refers to printing as "an agency of change." The author stated clearly in his introduction that he had "benefited from [Eisenstein's] framework as a guide to the observation, documentation and discussion of the various effects of print-

---

38. Roper, "Arabic Printing in Malta 1825–1845: Its History and Its Place in the Development of Print Culture in the Arab Middle East" (Ph.D. thesis., Univ. of Durham, 1988), esp. 1–5, 260–9, 325–9.

39. Roper, "Fāris al-Shidyāq and the Transition from Scribal to Print Culture in the Middle East," in Atiyeh, *Book in the Islamic World,* 209–31.

40. Roper, "National Awareness, Civic Rights, and the Rôle of the Printing Press in the 19th Century: The Careers and Opinions of Fāris al-Shidyāq, His Colleagues and Patrons," in *Democracy in the Middle East: Proceedings of the Annual Conference of the British Society for Middle Eastern Studies, 8–10 July 1992, Univ. of St Andrews, Scotland* ([Durham]: BRISMES, 1992).

41. Nadia al-Bagdadi, "Print, Script, and the Limits of Free-thinking in Arabic Letters of the Nineteenth Century: The Case of Al-Shidyāq," *Al-Abhath* 48–49 (2000–1): 99–122. See further discussion in the next section.

ing technology in Morocco." His Eisensteinian approach informs the whole structure of his study, and he also explicitly compared and contrasted the role of printing in the European Renaissance, drawing on Eisenstein, with the equivalent transformation of Morocco in the nineteenth century. After tracing the different strands of intellectual, social, and political change as affected by the printed word, he concluded by asserting that "printing was not only an agent to preserve knowledge, but also an agent of change which contributed to the shaping of Moroccan history." [42] This work, while remaining unpublished in English, was translated into Arabic and published in Morocco in 1996. [43]

Eisenstein's direct influence can also be found in some smaller-scale studies from the 1990s. Francis Robinson's inaugural lecture as Professor of the History of South Asia at the University of London in 1992 deals with the impact of print on religious change in Islam, and he starts off by drawing parallels with the European Christian Reformation and Counter-Reformation, citing Eisenstein's analysis of the conflicting trends of "Erasmian" humanism and modernism on one hand and orthodox Biblical fundamentalism on the other. "Clearly," Robinson says rather ambivalently, "print has a lot to answer for." [44] He goes on to trace how printing "struck right at the heart of" traditional textual communication in Muslim society and thereby had a revolutionary impact, leading to the emergence of a kind of "Protestant or scriptural Islam," promoting pan-Islamic sentiments, undermining the traditional clerics (*'ulamā*), and eventually giving rise to the conflicting currents of modernism and fundamentalism. His main focus is on South Asian Islam, but his Eisensteinian insights have considerable relevance to other Muslim societies, including the Arab world.

A more specialized study of the use of *fatwās* (promulgated legal opinions) in nineteenth-century Egypt, by the Danish scholar Jakob Skovgaard-Petersen, appeared in 1997. In this connection he examined the use of the new print medium by Egyptian clerics (*'ulamā*) and jurists (*fuqahā*). Like Robinson, he was struck by the parallels with the European Reformation period and remarked that "although often accused of techno-determinism, Elizabeth Eisenstein's book *PPAC* contains a number of suggestions worthwhile reflect-

42. Abdulrazak, "The Kingdom of the Book: The History of Printing as an Agency of Change in Morocco between 1865 and 1912" (Ph.D. diss., Boston Univ., 1990), 5, 117–8, 257.

43. Fawzī 'Abd al-Razzāq, *Mamlakat al-kitāb: tārīkh al-ṭibā'a fī 'l-Maghrib 1865–1912* [*The Kingdom of the Book: The History of Printing in Morocco, 1865–1912*], trans. Khālid al-Ṣaghīr (Rabat, Morocco: Jāmi'at Muḥammad al-Khāmis, Kullīyat al-Ādāb wa-'l-'Ulūm al-Insānīya, 1996).

44. Robinson, "Technology and Religious Change: Islam and the Impact of Print," *Modern Asian Studies* 27.1 (1993): 232.

ing upon in this much later Egyptian context." The spread of printing, he observes, coincided with an important reformation in Islamic thought, and printing gave it permanence, unlike earlier ones, just as Eisenstein observed of sixteenth-century Europe. Furthermore, printing also eventually strengthened both uniformity of belief and a sense of personal responsibility and individual understanding of scripture—another Eisensteinian finding. He concludes that "the period 1850–1900 is hardly understandable without due consideration of how thoroughgoing were the changes in Egypt's cultural production," an assertion hardly to be found in the pre-Eisenstein era.[45] The French scholar Yves Gonzalez-Quijano studied a later era of Egyptian book production in his book on publishing and intellectual culture in the republican period (i.e., since 1952). His delineation of the culture of printed books, and its part in creating an autonomous role for both authors and readers, also shows the influence of Eisenstein, whose work appears in his bibliography.[46]

Another writer who invoked Eisenstein was the American Muslim professor of mass communication studies Abdullah Schleifer, although he took a rather different view of the print culture she analyzed. "As Eisenstein has so clearly documented," he wrote, "the printing press was inevitably the most potent weapon of every subversive (or 'progressive') force in the West; of worldliness, licentiousness and secularism, . . . of a plethora of sects splintering religious unity, . . . of the Enlightenment philosophers who banished God from social and scientific discourse," leading to the evils of the French Revolution. A similar fate awaited Muslim society from the nineteenth century on. But it was not just a question of the presses falling into the wrong hands, important though that was: another "inescapable component" of mass communication through printing is the desacralization of the word, in particular the word of God in the Qur'ān and the Names of God. It leads even to desecration, through the unthinking disposal of unwanted printed matter.[47] Here we find an author who accepts Eisenstein's analysis, only to stand it on its head by using it to reject the values of the print culture whose role in human progress is her central theme. Schleifer brings to this rejection the ardor of the religious convert. But other writers, too, both Muslim and non-Muslim, have been ambivalent in their attitude toward Eisensteinian print

45. Skovgaard-Petersen, *Defining Islam for the Egyptian State: Muftis and Fatwas of the Dār al-Iftā* (Leiden: Brill, 1997), 51–6.

46. Gonzalez-Quijano, *Les gens du livre: Édition et champs intellectuel dans l'Egypte républicaine* (Paris: CNRS Éditions, 1998).

47. Schleifer, "Mass Communication and the Technicalization of Muslim Societies," *Muslim Education Quarterly* 4.3 (1987): 4–12.

culture and toward the postulates of her formulation of the concept. To these we now turn.

Problems with the Eisenstein Model in the Arab World

The influence of Eisenstein on studies of Arab printing history and cultural modernization is undeniable, and she can fairly be said to have transformed the concepts of a significant number of scholars of the early modern history of the Middle East, as elsewhere. Nevertheless, there has been some reluctance to embrace in toto her model of print-induced modernity, and a tendency in some quarters to seek at least partial alternatives. This is true even of some of the scholars mentioned earlier who have been influenced by her.

A few scholars have given preference to alternative or variant European approaches, such as those of Roger Chartier. This is true, for instance, of Gonzalez-Quijano, although, as we have seen, he does not ignore Eisenstein. He places some emphasis on Chartier's view of the role of the book (and of writing and printing generally) as a social instrument, and in his study of Egyptian "book people" develops this view in the direction of the notion of a print-enabled "public space," in sociopolitical terms, using a concept of Jürgen Habermas.[48] The latter is also taken up by Juan Cole, in his 2002 article, who likewise uses the concept to extend and partly qualify the application of Eisenstein's frameworks to areas south and east of the Mediterranean.[49] Chartier's emphasis on "the many uses and plural appropriations" of print[50] is also one that has appealed to some historians of Arab print culture because the printed book, at the level of the learned culture on which Eisenstein concentrated, has never been quite as significant among Arabs and Muslims as it has been in Europe. Popular devotional texts, pamphlets, "pavement literature," and, above all, newspapers and journalism, tended to loom larger in the Middle East in the print era, as Gonzalez-Quijano suggests.[51]

There has also been, among some Middle East historians, a resistance to the "technological determinism" that has been unfairly attributed to Eisenstein. Some instances of this resistance have been noted already, but the question whether culture determines technology or technology determines

---

48. Gonzalez-Quijano, *Les gens du livre*, 8, 16.

49. Cole, "Printing and Urban Islam in the Mediterranean World, 1890–1920," in *Modernity and Culture, from the Mediterranean to the Indian Ocean,* ed. Leila Tarazi Fawaz and C. A. Bayly (New York: Columbia Univ. Press, 2002), 345–6, 358–9.

50. Chartier and Alain Boureau, *The Culture of Print: Power and the Uses of Print in Early Modern Europe,* trans. Lydia G. Cochrane (Princeton, NJ: Princeton Univ. Press, 1989), 2.

51. Gonzalez-Quijano, *Les gens du livre*, 11, 124, 174, 190–3, 196–7.

culture has particularly exercised scholars concerned with this part of the world. The German Ottomanist Klaus Kreiser, for instance, points out that the introduction of printing by İbrahim Müteferrika to Ottoman Muslim society in the eighteenth century "did not create a fundamental break with the past as induced by the new technology in Europe," [52] citing Eisenstein in his discussion. Others too have attributed a decisive role to Muslim culture in the way printing was introduced and received in the Middle East, which meant that printing itself did not play such an important role in modernization: its effects were mediated by local patterns of intellectual production and authority, and the modernizing influences came from without.[53]

Nadia al-Bagdadi has used a study of part of the career and output of Fāris al-Shidyāq (the celebrated nineteenth-century Arab renaissance writer who spanned the transition from scribal to print culture) to "take up the debate among the main representatives of the 'Eisenstein school' and scholars refuting the approach laid down in Eisenstein's work, most prominently Roger Chartier." [54] In particular, she questions the idea that there could be "no *nahḍa* [Arab renaissance] without the printing press" and asks whether technology really accounts for the substantive nature of literature. To support this challenge, she considers the use made by Fāris of scribal as well as print transmission, particularly of texts that might upset religious sensibilities, such as his critique of the Christian Gospels, *Mumāḥakāt al-ta'wīl fī munāqaḍāt al-Injīl* [Disputations of interpretation in criticisms of the Gospel].[55] In her view, this indicates "sharply diverse strategies in the production and dissemination of knowledge" and typifies the co-existence of print and manuscript in nineteenth-century Arab culture. This co-existence in turn creates a "need to reconsider some of the assumptions concerning print" in relation to the Arab renaissance.[56] Beyond this one case, however, she does not produce any general or quantitative data to support her challenge. But her treatment of Fāris al-Shidyāq, while not invalidating earlier studies, including my own,[57] provides an interesting variation of emphasis, away from the Eisenstein model.

The partial shift away from Eisenstein or the limits placed on the applica-

---

52. Kreiser, *Beginnings of Printing*, 16.

53. Cf. Schulze, "Mass Culture"; and Timothy Mitchell, *Colonising Egypt* (Cambridge: Cambridge Univ. Press, 1988), among others.

54. Bagdadi, "Print, Script, and the Limits," 99 n. 2.

55. This work survived only in a manuscript copy kept in the Awqāf Library in Baghdad. Since the destruction of that library following the U.S. invasion in April 2003, it may now be completely lost.

56. Bagdadi, "Print, Script, and the Limits," 103, 118; the argument is further developed throughout the essay.

57. Roper, "National Awareness, Civic Rights," and "Fāris al-Shidyāq."

tion of her model to the Arab and Muslim domains are mainly attributable to three major problems in the history of Arabic textual transmission and book culture.

The Late Arrival of the Printing Press

The Arabs used printing as early as the tenth century CE, five hundred years before Gutenberg.[58] But this was to produce block-printed amulets, and it was certainly not an "agent of change." Book production remained firmly in the hands of scribes until the eighteenth century. It did not become a normal method of text transmission among Arab Muslims until the second half of the nineteenth century, despite the much earlier triumph of the print revolution elsewhere. This is a major problem for cultural historians, and, in the words of the German Arabist Hartmut Bobzin, "until today [the] Islamic world's delay in employing one of the greatest achievements of Western technology . . . has not been explained convincingly."[59] Much attention has, however, been given to the problem. In 1954 André Demeerseman, a French scholar based in Tunisia, explored the issue in an extended article. He drew a distinction between superficial (and false) reasons, such as resistance to progress, aversion to culture, inwardness, inertia, and formalism, on one hand, and essential reasons—cultural, artistic, social, moral, doctrinal, economic, political—on the other.[60] While this distinction is certainly helpful, each of these "essential reasons" requires extended treatment in itself. Others have followed these lines of inquiry, most recently Lutz Berger at the Bamberg conference in 2001. He likewise pursues sociocultural, economic, and aesthetic lines of inquiry but ends by lamenting that the "eloquent silence" of Islamic sources on the subject renders attempts to reconstruct the earlier Muslim viewpoints premature.[61]

This still unsolved problem seems not susceptible to an Eisensteinian analysis. If the printing press was such a powerful agent of change in early modern Europe, why did it not have a significant impact on the Arab world for another four centuries? It is not surprising that inquirers in this field have

58. Karl R. Schaefer, *Enigmatic Charms: Medieval Arabic Block Printed Amulets in American and European Libraries and Museums* (Leiden: Brill, 2006).

59. Bobzin, *Between Imitation and Imagination: The Beginnings of Arabic Typography in Europe* (Beirut: Orient-Institut der Deutschen Morgenländischen Gesellschaft, 1997), 3.

60. Demeerseman, *L'imprimerie en Orient et au Maghreb: Une étape décisive de la culture et de la psychologie islamiques* (Tunis: Nicolas Bascone & Sauveur Muscat, 1954), previously published in *IBLA* 17 (1954).

61. Berger, "Zur Problematik der späten Einführung des Buchdrucks in der islamischen Welt," in Marzolph, *Das gedruckte Buch im Vorderen Orient*.

tended to pursue cultural and social reasons for technological change (or lack of it) rather than seeing the technology of the printing press as itself an agent of change.

Lithography

Another feature of Arabic-script printing history that has no counterpart in earlier European experience is the prevalence for much of the nineteenth and early twentieth centuries, in areas as far apart as Morocco and Indonesia, of a hybrid method of book production: lithography. Whereas in Europe this technique was used almost entirely for pictorial and cartographical illustration, Muslims used it to reproduce entire texts written by hand. In this way they could retain most of the familiar features of Islamic manuscripts, and the calligraphic integrity of the Arabic script, and avoid expensive investments in movable types.[62] But this means that Eisenstein's insights into the conscious and subliminal effects of the standardization of text presentation, and the emergence of a new print-induced *esprit de système,* do not really apply to those societies where this method was prevalent. Yet, the effects of the much wider dissemination of these texts—mainly traditional and classical ones—was very considerable, and, as Proudfoot says, "ushered in the print revolution."[63] Hence the ambivalence—part acceptance, part rejection—of Eisensteinian analyses among those who have studied this important phase in the development of Arab and Muslim print culture.

The Relationship between Modernization and Westernization

An even more serious historiographical problem is that the widespread adoption of printing in the Arab Middle East came in the wake of major European incursions in the military, economic, and cultural domains. Modernization has often been equated with westernization, and printing treated as an aspect of the latter. An adequate assessment of this problem cannot be attempted here. Suffice it to say that this equation has led some scholars to take a negative view of the effects of the print revolution on Arab and Muslim society

---

62. Cf. Demeerseman, "Une étape importante de la culture islamique: Une parente de l'imprimerie arabe et tunisienne, la lithographie," *IBLA* 16 (1953): 347–89, also published separately in Tunis, 1954; Karl Klaus Walther, "Die lithographische Vervielfältigung von Texten in den Ländern des Vorderen und Mittleren Orients," *Gutenberg-Jahrbuch* 65 (1990): 223–6; Brinkley Messick, "On the Question of Lithography," *Culture & History* 16 (1997): 158–76; and Ian Proudfoot, "Mass Producing Houri's Moles, or Aesthetics and Choice of Technology in Early Muslim Book Printing," in *Islam: Essays on Scripture, Thought, and Society,* ed. Peter G. Riddell and Tony Street (Leiden: Brill, 1997), 161–84, among others.

63. Proudfoot, "Mass Producing Houri's Moles," 182.

and culture. Timothy Mitchell, for instance, considered that, because of the partly oral nature of Islamic scholarly and literary communication, and of the Arabic language and script through which it was mediated, "writing could never unambiguously represent an author's unambiguous meaning [and therefore] no proper Arab scholar would have been interested in the power of the printing press. The problem of the author's presence in writing, furthermore, corresponded to a problem in the presence of political authority in society." But in mid-nineteenth-century Egypt, Europeans effectively colonized Muslim thought by promoting a medium — print — in which "words were to lose their power" and traditional authority was to be replaced by "an apparent certainty — the effect of an unambiguous meaning — made possible by modern methods of representation."[64] The printing press was thus certainly an "agent of change" but in the direction of dependency and peripheralization, rather than autonomous modernity. Some of the writers mentioned previously in this essay have also associated the print revolution with westernization, although not always quite so negatively.[65]

I and a few others, however, have taken a different, more Eisenstein-oriented view. Regardless of its origins, I wrote in 1988, "printing has its own direct effects, as Innis, McLuhan, Febvre and Eisenstein have shown. These operate, as they have demonstrated, both on the cognitive plane, and on the socioeconomic plane. The systematic investigation of these factors might shift the historical perspective somewhat: westernization might then perhaps seem a less direct cause of some of the changes in Middle Eastern thought and society in the nineteenth century."[66] I stand by these words, and call upon my colleagues, in the spirit of Eisenstein, to devote more effort to that systematic investigation.

---

64. Mitchell, *Colonising Egypt,* 150–3.
65. Cf. Gdoura, *Le début de l'imprimerie;* Schulze, "Mass Culture" and "The Birth of Tradition"; Abdulrazak, *The Kingdom of the Book;* and Robinson, "Technology and Religious Change," among others.
66. Roper, "Arabic Printing in Malta" 4–5.

Chapter 13

Print and the Emergence of Multiple Publics in Nineteenth-Century Punjab

VIVEK BHANDARI

Harsukh rai and Dayal Singh Majithia, two prominent personalities of late-nineteenth-century Punjab (in North India), came from radically different backgrounds. Harsukh Rai was a Bhatnagar Kayastha (a caste
of scribes) from Bulandshehr whose father had been appointed municipal
commissioner by the British. With the help of the colonial government, Rai
moved to Punjab and established a printing press in Lahore immediately after
the British annexation of Punjab in 1849.[1] Dayal Singh Majithia was the son
of Sardar Lehna Singh, a prominent lieutenant of Ranjeet Singh, the ruler
of Punjab province until 1849. On his father's death, Dayal Singh inherited
one of the largest and wealthiest estates of the province. In 1883–4 he was
appointed honorary magistrate of Amritsar and subsequently went on to join
the Indian National Congress as a spokesman for the Punjabi region.[2] Both
of these men, each in his own way, deployed their literary talents and political
skills as self-appointed publicists for their personal social constituencies. They
adopted ideological postures inspired by Western liberalism but adapted them
to suit their shifting contexts, and by participating in diverse publics, they
addressed a wider social base than had ever been possible in the past. These
men shared the distinction of establishing two of the earliest and most widely
read newspapers of the Punjab—the *Kohinoor* (in Urdu) and the *Tribune* (in
English). These newspapers reached impressive circulation figures and had a
profound social impact by encouraging lively debate on a wide range of issues.
As early as 1856, for instance, Rai expressed strong views on the freedom of
the press (perhaps for the first time in colonial Punjab) and went on to influence a whole generation of publicists. What these men were articulating was
a heightened awareness that they were members of a distinct, regional urban

---

1. Imdad Sabri, *Tarikh-i Sahafat-i Urdu* (New Delhi, 1953), 417–25.
2. Prakash Ananda, *A History of The Tribune* (New Delhi: Tribune Trust, 1986), 1–2, 3–4.

culture in flux and steeped in practices of debate and argument. A product of dramatic shifts in the political economy of the region following the British annexation of Punjab in 1849, this social formation set the parameters for how groups in India viewed questions of justice, loyalty, freedom, reform, literary production, and indeed their own subject position in relation to the wider world. Because of their scope, these shifts had far-reaching effects on the contours of nationalist discourse as it emerged in the last decades of the nineteenth century.

This essay describes how the emergence of new forms of communication (specifically those associated with print and oratory) created an urban environment that fostered cosmopolitan debate, reform, and social mobilization in nineteenth-century Punjab. Elizabeth Eisenstein's pioneering work on the ways in which the transformations associated with print shaped a culture of cosmopolitanism gives us a starting point for unearthing how the growth in uses of print shaped urban culture in Punjab. Eisenstein points out that although "a reading public was not only more dispersed; . . . more atomistic and individualistic than a hearing one, . . . vicarious participation in more distant events was . . . enhanced; and even while local ties were loosened, links to larger collective units were being forged."[3] By the last quarter of the nineteenth century, this cosmopolitan attitude was an important facet of city life in the region, and the politics of Punjab province was increasingly shaped by the activities of a group of individuals who came from different backgrounds but were beginning to converge in a plethora of associational "publics," variously described as *samajes, sabhas,* and *anjumans* (loosely translated as "societies," "congregations," and "gatherings," respectively). This activity produced a class of publishers, booksellers, and publicists that was able to use the existing, deeply drawn lines of communication within society to which the colonial authorities had only minimal access, to fashion a public culture based primarily on the uses of oratory, performance, and print.

The Origins of Print in South Asia

In a recent essay, Vinay Dharwadker argues that colonial South Asia witnessed the first "fully formed" print culture to appear in the world outside Europe and North America, "distinguished by its size, productivity, and multilingual and multinational constitution, as well as its large array of Asian languages and its inclusion of numerous non-Western investors and producers among

---

3. Eisenstein, *PPAC,* 132.

its active partipants." [4] For many scholars, deciphering this cultural formation has posed a formidable challenge, not least because of the Indian subcontinent's size, diversity, and cultural plurality. It is therefore necessary to clarify that my essay attempts to locate the contours of print culture in nineteenth-century Punjab, a province of northwestern India (a sizable portion of which is in present-day Pakistan) within the larger history of public culture in the subcontinent. [5]

Printing originated in India in the summer of 1556 when the first printing press arrived from Lisbon with a group of Jesuits, who set it up at the College of St. Paul in Goa, the Portuguese colony on the west coast of the Indian peninsula. Dharwadker points out that for the next two and a half centuries, Catholic and Protestant missions from Europe, working in the coastal areas of the subcontinent, extensively used print technology. By 1578 the Jesuits had installed a press at Quilon, on the Malabar coast; between 1706 and 1715 the Danish Lutheran Mission, in conjunction with the Society for the Promotion of Christian Knowledge, established a press, a type foundry, and a paper mill at Tranquebar, near Madras; in the following decade, the Dutch East India Company and the mission of the Dutch Reformed Church jointly set up the Hollander Press in Colombo, Sri Lanka. [6]

According to Dharwadker, in 1800 two momentous cultural interventions had the effect of accelerating the use of print, and simultaneously altering Europe's self-image as well as its understanding of East Asia. The first was "Lord Wellesley's establishment, in April 1800, of Fort William College in what is now southern Calcutta, for the professional education of the company's officials, including their training in Indian languages. The college created the first professors of Arabic, Persian, Sanskrit, Bengali, Hindi-Urdu, Marathi, and other languages, and a curriculum in the literature, histories, and cultures of a dozen major regions of India, a full twenty-eight years before an English university created the first professor of English language and literature." [7] This pioneering college press published some of the first introductory and advanced textbooks, grammars, and dictionaries in Arabic,

---

4. Dharwadker, "Print Culture and Literary Markets in Colonial India," in *Language Machines: Technologies of Literary and Cultural Production,* ed. Jeffrey Masten, Peter Stallybrass, and Nancy Vickers (London: Routledge, 1997), 112.

5. For a recent collection of essays on the vagaries of book history and print culture as they have shaped different parts of India over the past two centuries, see Abhijit Gupta and Swapan Chakravorty, eds., *Print Areas: Book History in India* (Delhi: Permanent Black, 2004). Of particular interest are the essays in this collection by Anindita Ghosh, Francesca Orsini, and Veena Naregal.

6. Dharwadker, "Print Culture and Literary Markets," 108–14.

7. Ibid., 110.

Bengali, Burmese, Chinese, Hindustani (Hindi-Urdu), Kannada, Marathi, Oriya, Punjabi, Persian, Sanskrit, and Telugu.[8]

The other cultural intervention of the time was the establishment of the Serampore Mission Press, funded by Baptist churches and founded in January 1800 in Serampore (Srirampur, north of Calcutta), under the protection of the Danish mission in a politically independent pocket within British India. Dharwadker says that over the first two decades of the nineteenth century, this mission became the site for the largest and most specialized press and type foundry in Asia. His research has shown that between 1800 and 1840 this press printed 212,000 items in forty languages, including books in thirty Indian languages and dialects, as well as books in Arabic, Armenian, Burmese, Chinese, Javanese, Malay, Maldivian, Persian, Singapuri, and Thai.[9] Over the course of its existence, the Serampore press published the Bible in forty-five languages in all, translations into thirty-eight of these languages produced by scholars working in Serampore and Calcutta.[10] The Calcutta region, as it must have been between about 1760 and 1845, was probably the single most important center for the translation of Asian languages from the media of voice, palm-leaf, and scroll to the medium of print, and for the transposition of print culture from Europe into Asia.[11]

Print Culture and Colonialism: A "Limited Hegemony"?

Despite these early beginnings, print did not dramatically alter the cultural life of India until well into the nineteenth century, something that is not easily explained, especially in the Eisensteinian context of the revolutionary power of print. Put differently, it is not entirely clear why it took so long for a culture of cosmopolitan debate and associational life to emerge after the early

---

8. For information about Fort William College and its press, see B. S. Kesavan, *History of Printing and Publishing in India: A Story of Cultural Reawakening* (New Delhi: National Book Trust, 1985), 391–400; David Kopf, *British Orientalism and the Bengal Renaissance: The Dynamics of Indian Modernization, 1773–1835* (Berkeley and Los Angeles: Univ. of California Press, 1969); and R. S. McGreggor, *Hindi Literature in the Nineteenth and Early Twentieth Centuries,* vol. 8, fasc. 2 of *A History of Indian Literature,* ed. Jan Gonda (Wiesbaden: Otto Harrassowitz, 1974). These references are given by Dharwadker, in "Print Culture and Literary Markets," 128.

9. See Kesavan, *History of Printing and Publishing in India,* 237–46, 381–8; Sisir Kumar Das, *A History of Indian Literature, 1800–1910, Western Impact: Indian Response* (New Delhi: Sahitya Akademi, 1991), 32–3; and Dharwadker, "Print Culture and Literary Markets," 110. On the linguistic diversity of India in the post-Independence period, which places the nineteenth-century situation and the accomplishments of the Serampore Mission Press in perspective, consult Paul R. Brass, *Language, Religion, and Politics in North India* (New York: Cambridge Univ. Press, 1974).

10. Kesavan, *History of Printing and Publishing in India,* 237–63.

11. Dharwadker, "Print Culture and Literary Markets," 111.

arrival of print in different parts of the subcontinent. Historians have speculated on a large number of reasons to explain why the presence of printing technology in the coastal areas of the subcontinent (where European traders were based) did not trigger a revolution as it did in other times and places. These speculations have concluded that the bazaar writers maintained a monopoly and their product was cheap; that there were strong ritual objections to printing texts, which alone would have made the press economically unviable; that Persian script proved difficult for lithographers;[12] and, finally, that indigenous rulers were hostile to the press on political grounds. None of these possible reasons explains the answer to a question posed by C. A. Bayly: Why did all these alleged impediments break down so rapidly in the first half of the nineteenth century in India, at least a century after print had acquired strong roots in the subcontinent?[13] The answer to this question is still a subject of considerable debate, perhaps because the question itself has been reframed as a result of important interventions in the fields of postcolonial criticism. The focus, for some time now, has been on the degree to which the very advent of colonial modernity has been the primary agent of change in Indian society.

This debate has far-reaching ramifications for discussion on how the cultural production and consumption of print made its presence felt. In a fascinating argument exploring the literary history of the subcontinent, Dharwadker has argued that one of the most far-reaching effects of print between about 1800 and 1835 was the more or less simultaneous invention of modern prose in various languages, including Bengali, Hindi, Marathi, Tamil, Telugu, and Urdu.[14] Some of these languages had centuries-old traditions of oral and written prose and were connected in different ways to their canonical roots in Sanskrit, Arabic, and Persian. All displayed a remarkable degree of resilience and adaptability by shifting to new lexicons and grammars, new principles of punctuation and syntax, and new discursive forms and styles.[15] Like the formation of the subcontinent's print culture as a whole,

---

12. Francesca Orsini has recently pointed out that this argument about the difficulties posed by the Persian script is belied by the boom in the printing of Urdu materials (which use the Persian inspired Nastaliq script) in the nineteenth century (Orsini, "Pandits, Printers and Others" in Gupta and Chakravorty, *Print Areas*, 138 n. 76). My findings on printing in nineteenth-century Punjab corroborate Orsini's clarification.

13. Bayly, *Empire and Information: Intelligence Gathering and Social Communication in India, 1780–1870* (Cambridge: Cambridge Univ. Press, 1996), 238–9.

14. Dharwadker, "Print Culture and Literary Markets," 112.

15. Indeed, the growing consolidation of the field of English literature by the late nineteenth century owed a great deal to the politics of empire, especially in the ways that processes of canon formation and the practices associated with literary study became central to the "civilizing mission"

the invention of modern Punjabi prose was a textured, multi-layered affair in which Europeans and Indians worked independently and together in response to the "new set of intellectual, social, and economic requirements" that the medium of print had imposed on writing and cultural production.[16] Dharwadker argues that by the 1830s the evolving pastiche of writing, print, prose, journalism, education, and social and religious reform had become the locus of a long revolution in everyday Indian life, one that occurred, as Partha Chatterjee notes, "*outside* the purview of the [colonial] state and the European missionaries."[17] According to Dharwadker, "The particular intersection of modes, mediums, and domains of representation with this metamorphosing multiplex had irreversible consequences for the life of the empire on the subcontinent. This intersection metaphorically defined the space in which writing, print, and education converged to constitute the Indian colonial subject."[18]

Recent discussions on the effects of entrenched "colonial forms of knowledge," to borrow the anthropologist-historian Bernard Cohn's phrase, have important ramifications for our understanding of the impact of print as an agent of change in Punjab.[19] Gayatri Spivak's treatment of colonialism, for example, as the scholar of minority literature and culture Henry Louis Gates Jr. observes, suggests that "there is nothing outside (the discourse of) colonialism" and, in an even stronger form, that "all discourse is colonial discourse." Dharwadker points out that such a perspective implies that the Indian colonial subject through the use of print constituted a reproduction of the autonomous, rational subject of the European Enlightenment, or what Spivak calls "the subject of the West, or the West as Subject."[20] In Spivak's

---

under British rule. Gauri Vishwanathan's seminal study of "English studies" in nineteenth-century India shows the degree to which the institutionalization of English in India and the exercise of colonial power were inextricably linked. See Vishwanathan, *Masks of Conquest: Literary Study and British Rule in India* (New York: Columbia Univ. Press, 1989).

16. Das, *History of Indian Literature,* 67–75; Das quotes the last phrase from Muhammad Sadiq, *A History of Urdu Literature* (Delhi: Oxford Univ. Press, 1974), 291.

17. Chatterjee, *The Nation and Its Fragments: Colonial and Postcolonial Histories* (Princeton, NJ: Princeton Univ. Press, 1993), 7. Also see the excellent local, regional, and subcontinental surveys and case studies in Kenneth W. Jones, ed., *Religious Controversy in British India: Dialogues in South Asian Languages* (Albany: State Univ. of New York Press, 1992), chaps. 1–3, 6, 8–10.

18. Dharwadker, "Print Culture and Literary Markets," 113. For a nuanced discussion of this process, especially as it shaped the emergence of religious nationalisms in Punjab, see Harjot Oberoi's fine study, *The Construction of Religious Boundaries: Culture, Identity, and Diversity in the Sikh Tradition* (Delhi: Oxford Univ. Press, 1994).

19. Cohn, *Colonialism and its Forms of Knowledge: The British in India* (Princeton, NJ: Princeton Univ. Press, 1996).

20. Quoted in Dharwadker, "Print Culture and Literary Markets," 113.

formulation, the Indian subaltern subject cannot be located in discourse and hence cannot "speak." [21] The influential writings of Benedict Anderson, who describes the nation as an "imagined community" created in part by the forces of "print capitalism," contain the implicit claim that the Indian colonial subject, constituted on the ground of print, mimicked the romantic nationalism of modern Europe. In this perspective, anticolonial nationalisms in the non-Western world were modeled on European nationalisms that gave rise only to a "derivative discourse" of postcolonial nationhood. Or, as Partha Chatterjee puts it, "Nationalisms in the rest of the world have to choose their imagined community from certain 'modular' forms already made available to them by Europe and the Americas." [22]

Such arguments, although valid for some as aspects of colonial discourse, sometimes privilege notions of cultural essentialism that are deeply ahistorical, and as far as our discussion of print is concerned, display a certain degree of technological determinism. They assume, as Dharwadker puts it, that "print is controlled completely by its origins, transcends the specificity of cultural (re)location and historical (dis)articulation, and therefore homogenizes all the objects it encounters." The multiplicity of forces at work in the creation of print culture in India could not have reproduced the "conditions, processes, and outcomes that accompanied the Enlightenment, print capitalism, or romantic nationalism of Europe." [23] The numerous historical connections between Europe and India and the obvious continuities have not been sufficient to render the two cultures homogenous or identical. Indeed, at no stage was colonial hegemony total, and my findings reinforce Ranajit Guha's claim that colonial rule was at best an exercise in "dominance without hegemony." [24]

In the Punjab, the lives of men like Rai and Majithia exemplify the ways in which colonial subjects made strategic use of the new opportunities available to them. Joseph Warren, a Presbyterian missionary working in the region in the 1850s, commented that despite the early hostility of the Sikh rulers, by the early 1850s "little lithographic presses have sprung up all over the country

---

21. Spivak, "Can the Subaltern Speak?" in *Colonial Discourse and Postcolonial Theory: A Reader*, ed. Patrick Williams and Laura Chrisman (New York: Columbia Univ. Press, 1994), 66.

22. See Anderson, *Imagined Communities: Reflections on the Origin and Spread of Nationalism* (London: Verso, 1983). The phrase "derivative discourse" comes from Partha Chatterjee, *Nationalist Thought and the Colonial World: A Derivative Discourse* (1986; Minneapolis: Univ. of Minnesota Press, 1993). The quotation is from Chatterjee, *Nation and Its Fragments*, 5.

23. Dharwadker, "Print Culture and Literary Markets," 114.

24. This phrase is the title of Guha's enormously influential book on the subject: *Dominance without Hegemony: History and Power in Colonial India* (Cambridge, MA: Harvard Univ. Press, 1997).

in great numbers for printing Urdu and Persian books." These "grew up like mushrooms and often fail like them too."[25] Harsukh Rai experimented with several newspapers (most notably the *Riyaz-i-Noor* and the *Lahore Gazette*) in addition to the *Kohinoor*. Warren's narrative describes evocatively the range and depth of the conversations triggered by the dissemination of ideas through such publications. Public instruction, along with small books and newspapers, the vogue for statistics, and debates over the definition of rights, changed the face of government and created new knowledge communities among Indian elites. Disenchanted by chronic economic depressions, expatriate businessmen, for example, attacked Indian merchants and government officials in newspapers and at public meetings; and Indian government spokesmen argued in response. Bayly points out that these changes were, however, most uneven in their effects. While they created arenas in which new publicists ultimately came to the fore, existing authorities, sectarian leaders, and magnates were often able to enhance and expand their influence. Yet though there were as many losers as winners, public instruction, the new media, and the diffusion of western knowledge had unsettled society.[26]

The British were generally ambivalent about the virtues of press freedom, especially after the Rebellion of 1857. On one hand, they were still hopeful of using it to gain insights into Indian opinion and spreading Western "enlightenment."[27] On the other hand, they were now much more suspicious of its potential for sedition, especially after the unsettling events of 1857. The favor with which Indian newspapers had been viewed in the time of Governor-General Lord Bentinck as disseminators of useful information evaporated after 1857. Many editors in North India were suspected of sympathy with the rebels and their vitriolic criticism of the authorities throughout the fighting was generally regarded as bordering on sedition.

One of the skills of the new generation of publicists and the rapidly expanding vernacular press was an ability to link together the older institutions of social communication with the newer associations and urban societies that had sprung up in different parts of the Punjab. The oratorical strategies and literary tactics adopted in these arenas were an extraordinary blend of precolonial and colonial. Sectarian battles among modernist and traditionalist Muslims, Sunnis, and Shias and between Ahmadiyahs and the orthodoxy were staged using hostile prose in the printed media; in these campaigns blows were

---

25. Joseph Warren, *A Backward Glance at Fifteen Years of Missionary Life in North India* (Philadelphia, PA: Presbyterian Board of Publication, 1856), 45.

26. Bayly, *Empire and Information*, 245–6.

27. Ibid., 340.

struck against British rule and the tyrannies of western civilization. To limit latent threats from the press without completely hamstringing it, the government introduced a series of severe but flexible controls. Editors were subject to the forfeit of large deposits if they went wrong.[28] Surveillance of vernacular newspapers was increased, with the "Reporter on the Native Press" making regular weekly extracts from newspaper comment on political, religious, and social matters. Whatever officials tried to do, by the mid 1860s the Indian press and other internal lines of communication were increasingly running beyond the government's control. The power of the publicist and newspaper proprietor was manifest years before formal nationalist organizations began to emerge. George Grierson, the scholar of Indian languages, noted: "There is now scarcely a town of importance which does not possess its printing-press or two. Every scribbler can now see his writings in type or lithographed for a few rupees, and too often he avails himself of the power and the opportunity."[29] Sources of news had proliferated and supplemented existing forms of information gathering. Describing news sources in the United Provinces, Bayly shows how some news reports were picked up through marriage connections and others from the reports of the yet larger numbers of pilgrims coming into Banaras and Allahabad by railway. As Bayly puts it, the press was, indeed, discovering India.

As the urban spaces of colonial Punjab became increasingly populated with newspapers, literary texts, vernacular tracts, textbooks, and inexpensive religious propaganda materials, the concomitant circulation of ideas triggered new kinds of associational life. The relations between communities became as contested an issue as the meaning of community itself. The hardening of religious boundaries owed a great deal to the essentializing quality of communal labels as these were used in public discourse. Many articles in the early Urdu newspapers invoked dubious statistics to demonstrate the imbalance between religious, caste, and regional groups in the expanding government offices. These "statistics" were used to lobby for new positions and for preferential treatment. It is said that Swami Dayananda Saraswati, the founder of the Arya Samaj, one of the most influential Hindu reform organizations founded in Punjab, was a sub-editor at one period. The men active in the public arena of the later nineteenth century had put together a powerful and flexible range of communications that informed them about a newly emerging India while maintaining their stake in regional society.[30] In the longer term, the formal,

---

28. N. Gerald Barrier, ed., *Banned: Controversial Literature and Political Control in British India, 1907–47* ([Columbia]: Univ. of Missouri Press, 1974), 1–6.

29. G. A. Grierson, *The Modern Vernacular Literature of Hindustan* (Calcutta, 1889), 45.

30. Bayly, *Empire and Information,* 350.

depersonalized massing of opinion in printed books and newspapers tended to stereotype social categories. Newspapers, by choosing one script or form of language, tended to identify themselves with one "community" or another (as was particularly true of the Devanagri, Nastaliq, and Gurmukhi scripts). In time, the technologies of communication and the transformed cultures of public contestation were to fracture social relations along fault lines derived from the culturally essentialist, deeply structured vision of the colonial state's disciplinary order. The most far-reaching ramifications of this process are apparent from the stridency of cultural nationalism in the early twentieth century.

The Rudiments of a Social Formation

In post-1849 Punjab, shifts in the political economy were triggered as much by the colonial government's efforts at large-scale irrigation reform as by the entrepreneurial energies of commercial elites and a growing urban intelligentsia. These transformations went hand in hand with radical changes in the ways that individuals viewed themselves in relation to other groups in terms of class, religious, regional, or caste identity. Roger Chartier's rich writings demonstrate the degree to which the concept of social representation[31] is a multi-layered affair. For Chartier, the concept operates at three levels: first, at the level of collective representations that embody, within individuals, the divisions of the social world and organize the schemes of perception by which individuals classify, judge, and act; second, at the level of the self-conscious stylization and construction of the identity that those groups or individuals hope will be recognized; and third, at that level of organization at which specific individuals or institutions are delegated to represent the social formation, and thus affirm the stability of the identity.[32] In this framework, the history of the construction of social identities becomes a history of the relations of symbolic force. In nineteenth-century Punjab, the arrival of new forms of communication and transmission of knowledge had far-reaching implications for the ways in which these representations were constructed. Those who wielded the conceptual vocabulary and cultural capital that endowed them with symbolic power in the eyes of their peers play a significant role in shaping the contours of power.

---

31. Chartier writes with reference to the work of Louis Marin. See Chartier, *On the Edge of the Cliff* (Baltimore, MD: Johns Hopkins Univ. Press, 1997). The work of Chartier has deeply influenced my arguments in this essay. See, in particular, the essays in Chartier, ed., *The Culture of Print: Power and Uses of Print in Early Modern Europe,* trans. Lydia Cochrane (Cambridge: Cambridge Univ. Press, 1989).

32. Chartier, *On the Edge,* 4–5.

Bayly has identified a particularly fascinating figure that illustrates this process as it unfolded in Punjab. This was the *munshi,* a member of the precolonial elite lettered class of North India whose transformation over the nineteenth century reveals the delicate ways in which precolonial forms of symbolic power were transformed in later years. The word *munshi* generally referred to the consciously conservative man of letters, someone usually drawn from the caste of Kayasthas. However, between roughly 1820 and 1850, a new type of *munshi* began to appear.[33] The older generation of *munshi*s, who had taught Persian to the British and conducted their Indian diplomacy for them, remained firmly rooted in the culture of the precolonial elites. The new *munshis,* likewise, were tied closely to British patronage, and by the 1850s most were educated in English. Many were employees of the Department of Public Instruction. But rather than drafting newsletters and the proclamations of Indian rulers, they translated early Victorian schoolbooks into Urdu and Hindi — and played a pivotal role in the dissemination of printed materials through new forms of publicity.[34]

Shahamat Ali was an example of the new *munshi.* He accompanied Claude Wade as secretary during his embassy to Ranjeet Singh in 1837–8 and went on to Kabul, a journey that he described in an English journal later published in London. Soon after, he was elevated to the position of *Mir Munshi* to Wade when he was resident at Indore, ending his career in the Bhil Agency in central India. Shahamat Ali had studied English in the English Department of Delhi College. Bayly demonstrates how the writing of an accurate English journal was deemed to be the critical breakthrough into the modern world. At Claude Wade's insistence, Shahamat Ali not only "improved" himself but "acquired a habit of writing a journal, and continued the practice in various missions" on which that officer was employed. He recorded routes, quantities, and populations. He wrote about the "despotic" character of Ranjeet Singh's government.[35] He bemoaned the meanness of this monarch who, having invested him with a ceremonial garment, then refused to have it delivered to him. He wrote of the glories of the Mughal buildings he had seen. As Bayly observes, all of these themes would have appeared in classical Islamic travelogues, but in Shahamat Ali's narrative, the tone is different, the landscape is no longer crowded with the relics of great kings, and Sufi shrines are rarely mentioned. The political moves of the British are at the core of the narrative.

---

33. Bayly, *Empire and Information,* 229–30.

34. For example, Munshi Sadha Sukh Lal; see R. Roseberry III, *Imperial Rule in Punjab: The Conquest and Administration of Multan* (Delhi, 1987), 119.

35. Shahamat Ali, preface to *The Sikhs and Afghans in Connection with India and Persia Immediately before and after the Death of Ranjeet Singh* (London, 1849), xi, 124.

Most suggestive is Shahamat Ali's attitude toward what he calls "superstition," by which he means popular Hinduism and Islam. One sees in men like Shahamat Ali, and other intellectuals like him, such as Sayyid Ahmad Khan later in the century, the influence of the reformism that was then sweeping the cities.[36] This reformism, especially prevalent in the circle of men like Dayal Singh Majithia, Harsukh Rai, and *munshis* such as Shahamat Ali, was a product of their ongoing struggle with processes of economic and institutional change that forced them to choose, to adopt positions in relation to members of their own caste, religion, and social class.

In the past, the social and political authority of such men was based on land ownership, but in the second half of the nineteenth century land ownership was no longer enough to ensure their high social status. The opportunities created by the colonial state were paralleled by the impact of reformist ideas of groups such as the Brahmo Samaj and Arya Samaj, especially after the 1850s, in Punjab.[37] Men such as Majithia and Rai, together with others of their generation such as Muhammad Azim and Mahbub Alam, were increasingly influenced by the ideas of such reformist groups whose mobilizations redefined the ways in which they viewed themselves in relation to the changing world around them. The status of these men as "notables," in Bayly's use of the term, depended on their ability to communicate through print and oratory, which they used to harness the capricious networks of their social world. At the best of times (and by no means often), their economic aspirations acquired a synergistic relationship with their cosmopolitanism. To quote Eisenstein, though in a completely different context, "It seems . . . accurate to describe many publishers as being *both* businessmen *and* literary dispensers of glory. They served men of letters not only by providing traditional forms of patronage but also by acting as press agents and as cultural impresarios of a new kind."[38] Majithia, who founded the English newspaper the *Tribune* (which remains popular in Indian Punjab to this day), was an enormously successful entrepreneur and urban "notable" of his day.

The government was not necessarily the prime moving force behind these motivations because these developments also reflected the growing use of paper for publicity, archives, lists, and information gathering by many groups in society: religious foundations and specialists, all-India sects, commercial corporations, and landholders. Bayly has argued that even in precolonial

---

36. Bayly, *Empire and Information*, 232–3.

37. Kenneth Jones, *Arya Dharm: Hindu Consciousness in 19th-Century Punjab* (Berkeley and Los Angeles: Univ. of California Press, 1976), 24.

38. Eisenstein, *PPAC*, 23. Emphasis in original.

times, India was increasingly a "literacy aware" society.[39] Letter writing, the circulation of official and semi-official newsletters, and a flexible postal system had kept the elites in touch with one another over great distances. Ordinary people also participated in a well-developed culture of oral communication, which habitually used these written instruments as points of reference. Between a "knowledge"-generating state and the more fragmented communicative populace, and reflecting on both, there existed what Bayly has called the north "Indian ecumene" — "a form of cultural and political debate which was typical of North India before the emergence of the newspaper and public association, yet persisted in conjunction with the press and new forms of publicity into the age of nationalism."[40] This was a routine of political debate and surveillance, which subjected both rulers and society to critique through meetings, discussions, placarding, and demonstration.

Multiple Publics and the "Indian Ecumene"

Historians agree that in the West the public sphere was a domain of communication given form by printed media and the market, although as the revisionist scholarship on the public sphere demonstrates, there is much debate about the texture of this sphere and exclusionary mechanisms employed by this space.[41] Until the influence of revisionist scholarship on the public sphere took hold, it was argued that the public sphere was absent from the North Indian scene before the introduction of lithography in the 1830s and 1840s, although the reasons for this absence remain obscure. Politics may have played a part; several Indian rulers at the turn of the nineteenth century continued to discourage the use of the printing press because it threatened their authority.[42] My evidence, along with the rich writings of Francesca Orsini, Veena Naregal, and Vasudha Dalmia,[43] among others, support an opposing view: that royal authority was already too fragile to support the burgeoning use of print, let alone control it.

---

39. Bayly, *Empire and Information,* 366–7.

40. See ibid., 182. For an elaboration of Bayly's use of the term, see 181 n. 6.

41. Jürgen Habermas, *Structural Transformation of the Public Sphere* (Cambridge, MA: MIT Press, 1991). For a good collection of revisionist essays on the public sphere, see Craig Calhoun, ed., *Habermas and the Public Sphere* (Cambridge, MA: MIT Press, 1992).

42. For examples from Punjab, see Emmett Davis, *The Press and Politics in British West Punjab, 1836–47* (Delhi: Manohar Publications, 1983), 16.

43. See Vasudha Dalmia, *The Nationalization of Hindu Traditions: Bharatendu Harishchandra and Nineteenth Century Banaras* (Delhi: Oxford Univ. Press, 1997); and Orsini, "Pandits, Printers and Others." Also, see Veena Naregal, *Language, Politics, Elites, and the Public Sphere: Western India Under Colonialism* (Delhi: Permanent Black, 2001).

This view, in turn, points to a wider reason for the late explosion of print-ing. In Bayly's formulation, strategically placed written media gained in popularity when they reinforced a powerful culture of oral communication; printing in this sense was not needed until society itself began to change more radically under colonial rule.[44] In these circumstances, shaped as much by shifts in the political economy and the emergence of an energized urban culture, written media and oral communication complemented each other. This relationship, between oral and written, shaped the ways in which publics proliferated in the nooks and crannies of urban Punjab. Francis Robinson has made a strong case for the dominance of oral exposition and the importance of the physical presence of the reputed teacher within the pre-print culture of Islamic North India.[45] Oral exposition, presence, and memory were no doubt critical in philosophical debate among Hindus and Jains no less than among Muslims. They were also important in poetic and aesthetic discussion. Written media were, nevertheless, an essential part of North Indian critical debate, and for our discussion on the place of print in colonial India—it is important that we recognize the role they played in shaping the tone and content of printed materials as these circulated later in the century.

The idea of the "Indian ecumene" is extremely effective at softening the sharp break between tradition and nationalist modernity in our discussions of the "impact" of print. It also allows us to locate public culture in a num-ber of arenas, seeping into what Michael Warner has recently described as "publics" and "counterpublics."[46] Excellent studies have shown that Indians passionately debated before the mid nineteenth century.[47] Other histories reveal how Indians represented shifts in political power through festivals and cultural performances.[48] Bayly has persuasively demonstrated that the "ecumene of Hindustani-writing literati, Indo-Islamic notables and officers of state (which included many Hindus) fought its battles with a well-tested arsenal of handwritten media."[49] The guardians of the ecumene represented the views of the bazaar people and artisans when urban communities came

---

44. Bayly, *Empire and Information,* chap. 5.

45. Robinson, "Technology and Religious Change: Islam and the Impact of Print," *Modern Asian Studies* 27 (1993): 229–51.

46. For a detailed discussion of the distinction between the idea of "a public" and multiple "publics," see Warner, "Publics and Counterpublics," *Public Culture* 14 (2002): 49–90.

47. Jones, *Religious Controversy in British India.*

48. See the contributions in Sandria Freitag, ed., "Aspects of the Public in Colonial South Asia," Special Issue, *South Asia* 14 (June 1991).

49. Bayly, *Empire and Information,* 199–201.

under pressure. Their connections spread across religious, sectarian, and caste boundaries, though they never dissolved them. These forms of expression carried over into the period of colonial rule. In a sense, they were closer in spirit to the groupings of philosophers, urban notables, and officials in the world of late antiquity—the Christian-Greek ecumene—than to Habermas's modern public. His public sphere is more sharply separated from the world of intimate social relations; people's judgment is represented through an impersonal, commercial print in an almost mechanical way. The Indian ecumene, however, does bear comparison to the modern European public in the sense that its leaders were able to mount a critical surveillance of government and society.

One of the most comprehensive concepts helpful for understanding the conventions governing social public discourse is *adab*. Originally identified with an Islamic ideal, the content of *adab* is cosmopolitan and is shared by different social constituencies. Broadly defined, *adab* describes "the proper discrimination of social order, behavior, and taste; it espouses breeding and nurture; and it is sustained by deference towards those who embody its norms." In other words, the concept of *adab* determined the norms and conventions that defined exchange of opinions in specific arenas. These norms carried over into colonial settings and were increasingly adapted to new settings and forms of discourse. In fact, the rule and directives that characterized *adab* had always been broadly defined and were capable of adapting to a "multiplicity of potential systems of values associated with social and occupational roles; ethnic and regional values; aesthetic, cosmopolitan, and scientific modes of thought; and even alternate ways of being religious." Most of the reformers and various other public figures of late-nineteenth-century Punjab were familiar with the normative directives laid down as *adabiyat,* and the forms of public articulation reveal this familiarity. However, by addressing a wider audience, a number of these publicists recognized the need to adapt their modes of articulation to new contexts, not by denying the relevance of *adab* norms but by modifying them. Referring to the relevance of *adab* in colonial society, David Gilmartin notes: "The reformers in the modern period . . . are less concerned with elites because it is not just the elites who provide the cultural basis for the political system; rather there are larger groups of people who are now involved. This becomes particularly important in the late nineteenth century . . . when the political system itself, as the British are devising it, becomes more and more democratic." The norms of *adabi* behavior were extremely diverse, and specific to particular settings. Richard Eaton demonstrates how the shrine of Baba Farid in Pakpattan (in Punjab) was characterized by extremely distinctive *adab* of Sufi shrines. This *adab* comprises "highly elaborate codes of etiquette and pageantry that both dazzled and integrated into its structure the subjects of the kingdom."[50]

Historically, the learned, the local officeholders, and the "honorable" (*ashraf*) had acted as a check on the ruling elites. These men, many of whom were officeholders, were drawn from the same families as the urban property-holders and traders. Their functions were not limited to matters of religion until the colonial powers restricted them to this role. They were doctors, healers of the mind, poets and writers, astronomers, and advisers of citizens. The elites kept up a constant conversation on matters of religious wisdom through ritual and official *darbars,* mosque schools, the Sufi orders, and private homes. There was also a long tradition of independent thinking and debate about the status of non-Islamic religion and culture. Congregational meetings among the Muslim community during the nights of the month of Ramadan provided a forum for wider discussions on matters concerning the community, and the consensus of these meetings might be conveyed to the rulers.[51] Alongside this, the educated maintained a debate on literature, language, and aesthetics through poetry-reading circles or *mushairas.*

These forms of public discourse did not disappear with the arrival of colonial rule but simply re-presented themselves under different forms of patronage. Thus, Harsukh Rai's earliest efforts at establishing himself as a patron involved his active promotion of a *mushaira,* only this time his efforts were actively publicized in his newspaper the *Kohinoor.* This meant, first, that he could reach out to a larger audience and, second, that his own conception of the limits of his social reach had changed. In other words, the *mushairas* that had always remained the preserve of an *ashraf* elite were now accessible to a larger social group. The *Kohinoor* regularly published considerable portions of poetry that had been read aloud at the *mushaira.* This decontextualized the poems from their performative aspect — an aspect that had always been a major component of the articulation of the poetry of the "Indian ecumene."

Print and the Making of a "Literary Mode of Production"

In what way does the preceding overview of the lives of men engaged in print culture such as Harsukh Rai and Dayal Singh Majithia help us to grasp the

---

50. Barbara Daly Metcalf, ed., *Moral Conduct and Authority: The Place of Adab in South Asian Islam* (Berkeley and Los Angeles: Univ. of California Press, 1984), 12–3, 17, 19, 355. Gilmartin is quoted on p. 19. Eaton's essay is entitled "The Political and Religious Authority of the Shrine of Baba Farid," 333–57.

51. Metcalf, *Moral Conduct and Authority,* 17–9.

relationship between print culture and associational life in the larger context of colonial modernity? A discussion of what cultural theorist Terry Eagleton has called the "literary mode of production" provides part of the answer. In his conceptualization, the literary mode of production is an apparatus that includes "the specific institutions of literary production and distribution (publishing houses, book shops, libraries, etc.), but also encompasses a range of 'secondary,' supportive institutions whose function is more directly ideological, concerned with the definition and dissemination of literary 'standards' and assumptions. Among these are literary academies, societies and book clubs, associations of literary producers, distributors and consumers, censoring bodies, and literary journals and reviews." [52] Eagleton's point is not only to underscore the importance of studies of institutions that have become common among both sociologists of culture and cultural historians but also to emphasize the form and content of the texts produced, to discover the categories that are emphasized and de-emphasized, and to determine the ways in which these categories illuminate or obscure features of social experience. Quite simply, publications—and the plethora of institutions producing, monitoring, consuming them—played an active part in instigating change because they were part of a larger apparatus that facilitated what Habermas calls public "communicative action" among a section of the urban bourgeois population. [53] In the formulations of both Eagleton and Habermas, acquiring a nuanced understanding of the process of class formation is a key element. For our purposes, the juxtaposition of the ideas of the "literary mode of production" and the "public sphere" allows us to clarify our understanding of the shifting social worlds of those shaping the contours of colonial Punjab's print culture.

Another portion of the answer builds on an insight provided by Anthony Giddens, who in his writings on historical sociology has made a useful distinction between "class awareness" and "class consciousness." [54] The former refers to the existence of the awareness and acceptance of similar attitudes and beliefs, linked to a common style of life among the members of the class. In other words, "class awareness" does not involve, first, a recognition that these attitudes and beliefs signify a particular class affiliation or, second, the recognition that there exist other classes characterized by different attitudes, beliefs, and styles of life; Giddens uses "class consciousness" to imply both of

---

52. Eagleton, *Criticism and Ideology: A Study in Marxist Literary Theory* (London: Verso, 1976), 56.

53. For Jürgen Habermas's detailed description of these ideas, see his two-volume study, *The Theory of Communicative Action* (Boston, MA: Beacon Press, 1984–7).

54. These terms are taken from Giddens, "Class Structuration and Class Consciousness," in *Classes, Power, and Conflict: Classical and Contemporary Debates,* ed. Giddens and David Held (Berkeley and Los Angeles: Univ. of California Press, 1982), 162–3.

these. My research suggests that in nineteenth-century Punjab, class identity was fragmented, lacking the type of coherence that the category of "class consciousness" presumes for modern societies. The process of class formation in nineteenth-century Punjab was characterized by at best a class "awareness" that is reflected in the attitudes of individuals who expressed themselves as "public aware" intellectuals and publicists who were engaging a plethora of "publics," not as spokesmen for specific class groups but rather for social constituencies that drew on a wide repertoire of social labels.

Contrary to the view that the public sphere was a bourgeois space that encouraged rational debate (in the normative, Habarmasian sense), I argue that the possibility of public debate generated discourses that engaged a wider social base through the institutional apparatus of a colonial "literary mode of production." By the second half of the nineteenth century, these discourses led to the emergence of an internally fractured social formation defined by its increasing participation in urban associational activities, which helped to produce institutions that set the stage for the politics of the twentieth century. Members of this social group participated (directly or indirectly) in the activities of the newly emerging public spaces and facilitated the emergence of new forms of knowledge on a wide range of subjects that they controlled. The development of these forms of knowledge, in some instances reinforcing the hegemony of colonialism and in others challenging it, shaped the trajectories of politics as they developed into the twentieth century. In this sense, the figure of the *munshi* embodies the attributes of the "public aware" agent of change who jousts in public with his pen and provokes action through his public presence.

Together with structural shifts in the administrative, civic, educational, economic, and religious life in colonial Punjab, the arrival of print media was a catalyst of social change that linked people with similar agendas and access to similar discourses in the urban centers of this province. In tune with the enumerative and classificatory strategies of the colonial state, languages and scripts were objectified as markers of social identity and eventually standardized, becoming weapons in an arsenal of sectarian and, later, nationalist contestation. This process undoubtedly accelerated the adoption of print that became, perhaps not the only but certainly one important agent of change, a distinction that Eisenstein makes to forestall any confusion on her position in the preface of her pioneering study on early modern Europe.[55] As a result, religion, politics, constitutional reform, medicine, the role of women, and a

---

55. For Eisenstein, this distinction is particularly important in the wake of Marshall McLuhan's legacy, from which she seeks a certain amount of distance. For a detailed discussion of this, see Eisenstein, *PPAC*, xv.

whole range of issues became subjects of debate and points of contention in new public arenas.

Several presses had been set up in the Punjab by the early part of the nineteenth century with missionary patronage, but after 1849 this support increasingly came from newly empowered urban groups. That a number of publications of this period thrived on the patronage of landed elites and rajas reinforces the sense that the rural and agrarian worlds were not very far apart. Most newspapers were unprofitable, but they continued to be published, partly because the press facilitated the emergence of a medium of communication that adapted to the requirements of the "Indian ecumene" and met the demands of social groups who lived in urban centers where they were in the process of negotiating modern ways of thought and colonial institutions. In such settings, these groups distanced themselves from their rural background and, in addition to pursuing their commercial and professional interests, occupied themselves by exercising critical surveillance over the state and other transformations of the time. Bayly's description of the process is entirely apt for Punjab: "Print itself did not create an information revolution. Rather, it speeded up the velocity and range of communication among existing communities of knowledge. It helped transform some actors within the old ecumene into leaders of a modern public, but it marginalized and subordinated others." [56] Despite the best efforts of the British to monitor and regulate the contours of public culture, the imperial machinery remained fairly ineffectual in its efforts, as the rise of nationalism by the last decades of the nineteenth century demonstrates. The multiplicity of publics and the diversity of literary spheres lend credence to Douglas Haynes's claim that British rule in India displayed at best a "limited hegemony." [57]

---

56. Bayly, *Empire and Information*, 243.

57. Douglas Haynes uses the phrase to argue that colonial notions failed to penetrate many areas of indigenous culture. See his *Rhetoric and Ritual in Colonial India* (Berkeley and Los Angeles: Univ. of California Press, 1991), 15.

Chapter 14

"Ki ngā pito e whā o te ao nei"
(To the four corners of this world)

*Maori Publishing and Writing for Nineteenth-Century
Maori-Language Newspapers*

JANE MCRAE

In 1842, early on in the colonizing of New Zealand, the British government launched *Te Karere o Nui Tireni* (The New Zealand messenger), the first newspaper published in the Maori language. Appearing nearly thirty years after the Maori language had acquired a written form, the paper marked the beginning of a long line of such publications. From the debut of *Te Karere o Nui Tireni* in 1842 to the early decades of the twentieth century, more than forty additional newspaper titles were published in the Maori language. Some were published by the government, others by churches or philanthropists, and still others by Maori themselves. Within the pages of these papers are the traces of how the traditionally oral Maori became writers and publishers. Pieced together, these traces afford print scholars an opportunity to examine interactions between print and orality and the transformative effects of these exchanges.

In *The Printing Press as an Agent of Change: Communications and Cultural Transformations in Early-Modern Europe* (*PPAC*), Elizabeth Eisenstein emphasizes the complexity surrounding the emergence of what Marshall McLuhan termed "the typographical man" and urges historians to think "more historically and concretely about the sorts of effects that were entailed and how different groups were affected" by this emergence.[1] Reading early Maori newspapers with the history of print in mind underscores the wisdom

---

1. Eisenstein, *PPAC*, 129. On the need for detailed historical and ethnographic information on how literacy takes root in society, cf. Niko Besnier, *Literacy, Emotion, and Authority: Reading and Writing on a Polynesian Atoll* (Cambridge: Cambridge Univ. Press, 1995) 5, 173, 176; also Adrian Johns's call for a richly detailed historical approach to the book in *The Nature of the Book: Print and Knowledge in the Making* (Chicago: Univ. of Chicago Press, 1998), 623.

of her advice. Through their experience as readers, writers, and producers of newspapers, Maori made the kind of adjustments Eisenstein chronicles for a much earlier period and quite different societies—the movement "from a hearing public to a reading public,"[2] indeed from an oral to a literate culture. The forty-plus newspapers produced by and for Maori during these decades record such adjustments.[3] Drawing from titles of each major publisher, I recount this first and very active use of print by Maori. In the process I elucidate what Maori learned about literacy, print, and journalism; what they wrote; how, impressed by the far-reaching voice of a newspaper, they romantically conceptualized the press; and how, combining oral and literate practice, they used the press to challenge the colonizers.[4] This select view of Maori print history is emblematic of the differences between oral and literate mentalities.[5]

AFTER OBSERVING Maori in Auckland on days that the *Te Karere o Nui Tireni* was published, a mid-nineteenth-century European described their approach to reading the paper: "One native of a party is generally selected to read the news aloud: when he takes his seat upon the ground, a circle is then formed, and after the reader has promulgated the content, the different natives, according to their rank, stand up and argue the different points contained; which being done, they retire home, and answer the different letters [articles, letters, or editorials] by writing to the editor."[6] The listeners' eager and studied attention is apparent in this description, from their gathering around the reader to their ensuing debates. This scene no doubt was common. Many Maori were not literate and, because of their oral tradition, may have preferred listening to someone read aloud. *Te Karere,* the paper Maori read and listened to in Auckland and elsewhere, was a proper newspaper,

---

2. Eisenstein, *PPAC,* 129.

3. Supporting David D. Hall's contention that the utilitarian newspaper can contribute to "the makings of a history of the book," *Cultures of Print: Essays in the History of the Book* (Amherst: Univ. of Massachusetts Press, 1996), 28.

4. For publication history of the newspapers and articles about content, see Jenifer Curnow, Ngapare Hopa, and Jane McRae, eds., *Rere atu, taku manu! Discovering History, Language, and Politics in the Maori-language Newspapers* (Auckland, NZ: Auckland Univ. Press, 2002). The newspapers (some with translation to English) and English abstracts of the contents of several titles can be read at http://www.nzdl.org/niupepa.

5. See, for example, Walter Ong's arguments about the oral mentality in *Orality and Literacy: The Technologizing of the Word* (London: Methuen, 1982), and, with specific reference to Maori, those of Norman Simms in *Points of Contact: A Study of the Interplay and Intersection of Traditional and Non-traditional Literature, Culture and Mentalities* (New York: Pace Univ. Press, 1991).

6. W. Brodie, *Remarks on the Past and Present State of New Zealand* (London: Whittaker & Co., 1845), 110.

with editorials, letters, articles about local, national, and international news, notices, advertisements, and obituaries. Because of the times, the 1840s, and because the paper's publisher was the government, its tone was highly didactic and its content circumscribed. But Maori were to write independently to this paper, and their writing would testify to close and questioning reading of issues.[7]

Te Karere's first editorial invited Maori who were concerned about or opposed to the governor's rulings presented in its pages to submit their opinions "so that they can be printed in this paper for all people to see."[8] While this invitation encouraged public debate, a notion well known to Maori oral society, the extraordinary audience it offered was new to Maori, and they responded with enthusiasm. Up until this point their reporting on life had been confined to the localities of tribes. The *karere* (messenger) had run across the land with memorized copy but had not visited all villages or gone beyond the boundaries of the Maori world. Europeans were evidence of a world beyond, and newspapers brought that world closer by their foreign news and by a circulation that delighted Maori, who often enjoined editors, in what became a repeated expression, to send their article or letter "to the four corners of the world."

The aim of *Te Karere,* stated in the first and subsequent editorials, was to inform Maori about British law and European custom.[9] But the paper also gave voice to Maori opinions. In the first issue, for example, a report of the murder of a European family by a Maori included submissions from chiefs dissociating themselves from the killer and approving his treatment by the law[10]—as the governor would have wished. Though some submissions, such as chiefs' speeches to government and letters to the governor, were self-serving, others were more outspoken. One man wrote that he had given out copies of the paper to his tribe (probably a common means of distribution) so that they could read about European custom. He accepted that Maori be tutored in European ways, but in declaring his intention to tie up *Pakeha* (Europeans) who had been eating his pigs and take them to the courthouse,

7. This title ran from 1842 to 1846; subsequent government newspapers, under various titles and with a wealth of Maori contributions, ran until 1879. Two essays in Curnow, Hopa, and McRae, *Rere atu,* document the range and quality of this writing: Christine Tremewan, "Poetry in *Te Waka Maori,*" 115–33; and Lyndsay Head, *"Kupu pai, kupu kino:* Good and Bad Words in Maori Political Writing," 134–52.

8. *Te Karere o Nui Tireni,* January 1, 1842, 1. All translations from the newspapers are mine.

9. As stated in the first editorial, *Te Karere o Nui Tireni,* January 1, 1842, 1, and reiterated in others.

10. Ibid., 2–4.

he made the point that not only Maori needed such tutoring.[11] Another writer drew attention to the dilemma posed to Maori who, taking to heart an article's advice not to wear dirty clothes in town, wore their best outfits, only to have *Pakeha* suggest that they had stolen the clothes or mock their pretensions.[12]

While Maori may have considered the simplistic injunctions about appropriate behavior in this impressive and authoritative publication odd, they also saw in the paper an opportunity to put forth their own views "for all people to see." For this first newspaper in their language, they wrote about laws and bills before Parliament, the rights and wrongs of land sales, and military and political conflicts among tribes, settlers, and government. In addition, they used the paper to find work, advise of animals straying onto their properties, and advertise land, stock, or produce for sale.

In the pages of *Te Karere* Maori read articles on topics that ranged from English history to advice on land transactions to a life of Martin Luther. Quotations from the Bible—their primary reading material—appeared frequently in editorials and articles. And in those pages Maori encountered the authority, power, and conventions of print. A piece criticizing those who buried Bibles with the deceased taught that books were permanent possessions, while an announcement that correspondence of those Maori who formerly supported rebels but were now loyal to the government would be burned conveyed the power and authority of the written word. The editor counseled about selection, censoring, and writing: the newspaper would not print inaccurate information—such information "could be left on the lips of the many" (implying the truth of print and the falsity of talk)—nor would it print anonymous accusations. The wording of *waiata* (poetic songs) were to be suitable (for a Victorian sense of decency) and understandable to all, and correspondents were not to write in pencil but "in black ink so that the words are permanent." Maori meanwhile read with a critical eye. When they wrote to ask, for example, "Who will heed that newspaper?" or "Who will take up with those false and dishonest words?" the editor responded with a lengthy editorial to justify the reporting and counter the prevalent Maori attitude that print had no purchase on truth.[13] Although the Maori's oral and

---

11. The editor replied by expressing his approval but cautioned the writer to tie up the guilty and not the innocent. Ibid., December 1, 1842, 51–2.

12. Ibid., August 1, 1842, 33–4.

13. Ibid., January 1, 1845, 2–3; January 15, 1846, 1–2; July 15, 1845, 25; April 1, 1843, 16; November 1, 1843, 46; September 1, 1842, 38; August 1, 1844, 37–9. Cf. Johns, *Nature of the Book*, 378, that early readers recognized the "contestable status" of printed texts and defended their own knowledge in relation to them.

the *Pakeha*'s literate mentalities yielded contested meanings of print, Maori nevertheless greatly appreciated the newspaper as an avenue for opinions and news and a window on European life.

Moreover, Maori oral tradition found a place within the newspaper's pages: features typical of oral composition were adapted to a print context. Speeches by chiefs, for example, recorded verbatim, reflected their oratorical style. An excerpt from a speech about the history of a block of land in one issue captured the terse, rhythmical language of tribal oral histories, along with the episodic structure, and the traditional lists of geographic boundaries and genealogy.[14] Concluding with a warning that the land would not be given up for sale freely and a list of signatories, the speech reflected the contentious relations among Maori, settlers, and government officials over the sale of land along with the rhetoric of Maori interacting face to face in a tribal meeting. Similarly, Maori could read *waiata* with conventional phrases altered to fit a confrontation, for example, between the government and a rebellious chief.[15] On occasion print might also mock Maori oral heritage: one article classed the mythology of renowned cultural heroes as outmoded by comparison with the superior knowledge of Pakeha.[16]

The writing by Maori that was published in *Te Karere,* in conformance with the printed model and editors' requirements, was conservative, not least because the Maori had learned to read and write from Christian missionaries.[17] Newspapers, like books, provided lessons in literacy and faith. *Te Haeata* (1859–61) was the first Maori newspaper sponsored by a church. Although lean in contributions from Maori, this Wesleyan production encouraged the emerging reader and writer. God's words were written down, readers were told, so they could reach all people, a reminder of the capacity of print to make words and ideas widely accessible. And readers were urged to save the papers and bind them like a book for future generations, a reminder of the permanence of print.[18]

Te Haeata was filled with debates on doctrinal matters and descriptions of the Church's work in other countries, along with local and international news. But there seemed to be little scope for Maori opinion. The rigor of the printed religious and moral precepts may have deterred contributors. Also, the European editor was highly selective, though he had an eye for the Maori

---

14. *Te Karere o Nui Tireni,* December 2, 1844, 61.

15. Ibid., June 2, 1845, 24.

16. Ibid., July 1, 1844, 33–4.

17. For a list of their printed reading in the nineteenth century, see Phil Parkinson and Penny Griffith, *Books in Maori 1815–1900: An Annotated Bibliography* (Auckland, NZ: Reed Books, 2004).

18. *Te Haeata,* September 1, 1860, 3–4; April 2, 1860, 3–4.

reader. The imagery of the title, meaning "the light of dawn," was drawn from both Christian and Maori poetics, and the contents included *waiata* with Christian referents and the figurative political speeches of elders.[19] And Maori oral conventions appeared in the obituaries that opened with traditional farewells.[20] Maori writing did come to press, however, when, for example, it echoed the Church's disapproval of non-Christian customs, such as sorcery, or described the work of church monitors. *Te Haeata*—like *Te Karere,* an "instrument of domination"—was an example of an independent press as a vehicle for a particular viewpoint and demonstrated to Maori that a newspaper could be "an instrument of resistance."[21]

Maori soon sought the independence of their own newspapers. The first was produced by the Maori King Movement (an attempt to gain an influence equal to that of the British Crown by unifying the tribes under their own king), which followed an ancient royal tradition of defining itself "by the output of printed materials"[22]—when it published *Te Hokioi o Niu Tireni e Rere atu na* (The war-bird in flight to you).[23] The editor wrote that "the advantage of the press is that it carries our opinions to the peoples of the world,"[24] expressing the now familiar satisfaction with the reach of the printed word and the hope that the world's attention would be brought to their political aspirations. *Te Hokioi* was provocative. In a demonstration of the power of print, *Te Hokioi* suggested that a government newspaper, which had set up in direct opposition to and denigrated the King Movement, was "asking for a paper war."[25] Maori sympathetic to the movement stemmed its opposition by raiding the government premises and taking the press away.

The Maori newspaper *Te Wananga* (The forum), which began publication in 1874 and continued through 1878, demonstrated that the printed word had confirmed its place in Maori thinking about politics. The paper openly opposed the government press, which, ironically, in an early edition, had reminded readers that *Pakeha* had brought writing and print to Maori and that "one of the benefits of a newspaper such as this is to bring Pakeha and

---

19. See, for example, ibid., July 1, 1859, 2–3.

20. See examples in Yvonne Sutherland, "Church and Identity in the Wesleyan Newspaper, *Te Haeata,*" in Curnow, Hopa, and McRae, *Rere atu,* 103–12.

21. Besnier uses these terms in discussing how Nukulaelae Islanders used literacy to their own ends (*Literacy, Emotion, and Authority,* 178).

22. Eisenstein, *PPAC,* 135. They were also choosing print as "a means of asserting cultural independence" (Hall, *Cultures of Print,* 51).

23. On the press and its conflict with government, see Jenifer Curnow, "A Brief History of Maori-language Newspapers," in Curnow, Hopa, and McRae, *Rere atu,* 21–2.

24. *Te Hokioi o Niu Tireni e Rere atu na,* June 15, 1863, 1.

25. Ibid., April 2, 1863, 2.

Maori together."[26] Encouraged into print by government and church, Maori were using print, in David Hall's words, as an "agent of control" to legitimate their roles.[27] Nor was their bold, competitive harnessing of the press necessarily anticipated.[28]

Te Wananga was unashamedly Maori. The title refers to the learned teachings of the elders: a *wānanga* is a school of the oral tradition as well as a forum. The first issue proclaimed that the paper was "for the whole land, for the Maori people"; it was for all tribes and would bring them "together in one mind." Tribal independence, Maori had found, was a disadvantage in negotiations with the government and unity was an effective strategy—perhaps a key reason for the announcement that the subscription price would be set according to tribal agreement.[29] This newspaper was, in Alexis de Tocqueville's terms, an instrument of "action for an association";[30] in this instance the association was the society of individual tribes. The paper was also an agent for change in tribal alliances, providing, according to Eisenstein's perception, a new form of "group identity [that] began to compete with an older, more localized nexus of loyalties."[31] *Te Wananga* spoke clearly of its desire for such unity among Maori: "I, *Te Wananga*, am a press to reveal the words of each tribal group, whether it is Hauhau [a separatist religious group] or government; we are all Maori and *Te Wananga* will bring to light the pains that oppress the Maori people,"[32] but the editors invited opinion from opponents as well as supporters, and later even Pakeha, in pursuit of their cause.

As extant manuscripts reveal, Maori were prolific letter writers in the nineteenth century, and many of their letters went to the Maori-language newspapers. Numerous letters published in the early issues of *Te Wananga* indicate the exuberance with which the paper was welcomed, the expectations it embodied, and its efficacy for public announcement. One enthusi-

---

26. *Te Waka Maori o Ahuriri*, June 13, 1863, 1.

27. Hall, *Cultures of Print*, 51.

28. Cf. the Nukulaelae Islanders' use of literacy: *"empowering* the technology and giving it . . . a meaning that was related only remotely to the meaning that the agents of introduction intended it to have" (Besnier, *Literacy, Emotion, and Authority*, 66).

29. *Te Wananga*, August 5, 1874, 1; October 10, 1874, 30–1.

30. Tocqueville's discussion of the relation between newspapers in America and individuals, is cited in Hall, *Cultures of Print*, 29. See also Henri-Jean Martin, "The Use of Writing Cannot Develop Spontaneously Until Small Groups Fuse and Organize into a Society," in *The History and Power of Writing*, trans. Lydia G. Cochrane (Chicago: Univ. of Chicago Press, 1994), 507; and Thomas Habinek, *The Politics of Latin Literature: Writing, Identity, and Empire in Ancient Rome* (Princeton, NJ: Princeton Univ. Press, 1998), 40, in which Habinek makes the point that social cohesion was an important motif in early Latin literary history because of the struggle with Hannibal.

31. Eisenstein, *PPAC*, 132.

32. *Te Wananga*, September 4, 1874, 9.

astic reader proposed to write regularly.[33] Some anticipated that the paper would be a healer; others made known the lands they refused to sell. This was a forum where many writers "spoke" to their readers as if they were their tribe,[34] maintaining their oral rituals by beginning letters with lengthy greetings or making points in cryptic tribal sayings or concluding with a song or chant. In these letters Maori combined writing, which, as Thomas Habinek puts it, "implies distance," and oral performance, which "implies immediacy."[35] And in their writing down of the otherwise memorized oral tradition—which was largely composed by the repetition of and modification to fixed expressions that Walter Ong argues "form the substance of thought itself"[36]—we read the poetics and ideas of Maori thinking, or their oral mentality, of the time.

Maori had not replaced their personal, subjective way of communicating and thinking with the relatively impersonal objectivity of newspaper discourse.[37] Rather, they addressed the paper directly in many (often mixed) metaphors, likening it, for example, to a canoe with a freight of talk: "Greetings to you, the press for all the land. Greetings, *Te Wananga,* seek out the opinions of this whole land, to load aboard and to carry forth to the four corners of this world."[38] Maori used such traditional poetic imagery and formulaic phrases to conceptualize and familiarize themselves with this new object, which could communicate so much to so many.

Te Wananga also provided popular and necessary information: horse-racing events and results, market prices, opportunities for work, advertisements for goods. And it became an accepted messenger of death. One man who sought to have the paper publish details about the death of his wife, her character, his poetic lament for her, and a list of others who had died, twice implored the editor: "Don't be upset at the number of words and discard this, but take it on board for the relatives of this woman, these four children and three elders to see that they have died." After his second plea he added, "Soon I will send other freight for *Te Wananga.*"[39]

The "freight" was a burden to be balanced. When the conventions of the

---

33. Ibid., September 25, 1874, 13.

34. As Martin observes, "written discourse remains spoken when it is conceived to be recited in public" *(History and Power of Writing,* 163).

35. Habinek, *Politics of Latin Literature,* 153.

36. Ong, *Orality and Literacy,* 35.

37. Compare the learned oral composition, which is concise, cryptic, rhetorical, and subjective and reworks shared knowledge, with the learned written, which is detailed, explicit, critical, and objective and communicates new knowledge.

38. *Te Wananga,* October 24, 1874, 25.

39. Ibid., October 2, 1875, 257.

newspaper were explained, so too was its cost. Potential correspondents were advised that *Te Wananga* would not print objectionable material, would assume no responsibility for opinions expressed, and would like submissions to be as concise as possible for economy in printing. Advertisers were warned to describe land boundaries in sale notices succinctly to avoid being "dissatisfied with the cost." Readers sought clarification of advertising rates. One, inquiring whether a notice for lost cows and horses or any notice was two shillings an inch and whether that price was only for those who took the paper, was informed that all notices were to be paid for but reports of news were free. The cost of printed "talk" must have seemed curious to Maori. They must have been intrigued by the paper's journey abroad and its companion newspapers: "These are the titles of newspapers of many countries in the world to which *Te Wananga* is sent, and which are sent to *Te Wananga.*"[40]

In its own way *Te Wananga* was as homiletic as the government and church papers. Editors reflected in an early issue that the first English newspaper had had time to improve over 250 years, and that though new and unformed, *Te Wananga* aimed to "enlighten ourselves on matters unknown to us which, if known to us in the past, might have greatly benefited us, as in the difference in our thinking and that of the *Pakeha.*"[41] This was the crux of the matter. The political purpose of this newspaper was plain. It published parliamentary debates—especially those in which Maori members spoke—and articles on highly contested matters, such as land sales, the Native Land Court, and Maori representation in Parliament. The establishment of other Maori-owned papers prompted by politics suggests that in this topical writing, frequently opened by habitual greetings, Maori felt as prominently and effectively engaged as they did in their tribal gatherings.[42] *Huia Kotahi Tangata* (Unite the people; 1893–5) was, like its predecessors, established for "all the Maori tribes"; it arose out of a movement for a separate Maori Parliament, the establishment and proceedings of which were published in its successor, *Te Puke ki Hikurangi* (The hill at Hikurangi; 1897–1913).

Maori publishing of nineteenth-century newspapers was most active in seeking social and political change.[43] But it was also a witness to Maori

---

40. Ibid., August 14, 1875, 141; October 2, 1875, 257; August 14, 1875, 141.

41. Ibid., September 24, 1874, 27.

42. For a literature as "intervention" in society, see Habinek, *Politics of Latin Literature,* 3.

43. As D. F. McKenzie puts it, the essential motives were "economic, political and military." McKenzie, *Oral Culture, Literacy, and Print in Early New Zealand: The Treaty of Waitangi* (Wellington, NZ: Victoria Univ. Press with the Alexander Turnbull Library Endowment Trust, 1985), 20.

attitudes and culture.[44] *Te Puke ki Hikurangi*, for example, held an ancient story in its title. An ancestor, leaving by canoe for Aotearoa (or New Zealand, as it became) from the mythical Polynesian homeland of Hawaiki, was warned that his brother would later arrive as great waves and that their refuge would be the hill of Hikurangi. That association combined hill and canoe in contributors' and editors' minds: "Send in your words to load on our hill," one editor wrote, following it with the prosaic injunction "but write on just one side of the paper." For Maori, practically the newspaper was a bulwark against and refuge from the colonizing government, but emotionally it resonated with their cultural tradition, which allowed them to personify the press. Editors sometimes handed *Te Puke* the pen. On one occasion they offered words from "the heart of our pet" (a term of endearment often used for the papers). The message began, "My dear friends," continued with a long piece on politics and history, and signed off as the self, "Te Puke ki Hikurangi." The personified paper was not above asking for subscriptions, greeting supporters, blessing them in the name of the Lord (a practice learned from literature), and requesting them to send tickets to enable his journey by train or steamer to their homes. When Maori employed such language in their writing for the newspapers, they merged two contexts of compositional style and thought: the first familiar, oral, poetic, and grounded in tradition, and the second unfamiliar, literary, prosaic, and innovative. But this merger was also a mark of the pleasure and hopes they vested in "this great product of the Pakeha from which they do well."[45]

All Maori-language papers were doctrinal. An American philanthropist, evangelist, and advocate of temperance, W. P. Snow, founded *Te Korimako* (The bellbird; 1882–90). Yet Maori found their own use in it. Some supported the owner's persuasions; some complained that too much scripture was published. Others enjoyed the practicality or pride of public notice: warning about a wife who had absconded, announcing a new carved meeting-house, recording the occasion and ceremonial aspects of death; one two-page supplement described the death of a prominent chief, naming his esteemed visitors, reporting his dying words, and lauding his personal qualities.[46] Maori understood and took advantage of the political and economic opportunities of print. Individuals, tribes, and Maori members of Parliament wrote about disputes over land, tribal meetings, new railways, the government, and the

---

44. Perhaps, as Habinek has discussed, this was literature as a means of acculturation when preserving tradition (*Politics of Latin Literature*, 53–4).

45. *Te Puke ki Hikurangi*, December 21, 1897, 3; July 19, 1898, 1; November 8, 1898, 6; March 15, 1898, [4].

46. *Te Korimako*, September 14, 1882, 1; December 13, 1882, 3; Supplement, March 15, 1883, 1–2.

Native Land Court. Maori traders and buyers looked for information essential to their new economies and labor. They wrote to the paper asking for the price of products, such as iron, ploughs, or *kauri* gum; they complained when the regular commodity price lists were stopped; they sought the return of their lost stock; and they endorsed Pakeha traders' advertisements.

Maori were practical in this printed communication and discriminating as readers, but they were also romantic about *Te Korimako.* They spoke to it—"O bird, greetings to you, please takes my report to the four corners of the world"—and sent their subscriptions as "fragrant seeds for the bird." [47] In this paper as in those that preceded it, print captured their preference for the oblique and poetic as well as their cultural philosophy and ways of perceiving the world.

Te Korimako also tutored readers about newspaper publication, offering, for example, an article about the oldest paper in the world published in China, and a note that blacks in America produced 120 papers. A brief article about the history of the Maori newspapers explained that many had ceased to publish because of a lack of money, and it expressed concern that this fate would befall *Te Korimako.* This paper, like others, frequently published calls for proper payment (sometimes in response to complaints about costs of advertisement, lack of space for correspondence, or failure in delivery) and reminders that payment went to the printer but not to the managers and writers. [48]

The historical record, including the newspapers, confirms that many nineteenth-century Maori were very able readers and writers. Though D. F. McKenzie has argued that Maori literacy was partial if considered in relation to the hundreds of years that Western societies took to become fully literate, the newspaper literature suggests that McKenzie underestimated the quality and extent of their writing. [49] But it also shows that Maori were still anchored to oral tradition in their thinking and composing. A perceptible shift to a literate style and mentality by the turn of the century might be proposed, though not in detail here, on the basis of two newspapers sponsored by the Anglican Church.

Church doctrine was at the heart of *He Kupu Whakamarama* (Words of enlightenment; 1898) and *Te Pipiwharauroa* (The shining cuckoo; 1899–1913), but local and international news was also reported. The literacy of these

---

47. For discussion of the metaphor of the bird, see McRae, "'E manu, tena koe!' 'O bird, greetings to you': The Oral Tradition in Newspaper Writing," in Curnow, Hopa, and McRae, *Rere atu,* 42–59.

48. *Te Korimako,* January 15, 1883, 4; January 15, 1884, 6; August 15, 1883, 1–2; March 15, 1883, 1.

49. As Head, *"Kupu Pai, Kupu Kino"* also argues.

papers might be attributed to the Maori editors and their leading writers. Church ministers, doctors, members of Parliament, and tribal leaders, they were highly educated and well versed in literacy skills.[50] They had no doubt developed Henri-Jean Martin's "new sorts of connections in the reasoning process" and written expression that "gave priority to the concrete . . . to verisimilitude . . . to details of time and place."[51] They had moved, as Norman Simms labels it, from the "rhetorical" to "central" self.[52] Champions of the improved spiritual, physical, and intellectual health of Maori, they wrote articles about such topics as health and education that set out known wisdom and facts.[53] And they encouraged plain writing in their correspondents.[54] The rhetorical and highly allusive oral tradition was not eschewed, but the journalistic style predominated. Short on poetic, metaphysical, and localized knowledge, this explicit style made the writing accessible to a broad, diverse range of readers.

By the turn of the nineteenth century Maori had had over sixty years' experience with newspapers in their language. They had been energetic, pragmatic, and competent contributors, editors, and publishers. Tutored in writing for journalism, they nevertheless did not discard their long-held oral discourse. But when written out for publication, this discourse, of orators and speakers within a tribe, became a code of a small community, and was thus indecipherable by many readers. As Habinek writes, "Once the connection between performance and text, or between poet and traditional community, is broken, there is no easy way to localize the imagined community that replaces the real one."[55] In the effort to include the community of the "four corners of the world," it was inevitable that Maori would adjust their compositional style. Thus, to employ Hall's phrasing, their oral culture became "entwined with

---

50. Cf. Middle-class, higher educated publishers of African American journals in the same period in Michael Fultz, " 'The Morning Cometh': African-American Periodicals, Education, and the Black Middle Class, 1900–1930," in *Print Culture in a Diverse America,* ed. James P. Danky and Wayne A. Wiegand (Urbana: Univ. of Illinois Press, 1998), 129–48.

51. Martin, *History and Power of Writing,* 87, 165.

52. The rhetorical self is ritualized, oral, thinking outwardly through customs, seeking wisdom through rhythmic genres and ceremony; the central self is secular, literate, looking inward to personal experience, seeking wisdom by affirmation of ideas. See Simms, *Points of Contact,* 105.

53. Cf. Franz Bäuml's proposition that the existence of "facts" is dependent on literacy in his "Writing the Emperor's Clothes On: Literacy and the Production of Facts," in *Written Voices, Spoken Signs: Tradition, Performance, and the Epic Text,* ed. Egbert Bakker and Ahuvia Kahane (Cambridge, MA: Harvard Univ. Press, 1997), and the printing press as basis for modern science in Eisenstein, *PPAC,* 704.

54. The end of a line of editors calling for clarity in submissions; see, for example, Christine Tremewan's comments about poetry in "Poetry in *Te Waka Maori,*" 121, 129.

55. Habinek, *Politics of Latin Literature,* 101.

the world of print," and their newspapers chronicled a "continuum between print and oral modes."[56] Yet despite such adjustments, Maori confidently used the press for their own purposes.[57]

Nineteenth-century Maori would have understood Eisenstein's formulation of "the printing press as an agent of change." They certainly looked to the nineteenth-century newspaper as an agent *for* change. Whether it was an agent *of* change is subject for a different inquiry; it was certainly not their only strategy.[58] But they made print vital, their voice advancing their interests within and outside New Zealand in response to colonization.[59] To borrow from Elizabeth McHenry's comment on African Americans' use of literature, the use of print by Maori was "a public act, an assertion of cultural and political authority."[60]

Recognizing the complexity of print history, Eisenstein asked for concrete, historical examples of the effects and consequences of print for different groups. Detailed studies of literacy, print, and the book within particular societies have shown that fulfilling her request can be a fruitful pursuit.[61] Among the universal responses to this technology, the particulars and idiosyncrasies of culture, time, and place bring human interest to the history of print.

---

56. Hall, *Cultures of Print*, 84.

57. Besnier's characterization of the Nukulaelae Islanders' literacy as "incipient" compares, as does his summary of their active integration of literacy into their communicative repertoires (*Literacy, Emotion, and Authority*, 172–6).

58. As Eisenstein has noted, early printers were only effective in combination with other forces (*PPAC*, 703).

59. Cf. the creation of Latin literature as "survival strategies" after the Hannibal invasion in Habinek, *Politics of Latin Literature*, 39; also of that literature's preservation of Roman identity (60).

60. Elizabeth McHenry, "Forgotten Readers: African-American Literary Societies and the American Scene," in *Print Culture in a Diverse America*, 155. Cf. the African American periodical press in the early 1900s, which helped create and define their lives to others and to themselves; see Fultz, "The Morning Cometh."

61. See, for example, Johns's assertion that "cultures of the book were . . . local" and his conclusion that there is "no single revolution" associated with print but that it is different in "different cultural settings" (*Nature of the Book*, 30, 636); Hall's story of "ongoing exchanges and negotiations" (*Cultures of Print*, 5); and Besnier's premise that "literacy is a fundamentally heterogeneous phenomenon, whose shape can be determined by many aspects of the sociocultural context in which it is embedded" (*Literacy, Emotion, and Authority*, 3).

Part III

Agency, Technology, and the New Global Media Revolution

This book has stopped short in the age of the wooden hand press. . . . Nothing has been said about the railway tracks and telegraph wires which linked European capitals in the mid-nineteenth century, or about the Linotype and Monotype machines which went together with mass literacy and tabloid journalism. The typewriter, telephone, and a vast variety of more recent media have been entirely ignored. . . . Because contrary views have been expressed, however, it is necessary to point out that the process that began in the mid-fifteenth century has not ceased to gain momentum in the age of the computer print-out and the television guide. Indeed the later phases of an ongoing communication revolution seem altogether relevant to what is happening within our homes, universities, or cities at present.

—Elizabeth L. Eisenstein, *The Printing Press as an Agent of Change*

W<small>HEN</small> *The Printing Press as an Agent of Change: Communications and Cultural Transformations in Early-Modern Europe* (*PPAC*) was published in 1979, the "information superhighway" was still an unpaved road, and the desktop computer in its infancy, Radio Shack's Tandy, the Commodore PET, and the Apple II having been introduced to the world only a few years before.[1] Although the breadth of *PPAC*'s powers as a reactive agent was quickly evident, a recognition of its applicability to the current communications upheaval would need to wait roughly another fifteen years until the computer revolution had permeated nearly all facets of everyday life. Over the past decade or so, however, a diverse readership

---

1. For a comprehensive list of key developments in computer history, see the Computer History Museum Web site, especially the link to its online exhibition, "Timeline 1945–1990," http://www.computerhistory.org/.

has increasingly turned to Eisenstein's work as a means of assessing today's communications revolution and its potential long-term effects. Drawn to Eisenstein's arguments that print operated as an agent rather than merely a tool of change in the early modern period, students of late-twentieth-century electronic media have frequently viewed *PPAC*'s delineation of print's consequences—its revolutionary effects on knowledge production, cognitive processes, and cultural, intellectual, and social formations—as a template for charting the transformative capacity of new media in postmodern society. What have attracted less attention, however, are *PPAC*'s assertions about the ongoing, reverberating effects of print. Print, according to Eisenstein in 1979, was far from entering its final death throes but instead was continuing to function as an agent of change: "The process that began in the mid-fifteenth century has not ceased to gain momentum in the age of the computer print-out and the television guide. . . . Some of the unanticipated consequences . . . are now available for retrospective analysis. . . . Others are still unfolding" (*PPAC,* 704–5). That the effects of the initial European printing revolution persist to this day is a view Eisenstein has continued to express,[2] often doing so while simultaneously acknowledging the technological shifts of our own age.[3] It is clear that she sees print and electronic media as interacting with one another, with print maintaining its function as a reactive agent. Because of the potential usefulness of *PPAC* for understanding present transformations and the controversies surrounding its arguments, especially those related to manu-

---

2. As Eisenstein notes elsewhere, "Whatever the next turn of fortune's wheel may bring, it seems likely that certain cultural features introduced by printing are here to stay. . . . For this reason, if no other, it seems desirable to encourage more investigation of the communications revolution of the fifteenth century. Although the age of the wooden handpress has long been over, the cumulative process it set in motion still persists." Eisenstein, "From Scriptoria to Printing Shops: Evolution and Revolution in the Early Printed Book Trade," in *Books and Society in History: Papers of the Association of College and Research Libraries Rare Books and Manuscripts Section Preconference, 24–28 June, 1980, Boston, Massachusetts,* ed. Kenneth E. Carpenter (New York: R. R. Bowker, 1983), 40. And in our conversation with her that concludes this collection, Eisenstein asserts, "No doubt, we are in the midst of unprecedented transformations. But this does not mean that the printing revolution has ceased gathering momentum or is becoming irrelevant to our concerns."

3. That Eisenstein has not discounted a present communications revolution is also readily evident. In fact, commenting fifteen years later on the 1983 Boston preconference meeting, Robert Gross recalled that "only Eisenstein recognized the dawn of a communications revolution" in the digital era. Gross, "Communications Revolutions: Writing a History of the Book for an Electronic Age," *Rare Books & Manuscripts Librarianship* 13 (1998): 11.

scripts in the age of print, this interplay between the "old" media and the "new" calls for closely considering the analogies invoked to compare these two communication revolutions.

Comparisons between the changes wrought by print in the past and those now being generated by electronic media typically rely on analogies adhering to a general formula in which manuscript : print :: print : electronic formats. As James Dewar and Peng Hwa Ang remind us in Chapter 18, the soundness of the analogy—as well as the parallels deduced from it—will be affected by how the relationship between the terms within each set is perceived and the extent to which the two relational sets correspond to one another. If "printing's most revolutionary effect was on manuscript," as Peter Stallybrass postulates in Chapter 15, can the same be said of the impact electronic culture is exercising on print? And, if not, what comparisons can be made? In other words, to address the viability of the broader connections being proposed in comparing these two communication revolutions, we must consider how manuscript relates to print and how print relates to electronic media. Such considerations are addressed in various ways by the essays in this part. Tony Ballantyne, for instance, notes in Chapter 16 the necessity of better understanding how print has reacted with various phenomena at different times and in different places. Although his essay focuses on the colonial processes of the eighteenth and nineteenth centuries, his recognition of this need occurs, as his title indicates, within the context of today's globalized world, a globalization greatly accelerated by electronic media but still effected and affected by print. The historical roots of this globalization, moreover, extend back to interactions between print and manuscript.

With the invention of printing in the Renaissance, the word *manuscriptum* assumed new significance in the western European lexicon. Before the advent of printing, the need to distinguish between texts written by hand and those produced by another means was nonexistent. The hand, the physical embodiment of human ability to execute agency, and the hand alone (no matter the writing implement it wielded) governed textual production. The hand's agency in scribal production personalized the page in ways that its role in arranging type in a composing stick or manually pulling a bar to produce inked impressions of metal type characters on paper did not. Speaking of a later period, Robert Gross speculates in Chapter 19 about how the even-more-mechanized printing technology after the Industrial Revolution must have further depersonalized printed texts.

The etymological headnote to the *Oxford English Dictionary*'s entry for the noun "manuscript" helps elucidate this word's manifestation of the personal: "The post-classical Latin noun *manuscriptum* was used occasionally of documents which derived evidential value from being written by a particular person (e.g. a confession, a note of hand, a charter) until the late 15th cent., when the invention of printing gave it and the associated nouns *manuscripta* (a1475) and *manuscriptus* (a1567) wider currency, esp. in humanistic use."[4] While the handwriting of manuscripts connoted individual identity—a prominent example is the use of Algernon Sidney's unpublished manuscripts as a "witness" in his 1683 trial for treason—the advent of print intensified cultural assumptions about manuscript's role as such: "Placing a given manuscript against a printed text one may see much more clearly the idiosyncratic features of the individual hand of the scribe" (*PPAC,* 83). Moreover, the standardization that print achieved fostered the romanticization of manuscript as an embodiment of the personal: "Every hand-copied book, it is sometimes said, was a 'personal achievement,'" despite the reality that many such books were produced by diverse hands copying discrete sections; "even where a single hand runs from incipit to colophon and a full signature is given at the end, there is almost no trace of personality left by the presumably 'personal achievement'" (*PPAC,* 235). Gross makes a similar argument, pointing out that printed books were the product of a "collective" consisting of the many hands involved in a text's production and, as such, perhaps incapable of expressing the "personal" voice of the author.

Since *PPAC*'s publication, debates about the effects of printing's invention and spread throughout western Europe and the degree to which these

---

4. Nor is this phenomenon confined to England. The *OED* entry also offers the following overview of the word's linguistic heritage in Romance and Germanic languages: "Cf. Middle French, French manuscrit (1594 as adjective and noun), Italian manoscritto (a1601 as adjective, a1676 as noun), Catalan manuscrit (1638 as adjective), Spanish manuscrito (prob. early 17th cent. as adjective, 1650 as noun), Portuguese manuscrito (late 16th cent. as adjective, late 18th cent. as noun)."

effects were revolutionary have tended to conflate agency with personalization, obscuring this difference between manuscript and print, at times even replacing it with equations of technological determinism. Although the human hand's role in the production of electronic media — the touching of keys to create text, the pointing hand as a cursor on the computer screen — may seem akin to its status in printing, in fact, the new technology has recast notions of personalization and agency in wholly new ways.[5] On one level, as Barbara Brannon (Chapter 17) and Roger Chartier (Chapter 20) note, the new media enables any person with a computer and a printer or Internet access seemingly total control over the production process — a freedom that marks the arrival of the future for those who came of age when the IBM Selectric (the self-correcting typewriter) represented one great leap forward for creators of text. Yet at the same time, this leap forward also harks back to a pre-print past: "We seem to be in the midst of yet another publishing revolution that very well may undermine current notions of intellectual property rights and bring us closer to the medieval experience of everyman serving as his own scribe."[6]

Agency is not the only concept that straddles the old world of manuscripts and the new digital culture in ways that disrupt the symmetry of the manuscript-is-to-print-as-print-is-to-electronic-media analogy. Besides distinguishing a particular mode of textual production in the aftermath of Gutenberg's invention, the word "manuscript" also acquired additional meanings. With the spread of printing as a practical means of textual production, the term "manuscript" began to perform double linguistic duty by signaling not only a type of production but also a component in the manufacturing of printed works. Manuscripts were no longer necessarily the endpoint of publication — though they still could be and, in fact, often were well into the eighteenth century and beyond. Instead, they

---

5. A telling example occurred at the 2006 London Book Fair at which Margaret Atwood debuted the "LongPen." This device enables authors to sign books electronically from a site far removed from the physical book by "record[ing] handwriting digitally, then zip[ping] the information across the world to be emulated by a robotic arm." When asked whether fans would be dismayed by the lack of face-to-face meeting with authors, Atwood replied, "'The book is the interaction.'" Samson Spanier, "Theme of London Book Fair Is What Technology Can Do," *New York Times* online, March 7, 2006.

6. Eisenstein, "From Scriptoria to Printing Shops," 40.

formed an integral stage in the production of printed products. Within print culture, manuscripts operated in various roles: at times they were the documents written by authors seeking print publication; they were read in attempts to assess their commercial viability or political sensitivity; they found their way into print by agents other than authorial ones; and they were marked up for compositors. As printed works were produced and distributed, assumptions arising from this new sense of "manuscript" as part of the larger publishing process rather than its end goal were also subtly disseminated. Yet while manuscript achieved the status of an intermediate stage in print production, there was also a substantial realm of texts that continued to terminate in manuscript. Gross's mention of Thomas Jefferson as a coterie author of manuscript is only one example among many. These hand-produced texts shared many characteristics of printed texts, such as the potential for wide circulation and the facility of being edited, corrected, amended, and annotated, but they did not possess all of the traits of print. It is not that these texts lacked either currency or influence, especially within particular contexts; rather they lacked the preservative fixity of print as well as its capacity for essentially identical replication and widespread dissemination.

While the advent of print unquestionably altered the function and status of manuscripts, the changes effected were more complex than those suggested by usual interpretations of the analogy in which manuscript and print are treated as two, temporarily coexisting, yet never-intersecting cultures and the first term is rendered obsolete by the second. Historical and theoretical reconstructions of the relationship between the two based on such treatments have often obscured the role of manuscripts within early typographical culture as well as the revolutionary effects of print as a transformative agent. Although similar complexities characterize the ties between print and electronic modes and although print shows no signs of approaching obsolescence despite repeated predictions of its demise, the evolving relationship between the "old media" and the new differs in significant ways from that between manuscript and print. Indeed, from the vantage points of agency and the preservative effects of fixity, manuscript and electronic media share a kinship that positions print as the anchor term and posits a comparison in which manuscript : print :: electronic media : print. Notwithstanding the ability to "save" electronic copies and bookmark Web sites, the need to print copies of such material to help ensure the preservation of its content remains strong. An electronic file or Web site can be altered effortlessly with just a few keystrokes yet retain its original name; URLs disappear with regularity; and more frequently than not on any given Web site, at least one of the links no longer functions. The speed with which hardware, electronic readers, and platforms become outdated and superseded by newer forms of technology and the uncertain life span of storage devices such as CDs and DVDs (the current industry estimated life span for these devices ranges from thirty to, in rare cases, a few hundred years)[7] further underscore problems of textual preservation and fixity in the new media.

In short, despite possessing an exponential capacity for instantaneous, global dissemination as well as other capabilities distinct from those of print, electronic media at this stage in their history do not offer significant advances in the preservation of texts. Electronic formats, in fact, are arguably the least stable medium for recorded communications: "A piece of paper can last for centuries left alone in a dry, dark room. Nothing created by a computer has that kind of inherent longevity — nothing like it in fact. Computers and their contents only survive by the active and ongoing help of human beings."[8] Because "the life of an average website," absent human intervention, is "estimated to be around 44 days (about the

---

7. The Information Access Division of the National Institute of Standards and Technology (NIST) and the Preservation Directorate at the Library of Congress have conducted a study of the longevity of CDs and DVDs. As of September 29, 2006, the testing phase had been completed, and the results were being analyzed. For an overview of the project, see http://www.itl.nist.gov/div895/loc/overview.html. On February 14, 2004, the NIST Tech Beat Web site noted: "Most CDs and DVDs will last 30 years or more if handled with care, but many factors can slash their longevity," http://www.nist.gov/public_affairs/techbeat/tb2004_0213.htm. This life span does not refer to archival forms of these storage devices. At the January 2006 International CES/Defining Tomorrow's Technology trade show in Las Vegas, Memorex announced that it had developed vastly improved archival-quality, 24-karat gold CDs and DVDs: "These innovative discs are proven to last up to six times longer than traditional media with a CD archival life of up to 300 years and a DVD archival life of up to 100 years." "Memorex Adds 24-Karat Gold to Its Longest Lasting, Archival Grade CD and DVD Media," PR Newswire, January 4, 2006, http://www.prnewswire.com/cgi-bin/stories.pl?ACCT=104&STORY=/www/story/01-04-2006/0004242153&EDATE=. In contrast, the standard for paper now is five hundred years.

8. National Council of Archives, "Your Data at Risk: Why You Should Be Worried about Preserving Electronic Records?" (Richmond, Surrey: National Council of Archives, 2005), http://www.ncaonline.org.uk/materials/yourdataatrisk.pdf. During the preparation of this volume, several links on archival preservation associations' Web sites yielded the all-too-familiar "404 Not Found" message, surely an ironic comment on the ephemerality of Web-based information.

same lifespan as a housefly) there is a danger," as one national archiving association has recently warned, "that invaluable scholarly, cultural and scientific resources will be lost to future generations."[9] As archivists and computer scientists work toward long-term solutions for preserving the information created and disseminated through electronic media, individual users repeatedly rely on their desk-top printers, whose agency of change Brannon considers here, as the interim safeguard for capturing and preserving Web pages, e-mails, drafts, and final versions of documents that are digitally born. Print constitutes the retronymic "hard copies" of postmodern culture, maintaining its role as preservative agent even as we stare at computer screens, strike keyboards, click mice, and text message on cell phones.

The difference in the preservative capacities of print and those of electronic media points to an interdependency between the two that risks erasure if their dissimilarities are viewed solely as oppositional. Contrasts between the printed book and electronic text, for instance, have deflected attention from the substantive role electronic technology plays in contemporary production of print products. From its inception on a screen by an author to submission, editing, layout, and more, the printed text today is primarily a creation of electronic media. Electronic technology dominates the process, but print persists as the endpoint of much textual production — and not only that of books. Here again we should not forget the prevalence of printed ephemera both historically and currently. We receive e-tickets for travel, but we print out the e-mails confirming these electronic purchases and, once at the train station or airport, we receive printed paper boarding passes, if we did not print them earlier from a home computer. Similarly, while searches of electronic databases yield a broad range of texts deliverable as PDF files, this format is purposefully designed to end as printed text on paper.[10] In today's electronic culture,

---

9. "Project Overview," UK Web Archiving Consortium, http://info.webarchive.org.uk/. Members of the Consortium include the British Library (lead partner), National Library of Scotland, National Library of Wales, National Archives, and the Wellcome Trust.

10. That PDF files are created with print as an end goal is commonly recognized and often stated in user instructions. As Jakob Nielson, a former Sun Microsystems Distinguished Engineer and now leading expert on Web usability, has asserted: "Users get lost inside PDF files, which are typically big, linear text blobs that are optimized for print and unpleasant to read and navigate

Peter Stallybrass's "little jobs," the printed forms and other ephemera that are the subject of his essay here, are alive and well, and we have all become job-printers, or "little Gutenbergs" in the formulation of Paul Levinson, a prominent communications and media studies scholar.[11]

The symbiotic relationship that has arisen between print and electronic culture manifests itself in other ways as well. The recent Google Book digitization project is a ready example. Although Google's search engine allows users to locate references and passages in record time, its restricted access to selected full works and limitation on the number of viewable sequential pages, as well as the inability to print or download, encourages readers to seek out a copy of the printed work. While Google Book search in its current incarnation promotes a mutual dependence that appears driven, in part at least, by intellectual property issues, the Sony Reader, unveiled at the start of 2006, promotes a dependency that derives from marketing strategies aimed at ensuring a greater success for this latest e-book delivery system than its predecessors have had. Claiming to be "designed exclusively for immersive reading," promotional materials highlight the device's marriage of the still sought-after attributes of print with the benefits of new media: it employs advanced technology to create "a realistic print look that rivals traditional paper" and features " 'electronic ink,' " whose effect closely resembles "ink-on-paper," in a format "roughly the size of paperback novel, but thinner than most" and with a battery life that enables readers "to devour a dozen bestsellers plus *War and Peace*" without recharging.[12] Much as producers of incunabula replicated certain features of manuscript, Sony's integration of these qualities of print derive not from nostalgia but from a recognition of the existing needs and desires of readers. And much like the tactics of early printers who adopted running heads, title pages, indexes, and the like to harness the powers of print

---

online. PDF is good for printing, but that's it. Don't use it for online presentation." Summary, "PDF: Unfit for Human Consumption," Jakob Nielsen's *Alertbox,* July 14, 2003, http://www.useit .com/alertbox/20030714.html.

11. Paul Levinson, "The Future of the Printed Word," guest lecture, History of the Book: The Next Generation conference, Drew University, Madison, NJ, September 16, 2000. Levinson is also a science-fiction writer of note.

12. "New Sony Reader Puts a Library's Worth of Reading Material in Your Pocket," Sony Electronics press release, 2006 CES Conference: Defining Tomorrow's Technology, Las Vegas, NV, January 4, 2006, http://news.sel.sony.com/pressrelease/6394.

when it was a new medium, Sony's strategies in harnessing technological advances respond to the new requirements and desires that electronic culture has fostered by creating a device that takes searchability, portability, and readability (i.e., adjustable text size) to levels simply not possible with static ink-images impressed on paper. This technology echoes Gross's expression that "reading and experience become one."

This consideration of the relational correspondences between pairings of old and new media has touched on only a few of the attributes that link as well as distinguish manuscript, print, and electronic media from one another. Yet even this brief discussion indicates that the relationship within and between the traditionally paired terms is more complexly nuanced than ones suggested by analogies invoking obsolescence and supersession. Straddling both manuscript and electronic media, print has enjoyed a usually symbiotic, at times syncretic relationship with both. As Eisenstein notes in *PPAC,* "The effects of printing seem to have been exerted always unevenly, yet always continuously and cumulatively from the late fifteenth century on. . . . They have persisted, with ever-augmented force, right down to the present" (158). Adaptation and interaction, then, mark the current relationship between print and electronic media and present a basis for comparisons more compelling, as the essays in this part demonstrate, than analogies in which the advent of the new spells the disappearance of the old.

At first glance the essays in Part III might seem to bear little relationship to one another. On the surface they deal with disparate topics: the underappreciated preponderance of job printing and its products in early modern Europe and colonial America; a global view of print's agency in modern empire-building; the agency of the laser printer in altering relationships with written language and perceptions and construction of knowledge; the printing revolution as a guide in creating Internet policy; a proposed agenda for studying the history of "how people read and 'make meaning'"; and an analytical summary of print culture studies in the wake of *PPAC,* with remarks about this volume's contributions and recommendations for future work. Moreover, their range extends across a broad geographical and even temporal spectrum, with several essays appearing to address globalization and technological change only in passing, if at all.

Yet on closer inspection the topics presented here all prove to be integral facets of the typologies and relationships discussed earlier. Despite their dissimilarities, the contributions that follow speak to the adaptive and interactive qualities of current relationships between print and electronic media formats, as well as the attributes and potential force of the agency of print across time and space. These essays are further linked by their use of *PPAC* as a starting point for charting the unintended consequences of the symbiotic ties among a variety of media.

Prominent among these unintended consequences is the influence the interrelationship between print and new media exercises on print culture studies as a field. With electronic culture now pervading almost every aspect of daily (especially professional) life, scholars have observed phenomena of print from fresh angles. In the essay that opens this section, for instance, Peter Stallybrass reformulates the homologous relationship between manuscript and print, re-scripting its terms as handwriting and print and their correspondence as one of interaction and adaptation. Focusing on the age of imperial expansion, Tony Ballantyne examines the agency of print in the construction, collection, and dissemination of knowledge within and across global empires and its concomitant power in effecting political change. His reassessment of the reactive agency of print reorients its study from Eurocentric narratives of exportation to localized accounts of interaction and adaptation within a broader context of global imperialism. Evincing a meta-level of integration and adaptation, this reorientation itself is informed by today's globalized, technologically driven culture.

Alongside and in tandem with a re-envisioning of print culture studies, scholars have also begun to explore topics grazed but not extensively considered by Eisenstein in *PPAC,* as Gross demonstrates in his consideration of how reading has differed over time and how the reconstruction of its history needs to link textual encounters with lived experiences. Investigations of such topics raised but not pursued in *PPAC* often speak as much to the present as they do to the past. For example, what Gross postulates as the ability to transcend or transform existence through the act of reading corresponds to the ability of electronic media and its dissemination to render a similar effect. From MOOs to online book clubs, Internet interactive-game sites, chat rooms, virtual-tour Web sites, sports fantasy leagues, distance-learning courses, Internet porn, blogs, and much more, cyberspace enables users to access and participate virtually in all kinds of newly imagined communities. Encounters with such virtual worlds are altering lives in ways akin to those that Gross identifies in discussing print and its ability to change the lives of women and blacks in nineteenth-century America.

Just as lives changed by print and reading in the nineteenth century contributed to later, broader, and often profound alterations in the sociocultural, political fabric of the United States and elsewhere, so too are the changes being effected by new media yielding significant, global transformations. From business and commerce to the arts and sciences, from education and scholarship to government and religion, forms of new media are demonstrably altering the way people are experiencing life and the world. Offering many examples, the Internet has enabled con-stituencies for various movements, political and otherwise, to be created and mobilized without access to or reliance on traditional outlets. The unintended consequences of such formations can be witnessed in various phenomena and at a range of levels from the sporadic breakdown of geo-political nation-states to the instability of intellectual property rights as conventionally understood to the volatile status of authority in validating information and controlling its flow or the metamorphosis of grass-roots responses into international causes célèbres. Such effects, intended and unintended, are changing the way business is done, research is conducted, wars are waged, news is reported, causes are embraced, art is created and marketed, and much more.

The most potent yet elusive consequences of new media are arguably its cognitive effects. When Barbara Brannon queries, "Is it too much to imagine that digital technologies aim to duplicate the way people think?" she is quick to point out that the brain is simply a metaphor for the computer. Yet as Brannon, Gross, Dewar and Ang, and Chartier consider here, new media and their interactions with the reactive prop-erties of print are altering cognitive relationships with information. The seeming ease with which we can transmit large amounts of information or communicate instantaneously with many tells us that distance has shrunk, but this perception is not without false consequences. Programs that allow information in one language to be translated into another at the click of a mouse may appear to surmount linguistic boundaries, yet the resulting translations are rarely accurate or fluent. Images and texts can be downloaded and sent around the world with lightning speed, but their original context is often lost in the process, an occurrence lending added meaning to Dewar and Ang's characterization of the Internet as an "any-to-many" form of communication. Information without meaningful context, moreover, risks reducing "knowledge" to simply isolated bits of data. While opinions about the fate and future of knowledge in the "Information Age" range from effusively optimistic to dramatically dire, it is the cognitive processes used in reading and acquiring information that most affect the end result. In today's global, wired world, high-level literacy skills require integrating effectively the strategies governing the use of print and new media, and these strategies themselves are products of exchange and adaptation. Indeed, the "digital divide"—inequities in access to technology and in the acquisition of new literacy skills—has been fueled, in part, by the continued, symbiotic ties between print and new media and, as such, is yet another unintended consequence of the current communications revolution.

The adaptive and reactive capacities of print speak to its sustained relevancy as an agent of change in the twenty-first century. Understanding print and its history is thus more than simply a quest to understand a past communications revolution; it is also a means of better understanding our world as we negotiate the current communications revolution and anticipate its future. When Eisenstein published her monumental work in 1979, print culture studies did not exist as such, and historians, if they acknowledged the print revolution at all, did so only in passing. Commenting in *PPAC* on the oddness of such neglect, Eisenstein writes: "Because historians are usually eager to investigate major changes and this change [advent of print] transformed the conditions of their own craft, one would expect the shift to attract some attention from the profession as a whole" (3). After the appearance of Eisenstein's pioneering study, however, not only historians but a broad range of scholars, whether they agreed or took issue with her arguments, began to attend to print and its consequences. Today, with the conditions of historical scholarship and indeed of all intellectual labor being transformed through the symbiotic relationship print has with new media, it has become increasingly difficult to consider one without the influence of the other. Yet what seems far more difficult is imagining print culture studies today without *PPAC* as a foundational catalyst and without the reactive effects this work has exercised for over twenty-five years—and continues to exercise—across a diverse range of disciplines.

Chapter 15

"Little Jobs"

Broadsides and the Printing Revolution

PETER STALLYBRASS

The printed calendars and indulgences that were first issued from the Mainz workshops of Gutenberg and Fust . . . warrant at least as much attention as the more celebrated Bible.

—Elizabeth L. Eisenstein, *The Printing Press as an Agent of Change*

Printed Sheets

I BEGIN WITH a counterintuitive proposition: printers do not print books.[1] It is the process of gathering, folding, stitching, and sometimes binding that transforms printed sheets into a pamphlet or book. Certainly, some printers may have undertaken or paid for all of the latter processes. But that is not what printing is about. It never was. The first dated text that survives from Gutenberg's press is not a book but an indulgence. Most indulgences are printed on only one side of a single piece of paper. They were usually printed as multiple settings of the same text, which the compositor placed in a single

---

For Elizabeth Eisenstein and James Green.

1. I owe this formulation and much else to James Green, the Librarian of the Library Company of Philadelphia. See his "The American Bindings Collection of Michael Zinman," in *The Library Company of Philadelphia: 1999 Annual Report* (Philadelphia: Library Company of Philadelphia, 2000), 9, where he writes: "Printers print sheets, but books are made by binders." That printing is about sheets, not books, is a point repeatedly emphasized by Hugh Amory. See particularly "A Note on Statistics" in his *Bibliography and the Book Trade: Studies in the Print Culture of New England,* ed. David D. Hall (Philadelphia: Univ. of Pennsylvania Press, 2005), 163–70, where he notes the pitfalls of measuring printing by titles or number of pages. One of the many impressive features of *The Colonial Book in the Atlantic World,* vol. 1 of *A History of the Book in America,* ed. Hugh Amory and David D. Hall (Cambridge: Cambridge Univ. Press, 2000) is the insistence of the editors and the contributors on the sheet as the basic unit in printing. See particularly graphs 8a and 8b on p. 516. Hugh Amory and David Hall draw on the implications of D. F. McKenzie's work, particularly *The Cambridge University Press, 1696–1712: A Bibliographical Study,* 2 vols. (Cambridge: Cambridge Univ. Press, 1966).

forme; the printed sheet was subsequently cut up to make two, four, or more separate copies.

Gutenberg was already printing his great Bible when he stopped working on it to print 2,000 copies of his thirty-line indulgence in 1454–5. He undertook this work because it was paid for up front and brought an immediate cash return. The massive project of printing the Bible required a large investment of money, above all to buy paper. Gutenberg both kept afloat and subsidized his larger project by printing broadsides (that is, single sheets printed on one side only).[2] But Gutenberg's 1454–5 edition of 2,000 indulgences was only a foretaste of what was to come. In Augsburg in 1480, Jodocus Pflanzmann printed 20,000 certificates of confession, four to a sheet, and Johan Bämler printed 12,000 indulgences. In 1499–1500, Johann Luschner printed 142,950 indulgences for the Benedictine Monastery at Montserrat.[3] As Clive Griffin has shown, so profitable was the printing of indulgences that printers competed fiercely for the patents to print them. Successful printers sometimes had to set up new printing houses to cope with the work. Varela, for instance, set up a second house in Toledo where he printed indulgences from 1509 to 1514.[4]

As with Gutenberg, so with Caxton—the first surviving dated text that Caxton printed in England is an indulgence. The names of the recipients (Henry Langley and his wife) and the date (December 13, 1476) are written in by hand in the carefully placed blank spaces of the printed text.[5] Caxton

---

2. Albert Kapr, *Johann Gutenberg: The Man and His Invention*, trans. Douglas Martin (Aldershot, Hants.: Scolar Press, 1996), 189–90. See Keith Maslen, "Jobbing Printing and the Bibliographer: New Evidence from the Bowyer Ledgers," in his *An Early London Printing House at Work: Studies in the Bowyer Ledgers* (New York: Bibliographical Society of America, 1993), 141: "If we go back to the cradle of printing we find no . . . separation [of jobbing work from printing books]. Gutenberg's Indulgences of 1454–5 were necessarily printed and issued while his massive forty-two-line Bible was still slowly going through the press, not to be completed until 1456. His thirty-line *Indulgence . . .* may claim to be the earliest [surviving] product of the Western printing-press. It has many of the characteristics of its kind, ensuring neglect by librarians and scholars. It has no author as books do. It is a legal form, produced for an institutional customer, and serving an immediate social need. There is no point in keeping it once that need has been satisfied."

3. See John L. Flood, "'Volentes Sibi Comparare Infrascriptos Libros Impressos . . .': Printed Books as a Commercial Commodity in the Fifteenth-Century," in *Incunabula and Their Readers: Printing, Selling, and Using Books in the Fifteenth Century,* ed. Kristian Jensen (London: British Library, 2003), 139–51.

4. Clive Griffin, *The Crombergers of Seville: The History of a Printing and Merchant Dynasty* (Oxford: Clarendon Press, 1988), 52.

5. George D. Painter, *William Caxton: A Biography* (New York: G. P. Putnam, 1977), 83–4; N. F. Blake, *Caxton and His World* (New York: London House and Maxwell, 1969), 79, 232–3. Lotte Hellinga has shown that Caxton printed the 1476 indulgence while he was already at work on his edition of *The Canterbury Tales*. See Hellinga, *Caxton in Focus* (London: British Library, 1982), 81.

depended for his survival and success on an extensive patronage network for his more substantial projects,[6] but the ready money for the job printing of indulgences presumably appealed to him as a merchant. Other printers in England followed Caxton's lead. While only eight editions of indulgence documents by Caxton survive, nineteen editions were printed by Wynkyn de Worde and ninety-two editions by Richard Pynson. Eighty of Pynson's editions of indulgence documents were printed between 1500 and 1529, an example of the rapid increase in the production of indulgences in the early sixteenth century.

In England, indulgences or letters of confraternity were issued on behalf of an extraordinary range of institutions: excluding London, they were issued to the Confraternity of St. John in Beverley, the Church of St. Botolph in Boston, St. James's Chapel in Bosworth Field, the Hospital of Burton Lazarus, the Monastery of the Holy Cross in Colchester, the Hospital of St. Roch in Exeter, Hereford Cathedral, the Franciscan Convent in Ipswich, the Augustinian Priory in Kirkby, the Trinitarian Priory in Knaresborough, the Monastery of the Virgin Martyr and St. John the Evangelist in Langley, the Hospitals of St. Katherine and of St. Sepulchre in Lincoln, the Palmers of St. Lawrence in Ludlow, the Chapel of St. Mary in the Field in Newton (Isle of Ely), the Hospital of Pity in Newton (Suffolk), the Chapel of St. John the Baptist in North Newington, Christ Church and the Dominican Friars in Oxford, the parish church in Rickmansworth, the Collegiate Church of St. Wilfrid in Ripon, the Hospital of the Trinity and St. Thomas in Salisbury, the Guild of St. George in Southwark, the Monastery of the Blessed Virgin in Strata Marcella, the Hospital of St. Sepulchre in Suffolk, the Trinitarians in Thelsford, the Hospital of St. Sepulchre in Thetford, the Chapel of St. Margaret in Uxbridge, the Confraternity of St. John in Wakering, the Hospital of the Holy Trinity in Walsoken, the Confraternity of St. Cornelius in Westminster, the Confraternity of St. Mary of Mount Carmel and the Guild of Saints Christopher and George in York.[7] And dozens of other indulgences, indulgenced pictures, and licenses were issued in general or on behalf of specific individuals, continental institutions, or to raise money to fight the Turks or to ransom captives.[8]

England's contribution to the sale of printed indulgences in the fifteenth century, though, was small compared with that of the Holy Roman Empire

---

6. On Caxton's patrons, see Hellinga, *Caxton in Focus,* and *The Cambridge History of the Book in Britain,* vol. 3, *1400–1557,* ed. Hellinga and J. B. Trapp (Cambridge: Cambridge Univ. Press, 1999), 84–5, 213–14, 270–1.

7. *STC* (see Chap. 1, n. 38), 14077c.26 to 14077c.84a.

8. See *STC* 14077c.85 to 14077c.123.

from where thirteen editions survive for 1453, thirty editions for 1480, forty-three editions for 1481, thirty-six editions for 1482, thirty-three editions for 1488, eighteen editions for 1489, and twenty-six editions for 1490.[9] Paul Needham estimates that copies from at least six hundred editions of indulgences survive for the fifteenth century. But that number is the tip of a much larger iceberg. We know that more than two dozen editions of the 1479 Rhodes indulgence were printed in Germany, Switzerland, and the Low Countries. But of the thousands of copies from the six known English editions of the Rhodes indulgence, just nine copies survive, and four of the editions are known only through fragments that have been preserved as printer's waste reused in the binding of other books.[10] If the majority of copies have disappeared, so almost certainly have the majority of editions. In 1500 the Bishop of Cefalù paid for copies of more than 130,000 indulgences: not one survives.[11] And the 20,000 Spanish indulgences that Jacopo Cromberger printed in 1514 and the 16,000 that he printed two years later are recorded only in notarial documents. Again, not a single copy survives.[12] Because of how many editions survive in only one or two copies, it is statistically certain that hundreds of other editions have vanished without trace.

Tessa Watt notes that the survival rate of sixteenth-century English ballads is perhaps one in ten thousand copies and one in ten editions. She cites Folke Dahl's estimate of 0.013 percent of English newsbooks surviving from 1620 to 1642. Even for the slightly more substantial chapbooks, many editions (and even whole titles) were lost through use. The first surviving copy of William Perkins's chapbook *Deaths Knell* (1628) is labeled "9th edition"; had it not been announced as such we would have no knowledge of its popularity.[13] One in ten thousand copies and one in ten editions is probably too optimistic an estimate for fifteenth- and sixteenth-century indulgences.

Given the mass production of printed indulgences, Luther's Ninety-five Theses attacking indulgences must be read as a response to printing, and in particular to the campaign that was under way in Mainz, spearheaded by the pardoner Johann Tetzel, to sell huge numbers of indulgences to finance the

---

9. See Rudolf Hirsch, *Printing, Selling, and Reading 1450–1550* (Wiesbaden: Otto Harrassowitz, 1967), 122.

10. Paul Needham, *The Printer and the Pardoner: An Unrecorded Indulgence Printed by William Caxton for the Hospital of St. Mary Rounceval, Charing Cross* (Washington, DC: Library of Congress, 1986), 30, 33.

11. Ibid., 31.

12. Griffin, *Crombergers of Seville,* 51.

13. Watt, *Cheap Print and Popular Piety, 1550–1640* (Cambridge: Cambridge Univ. Press, 1991), 141, 259. On newsbooks, she cites Folke Dahl, *A Bibliography of English Corantos and Periodical Newsbooks 1620–1642* (London: The Bibliographical Society, 1952), 22.

rebuilding of St. Peter's in Rome.[14] But Luther initiated a new phase of printing in which the single sheets that Tetzel was offering would have to compete
against a remarkable proliferation of pamphlets. As Andrew Pettegree notes,
more than three-quarters of the ten thousand or so pamphlets printed in
Germany between 1500 and 1530 were printed in the six years between 1520
and 1526. Yet 50 percent of those pamphlets consisted of two sheets of paper
or less, usually in the form of the small quarto *Flugschriften,* in which two
sheets were folded to make sixteen pages.[15] Elizabeth Eisenstein, moreover,
is surely right to argue that we must see the thousands of Lutheran pamphlets within the context of the millions of Catholic printed indulgences.
As she notes, "a late medieval crusade" against the Turks in response to the
fall of Constantinople, not Florentine humanism or the Reformation, made
printing a form of mass production from its very inception. Though Luther's
Theses "received top billing in their day and are still making the headlines in
our history books," the indulgences and Bibles that came from Mainz in the
middle of the fifteenth century revealed the revolutionary possibilities of the
new technology. Eisenstein continues:

> If first things were placed first, it would . . . be noted that indulgences got
> printed before getting attacked. The first dated printed product from Guten-
> berg's workshop was an indulgence. More than half a century lapsed between
> the Mainz indulgences of the 1450s and Luther's attack on indulgences in 1517.
> During this interval the output of indulgences had become a profitable branch
> of jobbing-printing. 'When . . . Johan Luschner printed at Barcelona 18,000
> letters of indulgence for the abbey of Montserrat in May 1498 this can only be
> compared with the printing of income tax forms by His Majesty's Stationery
> Office.'[16]

---

14. See Falk Eisermann, "Der Ablass als Medienereignis: Kommunikationswandel durch
Einblattdrucke im 15. Jahrhundert; Mit einer Auswahlbibliographie," in *Tradition and Innovation in
an Era of Change / Tradition und Innovation im Übergang zur Frühen Neuzeit,* ed. Rudolf Suntrup
and Jan R. Veenstra, vol. 1 of *Medieval to Early Modern Culture / Kultureller Wandel vom Mittelalter
zur Frühen Neuzeit* (Frankfurt: Peter Lang, 2001), 99–128.

15. Andrew Pettegree, "Books, Pamphlets, and Polemics," in *The Reformation World,* ed. Pettegree (London: Routledge, 2000), 109–26, esp. 110–11. See also Mark U. Edwards Jr., *Printing, Propaganda, and Martin Luther* (Berkeley and Los Angeles: Univ. of California Press, 1994).

16. Eisenstein, *PPAC,* 178, 368, 375. The quotation is from S. H. Steinberg, *Five Hundred Years
of Printing,* rev. ed. (Harmondsworth: Penguin Books, 1961), 139. James Clark gives further evidence
that "long before the printing press became a servant of religious radicals in the 1520s, it had already
come to occupy an honoured position at the very heart of the clerical establishment." Clark, "Print
and Pre-Reformation Religion: The Benedictines and the Press, c. 1470–c. 1550," in *The Uses of Script
and Print, 1300–1700,* ed. Julia Crick and Alexandra Walsham (Cambridge: Cambridge Univ. Press,
2004), 71–92, 90. Compare Clark's account with David d'Avray's unsubstantiated claim for the
"mass" circulation of manuscripts before the advent of printing. Since he gives no figures, it is hard

Printer-publishers who did not undertake job printing such as indulgences to underwrite the expenses of larger projects were much more likely to fail. In late-fifteenth-century Ulm, Lienhart Holler attempted to survive by printing deluxe books for private consumption. As Martha Tedeschi has shown, he went bankrupt, while two other Ulm printers flourished by printing single-sheet broadsides.[17] Clive Griffin reaches the same conclusion:

> Spanish printers of the early sixteenth century were surrounded by evidence of colleagues who had failed to establish their operation on a sound economic foundation and who had collapsed. . . . There is evidence that printers had to engage in other commercial activities unless they were fortunate enough to corner the market in one of the few lucrative areas of jobbing printing. [Arnao Guillén de] Brocar, for instance, made his money not from the magnificent editions for which he is now remembered, but from the privilege which he enjoyed on the best-selling works of the grammarian, Antonio de Nebrija, and by his appointment as joint printer of the indulgences of the Santa Cruzada.[18]

Like Brocar, Gutenberg made his wealth less from his large undertakings than from job printing and the publication of small books, such as calendars and schoolbooks.[19]

As Elizabeth Eisenstein suggests, we can learn more about the printing revolution from indulgences than from the celebrated printing of Gutenberg's Bible or Caxton's Chaucer. Printers were businessmen, pursuing profit, and profit was rarely to be made by publishing huge folios that required major capital investments. Christopher Plantin, who ran one of the greatest printing houses of early modern Europe, almost bankrupted himself printing his most famous book, the Polyglot Bible, despite the official patronage of

---

to know what he is arguing. D'Avray, "Printing, Mass Communication, and Religious Reformation: The Middle Ages and After," in Crick and Walsham, *Uses of Script and Print*, 50–70.

17. Tedeschi, "Publish and Perish: The Career of Lienhart Holle in Ulm," in *Printing the Written Word: The Social History of Books, c. 1450–1520*, ed. Sandra Hindman (Ithaca, NY: Cornell Univ. Press, 1991), 67.

18. Griffin, *Crombergers of Seville*, 9 n.18.

19. Kapr notes that Gutenberg printed at least twenty-four editions of Donatus that survive, the most important of all medieval schoolbooks and "the most widely distributed book of the fifteenth-century." These schoolbooks, printed on vellum to stand up to wear and tear, comprised fourteen leaves or twenty-eight pages and were probably "the first books to be printed from type in Europe." But Kapr argues that Gutenberg interrupted the printing of Donatus to print even shorter items, assured of sale, such as calendars (*Gutenberg*, 148, 212). The only surviving copy of Gutenberg's Türkenkalender of 1454 comprises three sheets. See Eckehard Simon, *The Türkenkalender (1454) Attributed to Gutenberg and the Strasbourg Lunation Tracts* (Cambridge, MA: Medieval Academy of America, 1988).

Philip II of Spain.[20] The Bible took him four years of hard work to publish and he never had adequate financial support for the immense quantities of paper and parchment that he had to buy in advance. Indeed, so bad was his situation that he was forced to sell some of the paper that he had acquired even before he had begun the printing. As Colin Clair concludes, though the Polyglot Bible brought Plantin fame, "it left him burdened with crippling debts which were covered neither by the sales nor by the King of Spain."[21]

No doubt the economic failure of his greatest publication led Plantin to experiment with publication by subscription. On November 14, 1574, two years after the publication of the Polyglot Bible, Plantin submitted to the Synod of Louvain a proposal for printing an enormous *Graduale*.

> The plan was that the abbots of the archdiocese should each subscribe to a fund for the publication of the *Graduale*. The abbot of Averbode would contribute 500 fl., his colleague at Perk 400 fl., the abbot of St. Peter's Ghent 1,000 fl., and so on. As security for the repayment Plantin offered to pledge books to each subscriber to the value of his contribution, or to guarantee the total sum invested with the estimated 15,000 fl. worth of books he had stored at the Carmelite monastery in Antwerp.

The abbots were not interested in the plan, and the *Graduale* was never printed.[22]

In England, printing John Minsheu's *Ductor in Linguas* posed some of the same problems as Plantin's Polyglot Bible, since it required Greek, Anglo-Saxon, and Hebrew typefaces, in addition to roman, black letter, and italic. John Barnard notes that Minsheu started work on his dictionary in 1599 and was given a royal patent in 1611:

> Minsheu, however, was unable to raise the capital to publish the book until 1617: in doing so, he sought the support of the two universities, the Inns of Court, and 'diuers Honorable and Right Worshipfull Personages, Bishops, and others,' including merchants and London citizens: even so money ran out in the course of the printing and the work was done at different times by two different printers. It was this difficulty that led to the publication of the second edition in 1625 by subscription, the first English example of this practice, one revived in the 1650s and taken up by the trade in the 1670s and 1680s.[23]

---

20. Leon Voet, *The Golden Compasses: A History and Evaluation of the Printing and Publishing Activities of the Officina Plantiniana at Antwerp*, 2 vols. (Amsterdam: Vangendt, 1972), 2:296–7.

21. Clair, *Christopher Plantin* (London: Plantin Paperbacks, 1987), 64, 74–5, 83–4.

22. Voet, *Golden Compasses*, 2:297.

23. Barnard, introduction to *The Cambridge History of the Book in Britain*, vol. 4, *1557–1695*, ed. Barnard and D. F. McKenzie (Cambridge: Cambridge Univ. Press, 2002), 9.

Publication by subscription, however, was a belated response to the problems that English publishers had repeatedly experienced when they ventured too far from broadsides, pamphlets, small books, and the few large books that had a guaranteed market (e.g., Bibles and law books) or that were paid for up front by governments, patrons, or authors. In 1582 Christopher Barker, the King's Printer, claimed that even if one held a monopoly on a large book, one was still likely to be impoverished or bankrupted by printing it. He argued, for instance, that Henry Bynneman's patent for publishing dictionaries was "more Dangerous to the Patentee than profitable" and calculated that the dictionary required at least £10,000 capital ("equivalent to over £1,500,000 in today's currency," as Barnard notes). Although Barker's argument was self-interested since he was defending his own monopolies, he was right. When Bynneman tried to publish Morelius's Latin and Greek dictionary in the early 1580s, it was a financial disaster.[24]

Even a book that was as popular and influential as John Foxe's *Actes and Monuments* was not at first a financial success because of the massive quantities of paper that had to be bought before the printing could even begin and because of the expenses and complications of type, layout, and woodcuts. Foxe's Book of Martyrs would never have been published at all if John Day, who printed it, had not subsidized the enormous task with the profits he made as patentee of the best-selling ABCs. In this, Day was no different from Plantin, who complained to one of his patrons that he would have been ruined by the Polyglot Bible if he had not subsidized it through the sale of his best-selling breviaries.[25] Reprints and job printing had to support the deluxe volumes. But the deluxe volumes, surviving in substantial numbers, dominate accounts of the history of printing, while the great majority of broadsides, almanacs, pamphlets, and schoolbooks have disappeared completely. Later editions of *Actes and Monuments* were printed only when the capital involved was put up by publishing groups, later known as congeries. John Barnard notes that "the 1596 edition was financed by a group of ten trade partners, and when the stationers gained the rights to Foxe's work in 1620, they experienced serious difficulties in providing a subsequent edition, a problem only solved when no fewer than sixteen men agreed to share the risk of a new three-volume folio edition (1632)."[26] Like Plantin, although by a different means, Foxe's later publishers learned how to spread the risk in such a large undertaking.

---

24. Ibid., 7–8.
25. Clair, *Plantin*, 74–5.
26. All of the information about Foxe is taken from Barnard, introduction to Barnard and McKenzie, *Cambridge History of the Book*, 4:8–9.

Printers throughout early modern Europe thought of books in terms of the number of sheets required both because of the cost of paper and because of the frequency with which they printed only parts of a book. The 1632 edition of Foxe was put together from the sheets of two different printers. If it is possible to generalize from Peter Blayney's findings, nearly a third of all books published in early-seventeenth-century England involved shared printing, often between more than two printers, regardless of what the title pages claim. Blayney has further discovered that of the twenty-one printers working in London in 1605–9, Nicholas Okes shared printing of books with no less than eleven other printing houses. And of all the contemporary printers, Blayney has found only one who did not undertake shared printing: Robert Barker, the King's Printer, who nevertheless "certainly shares his *work,* since he sometimes had complete books printed for him by 'assigns' or 'deputies.'" [27] Shared printing was particularly important for large editions that needed to be printed in a hurry, such as almanacs, but it was also a way of coping with the strains of printing large books in a timely fashion. If one believed the title page of "The Fifteenth Edition" of Isaac Watts's *Hymns and Spiritual Songs,* the book was entirely the work of Benjamin Franklin, who "Printed and Sold" it in Philadelphia in 1741. In fact, the title page conceals not just shared printing but a publication that draws on the resources of three different cities. Franklin printed only the first and last sheets of the book in Philadelphia. In New York, James Parker printed the other ten sheets. Franklin and Watts then sent the sheets they had separately printed to Boston, where Charles Harrison bound the sheets to make what the *Boston Evening Post* described as "a small pocket volume." [28] It is difficult to think of a more striking example of the difference between the printing of sheets and the making of a book. Neither Franklin nor Parker was involved in any way in the transformation of the sheets they printed into a book. In this exceptional case, the difference between printing sheets and making books is clarified by the fact that the printing was done in Philadelphia and New York, while the books were made in Boston.

In the era of the handpress, shared printing was undoubtedly a common practice. In his *Autobiography,* Benjamin Franklin wrote that he and his

---

27. Blayney, "The Prevalence of Shared Printing in the Early Seventeenth Century," *Papers of the Bibliographical Society of America* 67 (1973): 437–42, and *The Texts of "King Lear" and Their Origins,* vol. 1, *Nicholas Okes and the First Quarto* (Cambridge: Cambridge Univ. Press, 1982), 49–50.

28. C. William Miller, *Benjamin Franklin's Philadelphia Printing* (Philadelphia, PA: American Philosophical Society, 1974), no. 266, 130–1. See also James N. Green, "Benjamin Franklin as Publisher and Bookseller," in *Reappraising Benjamin Franklin,* ed. J. A. Leo Lemay (Newark: Univ. of Delaware Press, 1993), 98–114, and "The Middle Colonies 1720–1790: English Books and printing in the Age of Franklin," in Amory and Hall, *Colonial Book in the Atlantic World,* 248–98.

partner, Hugh Meredith, procured the printing of "Forty Sheets" [29] of the third edition of William Sewel's *History of the Rise, Increase, and Progress, Of the Christian People called Quakers,* although the title page only says "Printed and Sold by Samuel Keimer." [30] Franklin composed a sheet a day, while Meredith did the presswork. The speed with which they worked is explained by the fact that Keimer, who did the bulk of the printing, had been working on the book for five years. The Quakers, who were financing the publication, were understandably frustrated at Keimer's slow rate of progress. So it was not difficult for Franklin to siphon off some of the printing in order to speed up the completion of the work. Franklin writes: "so determin'd I was to continue doing a Sheet a Day of the Folio, that one Night when having impos'd my Forms, I thought my Day's Work over, one of them by an accident was broken and two Pages reduc'd to Pie, I immediately distributed & compos'd it over again before I went to bed." [31] This passage has frequently been commented on as an example of Franklin's histrionic display of virtue. He was eager that his "Industry" should be visible to his neighbors to give the printing house "Character and Credit." What has not, I think, been noticed is the prior passage in which Franklin explains why, even without the dropping of forms, such large projects were repeatedly delayed. For like Gutenberg, Franklin never refused job printing even (or particularly) when he was working on large jobs. As he casually puts it: "The little Jobs sent in by our other Friends now and then set us back." [32] The "little Jobs" took precedence over prestigious folios, because the "little Jobs" regularly injected cash into the notoriously undercapitalized book trade.

It is now well established that printing houses of any size usually undertook several tasks concurrently. [33] But that large jobs were interrupted by smaller jobs is the clear implication of the contract that John Palsgrave, a prebendary at St. Paul's, drew up with Richard Pynson for his book on how to speak "trewe frenche." The contract stipulates that "the sayde richard schall imprint

---

29. In fact, forty-four sheets and, in addition, the title page.

30. Miller, *Franklin's Philadelphia Printing,* no. 1, 1–2.

31. Benjamin Franklin, *Benjamin Franklin's Autobiography: An Authoritative Text, Backgrounds, Criticism,* ed. J. A. Leo Lemay and P. M. Zall (New York: Norton, 1986), 49.

32. Ibid.

33. See Charlton Hinman, *The Printing and Proof-Reading of the First Folio of Shakespeare,* 2 vols. (Oxford: Clarendon Press, 1963), 1:16–24; D. F. McKenzie, "Printers of the Mind: Some Notes on Bibliographical Theories and Printing-House Practices," in *Making Meaning: "Printers of the Mind" and Other Essays,* ed. Peter D. McDonald and Michael F. Suarez (Amherst: Univ. of Massachusetts Press, 2002), 25–6. Peter Blayney argues in his magnificent *Texts of "King Lear"* that "the basic pattern" of a smaller printing house with a single press would be more likely to be "one of interruption rather than of concurrency," whereas "any printer commonly using two or more presses would probably diversify the nature of his output, and would thus be more likely to choose concurrent printing as the solution to problems of organization" (54).

euery hoole workyng day for the more speding off the saide work a shete off paper on bothe the sides. and not to cesse for none occasion except the kynges grace haue any thyng to be prynted tyll the hole worke be full fynyshyd." Palsgrave further stipulated that "all the sayde bokys" should "amountt vnto the holle nombre of vij c and ffyftye . . . complete bookes fullye and entyerlye accomplysshyd and ffynyshyd." [34] Given concurrent printing, there was every reason why the printing of 750 copies of a book of over five hundred leaves should be interrupted by other work. Even if Pynson had worked on nothing else, he would have had to spend more than 250 days on this one book. But in fact he worked on more than a hundred other surviving projects before he died six years later in 1529 with Palsgrave's book still not completed. When *Lesclair-cissment de la Langue Francoyse* was finally published, the book included the information that John Hawkyns had "fynysshed" printing it on July 18, 1530, more than seven years after the original contract had been drawn up.

If Pynson did not finish Palsgrave's book, it was partly because of the extensive job printing for the government that his contract allowed. This work included proclamations, statutes, and thirty-seven editions of legal year-books. But Pynson also undertook job printing for all sorts of other institutions that were explicitly excluded by the contract. The following are just the institutions for which we have surviving indulgence documents printed by Pynson between 1523 and his death:

1523: the Monastery of the Holy Cross, Colchester (two editions of indulgences)
1524: the Augustinians (certificates of confession and absolution)
1526: the papal commissioners (two editions of indulgences for the reconstruction of St. Peter's, Rome)
1527: the Trinitarian Order (letters of confraternity to ransom captives from the Turks)
1528: the Monastery of the Crutched Friars, London (two editions of letters of confraternity) and the Monastery of the Blessed Virgin of Strata Marcella, Montgomeryshire (letters of confraternity)[35]

Every copy of these indulgence documents was a single sheet or less, printed on one side. In fact, only the letter of confraternity for the Trinitarians consisted of a whole sheet. The other editions consisted of individual copies of a half or a quarter of a sheet.

---

34. Quoted in Percy Simpson, *Proof-Reading in the Sixteenth, Seventeenth, and Eighteenth Centuries* (London: Oxford Univ. Press, 1935), 46–7.

35. *STC* 14077c.2, .39, .40, .55, .76, .101A, .101B, .122.

So rarely do these "little Jobs" survive, though, that it is usually impossible to reconstruct how printers moved back and forth between printing books and jobbing. Take, for instance, William and Isaac Jaggard (father and son), the printers and part-publishers of Shakespeare's First Folio. As Charlton Hinman and Peter Blayney have shown, the printing of the First Folio was slowed down (in the usual way) by the concurrent printing of Thomas Wilson's *Christian Dictionary* and Augustine Vincent's *Discouerie of Errours.*[36] While the *Discouerie* was being worked on intensively, Jaggard started work on another large book, André Favin's *The Theater of Honour and Knight-hood,* also a folio, but both the Favin and the First Folio were further pushed back when Jaggard began to print William Burton's *Description of Leicester shire,* yet another folio, which he probably completed between July and October 1622. Burton's book was no risk to Jaggard, since he was printing it, according to its title page, "for Iohn White." The book, in other words, was financed by John White, the publisher, rather than by Jaggard, the printer, and the money that the book brought in to Jaggard as printer would have helped to capitalize his own work as a publisher. But the First Folio remained a serious financial risk. So it is not surprising that the Jaggards decided to share its costs. Although the title page declares that the First Folio was "Printed by Isaac Jaggard and Ed. Blount," the colophon states that the book was published "at the charges of W. Jaggard, Ed. Blount, J. Smithweeke, and W. Aspley." In other words, the Jaggards shared their risk with three other publishers.

With printers like the Jaggards, it is important to be clear about the extent to which they undertook work as publishers. As David Scott Kastan observes: "For a printer, the size of the job would be of little concern, assuming his rates were set appropriately; indeed a large job would be an advantage, assuring consistent work. The publisher, however, assumed the financial risk of the project, fronting the costs for producing and wholesaling the books; for the publisher, then, the larger the project the greater the risk."[37] However large and successful a firm the Jaggards were, they were above all printers, undertaking work that had been paid for by others. That work included lengthy books such as Burton's *Description of Leicester shire,* but it also consisted of innumerable "small Jobs," for which William held three patents.[38] At the beginning

36. Hinman, *Printing and Proof-Reading of the First Folio,* 1:16–24; Peter W. M. Blayney, *The First Folio of Shakespeare* (Washington, DC: Folger Shakespeare Library, 1991), 5–8; Andrew Murphy, *Shakespeare in Print: A History and Chronology of Shakespeare Publishing* (Cambridge: Cambridge Univ. Press, 2003), 46–8.

37. Kastan, *Shakespeare and the Book* (Cambridge: Cambridge Univ. Press, 2001), 141 n. 13.

38. Keith Maslen observes that Hinman, who was aware that even "well-established firms like Jaggard's . . . evidently valued job work," considers just "the 'other Jaggard books' that went through the press with the Shakespeare First Folio. His only piece of related jobbing, and one brought late to

of his career as a printer, Jaggard acquired the rights to print playbills, which would be paid for by the acting companies. One might have thought that such a monopoly was a small matter were it not for the fact that it became the central concern of the Stationers' Company for more than a decade, involving the king, the archbishop of Canterbury, the secretary of state, the lord keeper, the lord chief justice, privy councilors, the earl of Holland, Viscount Rochester, the bishop of London, the mayor of London, the Court of Aldermen, the House of Commons, the House of Lords, the Committee of Grievances, the King's Bench, the Star Chamber, and the Court of Chancery.[39]

In 1619, James I granted a monopoly to Marin de Boisloré, "esquire of the body to his Maiestie," for his "acceptable service." The monopoly was for thirty-one years and, according to the stationers' complaint to the House of Commons, gave to Boisloré and his assignees, Roger Wood and Thomas Symcock, the sole rights

> to imprint, utter, and sell, all and all manner of Briefes of Letters Pattents for losses by fier or water, all Indentures for Apprentices, all indentures for waterworkes, all bonds and Recognizances, all licenses to gather by, licenses to marry, licenses for Victualers, all acquittances, all articles for visitacions of Bishops and Officials, all billes for teaching schollers, billes for Phisitions, and all play-billes, all pasports, Charts, Epitaphs, portractures and pictures whatsoever, and all other things printed, and hereafter to be printed upon one side only of a sheete or sheetes of paper, or a skin or skinnes of parchment, as more at large . . . may appeare.[40]

The monopoly appeared to cover just about all broadsides ("printed upon one side only of a sheete or sheetes of paper, or a skin or skinnes of parchment"). In their response, the monopolists, while claiming that their patent was a "small thing," make clear how much is at stake. They assert that the "22 Master Printers," "great rich men," have engrossed all the lucrative job printing to themselves.[41]

[Hinman's] notice, is a Heralds' Visitation Summons printed about August 1623 with the same types as the Folio. Yet the Jaggards, father and son, both concerned with the Folio, were Printers to the City of London, authorised to print 'proclamations, acts of common council and other matters for the service of this city.'" Maslen, "Jobbing Printing," 141.

39. See William A. Jackson, introduction to *Records of the Stationers' Company, 1602–1640* (London: Bibliographical Society, 1957), xvi–xxii; and W. W. Greg, *A Companion to Arber* (Oxford: Clarendon Press, 1967), 59–66, 75, 164–75.

40. Guildhall Library, Broadside 23:115, in Wallace Notestein, Frances Helen Relf, and Hartley Simpson, eds., *Commons Debates 1621,* 7 vols. (New Haven, CT: Yale Univ. Press, 1935), 6:535.

41. On the central importance of monopolies to the development of copyright in seventeenth-century England, see Joseph Loewenstein's impressive analysis in *The Author's Due: Printing and the Prehistory of Copyright* (Chicago and London: Univ. of Chicago Press, 2002).

Of these "great rich men," Boisloré and his assignees single out for particular mention "foure rich Printers," who, they argue, were the real instigators of the complaint:

> viz. Master Lownes, Mater Purfoote, Master Iaggard, and Master Beale. Master Lownes now Maister of his Company, a man of great woorth, when he was made Warden foure yeares agoe or thereabouts . . . procured an ordinance for the Company for the sole printing and selling of all Indentures for Apprentizes. Master Purfoote procured all Briefes for collections in like manner, Master Iaggard all Play-bills, and Master Beale all Bonds and Recognizances for Victualers. And if any poore Printer who had heretofore usually printed these things did print any of them, these foure rich Printers being men of great worth, and all of them of the Livorie of their Company, presently caused the poore Printers Presse and Letters to be seised, and the party either imprisoned or fined at their pleasures . . . by which meanes they enioy the sole printing and selling of these thinge.[42]

In other words, William Jaggard and his associates are accused of making their wealth from printing broadsides and of jealously protecting the monopolies that have enriched them.

We do not need to believe the claims of the new monopolists that they were charitably going to distribute the printing of broadsides among "the poore Printers" to accept their claim that the wealthiest members of the Stationers' Company had taken over the richest pickings of the trade: job printing. Ten years after the new monopoly had been granted, and despite the fact that first Wood and Symcock and then Symcock alone appear to have had minimal success in enforcing their claims, Humphrey Lownes, Clement Knight, Thomas Purfoot, and John Beal petitioned the king, representing themselves as "poor printers," though one of their opponents said that they were worth £4,000. Three months earlier, on February 12, 1629, the stationers had ordered John Beale, Miles Flesher, Robert Young, William Jones, John Wright, and Richard Shorlayker "to follow the busines" and they petitioned both the House of Commons and the House of Lords. As William Jackson notes, the selected petitioners were all interested parties: Beal had a patent for indentures and recognizances; Flesher had a patent for prison petitions; Young had a patent for a wide variety of indentures; Jones had a patent for recognizances; Wright was one of the ballad partners; and Shorlayker was a major dealer in prints.[43]

---

42. Guildhall Library, Broadside 24:3, in *Commons Debates 1621,* 6:537–8.
43. Jackson, introduction to *Records of the Stationers' Company,* xxi, xxi n. 4.

The major dispute of the Stationers' Company in the early seventeenth century was thus not about books at all: it was about sheets of paper or parchment printed on one side only. A final irony of the dispute about sheets printed on only one side is that it was conducted through sheets printed on only one side. The broadside abstract that proclaimed the patent granted to Boisloré and his assignees (*STC* 8615) was answered by the stationers' broadside addressed to the House of Commons (*STC* 16786.6), which was in turn answered by the broadside with which Boisloré responded (*STC* 3217.5). And in 1628, Thomas Symcocke asserted his sole claim to the monopoly in a further broadside (*STC* 8903). Printing had become a standard means of conducting legal, economic, and political campaigns.

In 1621, the same year that the stationers published their first complaint, the bookbinders printed a petition against the monopoly of the goldbeaters, the brewers printed a petition for tax relief, the London brokers printed a petition against foreign brokers, the carpenters printed a petition against the restrictions of the building commissioners, the cloth-workers printed a petition for a restriction on the export of undyed cloth, the customs-house clerks printed a petition against a new monopoly, the cutlers printed a petition against the monopoly of goldbeaters, the dyers printed a petition against abuses in dyeing and requesting a prohibition on the use of logwood, the felt makers printed a petition against the importation of felts and hats, the fustian makers printed a petition against export taxes, the goldbeaters printed a petition in answer to the cutlers' petition, the hot pressers printed a petition against a new monopolist, the merchants of the staple printed a petition against the merchant adventurers, church ministers printed a petition for equitable assessments, the shipwrights printed a petition on the governance of their company, the tilers and bricklayers printed a petition against unlawfully made bricks, the watermen printed a petition on the reasons for forming a company, the water-tankard-bearers printed a petition against the opening of private branches and cocks, the Wharfingers printed a petition against the woodmongers, and the woodmongers printed a petition justifying their practices.[44]

In the broadside defending Boisloré's patent, William Jaggard is named as one of the "foure rich Printers" with a particular concern for sheets printed on only one side because of his monopoly on "all Play-bills." In fact, playbills were not the only broadsides on which Jaggard held a monopoly. On May

---

44. The list of all the surviving London petitions can be found in *STC* 16768.4 to 16787.14. It should be noted that a disproportionate number were either printed in 1621 or have been preserved from that year.

26, 1604, James I had issued a warrant ordering that "in euery Church and chappel a Table of Ten Commandments may be set up by William Jaggard his deputies or assignes at the charge of the parish and that the said Jaggard nor his deputies take above xv d. sterling for euery of the said tables."[45] While the patents for these broadsides had indeed helped to make him a rich printer, Jaggard was probably more alarmed about Boisloré's threat to another part of his business that must have been more lucrative than either of these patents: the broadsides for which he had a monopoly as a result of his appointment as Printer to the City of London in 1610, a position that he held until his death in 1623 and that he passed on to his son Isaac. The job printing for the city would have guaranteed a steady flow of cash.

Although only a fraction of the Jaggards' broadsides survives, it is enough to show the variety of work that they undertook, even, or especially, when they were printing and publishing large books. For the three years from 1621, just before they began the First Folio, to 1623, the year of the folio's completion, the following single sheets or two-leaved folios survive:

FOR THE CITY OF LONDON:

"The order of my lord maior, the aldermen, and the sheriffs, for their meetings" (*STC* 16728). Single sheet

"An act for reformation of the negligences of constables" (*STC* 16728.3). Two-leaved folio

"An act. . . . made for the preuention of theft" (*STC* 16728.5). Single sheet

"Orders regarding Blackwell-hall" (*STC* 16728.7). Two-leaved folio

"An acte of common councell, concerning the preseruation and clensing of the river of Thames" (*STC* 16728.9). Single sheet

FOR THE KING:

"An abstract of his maiesties royall priuiledge, graunted to G. Wither" (*STC* 8704.5). Single sheet: commanding that Wither's *Hymns* should be bound with all copies of the metrical psalms

FOR THE COLLEGE OF HERALDS:

"To the high-constables of the towne of ———— or to any of them, greeting . . ." (*STC* 16768.32). Single sheet: a blank form summoning the gentry to present evidence of their claims to gentility to R. Treswell and A. Vincent

---

45. PRO, SP 38/7, quoted in Edwin Eliott Willoughby, *A Printer of Shakespeare: The Books and Times of William Jaggard* (London: P. Allan and Co., 1934), 66.

FOR THE TOWN OF TEWKESBURY:

"Reasons, why the county of Glocester, ought to joyne with the towne of
Tewkesbury, in repayring of a decayed bridge" (*STC* 23918.5). Single sheet:
a petition presented to parliament by the town of Tewkesbury

FOR PHILLIP PAGE:

"To the right reverend. . . . the Lords spirituall and temporall, in Parliament.
An abstract of the greeuances of P. Page against Foxwell, Hutton, Sherbon,
Day, and Cason" (*STC* 19087.7). Single sheet: a dispute over land, in
which Page accuses Sherburn and Day, servants of Lord Chancellor
Bacon, of accepting bribes.

The printers of the First Folio proudly proclaimed themselves "Printer[s]
to the Honourable Citie of London." But that they also printed a petition
from a town that wanted help repairing a bridge, a blank form for the College of Heralds, and a complaint of corruption by a private citizen reminds
us of the ubiquity of job printing. Every branch of central and local government, every town, every diocese, and institutions such as the universities and
the Inns of Court required an endless series of "small Jobs." But merchants,
shopkeepers, and hundreds of other individuals also ordered printed documents, receipts, labels, and tickets. And just as English printers competed
with each other and paid good money for patents for such "small Jobs," so
did Parisian printers. As Henri-Jean Martin observes, "we know from the
bitter rivalries between printers for the privilege of printing [broadsides]
that the business was highly prized, both for its status and profitability."[46]
Martin's reference to the "status" of job printing may seem surprising. But
in job printing, whether for royal proclamations or commercial advertisements, printers could display the full range of their art, their images, and
their type faces. The first printed proclamation in England is a broadside
beginning with a magnificent decorative initial *H* that is over a third the
height of the sheet. And the proclamation makes use of three different sizes
of type, an ornamental border, six woodcuts of different coins, and another
decorative initial.[47] Such broadsides reached a massively greater readership
or viewership than books, since they were "distributed, proclaimed, and
posted throughout the realm."[48] At the same time, according to a much later

46. Martin, *Print, Power, and People in Seventeenth-Century France,* trans. David Gerard
(Metuchen, NJ: Scarecrow Press, 1993), 161–75, esp. 165.

47. *Henricus dei gracia* (London: William Faques, 1504), *STC* 7760.4.

48. See Pamela Neville-Sington, "Press, Politics, and Religion," in *The Cambridge History of the
Book in Britain,* vol. 3, *1400–1557,* 580 and fig. 28.1.

account, compositors were paid more for job work than for their regular work on books.[49]

Though the Jaggards were proud of their status as Printers to the City of London, it is unlikely that they were as eager to promote themselves as printers of the First Folio. As David Scott Kastan suggests, they may have become the printers of Shakespeare's plays by default, simply because they were "willing to do it": "Few stationers would have been eager or even able to undertake a project the size of the Shakespeare folio. The commitment of resources and the impossibility of any quick profits would have made it an unattractive venture for any but the most ambitious publishers."[50] Undertaking the First Folio was ambitious as a publishing venture in which capital was risked, not as a piece of printing in which technical skill was displayed. As Colin Clair laconically remarks, "One cannot help regretting that so famous a book should be so poorly printed." As a specimen of the printer's art, the First Folio does not begin to compare with William Jaggard's 1608 edition of Robert Glover's *Nobilitas Politica vel Civilis,* with its engraved costume plates and variety of fonts.[51] Nor is it visually impressive like such job printing as Jaggard's 1621 edition of an "Act for Reformation of the Negligences of Constables, and of the Abuses and Misdemeanors of Apprentices, Carmen, and Others, and for the Better Apprehension of Offenders," with its heraldic cuts.[52] But there is no way of comparing the First Folio to the playbills and tables of the commandments for which Jaggard held patents: not one of his playbills or tables survives.[53]

We have only fragments of job printing before 1640, but our picture of job printing after 1640 is about to be radically changed by the groundbreaking work of Jason Peacey. In 1641, a single London bookseller, George Thomason, began to collect printed material on a massive scale. In the process, he created an extraordinary problem for modern scholars: how to account for the fact that between 1588 and 1639, the number of printed items ranged from 211 to 695 surviving titles a year, whereas in 1641 there are 2,042 titles and in 1642 an astonishing 4,038? Joad Raymond, from whom I take these figures, notes that in 1661, Thomason's library consisted of 22,000 items, mainly "pamphlets, newsbooks, broadsides, sermons, theological treatises,

49. Maslen, "Jobbing Printing," 144, quoting William Savage's 1841 *Dictionary of the Art of Printing.*

50. Kastan, *Shakespeare and the Book,* 59–60.

51. Clair, *A History of Printing in Britain* (London: Cassell, 1965), 136.

52. *STC* 16728.3.

53. A point noted by Blayney in *Texts of "King Lear,"* 1:37–8.

and books of poetry."[54] But as D. F. McKenzie has pointed out, we have no idea whether the total volume of printed material increased at all in the 1640s unless we can calculate the total number of sheets printed in any one year.[55] And how could the total number of printed sheets increase so astronomically when there is no evidence that there was a comparable explosion of presses or, more importantly, of compositors and pressmen to run the presses? And where would massive new supplies of paper have come from?

One way of addressing the problem has been to note that there must have been a major increase in printing small pamphlets and newspapers at the expense of larger volumes during the revolutionary period. This conclusion is undoubtedly true, but since pamphlets and newspapers were staple fare in the 1630s, it still does not address the astronomic increase in titles. What Jason Peacey brilliantly illuminates in his new work is that the term "broadside" is totally inadequate to get at what, because of Thomason, is preserved for the first time in history: a massive collection of single pieces of paper, ranging from full sheets to tiny lottery tickets. If we deduct this job printing from Thomason's 22,000 items, the increase in items printed looks far less impressive. The Thomason collection, in other words, allows us to see materials that had always been a fundamental part of printing but that would otherwise have been entirely lost. As Peacey shows, these materials include invitations to meetings, lottery tickets, petitions, and a mass of blanks (printed forms, like indentures, with spaces left to fill in by hand). This bewildering variety of printed forms was printed in a bewildering variety of quantities. Who today would imagine printing petitions when soliciting for a job? But on February 7, 1728, a customer named Dr. Cradock paid for 250 copies of the list of governors of Guy's Hospital; ten days later, he ordered 100 copies of a petition to be made surgeon of the hospital; nine days later, he ordered another 100 copies of the petition. And a month after his first purchase, he ordered 1,000 copies of the petition. Even more surprising are the 34,000 petitions that Edward Umfreville ordered in his campaign to become the Middlesex coroner.[56] Petitioning on such a scale would be inconceivable without printing. But prior to Thomason's collection, we only rarely get a glimpse of such job printing as John Beale undertook on May 3, 1609, when he agreed to print 1,900 "Recognizances for Alehouse Keepers," half of them on parch-

---

54. Raymond, *Pamphlets and Pamphleteering in Early Modern Britain* (Cambridge: Cambridge Univ. Press, 2003), 161–5.

55. McKenzie, "The London Book Trade in 1644," in McDonald and Suarez, *Making Meaning,* 130.

56. Maslen, "Jobbing Printing," 50, 147.

ment.[57] Though quantity was a crucial part of printing, so was speed when it came to job printing as opposed to the printing of large books. In 1572, the duke of Alva put in an order to Plantin for a broadside justifying the sacking of Malines by his troops on October 2–4 of that year. Alva delivered the order for 150 copies in Dutch and 100 in French at 9 A.M. and Plantin delivered them "aprèsdisnée" on the same day. Similarly, in 1577 Plantin received an order to print German passports at 11 A.M. and he completed them by 4 P.M. the same day.[58]

In his foundational article on job printing, Keith Maslen summarizes the little that we know and gives a detailed account of the role of jobbing in the large Bowyers' printing house in eighteenth-century London.[59] If one looks just at the jobs that Maslen mentions in his article, one is immediately struck by the sheer number and variety both of its customers and of the jobs it undertook. Its customers included Henry Lintot, bookseller; Thomas Woodward, bookseller; Fletcher Gyles, bookseller; John Whiston, bookseller; Thomas Trye, bookseller; Henry Plowman, stationer; Alexander Hamilton, solicitor; Edward Umfreville, solicitor; members of Parliament; the Society of Antiquaries; the post office; the customs house; the excise office; London Common Council; Marylebone Council; St. Andrew's parish; the bishop of Exeter; the archdeacon of St. Albans; St. George's Chapel; Bridewell Hospital; Bethlehem Hospital; Guy's Hospital; St. Bartholomew's Hospital; the Westminster Infirmary; Felstead School; Dr. Busby's Charity; the Bedford Level Corporation; Shadwell Water Works; the New River Water Company; the Amicable Society for Perpetual Assurance; the coopers; the fishmongers; the haberdashers; the mercers; the plumbers; the stationers; the apothecaries.

The jobs included 1,400 advertisements (each consisting of an eighth of a sheet); 200 bills for a house to let; 100 catalogues of books (half a sheet); 500 catalogues of books (three and a quarter sheets); 1,000 summonses to master printers to meet at a tavern (an eighth of a sheet); 250 proposals for a book of poems (half a sheet); 500 lists of subscribers (half a sheet); 550 summonses for nonpayment of arrears (500 with "Sir," 50 with "My Lord"); 3,800 messages to members of the Commons over a period of two months, with enough copies of each message for every member; 34,600 petitions to become a coroner (over a year and a half); 1,000 directions to postmasters; one ream of tide surveyors' bills for rummaging; 150 instructions to the surveyors of the customs; 1,006 advertisements for a customs house sale; 8,000 summonses for persons

57. Jackson, ed., *Records of the Stationers' Company,* 109.
58. Voet, *Golden Compasses,* 2:302 and 302n.
59. Maslen, "Jobbing Printing," 139–52.

refusing to pay excise; 2,000 advertisements of a "job for Common Council Men" (a quarter of a sheet); 250 licenses for ale houses; 500 certificates for burying; 500 blank receipts (half a sheet); 400 lists of the apothecaries (half a sheet); 1,000 notices for the improvement of the Chelsea physic garden (one sheet); 14,000 briefs "for the relief of the poor episcopal reformed churches" in Poland and Transylvania; 250 citations of clergymen (a quarter of a sheet); 500 citations of churchwardens (a quarter of a sheet); 1,000 receipts for tithes; 3,500 petitions for a living; 104 separate editions of hymn sheets between 1710 and 1757; 250 lists of the governors of a hospital (half a sheet); 100 petitions (half a sheet); 100 petitions (a quarter of a sheet); 1,000 petitions (one eighth of a sheet); 500 rules for school masters and school mistresses; 150 tickets for a school feast (a quarter of a sheet); 1,000 orders of the trustees of a charity (a quarter of a sheet); 300 sales of timber; 6,000 bills for Bateman's Spirits of scurvy grass; 50 Ealing coach bills; 1,000 shop bills for nets, fishing tackle, and the like (an eighth of a sheet); 1,000 notices of sale of hogs and pigs (a quarter of a sheet); 100 bills for a play (a quarter of a sheet); 300 tickets for a play (an eighth of a sheet). In addition, the Bowyers undertook 130 different jobs for the Excise, including abstracts, bills for low wine, certificates of having taken oaths, commissions for seizing the goods of tallow chandlers, diaries for brewers and for brewery surveyors, brewers' discharges, candle and soap entries, informations against officers of the excise, malt books, and receipts for paying excise.

How many historians of the book today, let alone anyone else, have seen a fraction—or even any—of these ephemera? [60] Yet in 1731, the Bowyers undertook 137 jobs compared with 86 books and pamphlets. (My numbers differ from Maslen's here because he counts the 76 issues of the *Votes of the House of Commons* as a single job, despite the fact that they were printed over a period of three and a half months.) It must be acknowledged, however, that jobbing did not necessarily require the quantities of paper that went into printing books. However extensive the Bowyers' job printing, it accounted for only 25 percent of the sheets they printed in 1731. In other words, the Bowyers were certainly not "jobbing printers," any more than Gutenberg or Caxton were. They were printers who tried to balance the rapid cash flow that came from job printing against the speculations they made when printing books. [61]

---

60. For a magnificent survey of the sheer variety of job printing, mainly from a slightly later period, see Maurice Rickards, *The Encyclopedia of Ephemera: A Guide to the Fragmentary Documents of Everyday Life for the Collector, Curator, and Historian* (New York: Routledge, 2000).

61. In *Texts of "King Lear,"* Blayney convincingly argues that the larger printing houses, like the Jaggards', monopolized much of the job printing and that the smaller printers like Okes would have had a tough time competing for what was left. He further suggests that smaller printers like Okes

In England, the earliest records that survive that give any sense of the total output of a printing house are from Cambridge University Press and the printing houses of Charles Ackers and the Bowyers. If they give an adequate picture of the role that jobbing played in the economics of printing, my claims for the significance of "little Jobs" may seem inflated. Less than 25 percent of Charles Ackers's printing, for instance, consisted of job printing. But then Ackers could not be described as primarily a printer of books, either. In 1733, 271,625 of the 595,530 sheets that he printed for what McKenzie calls "book work" were for the monthly *London Magazine.* The magazine, McKenzie suggests, accounted for at least half of Ackers's profits that year since he was both the printer and the part-owner of it.[62] Is a magazine more like a book or a broadside? Even Cambridge University Press, which was established to publish learned books, "not admitting low & trivial things of quick sale to be printed at its press," undertook a wide range of job printing. Maslen notes that 120 of the 274 items that Cambridge printed between 1696 and 1712 were "small Jobs" of less than one sheet.[63]

To find eighteenth-century printers to compare with the Bowyers and Charles Ackers, we need to cross the Atlantic to Philadelphia, where Benjamin Franklin and his partner David Hall kept comparable records. In 1765, Franklin and Hall printed fifty-two editions of their weekly newspaper, the *Pennsylvania Gazette,* which consisted of a demy sheet, printed on both sides. In the same year, they printed a large quantity of unbound almanacs (James Parker, drawing up the Franklin-Hall accounts, records "9771 of Poor Richard's Almanacks for 1766 [i.e., printed in 1765] at 4d."); a sermon, made up of one and a half sheets; a number of broadsides for the legal bodies of Philadelphia and Pennsylvania (a single-sheet proclamation for the opening of trade with the Indians, a half sheet for the Proprietaries' Land Office, a half sheet for paving and cleaning the streets, and the like); and a half sheet for "The New-Year Verses of the Printers' Lads."[64] Franklin and Hall also printed the records of the General Assembly of Pennsylvania, which added up to a substantial folio volume when the parts, issued separately, were bound

---

"would not have allowed jobbing to cause *major* disruption in the flow of books" (38). With some trepidation, while accepting that this may be true for Okes, I would suggest that the examples of printing houses as diverse as Gutenberg's, Pynson's, the Bowyers', and Franklin and Hall's reveal a surprisingly high level of disruption in the printing of books as the norm.

62. McKenzie, "The Economies of Print, 1550–1750: Scales of Production and Conditions of Constraint," in *Producione e Commercio della Carta e del Libro sec. XIII–XVIII* (Prato: Le Monnier, 1992), 404.

63. Maslen, "Jobbing Printing," 141.

64. Miller, *Franklin's Philadelphia Printing,* nos. 842, 866, 835, 847, 848, 849, 843.

together. Apart from that book, which they undertook as the colony's print-ers, they printed only one other book that year: the catalogue of the Library Company of Philadelphia in an edition of four hundred copies.[65] Just two books, in addition to the newspaper, the almanacs, and the broadsides. What else did Franklin and Hall print? Their work book gives a detailed day-by-day account of the other work they undertook that year. In Lawrence Wroth's summary, it consisted of:

700 vestry notices
1,000 library notes
100 promissory notes
13,350 lottery tickets
2,500 advertisements
200 deeds on paper and 190 on parchment
1,000 bonds and certificates for loading foreign molasses (spread over the year)
300 venires
200 bonds for loading lumber
200 advertisements, desiring landlords to pave their footways
500 tickets for the charity school
100 advertisements for the sale of land
100 bills of health
1,000 way bills
200 certificates
50 invitation cards
100 advertisements for the sale of a plantation
200 receipts and 500 promissory notes for the library
200 proclamations on trade with the Indians
1,000 bills for sale of goods
200 advertisements for opening the land office
200 deeds "on best Pott Paper" and 112 on parchment
1,000 permits
60 advertisements for the sale of lands
1,000 "loose Advertisements, Folio Page, small Paper"
400 bonds and 200 certificates for loading iron and lumber (spread over
    the year)
100 articles of agreement
200 copies of "a Ship's Report Inwards"
100 copies of "a Ship's Report outwards"
500 advertisements
500 promissory notes

65. Ibid., nos. 810, 844–6. Despite the 1764 date on the title page of Library Company cata-logue, the printing was not finished until March 11, 1765.

1,000 copies of "Governor Franklin's Answer to some Charges against him" (a broadside)

100 copies of duties on foreign sugar

100 copies of duties on enumerated goods

100 advertisements for the sale of a house

100 "Single advertisements on a Half Sheet (very long)"

200 advertisements for a night school

200 notices for St. Paul's Church

200 permits for sailing

Four different promissory notes, 200 copies each

2,000 copies of John Dickinson's address to the inhabitants of Pennsylvania (a broadside)

1,000 certificates

100 certificates

100 copies of duties on foreign sugar

400 copies of John Galloway's "Vindication" (a broadside)

100 promissory notes for linen manufacture

300 notices about a meeting[66]

I make no apology for reproducing this list in full. Only twenty copies of ten editions of "little Jobs" of a sheet or less are recorded in C. William Miller's exhaustive bibliography.[67] Twenty copies of the 35,262 copies that Franklin and Hall record in their 1765 work book. In other words, nearly all of Franklin and Hall's job printing has disappeared. Paradoxically, twenty of over 30,000 is quite a high survival rate compared with that of fifteenth-century indulgences or seventeenth-century broadsides. David McKitterick notes that only a single imperfect copy survives of the sheet almanacs that Cambridge University printed before 1640. Yet we know that between 1631 and 1633 alone the press had printed nearly 30,000 such almanacs, none of which survives.[68] It is only because their records survive that we know that "small Jobs" were a substantial part of what Franklin and Hall undertook. In fact, as James Green has shown, Franklin's most important publications in terms of financial returns were, first, his newspaper (one or one-and-a-half sheets) and almanacs (mostly one-and-a-half sheets), second, government printing (including a variety of single sheets), third, job printing (excluding government work), and only fourth and last, pamphlets and books that he published at his own risk (about eighty works over nearly twenty years, only fifteen of

---

66. Lawrence C. Wroth, *The Colonial Printer* (New York: Grolier Club, 1931), 218–22.

67. Miller, *Franklin's Philadelphia Printing*, nos. 836–840, 843, 847–50.

68. McKitterick, *Printing and the Book Trade in Cambridge, 1534–1698*, vol. 1 of McKitterick, *A History of Cambridge University Press*, 3 vols. (Cambridge: Cambridge Univ. Press, 1992–2004), 203.

which were of ten sheets or more).[69] We can draw a simple conclusion from Green's analysis of Franklin's whole career: Franklin was a printer, but he was only marginally a printer of books and still more marginally a publisher of books. If we exclude the almanacs, Franklin and Hall printed only two books in 1765: the folio volume of the laws of Pennsylvania and the octavo *Charter, Laws, and Catalogue of Books, of the Library Company of Philadelphia* (consisting of eleven sheets). For neither book were Franklin and Hall the publishers. The laws were commissioned and paid for by the colony, and for "Paper and Printing 400 Catalogues," Franklin and Hall were paid £43 9s 0d by the Library Company.[70]

Despite the staggering variety of jobs that printers undertook, as I emphasized above, such jobs did not necessarily use up many sheets of paper. As Hugh Amory notes, Franklin's 14,000 lottery tickets were printed "seventy to a demy sheet in a composite run of 200 sheets."[71] By comparison, a single copy of the 1568 Bishops' Bible required 409 sheets, more than twice as many sheets as Franklin used for his 14,000 tickets. And a hypothetical edition of 1,000 copies of the Bishops' Bible would have required 409,000 sheets. But the cost of such massive undertakings as the Bible made job printing all the more important to the economics of printing, since it insured a regular flow of cash in an undercapitalized industry. At the same time, the fierce competition to gain monopolies on indulgences and other "sheets of paper or parchment printed on one side only" is a clear sign of the money to be made from this kind of printing.

Other profitable mainstays of the book trade included almanacs and reprints. The Bishops' Bible was itself essentially a reprint because there was already a known market for it. But securer profits were usually made on textbooks of one kind or another. This conclusion is suggested by the books that two of England's earliest printer-publishers produced as their regular staples. Between 1495 and 1534, Wynkyn de Worde printed or published 230 surviving editions of John Stanbridge's and Robert Whittinton's Latin textbooks. And the guaranteed market for legal books explains why Richard Pynson produced 92 editions of the folio yearbooks between 1496 and 1528. But we should remember that the size of the book and the collecting practices of lawyers guaranteed that numbers of copies from most editions of the yearbook would survive. By contrast, the format of the surviving editions of indulgences that

---

69. Green, "Benjamin Franklin as Publisher and Bookseller," 99.

70. Miller, *Franklin's Philadelphia Printing,* no. 810, 430–1.

71. Amory, "Note on Statistics," 168.

Pynson printed guaranteed that the majority of both copies and editions would vanish without trace.

Let me repeat the proposition with which I started: printers do not print books. They print sheets. If the printer is also the publisher, he or she will be financially involved in transforming those sheets into books. But in terms of printing, the sheets are what matter. It is even more important to emphasize how frequently printers were not even trying to make books. The conceptual gluttony of "the book" consumes all printing as if all paper was destined for its voracious mouth. In her response to Adrian Johns, Eisenstein has to emphasize yet again that her work is not "centrally about the history of books." The printing revolution that she describes "encompassed images and charts, advertisements and maps, official edicts and indulgences."[72] We will only begin to understand the printing revolution when we start looking at the millions of sheets of printed paper that, beginning with Gutenberg's indulgences, transformed the texture of daily life.

A final point worth stressing is that job printing transformed daily life without necessarily having any connection to reading. Our obsession with literacy rates has tended to obscure the extent to which many printed sheets fulfill their function without being read. I hand my passport to the immigration officer to be stamped—but I read my passport for the first time while writing this essay. Coins and paper money have writing on them, but such writing needs to be read only in the bizarre case of United States bank notes, where, in contrast to every other currency that I have handled, the different notes are all the same size and shape, whether they are for $1, $5, $10, $20, $50, or $100. Unable to understand a word of what a tax form says, I fill it in and affix my signature under the guidance of a tax lawyer. An indulgence served its function (or did not) whether or not the recipient could read the Latin or vernacular writing on it. And the laws that were issued through printed proclamations were (sometimes) put into effect whether or not anyone had heard or read them. We have tended to generalize the concept of "reading" so that we now read maps or read people or read societies.

Finally, although I cannot document my claim here, I would argue that printing's most revolutionary effect was on manuscript. If we define manuscript in terms of all writing by hand as opposed to the kind of manuscripts that have been the main object of study, we might begin to see that the history of printing is crucially a history of the "blank" (that is, of printed works designed to be filled in by hand). From indulgences to interleaved almanacs

72. Elizabeth Eisenstein, "Reply," in AHR Forum, "How Revolutionary Was the Print Revolution?" *American Historical Review* 107.1 (2002): 126.

to bills of lading to bank checks to those great twentieth-century bestsell-ers, the diary and the wall calendar, printing has become the great means (compulsory with tax and customs declaration forms) of eliciting writing by hand.[73] As we approach the United States by plane, the cabin crew hand out customs declaration forms. If we fail to complete the forms by hand (in pen, not pencil), we will be refused admission. In such situations we experience the immense power of printing to shape where we live, move, and have our being.

---

73. "Printing-for-manuscript" was the subject of my Rosenbach Lectures at the University of Pennsylvania in February 2006.

Chapter 16

What Difference Does Colonialism Make?

Reassessing Print and Social Change in an Age of Global Imperialism

TONY BALLANTYNE

THE RELATIONSHIP between print and colonialism has become increasingly important in scholarship over the past two decades, not just because of Elizabeth Eisenstein's bold argument about the revolutionary impact of the printing press on "Western Civilization" and the flowering of the "history of the book" in European history but also as a result of several historiographical shifts in the study of empires and colonialism. "Print culture" has emerged as a significant analytical concern for a small but significant group of historians whose research focuses on the history of communication within and between empires;[1] this concept has also moved to the heart of recent studies of the intellectual and literary history of colonial cultures, especially in South Asia.[2] Such work is a significant part of a larger series of debates over the sources, nature, and impact of European empire-building stimulated by Edward Said's *Orientalism;* the impact of the Subaltern Studies collective, which radically recast understandings of the history of colonial and postcolonial South Asia; and the rise of the "new imperial history," which drew on literary studies and anthropology as it foregrounded the centrality of cultural difference in shaping both colonial encounters and imperial culture.

---

1. C. A. Bayly, *Empire and Information: Intelligence Gathering and Social Communication in India, 1780–1870* (Cambridge: Cambridge Univ. Press, 1996); Leila Tarazi Fawaz and C. A. Bayly, *Modernity and Culture: From the Mediterranean to the Indian Ocean* (New York: Columbia Univ. Press, 2002); and the essays collected in *Modern Asian Studies* 27.1 (1993). Elizabeth L. Eisenstein, "An Unacknowledged Revolution Revisited," in AHR Forum, "How Revolutionary Was the Print Revolution?" *American Historical Review* 107.1 (2002): 88, and "On Revolution and the Printed Word," in *Revolution in History,* ed. Roy Porter and Mikuláš Teich (Cambridge and New York: Cambridge Univ. Press, 1986), 186–206.

2. Anindita Ghosh, "An Uncertain 'Coming of the Book': Early Print Cultures in Colonial India," *Book History* 6 (2003): 23–55; Priya Joshi, "Culture and Consumption: Fiction, the Reading Public, and the British Novel in Colonial India," *Book History* 1 (1998): 196–220.

Even though this "cultural turn" has been strongly resisted by some historians wedded to older economistic Marxist traditions of analysis and rejected by imperial historians skeptical of postcolonial theory, there is no doubt that a new vision of colonialism as a cultural project has crystallized. "Knowledge" has emerged as a key problematic for historians of empire, and much recent work has focused on the construction of colonial knowledge and the role of knowledge production in the creation and projection of colonial authority. Because printing was central to the working of modern colonial states, and because it stands at the junction of several key fields of historical analysis — the history of technology, economic history, religious and intellectual history, and the history of the modern state itself — it has become an important point of debate in the scholarship on modern empire building.

Where Elizabeth Eisenstein's substantial body of research has been concerned with the rise of the printing press and an attendant "print culture" that transformed "Western Civilization," this essay moves beyond early modern Europe to offer a thumbnail sketch of the place of print in an age of rapid empire-building, where the printing press (and its agents) became a crucial instrument for colonial administrators, missionaries, and social reformers, indigenous leaders and pioneering nationalists, and the members of international scientific, humanitarian, and political communities. From the 1760s, which witnessed a new imperial thrust by Britain as its Atlantic empire was plunged into crisis and its ongoing conflict with France became a global war, print culture was crucial in shaping the cultural projects of colonialism in the vast parts of Africa, Asia, and the Pacific newly opened to tentacles of European imperialism — both formal and informal.[3] European print culture, the product of the "long revolution" surveyed in Eisenstein's *The Printing Press as an Agent of Change* (*PPAC*), was not simply exported to these societies but was contested and reworked in each colonial context, assuming a specific position in the various forms of colonial modernity that emerged during the long nineteenth century. By examining the impact of print in the lands incorporated into the British Empire from the mid eighteenth century, the main body of this essay maps the role of printing in the development of colonial regimes, its function as an integrative force within the empire, and the ways in which various colonized groups engaged with the printing press. It then brings this material to bear on recent debates over Eisenstein's work,

---

3. On the significance of this period, see Tony Ballantyne, "Empire, Knowledge, and Culture: From Proto-Globalization to Modern Globalization," in *Globalization in World History*, ed. A. G. Hopkins (New York: W.W. Norton, 2002), 117–20; and C. A. Bayly, "The First Age of Global Imperialism, c. 1760–1830," *Journal of Imperial and Commonwealth History* 26.2 (1998): 28–47.

in particular the revolutionary impact of print and its ability to standardize and preserve texts, suggesting that print was in fact a powerful and often revolutionary force within colonial contexts. The essay concludes by arguing that print in non-European and colonized societies poses a profound challenge for work that sees printing as essentially European, or that uses Europe as the normative case for understanding the impact of print.

It is important to begin by underscoring that Eisenstein's vision of the history of printing is grounded in a belief that print played a primary role in the creation of modern "Western Civilization" and, as such, the narratives she has produced are fundamentally European in their orientation. Recent work on the history of printing and the book in Europe has sought to add nuance to the grand vision of *PPAC*, noting complex regional divergences, significant cultural patterns, and the differential significance of print for various fields of learning. Once our focus shifts outside Europe to examine the interconnections between the history of printing and imperialism, we have to grapple with an even more complicated story, one that resists easy generalizations and grand narratives. Not only are we confronted by the introduction of printing into a bewildering array of social structures and linguistic contexts (ranging from the host of nonliterate languages of Aboriginal Australia to China, which had a rich literary culture and its own tradition of printing that long predated Gutenberg) but we are also grappling with the transformative power of colonialism itself, a powerful complex of processes and social relationships that enacted momentous change.

Historians of imperialism who examine the history of printing and the development of colonial print cultures, therefore, have to assess the ways in which the precolonial linguistic history, the sociology of precolonial communication systems, literacy, and education, and the orthographic conventions of very different languages mediated the relationships between print and imperialism and molded resulting patterns of social change. These factors mean that the impact of Gutenberg's printing press appears very different if viewed from China[4] (as Kai-wing Chow makes clear elsewhere in this volume), the Islamic world surveyed by Geoffrey Roper, or, even more starkly, from nonliterate cultures, like the Maori communities examined in Jane McRae's essay, who were first exposed to books and printing during their first encounters with Europeans, and whose access to these technologies and skills occurred within

---

4. An interesting study of Chinese printing that engages with Eisenstein's work and explores both parallels and divergences between Chinese and European printing is Catherine M. Bell, "'A Precious Raft to Save the World': The Interaction of Scriptural Traditions and Printing in a Chinese Morality Book," *Late Imperial China* 17.1 (1996): 158–200, part of a special issue titled "Publishing and the Print Culture in Late Imperial China."

the unequal political relationships of colonialism. It is beyond the scope of this brief essay to offer any systematic summation of the interrelationship between print and imperialism, even within the British Empire during the long nineteenth century (1780–1914). But we can at least make two important observations that might be the basis for a broader synthesis that charts the relationships between print and British imperialism.

First, printing assumed a very important position both in the internal development of individual colonies and, more generally, in the operation of the larger imperial system. Recent scholarship on colonial encounters in Africa, South Asia, and the Pacific has stressed that the "textualization" of indigenous cultures was a crucial foundation of colonial rule in many if not all colonial contexts (in the Malay world, for example, colonial knowledge-gathering foundered from around 1820 to 1890).[5] While the creation of the archival basis of colonial rule depended on a host of processes that allowed colonial states to gather knowledge from a wide range of sources (from monumental remains to oral narratives and, where colonial rule encountered literate cultures, various forms of written records), printing was crucial to systematization and dissemination of colonial knowledge. This process of collecting and codifying local knowledge traditions typically culminated in the publication of edited texts, district gazetteers, settlement reports, censuses, government proceedings, and historical or ethnographic accounts of the "natives." These printed texts were the very basis of the day-to-day operation of colonial rule, but the processes by which they were created profoundly altered the knowledge they recorded, disembodying these traditions, wrenching them free of the traditional social contexts of knowledge transmission to revalue them as an aid to the operation of imperial authority. Colonial states also sponsored the production of a wide range of textbooks, moral tracts, and "improving literature" designed to inculcate the value of domesticity, work, Western learning, and science. Anxieties over the efficacy of these measures and fears of cultural backsliding meant that colonial regimes also policed the operation of presses controlled by colonized peoples. Even though many missionaries, orientalists, and proponents of "useful knowledge" believed that print was a crucial bridge between European and non-European knowledge traditions, indigenous printing was frequently feared as an agent of obscenity, resistance, and rebellion. Robert Darnton has recently suggested, for example, that after 1857–8 the British in India constructed a new regime of surveillance as they attempted to "catalogue everything" in South Asia, an enormous

---

5. On the Malay world, see T. N. Harper, "Globalism and the Pursuit of Authenticity: The Making of a Diasporic Public Sphere," *Sojourn: Journal of Social Issues in Southeast Asia* 12.2 (October 1997): 261–92.

exercise of imperial power that "depended on modern modes of information gathering—that is, on an endless flow of words on paper" and the careful monitoring of the books produced by and for Indians.[6]

These printed forms of colonial knowledge were central to the political systems and cultural life of the empire as a whole. Printed texts—whether newspapers, government records, anthropological and historical texts, religious literature, and nationalist tracts—were mobile and were exchanged widely within the empire, forming a crucial element in the construction of what Mrinalini Sinha has identified as the "imperial social formation," or what C. A. Bayly has termed the empire's "extended political arena," or what I have conceived as the "webs of empire."[7] The circulation of government reports, scientific texts, and periodical articles between colonies informed many policy-making decisions, including the formation of revenue-extraction regimes, the institution of measures to control nonwhite immigration, and the creation of forestry policy.[8] Many colonial officials, most notably Sir George Grey, accumulated vast libraries in the belief that large collections of manuscripts, periodicals, and books could simultaneously function as an aid to the colonial administrator and as a civilizing influence on future colonial generations.[9] Periodicals and pamphlets—which frequently distilled news and journalistic accounts from many far-flung points in the empire into a single text—were important educational and propaganda tools for missionary organizations, social reform movements, and feminist groups.[10] Learned institutions and philosophical societies across the empire depended on exchange policies and the global book trade to build up their libraries

6. Darnton, "Literary Surveillance in the British Raj: The Contradictions of Liberal Imperialism," *Book History* 4 (2001): 138. Also see Norman G. Barrier, "The Literature of Confrontation: An Introduction to Banned Publications in British Punjab," *Indian Archives* 21.1 (1972): 9–32; and Charu Gupta, "'Dirty' Hindi Literature: Contests about Obscenity in Late Colonial North India," *South Asia Research* 20.2 (2000): 89–118.

7. Sinha, *Colonial Masculinity: The "Manly Englishman" and the "Effeminate Bengali" in the Late Nineteenth Century* (Manchester: Manchester Univ. Press, 1995); Bayly, "Informing Empire and Nation: Publicity, Propaganda and the Press 1880–1920," in *Information, Media and Power through the Ages*, ed. Hiram Morgan (Dublin: Univ. College Dublin Press, 2001), 179; Tony Ballantyne, *Orientalism and Race: Aryanism in the British Empire* (Houndmills, Basingstoke, Hants.; New York: Palgrave, 2002).

8. For example, S. B. Cook, *Imperial Affinities: Nineteenth-Century Analogies and Exchanges between India and Ireland* (New Delhi; Newbury Park, CA: Sage, 1993); and Radhika Viyas Mongia, "Race, Nationality, Mobility: A History of the Passport," in *After the Imperial Turn: Thinking with and through the Nation*, ed. Antoinette M. Burton (Durham, NC: Duke Univ. Press, 2003).

9. Donald Kerr, "Xhosa Bibles and Black Letter Books: Sir George Grey's Book Collecting Activities in South Africa," *Bulletin du bibliophile* 3.1 (2003): 23–62.

10. Tony Ballantyne, "Print, Politics, and Protestantism: New Zealand, 1769–1860," in Morgan, *Information, Media, and Power through the Ages*, 152–79.

and to enable the comparative research that was at the heart of early colonial anthropology, while they raised crucial funds by selling journals internationally. Conversely, these "horizontal" connections between colonies were also crucial in nurturing anticolonial movements and nationalist ideologies. While Benedict Anderson demonstrated the fundamental role played by print, especially in the form of newspapers, in the "imagined communities" fashioned by anticolonial nationalists, the intricate transnational networks of information exchange and political connection that linked colonial nationalists are only just being brought into focus.[11] We are now aware that printing was crucial in fashioning the Buddhist and Theosophical networks that energized nationalism around the Indian Ocean, in drawing together both Egyptian and Irish nationalists with their Indian counterparts, and in providing Maori prophets and political leaders with a potent range of international examples, from the Indian rebellion of 1857–8 to the Haitian slave revolt.[12]

Second, if we focus on the role of print in transforming indigenous mentalities, we can note the divergent cultural responses to print, the different speed with which different colonized societies adopted the new technology, and the diverse ends to which they harnessed printing. Printing with movable type had limited impact in East Asia during the nineteenth century not only because significant portions of the region successfully resisted or contained European incursions but because they were "inoculated" against the new technology by a lengthy pre-existing tradition of printing and the continued technological superiority of traditional block printing for producing Chinese, Korean, and Japanese characters. Muslims, however, expressed far greater anxiety over the impact of printing. Recent research has made it clear that the technical problems posed by cursive scripts do not account for the slow adoption of printing within the Islamic world but rather reflect a powerful set of assumptions about the proper way in which valuable knowledge should be communicated. Although some Muslims within Europe and non-Muslims living within the *dar-al islam* (the Islamic lands) during the sixteenth century

---

11. Benedict R. Anderson, *Imagined Communities: Reflections on the Origin and Spread of Nationalism* (London: Verso, 1983).

12. For example, C. A. Bayly, "Ireland, India, and the Empire, 1780–1914," *Transactions of the Royal Historical Society,* ser. 6, 10 (2000): 377–97; Mark Frost, "'Wider Opportunities': Religious Revival, Nationalist Awakening and the Global Dimension in Colombo, 1870–1920," *Modern Asian Studies* 36.4 (2002): 937–67; Lachlan Paterson, "Haiti and the Maori King Movement," *History Now* 8.1 (2002): 18–22; and Lachlan Paterson, "Kiri Mā, Kiri Mangu: The Terminology of Race and Civilisation in the Mid-Nineteenth-Century Maori-Language Newspapers," in *Rere atu, taku manu! Discovering History, Language and Politics in the Maori-Language Newspapers,* ed. Jenifer Curnow, Ngapare Hopa, and Jane McRae (Auckland, NZ: Auckland Univ. Press, 2002), 78–97.

employed print, the new technology was not in wide use before 1850. The delay in the adoption of printing was, at least to a large degree, the result of the belief that printing challenged traditional systems of Islamic learning grounded in the memorization and oral recitation of the Qur'an and the person-to-person transmission of authoritative knowledge. Traditions of learning within the *dar-al islam* privileged the spoken word over the written, reflecting the belief that information and arguments were best derived from words spoken by the actual author or, if that was not possible, from a teacher whose *isnad* (chain of transmission from the original author) was reliable. Within this context, the vernacularizing and potentially democratizing consequences of printing were not valued in the same way as they were in Europe, and, in many instances, Muslims believed that printing "struck right at the heart of Islamic authority." [13]

Thus, in those parts of North Africa, Turkey, and Iran where Muslim political authority remained firm despite European imperial ambitions, print had comparatively limited influence until the close of the nineteenth century, when it took on a new significance amid widespread anxiety about the new wave of European imperialism. [14] Conversely, within those parts of the Islamic world that were colonized, such as South Asia, the technology of printing was adopted earlier and with greater enthusiasm. Established Muslim scribes found employment in and around the seats of colonial power and quickly discovered that their lithographic and publishing skills had significant commercial and political value. Not only was there money to be made in printing government notices and textbooks, but the colonial state's concern with "native opinion" and its attempts to define the boundaries and histories of colonized groups created a political context where print was a crucial tool for articulating both group identity and political interest. Not surprisingly, by the 1830s, publishers in South Asia discussed lithographic techniques to print Muslim newspapers that reached large audiences, and, after the rebellion of 1857–8, Muslim religious literature (including Persian and Urdu translations of the Qur'an), social commentary, and political tracts proliferated at great speed. But even as South Asian Muslims responded to the cultural challenge of colonialism, the products of Muslim-run presses remained heavily inflected by the idioms and concerns of long-established literary forms, from the lives of Sufi saints and revered teachers, to the *akhbarat* (newsletter) and the *ghazal*

---

13. Francis Robinson, "Technology and Religious Change: Islam and the Impact of Print," *Modern Asian Studies* 27.1 (1993): 239.

14. Serif Mardin, *Religion and Social Change in Modern Turkey: The Case of Bediuzzaman Said Nursi* (Albany: State Univ. of New York Press, 1989), 120; Adeeb Khalid, "Ottoman Islamism between the Ümmet and the Nation," *Archivum Ottomanicum* 19 (2001): 197–211.

(short Urdu verses).[15] By the close of the nineteenth century, South Asian Muslims had harnessed the press as a crucial tool for efforts aimed to "uplift" their community and had joined their Sikh, Hindu, and Christian neighbors in South Asia in fierce debates over community boundaries and the results of colonial policy.[16]

We can find similar divergences between the responses to print in nonliterate cultures. Very few Aboriginal Australians exhibited any sustained interest in printing and literacy before the 1930s, while across Polynesia, literacy had became a highly valued skill by the 1840s.[17] During the nineteenth century, Polynesian political systems, social structures, and mentalities underwent significant change as the region was opened up by trans-Pacific commercial networks, became an important site for European missionary efforts, and was incorporated into European imperial systems. Within this new context, the printed word was central to the religious and political lives of Polynesians, and literacy became an increasingly important skill for indigenous leaders.[18] Even as they struggled against the increasing disparities of power that characterized colonial New Zealand, Maori leaders and communities contested many of the political transformations that faced them after the signing of the Treaty of Waitangi in 1840, and found ingenious ways of using print to serve their interests, meet their spiritual needs, and forward their political aspirations. Most important, print and the Bible provided successive generations of Maori leaders with new skills and knowledge that could be turned against *Pakeha* (white settlers).[19] The radical potential of the Bible, particularly when wrenched free of missionary control, was clear; as one Maori bluntly stated in 1843, "This is my weapon, the white man's book."[20]

Even this cursory survey suggests that work on the intersection between printing and imperialism might help enrich and reorient much of the recent work on the history of printing in the "West." Certainly the very different

15. Bayly, *Empire and Information*, 240–3.

16. For example, Azra Asghar Ali, "The Emergence of Reformist Literature about Indian Muslim Women in Urdu Language (1857–1910)," *Pakistan Journal of History and Culture* 19.2 (1998): 27–41; and Kenneth W. Jones, ed., *Religious Controversy in British India: Dialogues in South Asian Languages* (Albany: State Univ. of New York Press, 1992).

17. G. S. Parsonson, "The Literate Revolution in Polynesia," *Journal of Pacific History* 2 (1967): 39–57.

18. Lyndsay Head and Buddy Mikaere, "Was 19th-Century Maori Society Literate?" *Archifacts* 2 (1988): 17–20; Ballantyne, "Print, Politics, and Protestantism."

19. *Pakeha* is the Maori word commonly used by New Zealanders to designate the non-Maori population, particularly people of European descent.

20. Cited in Peter Lineham, "'This Is My Weapon': Maori Response to the Bible," in *Mission and Moko: Aspects of the Work of the Church Missionary Society in New Zealand, 1814–1882,* ed. Robert Glen (Christchurch, NZ: Latimer Fellowship of New Zealand, 1992), 178.

responses to print recounted might bear directly on any discussions of the extent to which the printing press as a technology had an innate "revolutionary" quality. To date, the debates over the printing press's evolutionary or revolutionary impact among historians of printing have been largely focused on Europe or have taken Europe as the normative test case for assessing the cultural effects of print culture. By seeing these histories of print and colonialism as significant, in terms of both world history and the history of the book, print culture can no longer be only foundational to the emergence of early modern Europe (through the Renaissance-Reformation-Scientific Revolution) but is reframed in such a way that it is entangled with the rapid transformation of a host of cultures through the violence of colonialism and upheaval of conversion. In other words, if we take the role of print in colonialism seriously, we must question the tendency to see the "nature of the book" within the narrow frame of Europe or, more narrowly still, seventeenth-century Britain (in the manner of Eisenstein's critic Adrian Johns).[21]

Moreover, histories of print and colonialism may offer important insights into the debates over the standardization and preservation of texts in an age of print, or what Adrian Johns has framed as the "fixity" of texts.[22] Johns's argument in *The Nature of the Book* that the printing press did not result in a shift to textual standardization, as piracy and plagiarism created widespread anxiety about the reliability of printed texts,[23] hinges on an assumed cultural backdrop of a long-established and stable scribal culture. But if our cultural backdrop is not literate or host to an established scribal tradition, it is harder to discount the standardizing effects of print, even across widely differing social contexts. Eisenstein has also pointed out that Johns's work effaces the preservative role of print, an omission that seems all the more striking for a historian of colonialism.[24] There is no doubt that colonial administrators attached great importance to the ability of print culture to preserve valuable oral traditions and record local knowledge traditions, making the "native mind" legible and providing a secure basis for the operation of colonial authority. But in many instances, colonized peoples embraced the printed word's ability to preserve "tradition" through the recording of genealogies, the documentation of oral traditions, and the production of caste and tribal histories. These texts allowed colonized groups to record their understandings of the past and to articulate their vision of the future. In many cases, we should see this response to colonialism not as conservative or reactive but

---

21. Johns, *The Nature of the Book: Print and Knowledge in the Making* (Chicago: Univ. of Chicago Press, 1998).

22. Eisenstein, "Unacknowledged Revolution Revisited," 91–2.

23. Johns, *Nature of the Book*, 371.

24. Eisenstein, "Unacknowledged Revolution Revisited," 91.

rather as a creative and powerful response that turned the colonial state's fetishization of documents and history against itself.

THUS, within power-saturated colonial encounters, printing assumed great significance not only because it was a technology that was identified as an important marker of European power and modernity but because it had the power to recast the economic, social, and political relationships that conditioned the ways in which colonizer and colonized made sense of their place in the world. One of the implications of this essay, then, is that the "European" and "non-European" histories of the book and print culture need to be brought more firmly into dialogue. In studying the history of the book in colonized societies—whether settler colonies, plantation colonies, military-garrison colonies, or zones of informal imperialism—we can not simply transplant European models in an unproblematic manner to the colonized world. Beyond Europe, we encounter a plethora of languages, a host of manuscript traditions, a wide range of "information orders" that depart from the European patterns that are all too frequently seen as normative. Reflecting on print outside Europe, specifically in China between the Song and Qing dynasties, Roger Chartier has observed that these histories necessitate a "more careful evaluation of the importance of Gutenberg's invention," one that interrogates the unquestioned superiority attached to movable type (as opposed to the use of engraved wooden blocks that were the basis of early printing in East Asia) and the relationship between printing and what Chartier terms "textual culture."[25] By examining the history of printing outside Europe, we might find new perspectives that unsettle European narratives and also recognize the connectedness of the European and non-European histories. Empires brought previously distant lands and unconnected cultures into contact, forcing them into a highly uneven but integrative system that created new forms of cultural interdependence and exchange. In the light of this cultural enmeshment, one of the key thrusts of the "new imperial history" has been to undercut the rigid division between "European" and "colonial" histories in an age of imperialism, revealing the interconnectedness of these histories, and the constitutive role of empire-building in the creation of European culture itself.

I believe that these perspectives can offer a great deal to the histories of printing and print culture. At a moment when "studies in print culture are taking a more skeptical and self-critical turn,"[26] it seems striking that this

---

25. Roger Chartier, "Gutenberg Revisited from the East," trans. Jill A. Friedman, *Late Imperial China* 17.1 (1996): 1, 2, 4.

26. Nicholas Hudson, "Challenging Eisenstein: Recent Studies in Print Culture," *Eighteenth-Century Life* 26.2 (2002): 94.

turn remains largely restricted to studies of the book in the "West." Any survey of recent monographs, journal articles, and methodological essays on book history suggests that the field remains dominated by work on Europe and North America,[27] and, beyond some pioneering work in South Asia and D. F. McKenzie's much-cited essay on the Treaty of Waitangi,[28] historians of the book have been reluctant to grapple with printing and colonialism, or the place of books in imperial systems. Most of the work bearing on these issues has been produced by historians of empire interested in the history of communication and the development of "colonial knowledge" rather than by historians of the book. These two fields—the history of the book and the history of empires—need to be brought more firmly into dialogue. Such a truly two-sided conversation will allow historians of the book in the "West" to recognize that their "European" or "American" stories occurred within a cultural milieu profoundly shaped by empire-building and might also enable ideas, approaches, and theoretical questions to move from non-European contexts to Europe, reversing the well-worn track of frameworks exported form Europe to Africa, Asia, and the Pacific. So while the key questions about the interrelationships between technology and cultural change that Elizabeth Eisenstein explores in the *PPAC* remain highly relevant, historians need to pursue these questions with an awareness of the broad frameworks of world history and a sensitivity to the fundamental role of imperialism in fashioning the modern world.

---

27. In addition to Hudson's review essay, see Jared Jenisch, "The History of the Book: Introduction, Overview, Apologia," *Portal: Libraries and the Academy* 3.2 (2003): 229–39.

28. McKenzie, *Oral Culture, Literacy, and Print in Early New Zealand: The Treaty of Waitangi* (Wellington, NZ: Victoria University Press with the Alexander Turnbull Library Endowment Trust, 1985).

Chapter 17

The Laser Printer as an Agent of Change

Fixity and Fluxion in the Digital Age

BARBARA A. BRANNON

I TEACH the booksmiths of the coming generation in a laboratory space converted from the hard sciences to the pursuit of publishing. In this brick-walled room of tall windows and durable black countertops, gooseneck faucets, and disengaged gas-jet fittings, there is an apt melding of old and new, art and science, alchemy and craft. Books are made here: they are conceived, edited, set in type, paginated, reproduced, and bound. But nowhere in the studio is there a drop of ink to be found. There is no smell of solvent. No clink and clatter of metal types. Not even the reassuring music of a printing press.

My university undergraduates understand (at least they do if they have paid attention in class) what the historian Elisabeth Eisenstein cogently argued twenty-five years ago, before most of them were born: that print revolutionized the world.[1] By changing the ways in which books were produced, print created the very notion of science; it changed the way humankind conceived of politics, of religion, of philosophy, of knowledge itself. This they grasp even though print means something entirely different to them than it did in the mid fifteenth century, and fixity is an unnatural concept in their environment of fluid electronic Internet resources, online library catalogs, e-mail attachments, Web logs, and media downloads.

To these children of the digital age, "print" is the verb for the end process, the output, of their computers. Digital computers are their printing presses, their composing sticks, their type foundries, their wood blocks and engrav-

This essay was first presented as a paper at the 2001 conference of SHARP, the Society for the History of Authorship, Reading and Publishing, in Williamsburg, VA. A version of that talk that subsequently appeared in *Publishing Research Quarterly* 17.4 (2002): 3–8 has been revised and expanded here; I wish to thank *Publishing Research Quarterly* for allowing the original essay to be modified for the present collection.

1. Eisenstein, *PPAC.*

ing plates. These students inhabit a paradigm shift, half a millennium after Gutenberg, every bit as radical as that from manuscript to print. The shift to what we now call information technology roughly parallels their lifetimes. What I want to assess, as we close the door on what John Tolva has called the era of "digital incunabula," [2] is how this latest revolution in the history of books began some twenty years ago.

But I return first to Eisenstein, whose pioneering scholarship provides a springboard. In analyzing the effects of the first printing revolution on the world, she described and evaluated the ways in which the shift from manuscript culture to print culture caused—or contributed to—the sweeping intellectual and societal changes that followed. Paramount among these changes, she concluded, was a fixity of texts and knowledge that fueled nothing less than the Reformation and the Scientific Revolution.[3] The faithful replication of identical books, pamphlets, and maps, made possible by movable metal types, allowed wide and speedy dissemination of written ideas and data and created a common platform for the advance of scientific knowledge. The printing press became an agent of change in the right place, at the right time.

It is an understatement to say that the computer, in its time, is just as great an agent of change—this much we know from every aspect of our daily digital lives. Scholars and cultural critics have produced a hefty literature already on the changes wrought by such manifestations as the Internet, hypertext, user interfaces, networking, and electronic publishing, even while they are caught up in the midst of these developments.[4] But what I consider here is

---

2. John Tolva, "The Heresy of Hypertext: Fear and Anxiety in the Late Age of Print" (1995), http://www.ascentstage.com/papers/heresy.html. In a bit of cyber irony, the text of Tolva's original conference paper, widely cited as located at http://www.mindspring.com/~jntolva/heresy.html, is no longer accessible there. Tolva's commentary on his own work is available from his Web log, Ascent Stage, http://www.ascentstage.com.

3. In her chapter titled "Fixity and Cumulative Change," Eisenstein writes, "Of all the new features introduced by the duplicative powers of print, preservation is possibly the most important" (PPAC, 113). Adrian Johns's doubts in The Nature of the Book: Print and Knowledge in the Making (Chicago: Univ. of Chicago Press, 1998) regarding the extent to which texts were actually "fixed" notwithstanding, it is widely recognized that Eisenstein's study was the first to give thorough consideration to the complex factors in the print culture revolution; similarly, as James J. O'Donnell puts it, "No one would disagree that before the relative stability of printing, texts were often disconcertingly labile and unreliable." O'Donnell, Avatars of the Word: From Papyrus to Cyberspace (Cambridge, MA: Harvard Univ. Press, 1998), 44.

4. Many recent thinkers have attempted to isolate social, political, and technological cause-and-effect relationships, especially as the turn of the millennium approached. While the pioneers Marshall McLuhan and Walter Ong laid the theoretical foundations, Neil Postman, Technopoly: The Surrender of Culture to Technology (New York: Knopf, 1992), and Nicholas Negroponte, Being

the effect of computers as the mode of printing: that is, the laser printer as an agent of change.

Why the ubiquitous and utilitarian laser printer, you might ask? Doesn't it play a mere cameo role on a stage crowded by the stars of integrated circuits, transistors, microchips, operating systems, and sophisticated applications? Isn't it the shift to an "information age" in general that has so altered our world? Yes and no. Though the laser printer cannot be solely credited with launching the information age, it was the single invention that transformed several emerging technologies into a new way of thinking about printing, publishing, books, and, ultimately, the ways in which people interact with written language. The laser printer is no more single-handedly responsible for the current information revolution than was any one invention of Gutenberg's day: just as the printing press is commonly used today as a metonymy for the whole of the print culture revolution, the laser printer was the gathering point for a number of associated technologies and is used here as shorthand for the digital revolution. Its introduction marks the release of print from its five-hundred-year-old pattern of relative stability. As Oldrich Standera put it in the 1980s: "The arrival of digital typography represents a landmark in human written communication, and as such it has a profound impact on the human civilization." [5]

The laser printer, invented by IBM in 1975 but adapted for desktop use only in 1984 by Hewlett-Packard, is a useful, tangible milestone to encompass several advances that together, in the mid 1980s, created the endeavor we call desktop publishing. Like the printing press in its day, its success depended on the felicitous intersection of several other inventions: the miniaturization

---

Digital (New York: Knopf, 1995), considered emerging social trends in the 1990s. Paul Levinson surveyed the broad territory of technological change in *The Soft Edge: A Natural History and Future of the Information Revolution* (London and New York: Routledge, 1997); Brian Winston examined a host of inventions in minute detail in *Media Technology and Society: A History: From the Telegraph to the Internet* (London and New York: Routledge, 1998); and Charles T. Meadow wrote at length on changing media in *Ink into Bits: A Web of Converging Media* (Lanham, MD: Scarecrow Press, 1998). Alan C. Purves, *The Web of Text and the Web of God: An Essay on the Third Information Transformation* (New York: Guilford Press, 1998), and O'Donnell, *Avatars of the Word*, see hypertext as the emerging metaphor of communication; James A. Dewar, "The Information Age and the Printing Press: Looking Backward to See Ahead," a Rand Corporation paper (1998), http://www.rand.org/publications/P/P8014/P8014.pdf, points to networking as the defining characteristic of the information age; and Steven Johnson, *Interface Culture: How New Technology Transforms the Way We Create and Communicate* ([San Francisco, CA]: HarperEdge, 1997), considers the user interface as the major transformative factor.

5. Standera, *The Electronic Era of Publishing: An Overview of Concepts, Technologies, and Methods* (New York: Elsevier, 1987), 127. Standera's early survey was one of the first to present such a comprehensive assessment.

of processors to produce the affordable personal computer; the design of the WYSIWYG (what-you-see-is-what-you-get) graphical user interface that allowed the computer operator to view images and proportionally spaced text together onscreen; the concept of the mouse as a pointing device; and the PostScript language, which could tell a laser printer how to render fully scalable characters and pictures using mathematical vectors, or formulas. Until these technologies converged through such commercially viable products as Xerox's Ventura Publisher, Aldus Corporation's PageMaker, Adobe FrameMaker, the Apple Macintosh computer, and, a bit later, the Windows interface, the capability of digitally composing text and images together on a printable page was not widely available. On the brink of 1984, just as in the era of xylographic books that immediately preceded movable type, printers and publishers generally had to resort to a hybrid method of cobbling together clumsily generated text with separately prepared images. The laser printer and its associated developments put the power of easy page makeup and rapid replication into the hands of anyone with a few thousand dollars for hardware and software.[6]

More interesting, I propose, is the shift in the actual technology that made possible the change in technique. It is the fluid, *unfixed* nature of the assembly of tiny dots forming the shape of laser-printed letters that endows this invention with such transformative power. The ability to define the shape of a capital *A,* for instance, as a series of mathematically described paths filled in and converted—rasterized—by PostScript into an arrangement of discrete dots, presenting the illusion of an imprinted letter, allowed for infinite variety in design, size, and placement of typeset text. Moreover, the same mathematical principles for rasterizing character shapes could also be applied to illustrations and photographic images. Arranged within the page layout right alongside the type, nontext matter could be integrated and output with text, the whole represented by such a fine array of black dots on white substrate that it approximated the fidelity of traditional printing methods. The concept of forming the printed image from a series of points was suggested by the halftone method used for photographic reproduction—first developed

---

6. Information on the history of these technologies, here and below, is drawn largely from popular user manuals of the time: Ted Nace and Michael Gardner, *LaserJet Unlimited,* 2nd ed. (Berkeley, CA: Peachpit Press, 1988); and Roger Hart, *Inside the Apple LaserWriter* (Glenview, IL.: Scott, Foresman, 1989). Two later books are quite useful: Alan Freedman, *The Computer Desktop Encyclopedia,* 2nd ed. (New York: Amacom, 1999); and Paul Freiberger and Michael Swaine, *Fire in the Valley: The Making of the Personal Computer* (Berkeley, CA: Osborne/McGraw-Hill, 1984). The best technical guides for layperson or specialist are Frank J. Romano, *Professional Prepress, Printing, and Publishing* (Upper Saddle River, NJ: Prentice Hall, 1998); and William E. Kasdorf, ed., *The Columbia Guide to Digital Publishing* (New York: Columbia Univ. Press, 2003).

by William Henry Fox Talbot in 1852 and commercially implemented in the 1880s. Early attempts at using this approach to produce type were the coarse dot-matrix printer of the 1970s and 1980s, and, in the late 1970s, raster-based photographic typesetting.[7]

The benefits of desktop publishing were quickly realized and commercialized: imagine the possibilities if everyone could indeed be his or her own printer. Five hundred years ago, Eisenstein claims, the invention of rigid metal types helped to stabilize texts, and thus ideas, in the emerging modern world; today, I propose, the unfixing of typography creates an opposite movement, a destabilization of texts. Fluxion, and not fixity, is the salient characteristic of the digital revolution. I choose the archaic "fluxion" deliberately. When Enlightenment mathematicians employed the word to describe the movement that made a line from a point, they prefigured the relationship between the smooth flow of analog measurement and the either/or operations of digital computing. Calculus gave them the ability to see a world of variable curves and continuous lines in the language of specific functions anchored by discrete points. Eisenstein, in her analysis of epistemological changes in the post-Gutenberg world, demonstrated how the stable properties of the printed book allowed thinkers to clearly express, within their pages, emerging scientific certainties. She rightly observed that one of the most important byproducts of printing was what Hugh Kearney described as "the application of mathematics to the problems of the natural world" (*PPAC*, 686).

With that mathematical background in mind, let me bring the discussion back again to the laser printer. The first commercial models—the Xerox 9700, IBM's model 3800, the Siemens ND2—were all mainframe output devices, operating only in the largest and most advanced publishing systems. They supplemented the variety of impact printers that had been devised for the first digital computers, beginning with ABC in 1940 and ENIAC in 1943–5 and later the UNIVAC and the VAX mini-mainframe. These earliest output devices all used fixed-shape slugs to strike paper when moved into proper position—a sort of computer-driven typewriter that differed little in principle from hot-metal typesetting. Likewise, the printers with plastic daisy wheels that were introduced in the 1970s, though they were smaller and faster and provided changeable font wheels, still produced words by impressing inked, raised characters onto paper, just as Gutenberg's press had done.

The laser printer, by contrast, imitated the look of metal type even in

---

7. Matthew G. Kirschenbaum offers an overview of raster and vector technologies, from the history of printmaking to the introduction of the graphical user interface, in "Vector Futures: New Paradigms for Imag(in)ing the Humanities," http://www.otal.umd.edu/~mgk/docs/VectorFutures .pdf.

relatively coarse resolutions by forming type characters from a series of tiny light-generated dots, a raster pattern not unlike sampler embroidery or the pinpoint grid of a television screen. (The term "raster," in fact, first employed in English in the 1930s in relation to the operation of television cathode-ray tubes, is borrowed from the German word for the regular pattern of lines made by a rake.) The 9700 model printer introduced by the Xerox Corporation in 1977 cost $350,000, but it produced seven thousand lines of type per minute. Within six years Canon of Japan had figured out a way to miniaturize the mechanics of the printer engine and produce it on a more affordable scale, and in 1984 Hewlett-Packard brought out the first desktop-sized model, its LaserJet.

The last key refinement came the following year, when Apple Computer teamed up with Adobe Systems to incorporate PostScript, a computer language that describes type characters in terms of mathematical vectors (functions that define the outlines or boundaries of shapes such as letterforms). Fonts were now fully scalable and could be integrated on the same page with graphics. Within just a few years, major manufacturers of such high-end phototypesetting systems as Compugraphic, Linotype-Hell, and AGFA had seen the wave of the future and designed raster-image processing units to feed computer-coded pages into the same photoprocessors that had previously relied on optics to generate "repro" or "cold" type.

It did not take long for the printing and publishing industries to adopt the new technology. Though the first few years of the desktop generation were marked by the growing pains of incompatible software, conflicting digital fonts, limited storage media, and complicated requirements for preparing graphics files, by 1990 digital processing was everywhere. On the high end, at large commercial firms, such as book and magazine publishers, full-service job printers, and metropolitan newspapers, "electronic" became the standard. Overnight, it seemed, such operations had become home to sophisticated electronic prepress departments with designers fluent in PageMaker, Quark XPress, and Photoshop. On the low end, everyone from the smallest mom-and-pop copy shop to the church secretary was theoretically capable of producing readable, professional-looking newsletters, flyers, posters, programs, even whole books, complete with pictures. If large numbers of copies were not required, neither were the services of a job printer or even a photocopier. The power to publish resided right there on each desktop. The person at the keyboard maintained full control over content right up until the moment that the fuser unit in the laser printer solidified the electrically charged grains of toner onto the paper according to the pattern guided by the computer.

The larger intellectual consequences of such freedom and economy might not have been immediately apparent to any but the digerati, but fervent debate soon began to surface in popular cultural commentary. *Disintermediation,* that 1980s buzzword that economists used to describe the death of the middleman, found its way into popular parlance—applied to the very media that were the root of the word. What would happen to the intermediary role of the publisher when self-publishing became so easy?[8] Would knowledge advance more rapidly, or less so, when texts could be quickly designed, reproduced, disseminated, and updated? What about the reliability of texts, in a day when printed information could issue so prolifically from so many sources? And what would happen to the fixed rules of grammar, spelling, and other conventions of language if the collaborative system of publishing were to yield to isolated, idiosyncratic operations?

The virtual, nonprint platform of the Internet raised these questions to the next higher power. And though cyberspace diverges from print in obvious ways, electronic texts nonetheless derive from the same root concepts. Written communication, once freed from the fixed page, blossoms into new modes of expression. Beginning in 1993 with HTML (hypertext markup language, the digital language that makes the Internet widely accessible), readers could browse the World Wide Web for information in a reticulated, nonlinear environment where content formed, disappeared, and reformed as needed. SGML (standard generalized markup language) and XML (extensible markup language) provided powerful tools for structural organization and typecoding of texts, within a flexible architecture that allowed for multipurposing, or preparation of texts for output in many different formats or media, print and nonprint, from a single digital source. Adobe's PDF (portable document format) caught on widely as a vehicle for exchanging formatted documents in fixed or editable form over remote networks. Once again, the advantages of such flexibility were easily grasped: searchability of text; the capability of linking related information; the ability to copy, paste, and edit seamlessly; the ability to output the same data in different forms or in different locations according to particular need. Developments such as print-on-demand, variable-data printing, electronic paper, and direct-to-plate printing emerged rapidly wherever digital technology could be brought to bear on each new market opportunity.

The vocabulary of the new era of digital information flowed intuitively

---

8. The publishing entrepreneur Jason Epstein has become a vocal proponent of a print-on-demand model (see, for instance, his "Reading: The Digital Future," *New York Review of Books,* July 5, 2001, 46–7). William Kasdorf believes that electronic and print-on-demand publishing will prove the salvation of scholarly monographs and will radically affect publishing models in other media (see Kasdorf, *Columbia Guide to Digital Publishing,* chap. 1).

from its analog precedent. Words with concrete and specific meanings were adapted to express the new technology. Return to the verb "print," for example. The word whose Latin roots formerly implied the weight of physical pressure now described the smooth revolution of an electrically charged drum. The same word that meant the action of reproducing a document on a printing press also described the action of producing the camera-ready original from an output device. And what was the "printer," the person or entity doing the reproduction, or the machine that generated the original? Even "original" became harder to define, as every separate copy emanating from the computer, whether printed to paper or written to disk, constituted an identical first-generation rendering[9] — not to mention that "copy" could conversely refer to the raw manuscript from which the type was set. (At one point someone introduced the neologism "mopies" for multiple first-generation copies, but the term never really caught on.) John Tolva points to the confusion of digital "text," with its suitable roots in the Latin noun *textus,* "web" or "weave," but lacking a separate word to distinguish it from its precursor, the printed "text." We have found no term in English for the entity we mean by the collective category of "digital texts" that is as handy and simple as its predecessor "print."

The slipperiness of all these terms underscores the radical shift involved. The revolution's best symbolic representation, however, may be the common dot: the most frequent mark of punctuation in the Internet arsenal and a perfect icon for the digital era because it conjures up not only the fragmentation of virtual "domains" on the Internet but the discrete units, the bitmap, of rasterization. The nonlinearity it embodies is the overarching feature of the digital age: its tendency to form texts, and likewise ideas, that are networked, associative, and parallel — a reticulated assemblage of separate points. If Eisenstein delved into the consequences of fixity at hindsight, we might well connect the dots to the future and examine possible outcomes. Several futurists have posited ideas, and though James Dewar reminds us that "the future of the information age will be dominated by unintended consequences," sufficient consensus exists to recommend their consideration.[10]

How durable are recorded texts, for instance, in an environment that is necessarily unstable? While Eisenstein considered preservation the most important capability of print, today's information technologists are still unsure how to preserve digital texts. Librarians have warned of the dangers inher-

---

9. "Digital is original" is a maxim of the computer age.

10. Dewar, "Information Age," 3. Meadow's list of digital-information characteristics in *Ink into Bits,* chap. 15, while subjective and somewhat random, is particularly thought-provoking; O'Donnell, *Avatars of the Word,* and Johnson, *Interface Culture,* also contribute stimulating ideas.

ent in the ephemerality of digital media—of both the physical instability of the substrate and its electrical charge, and the ever-evolving form of the software, hardware, or media itself. Nicholson Baker's concern for preserving the paper-based libraries of yesterday pales in comparison to worries about how to preserve virtual libraries of today and tomorrow, as problems of "bit rot" and "web rot," host responsibility, and machine dependence emerge as the price we pay for digital power.[11]

The fixed, printed page remains unsurpassed, at this writing, in its accessibility as an interface for the majority of human readers. If digital texts are nearly universally available, they nonetheless require dedicated machines to retrieve and read them, as well as the proper series of connections between source and reading point and the proper formatting for retrieval. Additionally, while no particular skill other than the knowledge of reading is required to use most features of a printed book or paper document, computer-based texts require some level of training to use. At best this situation poses an inconvenience, at worst an insurmountable barrier to human comprehension.

Since its inception print has been considered an art and has provided a medium for creative expression and pleasingly functional design, but users are slower to think of digital texts in quite this way. The aesthetics and ergonomics of digital texts are an area of ongoing exploration. Professional and aesthetic standards have been rapidly emerging, though readers of digital texts have hardly rushed to embrace electronic media as wholeheartedly as their tactile, analog forms—nor have as many readers embraced the digital reading experience overall.

Leaving aside the purely practical benefits and disadvantages of digital communications, even more profound changes may occur in human perception and knowledge. While it is unwise to expect that every outcome of print culture will have its inverse in digital culture, such arguments provide a starting point. We have seen that even as the overall quantity of information has continued to grow, dissemination has often become increasingly fragmented and specialized (analogies exist in the "narrowcasting" of television to a fragmented cable audience, in selective formatting for radio markets, in proliferation of niche-interest magazine titles, and in customization of daily newspaper content to particular market segments).[12] If the flow of texts to readers is

---

11. Nicholson Baker's *Double Fold: Libraries and the Assault on Paper* (New York: Random House, 2001) provoked widespread debate about the disposal of newspapers in hard-copy form by major research libraries.

12. William J. Donnelley targeted the late-twentieth-century television culture that resulted from ubiquitous and lightweight media programming in *The Confetti Generation: How the New Communications Technology Is Fragmenting America* (New York: Holt, 1986); a similar leveling phenomenon may be at work in computer culture as well.

prescreened or is filtered using limited search strategies, how will such ways of encountering information affect ways of knowing? The fragmentation of the postfixity age could lead to isolated perceptions of the universe—as with the old story of the blind men who each described only one portion of the elephant. Or it might instead force a model of networked, nonlinear learning that improves on traditional ways of thinking. It could be argued that online search strategies yield only the precise snippets of data the researcher specifically seeks (amid a barrage of irrelevant results), shackling the serendipity of true discovery. But is it possible, with improved search engines, that such results could begin themselves to uncover unexpected connections? If so, only the process of discovery changes—but its possibilities, its capacities, are ever-present. Likewise, RSS (the trigram is most often expanded as Rich Site Summary, though geek-joke alternatives abound) feeds, customized homepages, and other online syndicating and digesting services might shield viewers from the full range of news and knowledge. Denizens of the digital environment must accept, however, that their information no longer comes exclusively from three network news broadcasts or the daily newspaper of their choice. In exchange, their global range is expanded exponentially, limited only by language and their own speed of comprehension.

How, then, does the reader judge the credibility of disparate information? While Eisenstein argued that increased confidence in scientific fact resulted from the first printing revolution, the instability of the digital environment might, conversely, lead readers to treat information with increased skepticism. The first waves of doubt surfaced early, as it became clear how easy it was to confuse variant versions of word processing files and other digital texts. More vexing problems arose as critics warned users to discern the difference between the "information overload" and useful knowledge, and as teachers warned students against overdependence on Internet sources in their research. As Internet users well know by now, the content of digital sources can change unexpectedly and imperceptibly. Texts may be deliberately or inadvertently modified, with results that, whether salutary or destructive, are not evident to the user of a previous version. Textual corruption has become more rampant now than in any pre-Gutenberg scenario.

A related question concerns the establishment of authority and authenticity in digital texts. It would be supremely naive in the digital age to take mere publication as evidence of reliability—"If you see it in the *Sun,* it's so" will no longer be sufficient validation. As I remind my students, the digital information they used in yesterday's paper may not even exist tomorrow: a Web site may be cited, never again to be sighted, if its links become outdated, its server fails, or its host removes or changes it. Adrian Johns asks us to consider how differently texts might be viewed if they or their creators were not deemed reliable—as with pirated texts or tabloid journalism.[13] A corollary to the print-enabled scientific method proves instructive as well: while conclusions may be drawn from empirical results of a Web search (counting, say, the frequency of "hits" on a certain term), the sources, inevitably, shift, and the experiment cannot be replicated.

Given the increased need to examine the trustworthiness of digital information, one challenge is that in the digital world, the identities of author and publisher cease to matter much, and place of publication becomes completely moot. Moreover, information becomes globalized and homogenized, with English as the lingua franca of the Internet. (Note that Eisenstein attributed a similar phenomenon of linguistic shift to the printing press, though the effect was an inverse of globalization; the rise of print "fixed" the major vernacular languages of a more nationalistic Europe while breaking up a more uniform Latin Christendom.) Ideas and information are reduced to undifferentiated "content."

Where it is necessary to validate the identity of author or reader, digital authentication and encryption schemes may be needed. As digital media make it easy to disguise identity, the validity and value of every discourse must come into question. Anonymity is both empowering and problematic, as evidenced by rampant spam, spoofs, and other virtual imposters, and the very real threat from Internet predators of all stripes. But on the lighter side, I am reminded of a favorite *New Yorker* cartoon, in which one canine at a keyboard slyly tells another, "On the Internet, no one knows you're a dog."

Physical geography and navigation are likewise reformed in the world of digital media. The appearance of texts may be changed on the fly, modified or customized (annotated, revised, enhanced), depending on interaction with the reader, with variable pathways and variable results. Linking capabilities reveal and enable relationships among texts (external hyperlinks) and among sections of the same text (internal hyperlinks).

Post-Gutenberg astronomers compared their discoveries by mapping the heavens on the two-dimensional plane of the printed page. In the digital world, scientists need no longer limit themselves to the print medium. Computers free them to model in three and four dimensions and more and to envision not only spherical bodies but the double helix of DNA, quantum physics, folded space—any concept that requires a complex, shared medium for expression. The illusion of reality becomes ever more convincing. Through

---

13. Johns, *Nature of the Book,* 3–4.

such digital "texts," scientific knowledge is advanced on an unprecedented scale.

If real space is converging and our world and universe are shrinking, so too are our accustomed forms of communication media. In print and nonprint publications, distinctions between aural, visual, and tactile content are being blurred. As multimedia applications for input, recording, storage, and output become more accessible and interchangeable, the idea of what constitutes a printed document becomes fuzzier. Witness e-books and print-on-demand books, Internet magazines, magazines-with-CD, downloadable audiobooks, Web sites with streaming video. Eisenstein described a shift from a hearing culture (which relied on memory and symbol to perpetuate knowledge) to a reading culture (which could apply reason and imagination to the printed corpus of knowledge). In what further, unimagined ways, we must wonder, will a multiperceptual culture disseminate, process, and add to knowledge?

New technologies of information, as Marshall McLuhan observed, imitate existing ones until new paradigms become evident through use. Eisenstein, again citing Kearney, recognized that in the 1450s the technology of printing arose as a way of duplicating the way people wrote (*PPAC* 159); in 1984 and beyond, is it too much to imagine that digital technologies aim to duplicate the way people think? I fully expect that my students, as they continue to explore making books in the digital environment, will discover applications and understand themselves in ways we have not yet thought to consider. A computer is not a brain, of course, as the communications historian Raymond Gozzi reminds us; it is a metaphor for one. The rasterization of text by the laser printer is not an epistemology; but it is an effective metaphor for one, and the extension of this metaphor gives us fresh ways of looking at how we learn.

These days, texts, the ideas they embody, and the vehicles by which they reach us are formed not by sequenced lines of metal type sorts but by the congruence of millions of pinpoints of carbon or light. These points are as numerous and mutable as the stars and planets the Renaissance astronomers first set out to map. And they will guide our human knowledge there.

Chapter 18

The Cultural Consequences of Printing and the Internet

James A. Dewar and Peng Hwa Ang

The primary value of Elizabeth Eisenstein's work is in understanding the cultural consequences of the printing press in late medieval and early modern Europe. But we also found her work useful for thinking about policy related to the Internet in today's world. Policy making, at its best, is more art than science, and policy making under conditions of serious uncertainty is doubly difficult. Such is the situation in policy making for the Internet. Not only is Internet use a new and rapidly changing social phenomenon, but the technology underlying the Internet itself is changing at the speed of Moore's Law,[1] with transmission speed and storage capacity doubling every twelve to eighteen months. Since one of the most reliable approaches to thinking about policy is to look for guidance in historical instances with similarities to the current situation, we turned to Eisenstein's seminal work.

Several observers have seen useful parallels between the Internet and more modern technologies, such as radio, the telephone, television, and the VCR. James Dewar, co-author of this essay, has argued, however, that a better set of parallels is between the Internet and the printing press and his argument relies heavily on Eisenstein's work.[2] Her work contributed most significantly to the literature on the impact of the printing press by implicating it in three of the most far-reaching changes of European history—the Reformation, the Renaissance, and the Scientific Revolution. If the Internet were to have anywhere near the impact the printing press has had, its importance would beggar

---

1. "In 1965 Gordon Moore, the co-founder of Intel, predicted that the number of transistors per square inch on integrated circuits would double every year and this came to be known as 'Moore's Law.' The silicon industry has followed this law and transistors have exponentially decreased in size since the 1970s." Belle Dumé, "Noise Threatens Moore's Law," *News, Physics Web,* December 18, 2002, http://physicsweb.org/articles/news/6/12/11.

2. Dewar, "The Information Age and the Printing Press: Looking Backward to See Ahead," RAND, P-8014, 1998, http://www.rand.org/publications/P/P8014/.

that of its more modern parallels, and devising appropriate policies—even early on—could become crucial. With that in mind, a presentation of the parallels between the Internet and the printing press makes the case for the printing press as a guide to thinking about policy for the Internet and high-lights the importance of Eisenstein's work in that thinking.

Among the important parallels between the printing press in early modern Europe and the Internet, three broad areas are worth discussing in detail: the technological breakthroughs that fueled the impact of the printing press and that is fueling the growing impact of the Internet; the several ways in which printing and Internet technologies enable important changes in the way that people deal with knowledge; and the unintended consequences of each of the technologies.

Technological Breakthroughs in Communications

The printing press enabled the first true one-to-many communications capability in Europe. Before the printing press, if one wanted to communicate the same message to a large number of people, one could gather the people around and make a speech that would then have to be remembered by each attendee. One could also write up a number of copies of the speech and distribute them, but this process was laborious and fraught with the possibility of errors for documents of any length. With the printing press, one could print up hundreds or, eventually, thousands of identical texts and distribute them widely. Much of the impact that Eisenstein claims for the printing press is associated strongly with this one-to-many communications breakthrough.

Until the Internet, there has been no comparable breakthrough in communications capability. Technologies such as radio and television certainly increased the speed and reach and bandwidth of one-to-many communications capabilities and increased (to a few-to-many) the number of people who could distribute messages. The telephone (basically a one-to-one communications medium) significantly increased the number of individuals who could communicate with each other. CB radios provide few-to-few communications capabilities, as did early radios that were both receivers and transmitters. The Internet, however, is the first true many-to-many communications medium (though we prefer to think of it as an any-to-many medium). For the first time, just about anybody can distribute the same message to hundreds or thousands of people, and do so very easily and inexpensively. As overhyped as the Internet often seems to be, there is a fundamental difference about it as a communications medium that has not been seen since the introduction of printing. Since the first expansive one-to-one communications medium (language) helped distinguish humans from apes and the first one-to-many communications medium helped make Europe the first modern society, what impact might the latest fundamental change in that chain (many-to-many) have?

Changes in How Knowledge Is Manipulated

An important aspect of Eisenstein's work is her recognition that the printing press enabled changes in how people manipulated knowledge and that these changes led to important changes in the culture. Whether the changes in how people manipulate knowledge made possible by the Internet will lead to cultural changes similar to those made possible by printing is a separate question, but one whose answer rests on the parallels between the changes enabled by the two technologies.

In the discussion that follows, we examine the following areas: preserving, updating, and disseminating knowledge; retrieving knowledge; owning knowledge; and acquiring knowledge.

Preserving, Updating, and Disseminating Knowledge

In scribal culture, manuscripts were produced laboriously by scribes, with each copy likely to be slightly different from the other copies. Errors in one manuscript were typically propagated to the next copy of that manuscript, and new errors were often added. The knowledge or thought that resided in a manuscript was available to very few to read or to own. As Eisenstein points out, the ability to make hundreds or thousands of identical copies of a text had an enormous effect on the way knowledge was preserved, updated, and disseminated. Thousands of copies of a single printed book virtually ensured its preservation and dissemination. The sheer numbers of books made them much more available to the general public. This increase in the ability to preserve and disseminate knowledge, Eisenstein argues, had a profound impact on the Reformation. Robert Kingdon summarizes her arguments:

> Scholars have long recognized the essential role of the press in spreading Protestant doctrine. Luther himself, in fact, claimed that the invention of printing was a gift from God to reform His church. But Eisenstein argues that print did more than spread the Protestant Reformation: in an important sense, print caused the Reformation. Without access to the printed editions of biblical texts and church fathers, and the worrisome variants on crucial dogmatic issues they contain, Luther might never have been stimulated to develop his revolutionary new theology. And without accessibility to print, Luther might never have spread his ideas not only in the Latin of the scholarly community but also in the vernacular German of the lay community.[3]

---

3. Robert Kingdon, review of *PPAC, Library Quarterly* 50.1 (1980): 140.

Updating the knowledge in books had a more subtle and interesting history. In the early stages, printed books still contained and propagated errors, but their wider availability slowly had a dramatic effect: "A printed book, unlike a handwritten manuscript, was a standardized product, the same in its thousands of copies. It was possible for publishers to solicit corrections and contributions from readers who, from their own experience, would send back a report—and this was common practice."[4] Eisenstein contends that this feedback reversed the slow degradation of recorded thought and ushered in the era of accumulation of thought on which the Scientific Revolution was built: "The advantages of issuing identical images bearing identical labels to scattered observers who could feed back information to publishers enabled astronomers, geographers, botanists and zoologists to expand data pools far beyond all previous limits. . . . The same cumulative cognitive advance which excited cosmological speculation also led to new concepts of knowledge. The closed sphere or single corpus passed down from generation to generation, was replaced by an open-ended investigatory process pressing against ever advancing frontiers."[5] Again, we cannot know the full impact that the Internet will have on preserving, updating, and disseminating knowledge, but we can at least discuss what kinds of changes the Internet enables in those areas. In preserving knowledge, packet switching—the underlying technology of the Internet—was created to allow a network to be less sensitive to the loss of some of its elements. That is, packet switching was created to be able to route around physical trouble in the network. But that same capability enables the Internet to route around intentional trouble, particularly censorship. It is very difficult to control the flow of information on the Internet, making the dissemination of even forbidden material easier than the dissemination of printed materials. In addition, with the increased availability of inexpensive storage devices, the preservation of text, pictures, sound, and moving images is leading to an astonishing accumulation of information, and that accumulation will only accelerate. At the same time, archiving and preserving information in electronic form presents a host of new issues and problems.

A well-documented book can do a creditable job of addressing all the knowledge and thought up to the time of its publication, but it cannot address even the reaction to itself, let alone the thoughts it provokes. Subsequent editions are used to correct this situation but are rarely published less than a year (more commonly three to twelve years for reference works) after the original.

---

4. Eric J. Leed, "Elizabeth Eisenstein's *The Printing Press as an Agent of Change* and the Structure of Communications Revolutions," review of *PPAC, American Journal of Sociology* 88.2 (1982): 421.
5. *PPAC*, 687.

At that point, parts of the first edition are obsolete, but there is no good way to so indicate on a first-edition copy. It is much easier on the Internet to maintain links to any new material that affects digitized knowledge. Links can be added to materials that discuss, attack, correct, or amplify an Internet text. To see how the Internet is affecting the dissemination of knowledge, one has only to consider how fast jokes and computer viruses propagate on the Internet.

Retrieving Knowledge

In the scribal era, the ability to retrieve information was largely dependent on an individual's capabilities of recall. There were numerous mnemonic devices to aid the individual memory. There were authorities available for consultation, but for instant recall, the individual had to rely primarily on his or her own memory. In the move to print culture, the ability to retrieve information took a significant jump.

Eisenstein argues that the printed book brought about many changes that led to a more orderly, systematic approach to the printed word: indexes, title pages, regularly numbered pages, punctuation marks, section breaks, running heads, tables of contents, and the like. All had obvious and subtle effects. Of an introductory "Tabula" that John Rastel provided to his *Great Boke of Statutes 1530–1533,* Eisenstein says, "He was not merely providing a table of contents: he was also offering a systematic review of parliamentary history—the first many readers had ever seen." [6] In addition, bibliographies, book catalogues, and encyclopedias flourished thanks to these systematic changes. These developments, in turn, contributed to the retrieval of and critical reflection on published works and the accumulation of knowledge that characterized particularly the Scientific Revolution. The Internet has taken the retrieval of information one giant step further. With the exponential accumulation of knowledge on the Internet and with search engines, such as Google and Yahoo, the ability to look up and retrieve information already surpasses anything from the print era and increases daily.

Owning Knowledge

Before printing, there was little ownership of intellectual property. The Bible is a classic example. The notion of literary property rights developed after the introduction of the printed book. In fact, the first rights were "privileges" and were granted not to authors but to printers. [7] (See Jean-Dominique Mellot's

---

6. Ibid., 105.
7. Ibid., 120 n. 239.

essay in Chapter 2 on the subject of privileges and the development of counterfeit texts in France.) Preserving intellectual property rights—through both
"privileges" and patents—was a notion that grew out of the one-to-many
power of the printing press. Eisenstein speculates that this pride of authorship
helped fuel the individualism of the Renaissance. She also argues that the title
page had promotional value for both author and printer and that control of
and the requirement for the publicity apparatus gave printers an important
role in the rise of capitalism.

Where books created the need for protecting intellectual property rights,
the Internet is destroying those protections. The ease with which Internet
materials can be retrieved, copied, and altered has caused serious problems
with copyrights. The forefront of this battle is being played out in the music
arena, but it is a battle that will have to be fought eventually over all intellectual property. The Internet may well require us to create a new system of
rights in the same way that the printing press did. As John Perry Barlow has
said about computer software: "Software piracy laws are so practically unen-
forceable and breaking them has become so socially acceptable that only a
thin minority appears compelled . . . to obey them. . . . Whenever there is
such profound divergence between the law and social practice, it is not society
that adapts." [8]

Acquiring Knowledge

One of the immediate and recognizable impacts of the printing press was
on how one learned. In educating the elite in scribal culture, manuscripts
were relatively scarce, learning primarily involved listening (to someone read
a manuscript or give a lecture), and memorization was paramount. Apprenticeship training and memorization—what Eisenstein terms "learning by
doing"—were the primary means of educating the great majority.

The printing press wrought significant changes in this system of learning.
As Eisenstein says: "Possibly no social revolution in European history is as
fundamental as that which saw book learning (previously assigned to old men
and monks) gradually become the focus of daily life during childhood, ado-
lescence and early manhood. . . . As a consumer of printed materials geared
to a sequence of learning stages, the growing child was subjected to a different developmental process than was the medieval apprentice, ploughboy,
novice or page." [9] The structural changes are clear. People shifted from being

---

8. Barlow, "Everything You Know about Intellectual Property Is Wrong," *Wired* 2.3 (March
1994), www.wired.com/wired/archive/2.03/economy.ideas.html.

9. *PPAC*, 432.

listeners to being readers. Such dramatic structural changes should lead to significant societal and cultural changes, but pinning those secondary changes down has been very difficult. Eisenstein found difficulties with the common theories about the social impact of the transition from listening to reading. Nonetheless, it is generally conceded that despite the ambiguity of its effects, this transformation to learning by reading was a fundamental change in a world that was shifting from medieval to modern. Further, despite the invention and widespread use of other potential education-affecting technologies, such as film, radio, and television, formal learning is still largely reading-based today.

Computers, too, have the potential to affect how people acquire knowledge. In the West, computers have inched their way into the curricula from kindergarten to graduate school. Their successes have been modest and their failures legion. Yet, even though we have not seen the full promise of networked computers, there are indications that they will enable a fundamentally different kind of interaction with knowledge.

In combination, full-text search, hypertext, multimedia, and similar technologies provide a capability to acquire knowledge in a way that was unattainable before computers. They provide a user access to knowledge that is multimedia and less sequential than the printed book. These are available on stand-alone computers and not dependent on networks, but a CD-ROM in this context is just a "superbook"—frozen at production. Connecting with the network adds three capabilities: access to a much wider array of knowledge, the potential for access to constantly updated knowledge, and online help. Serious questions asked on today's Internet rarely go unanswered. Consider the autodidact in the world of networked computers. These capabilities open up the possibility of just-in-time learning—having the ability to access information on a topic of immediate concern (the best time for learning) in ways that are self-paced and matched to different learning styles. It is not too far-fetched to talk about the shift from a "reader" of printed knowledge to a much more interactively involved "user" of knowledge, one in collaboration with other users (many-to-many).

Dominant Unintended Consequences

The third area in which Eisenstein's work has helped thinking about Internet policy is in the unintended consequences of printing and Internet technology. Every successful technology has unintended consequences. Sometimes the unintended consequences are an inconvenience—cellular phones have created a tremendous burden on forest rangers because of the number of hikers who call asking for directions or assistance. Sometimes the unintended consequences are more serious — microwave ovens can be fatal for people with heart pacemakers. And sometimes the unintended consequences dominate the intended ones. Edward Tenner, for example, writes of methods for preventing forest fires that have been so effective in preserving dry underbrush that wildfires are now enormous conflagrations, destroying forests that survived lesser fires for centuries.[10] We argue that the printing press belongs in that last class, and we are seeing some provocative, unintended consequences of networking technologies.

Before proceeding, it is worth pausing to discuss why this set of parallels might be important. Suppose that history eventually shows that the printing press and the Internet were similar in producing unintended consequences that dominated the intended ones. How would that affect policy making about the Internet today? Policy making generally involves generating policy options, projecting the intended consequences of each option were it to be implemented, and choosing an option based on its projected consequences. If unintended consequences are likely to dominate intended ones, policy makers lose their ability to accurately project consequences of policy options, and the policy-making paradigm breaks down. This is an oversimplified recitation of the policy-making process, but dominant unintended consequences do have serious implications for policy making. They suggest an entirely different policy-making approach — one that is more incremental, experimental, and adaptive. The Federal Communications Commission (FCC) successfully adopted such an approach in eventually allowing computers to be connected to the telephone system. And that enabled the Internet itself.

Eisenstein does not make much of the dominant unintended consequences, but she is clear about the consequences of the work of Copernicus and Erasmus, noting: "Copernicus . . . was cast in much the same role as was Erasmus who had set out to re-do the work of Saint Jerome. Both men set out to fulfill traditional programs: to emend the Bible and reform the Church; to emend the Almagest and help with calendar reform; but both used means that were untraditional and this propelled their work in an unconventional direction, so that they broke new paths in the very act of seeking to achieve old goals."[11] What can be said of the potential for dominating unintended consequences of the Internet? Again, we are hampered by our lack of historical perspective, but there are some tantalizing hints. Some come from the

---

10. Edward Tenner, *Why Things Bite Back: Technology and the Revenge of Unintended Consequences* (New York: Knopf, 1996).

11. *PPAC,* 693.

Internet technology itself. For example, in its original manifestation as the ARPANET, the Internet was intended as a means to share computer time at remote facilities—if a machine was not going to be in use by its owner, an ARPANET user could connect with that machine and use it. Designers added an electronic mail capability so that people could communicate about computer usage, and the electronic mail capability soon swamped all other uses of the ARPANET.

A more provocative possibility comes from the work of Christopher Kedzie.[12] He has argued that there are causative links between democracy and the many-to-many interconnectivity of the Internet. He shows evidence that dictatorial governments that try to ban the new information technologies to protect their monopoly on power do so at the peril of economic growth. He also shows evidence that governments that allow access to the Internet in order to be connected to the international economic system do so at the risk of losing control of the population. An interesting example is the former Soviet Union, which permitted new information technologies to proliferate for economic reasons and found those technologies played a role in supporting the emergence of democracy.

Eisenstein's work has helped us think about policy making for the Internet both strategically and tactically. Strategically, *PPAC* provides a broad framework in which to think about Internet policy and in which to place new information about the emerging impact of the Internet as it becomes available. Tactically, *PPAC* has helped us think about and argue for policy for specific problems related to the Internet.

Strategic Thinking about Policy

The sheer number of parallels between printing and the Internet as communications media has convinced us that in thinking about policy related to the Internet, the history of the printing press is more useful than more recent developments in communications technology, such as radio, television, and the telephone. But having chosen the printing press and its impact on Europe as an important historical analogy, a careful policy maker might want to "verify" the historical parallels by asking whether the history of the printing press in other parts of the world might amplify or contradict the chosen analogy.

One of the impacts of Eisenstein's seminal work has been to spur investigations of the cultural impact of printing in Asia. Though those investigations

---

12. Kedzie, *Communication and Democracy: Coincident Revolutions and the Emergent Dictator's Dilemma* (Santa Monica, CA: RAND, 1997).

were not as far along as Eisenstein's, there appeared to be sufficient materials to convene a small group of scholars to discuss what could be said of the general cultural impact of printing (to include xylography, or woodblock printing) and how that might relate to policymaking about the Internet.

In October 2000 we hosted experts on the social impact of printing and xylography in China and Korea, experts on the social impact of printing in Europe and the United States, including Eisenstein,[13] and experts on the spread of the Internet. Over two days we addressed several questions related to printing and the Internet:

How did the impact of printing vary by area?

Why did it vary?

What role did policy play in the variations?

What role did the one-to-many capability play?

In what area was the impact "best," in terms of desired outcomes?

What does this say about the potential impact of the Internet and related policy?

The discussions were fascinating and far-ranging. The story of the impact of printing worldwide is still being written, but two days produced some interesting insights.

The biggest question of the sessions was, "If printing leads to such profound changes in societies, why do we see those changes in Europe but not in Asia?" The typical responses to that question referred to the use of ideographs in Asian languages and the effects of governmental control of printing as the major reasons Asia did not see the same effects as Europe, though there were a host of other explanations.

The history of printing in Korea turned out to be the most interesting case. Korea had both *hangul*—a twenty-four-letter phonetic alphabet—and movable metal type in 1443, seven years before Gutenberg's Bible. Even before that, though, printing had had an important effect on Korean society. During the Koryo dynasty (918–1392), the first metal type for printing presses was invented, and it was used to increase literacy and to print the exams for government service that became open to every literate person in Korean soci-

---

13. It is interesting to note that every print scholar at the gathering acknowledged a debt to Eisenstein for opening the field of the social impact of printing to serious study. In addition to Eisenstein, two other contributors to this volume, William Sherman and Kai-wing Chow, participated in the conference. "New Paradigms and Parallels: The Printing Press and the Internet," a conference co-sponsored by RAND and Nanyang Technological University, Santa Monica, CA, October 5–6, 2000, http://www.rand.org/multi/parallels/.

ety. These exams eventually produced a meritocratic (rather than aristocratic) ruling class known as the Sadaebu, or "learned men." This is an astonishing development in Asian society and echoes some of the effects of printing in Europe. That meritocratic society was, unfortunately, short-lived, but its mere existence lends credence to the power of printing to have profound effects on a society.

Lessons for the Internet

Eisenstein's work has illuminated the important role that printing played in the transformations that took place in Europe during the fifteenth, sixteenth, and seventeenth centuries. The history of the social impact of printing in Korea, as well as other parts of Asia, though still in its infancy, is helping us understand better the conditions in Europe (and less in evidence elsewhere) that fueled those transformations. Understanding both the effects that printing had and the conditions that might have hindered or helped produce those effects are important in understanding policy related to the Internet.

We in the West tend to think that the transformations that took place in Europe in the fifteenth and succeeding centuries were salutary. Europe became a modern society and dominated the world scene. When we compare the effects of printing in Asia to those in Europe, we would tend to say that the conditions in late medieval Europe were favorable and led to the positive effects of printing. If we assume that the impact of the Internet will play out as did printing in Europe, we can divide the lessons learned from the history of printing into two groups—those that suggest what we might expect from the Internet and those that suggest what conditions we might want to encourage so positive effects are most likely to occur.[14]

Lesson 1: The full effects of printing were not seen until a century or more after the invention of the printing press. Likewise, even with the increased speed at which societal changes take place today, if the Internet has profound effects on society, those effects are not likely to be seen clearly for decades or more. Furthermore, because Internet technology is still evolving rapidly and is likely to continue to do so for some time to come, speculations about its societal impact carry further uncertainty. Finally, even though technology changes quickly these days, societies are still much slower to change. This, too, argues for tentative, adaptive policies related to the Internet.

---

14. This uncertainty has not kept scholars from speculating. Carl H. Builder, for example, argues that the Internet will significantly decrease the power of the nation-state in favor of the individual. Builder, "Is It a Transition or a Revolution?" *Futures* 25.2 (March 1993): 155–68.

Lesson 2: The potential for profound societal changes argues for exercising care and thought about Internet policies. Relying only on Eisenstein's work, we might conclude that the Internet will lead to profound and positive societal changes. The history of printing in Asia suggests that profound and positive changes are possible, but that the "right" conditions must be present.

One of those necessary conditions seems to be that the government should not have too much control over the Internet. In Asia, the governments kept control of printing, and this policy eventually led to very restrictive uses of or bans on printing. In the Middle East, strong governments outlawed printing until the nineteenth century, and the area suffered serious declines in those centuries. (Geoffrey Roper's essay in Chapter 12 affords a detailed overview of printing in the Islamic world.) In Europe, businessmen controlled printing, making it easier for printing and its effects to spread—and more difficult for governments to control (although they certainly tried). Recall Kedzie's arguments that the Internet puts controlling governments in an untenable position in the modern world.

Lesson 3: Because of the potential for dominating unintended consequences, policy making for the Internet ought to be more adaptive. In the United States, the FCC's handling of policy for connecting computers to the telephone system might be a good example of Internet policy making done right.

Tactical Thinking about Policy

Each of the parallels between the societal and cultural effects of printing and the changes enabled by the Internet can be examined for help in developing policy. For example, in the area of intellectual property, printing changed the prevailing situation and led to the development and codification of intellectual property rights. The Internet is similarly changing the prevailing situation and is upsetting the norms established for printing. The issue of intellectual property rights is hot right now, with much energy being spent on trying to "fix" copyright law to work for Internet technologies and capabilities. Policy-related discussions of intellectual property rights already pay attention to the detailed history of copyrights, and historical analogies are playing an important role. On a more strategic level, history suggests that something entirely new could take the place of copyrights and that this development might take decades to work out. In the meantime, a good deal of money rides on attempts to enforce copyrights within the Internet environment, so the tactical battle is likely to continue raging until the issue is resolved.

In general, the level at which the parallels between specific areas related to printing and Internet technologies are going to be useful for policy making will have to be much deeper than Eisenstein addressed in her work. Nonetheless, her work has pointed to several very useful parallels that such policy makers ignore at their peril.

Epilogue

As the first author of this essay, James Dewar, thought about proper policies for the Internet, he searched for historical analogies that might help him reason about the Internet and its future. Slowly, he winnowed out more modern technologies and began looking more seriously at printing as a potential analogy, narrowing his search to works that describe the impact in terms of the one-to-many dimension that printing brought to communication. The one work that kept recurring in searches and conversations was Eisenstein's work on the printing press as an agent of change in early-modern Europe. Her work became the backbone of a paper that argues for printing as an important analog for thinking about the future of the Internet.

Meanwhile, the second author, Peng Hwa Ang, saw a printing press from the thirteenth century in a museum in Korea and wondered what role censorship might have played in the impact of printing in Korea. When he subsequently came across Dewar's paper, a wider conversation began about what the more global impact of printing might have to say about the future of the Internet. Here, Eisenstein's work was again instrumental in progress because her work had spawned similar efforts to investigate the impact of printing in China, Korea, and Japan.

Finally, a collection of scholars that included Eisenstein herself took a serious look at the impact of printing and how it might help modern policy makers deal with the Internet. Eisenstein's work about a technology and a culture from the fifteenth century came to have an important impact on how two modern policy makers think about a technology and a world five centuries removed from her subject.

Chapter 19

Seeing the World in Print

Robert A. Gross

"So much of what I see reminds me of something I read in a book. . . . Shouldn't it be the other way around?" So Meg Ryan muses wistfully at the opening of the romantic comedy *You've Got Mail* (1998). Ryan plays Kathleen Kelly, owner of an old-fashioned children's bookstore on Manhattan's West Side, whose cozy world is shattered when Fox and Sons, a Borders-style superstore, opens just a few blocks away. The Shop around the Corner is a neighborhood fixture, where Kelly presides as "the Story Lady," reading aloud to children, greeting customers by name, and knowing just which book they would like. But how can she compete against the mammoth intruder, with its discount prices, espresso bar, and lively entertainment? In this battle of David and Goliath, Kelly faces off against her co-star Tom Hanks's Joe Fox, the aggressive scion of the commercial empire, who views business as war and takes no prisoners. It is no contest; despite Kelly's brave fight, the giant wins. The film's more compelling struggle is for the heart, and the fun lies in watching love conquer all.[1]

What brings Kelly and Fox together is a most modern matchmaker: e-mail. Having met in that lounge for lonely souls—the chat room—the two carry on an earnest, affectionate exchange of messages, unaware of each other's real identity. She is "ShopGirl," he "NY152," and the brightest spot of their day is the cheery news from AmericaOnline, "You've Got Mail!" Anonymity is the key to romance. The strangers employ the impersonal instrument of electronic communication to express the authentic feelings of the heart. E-mail proves as vital to courtship as ever were handwritten letters sealed with a kiss. Electronic technology, the high-tech agent of modern commerce, the secret weapon of mass retailing that enables Fox and Sons to crush

---

1. For information and excerpts from the film's dialogue, see http://youvegotmail.warnerbros .com/. Nora Ephron's cinematic indictment of chain bookstores is challenged in a recent essay by Brooke Allen, "Two—Make That Three—Cheers for the Chain Bookstores," *Atlantic Monthly,* July–August 2001, 288.

The Shop around the Corner, is simultaneously a transparent window into the soul.

"You are what you read," Kelly announces early on. On that principle she has run her little store and formed her life. *You've Got Mail* fosters that ideal of reading with a contemporary twist. Kelly, a saint of bookselling, carries the store as a cross, bequeathed by her beloved mother. Her working days are confined to the narrow limits of the shop, her evenings spent with a left-wing newspaper columnist whose hostility to computers—he collects old typewriters—is matched only by his eagerness for publicity. It is a companionable but passionless affair. Not that Joe Fox is doing any better. His longtime lover, a self-absorbed literary agent, pursues dollars as greedily as Joe's father and grandfather, who run the family firm. In the director Nora Ephron's vision, the whole world of print—authorship, journalism, publishing, and bookselling—has been corrupted by money and power. Only Kathleen Kelly and her devoted employees love literature for its own sake. Happily, through the auspices of AmericaOnline, she conveys that faith, Joe returns her sentiments, even reading *Pride and Prejudice* under her tutelage, and they fall in love. As the film brings the two together, reading and experience become one.

With its love of books and transcendent ideal of reading, *You've Got Mail* provides a convenient entryway to a subject that has been engaging scholars on both sides of the Atlantic since David D. Hall announced two decades ago, in an influential lecture that helped to generate the American branch of this international scholarly endeavor, "The history of reading and of readers is central to the history of the book." This was a summons to wide-ranging investigation. Who could read and write in the past? What titles and genres did they choose? What was "the process by which persons responded to a text"? Through such probes, Hall hoped to uncover the uses and meanings of literacy as a central theme in "the history of culture and society."[2] That goal remains, but in its pursuit, our scholarship has recently taken a distinct turn. Few students follow the lead of Kenneth Lockridge and quarry in official records for evidence of popular literacy—though everyone employs his finding that colonial New England achieved the highest rate of male literacy in the early modern world. Researchers are daunted no doubt by the tedious labor involved in counting signatures on wills and deeds and discouraged

---

2. Hall, "On Native Ground: From the History of Printing to the History of the Book," paper presented at the American Antiquarian Society, November 1983, as the inaugural James Russell Wiggins Lecture in the History of the Book in American Culture, and published in *Proceedings of the American Antiquarian Society* 93 (1983): 313–36. It is now available in David D. Hall, *Cultures of Print: Essays in the History of the Book* (Amherst: Univ. of Massachusetts Press, 1996), 30, 34.

even more by the ambiguity of the results. In the early modern world, we have learned, reading and writing were separate skills, and many more people acquired the former than the latter. Nor has the late William Gilmore's approach—surveying the records of book ownership, as indicated in inventories of estates, and charting the popularity of titles and genres—become a necessity of research. Such findings may disclose broad trends, such as the rise of the novel and growing curiosity about the contemporary world. But they are plagued by uncertainty. Private libraries—even a small collection of Bibles, sermons, almanacs, and primers—were the privilege of the propertied. Listed and valued at the time of death, they reveal not what was read in a lifetime but what was preserved in the home. It is no easy task to classify these holdings, characterize their intellectual bent, and identify them with particular social groups. In the final analysis, the fundamental mystery remains. How did people read and "make meaning" from these printed works? [3]

Elizabeth Eisenstein recognized this problem in *The Printing Press as an Agent of Change: Communications and Cultural Transformations in Early-Modern Europe (PPAC)*, only to sidestep it as too hard to handle in the state of knowledge current in 1979. The changes "associated with the consumption of new printed products" are "intangible, indirect," and riddled with uncertainty. Perhaps for that reason, Eisenstein concentrated her mind on the production and dissemination of print, whose broad consequences—extension of communications, proliferation of books, and rationalization of knowledge—have been at the center of historiographical debates over her work. Did printing foster the advance of learning, as she maintains, by generating uniform texts, open to correction and improvement, for a cosmopolitan community of scholars? Or, as her critic Adrian Johns insists, did the press, as conducted by cut-throat capitalists with no compunctions about plagiarizing and pirating, actually undermine the stability and authority of printed knowledge? In this contest of interpretations, the practice of reading has commanded little attention. The leading figures in Eisenstein's account approach books as did

---

3. Lockridge, *Literacy in Colonial New England: An Inquiry into the Social Context of Literacy in the Early Modern West* (New York: W. W. Norton, 1974); R. A. Houston, *Scottish Literacy and the Scottish Identity: Illiteracy and Society in Scotland and Northern England 1600–1800* (Cambridge: Cambridge Univ. Press, 1985), 187–92; Gilmore, *Reading Becomes a Necessity of Life: Material and Cultural Life in Rural New England 1780–1835* (Knoxville: Univ. of Tennessee Press, 1989). To trace the reassessment of quantitative studies of book history, see Hall, "Readers and Reading in America: Historical and Critical Perspectives," in *Cultures of Print*, 169–87; Roger Chartier, "Frenchness in the History of the Book: From the History of Publishing to the History of Reading (1987 Wiggins Lecture)," in *Proceedings of the American Antiquarian Society* 97 (1987): 299–329; James Raven, "New Reading Histories, Print Culture and the Identification of Change: The Case of Eighteenth-Century England," *Social History* 23 (October 1998): 268–87.

the Danish astronomer Tycho Brahe, who pored over texts as intently as he stared at the sky, comparing and contrasting reports with an alert eye for inconsistencies and an indefatigable will to fix precise observations in print. His was an exemplary exercise of critical reason, an instance of the new habit of "learning by reading" made possible by the printing revolution, and akin to Eisenstein's own method in her monumental book. Did others read the same way? The question goes unexplored in Johns's critique. Although he notes that anxiety over reading—notably, a fear of the disorderly passions it could unleash—inspired efforts to establish in England an authoritative realm of print, his interest, like Eisenstein's, centers on the production of knowledge. But how books were manufactured, whether by learned printers or by dishonest businessmen, does not reveal how meaning was made.[4]

Unable to answer that question by quantitative methods, researchers on both sides of the Atlantic have shifted direction. Today, the top agenda is reader response: the direct encounter between person and text. Witness the themes in recent scholarship: the codes and conventions of reading, the relation of author to reader, the personalization of print, reading and writing the self. This preoccupation is shared by specialists in literature and history alike. Among critics, it marks a decisive change in the interpretation of texts. No longer is meaning assumed to inhere in the poem or novel, as constructed by the author and deciphered by the scholar. The current credo is that readers create the text anew, "appropriating" characters, themes, images, phrases to serve their own needs and desires. As literary theory has taught us, language is indeterminate, its meanings multiple, and every effort to render a coherent world in words doomed to failure. In that very fluidity resides the creative force of books. Reading, as Janice Radway construes it, takes place in "a space between, a space neither ordered by the text itself nor controlled by the reader, but one born of that special act of ventriloquism whereby the reader speaks another's words in populated solitude."[5] A similar faith in individual agency animates historians. In the figure of Menocchio, the sixteenth-century Italian miller, Carlo Ginzburg reveals the fertile mind and tenacious character of a humble but uncommon man who fashioned an iconoclastic world-view from wayward reading and defended it fiercely before the Roman Inquisition, at the ultimate cost of his life. So, too, have feminist historians discerned, in diaries

---

4. Eisenstein, *PPAC*, 60, 61; Adrian Johns, *The Nature of the Book: Print and Knowledge in the Making* (Chicago: Univ. of Chicago Press, 1998); Elizabeth L. Eisenstein, "An Unacknowledged Revolution Revisited," and Adrian Johns, "How to Acknowledge a Revolution," in AHR Forum, "How Revolutionary Was the Print Revolution?" *American Historical Review* 107.1 (2002): 84–128.

5. Radway, *A Feeling for Books: The Book-of-the-Month Club, Literary Taste, and Middle-Class Desire* (Chapel Hill: Univ. of North Carolina Press, 1997), 360.

and letters of women readers, private dramas of resistance to patriarchal domination. "Reading provided space—physical, temporal, and psychological—that permitted women to exempt themselves from traditional gender expectations, whether imposed by formal society or by family obligations," Barbara Sicherman writes. "The freedom of imagination women found in books encouraged new self-definitions."[6]

On such presumptions of the "reader's liberty" the French cultural historian Roger Chartier has issued a manifesto for a field. Against the bleak Foucauldian view of individuals dominated by discourse, he sets the lovely metaphor, borrowed from Michel de Certeau, of readers as "poachers," slipping past the border guards of print and foraging freely where they may. "The book always aims at installing an order," but readers always retain the cunning to circumvent and subvert, if not entirely elude, that claim. Whatever its badges of authority—formidable size, lofty language, royal imprimatur—the book still requires the reader "to give it meaning." "This dialectic between imposition and appropriation" is the driving force of book history.[7]

It is tempting to endorse this stance, especially for an American. What better suits our point of view than a progressive insistence on the creativity of the mind and the capacity of people to resist authority?[8] Unwittingly, that outlook can turn history into a Whiggish contest between liberty and power. It assumes the contemporary ideal of reading—the quest for an authentic self through the written word—and projects it back onto the past. It dissolves the cultural meaning of a text or genre into a myriad of individual responses, all "equally plausible"; putting a premium on "fragmentation and interpretative freedom," James A. Secord cautions, this approach risks becoming "a celebration of Victorian values of liberal pluralism."[9] And it never doubts that books and reading are and have always been good things.

That wasn't what the father of cultural critic Sven Birkerts thought when he found the boy lounging with his head in a book. "What are you doing on

6. Ginzburg, *The Cheese and the Worms: The Cosmos of a Sixteenth-Century Miller,* trans. John Tedeschi and Anne Tedeschi (Baltimore, MD: Johns Hopkins Univ. Press, 1980); Robert A. Gross, "Reading Culture, Reading Books," in *Proceedings of the American Antiquarian Society* 106 (April 1996): 59–78.

7. Chartier, *The Order of Books: Readers, Authors and Libraries in Europe between the Fourteenth and Eighteenth Centuries,* trans. Lydia G. Cochrane (Stanford, CA: Stanford Univ. Press, 1994), vii–ix, 2; Michel de Certeau, *The Practice of Everyday Life,* trans. Steven Rendall (Berkeley and Los Angeles: Univ. of California Press, 1984), 165–76.

8. Paul Giles, "Reconstructing American Studies: Transnational Paradoxes, Comparative Perspectives," *Journal of American Studies* 28 (1994): 335, 344.

9. Secord, *Victorian Sensation: The Extraordinary Publication, Reception, and Secret Authorship of Vestiges of the Natural History of Creation* (Chicago: Univ. of Chicago Press, 2000), 521.

the couch in the middle of the day?" he erupted, as Birkerts recalls in *The Gutenberg Elegies,* a lament for a vanishing world of print. Idle reading was equally anathema to the long line of farmers, businessmen, and politicians who have scorned eggheads, exalted the school of hard knocks, and made anti-intellectualism an American tradition. To be sure, these practical men read newspapers omnivorously and consulted guides on how to raise larger crops and build better houses. And like most people today, they readily followed instructions when it served their interests. Who among us wants a user's manual, whether for car, computer, or VCR, open to creative reading?

There are, after all, many kinds of texts, addressed to varied ends, and no single theory can fit them all. "What did individuals read for?" the English historian James Raven asks. "Were they reading to learn and understand? Were they reading to remember something and then apply the skill? Were they reading to gather information or to take a decision? Were they reading, at least apparently, for simple entertainment?" Were they reading, I would add, to identify with elites, to affiliate with "imagined communities," or to adopt the manners and styles necessary for upward mobility? None of these "modalities of reading" need stir contests with authority or foster intense experience. They may, in fact, be the most common encounters we have with print.[10]

Even this pragmatic approach is too simple. It smoothes out the past into a familiar landscape, whose sensible inhabitants are extensions of ourselves. We are thus unprepared to find in the historical record individuals like the young tailor John Dane. Uncertain whether to emigrate from England to America, this future settler of Puritan Massachusetts turned to the Bible to tell his fortune. "I hastily toke up the bybell, and tould my father if whare I opend the bybell thare i met with anie thing eyether to incuredg or discouredg that should settle me. I oping of it, not knowing more then the child in the womb, the first I cast my eye on was: Cum out from among them, touch no unclene thing." On that authority, he booked passage for the New World. And what about the African American freed-woman whom a Scottish traveler encountered in the Reconstruction South? A pious Christian, she could identify only the symbols for Jesus in the Bible, but that was enough. Opening the New Testament at random, she would trace her finger through the scripture, word by word, page by page, until she came upon the sign for her Lord.

---

10. Birkerts, *The Gutenberg Elegies: The Fate of Reading in an Electronic Age* (Boston: Faber and Faber, 1994), 38; Richard Hofstadter, *Anti-Intellectualism in American Life* (New York: Vintage Books, 1963); Raven, "New Reading Histories," 286. For a parallel view of reader reception, see Jonathan Rose, "Rereading the English Common Reader: A Preface to a History of Audiences," *Journal of the History of Ideas* 53 (1992): 47–70.

"'And oh!' she said [according to the traveler], 'how dat name started up like a light in the dark,' and I say, 'Dere's e name of my Jesus!' It was de on'y one word I knew . . . but dat one word made me hunger for more.'" Such incidents reveal the past to be a foreign country, where familiar acts can assume unaccustomed meanings and forms. Robert Darnton has been pressing that insight in his widely read, but little imitated, essays. Reading is "a mystery," he observes. "Both familiar and foreign, it is an activity that we share with our ancestors yet can never be the same as what they experienced." The challenge is to shed "the illusion of stepping outside of time" and to recover the strangeness of the past. "A history of reading, if it can ever be written, would chart the alien element in the way man has made sense of the world." [11]

Seen in this light, the vision of reading in *You've Got Mail* and its nineteenth-century precursors is hardly universal. It constitutes one among many versions that have co-existed, competed, and commingled in American and Western culture from early on and still do. Reading is best seen as a cultural practice, carried out in particular settings and styles, linked to specific groups, and informed with ideological meanings. The challenge for the scholar is to recover such practices in their full richness, to track their trajectories across time and space, and to describe the patterns of continuity and change. A history of reading so conducted "becomes a study of cultural formation in action," to use the apt formulation of Secord. [12] That is a formidable task. Yet, I want to propose we do even more, that we step back and reflect on the conundrum that puzzled the cinematic bookseller Kelly: the relation between reading and experience. To that end, let me suggest a way of thinking about that problem. What does it mean to see the world through print? Reading is, most immediately, an experience in its own right, made accessible as cultural practice. But its impact on personal and collective existence remains unclear. "Books," Ralph Waldo Emerson once suggested, "are for the scholar's idle times. When he can read God directly, the hour is too precious to be wasted in other men's transcripts of their readings." The contemporary Canadian writer Alberto Manguel's mother put the matter more bluntly. "'Go out and live!' [his] mother would say when she saw [him] reading, as if [his] silent

---

11. David D. Hall, *Worlds of Wonder, Days of Judgment: Popular Religious Belief in Early New England* (New York: Alfred A. Knopf, 1989), 26; Grey Gundaker, *Signs of Diaspora, Diaspora of Signs: Literacies, Creolization, and Vernacular Practice in African America* (New York: Oxford Univ. Press, 1998), 141; Robert Darnton, "First Steps Toward a History of Reading," in *The Kiss of Lamourette: Reflections in Cultural History* (New York: W. W. Norton, 1990), 155, and "Readers Respond to Rousseau: The Fabrication of Romantic Sensitivity," in *The Great Cat Massacre and Other Episodes in French Cultural History* (New York: Vintage Books, 1985), 216.

12. Secord, *Victorian Sensation*, 3.

activity contradicted her sense of what it meant to be alive." [13] Such formulations sunder reading from living. That relation, we know, is more complex.
Aid to existence one moment, reading can confuse it the next. Books can
be refuge from life's pain, compensation for its deficits, enhancement of its
pleasure, barrier to its promise, threat to its survival. A history of reading,
then, is not just a chart of reader response. It must encompass both the social
organization of reading, particularly its patterning by race, gender, ethnicity,
and class, and its conduct among varied forms of work and leisure, ritual and
routine, and communication in the past. In that complex configuration, I
propose, lie important clues to the changing character of society and culture.

I can, of course, only illustrate this agenda for research with examples from
the area I know best, the United States. What follows is a short survey of
what I take to be two leading representations of reading in American culture,
which have endured and adapted to changing contexts from colonial times
to the present. When Kathleen Kelly stirred on film with passion for print,
she hardly resembled a seventeenth-century Puritan, certainly not in the figure of Meg Ryan. But the thrill she sought in the written word—rapturous
encounter with other realities, vital communication with other souls—had
its roots in the cultural practice of reading in colonial New England. To the
evangelical Christians who aspired to build a New Israel in the American
wilderness, the Bible, "the book above all books," was the living Word of
God, the utterance of "his own most hallowed lips." In the pages of scripture,
they heard the "voice" of Christ, speaking directly to the hungry soul. As
Saint Paul had assured them, the gospel had been "written not with ink, but
with the Spirit of the living God" and "not in tables of stone, but in fleshly
tables of the heart." Whether preached from the pulpit, written down in
manuscript, or printed in cold type, the holy text was the pure, unmediated
communication of the Holy Spirit. Consequently, Puritans invested the act
of reading with sacred purpose. Approach the text in a devout spirit, the New
England clergy advised; ponder the words slowly and carefully, literally chew
them over, like a cow with its cud, so as to absorb the goodness into the soul.
Underline passages you find "most relish in," or make notes in the margin
"that you may easily, and more quickly find them again." "Once or twice
reading over a booke is not enough." This was the style that has come to be
known to historians as "intensive reading," the reverent return to the same
sacred texts day by day, year by year, over the course of a life. Not just the
Bible but sermons, hymnals, and guides to devotion were treated the same

---

13. Emerson, "The American Scholar," in *Selected Essays,* ed. Larzer Ziff (New York: Penguin,
1982), 89; Manguel, *A History of Reading* (New York: Viking, 1996), 21.

way. As preachers of the Word, Puritan ministers claimed its divine aura for their own works: the Holy Spirit spoke through them. And so, too, might it touch ordinary men and women. Ultimately, reading was but the means to an end: the experience of divine grace. At stake was eternal life.[14]

Every aspect of communication—speaking and hearing, reading and writing—was thus fraught with blessings or perils for the soul. The human tongue could be "exceedingly good" or "excessively evil." Protestant reformers promoted godly speech both at the meetinghouse, where they developed a new style of plain preaching, and in daily life, where they aimed to "govern their tongues." All sorts of talk that enlivened early modern villages and embroiled them in conflict—scolding and libeling, bawdy jokes and blasphemous oaths—were subject to peer pressure and criminal sanction in New England. Puritan eyes as well as ears were shut to profane ballads and lewd jests. "When thou canst read," the Reverend Thomas White advised, "read no Ballads and foolish Books, but the Bible." Not everyone was listening, on either side of the Atlantic. "Alas!" the anonymous author of *The History of Genesis* (1690) lamented, "how often do we see Parents prefer Tom Thumb, Guy of Warwick, Valentine and Orson or some other foolish book, before the Book of Life." Although they never stopped inveighing against such popular tastes, the moral arbiters of New England had no more success keeping such chapbooks and "merriments" out of the region than out of the hands of idle youth.[15]

The sacred use of literacy could, at times, verge on superstition. John Dane, the Puritan emigrant, treated the Bible like a crystal ball. Many used it to pick names for their children. For one trusting soul, it was a talisman against evil. Amid an Indian attack on his village during King Philip's War, he sat in the town common calmly reading the good book—only to become the day's sole casualty. For most Puritans, the Bible was not a magical totem but a tabernacle of the spirit, which they longed to enter, and it was this vision of books and reading they bequeathed to later generations of Americans. The Reverend Cotton Mather, New England's most assiduous author, delighted in giving away copies of his books, and as he did so, he alerted recipients: "Remember, that I am speaking to you, all the while you have the Book before you!" As originating spirit, the author was one with the text, animating its every word. The ideal communication brought two souls together in intimate conversation.[16]

14. Hall, *Worlds of Wonder*, 21–31; Hall, *Cultures of Print*, 64; Jane Kamensky, *Governing the Tongue: The Politics of Speech in Early New England* (New York: Oxford Univ. Press, 1997), 31.

15. Kamensky, *Governing the Tongue*, 3–44; Hall, *Cultures of Print*, 51; Velma Bourgeois Richmond, *The Legend of Guy of Warwick* (New York and London: Garland, 1996), 167.

16. Jill Lepore, "Literacy and Reading in Puritan New England," in *Perspectives in American Book History*, ed. Scott E. Casper, Joanne D. Chaison, and Jeffrey D. Groves (Amherst: Univ. of

On these terms evangelicals have searched for salvation in every wave of revivals in American history. In the middle decades of the nineteenth century, they seized on the latest innovations in printing technology—the steam-powered press, the stereotype plate—to produce Bibles and tracts by the million in a crusade to convert every American to Christ. Armed with these pamphlets, college students traveled country roads to the "darkest corners of the land," peddling the word from door to door, and giving away books as freely as Cotton Mather. These were often the same texts that had circulated in Mather's time: the "steady sellers" of Protestant piety. And they were to be read in the same intensive spirit. "It is not he that reads most, but he that meditates most, that will prove the choicest, sweetest, wisest, and strongest Christian," one missionary newspaper urged in 1851.

Far from expiring in an expansive age of capitalism and democracy, the Puritan vision of literacy endured—contrary to the claim of historians, who have detected a shift from intensive to extensive reading in this era. The colonists, it has been argued, read the same books over and over because they had no choice. In an age of scarcity, books were few and costly. But the publishing revolution of the nineteenth century generated a new world of abundance. With access to a vast array of titles for every taste, Americans cast aside old habits, embraced diversity and choice, and began reading "extensively." The new economy was incompatible with the old piety. Evidently, nobody told the evangelicals. They still read the Bible the old way, even as their presses poured forth cheap tales of Christian conversion. In their view, mass printing was a gift from God—"a spiritual telegraph"—designed for sacred ends. Too often it was misused for base purposes, supplying "infidel" and immoral fare for the sake of commercial profit. But properly conducted, it was a boon to mankind. Thanks to modern technology, the Gospel with its universal promise of salvation could spread all over the globe. The medium was *not* the message. And so it has gone with every major advance in communications since. Radio put revivalism on the air waves; television has brought forth an "electronic church" and a Christian Broadcast Network. And the text of the Bible is available free on the World Wide Web.[17]

The sacred practice of reading left a lasting mark on American literary culture. In the first half of the nineteenth century, the Calvinism of the Puritan

---

Massachusetts Press; Washington, DC: Library of Congress, 2002, 17–46); Hall, *Worlds of Wonder*, 26; Michael D. Warner, *The Letters of the Republic: Publication and the Public Sphere in Eighteenth-Century America* (Cambridge: Cambridge Univ. Press, 1990), 20–22.

    17. David Paul Nord, "Religious Readers and Reading in Antebellum America," *Journal of the Early Republic* 13 (1995): 246, 255; David Edwin Harrell Jr., "Oral Roberts: Religious Media Pioneer," in *Communication and Change in American Religious History*, ed. Leonard I. Sweet (Grand Rapids, MI: William B. Eerdmans, 1993), 320–34.

fathers lost its hold on New England's leading intellectuals. But the ethic of "plain living and high thinking" remained. For all his talk of finding God in nature, Ralph Waldo Emerson, trained as a Unitarian minister, looked to books for intense, spiritual experience, just as his clerical forebears had done. "When the mind is braced by labor and invention," he proclaimed, "the page of whatever book we read becomes luminous with manifold allusion." Instead of salvation, Emerson sought epiphanies in texts: the illumination of truth in one mind by another. His ideal was an intimate exchange between author and reader — exactly what he found in the French essayist Montaigne. "[His] is the language of conversation transferred to a book. Cut these words, and they would bleed; they are vascular and alive." Similarly, Henry David Thoreau converted the act of reading into a strenuous exercise of the spirit. "It requires a training such as the athletes underwent," he declared in *Walden,* "the steady intention almost of the whole life to this object. Books must be read as deliberately and reservedly as they were written." It is tempting to think that such visions were confined to a narrow intelligentsia. Not at all. Young clerks in the countinghouses of Manhattan in the 1840s were eager for cultural experience, albeit on a less exacting plane. Attending lectures, joining in conversation, reading books: in such pastimes, they sought contact with other minds. A satisfying lecture stimulated thought and stirred emotions, a disappointing one lacked "depth and earnestness of feeling." So, too, with a good book, like Longfellow's *Hiawatha,* which one Boston clerk kept with him in a "side pocket," an ever-ready friend. "This little volume has since been a traveling companion with us for many hundred miles," he reported affectionately. "It has been read and re-read — read in silence, read aloud, read to the lady we love, and ladies we do not love." Likewise, the businessmen, professionals, and politicians who patronized the Richmond (Virginia) Library Company in the 1840s and 1850s threw themselves into the works of Walter Scott with the same intensity that evangelicals pored over the Bible and devotional texts. One Waverly novel was seldom enough; readers would go on "binges" with Scott, racing through four or five titles in a row — usually, one a week — and occasionally returning to favorites a few years later. Absorbed in a fictional world that afforded, in one admiring estimation, "all varieties of science, information, profession, and character," they were evidently eager to commune with "the man in the imagination, the cheerful, healthy, vigorous, sympathetic, good-natured and broad-natured Walter Scott himself." [18]

18. Emerson, "American Scholar," 90; Thomas Augst, *The Clerk's Tale: Young Men and Moral Life in Nineteenth-Century America* (Chicago: Univ. of Chicago Press, 2003), 85, 91; Thoreau, *Walden,* ed. William Rossi (New York: W. W. Norton, 1992), 68; Emily B. Todd, "Walter Scott and the

This ideal of "friendly reading," as Barbara Hochman calls it, shaped the conventions of fiction in nineteenth-century America. To read a novel was not just to meet the characters and follow the plot; it was also to converse with the author, as if sitting in a parlor among friends. When modernist writers in the late nineteenth and twentieth centuries refused that relation and withdrew from the text, readers felt betrayed. Fleeing the cold, impersonal world of experimental fiction, they found a warm welcome in the Book-of-the-Month Club, started in 1926. That "middlebrow" enterprise, as Janice Radway portrays it, was dedicated to books that could "capture the regard of readers" and compel their emotions. Its ethos was defined by Henry Canby, the editor and critic who led the selection committee. What he craved in books was "deep reading," total immersion in a text. "Reading for experience," he affirmed, "is the only reading that justifies excitement. . . . [It] is transforming. Neither man nor woman is ever quite the same again after the experience of a book that enters deeply into life." Deep reading was, in fact, a secular conversion experience. In the pages of a book, the reader is born again. Though Canby was choosing texts for the professional middle class in a corporate world, he was carrying on the tradition of Puritan preachers and of New England intellectuals. Appropriately, he wrote a biography of Thoreau. His ideal of reading, Radway tells us, guided Book-of-the-Month Club editors down through the 1980s. And it inspires film characters like Kathleen Kelly in *You've Got Mail* today.[19]

At the opposite pole from the "personalism" of the Book-of-the-Month Club is the style I call "rational reading," a cultural practice with equally deep roots in American life. As an ideal, it developed along with the printing press in early modern Europe. As Eisenstein has shown, early printing houses gathered learned men of diverse nations and faiths — Christians, Jews, Arabs — into cosmopolitan communities, where they collaborated on works of ecumenical scholarship. Though Reformation and Counter-Reformation disrupted such endeavors, that model of cooperation had enormous appeal, and in the eighteenth century, it inspired the conduct of learned culture. Through networks of correspondence that crossed the Atlantic, educated men shared the results of scientific research into the natural world. Their intellectual outlook was empirical; in the advancement of learning, they

Nineteenth-Century American Literary Marketplace: Antebellum Richmond Readers and the Collected Editions of the Waverly Novels," *Papers of the Bibliographical Society of America* 93 (December 1999): 495–517; Nina Baym, *Novels, Readers, and Reviewers: Responses to Fiction in Antebellum America* (Ithaca, NY: Cornell Univ. Press, 1984), 35, 144.

19. Barbara Hochman, *Getting at the Author: Reimagining Books and Reading in the Age of American Realism* (Amherst: Univ. of Massachusetts Press, 2001); Radway, *Feeling for Books*, 294.

pledged allegiance to facts and experiments, not authority and tradition. That commitment nurtured a "cool" sensibility, geared to logic and reason and detached from emotions, especially in religion. The goal of learning was, after all, to be "useful," to improve the condition of mankind. To that end, freedom of inquiry was indispensable. Men of learning required the right to pursue ideas for their own sake, without restraint by state or church. They had the obligation as well to rise above prejudice and assist fellow seekers of truth, whatever their country. All belonged, in principle, to an international Republic of Letters.[20]

For all its claim to be impartial and disinterested, this vision of learned culture had powerful political consequences. It challenged the old order of the eighteenth century with a new model of social organization. In the influential formulation of the German sociologist Jürgen Habermas, it brought into being a critical "public sphere," an autonomous realm, independent of state and church and separate from the household, in which men could share their thoughts about civic affairs. This forum arose in coffeehouses and taverns, in clubs and salons. It took shape as well in print culture, notably, in the newspapers springing up in leading cities throughout the Anglo-American world. As a medium of public debate, the press acquired fresh meaning. No longer would it radiate a personal spirit, human or divine. Rejecting that evangelical view, the champions of the public sphere recast print in impersonal terms. Its cold type carried abstract truth. Detached from specific persons, the newspaper was identified with a general public. In its pages, citizens followed the rule of reason. They discussed principles, not personalities; they forswore self-interest for the common good. Speaking for everyone in general and nobody in particular, the anonymous voice of the press could claim to represent a new force—public opinion—that was constituted in its columns of type. It thus embodied the sovereignty of the people. The republic was born in print.[21]

Such was the vision, according to Michael D. Warner, held by the Patriot elite that led the American Revolution and established a new nation under the Constitution. In its terms, the cultural practice of literacy was remade. In pamphlets and newspapers, critics of the mother country assumed the personae of virtuous statesmen from Greece and Rome and studded their essays with learned references to antiquity. Their duty, as they saw it, was to expose the

---

20. Eisenstein, *PPAC*, 99–101; David D. Hall, "Learned Culture in the Eighteenth Century," in *The Colonial Book in the Atlantic World*, ed. Hugh Amory and David D. Hall, vol. 1 of *A History of the Book in America* (Cambridge: Cambridge Univ. Press, 2000), 415–8.

21. Warner, *Letters of the Republic*, 34–117; Habermas, *The Structural Transformation of the Public Sphere: An Inquiry into a Category of Bourgeois Society*, trans. Thomas Burger (Cambridge: Cambridge Univ. Press, 1989).

danger of imperial measures, to set forth the causes and consequences of the crisis, and to lay out a reasoned plan of resistance. The responsibility of the public was to read and reflect—and ultimately to support the gentlemen who spoke in their name. Fired up by the republican mission, John Adams proclaimed in the *Boston Gazette,* "The people have a right, an indisputable, unalienable, indefeasible divine right to that most dreaded and envied kind of knowledge, I mean of the characters and conduct of their rulers." Let no one dare to take that away. Be not "intimidated . . . from publishing with the utmost freedom, whatever can be warranted by the laws of your country; nor suffer yourselves to be wheedled out of your liberty, by any pretences of politeness, delicacy or decency." [22]

Who read these essays, and in what cultural mode? For all the talk about "critical reason" as the key to the public sphere, we know little about its actual exercise. To judge from the newspapers, a large gap existed between ideals and practice. Initially, the gentlemen who penned the disquisitions on liberty for the press wrote for educated readers like themselves. Presumably, these privileged communications would be passed along to the common people by their "betters." "When I mention the public," the Virginian John Randolph explained in 1774, "I mean to include only the rational part of it. The ignorant vulgar are as unfit to judge of the modes, as they are unable to manage the reins of government." But in the course of the Revolutionary movement, the Patriot elite had to mobilize the lower orders—farmers, mechanics, laborers—for a fight that demanded force and numbers as well as reason. Politics was quickly popularized, with a rapid transformation of public rhetoric. No longer could gentlemen assume with Thomas Jefferson that the audience for their words would be "an assembly of reasonable men." Instead, they had to compete for public favor against upstarts with little education, who did not hesitate to exploit prejudice against "Aristocracy," accuse opponents of self-interest, and employ a fiery, emotional style in debate. Then again the political elite was willing to play the same game to get its way. In the campaign for the Constitution, Federalists jettisoned the ideal of anonymity. They invoked a "spectacle of names," urging voters to follow the lead of Washington and Franklin, and they closed the pages of their newspapers to contributors who declined to reveal their identities. Once their opponents were known to be mere "plowjoggers" and mechanics, Federalists expected,

---

22. Gordon S. Wood, "The Democratization of Mind in the American Revolution," in *Leadership in the American Revolution* (Washington, DC: Library of Congress, 1974), 63–88; John Adams, "A Dissertation on the Canon and the Federal Law" (1765), quoted in Richard D. Brown, *The Strength of a People: The Idea of an Informed Citizenry in America 1650–1870* (Chapel Hill: Univ. of North Carolina Press, 1996), 56–7.

nobody would take their opinions seriously. By the time the Constitution was ratified, the new nation was a far cry from a rational republic.[23]

The ideal of an informed citizenry endured, at least in the political elite. But the republicanism of the founders had to adapt to popular culture, and the result was the mass democracy of the Jacksonian Age. To his everlasting disappointment, Jefferson could not persuade the Virginia legislature to fund his scheme for tax-supported public education for all white men. Nor could George Washington, James Madison, or John Quincy Adams get Congress to establish a national university. The course of American politics would be guided not by an enlightened elite but by professional politicians at the helm of competitive parties. In the heyday of nineteenth-century politics, Democrats got out the vote with huge rallies, torchlight parades, and summons to battle in the party press; Whigs and then Republicans did the same. Nobody tried very hard to win over the other side with rational argument. That notion gained credence in American life, as the sociologist Michael Schudson has argued, only in the Progressive Era, when reformers successfully pressed measures—civil service, the Australian ballot, the referendum—to strengthen the role of the expert and to empower the independent citizen. Parties abandoned "spectacular campaigning" and concentrated on delivering their message through an ever-more professional press. Thanks to these changes, supporters of good government anticipated an age of informed citizens, rationally considering the issues, weighing the arguments of all parties, obtaining essential knowledge from a responsible press. Instead, Schudson notes, "the citizens themselves began a retreat from political activity, voter turnout dropped precipitously, and the fate of democratic rule seemed very much in doubt."[24]

This survey of rational reading in the public sphere is heavy on ideology, weak on practice. It highlights a tension between civic ideals and popular democracy, and in the process, subtly disparages the self-education of common people. In this model, elites—or at least a few intellectuals—discuss issues calmly and rationally, while the masses are moved only by passion and interest. That premise understates the powerful drive of women, blacks, and other groups to inform themselves and to challenge their traditional exclusion from suffrage and office. The privileged classes are no less prone to prejudice and selfishness than those they presume to rule.

A similar objection arises to the opposition I have posed between reading

---

23. Wood, "Democratization of Mind," 67, 72.

24. Warner, *Letters of the Republic,* 126–7; Brown, *Strength of a People;* Schudson, *The Good Citizen: A History of Civic Life* (Cambridge, MA: Harvard Univ. Press, 1999), 187.

practices. Are "personalism" and "rational reading" as incompatible in reality as they appear in principle? Must individuals decide between subjective immersion in texts and impartial encounters with disembodied ideas? So our history of reading inadvertently suggests, notwithstanding considerable evidence that people in the past saw no need for such choice. In the eighteenth century, sense and sensibility frequently went hand in hand. As Robert Darnton has shown, French readers could embrace the *Encyclopedists'* indictment of the ancien régime as contrary to reason and nature, even as they indulged the "delicious outpourings of the heart" in response to Rousseau's *Nouvelle Héloïse.* Thomas Jefferson, for one, had no problem with this logic. As a gentleman of letters devoted to Enlightenment ideals, he preferred to compose and circulate his manuscripts for select coteries, and when he did put his writings before the general public, he invariably sought to remain anonymous. So adroitly did he conceal the private personality behind the public man that Jefferson remains to this day an "American Sphinx." Nonetheless, America's philosopher-statesman cherished the heart as well as the head. In 1771, he drew up a list of books for the education of a gentleman, numbering 148 titles in all. Not surprisingly, politics, law, ancient and modern history, and natural philosophy comprise much of the collection. But it also included a good many works of poetry, drama, and fiction. For Jefferson, novels were a powerful instrument for promoting "the principles and practices of virtue." "We never reflect whether the story we read be truth or fiction," Jefferson advised the young man, Robert Skipwith, for whom he compiled the catalogue. "If the painting be lively, and a tolerable picture of nature, we are thrown into a reverie, from which if we awaken it is the fault of the writer. I appeal to every reader of feeling and sentiment whether the fictitious murther of Duncan by Macbeth in Shakespeare does not excite in him as great a horror of villainy, as the real one of Henry IV by Ravaillac as related by Davila." The ideal republican was a man of feeling and reason alike.[25]

Nineteenth-century Christians displayed their own breadth of interests and tastes. For many evangelicals, piety and intellect were allies in a common cause. Consider the case of Matthew Floy, a "devout Methodist" who yearned to bring the light of the Gospel to everyone, "even the most humble beggar." Living in lower Manhattan during the 1830s, he had his work cut out for him. By day, the young man, then in his twenties, still single and residing

25. Darnton, "Readers Respond to Rousseau"; Douglas L. Wilson, "Jefferson and the Republic of Letters," in *Jeffersonian Legacies,* ed. Peter S. Onuf (Charlottesville: Univ. of Virginia Press, 1993), 50–76; Thomas Jefferson to Robert Skipwith, August 3, 1771, in Merrill D. Peterson, ed., *Thomas Jefferson: Writings* (New York: Library of America, 1984), 741; Andrew Burstein, *The Inner Jefferson: Portrait of a Grieving Optimist* (Charlottesville: Univ. of Virginia Press, 1995).

in his parents' home, labored in the family nursery business; in leisure hours, he attended Methodist class meetings, taught Sunday school, and devoted much of his time to books. As he prepared himself for the duties of adult life, Floy sought models in his reading, a record of which he faithfully kept in a diary from 1833 to 1837. In that four-year period, he bought more than two hundred books and read over a hundred of them. To judge from some of his choices and comments, this denizen of Jacksonian America was still living in the colonial past. His reading fare consisted of the Bible, which he consulted daily in a pocket-size version he always carried with him, and such "steady sellers" of evangelical Protestantism as Philip Doddridge's spiritual biography of the "Christian soldier" James Gardiner, first issued in 1747. In these devotional texts, Floy sought examples of "ardent piety." He shunned altogether the popular genre of the novel—it was, in his view, a source of moral corruption, responsible for creating "a greater part of the prostitutes in the world"—and paid no heed to the emerging penny press, the tabloids of the day. Cotton Mather would have approved. Yet, Floy was also a man of his times, and driven by a "thirst for knowledge," he bought many contemporary books with a secular bent, particularly volumes of history and biography. In the interest of forming his character, he took up whatever he "conceived to be useful." One unlikely choice was the earl of Chesterfield's *Letters to His Son,* a late-eighteenth-century work suspect for its lax morals and cynical advice for getting ahead. Floy was appalled by Chesterfield's "wicked" counsel of hypocrisy, yet he was prepared to separate the wheat from the chaff. Intent on becoming a Christian gentleman, Floy was open to Chesterfield's lessons in "politeness," even as he aspired to put them to evangelical ends. In this instance and many others, Floy was ready to take advantage of diverse genres of print. Read in the proper spirit, godly and worldly books belonged on the same shelf.[26]

Only by grappling with such concrete details, as documented in diaries, letters, library circulation records, and inventories of estates, to name a few key sources, can we get beyond ideology and witness the actual practice of reading in everyday life. For this purpose, bibliographical skills are indispensable. How else to determine the meaning of an individual's reading but by reconstructing, title by title, the works she assembled and read? In this inquiry, the physical character of a book may matter as much as its contents.

---

26. Scott E. Casper, *Constructing American Lives: Biography and Culture in Nineteenth-Century America* (Chapel Hill: Univ. of North Carolina Press, 1999), 125–30; Scott E. Casper, "Antebellum Reading Prescribed and Described," in Casper, Chaison, and Groves, *Perspectives on American Book History,* 142–6.

Most students of reading have ignored that essential point. A book, after all, is more than a text, and it does not spring directly from its creator's head. Only through the collaborative effort of diverse agents — paper makers, compositors, pressmen, proofreaders, binders, publishers, shippers, and retailers, not to mention authors — do books actually make their way to readers. What impact does the material form of a book have on its cultural connotations? To take one example: can a collective product express a personal voice? Pious Christians have always thought so; God can speak in any medium, whether scroll or codex, manuscript or print, prayer, psalm, or burning bush. In practice, some forms can seem more appropriate than others. As Jean Ranson, a French Protestant enthusiast of Rousseau, informed his bookseller, the Bible should appear in a folio edition: "It is more majestic and more imposing in the eyes of the multitude for whom this divine book is intended." It was perhaps easy to conceive of books as personal expressions in the early modern period, when every aspect of their creation was done by hand. But how did the ideology of personalism survive in the industrial era? With great difficulty, according to the historian Paul Gutjahr, who argues that the Word of God lost its divine "aura" in the age of mass production by steam-powered machines. That seems unlikely, given that Amsterdam printers were already stereotyping the Bible in the seventeenth century, as the late Hugh Amory has observed, and churned out some three million copies in the eighteenth century. The links between form and content remain elusive.[27]

What, then, of the relation between reading and experience? The act of reading, as I suggest, is invested with diverse meanings by the larger culture, even as it takes shape in encounters with specific texts. No individual approaches a book as a tabula rasa. And no one is compelled to take dictation from an author. Modernist writers could not win readers whose tastes ran to "warm-blooded" narratives. However reading is constructed, it surely plays many roles in everyday life. It can, of course, enable individuals to imagine new worlds for themselves and thereby challenge constraints on their lives. That was clearly true for women readers, for blacks, and for restless young men on New England's farms. But is the conversion of reading into experience always a good thing? In the mid nineteenth century, Karen Halttunen informs us, a "pornography of violence" emerged as a literary genre, offering up graphic accounts of rape, torture, and murder to male readers in northern cities. Why this surge of blood-lust? One reason may be the new sensitivity to

---

27. Darnton, "Readers Respond to Rousseau," 222; Paul C. Gutjahr, *An American Bible: A History of the Good Book in the United States, 1777–1880* (Stanford, CA: Stanford Univ. Press, 1999); Amory, review of Gutjahr, *William and Mary Quarterly,* 3d ser., 57 (2000): 450–3.

pain and suffering in antebellum culture. Spurred by that impulse, Americans put an end to the carnival of the gallows, assigned the management of funerals to undertakers, and removed other physical functions from public view. Denied access to concrete experience, people embraced the lurid fantasies of the press. Or perhaps, the appeal of pornography was to beleaguered workingmen, whose autonomy at work was slipping as a result of industrialization, and whose traditional pastimes—hard drinking, cockfighting, boxing, and wrestling—came under attack by bourgeois reformers. Repressed in life, their manly passions rioted in texts. In this instance, it was surely a good thing readers did not put their reading into practice. Sadly, we cannot say the same for millions who have consumed racist stereotypes in the press and made them all too real. In such cases, rational reading takes on a moral imperative.[28]

Ultimately, neither the complexities of experience nor the contradictions of human nature can be captured in the pages of a book. No reading practice can overcome that gap. A history of reading thus needs not merely to log the response of individuals to texts but to assay the complex modes in which people connect textual encounters with the rest of their lives. It is surely only a happy moral for a Hollywood film to hope that reading and experience will always be one.

---

28. Halttunen, *Murder Most Foul: The Killer and the American Gothic Imagination* (Cambridge: Cambridge Univ. Press, 1998), 79–86; David M. Stewart, "Reading Violence: Toward a Recreational Male Identity," paper presented at annual meeting of the American Studies Association, Seattle, WA, November 1998.

Chapter 20

The Printing Revolution

A Reappraisal

ROGER CHARTIER

THE MAGNIFICENT set of contributions gathered in this volume permits us to assess the manifold influences long exercised by Elizabeth Eisenstein's great work. Furthermore, it leads to new assessments of the real issues behind hastily made critiques and overly abrupt objections in the midst of heated controversies — even the most recent ones.[1]

The first of these reassessments concerns the notion of print culture and one of the most fundamental effects that Elizabeth Eisenstein attributes to the "printing revolution": the distribution of texts on a level unknown in the time of manuscripts. This effect is indisputable. With Gutenberg's invention, more texts were in circulation and each reader was able to find a greater number of them. But what are these texts whose numbers were multiplied by printing? Books, of course. However, as D. F. McKenzie shows,[2] and as Peter Stallybrass further demonstrates in his essay here, books were often a fraction, sometimes a very small fraction, of the output of print shops between the fifteenth and eighteenth centuries. Print production comprised mainly libels, pamphlets, petitions, placards, forms, notes, receipts, certificates, and many other kinds of "ephemera" or "job printing," which represented the main source of income for these businesses. The consequences of this clarification are not trivial when defining "print culture" and its effects. In fact, the first of these effects is to revolutionize written culture itself, by making familiar objects and practices that were unknown or marginal in the manuscript era. In the cities at least,

---

This essay was translated from French by Genevieve Dell.

1. See the exchange between Elizabeth Eisenstein and Adrian Johns in AHR Forum, "How Revolutionary Was the Print Revolution?" *American Historical Review* 107.1 (2002): 84–128.

2. McKenzie, "The Economies of Print, 1550–1750: Scales of Production and Conditions of Constraint," in *Produzione e commercio della carta e del libro, secc. XIII–XVIII*, Istituto Internazionale di Storia Economica F. Datini, Prato, ser. 2, no. 23, ed. Simonetta Cavaciocchi (Florence: Le Monnier, 1992), 389–425.

printed matter takes over the walls, is read in public spaces, and transforms administrative and business practices.[3]

Hence the need to reformulate what has been a source of so many misunderstandings: the opposition between "scribal culture" and "print culture." With the work dedicated to manuscript publication in England,[4] Spain,[5] and France[6] over the past decade, no one today would argue that "this" (the printing press) killed "that" (the manuscript). Numerous kinds of texts (poetry anthologies, political libels or tracts, aristocratic books of conduct, newsletters, libertine and unorthodox texts, music scores, etc.) enjoyed a wide circulation through manuscript copies.[7] The reasons for the continued use of manuscripts are many: writing was cheaper than printing; handwritten texts eluded censorship more easily than printed ones; circulation could be restricted to an elite audience; and manuscript as a medium was more malleable in allowing additions and revisions. In short, it is now recognized that printing, at least for the first four centuries of its existence, did not lead to the disappearance of handwritten communication or manuscript publication.

Moreover, it led to new uses for handwriting. Peter Stallybrass describes many printed items with blank spaces and blank pages that invite their purchasers or other users to supply handwritten information. There are blank pages interleaved in almanacs, spaces waiting to be filled in on printed forms or under headings of commonplace notebooks, as well as wide margins or line spacing in publications, providing spaces for a reader's handwritten annotations. It would be easy to multiply examples for these printed items whose purpose is to engender and preserve writing by hand: editions of Latin clas-

---

3. Antonio Castillo Gómez, *Escrituras y escribientes: Prácticas de la cultura escrita en una ciudad del Renacimiento* (Las Palmas de Gran Canaria: Gobierno de Canarias y Fundación de Enseñanza Superior a Distancia de Las Palmas de Gran Canaria, 1997).

4. Harold Love, *Scribal Publication in Seventeenth-Century England* (Oxford: Oxford Univ. Press, 1993); Arthur F. Marotti, *Manuscript, Print, and the English Lyric* (Ithaca, NY: Cornell Univ. Press, 1995); H. R. Woudhuysen, *Sir Philip Sydney and the Circulation of Manuscripts, 1558–1640* (Oxford: Clarendon Press, 1996); and, more recently, David McKitterick, *Print, Manuscript, and the Search for Order, 1450–1830* (Cambridge: Cambridge Univ. Press, 2002).

5. Fernando Bouza, *Corre manuscrito: Una historia cultural del Siglo de Oro* (Madrid: Marcial Pons, 2001).

6. François Moureau, ed., *De bonne main: La communication manuscrite au XVIIIe siècle* (Paris: Universitas; Oxford: Voltaire Foundation, 1993); Miguel Benitez, *La face cachée des Lumières: Recherches sur les manuscrits philosophiques clandestins à l'âge classique* (Paris: Universitas; Oxford: Voltaire Foundation, 1996); François Moureau, *Répertoire des nouvelles à la main: Dictionnaire de la presse manuscrite clandestine XVIe–XVIIIe siècle* (Paris: Universitas; Oxford: Voltaire Foundation, 1999).

7. Roger Chartier, "Le manuscrit à l'âge de l'imprimé (XVe–XVIIIe siècles)," *La lettre clandestine* 7 (1998): 175–93.

sics used in sixteenth-century colleges,[8] the marriage charters used in some seventeenth-century dioceses in southern France,[9] or the first daily planners to feature the division of each day into various time segments, used in Italy since the eighteenth century.[10]

The convergence of handwriting and print is not limited to texts designed explicitly for combining the two. Readers in the past, particularly scholarly ones like those described by Ann Blair, often took up printed texts to correct errors and create useful lists of errata by hand; in some extreme instances (such as the biblical cross-referencing by the Ferrar family at Little Gidding, studied by Margaret Aston), readers created original books by interspersing handwritten references and commentary with cut-and-pasted printed fragments. These practices enable an extended, candid discussion about the standardization attributed to printing. Such an acknowledgment, however, does not imply ignoring all the processes that limit the effects of standardization: "stop-press corrections," which generate an array of possible combinations of corrected and uncorrected sheets within copies belonging to an edition, resulting in multiple states of the "same text"; handwritten "marginalia," which distinguishes the copy of a work through a particular reader's adaptations;[11] and the selection of particular texts, manuscript and print, chosen at will by a reader and then bound together to create a unique volume.[12]

As Harold Love emphasizes, the printed text is open to mobility, flexibility, and variation, if only because at a time when print runs were still limited (between 1,000 and 1,750 around 1680, according to a craftsman, the printer

---

8. Anthony Grafton, "Teacher, Text, and Pupil in the Renaissance Class-Room: A Case-Study from a Parisian College," *History of Unversities* 1 (1981): 37–70; Ann Blair, "Ovidius Methodizatus: The Metamorphoses of Ovid in a Sixteenth-Century Paris College," *History of Universities* 9 (1990): 72–118; Jean Letrouit, "La prise de notes de cours sur support imprimé dans les collèges parisiens au XVIe siècle," *Revue de la Bibliothèque nationale de France* 2 (1999): 47–56.

9. Roger Chartier, "Du rituel au for privé : Les chartes de mariage lyonnaises au XVIIe siècle," in *Les usages de l'imprimé (Xve–XIXe siècles)*, ed. Chartier (Paris: Fayard, 1987), 229–51; translated by Lydia G. Cochrane as "From Ritual to the Hearth: Marriage Charters in Seventeenth-Century Lyons," in *The Culture of Print: Power and the Uses of Print in Early Modern Europe, 15th–19th Centuries*, ed. Roger Chartier (Princeton, NJ: Princeton Univ. Press, 1989), 174–90.

10. Lodovica Braida, "Dall'almanacco all'agenda: Lo spazio per le osservazioni del lettore nelle guide del tempo italiane (XVIII–XIX seccolo)," *Acme: Annali della Facoltà di Lettere e Filosofia dell'Università degli Studi di Milano* LI, fasc. 3 (1998): 137–67.

11. See the essays collected in Sabrina Alcorn Baron, ed., *The Reader Revealed* (Washington, DC: Folger Shakespeare Library, 2001), and in "Le livre annoté," *Revue de la Bibliothèque nationale de France* 2 (1999).

12. Max W. Thomas, "Reading and Writing in the Renaissance Commonplace Book: A Question of Authorship?" in *The Construction of Authorship: Textual Appropriation in Law and Literature*, ed. Martha Woodmansee and Peter Jaszi (Durham, NC: Duke Univ. Press, 1994), 401–15.

Alonso Víctor de Paredes),[13] the success of a work implied several reprintings, which were never exactly identical to one another. Just as the production capacity of printing shops was far from being fully mobilized (at least for book printing), so too was the capacity of printing to reproduce a work whose individual copies were identical to one another, a potential that was not fully realized. Conversely, manuscript transmission does not necessarily entail textual alteration, especially when, as with the Bible or the Torah, the words are fixed and the text strictly controlled. Rather than a general, definitive diagnosis contrasting the permanence of print and the instability of handwriting, what matters is a comprehensive review of each textual transmission within its specific context.

Upon completing this first set of revisions, displaying the complex relationship between "scribal culture" and "print culture," we find the latter concept redefined. The comparison with Chinese printing introduced by Kai-wing Chow deepens this reevaluation. First, this comparison calls for a distinction between printing and Gutenberg's invention (or that of Füst or Coster according to sixteenth- and seventeenth-century accounts), because woodblock is also a printing technique and because the use of movable characters (of clay, wood or metal) does not imply the use of a press in the East, owing to the quality of paper. Such a comparison shows next that printed texts made with movable characters were not as rare in China as previously thought, even though wood carvings, or xylography, was the most commonly used technique because of its cost effectiveness (cheap labor, abundance of wood). Finally, this comparison demonstrates that it would be a grievous error to assume that typography is vastly superior to xylography, and the West more advanced than the East. On one hand, the technique of printing texts from woodblocks gave rise in China to a print culture very similar in its commercial organization and productions (encyclopedias, compilations, commonplace books, popular editions, etc.) to that of the West.[14] On the other hand, woodblock printing played a fundamental and enduring role in the West, as proved by both the continuity (wrongly questioned) in the fifteenth century between "block books" and incunabula and the continued, subsequent use of woodblock printing not only for illustrations and initials, but also for texts. Paradoxically perhaps, the fixity of texts associated with Gutenberg's invention no doubt is better exemplified by texts produced by

---

13. Alonso Víctor de Paredes, *Institución y origen del arte de la imprenta y reglas generales para los componedores,* ed. Jaime Moll (Madrid: Bibliotheca Literae, Calambur, 2002).

14. See the essays collected in *Late Imperial China* 17.1 (June 1996), and Kai-wing Chow, *Publishing, Culture, and Power in Early Modern China* (Stanford, CA: Stanford Univ. Press, 2004); and Cynthia J. Brokaw and Kai-wing Chow, eds., *Printing and Book Culture in Late Imperial China* (Berkeley and Los Angeles: Univ. of California Press, 2005).

engraved woodblocks, which could be used to print several thousand, even tens of thousands, copies.

The effects specific to Gutenberg's invention, however, are not those most often underscored. These concern the relationship between the works as texts and the forms taken by their material inscription. In the first place, if the printed book inherits basic structures from the manuscript book (i.e., the distribution of the text into gatherings and leaves specific to the codex, whatever the production or reproduction technique), it also introduces innovations that profoundly modify the relationship between the reader and the written text.[15] That is true of paratexts, or more precisely according to Gérard Genette's terminology, *péritextes,* which make up the book's threshold that William Sherman analyzes. Once printed, these paratextual items acquire an identity immediately perceptible by their particular signature marks (italics, vowels with tildes, symbols) that differentiate the preliminaries from other gatherings. The preliminaries were always printed (with the tables and the index) after the body of the book had been printed, and they were often prepared by the bookseller or printer rather than the author.[16] The architectural metaphors that during the sixteenth and seventeenth centuries designated these "porches" leading to the work itself, are strongly justified by the typographically marked separation between the work and the "vestibule" (a word chosen by Jorge Luis Borges) leading in to it.

In addition, compared with the manuscript, the printed book renders more common the practice of collecting works by the same author in a single volume. This innovation is not unique, given that in the fourteenth century the works of certain vernacular authors began to be bound within single volumes consisting only of their individual compositions. But this practice of print broke with the dominant tradition in the manuscript era, that of the miscellany, in which texts belonging to many different genres, dates, and authors were gathered together.[17] The 1616 Folio collected edition of Ben Jonson's works, composed by Jonson himself, or the 1623 First

---

15. For an example of the effect of typographic forms (format, layout, punctuation) on literary meaning, see the pioneering study of D. F. McKenzie, "Typography and Meaning: The Case of William Congreve," in *Buch und Buchhandel in Europa im achtzehnten Jahrhundert,* ed. Giles Barber and Bernhard Fabian (Hamburg: Hauswedell, 1981), 81–125, reprinted in McKenzie, *Making Meaning: "Printers of the Mind" and Other Essays,* ed. Peter McDonald and Michael F. Suarez, S.J. (Amherst: Univ. of Massachusetts Press, 2002), 198–236.

16. Philip Gaskell, *A New Introduction to Bibliography* (Oxford: Clarendon Press, 1972), 7–8; Juan Caramuel, *Syntagma de Arte Typographica* (Lyon, 1664), ed. Pablo Andrés Escapa (Salamanca: Instituto de Historia del Libro y de la Lectura, 2004), 134–43.

17. Gemma Guerrini, "Il sistema di communicazione di un corpus di manoscriiti quattrocenteschi," *Scrittura e Civiltà* 10 (1986): 122–97; Armando Petrucci, "Del libro unitario al libro miscellaneo," in *Tradizione dei classici, trasformazioni della cultura,* vol. 4 of *Società romana e impero*

Folio collection of Shakespeare's works (which owes nothing to Shakespeare and everything to his old colleagues and stationers' owning or having bought the "rights in copy" to his plays), or even before, the editions of *Workes* by Heywood, Gascoigne, or Samuel Daniel are exemplary illustrations of the link forged between the material aspect of the printed book and the concept of works supposedly complete.

It is the same for the notion of "national literature," as demonstrated by David Scott Kastan in his examination of the publishing initiative of the bookseller Humphrey Moseley, who, beginning in 1645, issued a series of texts introducing readers to the works of English poets and playwrights of his generation. The volumes follow a homogenous format (octavo for the poems, in quarto for the plays), the title pages share a similar arrangement, and the "frontispieces" offer a portrait of the author. At a time when neither the specificity of the word "literature" nor the dignity in writing for the theater was recognized, as demonstrated in the exclusion by Bodley and his librarians of such texts, the enterprise of the very royalist Moseley, publisher in 1647 of the folio collection of the works of Beaumont and Fletcher, brings coherence to a corpus that separates poetry and theater from other genres (history, narratives, travels, etc.) and builds a national canon that includes only English writers. Moseley's is not a singular instance, since at the same time in France, Charles Sorel introduces his *Bibliothèque française* (published in 1664–5),[18] which includes only those authors born in the kingdom or those naturalized by translations as in the case of "comic novels," which were nevertheless moral works, written by Spaniards.

In the course of debates centered on the printing revolution, two models have arisen in our understanding of historical phenomena, which are found also in this book. The first one emphasizes the dissemination of texts as well as presses. It analyzes practices that multiply publications and guarantee a larger circulation of texts and news: thus, the pirated editions (*contrefaçons*) in France that Jean-Dominique Mellot discusses or Elinor James's petitions regarding printing houses and the book trade in London between 1695 and 1715 Paula McDowell presents or even the publication of gazettes in Colonial America creating an "information system" that Calhoun Winton analyzes. Translations from one language to another;[19] the multiplication of antholo-

---

tardoantico, ed. Andrea Giardina (Bari: Laterza, 1986), 173–87; translated by Charles Radding as "From the Unitary Book to Miscellany," in Petrucci, *Writers and Readers in Medieval Italy: Studies in the History of Written Culture* (New Haven, CT: Yale Univ. Press, 1995), 1–18.

18. Charles Sorel, *La Bibliothèque françoise* (1664; repr., Geneva: Slatkine, 1970).

19. See, for example, Roger Chartier, "La Europa castellana," in *La España en tiempos del Quijote*, ed. Antonio Feros y Juan Gelabert (Madrid: Taurus, 2004), 129–58.

gies, excerpts or "libraries" of any kind;[20] the early invention of cheap editions meant for readers of mass popular works ("pliegos sueltos," broadside ballads, chapbooks, "Bibliothèque bleue");[21] as well as the "culture of reprinting" during the nineteenth century[22] should be added to the list of practices invented and multiplied by printing that lead to the acculturation of writing in Western societies from the fifteenth to the eighteenth century.

Moreover, such a model is also present in the essays illustrating the geography of the diffusion of printing shops in different parts of the world. As suggested by Antonio Rodríguez-Buckingham, Vivek Bhandari, Geoffrey Roper, Jane McRae, and Tony Ballantyne, the typology of this diffusion of Western printing technology involves several elements: the date of the installation of a first press (1539 in Mexico, 1798 in Egypt, 1821 [for the Maori language] in New Zealand); a prior knowledge of writing or a lack thereof in the cultures encountered by Europeans; the domination, be it colonial or not, exerted by Europeans on the newly discovered territories; the respective weight of locally printed productions and those of Europe. The Scottish example Arthur Williamson studies shows that even in Europe a map of the places of publication of texts and that of the origins of the books read in a particular area do not overlap. This divergence is even more obvious in colonial situations, where a great gap exists between the ultimately very few works printed in local shops and those arriving from the metropolis, brought by booksellers or private individuals.[23]

Intersections among these many elements depend on the uses and meanings assigned to printing outside Europe. Printing, within the framework of colonial empires, is an essential tool used for the purposes of administration, Christianization, and acculturation. But it is also the object of specific appropriations and uses by which a tool employed by colonizers to insure their dominance was turned against them. This duality is full of misunderstandings and ambiguity, as D. F. McKenzie shows in the well-known analysis

---

20. See also, for example, Barbara M. Benedict, *Making the Modern Reader: Cultural Mediation in Early Modern Literary Anthologies* (Princeton, NJ: Princeton Univ. Press, 1996); and Leah Price, *The Anthology and the Rise of the Novel: From Richardson to George Eliot* (Cambridge and New York: Cambridge Univ. Press, 2000).

21. For a comparison on a European scale, see Roger Chartier and Hans-Jürgen Lüsebrink, eds., *Colportage et lecture populaire: Imprimés de large circulation en Europe, XVIe–XIXe siècles* (Paris: IMEC Editions and Editions de la Maison des Sciences de l'Homme, 1996).

22. Meredith L. McGill, *American Literature and the Culture of Reprinting, 1834–1853* (Philadelphia: Univ. of Pennsylvania Press, 2003).

23. Carlos Alberto González Sánchez, *Los mundos del libro: Medios de difusión de la cultura occidental en las Indias de los siglos XVI y XVII* (Seville: Deputación de Sevilla; Universidad de Sevilla, 1999).

of the Waitangi Treaty (1840), illustrating the different, even contradictory meanings given by the Maori chiefs and the colonizers to the words, the written document, and the act of signing.[24] The emphasis placed on the diffusion of Western techniques permits us to situate the history of printing within the "connected stories" that, today, are giving a new appearance to the project of global history.[25] But it also requires that particular attention be given to the representations and practices that invest the same technique with such diverging meanings.

From this stance, the "dissemination" model in our understanding of print culture is not necessarily opposed to the "constructivist" one, which underscores that there are no properties intrinsic to typography. These properties, according to Adrian Johns, are always constructed based on the representations and conventions that make it possible to have confidence, or lack of it, in the book entrepreneurs; to judge the authenticity of texts or the value of editions; or even to credit the knowledge transmitted by printed texts.[26] In the Spanish Golden Age, Cervantes, Lope de Vega, and Quevedo echo all those who denounce the dishonesty and tricks of the booksellers and publishers, the multiplication of useless books, and the denaturation of knowledge given to readers unable to understand it.[27] In establishing, though not without conflicts or differences, shared rules to detect corrupted texts and false knowledge, members of the book trade are attempting to counter the discredit so firmly affixed to both printed books and their publishers.

The attention given to the collective practices according authority to printed matter places "print culture" in the paradigm governing a new history of sciences. This history gives special weight to three processes: negotiations fixing the conditions under which experiments are replicated, thus allowing results to be compared or cumulated; conventions defining the credit that can be granted or refused to the certification of discoveries based on the quality and condition of the witnesses and their capacity to tell the truth; and controversies arising not only from antagonistic theories but even more

---

24. McKenzie, "The Sociology of Texts: Orality, Literacy, and Print in Early New Zealand," *The Library,* 6th ser., 6 (1984): 333–65, reprinted in McKenzie, *Bibliography and the Sociology of Texts* (Cambridge: Cambridge Univ. Press, 1999), 77–130.

25. Patrick Karl O'Brien, "Perspectives on Global History: Concepts and Methodology / Mondialisation de l'histoire: concepts et méthodologie," *Proceedings, 19th International Congress of Historical Sciences / Actes, XIXe Congrès International des Sciences Historiques* (Oslo, 2000), 3–52.

26. Johns, *The Nature of the Book: Print and Knowledge in the Making* (Chicago: Univ. of Chicago Press, 1998).

27. Fernando Bouza, "Para qué imprimir: De autores, públicos, impresores y manuscritos en el Siglo de Oro," *Cuadernos de historia moderna* 18 (1997): 31–50. See also Ann Blair, "Reading Strategies for Coping with Information Overload," *Journal of the History of Ideas* 64 (2003): 11–28.

from conflicting conceptions about which social and epistemological conditions should control the production of scientific discourse about the natural
world.[28] This intelligibility model provides a pertinent account of the multiple transactions conceding, or tending to concede, authority to all texts and
all books governed by the distinction between what is true and what is false.
Books of natural philosophy, as well as theological works or travel narratives,
produce truths requiring accreditation from different mechanisms, inside or
outside the texts.

Is this true, however, for all of printed matter, of which a large part, perhaps a majority, is dedicated to texts that are not dependent on the criteria of
veracity? A ready example is given by works of fiction whose reception is not
governed by the conventions specific to the discourses of knowledge. In the
theater, for instance, the respect for the "right in copy," which trade courtesy
dictates must be given to the bookseller who first enters the title of a given
text in the Stationer's Company register, does not imply a similar respect for
the authenticity of that text or the accuracy of its printing.[29] The desire to
read a play or the pleasure in reading did not depend, in this instance, on the
recognition given to the edition, nor the trust accorded to its publisher.

Just as the many meanings given to Gutenberg's invention cannot be
deduced from its technical mechanism, the meaning of the texts propagated
by such an invention is not intrinsic to them. It is shaped by the readers—and
by readers who share codes and reading strategies. As Robert Gross indicates
in his essay here, they can create specific and long-lasting relationships with
what is written as well as specific links between reading and experience. Therefore, for Gross, the Puritan conception of the book characterizes American
culture between the seventeenth and nineteenth centuries, as does critical
and rational reading from the eighteenth century on—without excluding
a possible association between the two ways of reading, between piety and
understanding.

Robert Gross juxtaposes this necessary inventory of "reading modalities"
to the overly simple and anachronistic thesis (which would be mine) that
freedom is a universal and essential characteristic of reading, which would
entail breaking up all acts of reading into an infinite fragmentation and holding all interpretations as equally plausible, or comparable. That is not my
position, even if some overly definite formulations would lead one to think so.

---

28. Simon Schaffer and Steven Shapin, *Leviathan and the Air-Pump: Hobbes, Boyle, and the
Experimental Life* (Princeton, NJ: Princeton Univ. Press, 1985); Steven Shapin, *A Social History of
Truth: Civility and Science in Seventeenth-Century England* (Chicago: Univ. of Chicago Press, 1994).
29. David Scott Kastan, *Shakespeare and the Book* (Cambridge: Cambridge Univ. Press, 2001).

The emphasis placed on the reader's poaching[30] was inspired by the desire to distance the reader from the text and to assert, contrary to a purely linguistic approach, that meaning is born not of textual machinery but of the relationship between what is read and the reader. But, as opposed to the phenomenological perspectives describing the act of reading in its double individual and universal dimension,[31] historicization of categories such as "interpretive community" (found in Stanley Fish's work) and "appropriation" (borrowed from both Foucault and hermeneutics) are reminders that each reader is constructed by the conventions, norms, interests, and practices that socially and culturally characterize the different ways of reading. These common codes are both classificatory principles and internalized judgments, ruling the relationship with what is written (or decoding the social world) for all those who share the same trajectories and experiences. This is not at all about dissolving the cultural meaning of texts or genres appropriated by readers in a myriad of universal responses; on the contrary, this is about locating the preferences and reading practices that a reader adopts—or that are imposed on him or her—within the systems of constraints defined by the reader's social identity and the textual as well as material forms of the written text.

The capacity of Elizabeth Eisenstein's significant book to provoke much thought has not waned with time. As proof, consider its presence in reflections that, like those of Barbara A. Brannon or James A. Dewar and Peng Hwa Ang here, try to bring about a more assured diagnosis of our present-day revolution: the digital revolution. An analogy between the printing revolution and the Internet is tempting. Nor is it without validity since both concern a technical innovation that proposes (or imposes) a new technique for transmitting text and images. It is therefore legitimate to use this comparison to locate fundamental mutations introduced by electronic text. On one hand, the digital revolution replaces printed fixed texts (at least partially) with open, mobile, and malleable texts. Texts and hypertexts assembled on the screen by the reader's preference are by nature ephemeral and, unless secured, can be cut, increased, moved, and recompiled at will. On the other hand, unlike the multiple and successive operations and decisions associated with printed publication—distributed among editors, publishers and booksellers,

---

30. Michel de Certeau, "Lire: Un braconnage," in *L'invention du quotidian* (Paris: U.G.E., 1980; rev., 1990), 239–55; translated by Steven F. Rendall as "Reading as Poaching," in *The Practice of Everyday Life* (Berkeley and Los Angeles: Univ. of California Press, 1984), 165–76.

31. Wolfgang Iser, *Der Akt des Lesens: Theorie ästetischer Wirkung* (Munich: Wilhelm Fink, 1976), translated by the author as *The Act of Reading: A Theory of Aesthetic Response* (Baltimore, MD: Johns Hopkins Univ. Press, 1978); Susan R. Suleiman and Inge Crosman, eds., *The Reader in the Text: Essays on Audience and Interpretation* (Princeton, NJ: Princeton Univ. Press, 1980).

master printers, typesetters, proofreaders, and pressmen—desktop publishing enables each author to be his or her own potential publisher, editor, and bookseller. Hence, it is useful to reflect on the effects of the "print revolution" to understand, by seeing the similarities or differences, what is to be expected in this new mutation of written culture.

It seems to me, however, that it would be an error to limit the comparison of the present and the past only in those terms. In fact, the digital revolution enables texts to be read on a new surface (the screen and no longer the page) and from a new object (the computer and no longer the book or other printed artifacts). These changes fundamentally alter both the methods of textual inscription and the readers' intellectual and physical relationship with what is written. This disruption is not at all comparable with Gutenberg. The printed book remained identical in its fundamental structures (gatherings, leaves, pages) to the manuscript book. And the new objects (libels, posters, forms, etc.) multiplied by printing did not undo the essential characteristic of written culture—that is, the link immediately visible between genres of text, classes of objects that are distinct from one another, and types of uses of the written word. By contrast, in the digital world, all texts, no matter their own identity, are displayed on the same medium, the computer screen, and in very similar forms and dispositions. In that sense, the break in the twentieth century is much more radical than that in the fifteenth century.[32]

If one is to find an analogy in a *longue durée* history of writing and reading, one should look at the invention of the codex. By replacing the scroll with a new book form, this revolution, largely forgotten or unacknowledged except by specialists, is the one that led to practices that are still ours today and that were completely impossible with the scroll: for example, leafing through a book, quickly locating a passage, using an index, and writing while reading.[33] Between the second and fourth centuries, a new book form became predominant and was inherited by Gutenberg, Füst, and Coster. Despite the title of the aptly famous work by Lucien Febvre and Henri-Jean Martin,[34] books did

---

32. Roger Chartier, "Languages, Books, and Reading from the Printed Word to the Digital Text," *Critical Inquiry* 31 (Autumn 2004): 133–54.

33. Guglielmo Cavallo, "Testo, libro, lettura," in *La circolazione del testo,* vol. 2 of *Lo spazio letterario di Roma antica,* ed. Cavallo, Paolo Fedele, and Andrea Giardina (Rome: Salerno Editrice, 1989), 307–34, and "Libro e cultura scritta," in *Caratteri e morfologie,* vol. 4 of *Storia di Roma,* ed. Aldo Sciavone (Turin: Einaud, 1989), 693–734. See also Alain Blanchard, ed., *Les débuts du codex* (Turnhout: Brepols, 1989).

34. Lucien Febvre and Henri-Jean Martin, *L'apparition du livre* (Paris: A. Michel, L'Evolution de l'Humanité, 1958; reissued Paris: A. Michel, 1999); translated by David Gerard as *The Coming of the Book: The Impact of Printing, 1450–1800,* ed. Geoffrey Nowell-Smith and David Wootton (London: N.L.B., 1976; reissued London: Verso, 1990).

not make their first appearance with printing, nor with the codex. One must therefore be careful not to attribute to printing and to movable type the textual inventions (index, tables, cross-references, numbering, and pagination) that were part, more than ten centuries before, of the new materiality of the book which made them possible—or necessary. Therefore, to understand the effects on texts and reading engendered by the transformation of the modalities of their publication and diffusion, we must broaden our chronological perspective and also examine the codex revolution as well as the print revolution. And we are invited to do precisely that by the eternally young Elizabeth Eisenstein's book, more than twenty-five years after its publication.

A Conversation with
Elizabeth L Eisenstein

In lieu of a formal afterword, we conclude this volume with a short conversation with Eisenstein, in which we posed to her some questions we have not seen answered elsewhere.

Editors: What were the challenges you faced in undertaking such an ambitious project on a topic generally viewed at the time as arcane?

Eisenstein: The main challenge was how to present my ideas in an acceptable form. After publishing "Clio and Chronos," I had written a long letter to Robert K. Merton about his book, *On the Shoulders of Giants,* explaining why I thought the aphorism in his title had different meanings for those who lived before and those who lived after the advent of printing.[1] Merton wrote back that he had never considered the significance of printing in this light. He urged me to publish a fuller account of my views, even though they were still somewhat inchoate, under the heading of a "preliminary report." Encouraged by his advice, I turned out a long article, cautiously titled "Some Conjectures." Its acceptance by the *Journal of Modern History*[2] paved the way for subsequent articles and eventually for the two-volume book.

I never thought my work dealt with an "arcane topic." Rather I thought of it as a way of tackling some long-standing, major problems in early modern European history. I had long been dissatisfied with conventional treatments of the Renaissance, the Reformation, and the so-called Scientific Revolution.

---

1. Eisenstein, "Clio and Chronos: An Essay on the Making and Breaking of History-Book Time," *History and Theory* 6, Beiheft 6: History and the Concept of Time (1966), 36–64; Merton, *On the Shoulders of Giants: A Shandean Postscript* (New York: Free Press, 1965).

2. Eisenstein, "Some Conjectures about the Impact of Printing on Western Society and Thought: A Preliminary Report," *Journal of Modern History* 40.1 (1968): 1–56.

After I started teaching and had to discuss such developments regularly with students, my dissatisfaction increased. It occurred to me that by considering possible changes wrought by printing, a topic that had been neglected in my own undergraduate and graduate studies, some familiar problems could be tackled more successfully. This consideration meant engaging with the sort of "grand narrative" that has fallen out of fashion in recent years. Fashionable or not, narratives pertaining to the course of Western civilization continue to provide agreed-upon reference points for most humanists and social scientists. Historians have a special responsibility for maintaining such guidelines in good working condition.

Editors: What was it like trying to make your way in what, when you began your career, was an overwhelmingly male profession? Did your situation have any effects on your work?

Eisenstein: In the early 1950s I had been unable to obtain even a part-time job at either of the two universities (in Madison, Wisconsin, and State College, Pennsylvania) where my husband, a physicist, served on the faculty. I had no more luck after we moved to Washington, DC, in 1956–7. By then I had obtained a Harvard Ph.D. and had a book accepted by the Harvard University Press.[3] I applied to several institutions: Georgetown, George Washington, Howard, Catholic Universities, and the University of Maryland. All seemed reluctant to hire a woman historian. Finally, I landed a job as a part-time "adjunct lecturer" at American University. I was hired to teach a required survey course in "Western Civ" to two sections of a captive audience of 120 students. Although frustrating at the time, I now realize that handling a survey course was not without benefit: it forced me to go over and over the problems mentioned above in a way that increased my dissatisfaction with conventional treatments.

The experience of being marginalized as a woman scholar during the 1950s and 1960s may have some bearing on why I tend to adopt a skeptical, even iconoclastic, attitude toward views that are accepted by most of my colleagues. This tendency was evident in my earlier work in the field of French studies, where I challenged the accepted (quasi-Marxist) interpretation of the origins of the French Revolution.[4] It also was manifested in *The Printing Press as an Agent*

---

3. Eisenstein, *The First Professional Revolutionist: Filippo Michele Buonarroti (1761–1837): A Biographical Essay* (Cambridge, MA: Harvard Univ. Press, 1959).

4. Eisenstein, "Who Intervened in 1788? A Commentary on *The Coming of the French Revolution,*" *American Historical Review* 71.1 (1965): 77–103. See also Jeffrey Kaplow, "On 'Who Intervened in 1788?'" in "Class in the French Revolution: A Discussion," *American Historical Review* 72.2 (1967): 497–502.

of Change (*PPAC*), as was noted, with disapproval, by several reviewers. That I expressed disagreement with some views set forth in major works by distinguished scholars was taken as a sign of overreaching. When I cited relevant passages from the most authoritative works by the most distinguished historians, I did so, not to question their undoubted mastery of their craft, but, rather, to demonstrate a general failure to make room for changes wrought by printing.

EDITORS: You have discussed elsewhere the circumstances surrounding the inception of *PPAC,* but we don't know about the years you spent researching and writing. Can you say something about that?

EISENSTEIN: I spent most of my time in the 1960s and 1970s trying to become familiar with recent work in the diverse fields covered by my book. Gaining this knowledge entailed reading many monographs and special studies while attending seminars and conferences at rare-book libraries and affiliated societies. I sought bibliographical guidance from medieval codicologists and Renaissance historians, from the authors of studies on early printers (notably Robert Kingdon and Natalie Z. Davis), and history of science specialists.

   In the hope of receiving useful feedback, I also gave papers at numerous conferences here and abroad and published several articles. I was disappointed by the lack of response. Apart from a single article that questioned my approach to the problem of the Renaissance,[5] there was little to indicate how my views were being received. The contrary was true after the publication of my book, which was widely reviewed.

EDITORS: As you say, your book was widely reviewed, generally, though not uniformly, favorably. How did you imagine your book would be received? What was your reaction to the criticism?

EISENSTEIN: The sheer number of journals that ran reviews surprised me. So did the variety of specialties represented by the reviewers. (They ranged from cartographers and library scientists to anthropologists and media analysts.) Of course I was heartened by positive reviews and disheartened by negative ones. Probably the most influential piece was Anthony Grafton's informative review essay.[6] Among other criticisms, Grafton took me to task for devoting too much attention to secondary accounts while failing to consult the early

---

   5. Theodore Rabb and Elizabeth L. Eisenstein, "Debate: The Advent of Printing and the Problem of the Renaissance," *Past & Present* 52 (August 1971): 135–44.
   6. Grafton, "The Importance of Being Printed," *Journal of Interdisciplinary History* 11.2 (1980): 265–86.

printed books that presumably constituted my sources. Others have often echoed this complaint. Probably I should have pointed out more emphatically that my work was intended to be a critique of historical literature and was not aimed at listening to the voices of the past.[7]

EDITORS: Your book seems to have had an especially strong influence on English literary studies. Does this surprise you? What effect do you think the book has had in your own fields of history and French studies?

EISENSTEIN: As is true of the editors of this collection, I've spent recent years working in the Folger Shakespeare Library, which holds special attractions for literary scholars engaged in research on early modern English topics. Thus, we are all especially familiar with work in this field. Still, there are several scholars who have applied some of my views not to English but to early modern French literature.[8] And there are numerous other groups concerned with such topics as technology and culture, nationalism, and media and communications that have also made use of my book.[9] During the years I spent as a fellow at the Center for Advanced Study in the Behavioral Sciences (1981–2; 1991–2) interest in my work was exhibited by many other fellows, none of whom were literary scholars or concerned with early modern England.

I have also traveled abroad sufficiently to observe wider repercussions. As an invited guest to conferences held by diverse groups in Greece, Portugal, Italy, Israel, Norway, Ireland, Australia, I've encountered colleagues who work on diverse non-English topics. Among the contributors to this volume, I first met Jean-Dominique Mellot at a conference in Lisbon and Tony Ballantyne at another in Cork. My large book was translated into Italian. The abridged version has been issued in numerous translations, including French, Greek, Japanese, Polish, and Portuguese.[10] As a member of the Society for French

---

7. Roland Crahay's review in *Bibliothèque d'humanisme et Renaissance: Travaux et documents* 42 (1980): 700–703, used the helpful phrase "historical epistemology." In his *Times Literary Supplement* review, June 24, 1983, 679, Nicolas Barker also recognized that my chief concern was with the way history was being written.

8. Cynthia Brown, *Poets, Patrons, and Printers: Crisis of Authority in Late Medieval France* (Ithaca, NY: Cornell Univ. Press, 1995); and Adrian Armstrong, *Technique and Technology: Script, Print, and Poetics in France, 1470–1550* (New York: Oxford Univ. Press, 2000) are two titles that come to mind.

9. See, for example, references in "Technology and the Rest of Culture," *Social Research* 64.3 (1997), a special issue of the journal containing all versions of presentations given at the Technology and the Rest of Culture conference held at the New School in January 1997. See references to Patrice Flichy and Bruno Latour in nn. 17 and 18. Benedict Anderson, *Imagined Communities: Reflections on the Origin and Spread of Nationalism* (1983; rev. and extended edition, London and New York: Verso, 1991) is probably the most often cited study of nationalism that makes use of my work.

10. For details, see Appendix A. Most recently, Al Hiwar Athaqafi Publishers has contracted for an Arabic-language edition.

Historical Studies and as a beneficiary of the University of Michigan history department's faculty-exchange program, I have long enjoyed cordial relations with many French scholars. During a term spent in Paris, I served as a visiting professor (*maître d'études*) at the École Pratique des Hautes Études en Sciences Sociales. One of my preliminary articles was published in the *Annales*.[11] The same journal published an extended review essay that discussed my work.[12] Controversies about it were surveyed in *Le débat*.[13] I've contributed to the history of the book in France (*Histoire de l'édition française*),[14] to two essay collections on French press history,[15] and to a festschrift in honor of Henri-Jean Martin.[16] Patrice Flichy, the editor of *Reseaux*, a French journal sponsored by the National Center for Telecommunications, reviewed my work in a special issue on new approaches to communications.[17] In France, also, my treatment of scientific communications caught the attention of Bruno Latour, whose controversial account of what he calls "immutable immobiles" originated from his reading of my book.[18]

With regard to history "as a discipline at large," current fashions tend to favor the adoption of a "micro" rather than a "macro" approach to the past. Insofar as sweeping syntheses are being attempted, the vogue for world history has tended to eclipse earlier, more circumscribed accounts. Thus, my approach is vulnerable to the charge of being too Eurocentric. Nevertheless, as is shown by this collection, many of the issues I discuss are relevant to developments that occurred outside the Western world.

---

11. Eisenstein, "L'avènement de l'imprimerie et la Réforme: Une nouvelle approche au problème du démembrement de la chrétienté occidentale," *Annales: Économies, sociétés, civilisations* 26.6 (1971): 1355–82.

12. Roger Chartier, "L'ancien régime typographique: Réflexions sur quelques travaux récents," *Annales: Économies, sociétés, civilisations* 36.2 (1981): 191–209, esp. 207–8.

13. Jacques Revel, "La culture de l'imprimé," *Le débat* 22 (November 1982): 170–92.

14. Eisenstein, "Le livre et la culture savante," in *Le livre conquérant: Du moyen âge au milieu du XVIIe siècle,* vol.1 of *Histoire de l'édition française,* ed. Henri-Jean Martin and Roger Chartier (Paris: Promodis, 1982), 563–83.

15. Eisenstein, "The Tribune of the People: A New Species of Demagogue," in *The Press in the French Revolution,* ed. Harvey Chisick with Ilana Zinguer and Ouzi Elyada, Studies on Voltaire and the Eighteenth Century 287 (Oxford: Voltaire Foundation, 1991), 145–59, and "Le publiciste comme démagogue: La *Sentinelle du peuple* de Volney," in *La révolution du journal: 1788–1794,* ed. Pierre Rétat (Paris: Centre National de la Recherche Scientifique, 1989), 189–95.

16. Eisenstein, "The Libraire-Philosophe: Four Sketches for a Group Portrait," in *Le livre et l'historien: Études offertes en l'honneur du Professeur Henri-Jean Martin,* ed. Frédéric Barbier et al. (Geneva: Droz, 1997), 539–50.

17. Patrice Flichy, "La question de technique dans les recherches sur la communication," *Réseaux: Communication, technologie, société* 50 (1991): 53–62.

18. Latour was largely responsible for arranging for a French translation and getting the first French edition of my abridged version published. On the "immutable mobiles" controversy, see Michael John Gorman, "The Elusive Origins of the Immutable Mobile," http://www.stanford.edu/group/STS/immutablemobile.htm.

I have long believed that questions pertaining to printing and its effects are especially well suited to comparative study.[19] The enthusiastic reception of printing by Western churchmen seen in tandem with the prolonged rejection of printing by Islamic authorities is just one of many intriguing contrasts that are worth further exploration. In my big book, I paused over the difference between Christian and Muslim sacred texts and noted that the Koran lent itself to transmission by means of oral recitation much better than did the larger polyglot Bible. The latter was much more vulnerable to changes wrought by printing partly because of the difficulty of transmitting it by word of mouth.[20]

Another intriguing comparison, between Chinese and Western printing, is explored by Kai-wing Chow and discussed by Roger Chartier in this collection. Chartier brings out the advantages of xylography for fixing texts but stops short of noting the significance of combining woodblock illustration with letter-press printing and connecting the two with various devices as is exemplified by Vesalius's *De Fabrica.* As noted in *PPAC,* the hiring of illustrators to make fresh woodblocks and engravings for the purpose of illustrating newly printed ancient texts contributed to a reappraisal of inherited technical literature.[21]

EDITORS: You have been criticized for your treatment of "standardization" and "fixity," terms that figure largely in your discussion of print culture. How do you respond to this criticism?

EISENSTEIN: Granted that the terms in usage are less than rigorous, I regret the way critics tend to discuss standardization and fixity as if these two terms were interchangeable. Standardization represents a synchronic aspect of print culture: it entails the publication of numerous copies of the same text or the same image, chart, map on the same date. "Print spread texts in a different way from manuscript; it multiplied them not consecutively but simultaneously."[22] This synchronic aspect can be illustrated by the way the Declaration

---

19. See my remarks as a commentator at a session at the January 5, 1997, annual meeting of the American Historical Association in New York sponsored by the Society for the History of Authorship, Reading and Publishing (SHARP): "Printing as an Agent of Change outside Europe." The papers dealt with printing in colonial Virginia, in Egypt under the Ottomans, and in Meiji Japan.

20. See *PPAC,* 334–45. In his essay in this volume, Chartier couples the Bible with the Torah as being amenable to strict control and being "fixed" by scribal transmission. Although this seems to be true of the Koran, it is not in accord with most studies of changes undergone by manuscript versions of the Vulgate.

21. *PPAC,* 54, 264–7.

22. Introduction to *The Uses of Script and Print, 1300–1700,* ed. Julia Crick and Alexandra Walsham (Cambridge: Cambridge Univ. Press, 2004), 20.

of Independence was first issued in printed form so that copies could be made immediately available to all thirteen colonies. Only later was a hand-inscribed presentation copy produced.[23]

Fixity (or preservation) points to a diachronic aspect. Copies of a given text (image, etc.) were issued in sufficient quantities to preserve it (as manuscripts had not been preserved) over the long *durée*, making it available to successive generations for reconsideration and augmentation. The preservative powers of print account for the way the number of known plants went from six hundred in the fifteenth century to some six thousand two centuries later. They also explain why previously lost languages once decoded were not lost again or why bibliographies kept expanding to the point where bibliographies of bibliographies became necessary. Preservation by means of duplication set the knowledge industry on a path that led from an economy of scarcity to one of abundance and glut.

Features such as standardization and preservation ought to be regarded as relative not absolute phenomena. Recent studies show this point is worth more emphasis. It seems especially pertinent to questions raised by Adrian Johns with regard to standardization. To say that early printed products were more standardized than were late medieval manuscripts is not to deny that they were also more multiform than were the later products of mechanical presses, or of lithography or photography. Far from denying this point, I warn against ignoring it. Yet Johns seems to believe he is refuting my arguments when he devotes much of his massive study of scientific publication in early modern England to documenting the multiformity of early printed output. That "exactly repeatable" pictorial images were often reproduced inexactly is evident from my own reference to "reversals, misplacements, and the use of worn and broken blocks." Many more examples are cited by Johns. They all confirm that the output of the handpress fell short of meeting modern standards. But they do not contradict the point that early printed products were more standardized than were hand-copied ones.[24]

To dwell on the incapacity of the handpress to meet modern standards, moreover, is to assume an anachronistic posture. Johns is so intent on contrasting early printed products with modern ones that he often forgets this contrast was unavailable to early modern Europeans. "Contemporaries had good reason to be wary," he writes, since "their editions of Shakespeare, Donne, Sir Thomas Browne were liable to be dubious." The First Folio of

---

23. Thomas Starr, "Separated at Birth: Text and Context of the Declaration of Independence," *Proceedings of the American Antiquarian Society* 110, pt. 1 (2002): 152–90.

24. McKitterick acknowledges that there was a "greater measure of standardization in the printed book" but at the same time seems to object to my asserting that this was the case. McKitterick, *Print, Manuscript, and the Search for Order* (Cambridge: Cambridge Univ. Press, 2003), 99–100.

Shakespeare contained "non uniform spelling and punctuation. . . . No two copies were identical. . . . In such a world, questions of credit took the place of assumptions of fixity."[25] Concern about non-uniform spelling and about variants in a Shakespeare folio was not characteristic of the early modern world. The erratic spelling of seventeenth-century English writers would have appalled modern schoolteachers but was accepted as common practice at the time.[26] Contemporaries were surely not bothered by "variants" in the First Folio since the device used to uncover and count them was not developed until the twentieth century.

However relative was the degree of standardization obtained by the hand-press, the fact remains that early modern Europeans were much better able than their forebears had been to consult more or less the same text, chart, or table at more or less the same time and to correspond with one another about the same items on the same page.[27] Even polemical pamphlet controversies showed a capacity on the part of participants to refer to identical passages when carrying on an argument.

EDITORS: *PPAC* is usually credited with playing a significant role in the creation of a new field, that of the history of the book, yet you have said that you were not writing book history. Could you comment on this and also say something about how you conceive of the relationship between book history and print culture studies?

EISENSTEIN: The chief problem I have with "book history" is suggested by Peter Stallybrass's essay in this collection.[28] When Daniel Boorstin first proposed creating a "center for the book" in the Library of Congress, I objected that the title implied exclusion of newspapers and all the other nonbook printed materials housed in the Library. Of course, the Center for the Book has flourished, and Boorstin was probably right to waive aside my seemingly pedantic objection.

---

25. Adrian Johns, *The Nature of the Book: Print and Knowledge in the Making* (Chicago: Univ. of Chicago Press, 1998), 30.

26. Philip Gaskell, *A New Introduction to Bibliography* (Oxford: Oxford Univ. Press, 1972), 344.

27. See, for example, exchanges concerning Copernicus's *De Revolutionibus* in Robert Westman, "Three Responses to the Copernican Theory," in *The Copernican Achievement,* ed. Robert Westman (Berkeley and Los Angeles: Univ. of California Press, 1975), 285–345.

28. On this point, see my reply to Adrian Johns in the AHR Forum, "How Revolutionary Was the Print Revolution?" *American Historical Review* 107.1 (2002), 126, where I deny that my work is "centrally about the history of books." See also the new afterword in the 2nd ed. of Eisenstein, *The Printing Revolution in Early Modern Europe* (Cambridge and New York: Cambridge Univ. Press, 2005), 317.

Nevertheless, current concern with the book, as both Stallybrass and Chartier observe, often results in neglect of many other historically significant printed products. One regrettable outcome is that books and periodicals are encouraged to go their separate ways despite their natural affiliation.[29] Furthermore, book historians are likely to regard the changes that came after the adoption of printing as relatively insignificant in view of all the other major changes (word separation, adoption of half uncials, commercial copying, etc.) evidenced in the manuscript book after codex replaced scroll. Book historians have good reason to cite M. B. Parkes's thought-provoking comment that "the late medieval book differs more from its early medieval predecessors than it does from the printed book of our own day."[30]

Because "book history" encourages the view that nothing much changed after printer replaced scribe, I think the frame provided by this label is too restrictive. Other historical disciplines tend to be more accommodating. Economic historians, for example, have long made ample room for the innovative aspects of early printing. From their perspective, the early printer belongs in the company of other entrepreneurs and early capitalists. Social historians are unlikely to confuse scriptoria with printing shops or the earlier occupational culture with the later one. Within western Europe, the book-as-object goes back to the era of the codex, whereas the fifteenth-century printer is generally acknowledged to be a "new man" (or woman — *pace* Paula McDowell).

It is possible, of course, to regard "print culture studies" as a "subset" of book history. I prefer to think of such studies as a subset of a broader history of communications, although, to be sure, communications as a historical field of study is still in an amorphous state. The labels and categories that are used within such a field are bound to be untidy. The catch-all title of the Society for the History of Authorship, Reading and Publishing[31] is less than rigorous. Yet it has the advantage of being capacious and as a result has been serving its membership rather well.

With regard to labels and categories, something needs to be said about the use of such terms as "scribal culture" and "print culture." These terms seemed helpful for describing the large concatenation of activities entailed in duplicating and distributing written materials before and after the use of the

---

29. See relevant discussion in Eisenstein, *Grub Street Abroad: Aspects of the French Cosmopolitan Press from the Age of Louis XIV to the French Revolution,* Lyell Lectures, 1989–90 (New York: Clarendon. Press, 1992), 10–12.

30. M. B. Parkes cited by McKitterick in *Print, Manuscript,* 11.

31. For information about the society, see http://www.sharpweb.org/.

wooden handpress.[32] This large concatenation of activities was fundamentally changed after the establishment of printing shops. An eminent authority on punctuation in manuscripts makes it clear how hand-copying practices themselves came to be dominated by printed ones:

> New conventions became established and were disseminated more quickly through printed books than through manuscripts because of the number of identical copies produced through the new process. . . . Practices established by printers soon began to appear in manuscripts. . . . The written word had become associated in the minds of readers with the printed word and the conventions of written language had become dominated by those employed in printed texts.[33]

In this sense, it seems fair enough to say that scribal culture had come to an end. It is in this sense that I refer to a shift from script to print. But this does not mean that manuscripts were no longer being produced or that copyists had stopped plying their trade. To say, as Parkes does, that manuscripts followed conventions employed in printed books is obviously not to deny that manuscripts continued to be produced. The same point applies to Curt Bühler's finding that scribes soon began copying from printed books.

Since my first edition was published, the fallacy of doctrines of "supersession" has been brilliantly illuminated by Paul Duguid and Geoffrey Nunberg.[34] Elsewhere I've made clear my agreement with their position while also questioning recent doomsday pronouncements about the supersession of print.[35] Here, let me simply reiterate: printed texts did not supersede manuscripts any more than engraving and woodcut superseded drawing and painting. Nevertheless, the introduction of printing did arrest and then reverse the process of loss, corruption, and erosion that had accompanied the hand copying of texts and images. After printing, the output of manuscripts, however large or small, far from arresting the increase in book production, augmented it.

One more comment about terminology: it is a good idea to distinguish

---

32. Adrian Johns's definition of print culture comes close to agreeing with mine: "a vast array of representations, practices and skills which extended from the printing shop through the bookshop and marketplace to the . . . study . . . and home—and thence back to the printing house again" (*Nature of the Book,* 58).

33. M. B. Parkes, *Pause and Effect: An Introduction to the History of Punctuation in the West* (Berkeley and Los Angeles: Univ. of California Press, 1993), 56.

34. Geoffrey Nunberg, introduction to *The Future of the Book,* ed. Nunberg (Berkeley and Los Angeles: Univ. of California Press, 1996), 9–20; Paul Duguid, "Material Matters," in ibid., 66–73.

35. Eisenstein, "From the Printed Word to the Moving Image," *Social Research* 64.3 (1997): 1049–66.

between hand copying, which persisted after printing but did so in a diminished form, and handwriting, which flourished after printing at least until the invention of the typewriter, as numerous printed manuals on penmanship and letter writing suggest.

EDITORS: Do you see any points of comparison between the printing revolution you describe and the communications revolution progressing as we speak?

EISENSTEIN: The "electronic age" encompasses too many changes affecting communications (from radio and telephone to photocopying and computers) for any simple comparisons with the fifteenth-century revolution to be drawn. Moreover, such comparisons tend to relegate printed communications to the past or at least to overlook the significance of their persistence at present. This tendency is demonstrated by numerous gloomy prophecies about the "end of the book." Yet just as handwriting coexisted with the printed word, so too, I think, the printed word is likely to coexist with electronic communications. No doubt we are in the midst of unprecedented transformations. But this does not mean that the printing revolution has ceased gathering momentum or is becoming irrelevant to our concerns. Librarians make full use of electronic databanks not to dispense with printed materials but rather to locate them more efficiently. Moreover, librarians are still concerned about the increased output of printed books and the persistent shortage of bookshelf space. Even while the preservative powers of print continue to pose problems, they also serve as a safeguard against losing completed texts in cyberspace. Indeed, the fluidity of texts on screens enhances the value assigned to the fixity of hard copy. I see that I have reached a point where I'm repeating myself—a sure sign that it is time to bring this conversation to a close.

Appendix A

Publications by Elizabeth L. Eisenstein

Books

The First Professional Revolutionist: Filippo Michele Buonarroti (1761–1837): A Biographical Essay. Cambridge, MA: Harvard Univ. Press, 1959.

The Printing Press as an Agent of Change: Communications and Cultural Transformations in Early-Modern Europe. 2 vols. Cambridge and New York: Cambridge Univ. Press, 1979. Reprinted in 1-volume paperback edition, 1980.

The Printing Revolution in Early Modern Europe. New York: Cambridge Univ. Press, 1983.

La rivoluzione inavvertita: La stampa come fattore di mutamento (Italian translation of *PPAC*). Translated by Davide Panzieri. Bologna: Il Mulino, 1985.

Grub Street Abroad: Aspects of the French Cosmopolitan Press from the Age of Louis XIV to the French Revolution. Lyell Lectures, 1989–90. Oxford and New York: Clarendon Press, 1992.

The Printing Revolution in Early Modern Europe. 2nd ed., with new afterword. Cambridge and New York: Cambridge Univ. Press, 2005.

Translations of *The Printing Revolution in Early Modern Europe*

Insatsu kakumei. Translated by Sadanori Bekku. Tokyo: Misuzu Shobo, 1987.

La révolution de l'imprimé à l'aube de l'Europe moderne (cover title: *La révolution de l'imprimé dans l'Europe des premiers temps modernes*). Translated by Maud Sissung and Marc Duchamp. Paris: Éditions La Découverte, 1991.

La revolución de la imprenta en la edad moderna Europea. Translated by Fernando Jesús Bouza Alvarez. Madrid: Akal, 1994.

Le rivoluzioni del libro: L'invenzione della stampa e la nascita dell'età. Bologna: Il Mulino, 1995.

Die Druckerpresse: Kulturrevolutionen im frühen modernen Europa. Vienna and New York: Springer, 1997.

A revolução da cultura impressa: Os primórdios da Europa moderna. Translated by Osvaldo Biato. São Paulo: Editora Atica, 1998.

Hē typographikē epanastasē otis aparkhes tēs neoterēs Eurōpēs. Translated by Vassilis Tomanas. Thessaloniki: Typophilia/Mastoridis, 2004.

Rewolucja Gutenberga. Translated by Henryk Hollender. Warsaw: Prószyński i S-ka, 2004.

Published Lectures, Journal Articles, and Chapters in Collaborative Works

"Who Intervened in 1788? A Commentary on *The Coming of the French Revolution.*" *American Historical Review* 71.1 (1965): 77–103.

"Clio and Chronos: An Essay on the Making and Breaking of History-Book Time." *History and Theory* 6. Beiheft 6: History and the Concept of Time, 1966, 36–64.

"A Reply." "Class in the French Revolution: A Discussion." *American Historical Review* 72.2 (1967): 514–22.

"Buonarroti, Filippo." In *International Encyclopedia of Social Sciences,* edited by David L. Sills, 2:202–3. New York: Macmillan and Free Press, 1968.

"Some Conjectures about the Impact of Printing on Western Society and Thought: A Preliminary Report." *Journal of Modern History* 40.1 (1968): 1–56.

"The Advent of Printing and the Problem of the Renaissance." *Past & Present* 45 (November 1969): 19–89.

"The Advent of Printing in Current Historical Literature: Notes and Comments on an Elusive Transformation." *American Historical Review* 75.3 (1970): 727–43.

"The Advent of Printing and the Problem of the Renaissance: A Reply." *Past & Present* 52 (August 1971): 140–4.

"L'avènement de l'imprimerie et la Réforme: Une nouvelle approche au problème du démembrement de la chrétienté occidentale." *Annales: Économies, sociétés, civilisations* 26.6 (1971): 1355–82.

"The Advent of Printing and the Protestant Revolt: A New Approach to the Disruption of Western Christendom." In *Transition and Revolution: Problems and Issues of European Renaissance and Reformation History,* edited by Robert M. Kingdon, 235–70. Minneapolis, MN: Burgess, 1974.

"In the Wake of the Printing Press." *Quarterly Journal of the Library of Congress* 35.3 (1978): 183–97.

"The Emergence of Print Culture in the West." *Journal of Communication* 30.1 (1980): 99–106.

"The Early Printer as a 'Renaissance Man.'" *Printing History* 3.1 (1981): 6–17.

"The Fifteenth Century Book Revolution: Some Causes and Consequences of the Advent of Printing in Western Europe." In *Le livre dans les sociétes pré-industrielles: Actes du premier colloque international du Centre de Recherches Néohelléniques / To vivlio stis proviomēchanikes koinōnies: Praktika tou A' Diethnous Symposiou tou Kentrou Neoëllēnikōn Ereunōn,* 57–76. Athens: Kentron Neoellenikon Ereunon, Ethnikon Hidryma Ereunon, 1982.

"Le livre et la culture savante." In *Le livre conquérant: Du moyen âge au milieu du XVIIe siècle.* Vol. 1 of *Histoire de l'édition française,* edited by Henri-Jean Martin and Roger Chartier, 563–83. Paris: Promodis, 1982.

"From Scriptoria to Printing Shops: Evolution and Revolution in the Early Printed Book Trade." In *Books and Society in History: Papers of the Association of College and Research Libraries Rare Books and Manuscripts Preconference, 24–28 June, 1980, Boston, Massachusetts,* edited by Kenneth E. Carpenter, 29–42. New York: R. R. Bowker, 1983.

"On the Printing Press as an Agent of Change." In *Literacy, Language, and Learning: The Nature and Consequences of Reading and Writing,* edited by David R. Olson, Nancy Torrance, and Angela Hildyard, 19–33. Cambridge: Cambridge Univ. Press, 1985.

"L'invenzione della stampa: Il libro e la nuova circolazione delle idee." In *L'età moderna: La vita religiosa e la cultura.* Vol. 4 of *La storia: I grandi problemi dal medioevo all'età contemporanea,* edited by Nicola Tranfaglia and Massimo Firpo, 1–60. Turin: Unione Tipografico-Editrice Torinese, 1986.

"On Revolution and the Printed Word." In *Revolution in History,* edited by Roy Porter and Mikuláš Teich, 186–206. Cambridge and New York: Cambridge Univ. Press, 1986.

Print Culture and Enlightenment Thought. Sixth Hanes Lecture. [Chapel Hill]: Hanes Foundation, Rare Book Collection / University Library, University of North Carolina at Chapel Hill, 1986.

"Le publiciste comme démagogue: La *Sentinelle du peuple* de Volney." In *La révolution du journal, 1788–1794,* edited by Pierre Rétat, 189–95. Paris: Centre National de la Recherche Scientifique, 1989.

"La invención de la imprenta y la difusión del conocimiento científico." In *La ciencia y su público: Perspectivas históricas,* edited by Javier Ordóñez and Alberto Elena, 1–42. Madrid: Consejo Superior de Investigaciones Científicas, 1990.

"The Tribune of the People: A New Species of Demagogue." In *The Press in the French Revolution,* edited by Harvey Chisick with Ilana Zinguer and Ouzi Elyada, 145–59. Studies on Voltaire and the Eighteenth Century 287. Oxford: Voltaire Foundation, 1991.

"The End of the Book? Some Perspectives on Media Change." *American Scholar* 64.4 (1995): 541–55.

Printing as Divine Art: Celebrating Western Technology in the Age of the Hand Press. Harold Jantz Memorial Lecture, November 4, 1995. [Oberlin, OH]: Oberlin College, 1996.

"From the Printed Word to the Moving Image." *Social Research* 64.3 (1997): 1049–66.

"The Libraire-Philosophe: Four Sketches for a Group Portrait." In *Le livre et l'historien: Études offertes en l'honneur du Professeur Henri-Jean Martin,* edited by Frédéric Barbier et al., 539–50. Geneva: Droz, 1997.

"Bypassing the Enlightenment: Taking an Underground Route to Revolution." In *The Darnton Debate: Books and Revolution in the Eighteenth Century,* edited by Haydn T. Mason, 157–77. Studies on Voltaire and the Eighteenth Century 359. Oxford: Voltaire Foundation, 1998.

"Gods, Devils, and Gutenberg: The Eighteenth Century Confronts the Printing Press." 1996 Clifford Lecture. *Studies in Eighteenth-Century Culture* 27 (1998): 1–24.

"An Unacknowledged Revolution Revisited" and "Reply." AHR Forum: "How Revolutionary Was the Print Revolution?" *American Historical Review* 107.1 (2002): 87–105 and 126–8.

Book Reviews

Jacques Mallet-Du Pan, by Nicola Matteucci. *American Historical Review* 63.4 (July 1958): 970–1.

Questioni di storia del socialismo, by Leo Valiani. *Journal of Modern History* 32.2 (1960): 175–6.

Gilbert Romme: Storia di un rivoluzionario, by Alessandro Galante Garrone. *Journal of Modern History* 32.3 (1960): 287–8.

Massimo d'Azeglio: An Artist in Politics, 1798–1866, by Ronald Marshall. *American Historical Review* 72.2 (1967): 636.

Roland de la Platière: A Public Servant in the Eighteenth Century, by Charles A. Le Guin. *American Historical Review* 72.4 (1967): 1405.

L'histoire sociale: Sources et méthodes: Colloque de l'école normale supérieure de Saint-Cloud (15–16 mai 1965). American Historical Review 73.1 (1967): 145–6.

Les almanachs populaires aux XVIIe et XVIIIe siècles: Essai d'histoire sociale, by Geneviève Bollème. *French Review* 44.4 (1971): 777–8.

Histoire générale de la presse française, by Claude Bellanger, Jacques Godechot, Pierre Guiral, and Fernand Terrou. *American Historical Review* 76.2 (1971): 510–1.

Jacobin Legacy: The Democratic Movement under the Directory, by Isser Woloch. *French Review* 44.5 (1971): 946–7.

The Mythology of the Secret Societies, by J. M. Roberts. *American Historical Review* 78.4 (1973): 1049–50.

Essays on Manuscripts and Rare Books, by Cora E. Lutz. *Sixteenth Century Journal* 7.2 (1976): 125–6.

France and North America: The Revolutionary Experience, edited by Mathé Allain and Glenn R. Conrad. *Eighteenth-Century Studies* 10.1 (1976): 127–9.

The Coming of the Book: The Impact of Printing, 1450–1800, by Lucien Febvre and Henri-Jean Martin. *Journal of Modern History* 50.3 (1978): 490–3.

Victims, Authority, and Terror: The Parallel Deaths of d'Orléans, Custine, Bailly, and Malesherbes, by George Armstrong Kelly. *Journal of Modern History* 55.4 (1983): 736–8.

Essays on the Heritage of the Renaissance from Homer to Gutenberg: The Growth of Knowledge and Its Transmission through the First Printed Books, by Margaret Bingham Stillwell. *Papers of the Bibliographical Society of America* 78.4 (1984): 504–7.

The Damiens Affair and the Unraveling of the Ancien Régime, 1750–1770, by Dale K. Van Kley. *Journal of Modern History* 57.4 (1985): 748–50.

The Cultural Uses of Print in Early Modern France, by Roger Chartier. *Sixteenth Century Journal* 20.1 (1989): 130.

Press and Politics in Pre-Revolutionary France, edited by Jack R. Censer and Jeremy D. Popkin. *American Historical Review* 94.2 (1989): 456–7.

Le livre dans l'Europe de la Renaissance: Actes du XXVIIIe colloque international d'études humaniste de Tours, edited by Pierre Aquilon, Henri-Jean Martin, and F. Dupuigrenet Desrousilles. *Renaissance Quarterly* 42.3 (1989): 540–3.

Revolution in Brussels, 1787–1793, by Janet L. Polasky. *Journal of Modern History* 61.4 (1989): 829–32.

Histoire et pouvoirs de l'écrit, by Henri-Jean Martin. *American Historical Review* 95.5 (1990): 1487–8.

La Réforme et le livre: L'Europe de l'imprimé (1517–v. 1570), by Jean-François Gilmont. *Sixteenth Century Journal* 22.3 (1991): 583–4.

In the Public Eye: A History of Reading in Modern France, 1800–1940, by James Smith Allen. *Technology and Culture* 34.1 (1993): 140–2.

Printing the Written Word: The Social History of Books, circa 1450–1520, edited by Sandra L. Hindman. *Renaissance Quarterly* 47.1 (1994): 155–7.

Revolutionary France, 1770–1880, by François Furet. *American Historical Review* 99.4 (1994): 1323–4.

Print, Power, and People in Seventeenth-Century France, by Henri-Jean Martin. *Renaissance Quarterly* 48.3 (1995): 626–8.

Printing, Propaganda, and Martin Luther, by Mark U. Edwards Jr. *Renaissance Quarterly* 49.2 (1996): 396–7.

The Future of the Book, edited by Geoffrey Nunberg. *Papers of the Bibliographical Society of America* 91.2 (1997): 256–61.

Sir Philip Sidney and the Circulation of Manuscripts, 1558–1640, by H. R. Woudhuysen. *American Historical Review* 103.1 (1998): 173–4.

The Marketplace of Print: Pamphlets and the Public Sphere in Early Modern England, by Alexandra Halasz. *Sixteenth Century Journal* 30.1 (1999): 169–70.

The Evolution of the Book, by Frederick G. Kilgour. *Journal of Interdisciplinary History* 30.4 (2000): 635–6.

The Nature of the Book: Print and Knowledge in the Making, by Adrian Johns. *Isis* 91.2 (2000): 316–7.

The Cambridge History of the Book in Britain, edited by Lotte Hellinga and J. B. Trapp, vol. 3, *1400–1557. Journal of Ecclesiastical History* 52.4 (2001): 737–8.

Books and the Sciences in History, edited by Marina Frasca-Spada and Nick Jardine. *American Historical Review* 106.5 (2001): 1745–6.

Appendix B

Reviews of *The Printing Press as an Agent of Change*

This list aims at completeness in reviews appearing in British and American scholarly journals. Reviews in British and American newspapers and magazines and reviews in continental European journals are included without any claim to completeness.

Ahern, John. "The Revolution of Print." *Commonweal* 106.10 (1979): 309–10.

Atwood, Roy. *Media, Culture, and Society* 2.2 (1980): 189–93.

Barker, Nicolas. "Spreading the Word." *Times Literary Supplement,* no. 4186 (June 24, 1983): 679.

Blouin, Francis X., Jr. *American Archivist* 44.2 (1981): 157–8.

Bouwsma, William J. *American Historical Review* 84.5 (1979): 1356–7.

Broadus, John R. *Library Journal* 104.3 (1979): 400.

Burke, Peter. "Renaissance Studies." Review of *PPAC* and twelve other books. *Historical Journal* 22.4 (1979): 975–84.

Censer, Jack R. "Publishing in Early Modern Europe." Review of *PPAC;* Febvre and Martin, *Coming of the Book;* and Darnton, *Business of Enlightenment. Journal of Social History* 13.4 (1980): 629–38.

Chartier, Roger. "L'ancien régime typographique: Réflexions sur quelques travaux récents." Review of *PPAC;* Lowry, *World of Aldus Manutius;* Grendler, *Roman Inquisition and the Venetian Press;* Darnton, *Business of Enlightenment;* and Barbier, *Trois cents ans de librarie et d'imprimerie. Annales: Économies, sociétés, civilisations* 36.2 (1981): 191–209.

Choice 16.7 (1979): 808.

Crahay, Roland. *Bibliothèque d'humanisme et Renaissance: Travaux et documents* 42.3 (1980): 700–3.

Davis, Donald G., and Betsy Vantine. "The Significance of the Printing Press in the West." *Fides et Historia* 13.2 (1981): 82–7.

Dennis, Nigel. "Ah, the Magic of the Printed Word." *Sunday Telegraph,* May 20, 1979, 12.

Duffy, Shannon E. "The Unacknowledged Revolution." *H-Ideas,* June 2000. http://www.h-net.msu.edu/reviews/showrev.cgi?path=24899962821867.

Erdel, Timothy Paul. *Christian Scholar's Review* 10.1 (1980): 66–8.

Fahy, Conor. *Italian Studies* 36 (1981): 94–5.

Feld, M. D. *New Republic* 180.12 (March 24, 1979): 34–7.

Freeman, Eric J. *Medical History* 25.4 (1981): 423–6.

Gingerich, Owen. *Papers of the Bibliographical Society of America* 75.2 (1981): 228–30.

Golden, Richard M. "Print Changed History; But Is It Sensibly Used?" *Birmingham (AL) News,* July 29, 1979.

Grafton, Anthony T. "The Importance of Being Printed." *Journal of Interdisciplinary History* 11.2 (1980): 265–86.

Grannis, Chandler B. *Publishers Weekly* 216.6 (August 6, 1979): 56.

Hafter, Daryl M. *Michigan Academician* 13.4 (1981): 506–7.

Haile, H. G. *Michigan Germanic Studies* 6.1 (1980): 120–9.

Hay, Denys. "The Permanent Revolution." *New Statesman* 98, no. 2526 (August 17, 1979): 244.

Hollender, Henryk. *Kwartalnik Historii Nauki I Techniki* 28.1 (1983): 220–4.

Hunter, Michael. "The Impact of Print." Review of *PPAC* and Capp, *Astrology and the Popular Press. Book Collector* 28.3 (1979): 335–52.

Jacob, J. R. "The Medium and the Message in Early Modern Europe." Review of *PPAC;* Ferguson, *Clio Unbound;* Appleby, *Economic Thought and Ideology in Seventeenth-Century England;* and Hayes, *Winstanley the Digger. Annals of Scholarship: Metastudies of the Humanities and Social Sciences* 1.2 (1980): 113–23.

Jowett, Garth S. *Journalism Quarterly* 58.1 (1981): 117–9.

Kelley, Donald R. *Clio: A Journal of Literature, History, and the Philosophy of History* 10.2 (1981): 213–6.

Keunecke, Hans-Otto. *Buchhandelsgeschichte* 2.9 (1981): B532–4.

Kingdon, Robert M. *Library Quarterly* 50.1 (1980): 139–41.

Knight, David M. *British Journal for the History of Science* 13, pt. 2, no. 44 (1980): 164–6.

Krummell. D. W. *Journal of Library History, Philosophy, and Comparative Librarianship* 15.2 (1980): 205–9.

Laslett, Peter. *Renaissance Quarterly* 34.1 (1981): 82–5.

Leed, Eric J. "Elizabeth Eisenstein's *The Printing Press as an Agent of Change* and the Structure of Communications Revolutions." *American Journal of Sociology* 88.2 (1982): 413–29.

Lovett, A. W. *Irish Historical Studies* 22 (1980): 184–5.

Maffei, Domenico. *Journal of Ecclesiastical History* 32.3 (1981): 357–9.

Mander, Mary S. "Vision of a Hedgehog." *Journal of Communication* 30.2 (1980): 217–8.

Marvin, Carolyn. *Technology and Culture* 20.4 (1979): 793–7.

McConica, James. Review of *PPAC* and Eisenstein, *Printing Revolution. English Historical Review* 100.395 (1985): 342–4.

McLuhan, Marshall. *Renaissance and Reformation / Renaissance et Réforme,* n.s., 5.2 (1981): 98–104.

Mills, Geofrey T. Review of *PPAC* and Grendler, *Roman Inquisition and the Venetian Press. Cithara-Essays in the Judeo-Christian Tradition* 22.2 (1983): 77–9.

Mitchison, Rosalind. "Books Do Furnish a Continent." *Listener* 103, no. 2644 (1980): 58–9.

Montagu, Ashley. "The Power of the Press." *Sciences* 20.7 (1980): 20–1.

Murphy, James J. *Quarterly Journal of Speech* 67.2 (1981): 239–40.

Nauert, Charles G., Jr. "The Communications Revolution and Cultural Change." *Sixteenth Century Journal* 11.1 (1980): 103–7.

Needham, Paul. *Fine Print* 6.1 (1980): 23–5, 32–5.

Neuberg, Victor E. "Printing and Society." *British Book News,* August 1979, 625.

O'Day, Rosemary. *Wilson Quarterly* 4.1 (1980): 158.

O'Driscoll, Sean. *Leonardo* 18.2 (1985): 122.

Overmier, Judith. *Journal of the History of Medicine and Allied Sciences* 37.4 (1982): 462–3.

Poole, H. E. *Book Auction Records* 76 (August 1978–July 1979): xix–xx.

Porter, Roy. "Printing and Change." *Books & Issues* 1 (1979): 10–1.

Quinn, David B. Review of *PPAC* and Febvre and Martin, *Coming of the Book. Terrae Incognitae* 12 (1980): 115–20.

Reeds, Karen. "Recent Books on the History of the Book." Review of *PPAC; Winckler, History of Books and Printing;* Lowry, *World of Aldus Manutius;* Darnton, *Business of Enlightenment;* Carpenter, *Books and Society in History;* Hindman, *Early Illustrated Book;* and *Histoire de l'édition française,* vol. 1. *Scholarly Publishing* 15.4 (1984): 327–34.

Robinson, Fred C. "Print Culture and the Birth of the Text." Review of *PPAC;* Chappell, *Short History of the Printed Word;* and Cressy, *Literacy and the Social Order. Sewanee Review* 89.3 (1981): 423–30.

Rosaldo, Renato. "The Cultural Impact of the Printed Word: A Review Article." *Comparative Studies in Society and History* 23.3 (1981): 508–13.

Schlatter, Richard. *Journal of the Rutgers University Libraries* 42.1 (1980): 47–50.

Schmitt, Charles B. *Journal of Modern History* 52.1 (1980): 111–3.

Schoeck, R. J. *English Language Notes* 20.1 (1982): 109–11.

Schwartz, Hillel. *Religious Studies Review* 5.4 (1979): 286–7.

Schwiebert, Ernest G. *Church History* 49.1 (1980): 84–5.

Shaw, David. *The Library,* 6th ser., 3.3 (1981): 261–3.

Smith, C. N. Review of *PPAC* and Barbier, *Trois cents ans de librairie et d'imprimerie. Journal of European Studies* 11, pt. 3, no. 43 (1981): 212–4.

Sokolov, Raymond A. *New York Times Book Review* 84.12 (March 25, 1979): 16.

Sonne, Niels Henry. *Historical Magazine of the Protestant Episcopal Church* 50.1 (1981): 99–102.

Teichgraeber, Richard, III. "Print Culture." Review of *PPAC* and Darnton, *Business of Enlightenment. History of European Ideas* 5.3 (1984): 323–9.

Thompson, Lawrence S. *American Notes and Queries* 17.9 (1979): 149–50.

Thompson, Susan Otis. Review of *PPAC* and Parkes and Watson, *Medieval Scribes, Manuscripts, and Libraries. American Book Collector,* n.s., 1.5 (1980): 49–51.

Traister, Daniel. *Printing History* 4, nos. 7–8 (1982): 71–3.

Turchetta, Gianni. Review of Italian translation of *PPAC. Belfagor: Rassegna di varia umanità* 41.6 (November 30, 1986): 735–6.

Van Deursen, A. T. *Tijdschrift voor Geschiedenis* 94.1 (1981): 105–7.

Viner, George. "Following On from Old Gutenberg." *Media Reporter,* December 1979, 47.

Walker, D. P. "The Power of the Press." *New York Review of Books* 26.16 (October 25, 1979): 44–5.

Walsh, Michael J. *Heythrop Journal* 21.4 (1980): 461–2.

Westman, Robert S. "On Communication and Cultural Change." *Isis* 71.3 (1980): 474–7.

Winger, Howard W. *College and Research Libraries* 41.4 (1980): 356–8.

Woodward, David. "The Printing Press as an Agent of Change." *Imago Mundi* 32 (1980): 95–7.

Yates, Frances. "Print Culture: The Renaissance." *Encounter* 52.4 (1979): 59–64.

Notes on Contributors

Peng Hwa Ang is vice dean and associate professor at the School of Communication and Information, Nanyang Technological University, Singapore. His research interests lie in Internet law and policy, for which he has consulted with the Bertelsmann Foundation, the European Union, and the United Nations Development Program. A board member of the Internet Content Rating Association, he was a Fulbright fellow at the Kennedy School, Harvard University, in 2000 and a visiting scholar at Oxford in 2001.

Margaret Aston's many publications include *Lollards and Reformers: Images and Literacy in Late Medieval Religion* (1984), *England's Iconoclasts: Laws against Images* (1988), and *The King's Bedpost: Reformation and Iconography in a Tudor Group Portrait* (1994). Her work on English woodcuts includes study of the illustrations in Foxe's Book of Martyrs for the online edition of the British Academy's John Foxe Project.

Tony Ballantyne is a lecturer in history at the University of Otago (New Zealand). He specializes in transnational history, with a particular emphasis on the intellectual and cultural networks that reshaped Asian culture in the long nineteenth century and the region's place within a larger imperial system of exchange and mobility. His publications include *Orientalism and Race: Aryanism in the British Empire* (2002) and *Bodies in Contact: Rethinking Colonial Encounters in World History* (edited with Antoinette Burton, 2005).

Sabrina Alcorn Baron is a lecturer in history at the University of Maryland. She has published on censorship, book collectors, the book trade, and news writing, as well as the culture of publication in early seventeenth-century England. Baron co-edited (with Brendan Dooley) *The Politics of Information in Early Modern Europe* (2001). Also in 2001 she was guest curator for the Folger Shakespeare Library Exhibition, *The Reader Revealed*, and she compiled and edited the exhibition catalogue of the same name. Baron was a Fulbright scholar in Albania (1997–8).

Vivek Bhandari is an associate professor of history and South Asian studies at Hampshire College, Amherst. After graduate work at the University of Delhi, he completed his Ph.D. at the University of Pennsylvania with a dissertation on the historical impact of print on public culture in colonial South Asia. His ongoing research addresses the historical relationship between public culture, civil society, and the construction of sociopolitical identity, especially as it pertains to democratic practices and institutions in postcolonial India.

ANN BLAIR, a 2002 MacArthur Fellow, is a professor of history at Harvard University. She is the author of *The Theater of Nature: Jean Bodin and Renaissance Science* (1997) and co-editor, with Anthony Grafton, of *The Transmission of Culture in Early Modern Europe* (1990). Her current research explores the strategies that scholars used to adjust to the information explosion during the Renaissance. Showing that methods of medieval manuscript culture played just as influential a role in responding to this crisis of information as did the new technologies of mechanical reproduction, she documents historical responses to challenges that, in many ways, resonate with contemporary times.

BARBARA A. BRANNON, whose twenty-five years in book publishing have encompassed graphic design, desktop publishing, marketing, and editorial functions, is the director of the Publishing Laboratory at the University of North Carolina, Wilmington, where she teaches editing and publishing. An officer of SHARP (Society for the History of Authorship, Reading and Publishing), she is a specialist in twentieth-century American bookselling and publishing.

ROGER CHARTIER is Directeur d'Études at the École des Hautes Études en Sciences Sociales in Paris and Annenberg Visiting Professor in History at the University of Pennsylvania. His most recent book is entitled *Inscrire et effacer: Culture écrite et littérature, XIe–XVIIIe siècles* (2005), which will be translated and published by the University of Pennsylvania Press in its Material Texts series. In 2005 he was elected to the Chair of History at the Collège de France, the highest academic honor in France.

KAI-WING CHOW is a professor of East Asian languages and cultures at the University of Illinois. His study of the impact of printing on cultural production in sixteenth- and seventeenth-century China was published as *Publishing, Culture, and Power in Early Modern China* (2004). With Cynthia Brokaw, he has edited a conference volume, *Printing and Book Culture in Late Imperial China* (2005). Other interests include the politics of identity formation, power relations in cross-cultural translation, and the politics of knowledge making.

JAMES A. DEWAR is director of the RAND Frederick S. Pardee Center for Longer Range Global Policy and the Future Human Condition and is also the Frederick S. Pardee Professor of Long-Term Policy Analysis at the RAND Graduate School. He has written extensively on strategic planning and is the author of *Assumption-Based Planning: A Tool for Reducing Avoidable Surprises* (2002).

Robert A. Gross is the James L. and Shirley A. Draper Professor of Early American History at the University of Connecticut. He has also taught at the College of William and Mary, where he was director of American Studies and book review editor of the *William and Mary Quarterly,* and at Amherst College. His books include *The Minutemen and Their World* (1976; twenty-fifth anniversary edition, 2001) and *Books and Libraries in Thoreau's Concord* (1988). He served as chair of the American Antiquarian Society's Program in the History of the Book in American Culture from 1993 to 1999 and is co-editor with Mary C. Kelley of *An Extensive Republic: Books, Culture, and Society in the New Nation, 1790–1840,* vol. 2 of *A History of the Book in America* (forthcoming).

David Scott Kastan is the Old Dominion Foundation Professor in the Humanities at Columbia University. His most recent book is *Shakespeare and the Book* (2001). He is also the author of *Shakespeare after Theory* (1999) and *Shakespeare and the Shapes of Time* (1982). He serves as general editor of the Arden Shakespeare as well as general editor for the forthcoming *Oxford Encyclopedia of British Literature;* in 2005, he published editions of Marlowe's *Doctor Faustus* and Milton's *Paradise Lost.* He is currently working on a book called "The Invention of English Literature," a project for which he was awarded a Guggenheim Fellowship for 2004.

Eric N. Lindquist is a librarian at the University of Maryland. He has published articles on seventeenth-century English parliamentary history in the *Historical Journal,* the *English Historical Review,* and elsewhere and co-edited and contributed to *Who Wants Yesterday's Papers?: Essays on the Research Value of Printed Materials in the Digital Age* (2005). His research interests include King James VI and I as reader, writer, and controversialist and aspects of print culture in early modern Britain.

Harold Love is emeritus research professor of English in the School of Literary, Visual, and Performance Studies at Monash University, Melbourne. He is the author of a long list of articles, chapters, editions, and books, including *Scribal Publication in Seventeenth-Century England* (1993), *The Works of John Wilmot, Earl of Rochester* (1999), *Attributing Authorship: An Introduction* (2002), *English Clandestine Satire 1660–1702* (2004), and (edited with Robert D. Hume) *Plays, Poems, and Miscellaneous Writings Associated with George Villiers, Second Duke of Buckingham,* 2 vols. (2006).

Paula McDowell is an associate professor of English at New York University. She is the author of *The Women of Grub Street: Press, Politics, and Gender in the London Literary Marketplace 1678–1730* (1998) and of articles on subjects ranging from Henry Fielding to the history of the book. She has also published an edition of the more than ninety broadsides and pamphlets of London printer-author Elinor James (fl. 1681–1716), *The Early Modern Englishwoman: Essential Works: Elinor James* (2005). Her current book project, *Fugitive Voices: Literature and Oral Culture in Eighteenth-Century England,* argues for the continuing centrality of oral culture after the commercialization of print.

JANE MCRAE is a lecturer in Maori oral literature in the Maori Studies Department of the University of Auckland. She has written on the history of the transition from Maori orality to literacy in *Book and Print in New Zealand* (1997) and *A Book in the Hand* (2000). She has also contributed to and co-edited *Rere atu, taku manu! Discovering History, Language and Politics in the Maori-Language Newspapers* (2002) and edited *Nga Moteatea-The Songs: Part Two* (2005).

JEAN-DOMINIQUE MELLOT is senior curator in the Bibliothèque nationale de France, in charge of early collections, and is a lecturer in the École pratique des hautes études (Paris, Sorbonne), department of historical sciences. A graduate of the École nationale des chartes, Paris, he earned his doctorate in history from the Sorbonne. The author of several articles on the history of the book and various works concerning cultural practices during the French ancien régime, he is co-editor of the *Revue française d'histoire du livre* and currently in charge of the *Dictionnaire encyclopédique du livre* (Éditions du Cercle de la Librairie, 2 vols.).

ANTONIO RODRÍGUEZ-BUCKINGHAM is a professor in the School of Library and Information Science at the University of Southern Mississippi. He has published articles on early printing and books in Spanish America in the *Harvard Library Bulletin, Libraries and Culture,* and elsewhere. His other interests include the digitization of rare books and documents.

GEOFFREY ROPER, recently retired, was a compiler/indexer at the Islamic Bibliography Unit of Cambridge University Library, and now serves as advisor and consultant to various bibliographic projects. He has co-edited the *Index Islamicus on CD-ROM: A Bibliography of Publications on Islam and the Muslim World since 1906* (1998). His other relevant publications include "Faris al-Shidaq and the Transition from Scribal to Print Culture in the Middle East," in *The Book in the Islamic World: The Written Word and Communication in the Middle East* (1995). In 2005 he was the first recipient, along with John Eltis, of the Partington Award in recognition of outstanding contributions to the field of Middle Eastern librarianship.

WILLIAM H. SHERMAN is professor of Early Modern Studies and co-director of the Centre for Renaissance and Early Modern Studies at the University of York. He is the author of *John Dee: The Politics of Reading and Writing in the English Renaissance* (1995) and articles on early modern travel writing, Renaissance drama, and the history of reading. With Peter Hulme, he edited *"The Tempest" and Its Travels* (2000), and he has also published a Norton Critical Edition of *The Tempest* (with Peter Hulme, 2004) and *On Editing* (with Claire MacDonald, 2002). His edition of *The Alchemist,* with Peter Holland, for *The Cambridge Works of Ben Jonson* is forthcoming.

ELEANOR SHEVLIN, a 2005–2006 Kluge Center Fellow (Library of Congress), teaches in the English Department at West Chester University of Pennsylvania. Her articles have appeared in *Eighteenth-Century Fiction, Book History, Modern Fiction Studies,* and elsewhere. Currently the Public Affairs Director for SHARP (Society for the History of Authorship, Reading and Publishing), she is working on a monograph titled "Harrison and Co.: Cultural Production, Economies of Print, and the Making of the English Novel."

PETER STALLYBRASS is the Walter H. and Leonore C. Annenberg Professor of the Humanities at the University of Pennsylvania, where he directs the History of Material Texts seminar and co-edits the series Material Texts for the University of Pennsylvania Press. His most recent publications are *O Casaco de Marx* (Marx's coat), published in Brazil in 1999, and *Renaissance Clothing and the Materials of Memory* (with Ann Rosalind Jones, 2000), which won the James Russell Lowell Prize from the Modern Language Association in 2001. In 2006, he delivered the Rosenbach Lectures at the University of Pennsylvania, entitled, "Printing-for-Manuscript." At present he is working on a material history of reading and writing.

ARTHUR WILLIAMSON is a professor of history at California State University, Sacramento. His numerous publications include *Scottish National Consciousness in the Age of James VI* (1979), *The Expulsion of the Jews: 1492 and After* (with Raymond B. Waddington, 1994), *George Buchanan: The Political Poetry* (with Paul J. McGinnis, 2000), and *The British Union* (with Paul J. McGinnis, 2002). He has also produced a sixteen-lecture video for the Teaching Company, entitled *Apocalypse Now, Apocalypse Then: Prophecy and the Modern World.*

CALHOUN WINTON, professor emeritus in the department of English at the University of Maryland, is the author of a two-volume biography of Richard Steele (1964, 1970) and *John Gay and the London Theatre* (1993). He has also published a number of articles on printers and the book trade in colonial British America. Recent publications relevant to this volume include a chapter entitled "The Southern Book Trade in the Eighteenth Century," in *The Colonial Book in the Atlantic World* (2000), vol. 1 of *A History of the Book in America,* and articles on the printers Samuel Keimer and William Bradford in the *Oxford Dictionary of National Biography* (2004).

Index

Page numbers in *italics* refer to illustrations.